D0616914

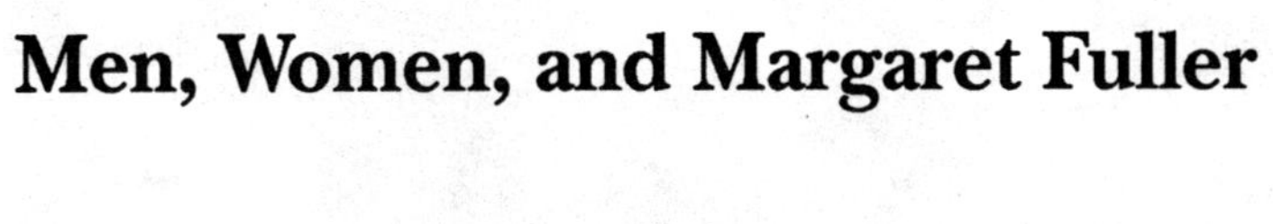
Men, Women, and Margaret Fuller

Ralph Waldo Emerson

Lidian Emerson

Giovanni Angelo Ossoli

Waldo Emerson Jr.

Henry David Thoreau

Nathaniel Hawthorne

Bronson Alcott

Margaret Fuller Ossoli

Elizabeth Hoar

Carolyn Sturgis

Harriet Martineau

Julia Ward Howe

Ellen Fuller

Edgar Allen Poe

Thomas Carlyle

Horace Greeley

Samuel Grey Ward

Men, Women, and Margaret Fuller

by Laurie James

The truth that existed between Margaret Fuller and Ralph Waldo Emerson and their circle of Transcendental friends.

Volume 3
in a series on the life and work of
Margaret Fuller Ossoli (1810-1850)

Golden Heritage Press, Inc.
New York
1990

Selections from the following works were made possible by the kind permission of the authors, publishers and/or representatives:

Manuscripts, papers and letters of Margaret Fuller. Reprinted by permission of the Houghton Library.

Margaret Fuller's *1842 Journal.* Reprinted by permission of Harvard University Library and Joel Myerson.

Margaret Fuller's *1844 Commonplace Book*, on deposit at the Massachusetts Historical Society. Reprinted by permission of Allie Perry.

The Letters of Ralph Waldo Emerson, ed. Ralph L. Rusk, 6 Vols., New York, Columbia University Press, 1939. Reprinted by permission of Houghton Library.

The Journals and Miscellaneous Notebooks of Ralph Waldo Emerson, ed. W.G. Gilman et al., 14 vols., Cambridge, Mass., Harvard Belknap Press, 1960-1978. Reprinted by permission of the Ralph Waldo Emerson Memorial Association and of the Houghton Library.

The Life of Lidian Jackson Emerson, by Ellen Tucker Emerson, edited by Delores Bird Carpenter, Boston, Twayne Publishers, 1980. Reprinted by permission of Delores Bird Carpenter.

Waldo Emerson by Gay Wilson Allen, Penguin Books, The Viking Press, 1981. Reprinted by permission of Viking Penguin Inc.

Designer and Compositor: Richard Scillia, Creative Abilities, Wantagh, New York.

Body text set in ITC New Baskerville® 10/12 using Macintosh™ computers and an Apple LaserWriter.® Cover pages output on a Linotronic® L300.

Printed in the United States of America

Library of Congress Catalog Card Number 89-83247

ISBN 0-944382-00-2 (Volume 1)
ISBN 0-944382-01-0 (Volume 2)
ISBN 0-944382-02-9 (Volume 3)
ISBN 0-944382-03-7 (Volume 4)
ISBN 0-944382-04-5 (4 Volume Set)

This book is dedicated to
the millions
who are not Margaret Fuller fans...

in the hope
they will read this
and become Margaret Fuller fans.

"humanity can be divided
into three classes —
men, women, and margaret fuller."

— edgar allen poe

Author's Acknowledgment

I am indebted to all of you who have over the years seen my dramas on Margaret Fuller,* and who have asked questions afterwards. You are the ones who initially spurred my interest to write books on Fuller and showed me the need for them.

I am indepted to Councils on the Humanities in the states of New York, Massachussetts, Wisconsin, Maine, and Pennsylvania for awarding me grants to tour my drama, as well as to artistic directors such as Anne Forman** and Edith O'Hara*** who have so encouraged me by their abiding faith and kindnesses, and to program coordinators and administrators, such as Rosemary Matson, Gwen Harper, Alexa Payan, and others throughout the United States, Mexico and Hong Kong, who have helped to bring my drama to their audiences.

A special recognition goes to Ramona Barth who is proud to have no official title or resume attached to her name but whose expert and offbeat grassroots promotion has done more than anyone to spread the name of Margaret Fuller.

I am indebted to the New York Foundation for the Arts for awarding me a 1989 Artists' Fellowship which has enabled the publication of this book.

I am indebted to the eminent scholars who have preceded me, who have evaluated original materials and written the works that now exist. Especially, the acknowledgment is forwarded to Robert N. Hudspeth, Joel Myerson, Bell Gale Chevigny, Paula Blanchard, Joseph Jay Deiss, and Ralph L. Rusk. Due to their excellent work, I have not felt I had to "reinvent the wheel" and pour over every piece of

---

* The title of my solo drama, *Still Beat Noble Hearts* was changed to *Men, Women, and Margaret Fuller* in 1988. The title of my drama on Margaret Fuller and Ralph Waldo Emerson is *O Excellent Friend!*

** Artistic Director of Wantagh Cultural Arts Program, Wantagh, New York.

*** Artistic Director of The Thirteenth Street Repertory Theater.

original paper, albeit I have examined much. It would take most of the rest of my life if I were to attempt to decipher all the quill pen scratchings. My bibliography attests to the depth of my research. I will echo Margaret Fuller who said when she was working on the life of Goethe, "I intend to content myself with doing it inadequately rather than risk living so long in the shadow of one mind."*

I am indebted to all feminist theory and feminist groups and many individuals (and, of course, to Margaret Fuller herself) for helping me gain a broadened perspective other than what patriarchal society brainwashed me with as a child and young adult.

I am indebted to my mother for her inspiration and her early teaching me the art of writing, and I am indebted to my father who sent me to drama teachers and drama school in New York.

I am indebted to my husband for his continued encouragement and understanding, and for pushing me off to perform at the Edinburgh Fringe Festival.

A thank you goes to my grown children, Mary, Lynn, Hardy, Winkie, Mike, and my sons through marriage, Andy and Bob, for their solid support and, yes, advice, and for not making too many jokes about a driving interest that has consumed me for many years. I especially bow in appreciation to Mary, Lynn and Mike who often got involved technically in my drama and who showed up when asked, whether they wanted to or not, and often for free.

I am indebted to modern technology without whose computer this book could never have been written.

* Letter to Ralph Waldo Emerson, June 3, 1839.

Contents

L.J.

Did Margaret Fuller and Ralph Waldo Emerson have sex?

This may seem a blatant question, but it is one that is on people's minds after seeing my drama, *O Excellent Friend!*, because they have heard some divinely cryptic words.

I save everything in print on Fuller* and Emerson, but I've thrown into trash articles that flippantly drop comments that they were seen slipping behind bushes at Brook Farm (one of America's first communes). Such statements have no factual basis.

The complexities of the relationships may shock. All could easily be satirized or treated like soap opera. But the stature of our characters, plus our cultural legacy, demand that depth of literary and historic sensitivity and taste be accorded.

The truth is there was a hot/cold relationship between Emerson and Fuller. In his journals Emerson writes, "...these strange, cold-warm, attractive-repelling conversations with Margaret, whom I always admire, most revere when I nearest see, and sometimes love, yet whom I freeze & who freezes me to silence, when we seem to promise to come nearest."[1]

No writer has brought the truth vibrantly to life within the context of daily life and social circle. A few contemporary biographers have attempted to tell the story, but only a couple have understood it without blinders, and these authors have so blocked their manuscripts into categories, for purposes of their own, that the full impact has been blurred.

---

* The name "Fuller" is used throughout this book in preference to "Ossoli" because this was her pen name and therefore the name by which Americans knew her.

If past biographers allude to the love angle at all, it seems a dull platonic association. Fuller is usually featured as an ugly, ridiculous spinster who is aggressively domineering, and Emerson, safely married, is esoterically lofty, benignly reluctant to recognize Fuller's advances. Fuller is sexually frustrated and Emerson is never attracted to women other than his wives. His marriages, if dealt with at all, are generally pictured as satisfactory, especially the first. The one recent biographer who attempted the truth misses by writing a one-perspective story that leaves out relevant facts; therefore, he misunderstands and badly denigrates the second wife.

Contrary to the impression left posterity, Emerson needed women around him, as do many men. He promoted, relied and drew on women, as Fuller promoted, relied and drew on men.

He baited Fuller as much as she baited him. Emerson may have held off Fuller's earliest advances, but it was Fuller who rejected Emerson's final advances, not vice versa, as most biographers would have us believe. Both remained friends, thanks to Fuller.

The game playing lasted their entire lives; it lasts even until this day. If you dig for it — if you read between the lines — if you latch onto certain papers or certain scholarly works available in certain libraries — you will find it out.

Margaret Fuller was an equal combatant. She was one of the few who could command Ralph Waldo Emerson's interest and respect. Her repartee was so sharp that she often left Emerson feeling uneasy. "She makes me laugh more than I like," he wrote after he first met her. He wrote that she was eternally enriching him: "Of personal influence… she had an extraordinary degree; I think more than any person I have known."

Fuller asked for invitations to visit the Emersons and she stayed for weeks at the "mansion of peace." Togetherness routinely consisted of afternoon teatimes, dinners, carriage rides, walks in woods, talks in Sleepy Hollow Cemetary. They also attended the ballet, concerts, art exhibits in Boston and visited Brook Farm together. There were arrangements to see each other, and both were admiring and critical of each other.

Their ideas often differing, Fuller often served as catalyst. They debated and corresponded about, with great wit and wisdom, Goethe,

Carlyle, George Sand, Henry David Thoreau, and other literary figures, art, poetry, metaphysics, the Divine Spirit, the celestial, the universe, the ideal, genius, beauty, nature, the weather, writing habits and struggles, joys and pains of editing *The Dial Magazine*, the growth of Waldo Jr., the psychological ramifications of marriage, love, friendship.

Not only did Fuller inspire, but she provided Emerson with material for essays and poems.* In fact, they used *The Dial Magazine* to communicate to each other. In his poems, "To Rhea" and "The Visit," Emerson offered his Platonic advice. In her articles, "Bettine Brentano and Her Friend Gündenode" and "Dialogue," she re-enforced to him her philosophy of friendship. She addressed her advice, privately, in several unpublished poems. (See Appendix and Chapters IV and V.)

Not only did they mail fascinating witty letters back and forth, but habitually they sent each other books, prints, gifts. They shared their writings, parts of their private journals. They performed favors for each other. They reciprocated opinions, stories, confidences, frustrations, grievances, silences.

Emerson read his first book, *Nature*, aloud to Fuller, and tested in like manner several essays and poems before publication. Later Fuller mailed duplicates of all her poems to Emerson to keep "in case of death."

Emerson sent Fuller tickets to his lectures and if she couldn't attend, he'd send her the manuscripts to read.

Both collected prints of the Sistine frescoes from the Boston Athenæum and hung them on their walls.

Early on Fuller tried to teach Emerson German so he could read Goethe whose works were not yet translated into English. She impressed upon him the importance of German literature, and even made short translations for his personal reading.

---

* Scholar Carl Staunch states, "About 20 poems were illuminated when examined in juxtaposition with the letters. 'Etienne,' 'The Park,' 'Destiny,' 'Rubies,' and 'To Rhea,' were entirely inspired by Emerson's relation with Fuller, and the others owe something to her in varying degrees." As Staunch asserts, these poems revealed "a more humane Emerson."[2]

Fuller introduced Emerson to her wide circle of friends who offered an intellectual match; thus, she enlarged his limited social terrain. It was these people, Fuller, Caroline Sturgis, Anna Barker and Samuel Ward that infused Emerson's long term thinking on the subjects of friendship and love that resulted in his essays, "Friendship" and "Love"— though his ideas on the subject are in opposition to Fuller's and, probably, to theirs.

Emerson helped Fuller get her first job as teacher by introducing her to the innovative educator Bronson Alcott. He encouraged her to write, especially on Goethe. He helped to see that her first book was published. He admitted her as one of the first women to the Transcendental Club meetings. He appointed her first editor of *The Dial Magazine.* When she went to Europe, Emerson gave her a letter of introduction to Thomas Carlyle, and later promised to help with a publisher for her Italian history. He did, finally, organize the writing and publication of her *Memoirs,* thus becoming her first biographer.

Once Emerson looked for Fuller's lost eyeglasses, and once he sent by messenger the shoes she left under his entry table.

Once Emerson gave her Thomas Carlyle's latest book as a birthday present. A seven year span between their ages, their birthdays were two days apart: his May 25, hers, May 23. For his birthday present she gave him a pouch handmade by a Seneca Indian woman and told him facetiously that he could hang it on his bedpost and dream of Niagara (where she bought it) or he could use it as a purse for collecting dollars for needy poets and philosophers (as he was prone to do).

While at the Emerson's, Fuller would work in the downstairs bedroom while he would work across the hall in his study. There were times when they couldn't speak to each other and both would confine themselves to their rooms and send notes back and forth via four year-old Waldo Jr.

Fuller played with Waldo Jr. She adored him as her own. When he died at the age of five, Fuller was one of the first persons Emerson notified; she mourned as much as the father and mother. They consoled one another with remembrances of him.

For four years they worked together on *The Dial Magazine,* exchanging evaluations of submitted articles and poetry. Finally, in the last issue of *The Dial,* both conveyed farewell messages to each other through its pages.

They criticized each other's work frankly and honestly. He judged her popular book by prevailing standards and called it a "fine manly work" — presumably a compliment.

Emerson thought Fuller lost herself in sentimentalism and that her personal feeling colored her judgment. He scornfully remarked, "Her pen is a non-conductor."

Fuller, as a well paid front-page literary critic on *The New-York Daily Tribune,* wrote about his collected poems: "...while they charm the ear and interest the mind (they) fail to wake far-off echoes in the heart."

Of his second series of *Essays,* she wrote: "We miss what we would expect from the great poet or the great philosopher.... We doubt this friend raised himself too early to the perpendicular and did not lie along the ground long enough to hear the secret whispers of our parent life."

Emerson was so dependant on Fuller for intellectual stimulation that when he failed to receive letters and packets from her, he complained.

He created elaborate, imaginative names for Fuller and used them in letters to her.

He beseeched Fuller to live near him in Concord, and at her suggestion he made inquiry of an appropriate house for her.

He was upset, disappointed and disgusted when Fuller left the Boston area to conquer new fields in New York.

When she was in Italy, he wrote from Paris and London, asking her to meet him and return to Concord with him and to live either with him and his wife or in Lidian's sister's house across the road.

He was crushed to hear rumors that in Europe the famous national Polish poet, Mickiewicz, had wanted a divorce to marry Fuller. He was equally hurt to learn that the revolutionary leader, Mazzini, had offered marriage. He was numbed to silence when informed that she had married an Italian nobleman with whom she'd had a child.

The truth is that Fuller was able to touch, converse with and reach people in a way Emerson never could. People were her priority. Her investment was life and heart above intellect.

Clearly, the complex friendship and love of S. M. F. and R. W. E. is one of the great literary relationships, still relevant today.

Here are two brilliant non-conformist, non-violent revolutionaries and visionaries who were in the forefront of the new wave of the century. They were challenging the status quo in our country, shaping philosophy, theology, literature, education, and self-reliance and self-confidence. Their keen insights have weathered more than a century and are so fresh and alive today that one could think time has stood still.

Both were out-of-the-mainstream innovators — neither seeking applause or praise. Both stirred controversy.

Emerson wrote: "Whoso would be a man must be a non-conformist." [3]

Fuller wrote: "Gentleness is dignified, but caution is debasing." [4]

Emerson wrote: "I like the Sayers of No better than the Sayers of Yes." [5]

Fuller wrote: "If a worthy resistance is not made by religious souls, there is danger that all the light will soon be put under bushels...." [6]

Both intoxicated, enthralled and dominated their audiences, and both attracted circles of admirers and worshipers.

Both felt an obligation to the community of humanity. Both stood as role models for the young, for intellectual radicals, and for working individuals.

Both saw the promise and need of a new and better world. "There is nothing wanting but preparation of the soil, and freedom in the atmosphere, for ripening of a new and golden harvest," Fuller wrote. "By use of (the truth), we harrow the soil and lay it open to the sun and air." [7]

Emerson wrote, "I unsettle all things. No facts are to me sacred; none are profane; I simply experiment, an endless seeker, with no Past at my back." [8]

Both searched for alternative structure. Emerson wrote, "Build therefore, your own world." [9] Fuller wrote, "If nations go astray, the narrow path may be found by the individual man." [10]

Both believed in the dignity and beauty of the ordinary, the everyday, the simple. Emerson preached the values of the agrarian way of life, with manual labor affording a wisdom. "The advantages of riches remains with him who produces them, not with the heir." [11] Fuller wrote, "The man who clears the barnacles from the keel is more essential than he who hoists the pennant on the lofty mast." [12]

Both admired the spoken and written word. Emerson especially used aphorisms and epigrams: "Hitch your wagon to a star."... "Things are in the saddle and ride mankind."... "When half-gods go, the gods arrive."... "Fired the shot heard round the world."... "A foolish consistency is the hobgoblin of little minds."

Fuller created: "Let them (women) be sea captains, if they will!"[13] ... "Truth is the nursing mother of genius."[14] ... "Only a noble fearlessness can give wings to the mind."[15] ...She quoted: "Tremble not before the free man but before the slave who has chains to break."[16] Opening her major book with the familiar quote: "Frailty, they name is Woman, The Earth waits for her Queen," she pointed out how this quote would be unacceptable if reversed to read, "Frailty, they name is Man. The Earth waits for its King."[17]

Both began as literary catalysts; both advanced to being political catalysts, though each in his/her own way. Neither was a political activist to the extent of striking, carrying signs, wearing special clothes or hair styles, collecting petition signatures, mailing mass propaganda, bashing in windows.

At a time when literature in American culture was gaining its first foothold, both wanted to see a fresh, organic literature with a national style and a national destiny that would spring from the heart of the country rather than the continuance of the prevailing imitation of English and European work. Fuller foresaw that a genius could be advanced from our country's soil. Americans had "abundant opportunity to develop a genius wide and full as our rivers... impassioned as our vast prairies, rooted in strength as the rocks on which our Puritan Fathers landed."[18]

Both felt the profundity of the universe. Both believed in the harmony and diversity of nature. Both believed in the conservation of environment and earth, the spirituality and perfection of reason, mind and heart. Both believed that God, the Divinity, the Universal Being, the omnipotent, was in the self, the impulse of Soul, the Indwelling Spirit.

"It was not meant that the soul should cultivate the earth, but that the earth should educate and maintain the soul," Fuller wrote. "Only by emotion do we know thee, Nature. To lean upon thy heart, and feel its pulses vibrate to our own; — that is knowledge, for that is love, the love of infinite beauty, of infinite love. Thought will never make us be born again."[19]

Emerson wrote: "Standing on the ground — my head bathed by the blithe air, and uplifted into infinite space — all mean egotism vanishes. I become a transparent eye-ball. I am nothing. I see all. The currents of the Universal Being circulate through me; I am part or particle of God."[20]

Both conceived of a day-by-day living faith, in flux, renewed. Both believed that the religious spirit did not require rituals, rites, sacraments. Church was in the Self. "Let my life be a church," Fuller wrote.[21]

Both had similar views of Jesus and the miracles, in the forefront of discussion and revolution. No mediator was needed to approach God, who could be approached directly. Emerson wrote: "Dare to love God without mediator or veil."[22]

Both respected tradition but they opposed the Calvinist belief that man was a "puppet" in God's universe, a sinner, possessed of the devil. To both the soul was an "infinite spiritual estate." Self-reliance is reliance on God. Emerson preached his theory of the Ultimate Perception — or intuition. Fuller claimed to have had two or three mystical experiences. She saw symbolic qualities in the carbuncle and other gems, as also in flowers which she regarded as the highest expression in nature. She found music deeply spiritual.

Fuller wrote: "Let men preach for the open air, and speak now thunder and lighting, now dew and rustling leaves...I feel that a great truth is coming...We shall reach what we long for, since we trust and do not fear, for our God knows not fear, only reverence, and his plan is All in All."[23]

Emerson said: "Look at it how we will, the most wonderful fact in history is Christianity; the fact that ten or twenty persons, or, if you please, twice so many did receive consciously or unconsciously, the revelations of the moral sentiment, with such depth and tenacity to live and die for them."[24]

Both believed that evil and misery merged into temporary harmony, transcended into a final restoration. Fuller wrote: "Make each discord harmony, by striking again the key-note; forget the imperfect interviews, burn the imperfect letters, till at last the full song bursts forth."[25]

Emerson wrote: "As when the summer comes from the south, the snow-banks melt, and the face of the earth becomes green before it, so shall the advancing spirit create its ornaments along its path, and carry with it the beauty it visits, and the song which enchants it; it shall draw beautiful faces, and warm hearts, and wise discourse, and heroic acts, around its way, until evil is no more seen."[26]

Both had rebelled against their Unitarian backgrounds; both came to be considered leaders of the Transcendentalist movement which they saw as being a state of mind in which each individual could see afresh, could envision more, could be empowered to rely on truth and intuition to control and transcend the circumstances of their lives.

Both disliked the label of Transcendentalist since it seemed a nickname inferring a pseudo way of looking beyond.

Each was independent, truthful to herself/himself.

If men thought rightly, Emerson believed, they would live rightly. Every person can be Man Thinking, Emerson stated.

His *Representative Men* was a search to find and describe the ideal which all men should strive to live up to. His geniuses were male: Shakespeare, Plato, Swedenborg, Montaigne, Napoleon, Goethe.

Fuller read "man" to include women. She envisioned a perspective of human perfection that encompassed women. It was imperative to broaden and stimulate women's minds as well as to give them self-confidence. She championed education and opportunities for women equal to men.

In her book she specifically clarified: "By man, I mean both man and woman: these are the two halves of one thought...I believe that the development of the one cannot be effected without that of the other."[27]

She named and discussed heroines throughout the ages, Elizabeth of England, Catharine of Russia, Sappho, Sita in the *Ramayana*, the Egyptian Isis, the women in Greek, Spanish, German legend literature, Shakespeare's Portia, and others, both known and unknown. "Let every arbitrary barrier be thrown down, every path laid open to woman as freely as to man!"[28]

Because their ideas often diverged, Emerson and Fuller met head-on and a rift in their admiration for one another was inevitable.

"Emerson, you are intellect!" Fuller once wrote. "I am life."[29]

Emerson called the gulf between them "a war of temperaments" that "could not be reconciled by words.... It was necessary to fall back on those grounds of agreement which remained and leave the differences henceforward in respectful silence."[30]

The question at the heart of Fuller's thinking was: "Is it not nobler to live than to think?"

Emerson felt: "A man's solitude is more beneficent than the concert of crowds."

Fuller pointed out: "It is not half so dangerous to a man to be immured in a dungeon alone with God and his own clear conscience, as to walk the streets fearing the scrutiny of a thousand eyes, ready to veil, with anxious care, whatever may not suit the many-headed monster in its momentary mood."[31]

Like most human beings, Fuller's most throbbing desire was to find love. She had no inclination to repress her natural feelings, as so many women of her day were brainwashed into doing. She had been searching for a physical relationship with a man from her teen-age years on.

One can go into a Freudian analysis of Fuller's relationship with her father, Timothy, who — no matter how well his daughter recited lessons to him — seldom expressed his love for her. One can speculate that Fuller's prayers to God, especially those after Timothy died, were in fact prayers to a father-substitute. One can imagine that she saw in Bronson Alcott, at least at first, a father's outstretched warmth. One can look at her liaisons with the Harvard graduates, George Davis, Sam Ward, James Freeman Clarke and others, and see her in search for a like-minded soul. And when one reads her letters to James Nathan, one becomes aware of the desperate, passionate, unfulfilled heart of Margaret Fuller. She had been rejected time and time again.

Did Emerson and Fuller love one another?

If you read Fuller's letters you will feel that she loved Emerson in varying degrees and ways from the time she met him until she went to New York in 1844. After that, on her part, it was a friendship.

If you believe the Emerson biographers, you will conclude that he was contentedly married and his morals were constantly impeccable, but if you read his private letters and journals, you will feel that Emerson loved Fuller all the years he knew her. You will also find out that Emerson was infatuated with the beauty of Anna Barker, was drawn to and needed the support and spirituality of Elizabeth Hoar, and warmly loved Carolyn Sturgis — at least for a time. He never actually states his feelings of love to these women.

Emerson claimed time and again in his private journals that he lacked "animal spirits," that he was cold in relationships. Still, there are confessions of his insistent sexuality. Like other human beings, as he himself admitted, he had "organs."

> The love of one (woman) should make him (one man) indifferent to all others...But now there is in the eye of all men a certain evil light, a vague desire which attaches them to the forms of many women, whilst their affections fasten on some one. Their natural eye is not fixed into coincidence with their spiritual eye. [32]

> I have organs also & delight in pleasure, but I have experience also that this pleasure is the bait of a trap. [33]

No matter how Emerson persisted in keeping stimulating, attractive women around him, there was reason for him to back away from any relationship that bordered on the physical with any woman other than his wife to whom he also skirted the subject of love. Furthermore, he put on "blinders" and refused to see triangles develop. So did Fuller, for that matter.

As to Fuller's sexuality, her friend/biographer William Henry Channing thought she was a virgin in the years he knew her, until she left for Europe at the age of thirty-six: "She had never met one who could love her as she could love; and in the orange-grove of her affections the white perfumed blossoms and golden fruit wasted away unclaimed.... No equal had recognized the rare beauty of her spirit. She was yet alone." [34]

Before she left for Europe Fuller wrote: "I think I may say, I never loved....As in a glass darkly, I have seen what I might feel as child, wife, mother, but I have never really approached the close relations of life. A sister I have truly been to many — a brother to more — a fostering nurse to, oh how many! The bridal hour of many a spirit, when first it was wed, I have shared, but said adieu before the wine was poured out at the banquet... And I am isolated...."[35]

When the highly sensitive Adam Mickiewicz, the national poet of Poland, met the thirty-six year-old Margaret Fuller in Paris, he thought she was a virgin and he encouraged her to aggressively seek and express herself in physical love in Italy, which she did.

Whether or not S.M.F. and R.W.E. had sex seems irrelevant. No one can prove that they did or did not. What matters is the complexity of feeling, the emotional dimension, the shifting consciousness they had for one another.

Let's examine where everyone was coming from.

S.M.F.

Sarah Margaret Fuller grew up to learn to behave in a manner that elicited the remark from educator Horace Mann that she "had the disagreeableness of forty Fullers."

Many people agreed with him.

The Fuller men had always been independant, feisty high achievers. These qualities were well admired in men, but they were not seen as particularly favorable in women. It was not that she did not grow up with advantages or in the arms of a loving family.

Life for Fuller was privileged and full of warmth. Her father was a professional with status, who could afford, if not every luxury, at least all comforts; his wife occupied that ultimate of positions. She did not have to work for money. Both parents loved their daughter dearly.

But early on Father opened Pandora's Box and offered goals effectual in the male world. Daughter toed the mark.

Psychologists today show us that gender identity and differentiation develop throughout the early growing years. Both boys and girls identify with the mother, the primary caretaker, to begin with, then boys eventually separate from the mother to identify with the father, thus realizing their own gender identity.

Early on Fuller was connected normally with the female world, but since her father served as dominate caretaker she also identified with the male world of action, reason, and objectivity. She was to be trained and to internalize early that she was capable of tasks considered in nineteenth century America to be within "woman's sphere" as well as those within the male spectrum. This acculturalization process of double message caused in the super talent of Margaret Fuller an internal conflict and torn soul that she would never be able to resolve or overcome. Of course, child behavior had not yet become a science.

Perhaps Timothy had hoped for a boy, but he'd celebrate even though the baby was a girl. Ecstatically he honored her birth on May 23, 1810 by planting two elms in front of his three-story yellow Cambridgeport house on the corner of Cherry and Eaton Streets, not far from the few brick buildings of Harvard College.

His lovely wife was well and bonding delightfully with daughter. Overwhelmed, he took special interest; he found a newborn endlessly fascinating, growing every minute, amazing to hold and watch, a joy.

In a day when child rearing was largely a matter of alternating a Bible with birch rod, he did not think he need break her will in order for her to achieve God's grace. He had long been a Unitarian and none of these traditional beliefs effected him or his wife. Timothy played with her lovingly, chose her dresses, supervised her care. Sarah Margaret was doted on by parents, aunts, uncles and grandparents. Life was fun.

Early on "Papa," as Sarah Margaret called him, must have noticed she could learn more quickly than others of her age. It must have been a real boost to his ego, exciting to see how much of what he gave her she could assimilate. Most parents did tutor their children until the age of seven, when girls (whose families could afford it) were sent on to private classes set up by local graduates, or to neighboring private schools or academies where extensive reading, languages, recitations were not required.

Not for precocious Sarah Margaret would there be ignorant or uncaring teachers. Timothy set up a daily plan. His teaching experience gave him solid footing.

"Mama," who had also been a teacher, was commissioned to see that Timothy's assigned daily lesson was strictly carried out. There was no slighting of reading or evening recitations. If her father was delayed at the office, she was kept up past bedtime so her lesson was never missed. She recited so well that "Papa" kept increasing the pace.

At the age of three Sarah Margaret had her earliest memory — the trauma of the sudden death of her one year-old sister. Sarah Margaret came home, met the nursery-maid with face streaming with tears, and was led into the chamber wherein her dead sister lay. The loss affected deeply. She later wrote: "She who would have been the companion of my life was severed from me, and I was left alone. This has made a vast difference in my life."

Again, Sarah Margaret became an only child — the child on which Timothy would focus his attention. It would be five years before another baby was born, Eugene, too young and the wrong sex to be the needed close companion.

Timothy had now become a Senator and spent long periods in Washington D. C., but he always stayed closely in touch with his family and he mailed off instructions for Sarah Margaret to his wife. He ended his letters with such comments as: "My love to the little Sarah Margaret. I love her if she is a good girl and learns to read."

At the age of four she could read.

She was also learning to sing and was encouraged to absorb the basics of sewing, cooking and caring for the house. Her mother's teaching conformed with what most girls received at that age, but Timothy insisted that his daughter keep to her books.

Timothy Fuller was a Jeffersonian Democrat...a liberal with sagacious energy. A lawyer and politician he supported unpopular and radical causes. He graduated from Harvard, class of 1801, with second honors when he should have had first, because he was penalized for leading a student protest. As a youth he'd admitted to being Unitarian, outrageous. When Sarah Margaret was growing up he admitted to being an abolitionist — a word not yet in some vocabularies. He had a scholarly interest in the classics and history, was well read in English and French literature, a Queen Anne's man.

He'd come from a long line of opinionated Fullers, stemming back to the 1630's in New Salem, Massachusetts, where Thomas Fuller, who had for some reason a title of "Lieutenant," had arrived from England to survey the wilderness and, after listening to a Cambridge minister, was vitalized into the Puritan faith. This Fuller appreciated the greatness of a country which offered freedom of religion, and he settled as farmer or blacksmith with land and house near a stream below Middleton Pond, which later became Middleton. Later he moved his family to Woburn, acquiring a farm which he left to his youngest son, Jacob, who lived on it with wife Mary Bacon and five children until he died in 1731. The fifth son, named Jacob, married Abigail Holton and they had ten children, one of which was Timothy (grandfather of Sarah Margaret Fuller). This first Timothy Fuller worked his way through Harvard in 1760 and became the first minister in Princeton, Mass., settling with five hundred acres and a bride, Sarah Williams of Sandwich (grandmother of Sarah Margaret Fuller, for whom she was named).

At the beginning of the American Revolution this first Timothy preached a sermon to the minute men in which he maintained that our country needed better preparation before taking on a war. He based his sermon on the text 1 Kings xx. 11, "Let not him that girdeth on the harness boast himself as he that putteth it off." This was not a popular view. For this, and because he failed to call a day of fast when the British blocked Boston Harbor, he was voted out of his parish. He sued the town for his salary, lost his case, paid costs, left Princeton for Martha's Vineyard, later returned to Princeton and bought another five hundred acres at the foot of Wachusett Mountain. Somehow he redeemed himself with the community.

After the American Revolution, he served as representative in the state convention where he voted against ratifying the Constitution of the United States because it recognized slavery. His wife's father had emancipated his slaves and wrangled a promise from his children to lend their support in event of need; therefore, wife Sarah fully complied with his actions.

This singleminded couple, grandparents of Margaret Fuller, had ten children, five of which were sons. The object of life was not wealth but to send sons to Harvard. Sarah Margaret Fuller was to write at the age of thirty, "To be an honored citizen, and to have a home on earth, were made the great aims of existence. To open the deeper fountains of the soul, to regard life here as the prophetic entrance to immortality, to develop his spirit to perfection...The result was a character, in its social aspect of quite the common sort. A good son and brother, a kind neighbor, an active man of business — in all these outward relations he was but one of a class, which surrounding conditions have made the majority among us."

The fourth child and eldest son, the second Timothy (Margaret Fuller's father), born in Chilmark, Martha's Vineyard, 1778, was to be as stubbornly independent and was to be the greatest achiever of the five successful lawyer brothers, all known for high Harvard scholarship, ready wit and satire, keen and cool minds.

After Harvard graduation in 1801, Timothy, Phi Beta Kappa — who worked his way through by teaching — became a preceptor at nearby Leicester Academy with teen-age girls as pupils, but he soon left to study law at the office of Hon. Levi Lincoln, of Worcester, and eventually opened his own office in Boston, became known for his eloquence and powers of reasoning, and attracted a large practice. He bought a house within commuting distance, in Cambridgeport and, two years later, 1809, married Margarett Crane. He begrudged the hours he needed for sleep.

He believed in freedom, the rights of man, democracy, was anti-British, a Democratic Republician. In his father's tradition, he took issue with the Constitution because it condoned slavery and was avidly against the Missouri Compromise which extended slavery. He had objected to Napoleon's actions, but protested his overthrow because he perceived that the Allied Powers had selfish motives. He claimed that "none but just wars can ever be waged by a free country." He respected the English judiciary system and therefore kept quiet about the John Jay Treaty which compromised the position of the English in America. Bolivar was a hero of his. And he was to support John Quincy Adams for president.*

Timothy had intelligence and energy but humor was desired. Compassion for the frailties of human nature seems to have been a void. Praise was something he didn't think to offer. He has been variously described as an authoritarian, a bully, arrogant, rigid, vain, but at the same time as loving, warm, liberal, and vulnerable. Regularly in winter he slept with a window open, practiced cold water bathing in a cold room, and his son Richard wrote he "occasionally ran barefoot a considerable distance in the snow."

---

*Timothy Fuller's published speeches were "An Oration delivered at Watertown, July 4, 1809", "Address before the Massachusetts Peace Society, 1826," "The election for the Presidency considered, by a Citizen;" and speeches on the Seminole War, Missouri Compromise.

Margaret Fuller was to write, "His love for my mother was the green spot on which he stood apart from the common-places of a mere bread-winning, bread-bestowing existence. In the more delicate and individual relations, he never approached but two mortals, my mother and myself...."

His views on women were stereotypical — except he held the outlandish opinion that women needed to acquire the highest of education to best fit the role of wife and mother. When he'd taught teen-age girls at Leicester Academy he'd read and re-read Mary Wolstonecraft's *A Vindication of the Rights of Women.* But he was not such an independent thinker as to believe that women were suited for any other career than that of governess. And he believed they should take on such work only if they could not find a husband.

Timothy had written that what he looked for in a wife was docility and modesty. Margarett was blessed with these characteristics and acquiesced in the lifestyle husband geared. She was not an intellectual match, but she handled social amenities better, was unaffected, simple, a good dancer, liked pretty clothes and had them, loved flowers and grew them in the back of the Cherry Street house in a garden which was her daughter's delight and refuge. In years to come, as the Fullers moved from house to house, they moved plants with them. One family of lilies was perpetuated for a quarter of a century, and Margarett bequeathed them to her children.

Timothy had met his future bride on one Sunday in Cambridge at church. She was a school teacher in Canton. They were married when she was twenty; he was thirty. Thereafter, in typical nineteenth century pattern, Margarett Crane Fuller was dependant first on Timothy, later on her eldest daughter, and still later on her sons.

Margaret Fuller once wrote a work of fiction that seems to pattern the husband/wife relationship: "...her marriage was the not uncommon one of a lovely young girl, ignorant of herself, and of her capacities for feeling, to a man of suitable age and position because he chose her. He was an honorable, kind hearted, well-educated (as it is called) and of good sense, but a mere man of business who had never dreamed what such a woman as she needs in domestic life. He kept her in a good house, with a good wardrobe, was even in temper, and indulgent to her wishes, but he did not know what it was to be companionable, the friend, much less the lover, and if he had he would not have had time, for his was the swift crowded course of an American business life. So she pined and grew dull, she knew not why, something was wanting she could not tell what, but there was a dreariness, a blank, she tormented herself that she was so ungrateful to a kind Providence, which had given her so much for want of which the many suffer."

Daughter, years later, compared her mother to a flower: "...so fair a blossom of the white amaranth." Again later, "...one of those fair and flower-like natures, which sometimes rises up even beside the most dusty highways of life — not to be shaped into a merely useful instrument, but bound by one law with the blue sky, the dew, and the frolic birds. Of all persons whom I have known, she had in her most of the angelic — of that spontaneous love for every living thing, for man and beast and tree, which restores the golden age."

Clearly, there was a warm mother-daughter relationship throughout the growing years and the mother's influence was assuredly considerable, though different from that which was generated by father.

If we ferret through obscure material, we do find information on Margarett Crane who outlived both her husband and daughter by many years, to whom all biographers have unfortunately devoted considerably less printed space in the mistaken notion that she exercised less influence over her family and genius/daughter.

She was the dowryless daughter of Major Peter and Elizabeth Jones Weiser Crane of Canton, Mass. He was an artisan of moderate circumstances, somewhat scholarly according to the standards of the day, though untutored, had an original mind. What others thought of him was of no concern to him. He'd served in the Revolutionary War and once substituted for the chaplain, but never called one religion his own. The only ready information to be found on his wife (Margarett Crane's mother and Margaret Fuller's maternal grandmother) is that she was a sweet, pious woman with a sunshiny disposition.

Margarett Crane Fuller was tall, slender, blue-eyed, with a rich complexion — with a sweet "madonna-like" expression when young — but awkward rather than graceful. She was shy, loving, even-going, cheerful, undemanding, domestic, self-sacrificing, saintly. Other descriptions have been "sweet," "amiable," "gifted, yet unpretending, with a rare intellect and ardent imagination, with warmth of sentiment and affectionate benignity of heart, together with tender susceptibilities.... Her life was one of habitual self-denial and devotion to duty in the various relations of her lot...." She never made an enemy.

Richard (Margaret's brother) wrote a personal memoir which gives us a good picture though it may be sentimental and heavy in describing her cheeks:

> In childhood and youth, my mother was marked not only for rare bloom and personal beauty, but for an almost irrepressible gayety and buoyance of temper. She was as full of the elasticity of life, and her heart as overflowing with the music of nature, as the early songsters of spring. She was above the medium height of woman, being in stature about five feet and nine or ten inches, and considerably taller than my father. She had blue eyes, a fair, white complexion, not liable to tan or freckle, and a rich bloom, like that of the peach, in her cheeks. This bloom was a very marked characteristic of her face, and one that she retained to quite mature life. It was transmitted to her daughter Ellen, and its rose has reappeared undiminished in the blooming cheeks of some of her grandchildren....
>
> As a child and maiden, she had a wild exuberance of spirits, regulated, however, by as strong a benevolence, and a tenderness of feeling and sympathy, which made her generally beloved.... [1]

Son Richard furthered his description that "she had a good store of refined fancy and delicate feeling...coupled with a ready hand and a willing mind for useful effort, graced by uninterrupted benignity and sweetness...." He wrote:

> A picture of her is very prominent in my mind, as she stooped over her flower-bed, and toiled long sunny hours over its extensive border. Her unwearied labors in the heat attracted the admiration even of the hardy farmers. Her expression, as she knelt by the flower bed and bent her nearsighted gaze close to a plant, and, discovering some new unfolding promise of beauty, turned round to announce it with a child-like simplicity and a delighted smile I think can never fade from the memories of her children. This image has often been renewed; and though latterly her hair, no less beautiful than before, has been

> gray, yet never thinned by years, her smile has gleamed ever with the same sunshiny, child-like triumph, her countenance never hardened or saddened by life's experience, nor her joy abated with the declining vigor of life. The flowers were ever new and ever young, and they kept her spirit still child-like in freshness of sentiment, simplicity of taste, and purity of soul, showing her ever guiless, single-hearted, and such as are of the kingdom of heaven...She never spoke against others — dwelt much upon their virtues, gently and charitably upon their faults ... duty was her daily food - not a burden, nor an artificial action, but the spontaneous movement of her life...Prayer was habitual — a frequent, regular, and delightful exercise to her. God was her best friend." [2]

In Cambridge she was active in the Unitarian church, sometimes taught Sunday School, and helped to form the Lee Street Church and Society. She loved sacred music, especially hymns and taught the children to sing and pray and took them on trips to Canton to visit her family.

In Washington D. C. when her husband was in Congress she was much admired and had good conversational powers "a lively fancy and a well-stored mind, which made her society much valued by the educated and the gifted."

In most instances Margarett, the mother, complied with the commands of her husband in true nineteenth century role pattern, but was sometimes independent enough to disregard his advice and follow her own instincts, as when once he was on an extended stay in Washington D.C. he asked her to date and number her letters consecutively so that he would be sure he received them all — she often "forgot."

No matter how much the young Sarah Margaret may have hated the ugly square yellow house in which she lived and the dusty roads on which she walked, there were advantages in being in America's intellectual heartland. Cambridgeport was a new settlement, developed to compete as a port — just as across the Charles River, Boston was a port, fourth largest of all American cities with a population of twenty five thousand. North of Cambridge, up one dirt road, was Concord (Emerson's part-time childhood environment).

Cambridge was divided into three villages, about twenty three hundred inhabitants at Fuller's birth and would triple its size by the time she was twenty. Rural life went on admist the pastures and marshes and frame houses with gardens and orchards and chickens and cows and pigs. Some men, like Sarah Margaret's father, commuted daily by stagecoach to Boston; others worked in the nearby "Soap Works."

Harvard Square represented the center of community, with its row of stores, town pump, First Parish Church and four brick buildings which comprised the College.

Harvard not only symbolized the cream of thought and leadership of the day, it was the institution to which the best, the most important, the greatest came from, worked out of and returned to. Women of course were not allowed admittance.

Harvard had been dominated since 1805 by Unitarian elite, and was dynamic enough to attract instructors from Europe, Charles Follen, Charles Beck, Pietro Bianchi, Francis Sales, and later Louis Agassiz.

During Margaret's growing up years the College took pride in claiming Henry Ware, Hollis Professor of Divinity, Edward Everett in Greek, Edward Tyrrel Channing in English and trainer of many an author, Judge Joseph Story in law, Thomas Nuttall, known for his works on botany and ornithology, supervising the Botanic Garden, John Quincy Adams as Professor of Rhetoric and Oratory, Levi Hedge as Professor of Logic and Metaphysics, George Ticknor in modern languages, George Bancroft in history, and Andrews Norton, as impeccable Professor of Sacred Literature. To drop a few more names: Joseph Green Cogswell, Washington Allston, Jared Sparks.

Fuller's neighbors were the Holmes, of whom the Rev. Abiel was pastor of the First Church and author of *The Annals of America*, and whose two sons were writers, Oliver Wendell and John. There were the Wares, all writers, including the two Henrys, John, William John F. W., and George. There were the Danas, of whom Richard Henry was a poet and his son of the same name became author of *Two Years Before The Mast*. The Channings, were a family of eminence, with the "Great Father," The Rev. William Ellery Channing, challenging New England orthodoxy and Calvinism. His nephew of the same name was to become a poet and another nephew was William Henry who was to become a minister and champion of social causes. There were The

Rev. Charles Lowell and family whose sons would be authors, Rev. R. T. S., and poet James Russell.

The Storys were headed by Judge Joseph, a distinguished legal writer whose son, William Wetmore had a future of being a sculptor and author. His son-in-law, George Ticknor Curtis, would be a legal writer and historian. The college librarian was Benjamin Pierce who happened to be father of the celebrated mathematician of the same name. There was John G. Palfrey who was a historian of New England whose sons were to be high achievers in military history and whose daughter would write poetry and fiction under the pen name of "E. Foxton." Charles Eliot Norton raised standards in literature. Also, growing up in Cambridge was Thomas Wentworth Higginson, who years later would become related to Fuller through the marriage of her sister and would be inspired to write a good biography of Fuller, refuting many of Emerson's evaluations. (See Volume II of this series, *Why Margaret Fuller Ossoli Is Forgotten.*) Higginson came to be, in even later years, friend and correspondent of Emily Dickinson.

Not only did the young Sarah Margaret immingle within this environment, she matured at a time in history when new ideas were exploding, when dissent and individualism were on docket. (So did Emerson.) Reformers were exposing conditions and seeking solutions by promoting the abolitionist movement, the peace movement, the temperance movement, free public schools, missions, the communitarian movement, prison and other institutional reforms, repentance, the woman's rights movement, the Graham Diet, phrenology, spirituality, hydropathy, the formation of unions and labor strikes.

People discussed these conditions, plus the banks, the tariff, the Boundary wars, the treatment of Indians, ignorance, competition, materialism, poverty, the exploitation and oppression of women and children.

These were the years the Unitarian controversy was brewing. There was a reserved and soft-spoken minister at the Federal Street Church — Fuller's neighbor — Rev. William Ellery Channing who preached about a God whose goodness and justice was within every man. (Presumably he also meant God was within every woman.) Man had *within himself* the power to achieve perfection and he must take the responsibility to develop the divinity within himself. Many were following him and wanted to seek change within themselves; others thought he spoke nonsense. Most adhered to Calvinist doctrine of sin, depravity and destiny.

Like osmosis, these controversies and conditions were absorbed by Sarah Margaret. When she was five, her mother's attention to her diminished as she was busied with her infant brother, Eugene. Sarah Margaret had her books and refuge in her mother's garden:

> ...Here I felt at home. A gate opened thence into the fields....This gate I used to open to see the sunset heaven....How exquisitely happy I was in its beauty and how I loved the silvery wreaths of my protecting vine! I never would pluck one of its flowers at that time....what I owe to that garden, where the best hours of my lonely childhood were spent... There my thoughts could lie callow in the nest, and only be fed and kept warm, not called to fly or sing before my time. I loved to gaze on the roses, the violets, the lilies, the pinks....my mother's hand had planted them, and they bloomed for me. I culled the most beautiful. I looked at them on every side. I kissed them, I pressed them to my bosom with passionate emotions, such as I have never dared express to any human being. An ambition swelled my heart to be as beautiful, as perfect as they.... [3]

When Sarah Margaret was six, her father taught her Latin and English grammar at the same time. Shortly, he set her to memorizing Virgil.

> I was put at once under discipline of considerable severity, and, at the same time, had a more than ordinarily high standard presented to me....He hoped to make me the heir of all he knew....At the very beginning, he made one great mistake....He thought to gain time, by bringing forward the intellect as early as possible. Thus I had tasks given me, as many and various as the hours would allow, and on subjects beyond my age; with the additional disadvantage of reciting to him in the evening, after he returned from his office. As he was subject to many interruptions, I was often kept up till very late; and, as he was a severe teacher, both from his habits of mind and his ambition for me, my feelings were kept on the stretch till the recitations were over. Thus frequently, I was sent to bed several hours too late, with

nerves unnaturally stimulated. The consequence was a premature development of the brain, that made me a "youthful prodigy" by day, and by night a victim of spectral illusions, nightmare, and somnambulism, which at the time prevented the harmonious development of my bodily powers and checked my growth, while, later, they induced continual headache, weakness and nervous afflictions, of all kinds.

No one understood this subject of health then. No one knew why this child, already kept up so late, was still unwilling to retire. My aunts cried out upon the 'spoiled child, the most unreasonable child that ever was....who was never willing to go to bed.' They did not know that, so soon as the light was taken away, she seemed to see colossal faces advancing slowly towards her, the eyes dilating, and each feature swelling loathsomely as they came, till at last, when they were about to close upon her, she started up with a shriek which drove them away, but only to return when she lay down again. They did not know that, when at last she went to sleep it was to dream of horses trampling over her, and to awake once more in fright; or, as she had just read in her Virgil, of being among trees that dripped with blood, where she walked and walked and could not get out, while the blood became a pool and splashed over her feet, and rose higher and higher, till soon she dreamed it would reach her lips. No wonder the child arose and walked in her sleep, moaning all over the house, till once, when they heard her, and came and waked her, and she told what she had dreamed, her father sharply bid her "leave off thinking of such nonsense, or she would be crazy," — never knowing that he was himself the cause of all these horrors of the night. Often she dreamed of following to the grave the body of her mother, as she had done that of her sister, and woke to find the pillow drenched in tears. These dreams softened her heart too much and cast a deep shadow over her young days; for then, and later, the life of dreams — probably because there was in it less to distract the mind from its own earnestness — has often seemed to her more real, and been remembered with more interest, than that of waking hours.

Poor child! Far remote in time, in thought, from that period, I look back on these glooms and terrors, wherein I was enveloped, and perceived that I had no natural childhood. [4]

Dreaming and somnambulism stayed with Fuller until about the age of twelve. "But little notice was taken of it...I thought other children felt the same for I knew they generally dreaded going to bed and Mother seemed ashamed of my sleepwalking and I had an idea something ridiculous was attached to it. I was twice found in convulsions in consequence of dreadful dreams."

> In Latin...I was trained to quite a high degree of precision. I was expected to understand the mechanism of the language thoroughly, and in translating to give the thoughts in as few well-arranged words as possible, and without breaks or hesitation — for with these my father had absolutely no patience.
>
> Indeed, he demanded accuracy and clearness in everything: you must not speak, unless you can make your meaning perfectly intelligible to the person addressed; must not express a thought unless you can give a reason for it, if required; must not make a statement, unless sure of all particulars — such were his rules. "But," "if," "unless," "I am mistaken," and "it may be so," were words and phrases excluded from the province where he held sway....He had no belief in minds that listen, wait, and receive. He had no conception of the subtle and indirect motions of imagination and feeling. His influence on me was great, and opposed to the natural unfolding of my character, which was fervent, of strong grasp and disposed to infatuation, and self-forgetfulness.... I did not go mad, as many would do, at being continually roused from my dreams. I had too much strength to be crushed....My own world sank deep within, away from the surface of my life; in what I did and said I learned to have reference to other minds. But my true life was only the dearer that it was secluded and veiled over by a thick curtain of available intellect, and that coarse, but wearable stuff woven by the ages — Common Sense. [5]

Domestic responsibilities deceased; singing and piano lessons were added. Her greatest admiration was for the great Romans:

> ...whose thoughts and lives were my daily food...The genius of Rome displayed itself in Character...Who, that has lived with those men, but admires the plain force of fact, of thought passed into action?...Everything turns your attention to what a man can become,

> not by yielding himself freely to impressions, not by letting nature play freely through him, but by a single thought, an earnest purpose, an indomitable will, by hardihood, self-command, and force of expression...Man, present in nature, commanding nature too sternly to be inspired by it, standing like the rock amid the sea, or moving like the fire over the land, either impassive, or irresistible; knowing not the soft mediums or fine flights of life, but by the force which he expresses...It is degeneracy for a Roman to use the pen; his life was in the day....
>
> I steadily loved this ideal in my childhood and this is the cause probably, why I have always felt that man must know how to stand firm on the ground, before he can fly. In vain for me are men more, if they are less, than Romans....
>
> Reading became a habit and a passion.... I thought with rapture of the all-accomplished him of the many talents, wide resources, clear sight, and omnipotent will. A Caesar seemed great enough. I did not then know that such men impoverish the treasury to build the palace. I kept their statues as belonging to the hall of my ancestors, and loved to conquer obstacles, and fed my youth and strength for their sake. [6]

Timothy was only pressuring with the kind of education any advantaged boy would receive if he were being groomed to enter Harvard where examinations were taken between the ages of thirteen through sixteen.* For instance, Frederic Henry Hedge had memorized Virgil by seven, had read half of all Latin literature by eleven and therefore qualified to enter Harvard. Henry David Thoreau entered at sixteen while Edward Everett graduated at that age. (Not Emerson.)

---

* Youngsters born to poor families commonly had no school at all because their families could not pay fees, and the prevailing attitude was that long years of schooling were not particularly necessary for a productive life. Conscientious parents who did not live in the proximity of the Boston Public Latin School — and especially those with more than one child — would set up their own school, along with one or two other families — and would share the teacher's salary. It was not until the 1830s and 1850s, with Boston and New England leading the way and serving as model, that public education was organized with a system of elementary and high school divisions, with teacher training, and truancy laws.

Sometimes Sarah Margaret Fuller played outdoor games with Cambridgeport youngsters, but the neighborhood children found her different, remote. She had that strange habit of half-closing her eyes (probably because she was nearsighted).

Playing by herself, she developed a great game in which she imagined herself an orphan left on a doorstep, or a European princess stolen away at birth. Other times she would be a queen, or "The Duchess of Marlborough." If her younger brother were with her, (William Henry had also been welcomed into the family), he would be "The Prince of Savoy" or a king. Sometimes, alone, she would talk to the flowers in her mother's garden. To them she could divulge her feelings.

Fuller later wrote:

> My mother was in delicate health, and much absorbed in the care of her younger children. In the house was neither dog nor bird, nor any graceful animated form of existence. I saw no persons who took my fancy, and real life offered no attraction. Thus, my already over-excited mind found no relief from without, and was driven for refuge from itself to the world of books.... [7]

Upstairs in her Papa's closet were copies of Smollett, Fielding, Molière, and Cervantes, but she was allowed to take these books off the shelves only when the daily lesson was completed.

She attended the Unitarian church, but more often than not fell dozing during the dulling sermon. Much of what she saw at church seemed superficial. One Sunday Sarah Margaret's attention was drawn to an older woman:

> ...a face most fair, and well-known as it seemed at first glance — for surely I had met her before and waited for her long. But soon I saw that she was a new apparition foreign to that scene, if not to me. Her dress — the arrangement of her hair, which had the graceful pliancy of races highly cultivated for long — the intelligent and full picture of her eye, whose reserve was in its self-possession, not in timidity — all combined to make up a whole impression, which, though too young to understand, I was well prepared to feel.

> She was an English lady, who, by a singular chance, was cast upon this region for a few months. Elegant and captivating, her every look and gesture was tuned to a different pitch from anything I had ever known. She was in various ways accomplished, as it is called, though to what degree I cannot now judge. [8]

The impressionable seven year-old projected onto Ellen Kilshaw, daughter of a wealthy Liverpool manufacturer, John Kilshaw, all the unarticulated, imaginative longings that had surged within her: "I saw in her the storied castles, the fair stately parks and the wind laden with tones from the past, which I desired to know."

Timothy and Margaret approved the relationship. They liked Ellen Kilshaw and felt she would serve as the needed positive role model of feminine grace, and apparently she did. In turn, Ellen seemed to be fascinated by this gifted girl who could speak with such a grown up vocabulary on so many subjects, yet who was childish and immature. They went on long walks together, and Sarah Margaret happily watched her paint pictures and listened to her play the harp.

This is the same year Sarah Margaret asked to drop the "Sarah." She said it was "an old maid's name." "I will not be content to be called by it till I am sixty years old." Then "I will knit stockings look cross and be called Miss Sarah Margaret Fuller for the rest of my life." Timothy was not supportive. But Ellen was.

Then a premonition came upon her. Ellen, "first angel of my life," would return to England and Margaret would be left alone once again. And this happened: "My English friend went across the sea. She passed into her former life and into ties that engrossed her days...I fell into a profound depression...I knew not how to exert myself, but lay bound hand and foot. Melancholy enfolded me in an atmosphere as joy had done.... We wrote to one another for many years; — her shallow and delicate epistles did not disenchant me."* [9]

---

*In England Ellen Kilshaw's father suffered financial reverses; she considered a marriage proposal that was loveless, but the gentleman's relative thwarted the relationship. Kilshaw was forced to accept a position as governness in Ireland. Later, she married and had children and wrote to the Fullers that she had grown fat. Mrs. Fuller named her next daughter after her, Ellen, born in 1820.

Margaret was not to be consoled. Headaches resumed; lethargy developed. "'I am to blame,' said my father, 'in keeping her at home so long, merely to please myself. She needs to be with other girls, needs play and variety. She does not seem to me really sick, but dull rather. I see she grows thin. She ought to change the scene.'"

> I was indeed dull. The books, the garden, had lost all charm. I had the excuse of headache, constantly, for not attending to my lessons...All joy seemed to have departed with my friend, and the emptiness of our house stood revealed...I avoided the table as much as possible, took long walks and lay in bed, or on the floor of my room. I complained of my head, and it was not wrong to do so, for a sense of dullness and suffocation, if not pain, was there constantly.
>
> But when it was proposed that I should go to school, that was a remedy I could not listen to with patience for a moment. The peculiarity of my education had separated me entirely from the girls around, except that when they were playing at active games, I would sometimes go out and join them. I liked violent bodily exercise, which always relieved my nerves. But I had no success in associating with them beyond the mere play. Not only I was not their school-mate, but my book-life and lonely habits had given a cold aloofness to my whole expression, and veiled my manner with a hauteur which turned all hearts away. Yet, as this reserve was superficial, and rather ignorance than arrogance, it produced no deep dislike. Besides, the girls supposed me really superior to themselves, and did not hate me for feeling it, but neither did they like me, nor wish to have me with them. Indeed, I had gradually given up all such wishes myself; for they seemed to me rude, tiresome, and childish, as I did to them dull and strange. This experience had been earlier, before I was admitted to any real friendship; but now that I had been lifted into the life of mature years, and into just that atmosphere of European life to which I had before been tending, the thought of sending me to school filled me with disgust.
>
> Yet what could I tell my father of such feelings? [10]

She withdrew further into the world of reading. The lyric poetry of Goldsmith, Cowper, Thompson and Gray, and Scott were always available. Discouraged were novels and narrative poetry but sometimes she could read them — but never on Sunday. Unitarians still observed the Sabbath with church services and Bible reading. One Sunday she dared to read the forbidden Shakespeare:

> This Sunday — I was only eight years old — I took from the bookshelf a volume lettered Shakespeare...I held in my hand *Romeo and Juliet* long enough to get my eye fastened to the page. It was a cold winter afternoon. I took the book to the parlor fire, and had there been seated an hour or two, when my father looked up and asked what I was reading so intently. "Shakespeare," replied the child, merely raising her eye from the page. "Shakespeare — that won't do; that's no book for Sunday; go put it away and take another." I went as I was bid, but took no other. Returning to my seat, the unfinished story, the personages to whom I was but just introduced thronged and burnt my brain. I could not bear it long; such a lure was impossible to resist. I went and brought the book again. There were several guests present, and I had got half through the play before I again attracted attention. "What is that child about that she don't hear a word that's said to her?" quoth my aunt. "What are you reading?" said my father. "Shakespeare," was again the reply, in a clear, though somewhat impatient, tone. "How?" said my father angrily — then restraining himself before his — "Give me the book and go directly to bed." [11]

Looking back at the age of thirty, Margaret Fuller wrote:

> It will be seen that my youth was not unfriended, since those great minds came to me in kindness. A moment of action in one's self, however, is worth an age of apprehension through others; not that our deeds are better, but that they produce a renewal of our being...They (the books) did me good, for by them a standard was early given of sight and thought, from which I could never go back...They did me harm, too, for the child fed with meat instead of milk becomes too soon mature...Certainly I do not wish that instead of these masters I had read baby books, written down to children...but I do wish that I had read no books at all till later — that I had lived with toys, and played in the open air. Children should not cull the fruits of reflection and observation early, but expand in the sun, and let thoughts come to them...With me, much of life was devoured in the bud. [12]

The eight year-old searched everywhere for a friend, like the strong Roman or Shakespeare figures of her imagination:

> The puny child sought everywhere for the Roman or Shakespeare figures, and she was met by the shrewd, honest eye, the homely decency, or the smartness of a New England village on Sunday. There was beauty, but I could not see it then; it was not of the kind I longed for. [13]

The precocious young girl steadily felt a growing awareness of mysterious spiritual forces and fates beyond her control. Her headaches, somnambulism and nightmares continued, and the stories of Roman and Greek gods and goddesses filled her imagination. Gazing into the lights of her ruby ring was fascinating; she saw never-ending depths transporting her into unexplored spheres.

When Margaret was eight, Timothy was off to Washington D. C. to serve a term as Congressman. The family went to Canton to stay the winter with Mrs. Fuller's parents and sisters. Pressure for rigid study was off Margaret, even though Timothy tried via mail to direct progress and correct faults.

Sprouting upwards, her most persistent question this year was: "Whether my manners ought to increase with my growth or with my years." She wrote her father: "Mama says people will judge of me according to my growth. I do not think this is just for surely our knowledge does not increase because we are tall."

(This season he had the idea [never activated] of buying Margaret a drum which, strapped around her shoulders, she could beat for awhile and thereby improve her posture.)

In the spring when Congress was over, the Fullers returned to Cambridgeport and nine year-old Margaret, who was reaching the height of a thirteen year-old (almost five feet two inches) and who was still plagued with headaches and somnambulism, was enrolled in the Port School in Cambridge.* Also, she studied Greek with her Uncle

---

*The Cambridge Port Private Grammar School was a private institution with a good reputation to which the well-to-do in Cambridge sent their children and in which Timothy Fuller held some influence due to his political stature and connections.

Elisha, Timothy's keenly perceptive and vivaciously witty youngest brother, newly graduated from Harvard, who was a Unitarian minister and was later to become a lawyer. She also studied music and penmanship with other tutors. She translated Oliver Goldsmith's poem, "The Deserted Village," into Latin.

Her schoolmate, Oliver Wendell Holmes, remembered her:

> Her air to her schoolmates was marked by a certain stateliness and distance, as if she had other thoughts than theirs and was not of them...was tall, fair complexioned, with a watery, aqua-marine luster in her light eyes, which she used to make small, as one does who looks at the sunshine. A remarkable point about her was that long, flexile neck, arching and undulating in strange sinuous movements, which one who loved her would compare to those of a swan, and one who loved her not to those of the ophidian who tempted our common mother. Her talk was affluent, magisterial, *de haut en bas*, some would say euphuistic, but surpassing the talk of women in breadth and audacity. Her face kindled and reddened and dilated in every feature as she spoke and, once I saw her in a fine storm of indignation at the supposed ill-treatment of a relative, showed itself capable of something resembling what Milton calls the viraginian aspect. [14]

He told the story that at school she had once belittled the opening of a theme with the exclamation, "It is a trite remark!" Since Holmes did not know the meaning of the word "trite," he was chagrinned with his inferiority. "How could I ever judge Margaret fairly after such a crushing discovery of her superiority?"

Timothy controlled his daughter's existence. She had friends her own age such as Elizabeth Randall, Harriet Fay and Amelia Greenwood, but if she had an invitation, he would decide if she should accept, what she should wear. If she wanted friends to come to her home, he made out the list and was there to receive them. Her mother stayed in the background.

When Margaret asked her father to correct her Latin translation of The Lord's Prayer, he responded: "I would not discourage you, my girl, by being too critical and yet I am anxious to have you admit to one fault, which you will remember I have often mentioned, as the source, the very fountain of others — carelessness."

She begged her father to let her read Mrs. Ross's *Hesitation: or, To Marry, or Not to Marry?* But her father commented that she should acquire a taste for books of higher order. Margaret argued that novels were not trifling or silly, there was good reasoning in them. A person was "illiberal who condemns Sir Walter Scott's and (Maria) Edgeworth's novels."

When Congressman Timothy returned to Washington in the fall of 1821, his wife went with him. The new baby sister, Ellen, and the other children returned to Canton. Eleven year-old Margaret went to Boston to attend Dr. Park's school. She stayed at the home of her distinguished Uncle Henry, her father's brother and law partner who'd won second honors at Harvard and who had a reputation for creating entertaining courtroom scenes of ridicule and satire. A sparkling conversationalist, he not only wore old-fashioned clothes, but habitually wore his beaver hat with the fur brushed the wrong way.

The progressive curriculum at Dr. Park's school included French, Latin, Italian, composition, ancient and modern history, arithmetic, geometry, trigonometry, natural history, and geography. This level of study was elementary for Margaret. Right away she stole top honors from the daughter of the eminent Channing.

She talked like a book. She wasn't pretty. Susan's brother, William Henry Channing, remembered her as a girl who "was a butt for the ridicule of frivolous companions." From time to time he saw her at various events as "plain" but "dashing." She was always in the center of a listening group, being witty, but he shunned to meet "one so armed from head to foot in saucy sprightliness."

Subtle changes occured when her parents gave permission for her to take dancing lessons which she enjoyed. Up to this time she had been encouraged to learn facts, to speak boldly in generalities and abstractions, to be accurate, to compete and win. Now, the exact opposite message would begin to hone in: be sociable, mannerly, modest, prepare for marriage.

In March during a brief break in school she went to Canton with family. Her siblings had contracted the measles and her mother had had to leave Washington D. C. In a letter to her father Margaret noted that brother William Henry was not at the head of his class: "I am glad

I have not little children to teach, 'tis in my opinion a disagreeable occupation to repeat twenty times to a stupid child A B C and at last not to have him remember it in all probability."

Never would she write to her father about her headaches and sonnambulism. Her latest resolve was to be ugly and brilliant.

In December 1822 Timothy pulled his twelve year-old out of Dr. Park's school. She stayed at home in Cambridgeport, helped with household and new baby, Arthur, and studied on her own. She complained about weak eyes, but this didn't stop her from reading her father's speeches — he'd just spoken on the floor of the House supporting a bill that would provide enough ships to suppress piracy in the Gulf of Mexico; also she was reading Washington Irving's *Bracebridge Hall: or, the Humorists*, Adam Smith's *An Inquiry into the Nature and Causes of the Wealth of Nations*, and was asking her father for Bacon's *Essays* and William Paley's *Natural Theology*. She was most anxious to begin a study of ethics.

All the while she was making awkward attempts at socializing. She loved cotillions and balls, and asserted herself wholeheartedly. Frederic Henry Hedge, a scholarly student at Harvard who had read Kant in the original, met her at about this age:

> ...so precocious in her mental and physical developments, that she passed for eighteen or twenty...as a lady full-grown...a blooming girl of a florid complexion and vigorous health, with a tendency to robustness of which she was painfully conscious....With no pretensions to beauty then, or at any time, her face was one that attracted, that awakened a lively interest, that made one desirous of a nearer acquaintance. It was a face that fascinated, without satisfying....You saw the evidence of a mighty force, but what direction that force would assume — whether it would determine itself to social triumphs, or to triumphs of art — it was impossible to divine...She seemed equal to anything, but might not choose to put forth her strength.... She escaped the reproach of positive plainness, by her blond and abundant hair, by her excellent teeth, by her sparkling, dancing, busy eyes, which, though usually half closed from near-sightedness, shot piercing glances at those with whom she conversed, and, most of all, by the very peculiar and graceful carriage of her head and neck, which all who knew her will remember as the most characteristic trait in her personal appearance. [15]

Her face was a cause of consternation. She contracted what she called "a determination of blood to the head. My father attributed it to my overheating myself, my mother to an unfortunate cold. Both were much mortified to see the fineness of my complexion destroyed. My own vanity was for a time severely wounded...My father...was always scolding me for getting my forehead so red when excited..."

This "very painful flush" stayed with her until her twenty-first year. Her hautiness and sarcasm were regarded by some people as negatives. Yet she would tell the truth regardless of consequence — a habit which some people regarded as a negative.

She loved mimicry and repartee and managed to attract those around her, managed at parties to dance with all the bright young Harvard men (including Ralph Waldo Emerson's brother, Edward Bliss), but her behavior was so deviant from the norm that her parents seriously considered keeping her more often at home.

Thirteen years old, she was begging for tutors. To her father, who had asked from Washington D.C. if she continued her study of Greek: "I do study it, but I could go much faster and with far greater ease if I had the aid of an instructor." She was learning a portion of Tacitus every day and writing a translation of Cicero.

She wanted to go to a school she'd heard was operated and taught by the Emerson brothers, Ralph Waldo and William. But Timothy Fuller preferred that his daughter be under the feminine influence of Miss Prescott in Groton. Timothy wanted his daughter to conform, to be like the women he revered, the woman he married, modest, unassuming.

Margaret countered, "I should very much prefer going to Mr. Emerson's on every account and if I go to Miss Prescott's I must be compelled to give up seeing you at all."

Timothy responded: "...a few months with a judicious country lady, who will be free & faithful in watching and correcting your faults...." He closed another letter: "Depend upon my undiminished affection, as long as you continue dutiful."

In the spring of 1824 Margaret Fuller became one of forty students at the Prescott boarding school, situated in rolling apple country where Timothy had grown up. After she settled in, she received word that her mother had given birth to her seventh child.* Fuller wrote home: "I hardly think he will rival my pet Arthur in my affections. As to a name for him, I like Frank best, Frederick next, and I wish he might have three names." The baby was named Richard Frederick and he became her favorite brother.

Not one subject challenged Fuller. Studies included reading, writing, orthography, arithmetic, grammar, geography, rhetoric, French, embroidery, history. "I feel myself rather degraded from Cicero's Oratory to One and two are how many," she wrote her father. Wouldn't he send copies of Milton's *Paradise Lost*, Levi Hedge's *Elements of Logic*, the Bible and newspapers.

There was trauma in trying to express warmth to girls she could hardly admire — Timothy had admonished that belief in the worth of schoolmates was basic to success.

On one undated paper, she wrote: "I was now in the hands of teachers who had not, since they came on earth, put to themselves one intelligent question as to their business there."

Teachers hurt students because they held that the object of study was "exercise of memory." In her opinion, education was not memorization. "I had known great living minds," she wrote at the tender age of fourteen. "I had seen how they took their food and did their exercise, and what their objects were. *Very early I knew that the only object in life was to grow.*"[16]

Years later she wrote a fictional account of what she might have gone through. The lead character in her story was a beautiful, rebellious girl who roughed her cheeks and drew attention to herself one evening by dancing dizzily in a fancy dress and by reciting wierd poetry. Schoolmates, to humiliate her, staged a scene at the dinner table — all had brightly roughed their cheeks in mockery. Coming to dinner late, the girl instantly was mortified, but somehow managed to keep her decorum. Afterwards, in the privacy of her room, she collapsed. The sensitive school matron found her crying in her room and comforted her by telling her how she'd once been humiliated, and had learned to deal with other people by anticipating their

* Fuller now had five younger siblings, Eugene, William Henry, Arthur, Ellen, Richard. One child had died at the age of one.

needs. How much of this story was autobiographical is not known, but Margaret returned home from the Prescott school matured, adoring Miss Prescott who was "gold without alloy."

Margaret, turning fifteen in the spring of 1825, had completed formal schooling.* Her male friends, who were planning professional lives, went on to Harvard. No high schools or colleges were open to women. Female friends lived with parents and awaited marriage.

Margaret Fuller settled back into the yellow Cambridgeport house. Her father was now Speaker of the Massachusetts House of Representatives and a member of the Executive Board. She set up her own daily routine of self-education and she confided her hopes and ambition to her beloved teacher, Miss Prescott:

> I rise a little before five, walk an hour, and then practice on the piano until seven, when we breakfast. Next, I read French — Sismondi's Literature of the South of Europe — till eight, then two or three lectures in Brown's Philosophy. About half-past nine I go to Mr. Perkins' school and study Greek until twelve, when, the school being dismissed, I recite, go home, and practice again until dinner, at two. Sometimes, if the conversation is very agreeable, I lounge for half an hour over the dessert, though rarely so lavish of time. Then, when I can, I read two hours in Italian, but I am often interrupted. At six I walk or take a drive. Before going to bed I play or sing for half an hour or so, to make all sleepy, and about eleven, retire to write a while in my journal, exercises on what I have read, or a series of characteristics which I am filling up according to advice. Thus, you see, I am learning Greek, and making acquaintance with metaphysics, French and Italian literature.

---

* In 1821, when Fuller was eleven, Emma Willard was enabled to open the Troy Female Seminary in Troy, N. Y. But evidently Timothy Fuller never heard of it, or he considered the distance a problem. (Later Elizabeth Cady Stanton attended this school.) Fuller was into her twenties when the first women's colleges began to open throughout the 1830s: Oberon, Mt. Holyoke, Ipswich Female Seminary, Bradford Academy, Abbot Female Academy at Andover, Wheaton Female Seminary and Maplewood Institute in Pittsfield, Mass. Willard believed in the study of higher mathematics, and in 1829 the first public examination of a girl in geometry caused a public outcry and storm of ridicule. In 1845 Willard promoted women as superintendents of public schools and teacher training in normal schools, thus Emma Willard was to carry out the cause Fuller envisioned and almost espoused when she taught in The Greene Street School.

> "How," you will say, "can I believe that my indolent, fanciful pleasure-loving pupil, perseveres in such a course?" I feel the power of industry growing every day, and, besides the all-powerful motive of ambition, and a new stimulus lately given through a friend. I have learned to believe that nothing, no! not perfection, is unattainable. I am determined on distinction, which formerly I thought to win at an easy rate; but now I see that long years of labor must be given to secure even the *"succes de societé"* — which however shall never content me. I see multitudes of examples of persons of genius, utterly deficient in grace and the power of pleasurable excitement. I wish to combine both. I know the obstacles in my way. I am wanting in that intuitive tact and polish, which nature has bestowed upon some, but which I must acquire. And, on the other hand, my powers of intellect, though sufficient, I suppose, are not well disciplined. Yet all such hindrances may be overcome by an ardent spirit. If I fail, my consolation shall be found in active employment. [17]

For Margaret the ideal man was still the Roman hero of nobility... a strong, disciplined realist who decisively met challenge and took bold action.

She also searched for ideal women. For at least a few hours, she treasured every word of Thomas Wentworth Higginson's mother. Then there was Higginson's aunt, Miss Ann G. Storrow, who was witty and brilliant; and there was Mrs. J. W. Webster, a well-manered charismatic person.

These women were busy with their own interests, but one, a successful novelist and editor eight years her senior, had time for her. Lydia Maria Francis, famous at the age of twenty three for her children's books, *Hobomok* and *The Rebels*, was a rarity, successful in her personal life and in her writing. She had a Yankee dry humor, a pure mind and was, as Margaret was to state, "a natural person — a most rare thing in this age of cant and pretension."

Francis had spent many of her growing up years isolated in a rural section of Maine, where her brother, encyclopedia-of-information Convers Francis, was minister of First Parish. Her brother's collection of books had saved her from loneliness; reading them she wondered why she couldn't write a novel.

She'd taught school in Gardiner, Maine and then returned to Watertown, Massachusetts, to open up her own private school. She and Fuller had common interests.

Together they read the work of a French novelist who'd been equated "harlot."* No longer living, Madame de Staël had stood against the onslaught of rumor for her unprecedented stories about women. Further, she advocated equality for women. Even Napoleon (who was thwarted in his love for her) had circulated ridiculous stories about her. (Finally, he exiled her from Paris.)

Francis and Fuller read *Corinne* and *Delphine*, both of which described highly gifted women; also they enjoyed *De l'Allemagne*.

"Had you rather been the brilliant de Staël or the useful (Maria) Edgeworth?" Fuller queried Miss Prescott.

Maria Edgeworth was a popular Irish novelist who also offered proof that women could achieve on a level of equality with men.

Fuller has often been compared to de Staël's fictional heroine "Corinne", a poet accorded the highest of acclaim, whose orations were awaited with anticipation in Rome. Parades were staged in her honor; she was crowned with laurels. Searching for love, she met a Scottish nobleman, "Oswald Nelvil," a man of average talent and sensitivity, not an intellectual equal. "Corinne" was faced with a decision that men are never forced to make. Should she give up her work and successful life in Rome for a love which would transfer her into sterile, rural Scotland? After much indecision, "Corinne" decided on love with "Nelvil" in Scotland, but by this time, he had married another woman, her half-sister, an ungifted domestic-type. In shock and bitterness, "Corinne" died of a broken heart.

The same questions "Corinne" faced obviously burned in the minds of Margaret Fuller and Lydia Maria Francis.

In 1826 Timothy moved his family to the Dana mansion, built by Judge Francis Dana in 1785, a lovely old-fashioned house crowning the hill which separated Old Cambridge from Cambridgeport. Set back from the road to Boston and overlooking Harvard and the Charles River, it commanded acres of landscaped grounds. Here was a fitting residence for a dinner and ball for honored guest, President John Quincy Adams, whom Timothy actively supported for a second term. He had high hopes his reward would be an ambassadorship.

*Ten years later Lydia Maria Francis Child wrote a biography of de Staël.

Costly and elaborate, it was the grandest ball Cambridge had seen in years. It is recorded that sixteen year-old Margaret was so tightly laced into a low-necked pink silk dress — in order to hide her stoutness — that she had to hold her arms back as if they were pinioned. Her hair was curled all over her head. She danced quadrilles awkwardly. Despite this she danced merrily most of the night. Unfortunately for Timothy, the evening turned out to be a fiasco because John Quincy Adams left immediately following dinner.

Margaret, though, was finding friends, mixing in. Her wit and sarcasm began to command attention. People could not help but respect her knowledge, even though her erudite manner might turn them off at first. Her faithfulness to the truth was evident, and underneath the arrogance they discovered an appealing warm, sympathetic young woman. She also had a listening ear. In her it was easy to confide thoughts and feelings.

Margaret still devoted hours to studying and reading. "I have not had my mind so exercised for months," she wrote Miss Prescott as she happily raced through the works of Sir William Temple, an English author, and John Russell's *A Tour in Germany and Some of the Southern Provinces of the Austrian Empire.* She was also reading Epictetus, Milton, Racine, and Castilian ballads, and the elder Italian poets, Berni, Pulci, and Politian. She spent "a luxurious afternoon, having been in bed from dinner till tea, reading Rammohun Roy's book," *The Precepts of Jesus, the Guide to Peace and Happiness.* (Roy was a Brahmin from Bengal who converted to Christianity.)

"I have felt a gladiatorial disposition lately, and don't enjoy mere light conversation," she wrote Miss Prescott, adding that "an agreeable book to read at night just before you go to bed" was one containing the letters and reflections of Prince de Ligne.

Fuller's routine included helping her mother with the house and younger children, writing journals and fiction — even poetry, which she composed "merely as vents for the overflowings of a personal experience." She entered with new enthusiasm and energy into the Cambridge circle of young men and women, which included members of the 1829 Harvard class, famous for graduates who became prominent.

Eliza Farrar appeared like a fairy godmother. Born in England, Eliza Farrar was married to a Harvard professor of astronomy. She was planning to write a book of etiquette for young women, to be entitled *The Young Lady's Friend*, which would be published in1836. In Margaret she probably saw a challenge, the Cinderella touch.

Eliza Farrar changed Margaret's hairdresser; she combed away the tight curls and chose a simple smooth style, parted in the middle. She guided a weight loss program, and showed her how to carry herself with grace. She found a new seamstress and created a new wardrobe that enhanced; she taught Fuller a sense of fashion and taste. She took her visiting. Farrar also counseled psychologically, helped her work through the double gender identity messages. And she brought onto the scene to be friend, mentor and model, her Quaker niece, Anna Barker, from New Orleans.

Anna Barker was the daughter of a prominent and wealthy businessman, Jacob Barker, who owned homes in New Orleans, New York, Boston, and Newport. Having grown up with the best that money could offer, Anna was extraordinarily beautiful and comfortable in the social amenities. She and Margaret went visiting together, to parties, they shared clothes, books, ideas.

Soon Margaret was operating rather smoothly in the social scene, but beauty was another matter. She never overcame the feeling that she was ugly. And the men confirmed her feeling. In the one youthful picture that exists of Fuller today, she does not seem unattractive. Yet she developed her defensive "cover-ups."

On her eighteenth birthday, her brother Edward was born. The family said Edward had to be Margaret's, due to the coincidence of the birth. She adored him. Sixteen months later, after she'd cared for him day and night during a severe illness, he died in her arms.

After the grieving period, Fuller and Anna Barker entered with new enthusiasm and energy into the Cambridge circle of young men and women. Marriage was the ultimate goal.

Though the young men had the privilege of sitting in Harvard classrooms, pursuits outside the curriculum occupied their time. Typically, the Harvard men amused themselves with tapping their feet against the chapel benches during morning prayers, with entertaining visitors in their rooms on the Sabbath with singing and wine, with hanging effigies in Harvard Yard, with going on duck hunting expeditions at dawn.

The college system awarded rank to those who delivered excellence in recitations, attended regularly, and observed good behavior. "But as the majority of the class soon found that they could not attain a high rank," the sanguine and good looking Harvard youth (Fuller's cousin) James Freeman Clarke wrote, "they ceased to try, and contented themselves with reciting well enough and behaving well enough to escape punishment. The assumption in those days was that young men's minds and hearts will not respond to generous motives, that they must be coerced, restrained, punished, and driven, not led by affection, by good-will, by the love of truth, by the desire for knowledge, by the ardor of attainment...They did not put their strength into college themes, but into articles for the 'Collegian.' They did not read Thucydides and Xenophon, but Maculay and Carlyle. We unearthed old tomes in the college library, and while our English professors were teaching us out of Blair's 'Rhetoric,' we were forming our taste by making copious extracts from Sir Thomas Browne, or Ben Jonson. Our real professors of rhetoric were Charles Lamb and Coleridge, Walter Scott and Wordsworth."

Conversation centered on freedom, destiny, progress, Kant, Fourier, Schiller, Lamb, Browne, Tieck, Körner, Novalis, Richter, Wordsworth, Coleridge and Carlyle and the young women in Cambridge.

Except for the last mentioned subject, these were areas in which Margaret Fuller could shine with the greatest of ease. Conversation was "that power of forcing the vital currents of thousands of human hearts into one current, by the constraining power of that most delicate instrument, the voice." If she were a man, she would prefer this skill of the voice over a more permanent influence.

Harvard student Frederic Henry Hedge described her ability:

> Her conversation, as it was then, I have seldom heard equalled. It was not so much attractive as commanding. Though remarkably fluent and select, it was neither fluency, nor choice diction, nor wit, nor sentiment, that gave it its peculiar power, but accuracy of statement, keen discrimination, and a certain weight of judgment, which contrasted strongly and charmingly with the youth and sex of the speaker. [18]

Hedge admired her sincerity. "Her judgments took no bribe from her sex or her sphere…Her yes and no were never conventional; and she often amazed people by a cool and unexpected dissent from the commonplaces of popular acceptation."

Light-hearted talk was just as appealing and she would launch with great gusto and gayness into entertaining descriptions of people she'd met, events she'd attended, experiences she'd had. Hedge said, "When she felt an interest, she awakened an interest." Her perception of character, sharp insight, her creative imagination, her dept of knowledge, her love of truth, plus her deep sense of humility, drew people to her.

Surely in all America there was one man for Margaret.

Intelligent and witty Lydia Maria Francis was not considered a beauty, but she had married David Lee Child, an 1817 graduate of Harvard, a lawyer with an office in Boston and they lived in a small house. Lydia was highly successful, editor of her own magazine, *Juvenile Miscellany*, the first major children's magazine in the country. The marriage seemed to be working. He told her that whatever she did was wise.

Among the men at Harvard, there was Frederic Henry Hedge, born to the Brahmin purple, son of Levi Hedge, Harvard professor of logic, finishing a four year stint in Divinity School, whose character can be revealed in the anecdote that upon being told that the facts were against him, replied, "so much the worse for the facts."

There was Oliver Wendell Holmes whose talent did not become known "till we were well through college," James Freeman Clarke wrote.

Cousin Clarke was "only thirty-seven degrees removed," Fuller declared. He was "a socialist by vocation, a sentimentalist by nature, and a Channingite from force of circumstances and fashion." Everyone associated Clarke with Havanna cigars and climbing and standing upright on seventy foot high masts.

Most attractive to Fuller was the charming and brilliant law student, George Davis, who had a prodigious memory and a penchant for humorous anecdotes and literary quotations. "His mirth unsettled all foundations," Fuller quipped. He could tear himself away from chess games and smoking circles to pay calls on a young woman whose mind was his match.

There was the thoughtful nephew of Dr. William Ellery Channing, William Henry Channing, who thought Fuller too intense, too imperious, affecting the part of a Yankee Corinna.

He typified those who felt intimidated by Margaret Fuller:

> At first, her vivacity, decisive tone, downrightness, and contempt of conventional standards, continued to repel. She appeared too intense in expression, action, emphasis, to be pleasing, and wanting in that *retenue* which we associate with delicate dignity. Then, again, there was an imperial — shall it be said imperious? — air, exacting deference to her judgments and loyalty to her behests, that prompted pride to retaliatory measures. She paid slight heed, moreover, to the trim palings of etiquette, but swept through the garden-beds and into the doorway of one's confidence so cavalierly, that a reserved person felt inclined to lock himself up in his sanctum. [19]

She inspired confidences from the young men. She knew these to be private, not-to-be-revealed confessions.

Friends, she thought, had the responsibility of telling the truth to one another, no matter how it might hurt. It was imperative to face faults and weaknesses. After that there could be genuine understanding. The friendship would be nobly strong, worthy to last a lifetime. She once wrote: "If I don't like what you say, let me say so. I have ever been frank as if I expected to be intimate with you good three-score years and ten. I am sure we shall always esteem each other. I have that much faith."

Once she wrote, "Undeserved regard could give me no pleasure; nor will I consent to practice charlatanism, either in friendship or anything else."

Introspective and self-conscious James Freeman Clarke could talk to her in detail about his loves and infatuations. To hear about a popular pretty blond who had a marvellous figure was quite a wrench to Fuller, especially since the girl, Elizabeth Randall, had been a close childhood friend whom she knew to be emotionally immature.

Together they walked amongst the lindens on the Fuller grounds, met at parties, rode horseback to Newton for tea with his grandparents, talked about their past lives, their struggles and conflicts, their hopes.

Clarke told her about the terrible inferior feelings that came upon him, especially as he tried to impress Elizabeth Randall — despite all his dynamic successes in climbing, gymnastics, football, baseball, fishing, fencing, hunting, and poetry. He could discuss his philosophical doubts and the universal questions of life and success that pained, plus the Transcendentalism that more and more intrigued.

To him she could be absolutely frank in exposing how she dealt with her inevitable feelings of superiority in relationships:

> Those who professed to seek my friendship, and whom, indeed, I have often truly loved, have always learned to content themselves with that inequality in the connection which I have never striven to veil. Indeed, I have thought myself more valued and better beloved, because the sympathy, the interest, were all on my side. True! such regard could never flatter my pride, nor gratify my affections, since it was paid not to myself, but to the need they had of me; still, it was dear and pleasing, as it has given me an opportunity of knowing and serving many lovely characters.[20]

It was Frederic Henry Hedge, whose father had sent him to Germany at the age of thirteen, who began to spread Goethe's reputation among the Harvard circle. He owned Goethe's books and lent them to Margaret Fuller and James Freeman Clarke so they could learn the language and read the masterpieces in the original German. Hedge was the kind of person who is remembered to have claimed you were stupid if you didn't understand the Germanic obscurity.

No woman read Goethe. Men did not read Goethe in America. Any man who did read Goethe might possibly be forgiven, especially if he was a clergyman or intellect who of forced necessity had to keep abreast of international literary currents. But a woman reader would immediately be branded with improprieties. Goethe may have been a great poet but he led an immoral life.

Many Americans who heard of him were appalled at stories of his open liaisons with the opposite sex and his luxurious life at Weimar. Americans saw him as dangerous, a sham, an opportunist, unpatriotic. His argument that new experience was beneficial was outrageous.

But James Freeman Clarke and Fuller felt that Goethe's philosophy and way of life was freeing and honest. Life and nature was an extension of the divine which was to be celebrated.

Within a year Fuller had absorbed much Goethe. His mind embraced the universe. His characters spoke to her. "He comprehends every feeling I have ever had so perfectly, expresses it so beautifully...."

Soon Fuller, who couldn't be admitted to Harvard because she was a woman, and Clarke, who was considered by his professors as a lazy who could do better if he would make an effort, set to work translating. Margaret translated Goethe's *Tasso* and Clarke concentrated on the first act of *Die Jungfraw von Orleans* and other pieces.

Faust was a work without parallel, an original in a class by itself. *Iphigenia* was unsurpassed in its own subject and style, while *Tasso,* somewhat inferior, revealed a poet's imagination and soul. The concept that in every man there was a dæmon who confused and limited a life was one Margaret Fuller could respond to. She had her own nagging dæmon.

At the age of twenty, she wittily summarized her accomplishments to her friend, Almira Barlow:

> I have neither fertilized the earth with my tears, edified its inhabitants by my delicacy of constitution, nor wakened its echoes to my harmony — yet some things have I achieved in my own soft, feminine style. I hate glare, thou knowest, and have hitherto successfully screened my virtues therefrom. I have made several garments fitted for the wear of American youth; I have written six letters and received a correspondent number; I have read one book — a piece of poetry entitled "Two Agonies," by M. A. Browne, (pretty caption, is it not?) and J. J. Knapp's trial; I have gained two friends, and recovered two; I have felt admiration four times — honor once, and disgust twice; I have been a journey, and shewed my penetration in discovering the beauties of Nature through a thick and never-lifted shroud of rain; I have turned two new leaves in the book of human nature; I have got a new pink bag (beautiful!). I have imposed on the world time and again, by describing your Lynn life as the perfection of human felicity, and adorning my visit there with all sorts of impossible adventure — thus at once exhibiting my own rich invention and the credulous ignorance of my

auditors (light and dark, you know, dear, give life to a picture). I have had tears for others' woes, and patience for my own — in short, to climax this journal of many-colored deeds and chances, so well have I played my part, that in the self-same night I was styled by two several persons "a sprightly young lady," and "a Syren!!" Oh rapturous sound! I have reached the goal of my ambition; Earth has nothing fairer or brighter to offer. "Intelligency" was nothing to it. A "supercilious," "satirical," "affected," "pedantic" "Syren"!!!! Can the olla-podrida of human nature present a compound of more varied ingredients, or higher gusto? [21]

When most of her women friends were readying their hope chests, Fuller was claiming that what America needed was a genius, a leader, and she envisioned this person being male. To the man who was writing poetry in the style of Goethe to her, James Freeman Clarke:

I have greatly wished to see among us such a person of genius as the nineteenth century can afford — i.e., one who has tasted in the morning of existence the extremes of good and ill, both imaginative and real. I had imagined a person endowed by nature with that actute sense of Beauty, (i.e., Harmony or Truth,) and that vast capacity of desire, which give soul to love and ambition. I had wished this person might grow up to manhood alone (but not alone in crowds); I would have placed him in a situation so retired, so obscure, that he would quietly, but without bitter sense of isolation, stand apart from all surrounding him. I would have had him go on steadily, feeding his mind with congenial love, hopefully confident that if he only nourished his existence into perfect life, Fate would, at fitting season, furnish an atmosphere and orbit meet for his breathing and exercise. I wished he might adore, not fever for, the bright phantoms of his mind's creation, and believe them but the shadows of external things to be met with hereafter. After this steady intellectual growth had brought his powers to manhood, so far as the ideal can do it, I wished this being might be launched into the world of realities, his heart glowing with the ardor of an immortal toward perfection, his eyes searching everywhere to behold it; I wished he might collect into one burning point those withering, palsying convictions, which, in the ordinary routine of things, so gradually pervade the soul; that he might suffer, in brief space, agonies of disappointment commensurate with his unpreparedness and confidence. And I thought, thus

> thrown back on the representing pictorial resources I supposed him originally to possess, with such material, and the need he must feel of using it, such a man would suddenly dilate into a form of Pride, Power, and Glory — a centre, round which asking, aimless hearts might rally — a man fitted to act as interpreter to the one tale of many-languaged eyes!
>
> What words are these! [22]

It was no ordinary man Margaret Fuller searched for.

The nagging inside Fuller was not exonerated when James Freeman Clarke tenderly confided in her that the woman he'd marry would be a silent, listening person, a "loved and loving one, twining her arms about me and gazing in my face with eyes full of passion and dependence."

But then there was fun-loving George Davis. He paid enough calls to the Dana mansion so that Fuller considered him a serious suitor. Wasn't the relationship deepening into love?

Fuller imagined her relationship with Anna Barker was such as Mme. de Staël had for Mme. Récamier, which had been a twenty year poetic loving friendship between two celebrated women that transcended gender and endured through work, separation, marriage, love affairs.

De Staël was the eldest, the most intelligent, the best conversationalist, the most dominant and aggressive, the most active, the mother, the worshiper. The charming Mme. Récamier was the beautiful, the feminine, the coquette, the receiver.

Margaret thought of herself as having within herself the power of a woman like de Staël. She had chosen the carbuncle as her own. In her projection she saw in the lights of this gem two sexes, the masculine which had its own light and the feminine which reflected light. Hers, she wrote, was the masculine.

Strong female friendships were common in nineteenth century America, and were encouraged. Female bonding, peer relationships, fulfilled an empty void in the lives of most women. Men were expected to compete and win in the harsh hierarchal system of urbanization and capitalism. They were not expected to express themselves emotionally or to be especially sensitive to women and their feelings, or to treat them equally. Women's "sphere" was so narrow and called for so many adjustments and sacrifices that women turned to each other and found the warmth and understanding they needed. They built a support network that they could never find in relationships with men.

Men seemed never to be able to really understand or want to listen to the feelings, sorrows, anxieties, pains and subtleties of women's experiences. Male friends did not return the favor of listening and nurturing. A close female would respond, share, empathize. A woman would not treat another woman friend as an inferior.

In a much later diary Fuller privately admitted to the depth of intimacy in her friendship with Barker. After being enchanted by the beauty of Mme. Récamier in a large engraving, she wrote in her 1842 journal:

> I have so often thought over the intimacy between (Mme. Récamier) and Mme. de Staël. It is so true that a woman may be in love with a woman, and a man with a man. It is so pleasant to be sure of it because undoubtedly it is the same love that we shall feel when we are angels when we ascend to the only fit place for the Mignon's where —
>
> "zie fragen nicht nach Mann und Weib"*
>
> It is regulated by the same law as that of love between persons of different sexes, only it is purely intellectual and spiritual, unprofaned by any mixture of lower instincts, undisturbed by any need of consulting temporal interests. Its law is the divine of the spirit to realize a whole which makes it seem in another being for what it finds not in itself. Thus the beautiful seeks the strong, and the strong the beautiful, the mate seeks the eloquent and the butterfly settles always on the dark flower. Why did Socrates love Alcibiades? Why did Horner love Schneider? How natural is the love of Wallenstein for Mase, that of Mme. de Staël for de Récamier, mine for Anna Barker.

---

*A quote from Goethe meaning: It is not a question of man or woman.

> I loved (Anna Barker) for a time with as much passion as I was then strong enough to feel. Her face was always gleaming before me, her voice was echoing in my ear, all poetic thoughts clustered round the dear image. This love was for me a key which unlocked many a treasure which I still possess; it was the carbuncle (emblematic gem!) which cast light into many of the darkest corners of human nature. She loved me, too, though not so much, because her nature was "less high, less grave, less large, less deep"; but she loved more tenderly, less passionately. She loved me, for I well remember her suffering when she first could feel my faults, and knew one part of the exquisite veil rent away, how she wished to stay apart and weep the whole day. Then again that night when she leaned on me and her eyes were a deep violet blue, so like night, as they never were before, and we both felt such a strange mystic thrill and knew what we had never known before. No being but myself would understand it. I do not love her now with passion, for I have exhausted her idea & she does not stimulate my fancy — she does not represent the beautiful to me now — she is only one beautiful object. Then, she has never had a chance to get a hold on my heart by the thousand links of intimacy, — we have been so little together, all was from the elective affinities. But still I love her with a sort of pallid, tender romance, & feel towards her as I can to no other woman. I thought of all this as I looked at Madame Récamier.... [23]

Not only have scholars and biographers crossed out Anna Barker's name in this passage, but they have consistently omitted or passed quickly over half of the above quote so as to purify Fuller and make the relationship seem only a passing or unimportant youthful infatuation, which it assuredly was in part. It is understandable that the issue be skirted since labelling someone as bisexual or lesbian without incontrovertible evidence is damning from the traditional heterosexual viewpoint.

Nineteenth century attitudes permitted passionate, flowerly wordflow and bonding between women, particularly during the romantic teen-age years. Sharing female relationships were considered innocent, were vital to woman's lives. That homosexual relations existed or were a possibility was never admitted.

It is true that later letters and incidents in Fuller's life seem to indicate that the Barker relationship might have been physical at least once. (See Chapter IV.) Reading through Fuller's correspondence and considering some of her early pressured education, her heroines and heroes, how she thought of herself, her actions, etc., it could appear that Fuller may have been bisexual. Her human needs were great. Her nature was passionate. It is hard to believe that this passionate idealist would have been as inhuman as to accede to the acceptance of celibacy as a way of life.

On the other hand, Fuller had a way of pouring out erotic or mystical overblown epistles to both women and men whom she most loved and admired — she even wrote in such a manner to her idol Beethoven. Because she wrote in this enraptured manner does not necessarily mean that she experienced sexual love with these persons. Certainly she was searching for an idealistic, poetic, close, sharing, relationship with another person and, as happens even in some lesbian and homosexual connections, such woman-to-woman and man-to-man attractions and friendships could have occurred with and/or without sexual involvement. There are only the existing letters and journals to go by and from our twentieth century hindsight one guess seems as good as another.

In the long run, whether she was chaste, heterosexual or bisexual hardly matters. What matters is that Margaret Fuller recognized the legitimacy of sexual duality. She was quite aware that nature did not exclude connections that transcended gender, of supportive, bonding, loving alliances between women, between men, between men and women. She was not afraid to give public voice to the subject at a time when it was daring to do so.

These perceptions she would echo in her book, *Woman in the Nineteenth Century,* even though she well knew that opening and probing this subject was sure to shock the American public, was sure to force controversy and bring criticism upon herself.

Large-minded Fuller was adamant about breaking through hypocrisy and pretence. If communication between the sexes were opened, if realities were ventilated, if options and opportunities were equalized, she believed that greater harmonies could be achieved that would generate greater rapport for all humankind.

At twenty, the realities of Fuller's future remained stark. Men often faced obstacles and burdens, but vast opportunity lay open to them.

For instance, the family of her friend James Freeman Clarke was facing personal misfortune with the paralyzing illness of his older brother who could no longer manage a store. Clarke was obliged to leave Harvard and find a paying job. But Fuller talked with her father who used his influence at Cambridgeport Public Grammar School to secure Clarke a position as master for a year. Then, when the family situation changed, by fall 1831, Clarke was back into Divinity School.

The friendship between Fuller and Clarke began to change. Clarke had become more knowledgeable, more self-confident, could see Fuller more objectively, could recognize her personal problems, and he pitied her. While both agreed with the German writers that mankind learns through experience, intuition, and the senses, he envisioned the new philosophy to raise man up to an ideal state of perfection. Fuller grounded her beliefs with Goethe's and maintained that what was natural in human beings was right. Clarke could not see it that way. Basically he was conservative, while she was radical in thought.

But something else was happening. He was becoming enraptured by Fuller's beautiful friend, Anna Barker, whose intellectuality left something to be desired.

Then, just as a political fight for presidency was being waged between John Quincy Adams and Andrew Jackson, Timothy Fuller moved his family out of the Dana mansion and into a smaller house, owned by his brother Abraham, built by Colonel Brattle before the American Revolution. The house was aligned with lovely linden trees and Margaret loved to walk in the formal, old-fashioned gardens with fish ponds, bridges, and spring-houses. Just a few steps from Harvard Square, it would be easier for George Davis to visit.

This was the year Goethe died. Fuller conceived an ambitious idea — to write the first biography. She felt capable of doing it. She had collected materials over the years, she could go to Germany for further research, could contact scholars and friends, could obtain reliable information on his personal life.

Then a devastating event sent her reeling into bed. George Davis announced his engagement to a friend of hers, Harriet Tidd Russell. They were to be married and move to western Massachusetts where

George was to start a law practice.* His feelings had been as false to Fuller "as those of Alcibiades."**

It was one thing to sublimate your feminity in study at the age of fourteen, but it was something else to face reality at the age of twenty-one. The throbbing headache would not cease. Finally, a doctor prescribed the traditional treatment — he bled her with leeches.

George Davis was going West, William Henry Channing was founding a Unitarian church in Cincinnati, and Frederic Henry Hedge was pioneering the new religious thought at the church in West Cambridge and considering a pastorate in Bangor, Maine. Her seventeen year-old brother Eugene was immersed in Harvard studies.

She could not do what Harvard men friends were doing — using education and talent to enter the professions. Yet she could not do what her Cambridge "lady" friends were doing — getting married. There were only two women she knew who seemed able to combine intellect and love. Eliza Farrar was polishing her etiquette book, *The Young Ladies Friend,* and Lydia Maria Child had just finished two best sellers, *The Frugal Housewife* and *The Mother's Book.* Such subjects hardly challenged Margaret Fuller.

Seven years later to Jane Tuckerman: "I have lived to know that the secret of all things is pain and that Nature travaileth most painfully with her noblest product."

She got out of her sick bed with the realization that she must accept the fact that with her men could be intimate to the point of sharing confidence and spiritual love, but would probably never offer her the love to match her great human need for physical passion.

On Thanksgiving Day, 1831 Fuller attended church or "exceedingly displease my father."

---

*George Davis became a journalist and a lawyer. He founded the *Franklin Mercury,* and practiced law in Greenfield. He later became a member of the Massachusetts Legislature and the U. S. House of Representatives. According to Thackeray, he was the "best conversationalist in America."

**Alcibiades, 450-404 B. C., was an arrogant and traitorous Athenian general who informed the Spartans of Athens' weak defences.

...to-day, more than ever before, the services jarred upon me from their grateful and joyful tone. I was wearied out with mental conflicts, and in a mood of most childish, child-like sadness. I felt within myself great power, and generosity, and tenderness; but it seemed to me as if they were all unrecognized, and as if it was impossible that they should be used in life. I was only one-and-twenty; the past was worthless, the future hopeless, yet I could not remember ever voluntarily to have done a wrong thing, and my aspiration seemed very high. I looked round the church, and envied all the little children; for I supposed they had parents who protected them, so that they could never know this strange anguish, this dread uncertainty. I knew not, then, that none could have any father but God. I knew not, that I was not the only lonely one, that I was not the selected Oedipus, the special victim of an iron law. I was in haste for all to be over, that I might get into the free air. [24]

Alone, for many hours, she wandered into the woods to try to recapture energy and spirit, and there she experienced a religious or mystical rejuvenation:

Suddenly the sun shone out with that transparent sweetness, like the last smile of a dying lover, which it will use when it has been unkind all a cold autumn day...I remembered how, a little child, I had stopped myself one day on the stairs, and asked, how came I here? How is it that I seem to be this Margaret Fuller? What does it mean? What shall I do about it? I remembered all the times and ways in which the same thought had returned. I saw how long it must be before the soul can learn to act under these limitations of time and space, and human nature; but I saw, also, that it MUST do it — that it must make all this false true, — and sow new and immortal plants in the garden of God, before it could return again. I saw there was no self; that selfishness was all folly, and the result of circumstance; that it was only because I thought self real that I suffered; that I had only to live in the idea of the All, and all was mine. This truth came to me, and I received it unhesitatingly; so that I was for that hour taken up into God. [25]

...My earthly pain at not being recognized never went deep after this hour. I had passed the extreme of passionate sorrow, and all check, all failure, all ignorance, have seemed temporary ever since. [26]

In her vision she came to realize how small were her problems when placed within the infinity of the universe. She was strengthened with the thought that she could welcome hardship for it could only bring greater growth, greater faith.

Seven years later she eloquently described this experience to Jane Tuckerman:

> I touched the secret of the universe, and by that touch was invested with talismanic power which has never left me, though it sometimes lies dormant for a long while...I saw how idol were my griefs...All the films seemed to drop from my existence, and I was sure I should never starve in this desert world, but that manna would drop from heaven, if I would but rise with every rising sun to gather it. In the evening I went into the church-yard; the moon sailed above the rosy clouds. That crescent moon rose above the heavenward-pointing spire. At that hour a vision came upon my soul, whose final scene last month interpreted. The rosy clouds of illusion are all vanished, the moon has waxed to full. May my life be a church, full of devout thoughts, and solemn music. I pray thus, my dearest child: "Our Father, let not the heaviest shower be spared, let not the gardener forbear his knife, till the fair hopeful tree of existence be brought to its fullest blossom and fruit!" [27]

On a Sunday evening during the "3rd hour of the most superb moonlight" she wrote friend James Freeman Clarke: "Why should not I have a vision? — O I have been so happy — have done and felt everything with such enjoyment...Such gorgeous light, such rich deep shadows — such sweet, sweet west wind!...lived it all through and set it to musick in my soul...this is such a sweet and strange composure...."

Just as Fuller was beginning to come to terms with her inward conflicts, the Fuller family circumstances worsened. In 1828 John Quincy Adams had lost the presidential election to the popular "Old Hickory," Major General Andrew Jackson, in the first smear campaign America had ever seen. Jackson officials had spread lies, charging Adams with corruption. Adams supporters had retaliated as best they could, but Jackson had rounded up the backwoods and popular votes, and Jacksonian Democracy, the age of the common man, was ushered into American life.

The Fullers had patiently waited out the Jackson term but he was re-elected for a second term in 1832. Thus, Timothy's ambitions for an ambassadorship were totally crushed. He decided to leave politics for the life of gentleman farmer.

As Timothy searched for the ideal land, Lydia Maria Child brought out another book. Entitled *A History of the Conditon of Women in All Ages and Nations,* it was the first of its kind in America, a storehouse of information, a description of the customs and mores of life for women in countries throughout the world. Written to be easily read by young as well as the mature, it was still pitched below the standard of Fuller's intellectual fare.

At about the same time two daughters of a wealthy South Carolina plantation owner took an unprecedented action. They emancipated their slaves and came North. The two women had in mind to do something to put a stop to the practice of slavery. Their names were Sarah and Angelina Grimke.

The abolitionists held three-day national conventions and formed national and regional anti-slavery groups. The Fullers were not really affected as they settled into a farm in the picturesque country where Timothy had been raised, Groton. To him life with a view of Mount Wachusett was perfect. He would work on his plan for an American history. But Margaret greeted their new home "with a flood of bitter tears." The move meant isolation from the stimulus of Cambridge. "The seemingly most pure and noble hopes have been blighted; the seemingly most promising connections broken."

James Freeman Clarke also moved. Having been ordained at the Second Church in Boston (where Ralph Waldo Emerson was minister), Clarke was off to the far West, to the challenge of a young Unitarian church in Louisville, Kentucky.

Farming for Timothy Fuller meant a stately house that was within reasonable commuting distance to Boston for he still had his law practice. The residence was smaller than what the family were used to. It'd been built by Judge Samuel Dana who had worked alongside Timothy in the Massachusetts House, and it was dignified, and many respected families lived nearby. For Timothy it was peace from the pressures of Washington D. C., but no one else in the family could find advantages. His wife was lonely. Her health made it hard for her to fend without servants who couldn't be found in the isolated region. Then the boys claimed not to like farming.

Many never-ending farm duties fell on the shoulders of she who was eldest at twenty three, unmarried. Also, she had the task of teaching her four younger siblings (plus a few neighborhood children) five to eight hours per day. Teacher's qualities of patience and gentleness were not natural to her, but she hoped to learn. She tried to make three languages, geography and history interesting by holding both indoor and outdoor classes with books and nature as lore. Her concern was to lay a strong foundation, to prepare them for further education. She wanted the younger boys, Arthur and Richard, to follow Eugene into Harvard. But it was exasperating. "I pour ideas into the heads of the little Fullers; much runs out," she wrote to her friend Almira Barlow.

In order to continue her personal reading and writing, she burned the midnight oil. She was now into Goethe's *Kunst und Alterthum* and *Campagne in Frankreich.* Also, she was opening up Uhland, Novalis, Tieck, and some volumes of Richter whom she liked so much that on every page she was "forced to pencil." Then there was Eichhorn and Jahn in the original, as well as Schiller, Heine, Alfieri, Bacon, Madame de Staël, Wordsworth, and Southey and Petrarch. To this list she added Carlyle's *Sartor Resartus* and some of his shorter essays, as well as books on European and American history.

Eleven year-old Arthur had a serious accident which almost blinded him — Margaret nursed him. The two oldest brothers left home after arguing with Timothy. Moreover, her grandmother came to live with them, and thus Margaret, whose headaches never seemed to desist, nursed her mother and grandmother, both plagued by ill health.

Even though Timothy built Margaret a special retreat in the woods, even though she somehow managed to study and carry on a spirited correspondence with her Cambridge friends, even though she could visit the newly opened Groton Athenæum for lectures, even though she did take short excursions into Cambridge, Boston, New York, and was promised a trip to Europe, Margaret felt despair. Outwardly, she remained cheerful, but inwardly she fought for diligence in heart. She tried her hand at writing fiction. She continued her reading in European history, and works by Goethe, Alfieri and Schiller. With her father, who was writing a history, she studied the life of Thomas Jefferson.

One of her articles was published in the *Boston Daily Advertiser.* Earlier an essay on Brutus had appeared in the *North American Review* written by prestidigous Harvard historian George Bancroft, who had studied in Germany and had known Schleiermacher. He was publishing the first of ten volumes on the history of the United States. Timothy encouraged Margaret to write a reply which she signed anonymously with the single initial *J*. Her article was printed and bought follow-up reaction. *J* was thought to be a scholarly *gentleman.* Margaret was amused and Timothy was high on satisfaction. But her high soon faded. She spilled out her hopelessness in letters to her best friends, Almira Barlow, Amelia Greenwood, Frederic Henry Hedge and to James Freeman Clark.

She would look up at Mount Wachusett and Peterborough Hills "towering to the sky, and feel that I, too, from birth, had longed to rise, and though for the moment crushed, was not subdued."

On a lovely Sunday in June 1833, after she had gone to church, Fuller had another vision or religious rejuvenation, probably her third such ecstatic experience.

Such experiences did not occur to everyone, but, on the other hand, at this time hundreds of people were being "saved" through spiritualism and evangelism. All was a part of a movement called "The Second Great Awakening." Though Fuller was weaned on Unitarianism which was in direct opposition to the preaching that the kingdom of God was imminent, she could respond to the idea that each person needed only an internal conviction, arrived through the heart, to be able to communicate directly with God, to bring his/her spirit in contact with nature and the infinite. Outpourings of her heart and prayers filled her journal, all of which helped to sustain her through morbid lows.

More and more she turned to her literary mentor, Goethe.

Her soul quested for knowledge. To the steadfast James Freeman Clark: "Every day I become more sensible to the defects in my education — I feel so ignorant and superficial. Every day hundreds of questions occur to me to which I can get no answer and do not know what books to consult." She queried him as to teaching possibilities in

Louisville, but he replied that the Kentucky folk allowed no room for liberal breathing.

From Boston she probably heard of the furor being created by Lydia Maria Child's latest book, *An Appeal in Favor of That Class of Americans Called Africans.* This book was received by the public with such abhorrence that it was banned in many places. Apparently, one lawyer used tongs to throw this obnoxious book out his window. Subscriptions to Child's children's magazine dropped. Her other works were also banned. The Boston Athenæum, which had earlier extended her library privileges, revoked her membership card. Some of her friends stopped calling on her.

Child had, in modest, unassuming prose, pleaded the negro cause by describing slavery as it was in America. Child answered every argument against the system and called for immediate emancipation without compensation to slave-owners. She stated she was fully aware of the unpopularity of this cause: "...though I *expect* ridicule and censure, I cannot *fear* them."

Child had met the radical abolitionist, William Lloyd Garrison, two years earlier. She and her husband had co-founded the New England Anti-Slavery Society. Both Dr. William Ellery Channing and Wendell Phillips had been criticized for remaining quiet on the subject but, after reading her book, both took public stands.

Isolated in Groton during the second winter snows, Fuller outlined a course of work for herself: the history and geography of modern Europe, the elements of architecture, an outline of history of our own country. She also wrote articles on writer/reformer, Hannah More, Edward Bulwer-Lytton, George Crabbe, and Henry Taylor's drama *Philip Van Artevelde,* but these were rejected, as well as inquiries about her translation of Goethe's *Tasso.* Her brother Eugene found an entry level position in the law office of George Frederick Farley, Esq., of Groton, and consideration was being given to enroll Arthur in the Leicester Academy.

Word had spread throughout the area about young Rev. Ralph Waldo Emerson who had resigned his Second Church ministry over a dispute about communion. He was, Fuller wrote to Almira Barlow, "that only clergyman of all possible clergyman who eludes my acquaintance." She was reading everything she could find that he'd written.

In 1834 she heard from Henry Hedge, who had the distinction of having written the first article on Coleridge in *The Christian Examiner* (which Ralph Waldo Emerson had called "a living leaping Logos"). Hedge told her that he had passed along her translation of Goethe's *Tasso* to his friend, Emerson.

Fuller responded: "I had two reasons (if they may deserve to be so called) for wishing him (Emerson) to see my *Tasso.* It gratified me that a mind which had affected mine so powerfully should be dwelling on something of mine even though 'twere only new dress for the thoughts of another — And I thought he might express something which would be useful to me. I should like very much his corrections...." Fuller loudly hinted to her Groton parson to invite the Rev. Emerson to preach.

Hedge had wanted to locate permanently in or near Boston with a church that could provide him with a substantial means of support, but somehow the timing was wrong, and it appeared he would have to accept the offing of the Unitarian Church in Bangor, Maine. Fuller wrote that she was "not wild" about his going "to that *meagre* domain of Maine at all....But ah! this money this money....Can you live near Boston on eight hundred a year?"

It was surely a problem Fuller could identify with.

Then she returned to his notation that Emerson wanted to meet her. "I am flattered that Mr. Emerson should wish to know me. I fear it will never be but 'tis pleasant to know that he wished it. I cannot think I should be disappointed in him as I have been in others to whom I had hoped to look up."

By March there was speculation about the Rev. Ralph Waldo Emerson's bride-to-be, Lydia Jackson. (His first wife had died.) Some of the Bostonian women Fuller knew had talked with her. Elizabeth Peabody said she was "unaffected but peculiar." Sarah Freeman Clarke responded that she was the equal of Emerson and Lydia Maria Child claimed that Emerson was to marry a Swedenborgian.

Fuller wrote Henry Hedge: "I should think (Miss Jackson) everyway calculated to make Mr. Emerson happy even on his own principle that it is not the quantity but the quality of happiness that is to be taken into consideration. How is it that men who marry a second time usually select a wife of character and manners entirely unlike their first...."

Meanwhile, Fuller worked on an outline for developing some historical tragedies and Hebrew romances and German tales. Hedge wrote about an idea for a new "periodical of an entirely different character of any now existing, a journal of spiritual philosophy in which we are to enlist all the Germano-philisophico-literary talent in the country." He wanted Fuller to write for it.

Fuller was charmed with the idea: "I shall feel myself honored if I am deemed worthy of lending a hand albeit I fear I am merely 'Germanico' and not 'transcendental'...." She meant that her background was literary with a German emphasis, rather than with religious philosophy. She asked to "know the facts about Goethe and Lili, can you give them me?.... I want to know did he give her up from merely interested (ie. selfish) motives."

She begged every knowledgeable person to give her the facts of Goethe's liaisons for her projected book, but could find no one who would discuss the subject with her; such things were not for women's ears.

Hedge's project for a journal faded into oblivion as he made his final decision to move away from the supports in Boston to new responsibilities in Bangor, Maine.

In Louisville, Kentucky, James Freeman Clarke began to produce a new publication, *The Western Messenger.* His object was to spread liberal religion in the West. Clarke solicited his friends for material and thus, two of Margaret's articles saw print. It did encourage.

A new project formed in Fuller's mind. She planned to write two tragedies on the history of Gustavus Adolphus.*

In April word came that her friend, William Henry Channing was engaged to Julia Allen, who was a sister of Mrs. Jared Sparks, and now he was off to Europe with his mother and sister.

In June 1835 Fuller, now twenty five, was invited to go on a trip up the Hudson to Trenton Falls with the Farrars and friends. She asked her father for an appropriate amount of money, and he obliged. One of the party was Samuel Gray Ward, a Harvard senior rooming with the Farrars. He was a handsome young man with curly brown hair and

* In 1840 her tragedies "are sleeping peacefully in my trunk."

even features. Seven years younger than Fuller, he was a distant cousin with unusual charisma, of Salem and Puritan stalk. He wanted to be an artist, but his wealthy mercantile father and family were steering him towards business. His father was American agent for the distinguished investment firm of Baring Brothers of England, also treasurer of the Boston Athenæum and of Harvard. Sam Ward moved effortlessly among the upper-social ruling echelon of Boston. Fuller was quite aware of the distinction.

Fuller saw immediately how sensitive and poetic Sam Ward was. She listened attentively to his conflicts while they shared a moonlit evening. They could sympathize with one another, share silences together. He had no interest in entering the business world. He saw himself as a student, a literary man. He was an excellent conversationalist, informed, refined, a gentleman with youthful energy. His intelligence was superior. His imagination was superlative. She dubbed him "Rafaello" after their favorite artist, Raphael, who was "a young seer of beauty, with eyes softly contemplative, yet lit with central fire."

Sam Ward, Fuller felt, had a future of statues, buildings, splendid landscapes. He had the touch, the divine spark to be the Painter of the Age, to translate the beauty of centuries.

Ward dubbed her "Mother."

Back in Cambridge, visiting the Farrars, Margaret met Harriet Martineau, an English writer and abolitionist who was touring the United States. Here was a woman, eight years older, who had cut through obstacles and was doing work she felt destined to do, earning a living by writing. Fuller gravitated to her.

Harriet Martineau had been an awkward fearful child, rejected and ridiculed by her family. She'd developed nightmares, chronic indigestion, depression, and any number of other illnesses such as "languor," and "muscular weakness." She was so deaf she had to use an ear trumpet. When her father died leaving the family destitute, her mother, sisters and she did needlework for income. Because her mother disapproved of women authors, Martineau wrote at night and hid her work by day. When her book, *Illustrations on Political Economy* was rejected by every publisher, she published it herself with her own money. Overnight it was a sensation.

When they talked about Carlyle, Fuller "was not quite satisfied with the ground she took, but there was no opportunity for full discussion," and "what she said of Hannah More and Miss Edgeworth grated upon my feelings." Then, Martineau tried to convert Fuller into becoming an abolitionist, but in a later hour "we passed the barrier that separates acquaintance from friendship, and I saw how greatly her heart is to be valued."

In her journal of 1835 she wrote:

> I sigh for an intellectual guide...How blest would it be to be... instructed in one's vocation! Anything would I do and suffer, to be sure that, when leaving earth, I should not be haunted with recollections of "aims unreached, occasions lost." I have hoped some friend would do — what none has ever yet done — comprehend me wholly, mentally, and morally, and enable me better to comprehend myself. I have had some hope that Miss Martineau might be this friend, but cannot yet tell. She has what I want — vigorous reasoning powers, invention, clear views of her objects — and she has been trained to the best means of execution. Add to this, that there are no strong intellectual sympathies between us, such as would blind her to my defects. [28]

Harriet Martineau would be returning to England and Eliza Farrar planned to go with her. Wouldn't Margaret like to accompany them? Fuller was overwhelmed when her father agreed to the idea. Excitedly she planned to meet Carlyle, Wordsworth, Coleridge in England; she would go to Germany and talk to scholars about Goethe. She would go to Greece and Rome. The trip was a childhood dream to come true within a few months.

That abolitionist groups were causing renewed fury in Boston was of lesser concern. Fuller's all-consuming mission was to write the first biography on the genius Goethe.

She was fully cognizant of the economic interests involved in the system of slavery. She, like many of the liberal and radical literati, tended to side with those who felt the problems so devastatingly complex that slavery would have to be irradicated gradually over a great many years. Supportive of motives of the abolitionists, she could not be supportive of the disruptive tactics. To her abolitionists seemed "tedious," "narrow," "rabid and exaggerated in their tone," even though she was well aware that the cause "was really something worth living and dying for, to free a great nation from such a blot, such a plague." But the violence, the mob hysteria was something she, like many, found difficult to tolerate.*

Abolitionists were regarded by the establishment as those "one could not ask to dine."** At this time during the early phases of the movement, they had reputations as being offensive, coarse, unworthy of respect, of no influence, of disputable deportment. They were denounced as "illiterate," "ill-mannered," "poverty-stricken," "crazy," "long-haired."

The first groups were seen to be harmful to the cause because they stirred riot and hatred instead of friendly discussion and human betterment. Slavery was an evil, but there were other problems as great. Emancipation could not happen overnight. Surely a bloodless solution could be found. Perhaps the government might buy the slaves outright rather than to have all this agitation. Wouldn't influence and leadership from the North break down resistance in the South? Surely humanitarian results could be obtained with the weapons of high-minded principles and moral sentiments.

When Margaret Fuller heard about the August 21 Faneuil Hall rally led by the mayor and chaired by Harrison Grey Otis that adopted five resolutions against abolitionists, she was concerned, but she was not in the thick of it as was Harriet Martineau.

In Groton Fuller submitted to the deadliness of the daily routine and made an attempt at writing a "George Sand" romance. Her short story was about the romantic triangle between Fuller's former suitor,

---

*In 1842 she was to be devastated when she entered Providence during the midst of the Dorr Rebellion and was to write: "There is little good, little cheer, in what I have seen: a city full of grown-up people as wild, as mischief-seeking, as full of prejudice, careless slander, and exaggeration, as a herd of boys in the play-ground of the worst boarding-school. Women whom I have seen, as the domestic cat, gentle, graceful, cajoling, suddenly showing the disposition, if not the force, of the tigress....These absurdities, of course, are linked with good qualities, with energy of feeling, and with a love of morality, though narrowed and vulgarized by the absence of the intelligence which should enlighten."[29]

**O. B. Frothingham made this statement.

George Davis, his fiance, Harriet Tidd Russell and a friend, Joseph Angier. James Freeman Clarke had confided all the details. Fuller had changed the names and sent it to a magazine, figuring, if published, her characters and plot would not be recognized. But it was published and the inevitable occurred. Mortified, she again fell ill with fever and pains in her head. Her family feared for the worst; they nursed her around the clock. Timothy, who never praised, now was full of high words: "You have defects, of course, as all mortals have, but I do not know that you have a single fault." This statement moved Fuller to tears; shortly she began to recover.

Just when father and daughter were developing a new bond, Timothy was stricken while working in a low lying meadow. He died within twenty hours. The cause of death was attributed to the epidemic of Asiatic cholera believed to have been brought into America by the influx of immigrants.

The family went into shock. Fuller felt life flow out of her. "My father's image follows me constantly," she wrote.

Her mother was "worn to a shadow." Like most women, she was ill-prepared to take charge. "She was as inapt for...the arithmetic of the business... as the lilies that neither toil nor spin," wrote Richard years later. He, ten years old, came down with fever.

Timothy had not left a will. Papers were misfiled, missing. Most of the Fuller assets were tied up in notes and real estate that was yielding small rentals. For the present the Fullers could expect an income of almost nothing.

"If I were an eldest son," Fuller wrote, "I could be guardian to my brothers and sister, administer the estate, and really become the head of my family. As it is, I am very ignorant of the management and value of property, and of practical details." She felt that her mind could have been as knowledgeable in these matters as any man's and she could have been enabled to advise and act in her family's best interests.

The estate by law and tradition, would be entrusted to some male in the family...the wife would have little to say in the matter. If all proceeded accordingly, the wife would receive about a third, and the other two thirds would be divided among family members. Timothy's lawyer brother, Abraham W. Fuller, who had made a fortune years earlier in mercantile life because an embargo had caused a great rise in prices, was hired as attorney to manage the estate.*

Abraham W. Fuller was the kind of bachelor who could watch Thomas Wentworth Higginson's mother darn stockings and tell her, a mother of ten children, "You do not know how to darn stockings; let me show you," and he'd take the needle from her.

Fuller felt the burden of a changed future falling around her. Could she make the writing profession pay? She penned her thoughts into her diary.

> I have always thought that I would not, that I would keep all that behind the curtain, that I would not write, like a woman, of love and hope and disappointment, but like a man, of the world of intellect and action. But now I am tempted, and if I can but do well my present work and show that I can write like a man, and if but the wild gnomes will keep from me with their shackles of care for bread in all its shapes of factitious life, I think I will try whether I have the hand to paint, as well as the eye to see...please fate, be just and send me an angel out of this golden cloud that comes after the pelting showers I have borne so long.[30]

Fuller had to plead with Uncle Abraham for money. He insisted that the children's education be cancelled. He insisted that her sister Ellen leave home to become a governess. He insisted that the youngest boy be adopted by a neighboring farmer. Margaret and her mother constantly fought these proclamations.

The winter was grim, even with the two eldest brothers away — Eugene tutoring in Virginia and William Henry working in a store in Boston. They cared for the farm as best they could. As the winter wore on, her mother and Richard were alternately sick. To survive the lean, cold months they were forced to slaughter a cow and two hogs.

This was about the same time that a beautiful young Polish woman

---

*It turned out that the family inheritance was to total about $21,000. This was less than anticipated. (It would in time yield Fuller's mother about five hundred dollars per year, an amount equal to the yearly earnings of a craftsman.)

who had been banned from her native country launched an unprecedented one-woman mission. The eloquent Ernestine L. Rose travelled throughout the North and the South lecturing on the right of married women to hold and control property, the right of woman's enfranchisement, religious rights, equal rights, slave rights. She organized audiences wherever she could, in barns, in parks, etc., and her skill drew crowds. During the winter of 1836-37 she visited every city in New York state. Furthermore, she continually sent petitions to the state legislature. She later wrote about her first experiences in gathering names for a petition: "I obtained five signatures. Some of the ladies said the gentlemen would laugh at them; others, that they had rights enough; and the men said the women had too many rights already. Woman at that time had not learned to know that she had any rights except those that man in his generosity allowed her…" * [31]

As Fuller struggled to deal with inheritance matters, most of the country heard about William Lloyd Garrison's capture in Boston. On October 21 a mob of respected propertied Boston citizens had broken up a meeting of the Boston Female Anti-Slavery Society and had dragged the shy, gentle, unassuming William Lloyd Garrison with a rope through the streets. Mayor Lyman had to commit him to the county jail in order to save his life. A man by the name of Bronson Alcott visited him in his cell that night and vowed to work for the cause. A day or two later the press was blaming the women for having convened the meeting.

Angelina Grimke, one of the young sisters who'd travelled from South Carolina to do something to end slavery, was so emotionally involved with the entire event that she wrote a sensitive and informed letter to Garrison in support of his actions. He admired it and published it in his abolitionist newsletter, *The Liberator.* The publication of Grimke's letter caused another storm of public controversy which Garrison had, of course, foreseen.

---

* It was due to the groundbreaking work of Ernestine Rose that caused Judge Hertell of New York to introduce the first bill on the married women's property law which would ensure women full rights to own, inherit and bequeath property independently of a husband. The bill failed; however, it attracted the attention of many legal minds and paved the way for its first passage in New York in 1848 with other states following suit in later years.

Fuller's friend, Dr. William Ellery Channing, felt pressured to take a public stand on slavery and in early December he distributed his pamphlet *Slavery.* Now all Boston, it seemed, was afire. Fuller read it with complete approval, writing to Clarke: "It comes like a breath borne over some solemn sea...."

Early in 1836 John and Eliza Farrar extended the invitation of the European trip to Sam Ward. He would go; he would study art and literature. Life opened before him.

For Fuller life seemed narrow as a straitjacket. She was ready for vigorous, sustained challenge, ready to birth a labor of value and originality. Two of her articles had generated dollars, one on Heinrich Heine and one on Sir James Macintosh. She mentally planned a series of articles interpreting the German writers and thought how grand it would be to translate Tieck's *Little Red Riding Hood* since it corresponded with exactly what she felt children's books should be. But inwardly she feared she faced stagnation: teaching.

Fuller's family begged her to borrow against her part of the inheritance and go to Europe — but her mother's health seemed daily to dissipate. "I pray to God ceaselessly that I may decide wisely," she closed a letter to her brother Eugene who was beginning law in Charlestown, Mass.

She visited the Farrars again in Cambridge and with Harriet Martineau she read the New Testament, trying to find strength for a decision on the European trip. Martineau, though, was soon to continue with her American tour.

The debate went on for three months. On April 17 she began a letter to Eliza Farrar: "If I am not to go with you I shall be obliged to tear my heart, by a violent effort, from its present objects and natural desires...."

To James Freeman Clarke she again bewailed the opportunity to learn more about Goethe: "How am I to get the information I want, unless I go to Europe?" She begged him to tell her "without scruple" if he knew anything about Goethe's life with his mistress, Christiane Vulpius, an affair that had scandalized Weimar court — no one in America dared mention it. She was "very destitute of what is commonly *called* modesty...."

By this time everyone had heard of the untimely death from

tuberculosis of the "golden boy" of Harvard, Charles Chauncey Emerson, Ralph Waldo's brother. It is unclear whether or not Fuller had ever met this brilliant young man, however she proceeded to write a poem in his memory.*

A few days later on her 26th birthday, she mailed off her final decision to Eliza Farrar:

> Circumstances have decided that I must not go to Europe, and shut upon me the door, as I think, forever to the scenes I could have loved. Let me now try to forget myself and act for others' sakes. What I can do with my pen, I know not. At present, I feel no confidence or hope. The expectations so many have been led to cherish by my conversational powers, I am disposed to deem ill-founded. I do not think I can produce a valuable work. I do not feel in my bosom that confidence necessary to sustain me in such undertakings — the confidence of genius. But I am now but just recovered from bodily illness, and still heart-broken by sorrow and disappointment. I may be renewed again, and feel differently. If I do not soon, I will make up my mind to teach. I can thus get money, which I will use for the benefit of my dear, gentle, suffering mother — my brothers and sister. This will be the greatest consolation to me, at all events. [32]

The Farrars, Harriet Martineau and Sam Ward left for Europe. Anna Barker was sailing from New Orleans to join them.

A fragment of what Fuller probably wrote exists: "All youthful hopes of every kind I have pushed from my thoughts — I will not, if I can help it, lose an hour in castle-building and repining...I have now a pursuit of immediate importance to the German language and literature I will give my undivided attention...Please God now to keep my mind composed...Teach me to think justly and act firmly — Stifle in my breast those feelings which pouring forth so aimlessly did indeed water but the desert...Thou art my only Friend...Vouchsafe then thy protection that I may 'hold on in courage of soul.'"

Never did she overcome the feeling that her potential was forever thwarted. Though she steadfastly held to the belief in the ideal of an

---

*Entitled "Lines on the Death of C. C. E.," it was published in the May 20, 1836 *Boston Daily Centinel and Gazette.*

ennobling long-term love inspired by a worthy person, she had little hope such aspiration could be hers.

Outwardly, she tried to suppress her inward feelings which seemed as isolated as her environment.

In Groton she moved from mundane task to mundane task. Daily and weekly she continued the German lessons with her sister Ellen, and Latin and composition with Richard. Sometimes she squeezed precious time for the needed reading and writing. As she later phrased it, someone must tread the path.

No woman in America had ever achieved what Margaret Fuller was convinced she was capable of achieving.

Society had nothing to offer her, a woman of superior intellect.

Her prospect was to live the life of a New England spinster. It was limiting, in employment, in income, in emotional fulfillment.

As she gazed at the Peterborough Hills and the Wachusett outside her door, she would cheer herself by declaring her demise "could never be...the good knight may come forth scarred and maimed from the unequal contest, shorn of his strength and unsightly to the careless eyes, but the same fire burns within and deeper than ever, and he may be conquered, but never subdued."

R.W.E.

Emerson grew up in a family that "rarely touched each other… Usually his mother kept her affections as secret as her silent talks with God.…Having a saint for a mother was a calming influence — at times depressing. From his father he inherited an unusually resonant voice and a sense of style in language; from his mother, an inhibited emotional life. Smiling would come easily to him, even when it concealed pain, but spontaneous laughter, seldom — and angry words only from moral, not personal, indignation." [1]

Oliver Wendell Holmes asserted that Emerson never laughed loudly: "When he laughed it was under protest, as it were, with closed doors, his mouth shut, so that the explosion had to seek another respiratory channel, and found its way out quietly, while his eyebrows and nostrils and all his features betrayed the 'ground swell'… of the half surpressed convulsion."

Julia Ward Howe confirmed: "I remember very rarely to have seen him moved to laughter; and when some touch of his fine humor thrilled his audience, and brought a pleasant ripple to the surface, I cannot remember that his countenance underwent any change."

Biographer Woodberry tells us: "He had hidden humor…he was amused in secret over many things; in his family he would joke after a scriptural fashion by perverse quotation of Bible texts.…"

His step-grandfather Ezra Ripley, a kindly Concord Calvinist pastor in whose home, the Old Manse, the young Ralph spent many hours is recorded to have said these words: "My children, you will never see anything worse than yourselves." Emerson is recorded to have repeated this sentence often.

Joseph Emerson, the great-grandfather, prayed each night that his descendants would not be rich, and great-great-grandfather, Samuel Moody, is said to have pursued his backsliding parishioners into the alehouse on Saturday nights and to have dragged them back to decency by the collar. He is also supposed to have given away his wife's only pair of shoes from her bedside, thinking they were his own.

The Rev. William Emerson, the great-grandfather, minister at Concord and purchaser of the Old Manse and its great meadows, slave owner, preached enthusiastic sermons which recruited minute men and either joined the minute men in the Concord battle of 1775 which took place on his property or watched from his window with his wife and six-year old son,* (accounts differ) but soon left to serve as chaplain to the Revolutionary army in Ticonderoga but there caught the fever that was spreading and died (after he'd liberated his slaves).

Cabot writes that Ralph's chief recollection of his Unitarian minister father was as "a somewhat social gentleman, but severe to his children, who twice or thrice put me in mortal terror by forcing me into the salt water, off some wharf or bathing-house; and I still recall the fright with which, after some of these salt experiences, I heard his voice one day (as Adam that of the Lord God in the garden) summoning me to a new bath, and I vainly endeavoring to hide myself." [2] There are several quotes that show Emerson grew up to be not admiring of his father.

Ruth Haskins Emerson, whose son Waldo bore her resemblance, came of solid English stock. She was the tenth of sixteen children of a distiller, John Haskins, who led half of the family to the Episcopal Church in Boston on Sundays and his wife led the other half to the Congregational Church. Ruth followed her father; later followed her husband, and converted to Unitarianism.

She'd supposedly been given the best of educations — which wasn't much for women (the author has found no record of what or how she was educated) — had been baptized in King's Chapel, had a careful religious and domestic training, and always kept the Book of

---

*Ralph Waldo Emerson's father, William.

Common Prayer close to her. English manners and traditions were central to her being, even though she'd lived on American soil. She did express herself well in letters and diaries, was refined, lively, graceful, cultivated. She was twenty-eight when she married the Rev. William Emerson of Harvard (the Massachusetts town) and was supposedly happy living in the rural setting, evidently never complaining of a heavy workload, never expressing dissatisfaction. To keep busy all of the time, she knitted when visitors called. It is reported that she cared for the silver communion plate, and ironed the bands for her husband's black silk gowns herself.

Cooke writes that she was "of great sensibility, modest, serene, and very devout. She was possessed of a thoroughly sincere nature, devoid of all sentimentalism and of a temper the most even and placid. One who knew how to guide the affairs of her own house, as long as she was responsible for that, with the sweetest authority, and knew how to give the least trouble and the greatest happiness after that authority was resigned. Both her mind and her character were of a superior order....Her sensible and kindly speech was always as good as the best instruction; her smile, though it was ever ready, was a reward. Her dark liquid eyes, from which old age could not take away the expression, will be among the remembrances of all on whom they ever rested."

Cabot quoted Ralph Waldo Emerson when he called Ruth the "whitest of women."

> ...her counsels of perfection... helped to bring a strain.... In the two elder (boys) it was alleviated by a certain impassivity of temperament and an admixture (in Ralph, at least) of what their father called "levity," and Ralph afterwards, in his college days, 'silliness,' — we may call it humor — the habit of detaching his impressions from himself, and looking at them from the outside as a by-stander. Possibly, in his case, seclusion from the companionships and the pastimes of boyhood may have supplied a needed check to what he calls, in one of his early journals, "my cardinal vice of intellectual dissipation...."[3]

Not only is Ruth depicted as a perfectionist and a firm disciplinarian who strained the home situation, (and it is once claimed that she was not fun-loving), but many biographers dismiss her influence simply by citing the active life of The Rev. William Emerson in paragraph after paragraph, whose achievements they also insist were comparatively modest and mediocre. Ruth is barely mentioned — she who outlived her husband by forty-two years, who raised and cared for Ralph and the other children, three who were unusually gifted, one who was retarded, and two who died in infancy — all largely without the help of her husband whose work and activities kept him away from the household most of the time. After The Rev. William Emerson died and left her with nothing, she had the strength to raise her sons by taking in boarders and by serving as a housekeeper. For about twenty years she lived with her eminent adult son who, from his teen-age years on, was always most especially concerned about his mother and made it a prime motive to provide for her and ease her life. As to the father who died when Ralph was eleven years old, he had a negative memory or two; otherwise he remained silent. Therefore, it seems reasonable to believe that Emerson had a far stronger bond with his mother than with his father. Surely, she was of some beneficial influence.

But biographers have dismissed her. For instance, Oliver Wendell Holmes gives Ruth Haskins Emerson one paragraph on page 13 of his biography, but William Emerson gets three pages, 10 through 13, and later eight more pages in a description of the brilliant circle of movers and shakers in which he moved.[4]

The usual reason given for slighting women's work and women's lives is because "they did nothing."

It is hard not to conjure up the true picture that Ruth was a noble spirit, busily managing with infants and young children with little help, on a small income, while her prominent Reverend husband spent a quarter of it on books, fine clothing, select wines, and was wined and dined and honored by the intellectual elite of Boston. We can surmise that since she had to "take out the garbage," she was probably reasonably tired, yet endured with strength and courage beside her husband who seemed almost proud that he had not provided for his family in the predictable event of his death (his lung condition indicated tuberculosis).

William's sister, Mary Moody Emerson (who was their matchmaker) is quoted by Cabot as saying: "I knew her to be without comparison.... Thought her books, words, actions, the sweetest, wisest, fittest, chastest of all.... She sustained any occasional trial of temper with a dignity and firmness and good sense that I shall ever respect, and obtained a greater influence than is common over one of the best of husbands."

On Election Day morning, May 25, 1803, in her gambrel-roofed house on Summer Street in Boston, amidst garden, orchards and pastures, Ruth Haskins Emerson would not think of interrupting husband's daily schedule so she bore alone the labor pains while The Reverend carried out his duties at the church, the Old Brick, which included hearing an Election Sermon, attending Anthology Club meeting at Mr. Phineas Adams, and having dinner at Govener Caleb Strong's. When he returned home that night he was presented with his fourth child. That night The Reverend entertained guests — Mrs. Emerson probably had made all arrangements from her bed and with the help of a local neighbor. William added a comment in his diary: "Mrs. E. well."

She was gracious, quiet, patient, dutiful. She believed in the absolute sovereignty of God, a God who punished or rewarded, and she never missed her hour of meditation after breakfast (after family prayers) during which no child dared disturb. Biographers write that her reserve and her restraint of emotion made her seem a distant, remote kind of person.

Cabot mentions this story of Ralph's mother to demonstrate that she was "so far from making them feel her tenderness that once, when he and William had wandered off upon some holiday and spent the day away from home, they were much surprised, on their return, at her exclaiming: 'My sons, I have been in an agony for you!' 'I went to bed,' Ralph says, 'in bliss at the interest she showed.'"

Ralph, who biographers describe as beginning life in the cradle in yellow flannel, and progressing to "a spiritual-looking boy in blue nankeen," was enrolled in a Dame School near the parsonage on Summer Street before the age of three. Dame Schools were similar to nursery schools, generally run by spinsters or widows in their homes, where youngsters learned ABC's. Two months after enrollment, Cabot tells us, The Rev. William wrote: "Ralph does not read very well yet."

Ralph was a worry to his handsome, scholarly father who was

minister of the oldest and most honored church in Boston, First Church, who was Chaplain of the state Senate, Chaplain of the Ancient and Honorable Artillery Company, founder of the Boston Philosophical Society as well as the Anthology Club, member of American Academy of Arts & Sciences and Massachusetts Historical Society, who loved books so well that he was to start a public library at Harvard and was to edit the prestigious *The Monthly Anthology* of the Boston Anthæneum, and was to see several of his sermons published. He was an Overseer of Harvard College and a member of the Boston School Committee. He lectured locally, and he worked on a history of his church.

He carried himself well. He was conscious of fashion and wore the best of outfits, which included black silk stockings. He always carried a gold-headed cane. One biographer infers he was considered a "Georgian fop." He preferred the sociability of church functions rather than theological considerations. In his diary he indicated his misgivings for lacking the seriousness befitting a minister.

The eldest son, William, and the two youngest, Edward and Charles, all demonstrated high academic achievement, but Ralph's work was average or mediocre. (Margaret Fuller was precocious.) The young boy had some ability to rhyme, and he wrote many verses in school and out, but he showed no interest in competing and seemed to like the outdoors better than his studies. By 1807 one sister and one brother had died (one sister was yet to be born who would live only three years), and so the family narrowed to five boys. Discounting one who was mentally retarded, Ralph was the one needing most help with his lessons.

A schoolmate, Edward Greeley Loring (who became a prominent judge) said that Ralph "was a good scholar because honestly studious, but was not eminent.... He was liked for his equable temper and fairness, but was not demonstrative enough to be eminently popular." He walked slowly and seemed to lack energy. Biographer Richard Garnett wrote, "He was not a school boy, but a boy at school."

The brothers had daily chores, such as stacking and carrying wood for stove, tending a garden, saying grace at table, and Ralph had to herd the family cow to pasture before going to school. The Rev. William Emerson supervised their lessons closely and demanded daily morning prayers and recitations (just as Timothy Fuller demanded of Margaret). In spare time the Emerson boys were expected to read — not novels — books of worth.

The Sabbath, which began Saturday night, was strictly observed; toys were put away, visitors were disallowed. On Sunday Ruth attended church, dressed prettily, and the children attended Sunday School; there were two church services. In the evening the Emersons entertained the deacons of the church with wine and good talk. Of course, it was routine for Ruth to prepare for this and to clean up afterwards.

On Thursdays there were lectures by various neighboring ministers and afterwards William brought them home for dinner. Ruth prepared, served and cleaned up after. On the Friday afternoon before Communion Mr. Emerson's First Church and Brattle Street Church united for a lecture and on other occasions the Emersons invited ministers for breakfast. Ruth staged the solo productions. On holidays they traded hospitality at the various family houses.

There were adventures of all kinds for young boys in and around Boston. The streets were crowded with people of all nationalities and from all walks of life and there was Faneuil Hall, the Statehouse, buildings, bookshops, meeting halls, museums, theaters, publishing houses. There was also Boston Common, which was the communal center offering not only pasture for cows, but ice skating, sledding, marble and ball games. There was plenty of space so boys could wander in orchards, and there were the wharfs with the excitement of ships, bells and sailors. Picking up shells, finding frogs, etc., could happily occupy hours.

But much time was spent within the fenced grounds of the parsonage because there were tough gangs of the Round Point who frequently passed by their house on their way to and from the Boston Common. Thus, a growing dependency and loyalty developed among the Emerson brothers.

Generally though, it is reported that the brothers did not play as other boys did. They memorized poems or Scripture and recited to one another. The Rev. Dr. William Henry Furness who grew up with Ralph, is quoted to have said, "from his earliest years he dwelt in a higher sphere...had his being in an atmosphere of letters."

Later Emerson wrote in his journal, "When I was thirteen years old, my uncle Samuel Ripley one day asked me, 'How is it Ralph, that all the boys dislike you and quarrel with you, whilst the grown people are fond of you?' Now I am thirty-six, and the fact is reversed: the old people suspect and dislike me, and the young people love me."

At the age of nine Ralph attended South Writing School on West Street, and also entered Boston Public Latin School which, in operation over fifty years, regularly prepared and sent graduates to Harvard. Here, as was customary in all schools at that time, there was no concern to motivate or interest a student's curiosity; education consisted in memorizing long passages and dull facts. The teacher's place was to listen and to dispense marks — not to explain or hold question-and-answer sessions. A system called emulation was in use, which was simply a division of those boys who could remember the lesson from those who could not. Anyone who made a mistake was made to change his seat to a position below a boy who could correct him. After several weeks about fifteen boys would be selected as best, all working on about the same level and they would be moved to another room to continue with another master, the same routine being repeated. The emphasis was on ancient languages and the classics, such as Ovid and Virgil. It was a system about which James Freeman Clarke was later to write: "It had a benumbing effect on the mind. It stupefied our faculties. It gave a distaste for study. Latin, Greek, and mathematics, taught in this way, inspired only dislike."

Frequently, Emerson daydreamed or read a book other than the assigned text, and he often played truant when he was supposed to be in transit between the two schools. Nevertheless, he read and memorized parts of Shakespeare, Milton, Addison, Pope, Young, and Voltaire.

To lend a helping hand, William's sister made long visits. The influence of Mary Moody Emerson was vital to the growth of Ralph Waldo Emerson.

Mary Moody Emerson had been essentially an orphan. Her father having died, she'd grown up with her grandmother, isolated in the rural setting of Malden. After her grandmother died, she'd lived with an aunt and uncle, caring for them as they aged, and again later, she cared for another aunt who'd become insane. She saw her mother who'd re-married Ezra Ripley and her brothers and sisters infrequently. She called herself "the puny pilgrim, whose sole talent is sympathy." In her Almanack she wrote, "There is a sweet pleasure in bending to circumstances while superior to them." Her mind-set encompassed eternity and her final triumph in life was so unique that Ralph Waldo later claimed she was both a saint and a genius. In fact, he was to draw from her philosophy and to quote her in his essays, and in 1869 he devoted a lecture on her which he delivered at the Woman's Club in Boston, prefacing his talk with a poem based on ideas from her diary.

Aunt Mary called herself "a goody." She clearly resented her disadvantaged life of narrow opportunity. She was a solitary, as Waldo was to become. She claimed, "I love to be a vessel of cumbersomeness to society." At first, she found taking care of five nephews a labor, then she became affectionately attached. She made them aware of their inheritance of eloquent clergymen, father, uncle, great-great uncle, grandfather, and great grandfather.

In her late thirties, she deliberately separated herself from marriage. She desired to be celibate and androgynous. She blessed God "for giving me to see the advantage of loneliness." But she had to fight for her solitude and God was "alternately her jailer and the goal of her liberation."

Yellow-haired and blue-eyed, she stood just over four feet high, wore a mob cap and kept an Almanack which she considered "a letter to me when unable to think...Private..." She called these books Almanacks because she was consciously projecting herself into eternity, chronicling "sun and moon's rising," to study divine relationship. She sought visionary power.

Uneducated, she read on her own the classics, poetry, philosophy, theology, the Bible, which she often quoted, found rapture and communion in nature, as did Waldo later, spent hours in meditation, could spend hours discussing metaphysics, was witty, bustled about at a speed greater than others, had a quick, sharp mind, quick temper, and was quick to criticize. Emerson wrote that she surprised, attracted, chided, and denounced her companions by turns, and pretty rapid turns. She could see through sham and pretence, made ministers uncomfortable because she often knew more than they, was bored by small talk and if bored, would often ask her companion to go on an errand for her. At least once she steered a mediocre person away from questions by asking, "How's your cat, Mrs. Tenner?"

She made sharp retorts like, "I am tired of fools," or "What a poet Byron would have been if he had been born and bred a Calvinist." She developed her own brand of Calvinism, mingling it with smatterings of Arminianism, Romanticism, Unitarianism and, later, Transcendentalism. Seemingly radical and iconoclast, her faith sprung out of her strong inner need for a paternal yet androgynous deity on whom she could rely.

"Alive with God is enough — 'tis rapture... joy, hope and resignation unite me to Him whose mysterious will adjusts everything." Prayers, fasts, retreats, and denials of human indulgences such as food, sleep, relaxation and social life were basic to her religious fervor.

Her eccentricities have been recorded and exaggerated; Emerson's biographers have mythologized her. Van Wyck Brooks opened his book with the image of her riding on horseback at midnight through Concord with her "shroud and a scarlet shawl thrown about her shoulders." Other biographers have told the story of how she carried a broomstick through Concord. These stories are probably false, though she probably did wear a long cloak and did carry a long staff when she roamed the Concord woods.

Evidently, she did have a flannel shroud made and, since it was a pity that the shroud would be left idle, she wore it night and day until it was worn out; then had another one made. Emerson and other biographers referred to it as a shroud for her grave, but it was probably a type of loose, comfortable garment or dress. Her bed, Emerson wrote, was the form of a coffin, and she talked of the grave so often that close friends would greet her with, "I wish you joy of the worm."

Because her mind dwelt in the Infinite, she felt her life was a preparation for death. Calvinist theory shown through. Man was a sinner, depraved. Man must accept his worthlessness. The goal of every life is to praise God. There is no happiness on earth. In 1822 she wrote in her Almanack, "we exist in eternity. Dissolve the body and the night is gone, the stars are extinguished, and we measure duration by the number of our thoughts, by the activity of reason, the discovery of truths, the acquirement of virtue, the approach to God." In Eternity there was "no deceitful promises, no fantastic illusions, no riddles concealed by the shrouds...."

She felt herself untalented.

In 1807, a few years before she came to help the widowed Ruth, she wrote, "Had I prospered in life, what a proud, excited being, even to feverishness, I might have been. Loving to shine, flattered and flattering, anxious, and wrapped in others, frail and feverish as myself...I weary of my pilgrimage...when will He let my lights go out....Oh for transformation!"

She had inherited a piece of land from her aunt, later sold it to acquire a share of an obscure farm in Maine which was called "Elm Vale" with her sister and Ralph Haskins. It was within sight of the White Mountains in the woods at the foot of a hill called Bear Mountain. She got up at dawn, did her housework, baked bread, then read the Bible, Milton, Marcus Aurelius or Puritan sermons.

She loved children. "Children must be obedient, industrious and show the proper reverence for God, but they need not do constant penance for their sins...."

Other maxims (which Emerson freely quoted) were "Scorn trifles," "Lift your aims," "Look high," "Do what you're afraid to do," "Do boldly what costs you the most," "Sublimity of character must come from sublimity of motive."

She stimulated discussion and incited the boys' curiosity. She believed that her nephews were "born to be educated." She encouraged them to be distinguished, yet she scorned a "frivolous desire for fame." In later years she considered Emerson a genius who could write a better *Paradise Lost.*

Many of Aunt Mary's words and ideas were to be echoed by Emerson in his idealism, his reach for eternal values, his search for purity of motive, independence, in his 'disinterested love,' in his desire for solitude, in his call for freedom and self-reliance.

Emerson began another correspondence with a twenty year-old friend of Aunt Mary's, a modest and brilliant woman whom the president of Harvard was to call "one of the most wonderful scholars of her time, or indeed of any them." This was the self-taught Sarah Alden Bradford who would in four years, due to Aunt Mary's skillful matchmaking, become the wife of the Rev. Samuel Ripley, half brother of Emerson's father. Her learning encompassed Latin, Greek, Italian, French, languages and literatures, philosophy, natural history, botany, science, metaphysics, algebra, geometry, trigonometry, and calculus. Congressman Samuel Hoar wrote of her, a mother of nine children (two died in infancy), as a "lovely, motherly woman...seated in a chair, rocking a baby's cradle with her foot, knitting children's stockings with her fingers, while with her voice she at once corrected and encouraged a small boy with his Virgil, a task she could easily perform, as she knew almost all the *Aeneid* by heart."

Because her husband, the Reverend at the First Congregational Church, was paid so small a salary, they had begun a boarding school in their home in Waltham and she not only raised her own family but tutored boys who were having difficulty at Harvard. As a young girl her scholar/sea captain father encouraged her to study anything she wanted and she helped herself to an attic of books. Marriage and increasing demands of household, parish and school caused an abrupt change in her life, and her journal writings admit to suffering, fatigue, headaches, yet she covered these frustrations with an even temper, patience and good humor.

Ralph had her to stimulate a thirst for knowledge. It was she who suggested Ralph write letters to her in Latin and Greek. He never did but he sent her verses. She was a friend always, a regular visitor of his home.

During these years religion in America was in ferment. Over the past century there had been quiet dissent against the rigidity of Calvinism which preached an angry, vengeful God, incarnation, predestination, atonement, fall, regeration, redemption and man's innate depravity.

The first sparks ignited when some individuals began to doubt the divinity of Christ. In 1785 The Rev. James Freeman (James Freeman Clarke's grandfather) braved criticism by revising the Prayer Book of King's Chapel, leaving out references to the Trinity.

With the turn of the century The Rev. William Ellery Channing at the Federal Street Church and Andrews Norton, Harvard's Professor of Sacred Literature, led the liberal contingent, holding beliefs that reflected the new age of individualization and westward expansion.

God need not be feared. He did not punish. He was ready to help individuals to a better life. These new thoughts were criticized as being vague, a compromise.

By 1805, Harvard was still technically non-denominational, but Calvinism lost its stronghold. It was weighted by leaders of the new liberalism, with Unitarian Henry Ware appointed to the Hollis Professorship of Divinity. The two men who wished to ease the controversy, The Rev. William Ellery Channing at the Federal Street Church and Professor Andrews Norton, declined to use the name "Unitarian." The new faith was "liberal and rational Christianity." Channing spoke about self-reliance, the inner soul, the inner life of each individual.

Within three years the Calvinists opened their own school in Newton.

The Rev. William Emerson was in the midst of this controversy that raged for years, but in 1811 when Ralph was eight — one year after Margaret Fuller was born — he died of a tumor. He was honored with a funeral accorded to first citizens, and was laid to rest in the burying ground of Kings Chapel. It was just three months after a black-eyed daughter had been born, adding to the family of five boys, the eldest being ten years old. William Emerson wrote his wife in the last days of his illness that he trusted to Providence.

Ruth Emerson was forty-three. Provisions for her children meant "their souls first, their minds next, their bodies last." For a time The First Church voted a stipend. Ruth's youngest brother, Ralph Haskins, whom she'd raised from infancy and after whom she'd named Ralph Waldo, became part-time surrogate father. This position was shared by her husband's half brother, The Rev. Samuel Ripley.

The family was split temporarily, with one brother sent to Maine to live with relatives and Edward sent to Concord to live with grandfather Ripley, where for a summer Ralph joined him.

From 1811 until Ralph went to Harvard, the Emerson's moved as necessary, Ralph's mother sometimes ferreting an existence for the family by living with relatives, his grandmother Phoebe Emerson*

---

*Phoebe Bliss Emerson had been wife to Ralph Waldo's great-grandfather William Emerson, pastor at the Concord Church. After he died the parishioners voted Ezra Ripley as clergyman; two years later he and Phoebe were married.

and step-grandfather Ezra Ripley at the grey-hewed, gamble-roofed Old Manse in Concord. (Waldo attended Concord Grammar School.) Other times, Ruth managed by taking in boarders. Only by great exertion and frugality did she manage. Cabot reports that at one point Ralph and Edward shared one overcoat. Only one could go to school when the weather was cold. Ralph read, skated, swam, and wrote verses, and studied French. He worked on building a protective shell that would keep him safe. As he grew up, Ralph was to long for wealth so that he could be free of struggle.

William, the eldest son, who'd borne the major strain of the family misfortunes, was first in Harvard with a scholarship from First Parish and with financial assistance from Ralph Haskins. At the same time, when possible, he taught when he could at his uncle's school, thus helping family finances.

In her Almanack, Mary Moody Emerson was projecting defeat in life and looked for release through death…"tremendous future"…to vindicate her life of tedium, weakness, miscalculation and stupidity. "Alas, no progress and no death," she wrote.

In his early teens, in 1816-17, Ralph began to experience normal sexual urges. Biographer Allen writes: "He was becoming increasingly aware of sexual urges, wet dreams, temptations to masturbate and waking sexual fantasies, which he had been taught, not only by Aunt Mary and his mother but by the whole of society, to suppress at all cost. It was wicked even to dream of sex. The Puritans had insisted that a man who even imagined carnal sin was already guilty of that sin, and Ralph was all too familiar with this doctrine. Unable to keep erotic images out of his consciousness, he felt guilty, disturbed, even at times terrified. He concealed this anxiety, but secretly he turned, in the words of his later journal entry on puberty, from 'omnivorous curiosity to anxious stewardship.'[5]

In the summer of 1817 it looked as though Ralph would have to wait a year to become one of four hundred at Harvard because his mother's boarding house was not profiting. Edward needed to return to Andover, and William had another year at Harvard.

Fortunately, The First Church allocated Ralph a stipend, and the president of Harvard, a former good friend of his father's, beneficently appointed him "president's freshman" (his messenger or orderly). Thus, tuition would be covered. He walked to Cambridge to take the examinations; at fourteen, he became youngest member of the class of '21. (Margaret Fuller lived only a few miles away in Cambridgeport. She was seven years old. Her father, giving her Virgil to read, was extremely proud of her quickness to learn.)

To help pay for board, Ralph worked as waiter in the dining hall, taught at his uncle's school in Waltham, and also tutored the president's nephew for a time.

The teaching method at Harvard was very like that at the Boston Latin School, with dull routines of recitation. The general program consisted of the classics, Livy, Horace, Cicero, Homer, and Adam's *Roman Antiquities.* Then there were courses in geometry, algebra, history, Hebrew, philosophy, rhetoric, chemistry, astronomy, and electricity and magnetism. One by one students recited the lessons and received marks from the teacher and each was thereby assigned his rank in class. But at Harvard there were only three hours of classes per day, as students were supposed to devote two hours in preparation for every hour in class. Also there was an hour for exercise, and the regular meal periods. Many students considered the methods and studies at Harvard a bore, something they had to get through in order to receive credit and graduate.

Allen describes Ralph as "a tall, lanky, pale, sandy-haired, blue-eyed shy, taciturn, youth who looked more precocious than he actually was...well drilled in Latin, with a smattering of Greek...but poor in mathematics...physically and emotionally, an immature adolescent. His dignified manners and almost forbidding reserve deceived strangers, but his brothers knew him for the dreamy, well-intentioned, but rather frivolous boy he was." [6] Cooke writes, "...in philosophy he did not get on very well." [7] Woodberry notes, "He was neither shy, nor proud, he was slow." [8]

Allen continues: "Ralph lacked the competitive spirit and for him sibling rivalry was either so faint or so well concealed that it appears to have been almost non-existent." [9] Harvard's president's nephew, whom Ralph tutored, Samuel Kirkwood Lothrop, said Ralph seemed "to dwell apart, as if a tower from which he looked upon everything from a loophole of his own." Another classmate stresses Ralph's wide knowledge of literature and how he knew Shakespeare almost by heart. "He was mirthful and, though never demonstrative or boisterous, keenly enjoyed scenes of merriment and his placid smile was as highly prized as would have been a loud explosion in some others." [10]

A series of journals served Ralph as outlets for thoughts and impressions. He referred to them as his commonplace books or "Wide World."

In his second year at Harvard he participated in a class protest concerning some suspended sophomores, whereupon all sophomores ultimately withdrew from college for a time, and this action resulted in a special feeling of comradeship and the classmates formed a group called "The Conventicle," in which it seems certain persons, particularly archbishops, were satirized. Emerson belonged to another literary organization, but the leading clubs did not offer invitations to him, probably because he was poor and because of his reserve. Conventicle members spent much of their time drinking, and somehow along about this time Emerson learned to smoke. (Years later he would smoke half a cigar at a time.) Ralph wrote ditties to be sung with the Conventicle members' consumption of wine.

In his Junior year he exerted his independence by dropping the name Ralph in favor of Waldo, thereby authorizing his first act of giving himself rights of name changing and name-calling that he was to freely exercise throughout his life. He expected to become a respected and distinguished Unitarian minister as had been his father and ancestors, but his secret ambition was to be in the power position of a poet, a king or a saint, but as he confessed to his "Wide World" in which he poured all his deepest feelings, he felt..."Too tired and too indolent to travel up the mountain path which leads to good learning, to wisdom and to fame, I must be satisfied with beholding with an envious eye the laborious journey, and final success of my fellows, remaining stationary myself, until my inferiors and juniors have reached and outdone me." Nevertheless, he wrote compositions, read widely in Bacon, Milton, Plato, Montaigne, Bryon and Scott, Kant, Schelling, Fichte, Jacobi.

Then, entries in his journal describe a growing obsession with an interesting face of a freshman who has been identified as Martin Gay from Hingham, Mass.

Emerson wrote that "a dozen times a day and as often by night I find myself wholly wrapped up in conjectures of his character and inclinations." [11] Yet they did not become acquainted with one another and biographer Allen, who mentions the possibility of Waldo's passing through a normal youthful phase of homosexuality, emphasizes "another peculiarity in Emerson's emotional-intellectual life. The subject of ideal friendship, either with man or woman, would occupy his thoughts for many years, and almost invariably he would prefer the ideal to the reality; indeed, at times, as with Martin Gay, he would seem to be afraid to test the reality against a cherished abstraction. This schoolboy infatuation was a forerunner of Emerson's later theorizing on love and friendship." [12] (But it would be Margaret Fuller who would catalyze his ideas and enlarge his circle of friends.)

As to his heart, he wrote: "A blank...I have not the kind affections of a pigeon, ungenerous and selfish, cautious and cold, I yet wish to be romantic; have not sufficient feeling to speak a natural, hearty welcome to a friend or stranger, and yet send abroad wishes and fancies of a friendship with a man I never knew. There is not in the whole wide Universe of God (my relation to Himself I do not understand) one being to whom I am attached with warm and entire devotion.... Not a being to whom I have joined fate for weal or woe, not one whose interests I have nearly or dearly at heart... a true picture of a barren and desolate soul." [13]

Emerson graduated thirtieth in a class of fifty-nine. His ranking would have been lower except that some of the young graduates had been demoted due to insupportable conduct.

Emerson was chosen class poet, but six or seven others had refused the office before he was appointed. His poem was not considered brilliant and, at commencement, it is recorded that he forgot his lines and had to be prompted. [14]

He was not elected into Phi Beta Kappa until years after graduation. He was second prize-winner in the Bowdoin competition. Years later Josiah Quincy, the classmate who beat Emerson out of first place for the Boylston prize for English composition, wrote that Emerson seems "to have given no sign of the power that was fashioning itself for leadership...." [15] (His younger brother Edward was to graduate as first scholar in his class and Charles was to be valedictorian. Eleven year-old Margaret Fuller was winning medals in school.)

Just before his nineteenth birthday, Waldo wrote in his journal: "Mine approaching maturity is attended with a goading sense of emptiness & wasted capacity, with the conviction that vanity has been content to admire the little circle of natural accomplishments....I must be satisfied with beholding with an envious eye the laborious journey & final success of my fellows, remaining stationary myself....If I hold (the position I now hold) longer I may quite as well resume the bauble & rattle, grow old with a baby's red jockey on my grey head & a picturebook in my hand, instead of Plato and Newton....And I am he who nourished brilliant visions of future grandeur which may well appear presumptuous and foolish now...." [16]

Another biographer, Porte, senses "a psychological or psychosexual element" and suggests that Emerson might wish to be unburdened "of manhood heavy because of the extravagance of his own expectations in the face of a strong sense of ineptitude." [17]

Then, Ralph failed to receive a coveted position at Boston Public Latin School. Teaching had been a stepstone to the ministries of his grandfather, his father, and his older brother, William. So, William employed Ralph as assistant in the school for girls he was profitably operating at his mother's rented house in Boston. Emerson wrote of this experience: "I was nineteen; had grown up without sisters, and, in my solitary and secluded way of living, had no acquaintance with girls. I still recall my terror at entering the school."

Allen writes: "He had no intimate friends except his brothers and he could only fantasize in secret about girls, accompanied, probably by urges to masturbate. In his journal he recorded and then heavily cancelled: 'I have a nasty appetite which I will not gratify.' Feelings of guilt over this appetite, which every moral authority he knew said was a sin, doubtless contributed to his somber mood."

His disturbing dreams at night continued.

And again: "Now he was a miserable schoolteacher, without even the satisfaction of believing that he performed his duties well.... He was... unsocial, and this in turn was the result of his introversion, lack of confidence, and inability to take the initiative in meeting young people of his own age.... His affections needed only exercise and his constant self-analysis was not healthy." [18]

Waldo and William had to support the family, so no matter that

Waldo wrote, "Better tug at the oar, dig the mine, or saw wood; better sow hemp or hang with it than sow the seeds of instruction...."

There was no quitting (just as twenty-five year-old Margaret Fuller could not quit teaching in order to sustain support of her family).

Waldo was struggling to build his own theology apart from his legacy of Unitarian liberalism and Calvinist piety. He wrote long letters of inquiry to his Calvinist Aunt Mary, soliciting her answers and encouragement, and found what she said nourishing. He was interested in the oriental religions, the German mystics, science and social economy, Greek, and he was reading Plato, Coleridge, Carlyle, Samuel Clark, Edwards, Priestley, Belsham, David Hume, and Francis Bacon. He absorbed conversations and lectures given by Dr. William Ellery Channing whose ideas on reliance on the soul impressed him. Channing, who over the years had been pressured to take a stand on the religious controversy, had at last preached a sermon that outlined basic beliefs of liberal Unitarians. His words were spoken at the ordination of Jared Sparks in Baltimore in 1819, when Emerson had been sixteen, and they had signified the final break. Channing asserted that Unitarians believed in the use of reason in interpreting the Scriptures, the unity and moral perfection of God, and the spiritual leadership of Jesus.

Emerson, influenced by Channing's thoughts and his own ancestry of ministers, decided (after much indeciveness) to become a minister, not because he felt a strong call, but because he loved oratory, because he had an inclination to spend his life for the betterment of humanity, and because he wanted to earn enough to provide a home and sustenance for his mother. The Church encompassed the highest of visions. Philosophy and science were not yet practical professions; careers in poetry or literature could not be depended on to generate adequate income. However, the humanitarian world was open to leadership.

Emerson, though, thought of himself as a poet, a worshiper of nature, and he wrote every night. His private goal was fame, but he still admitted to being "idol, vagrant, stupid, and hollow." In his journal he described his brothers and others that he knew, recorded bits about his walks in woods and a trip through the Connecticut Valley, included poems, and poured out his questions, confusions and doubts concerning theology and philosophy. His problems were with skepticism, revelation, immortality, and the miracles of Christ.

Allen writes, "Though Emerson's moods continued to fluctuate between despair — at times almost physical nausea for the world — and spiritual exhilaration, he became steadily more ascetic and idealistic in the philosophical sense (supremacy of mind over matter)." [19]

Stephen Whicher writes: "Admiring purposeful scholarship and consecutive reasoning, practical skill and personal forcefulness, all of which, he was convinced, were the only means to the preeminence he aspired to, he found himself sadly deficient in them all and alternated between a strained self-exhortation and rueful resignation. Though his early journals often show a manly courage and good sense, the dominant mood is a sense of impotence." [20]

Allen continues: "Emerson knew he had serious defects of character. He still believed himself deficient in 'common sympathies' and afflicted by 'a levity of the understanding.' Apparently what he meant by these phrases was impatience with the banalities of the average conversation and intolerance of the petty vanities of ordinary human nature. Because of his impatience and self-consciousness he was ill at ease with people, and sometimes laughed or snickered at embarrassing moments. He criticized harshly, and when he praised he often overdid it. These defects of character — today we would probably say personality — would disqualify him for the practice of law or medicine. 'But in Divinity I hope to thrive.'" [21]

Just before Emerson was to become twenty-one, he wrote: "...in my frequent humiliation, even before women & children I am compelled to remember the poor boy who cried out, 'I told you, Father, they would find me out.'" [22] Over and over again in his journals Emerson decried guilts, doubts, insecurities, inability to sustain human relationships.

Allen continues: "To make up for his deficiencies, Emerson resolved to train himself by diligence and self-discipline. He would eat sparingly, overcome his tendency to waste time, guard his speech, and try to compensate for lacking a warm heart. 'And I judge that if I devote my nights and days in form, to the service of God and the War against sin — I shall soon be prepared to do the same in substance.... My trust is that my profession shall be my regenerative of mind, manners, inward & outward estate....' Or at least it would be a starting point: he would put on eloquence and goodness like a robe. This is a remarkably revealing confession. Emerson's resolve to play the role of an ideal minister is a confession that he must force himself to be what he knows he is not...."[23]

There were three years of teaching in a Roxbury girls school opened by his brother Edward. (In Cambridge thirteen year-old Margaret was writing her father to enroll her in the Emerson young ladies' school, but her father wanted her to attend the Prescott School in Groton.)

The Emersons' school earned sizeable dollars, and enabled William to go to Göttingen, Germany to study theology (where he so questioned his faith that he conferred with Goethe who advised him to ignore his doubts and become a minister). Then it was foreseen that the family could manage without the girls' school and they closed it. With interest from a good investment and by borrowing, Waldo could enroll in Harvard Divinity School.

(Margaret Fuller was nearly fifteen years of age. By summer formal education would come to an end for her.)

As fate would decree, Waldo stayed at Harvard Divinity School only a few weeks due to rheumatism in a hip, to a chest problem and to an eye problem that led to an operation which blocked study for about a year. Because of his eye problem, he was excused from reciting at lectures and then he was excused from taking examinations. Finally, he left Divinity School altogether.

Biographer Woodberry writes, "It is plain that Emerson was scholastically ill prepared for his profession. His studies, pursued mainly in private, and broken in upon by ill health, and school tasks, must have been of the most superficial kind and intellectually flimsy. He was never grounded in theology or metaphysics. His principal intellectual acquisition was literary, lying in the region of poetry and the more ponderous English prose...."[24]

For a time Emerson returned to teaching as the family continued to depend on his financial help. Edward succumbed to a tubercular crisis and was sent off for a recovery in the Mediterranean. Buckeley's retarded condition began to deteriorate and to cause renewed concern. And William, now returned from Germany, announcing he would study *law!* This was a blow, for the family believed he would carry on the ministry in good family tradition.

In October 1826, at the age of twenty-three, Emerson was licensed to preach. His step-uncle, Dr. Samuel Ripley and his father, Ezra Ripley, (who had approved Emerson's father as minister) were members of the Middlesex Association of Congregational Ministers which gave the stamp of approval. Emerson is quoted as saying "If they had examined me, they probably would not have let me preach at all." [25]

Within a few days, in Waltham where his step-uncle was minister, Emerson delivered his first sermon to some acclaim. His family was there, including brilliant Aunt Mary. She — unschooled and unsupported by caring adults, who had so long desired to find an opportunity to communicate her fervent faith to a public, thwarted at every turn because she was a woman — watched and heard her protege nephew in the pulpit...with what conflict of heart we can only surmise.

Three months earlier she had written, "I pray to die, though happier myriads and mine own companions press nearer to the throne. His (God's) coldest beam will purify and render me forever holy."

Another entry: "I have no one to sympathize with, though I sympathize in general benevolence from the President to the Cat." (She meant from the nation's highest leader to nature's lowliest animal creature.)

Later she would write, "I am eminent for the non-advantages in this life.... I am glad I have nothing as I can't have much."

She moved frequently. She was a "troublesome boarder," as Waldo wrote in his journal. She wrote in her Almanack that it was difficult for a lady to find inexpensive board.

Now Waldo was a bonafide minister, and the problem reoccured with the "mouse in his chest." Some scholars have speculated that it may have been psychosomatic, since no doctor found symptoms of tuberculosis. Others have written of a life and death struggle. It was decided that Waldo should go south for a winter to Charleston and St. Augustine. His generous uncle, Samuel Ripley, gave him the money. There, for two and a half months he walked, sat, watched the ocean, continued with his journal, wrote poetry, sermons, and letters to his brothers and Aunt Mary, and silently continued his struggle with the problems of evil and other theological concepts. He even preached. As he felt his health returning, he began to be aware for the first time of the value of rest and relaxation and for the remainder of his life he took care to balance his time and energy.

In his journal he summarized his own constitution: "I am cold & solitary & lead a life comfortable to myself & useless to others. Yet I believe myself to be a moral agent of an indestructible nature & designed to stand in sublime relations to God and to my fellow men." [26]

On the voyage home he met and shared vibes with the nephew of Napoleon, Achille Murat, who was an atheist and skeptic. Discussing religion endlessly, they challenged each other's beliefs, and in turn both were stimulated. They parted in different directions, never-to-be-forgotten friends; a relationship and stimulus that broadened and made a deep impression.

With lungs still straining, Emerson stopped on the way home to preach in Washington, Philadelphia and New York. During the next year he tried to maintain a slow-pace, preaching only intermittently in New England pulpits, including his father's and his uncle's churches, receiving invitations via relatives and their networks. Sometimes he had to walk long distances to reach his destinations.

The beauty drained from his dynamic, high-achiever brother, Edward, who had easily won all honors at Harvard. So exhausted was he from heavy law study in Daniel Webster's office, plus tutoring Webster's sons, plus additional teaching, that he had suffered a mental and nervous breakdown and had to be confined to an institution. Emerson helped to nurse.

On many points Emerson and Aunt Mary no longer agreed. He called himself a "Seeker," an admirer of Plato. Following Channing's lead, he indicated he began to question the creditability of the story of the life and death of Jesus in the New Testament. He began to look at the Bible as being a great piece of literature written by human beings rather than God's word. He wrote that sentiment was "one of the feelings of modern philosophy...and that it were fitter to account every moment of the existence of the Universe as a new Creation and <u>all</u> as a revelation proceeding each moment from the Divinity to the mind of the observer." [27] He wanted to serve as spectator, recorder, poet, preacher, philosopher, and he felt he must reach ordinary people.

When he preached a sermon on domestic piety at the Unitarian Society in Concord, New Hampshire, he met the beautiful but frail, sixteen year-old Ellen Tucker, with whom he fell in love. He was twenty-four years old and had never sustained a relationship with a woman younger than his Aunt Mary or Sarah Alden Bradford Ripley. Indeed, he prided himself (as stated in his journal) that he had never loved.

Waldo had earlier wanted a friend, as evidenced by his journal entries — a male friend to whom he could look up to, with whom he could share ideas and thoughts. Allen points out he was in a Baconian frame of mind, meaning he sided with Francis Bacon on friendship, love and marriage. He copied these Bacon quotes into the part of his journal he called "Encyclopedia":

> "Beautiful women are seldom of any great accomplishments, because they for the most part study behavior rather than Virtue."
>
> "*Raro mulieres donare solent.*" (Rarely are women accustomed to give.)

Scholar Allen writes, "Puritanical Boston had taught (Emerson) to be wary of sexual love, and Bacon's cynicism reinforced the lesson: 'great spirits and great business do keep out this weak passion....For it was well said, <u>That it is impossible to love and to be wise.</u>'" [28]

Ellen, eight years younger, who respected and adored him, probably presented him with a combination of qualities that Emerson needed. The model for marriage in Victorian America was a strong dominant husband who would protect a submissive, gentle wife who would encourage and admire. Emerson is not described as dominating at this age, but his age and education gave him the needed "edge."

He seems to have been reserved, self-conscious, slow moving, slow speaking, essentially humorless, serious minded. However, he was attractive, standing six feet high with shoes, long legged and thin, weighing about one hundred forty pounds, with thick fine brown hair, a narrow face, high forehead, wide mouth, prominent nose and bright blue eyes with violet lights. Allen writes: "His great strength was hidden in his character, and his complete dedication of his mind and talents to the moral life."

Close friends and family knew he had wit and a sense of humor which he had revealed during his early childhood years. Much of the time Emerson spent with Ellen was full of merriment and fun.

It was a whirlwind romance. For a marvellous description of the emotions Waldo felt, you can read the first part of his essay, "Love." Here young love is enthusiastically seen from a male perspective. Emerson obviously thought he was writing universally and impersonally about love, but if so he would have had to include the feelings and experiences of women. For a young woman's view of love, Ellen's letters can be read.

Even if Emerson's flowerly style and use of gender is disallowed, since in the nineteenth century sentimentalism and the word "he" to denote both "he" and "she" were perfectly acceptable, there is no way women can identify with such passages as these:

> (Love) like a certain divine rage and enthusiasm, seizes on man at one period and works a revolution in his mind and body; unties him to his race, pledges him to the domestic and civic relations, carries him with new sympathy into nature, enhances the power of the senses, opens the imagination, adds to his character heroic and sacred attributes, establishes marriage and gives permanence to human society.
>
> ...who can avert his eyes from the engaging, half-artful, half-artless ways of school-girls who go into the country shops to buy a skein of silk or a sheet of paper, and talk half an hour about nothing with the broadfaced, good-natured shop-boy." [29]

The essay is shot through with this one-sided perspective.

As Emerson was falling deeply in love with Ellen, so was another — his dear brother, Charles, whose love seems to have been idealistic. Whether or not Emerson knew of it is not clear. On the twelfth day of Waldo's second visit to New Hampshire he proposed and Ellen accepted.

She was fashionable, beautiful, seventeen years old, the youngest daughter of a Boston merchant who had passed away, consumptive.

She was living with her mother and step-father, Colonel William A. Kent, prominent retired businessman and citizen, active in the Unitarian Society. She had dark curls, a pear-shaped face, long nose and small mouth. She was child-like, idealistic, religious, fond of music, flowers, various animal pets, horseback riding, skating, poetry, literature, and she spoke French, as did Waldo. Her health was a major problem, and she felt she would not live long. She had tuberculosis; her father and brother had died from this affliction, and her mother and sister both had symptoms. Waldo had had lung problems and he hoped she would recover. He told her about his poor financial situation, but she called money "The ugly subject." It was not of primary importance because she had an income from her father's estate.

Allen writes: "Waldo Emerson's engagement to Ellen Tucker affected him like a religious conversion, which actually it was. His whole world seemed suddenly flooded with God's benevolence. He had no doubt whatever that his finding Ellen was providential, and that her love for him was a holy blessing."

Then, the Second Church on Hanover Street in the North End in Boston* called him to serve as assistant to Dr. Henry Ware Jr., who was in ill-health (who would resign within two years). At his ordination, Emerson's step-grandfather Ripley gave the Charge; his step-uncle Ripley preached the sermon, Dr. Frothingham, paster of the First Church (which had been Emerson's father's church) gave the Right Hand of Fellowship, and Emerson's classmate Ezra Stiles Gannett, made the Address to the Society. Waldo was boosted by the Old Boys' Network.

Now Emerson had one of the most coveted pulpits along with the security he needed to support a wife and to help his mother and brothers. The marriage would wait until Ellen was fully recovered from recent set-backs. She playfully called her coughing "red wheezers." She wrote, "Sell my wealth for a healthy winter — yes, willingly."

---

* Formerly the church of Increase and Cotton Mather who preached stern Puritan theology.

Throughout their "golden courtship" as Ellen called it, they wrote ardent love letters, teased each other, sent original poems back and forth. Her muse, she said, was "A disobedient lady." They made up names for each other, "King," "Queen," "Ellinelli," "Grampa," "Gramdma," "Lady Penseroso," "Lady Frolick." They thought of their love as ennobling and spiritual, bringing them closer to Heaven.* She prefaced plans for the future with "if I live," and this was another reason for her fantasizing on the immortality of their love.

The engagement lasted eight months with Ellen alternately suffering relapses, then recovering. During this time there were periods of separation as Waldo carried out his duties at The Second Church, but these were overshadowed with warm, exhilarating, happy times together. They went on a long excursion with her mother into the White Mountains and Merrimack. At the end of this journey Emerson, with what seems predetermined foresight, suggested that Ellen make out a will which left him a bequest. Ellen — who seems to have hated money matters — complied.

The wedding was small and quiet, performed in the Kent household in Concord on September 30, 1829. The newlyweds lived first in a boarding house, later in their own house, first in Boston, next in Brookline and back again to Boston, and now Waldo could and did indeed invite his mother to join them — as housekeeper.

(Margaret Fuller, nineteen, was still living in Cambridge. She had advanced through Eliza Farrar's socialization plan, and had emerged a vivacious force within the Harvard circle.)

It was a year of great happiness for the newlyweds, but also of despair. There were weeks, even months, when they thought Ellen's lungs had improved, then there were set backs. Also, Emerson's mentally retarded brother, Bulkeley, had to be taken to an asylum, and tuberculosis so affected Edward that a trip to Puerto Rico seemed the solution. In December 1830, Waldo preached a sermon that death meant a new birth. (Shades of Aunt Mary.)

Emerson carried out all duties as minister, though some were burdensome, such as visiting the sick and officiating at funerals. In

---

*Later and only gradually, Emerson abandoned his belief in immortality.

January one Sunday he served as Visiting Preacher at Twelfth Church in Boston. Sitting in a pew was a young lady from Plymouth whose name was Lydia Jackson. She was enraptured by his sermon. He hardly knew she was there.

His pulpit presence and eloquence were being acclaimed. Some of the older parishioners felt he should have more to offer on doctrine, but younger people were satisfied. His oratory was simple, unconventional, untheological.

Some people criticized him as being vague, whimsical and incomprehensible. One young lawyer heard his sermon on memory, and said to a woman: "No real thought in it. I can't remember anything he said, can you? " She replied, "Yes, he said 'shallow brains have short memories.'"

At the Emerson home, the doctor daily prescribed medicine and exercise for Ellen, and Waldo was insistent that she conform with carriage rides no matter how freezing the temperature. In mid-January there was so much snow that Emerson cancelled Sunday services, since his parishioners could not venture out, but he made sure that Ellen had her outdoor excursion. Emerson drew up plans to head South when weather permitted, and Ellen asked in letters to Edward in Puerto Rico that he find a house for them there. Steadily she grew weaker.

Since their engagement she had delighted in writing love poetry and one poem reveals that she at some time felt there was a change, even an end, in Waldo's love for her:

> I will not stay on earth Waldo
> Unless thy love is mine....
>
> Sweeter the green sod for my bones
> The black earth for my head
> The wind, than thy cold altered tones
> Whence all of love had fled.

On February 8, 1831 she drew her last breath.

Allen writes: Ellen "died in such a way as to make her extremely religious husband feel it was a kind of final spiritual consummation of their marriage. Like Dante's Beatrice, she had led him up to a landing on the stairway to heaven."

Waldo was anguished, but he felt she was transformed, transcended; it was a saintly death.

Two hours after Ellen's release he wrote to his Aunt Mary:

> My angel is gone to heaven this morning & I am alone in the world & strangely happy. Her lungs shall no more be torn nor her head scalded by her blood nor her whole life suffer from the warfare between the force & delicacy of her soul & the weakness of her frame. I said this morn & do not know but it is true that I have never known a person in the world in whose separate existence as a soul I could so readily & fully believe & she is present with me now beaming joyfully upon me, in her deliverance & the entireness of her love.... I see it plainly that things & duties will look coarse & vulgar enough to me when I find the romance of her presence (& romance is a beggarly word) withdrawn from them all. But now the fulness of joy occasioned by things said by her in the last week & by this eternal deliverance is in my heart. [30]

Into his journals he wrote:

> Shall I ever again be able to connect the face of outward nature, the mists of the morn, the star of eve, the flowers, & all poetry, with the heart & life of an enchanting friend? No. There is one birth & one baptism & one first love & the affections cannot keep their youth any more than men. [31]

Here shines Emerson's theory of compensation: "An inevitable dualism bisects nature.... Every excess causes a defect; every defect an excess. Every sweet hath its sour; every evil its good. Every faculty which is a receiver of pleasure has an equal penalty put on its abuse...." The absolute balance of give and take, the doctrine that everything has its price.... Our strength grows out of weakness....Both Ellen and Emerson believed this... and so did Margaret Fuller.

In "Compensation" he wrote:

> We cannot let our angels go. We do not see that they only go out that archangels come in.

> We linger in the ruins of the old tent where once we had bread and shelter and organs, nor believe that the spirit can feed, cover, and nerve us again.... We cannot stay amid the ruins. The death of a dear friend, wife, brother, lover, which seemed nothing but privation, somewhat later assumes the aspect of a guide or genius; for it commonly operates revolutions in our way of life, terminates an epoch of infancy or of youth which was waiting to be closed, breaks up a wonted occupation, or a household, or style of living, and allows the formation of new ones more friendly to the growth of character.... [32]

Within twelve days of Ellen's death Waldo was back preaching in the pulpit, to the surprise of his parishioners, but it is recorded he dreamed of Ellen, wrote poems to her, prayed to her, walked to her as she lay in her grave at the cemetery in Roxbury, tried to commune with her. When she did not answer, he questioned whether or not he had been forgotten. He wrote his brothers — Charles was most deeply grieved — stating that death had become attractive to him. But at the same time he wrote that he would now probably be able to pay the costs of Bulkeley's confinement and that Ellen in death would continue to benefit the Emersons: "I please myself that Ellen's work of mercy is not done on earth, but she shall continue to help Edward & B. & Charles." [33] ("B" is Bulkeley, the retarded brother.)

By June 25, he was writing in his journal:

> No love without sympathy. Minds must be alike. All love a seeking in another what is like self. Difference of opinion separates, common thought ties us. If we find a person esteems excellence that we have we love him.... The fact that we both drink hyson tea or both walk before breakfast — or delight in swimming are low points of union that do not create any permanent kindness but that we are both admirers of a great & good man is a very strong bond. If we both love God we shall be wholly alike & wholly love each other. [34]

Five months after Ellen's death, Emerson wrote in his journal:

> Few men communicate their highest thoughts to any person. To many they cannot, for they are unfit receivers. Perhaps they cannot to any. Yet are these thoughts as much made for communication as a sex. Ellen wondered why dearest friends, even husband & wife did so little

> impart their religious thoughts. And how rarely do such friends meet. I sit alone from month to month filled with a deep desire to exchange thoughts with a friend who does not appear — yet shall I find or refind that friend? [35]

Waldo remained friendly to all of Ellen's relatives, but they began proceedings to fight his right to a part in her estate. (Within a year and a half sister and mother had followed Ellen to the grave, both succumbing to tuberculosis.)

Then, a new worry developed. Waldo's brother, Charles (whom Oliver Wendell Holmes knew and referred to as "the most angelic adolescent my eyes ever beheld,") suffered a weakness, a stupor, a depression. He, like the brilliant Edward, was a youth idolized, whose academic work had foreshadowed genius.

In religion there was "much sham." Emerson wrote in his journal: "The difficulty is that we do not make a world of our own but fall into institutions already made and have to accommodate ourselves to them to be useful at all...this accommodation, is, I say, a loss of so much integrity & of course so much power." [36] He was thinking about writing a book.

During the summer of 1832, as diarrhoea began to plague him, his parishioners found some of his beliefs hard to accept. They could go along with his concept that Jesus was a great spiritual leader and teacher rather than the Son of God — because the subject was controversial — but the concept that the Bible was written by men and that truth could be found in nature rather than in the Bible was a bit too radical.

One person told him, "Young man, you do not know your business; you had better go back to your home."

He wrote over a hundred sermons, he praised freedom of will, self-reliance, and the divinity of man. And he was beginning to feel that form or ritual were not needed for faith.

He latched onto Communion service as a tangible ritual that his parish members could comprehend. He was not original in his objection — his great-great granduncle, the Rev. Joshua Moody had been imprisoned in 1683 for refusing to administer Communion rites. Also, both his father and his brother William had had doubts; in fact, this was one reason William had turned to law.

Communion, with its concept of sacrifice and ceremony, was controversial. In the Quaker belief it had not been practiced for two hundred years. Emerson had discussed it with his non-conformist, deeply spiritual, New Bedford Quaker minister-friend, Mary Rotch.

Armed with the Quaker arguments, Emerson announced to his congregation that he could not administer the Lord's Supper with good conscience since it confused the idea of God. Performing the service was turning "back the hand on the dial." Ministers had no right to represent God.

Many church members were angered that Emerson raised questions. The Society of Proprietors eventually voted against Emerson's stance, even though one committee member was his cousin and two were good friends. Since the church had to be closed for six weeks due to repairs, Emerson and brother Charles went to Maine, visited Aunt Mary for a week, and headed into wood and river country, where Charles left Emerson as a boarder with a small family, alone except for two other travellers. There, admist a circle of woods, a peacock on a fence, and the books, *History of the Quakers* by William Sewal and Henry Tuke's *Memoirs of the Life of Fox,* (founder of Quakers), he struck his first No to his legacy and conformity.

His mother was disapproving. Aunt Mary stood firm. "A reformer!" she wrote to Charles, "...and begin at the wrong end?" Charles reacted the same way. William was more understanding, since he'd already renounced the ministry. Step-grandfather Ezra Ripley joined throngs who thought him "insane."

Emerson reacted in his journal: "I have sometimes thought that to be a good minister, it was necessary to leave the ministry."

Enduring the diarrhoea which brought on loss of weight, he stood young, isolated, empowered, assertive, in control.

In his journal he began a poem:

> I will not live out of me
> I will not see with other's eyes
> My good is good, my evil ill
> I would be free —I cannot be
> While I take things as others please to rate them
> I dare attempt to lay out my own road

That which delights in shall be Good
That which I do not want, — indifferent
That which I hate is Bad. That's flat
Henceforth, please God, forever I forego
The yoke of men's opinions — I will be
Lighthearted as a bird & live with God. [37]

He returned to Boston at the end of July but delayed returning to Second Church by inviting substitute ministers for three weeks; then he avoided Communion Sunday by arranging an exchange with another minister.

With his September 9 resignation sermon, Emerson led the split from the Unitarian faith and formed a new philosophy which would eventually be labelled Transcendentalism, a term to be defined in differing ways, according to individual taste, but which was centered on the ideals of truth, beauty, harmony, individualism, the revelation of nature, the free range of the questioning mind, self-reliance, and the divinity of the soul.

For a time, after leaving Second Church, Emerson felt liberated, then fell into a deep depression. Finally — despite constantly being on guard for his health (the diarrhoea kept recurring) — he sailed to Europe with four passengers on a small merchant brigantine which carried logwood, tobacco, sugar, coffee, beeswax, and cheese.

(Fuller family fortunes and expectations had now turned, and they moved to rural Groton, Mass.)

This was the year Aunt Mary Moody Emerson turned sixty. She wrote in her Almanack: "I have given up, the last year or two, the hope of dying."

(Finally, Emerson's diarrhoea disappeared.)

Scholar Staebler states: "In a sense, Emerson went to Europe to prove to himself something he had known all along — that it was not necessary to travel the world in order to learn human nature...."

Emerson had written: "My greatest want is the very one I apprehended when at home, that I never meet with men that are great or interesting." Emerson met Samuel Taylor Coleridge, William Wordsworth, Thomas Carlyle, Walter Savage Landor, and many other literati and artists, all of whom so stimulated and broadened him beyond the New England mentality that he could now perceive what his life's work must be about.

Though both Emerson and Thoreau stubbornly clung to the maxim that one can travel far in Concord, Emerson was to become one of the best travelled men in America. He was to leave Concord on lecture tours every winter for more than twenty years.* (His second wife was to stay home.)

Despite health problems, his stamina was rigorous enough to endure the hardships of nineteenth century transportation and despite the remarks he made that travelling was "the colera," his trips brought him a better understanding of himself and others, and his mind was opened to new developments in science, evolution, and natural history. It is reasonable to speculate that had he narrowed his opportunities as women have largely been acculturized to do, had he stayed in Concord all of his adult life, he could not have formulated the largeness of his thought and solidified his position as literary giant.

When he returned to New England in August, Emerson stayed

---

*He toured the New England states repeatedly, went South to New York and Virginia, ventured West to Philadelphia, Pittsburg, Ohio, Michigan, Wisconsin, Illinois, California. He crossed the frozen Mississippi three times. He went to Europe three times and to Egypt once. He was to take advantage of many a stimulating opportunity in London, Florence, Paris, Edinburgh, Glasgow. He travelled by carriage, railroad, boat, skiff, sleigh, even by foot, in all kinds of weather, often at twenty or thirty degrees below zero. He would stay at inns, mostly, some quite bad and one caught fire and Emerson escaped by dragging his trunk hurriedly through a corridor. On a Great Lakes cruise the boiler of his ship exploded and caught fire. Many nights he slept on the floor of a small craft; it wasn't unusual that he'd get the worst bed in a hotel or tavern because he'd arrive so late. He endured mistakes in schedules, unheated lecture halls, gas light power failures. He faced the fact that promoters would close the local skating rink so as not to give people an excuse not to attend his lecture or to offer his lecture on the same ticket as a popular ball. Often his audiences were sparse and in the West he lectured before people who were illiterate, people who were looking for a hearty laugh. They did not care about poetry or metaphysics — and some people walked out before he was finished even though Emerson tried to adapt and did add humor. Bliss Perry reported that one person said of his lecture, "I could not catch his meaning; ergo, there was no meaning." No sooner would he deliver his lecture, he would begin another journey — perhaps it would take two or three days to reach his next scheduled speaking date.

with his mother in Newton, Massachusetts and devoted himself to reading geology, chemistry, and physics. In December 1833 his brother William married Susan Haven in Portsmouth, New Hampshire, and they settled in New York City.

The next spring when Emerson, as itinerant minister, preached at the Old First Church in Plymouth, unbeknownst to him in one pew again sat the slender, dark-haired, deeply religious young woman known as the "Saint of Plymouth." With her features of classic beauty and her hair pulled back, she radiated a madonna-like impression. (Emerson's mother had also been referred to as "a saint.")

Lydia Jackson was the kind of person who always, before Communion or Last Supper services, stood up in her family pew and walked out. This represented her dissent to the ceremony.

So mesmerized was Lydia Jackson by Emerson's spring sermon, it is recorded, that when it was over she slipped out of the church quickly so that no one could interrupt her enraptured mood.

Their meeting came about, probably, after one of his Plymouth lectures. Sometime later, as she has told her daughter, she had a vision that she was Emerson's bride, and she saw herself, with him the groom, descending the stairs of her home, the Winslow House.

Religion was central to Lydia Jackson's life. She was a Unitarian with Calvinist rootage. Her ancestors had dedicated the Church. She'd always read scriptures, sang, memorized hymns, attended services. At the age of fifteen she'd passed through a period of religious doubt. At the age of twenty-three she'd visited her aunt in Wood's Hole and, alone on a hill behind the house, she experienced a religious transformation. Some time later she talked with a man from another town about Christ. Later, she would say, "Christ was shown to me." Life *was* rejuvenated; the Bible *had* renewed meaning. Hearing Emerson's words in church that spring day, Lydia felt spiritually akin.

In the summer of 1834 — after a long court battle fought by family lawyer Charles — Waldo received the first part of his $22,000 Tucker inheritance or $1200 per year.* While it did not amount to as much as he had hoped, it did provide a basis for security, and he could

*At that time about $500 per year provided a frugal living for one person.

supplement with lecture fees. Thus, he was enabled to help his mother and family.

From Puerto Rico a blow came in a letter that Edward had died from tuberculosis. There followed great sadness and a period of mourning; then Emerson and his mother moved in with the eighty-eight year-old Ezra Ripley at the Old Manse in Concord. Ruth served as housekeeper in the homey, old fashioned, dusty and dark rooms which had interesting nooks and crannies and closets, and Emerson spent his days reading, writing, walking. Here, in the small study on the second floor, admist bookcases and within view of willow tree, orchard and the Concord River, his forebears had composed their sermons. Here, within sight of the spot where the American Revolution started, Emerson again vowed "not to utter any speech, poem, or book that is not entirely & peculiarly my work."

At some point during the year he had picked up a manuscript and spent some time reading it — it was Margaret Fuller's translation of Goethe's *Tasso,* which Frederick Henry Hedge had loaned him after praising her superior work. (In Groton Margaret Fuller, now twenty-four years old, was reading everything she could find of Emerson's, and was desperately wanting to meet him.)

In January 1835, after he'd organized a series of five lectures in Boston under the title of "Biography" (about men who'd influenced him, Michelangelo, Martin Luther, John Milton, George Fox, and Edmund Burke), he took time out again to travel to Plymouth for another lecture. According to his journal, he returned home on the 23rd but made no mention of seeing or conversing with Lydia Jackson. However, on the 24th, he mailed off a proposal of marriage.

In Plymouth Lydia had had a second vision. Emerson had been standing close to her, gazing steadily into her eyes.

The next afternoon Lydia's maid brought her a letter:

> Concord
> 24 January 1835
>
> To Miss Lydia Jackson.
>
> I obey my highest impulses in declaring to you the feeling of deep and tender respect with which you have inspired me. I am rejoiced in my Reason as well in my Understanding by finding an earnest and

> noble mind whose presence quickens in mine all that is good and shames and repels from me my own weakness. Can I resist the impulse to beseech you to love me? The strict limits of the intercourse I have enjoyed, have certainly not permitted the manifestation of that tenderness which is the first sentiment in the common kindness between man and woman. But I am not less in love, after a new and higher way. I have immense desire that you should love me, and that I might live with you always. My own assurance of the truth and fitness of the alliance — the union I desire, is so perfect, that it will not admit the thought of hesitation — never of refusal on your part. I could scratch out the word ('refusal'?). I am persuaded that I address one so in love with what I love, so conscious with me of the everlasting principles, and seeking the presence of the common Father through means so like, that no remoteness of condition could much separate us, and that an affection founded on such a basis, cannot alter.
>
> I will not embarrass this expression of my heart and mind with any second considerations. I am not therefore blind to them. They touch the past and the future — our friends as well as ourselves, even the Departed. But I see clearly how your consent shall resolve them all.
>
> And think it not strange, as you will not, that I write rather than speak. In the gravest acts of my life I more willingly trust my pen than my tongue. It is as true. And yet had I been master of my time at this moment, I should bring my letter in my own hand. But I had no leave to wait a day after my mind was made up. Say to me therefore anything but no. Demand any time for conversation, for consideration, and I will come to Plymouth with a joyful heart. And so God bless you, dear and blessed Maiden, and incline you to love your true friend,
>
> Ralph Waldo Emerson. [38]

Emerson was now thirty-two; Lydia was eight months older. He barely knew her; he asked to be unreservedly loved by her. But he was reserved in expressing love for her. Yet he could not consider a hesitation or refusal.

Lydia's reaction was to suggest they meet and talk. The meeting was arranged. Years later daughter Ellen described it:

> Lydia shut her eyes while she told him that she foresaw that with her long life wholly aside from housekeeping she should not be a skillful mistress of a house and that it would be a load of care and

> labour from which she shrank and a giving up of an existence she thoroughly enjoyed and to which she had become exactly fitted, and she could not undertake it unless he was sure he loved her and needed her enough to justify her in doing it, and many questions she asked him. [39]

A proposal from The Reverend Ralph Waldo Emerson was quite an honor, but marriage would mean, for Lydia, a giving up of her present lifestyle which she found enjoyable and satisfying. She could only make this "sacrifice" if the man needed and loved her.

She was well indoctrinated as to the proper duties and expectations of nineteenth century wife. She would take the supportive role as healer and guardian, central in the home, needed as symbol to uphold family and moral forces.

Lydia was refined, witty, modest, loving, meticulous, sensitive, religious, a woman who never cried but wished she could, never cut her hair but put it up with a twist with a comb, never wore corsets in a day and age when all women wore corsets, whose stock phrases were "ingenuity of mischief," "main strength and ignorance," "mind the main chance," "abomination of desolation," "mysteries of mysteries," "ye powers! a sight for men and angels!"

She loved fresh air, gardening, horseback riding, dancing, playing whist which she considered afforded better results than medicine. She loved animals, especially cats, fed birds, wouldn't kill spiders nor wasps even inside the house, suffered when animals suffered.

She was an articulate conversationalist, was well read on current issues, philosophy, public affairs, politics, liked to tell anecdotes, and spark controversy. Here's the type of wit she was capable of dishing up: "It is not in the power of 'Sulphur' homeopathic to cure pride ugly pride but a good hymn is always a good medicine."

Emerson wrote to his brother William: "I announce my engagement in a very different feeling from that which I entered my first connection. This is a very sober joy. This lady is a person of noble character whom to see is to respect. I find in her a quite unexpected community of sentiment and speculation, and in Plymouth she is dearly prized for her love & good words."

He gave Lydia a diamond ring that had belonged to Ellen, and

Lydia asked that it be set into a pin; the jeweler did not correctly follow directions, and she never wore it.

Emerson's second love letter was written as follows:

Concord
1 February —

One of my wise masters, Edmund Burke, said, 'A wise man will speak the truth with temperance that he may speak it the longer.' In this new sentiment that you awaken in me, my Lydian Queen, what might scare others pleases me, its quietness, which I accept as a pledge of permanence. I delighted myself on Friday with my quite domesticated position & the good understanding that grew all the time, yet I went & came without one vehement word — or one passionate sign. In this was nothing of design, I merely surrendered myself to the hour & to the facts. I find a sort of grandeur in the modulated expressions of a love in which the individuals & what might seem even reasonable personal expectations, are steadily postponed to a regard for truth & the universal love. Do not think me a metaphysical lover. I am a man & hate & suspect the over refiners, & do sympathize with the homeliest pleasures & attractions by which our good foster mother Nature draws her children together. Yet am I well pleased that between us the most permanent ties should be the first formed & thereon should grow whatever others human nature will.

My mother rejoices very much & asks me all manner of questions about you, many of which I cannot answer. I don't know whether you sing, or read French, or Latin, or where you have lived, & much more. So you see there is nothing for it but that you should come here & on the Battle-Ground stand the fire of her catechism.

Under this mornings's severe but beautiful light I thought dear friend that hardly should I get away from Concord. I must win you to love it. I am born a poet, of a low class without doubt yet a poet. That is my nature & vocation. My singing be sure is very 'husky' & is for the most part in prose. Still am I a poet in the sense of a perceiver & dear lover of the harmonies that are in the soul & in matter, & specially of the correspondences between these & those. A sunset, a forest, a snow storm, a certain river-view, are more to me than many friends & do ordinarily divide my day with my books. Wherever I go

> therefore I guard & study my rambling propensities with a care that is ridiculous to people but to me is the care of my high calling. Now Concord is only one of a hundred towns in which I could find these necessary objects but Plymouth I fear is not one. Plymouth is streets; I live in the wide champaign.
>
> Time enough for this however. If I succeed in preparing my lecture on Michel Angelo Buonaroti this week for Thursday, I will come to Plymouth on Friday. If I do not succeed — do not attain until the Idea of that man — I shall read of Luther, Thursday & then I know not when I shall steal a visit. —
>
> Dearest forgive the egotism of all this letter Say they not "The more love the more egotism.' Repay it by as much & more. Write, write to me. And please dear Lidian take that same low counsel & leave thinking for the present & let the winds of heaven blow away your dyspepsia.
>
> Waldo E. [40]

It is clear Emerson felt they did have commonalities, but this was hardly a love-note of the kind he had written Ellen.

Straightaway, Emerson moved to change her name. Apparently, she submitted to Emerson's will without rebuke.

The assertion to name and to declare the importance of the name is of enormous significance in the balance of power. The namer asserts authority, control and possessiveness — often acting from ego needs — while the receiver acquiesces in receptiveness, believing the namer is benevolent and warmly concerned. One judges and prescribes and the other is obedient.

Emerson added an "n" to Lydia, and then changed the "y" to "i." According to biographers/scholars, he rationalized that when she would take the surname "Emerson," those with New England accents would put an "r" between the two vowels and call her "Lydia-Remerson."

Also, he began to call her "Queen" — note that this is the nickname he gave his first wife, Ellen. Namesmith that he was — (in his Encyclopedia or journal he quoted Goethe: "A man's name is like his skin; it just fits him.") — he elaborated on his nickname for Lydian with "Queenie," "Mother Queeny," "Queen of Sheba," "Sybil," "Angel Heart," his "Palestine," his "Asia."

The latter name Lidian didn't like.

It reflected Emerson's admiration and fascination with Oriental thought. In his essay on Plato he wrote that Asia was "the country of unity, of immovable institutions, the seat of a philosophy delighting in abstractions, of men faithful in doctrine and in practice to the idea of a deaf, unimplorable, immense fate." And "it realizes this faith in the social institution of caste." Scholar Erik Thurin points out that the name "Lydia" was originally applied to female slaves from that part of the world. The caste system is based on birth, a system designed to hold persons in their place (from which there was no escape). Asia is also the place where Paul was confronted with the worship of the Great Mother in the guise of the moon goddess, the Diana of the Ephesians.

According to Emerson, the genius of Europe is active and creative: it resists caste by culture; its philosophy is a discipline; it is a land of arts, inventions, trade, freedom.

Emerson identified the qualities of woman with Asia. He identified the qualities of man — including himself — with Europe.

Thus, in marriage Lydia lost her first name as well as her last.

It is recorded that Emerson wanted Lidian to call him "Waldo," but she insisted on "Mr. E." Her only deviation was when she spoke to the children of "Papa." Her choice indicates that she always regarded him with formality, distant from herself. It can be assumed that she regarded herself as being in a secondary or inferior position despite the fact that she was the eldest and provided a stronghold share of the money to the liaison.

Then there was the problem of where they would live. Concord represented family and historic roots to Waldo as his ancestor, Peter Bulkeley from England, had founded and named Concord for the peace he anticipated.* (Scholar Firkins tells us that Peter Bulkeley

---

* Peter Bulkeley along with Thomas Hooker headed the committee which banished Anne Hutchinson from the state of Massachusetts for her heretical teachings. Her heretical beliefs were similar to ideas Ralph Waldo Emerson would promote two hundred years later.

was feeble-minded, but other accounts differ.) Also, Emerson family members had seen, from Grandfather William Emerson's windows, the first shots fired in the American Revolution.

To Lidian, Plymouth represented family and historic roots. Her Cotton and Winslow ancestors had settled and developed Plymouth Colony in 1631. Her father was the late Charles Jackson, owner of merchant ships, and her mother was the late Lucy Cotton, descendant of the English dissident Rev. John Cotton, who had been a leader found guilty by the Church of England for preaching Puritanism.

Both of Lidian's parents died when she was in her early teens. She and her sister were left sizeable legacies (controlled by their uncle) and both had finished good schools. Lidian boarded first with uncles and aunts in Plymouth and then boarded and lived independently on her six hundred dollars a year which she used on clothing to dress handsomely, on furniture to live exquisitely, on books to read widely, and on people. Her uncle Thomas disagreed with her use of money and Lidian had to fight to get it. She was active in a set of young intellects and enjoyed her days reading, studying, gardening, socializing. She'd spent fifteen happy years of independent life in Plymouth.

Waldo won the housing debate by arguing that he must live "where I can possess my soul...For me to go to Plymouth would be to cripple me of some important resources." [41] Thus, Lidian was the one to relinquish her ties and adjust to the unfamiliar.

Emerson ended his letter, "So do love...Waldo E." [42] He did not mention his love for her.

Like many of the second sex, Lidian seems to have failed to recognize the sexual politics or the power struggle being waged — or if she did recognize it, she did not put up a fight.

Next, because of work on his lectures, Waldo could not travel to Plymouth to visit Lidian as often as he said he wished; then even his letter writing became less frequent.

Soon after the engagement, Lidian went to Concord to meet the Emerson family. They considered her refined and unaffected, not beautiful. Though she did not meet Margaret Fuller, she met her friends, Elizabeth Peabody, Sarah Freeman Clarke, and Lydia Maria Child.

It was three days after she had returned to Plymouth that Emerson noted in his journal: "There is nothing so easy as to form friendships & connections. Yet lies there an unseen gulf between every man & woman."

He did not mention that he saw Lidian or that she made the trip to Concord.

One month later, on March 19, he was writing, "I loved Ellen and love her with an affection that would ask nothing but its indulgence to make me blessed." [43] Clearly, Waldo saw his wife's role in life was to "make him blessed" or to cater to his interests.

During the eight month engagement Emerson briefly mentioned Lidian in his journal twice. Nor did he express warmth to her in any way. In fact, during the same week that he wrote "I loved Ellen," he revealed his perspective of the interaction between men and women:

> There is no greater lie than a voluminous book like Boccaccio. For it represents the pleasure of appetite which only at select & rare intervals a few times in a lifetime are intense, & to whom accrue continence is essential, as frequent habitual, & belonging to the incontinent. Let a young man imagine that women were made for pleasure & are quite defenseless, & act on that opinion, he will find the weakest of them garrisoned by troops of pains & sorrows which he who touches her, instantly participates. He who approaches a woman unlawfully thinks he has overcome her. It is a bitter jest of nature. He will shortly discover that he has put himself wholly in the power of that worthless slut. Montaigne, coarse as he was, is, yet true. [44]

A few days later it was wisest, and happiness, to live alone:

> Alone is wisdom. Alone is happiness. Society nowadays makes us lowspirited, hopeless. Alone is heaven.

The next entry reveals again his sexuality:

> The wild delight runs through the man in spite of real sorrows. Nature says he is my creature & spite of all his pertinent griefs he shall be glad with me. Almost I fear to think how glad I am. I went by him in

> the night. Who can tell the moment when the pine outgrew the whortleberry that shaded its first sprout.* [45]

Before the marriage Waldo chose and purchased for $3500 two acres of land with brook, meadow and the two story John Collidge House (which tourists to Concord may visit today) which was sheltered by a grove of woods within easy view of the peaks of Wachusett and Monadnock. It bordered on Cambridge Turnpike on which stages travelled seventeen miles to Boston in three hours (now Lexington Road) — the Great Road on which British troops marched on their retreat from Concord in 1775. All was within easy walking distance to Walden Pond. Emerson had reservations about the low lying land, but was pleased with its accessibility.

Concord was fields, woods, hills, ponds, two thousand inhabitants, and the narrow, shallow, slow Concord River. It had woody and rocky soil, white wooden cottages, sheds, hen houses and pigeon-houses, and stone pig sties, vegetable gardens, orchards of apples and pears and cherries and peaches, bushes of blackberries and blueberries and whortle-berries and currents, streams with perch and eels and black mud-turtles, scarlet cardinal-flowers, trailing clematis, violets, fringed gentians and a variety of wildflowers, six months of snow followed by torrid heat, followed by Indian summer. The people were hard-workers, not rich, though some were to become comfortable with many of the luxuries of the well-to-do and many were cultivated and self-taught.

He planned that his younger brother Charles and fiance, the lovely and intelligent Elizabeth Sherman Hoar, would also live in a wing which he planned to build. Charles was now working in Squire Hoar's law office in Concord and Elizabeth was his "sunshine." Emerson had known her well since years earlier he had been substitute teacher for her Greek lesson when regular teacher, Ezra Ripley, had been absent.

The Hoars were called the "Royal Family of Concord." They lived

---

*These lines can also be found in Emerson's *Nature.*

in a lovely white colonial home in the heart of the village on Maine Street with barn, garden and orchards. Elizabeth (the oldest of six children) was daughter of the strict and no-nonsense disciplinarian, lawyer and Congressman, Squire Samuel Hoar (with whom the Emersons had blood ties). She and her brothers and sister inherited the pride and wealth of an American ancestry of nationally known politicians, mayors, governors, senators; her grandfather had signed the Declaration of Independence, and one forefather had been president of Harvard in 1672. All the Hoar men, of course, were Harvard graduates. The women were expected to fulfill their roles. Elizabeth was expected to manage the household, especially when her parents were away. Her father was a regular old Roman, strict, formal, cold, a classical scholar. Her mother was patterned from the same cloth.

Elizabeth grew up next door and, later, across the street from the Thoreaus. She and her brothers were schoolmates of Henry David Thoreau at the Concord Academy which her father had founded — he was a firm believer in education for both women and men, and the curriculum was the same for girls as for boys. Her best loves were drawing, reading poetry and stories, playing the piano and singing which she regularly enjoyed with Henry David Thoreau's sister, Helen. She read Greek with friends Sarah Bradford Ripley and Francis Prichard. Loving and pure, yet with the insecurity of the young, she suffered migraine headaches, yet still had a fine sense of humor, a lively spirit, a sense for fashion and "daguerreotyping eyes," as Emerson later described them. Charles described her during the courtship as "fairer than spring flowers & (she) droops not with leaves of autumn." Her only fault, he told her, was that she allowed herself to be acted upon by other people. She should be mistress of herself and not depend upon him for happiness.

Elizabeth and Charles had been engaged over two years; her father had demanded a long engagement. Both had boarded in Boston and had enjoyed a lively social life of balls, parties, lectures, etc., while she attended school. Her father made the offer that Charles take over his Concord law office while he took off to Washington D. C. as Congressman. Thus, Charles moved to a boarding house in Concord, but ate meals at the Old Manse with his mother. Here Lydia Jackson visited for a week.

Whether Lidian was consulted on the plan to have Charles and Elizabeth live with them is not known; however, she did not help to select, she did not even see the house that she was to live in until she moved in the day after the marriage.

(This is the summer Margaret Fuller travelled to Trenton Falls, New York, with her wealthy Cantabridgian friends, John and Eliza Farrar, and the charismatic Samuel Gray Ward, with whom she spent the lovely moonlit evening.)

And this was the summer that Aunt Mary Moody Emerson, now nearing sixty-four years, wrote in her Almanack: "O, I've yearned to open some page; — not now, too late. Ill health and nerves.... I am resigned to being nothing, never expect a palm, a laurel, hereafter...." But Mary was fated to live longer.

Emerson made the power decision to delay the wedding. He was asked to deliver the keynote address at the two hundredth anniversary celebration of Concord; therefore, he would be overloaded with research. Lidian adjusted.

Now thirty-two years of age Emerson had another problem. On August 1 he confessed into his journal: "After thirty a man wakes up sad every morning except perhaps five or six until the day of his death."[46]

Nevertheless, after his "Historical Discourse," Emerson found enough energy on September 13 to begin the drive to Plymouth in a rented chaise and horse which had been decked out with yellow reins in honor of the Bicentennial. He found this too decorative and changed them to green reins. He spent the night in Boston where an abolitionist rally was causing trouble, but this wasn't a concern of the groom who arrived in Plymouth at four in the afternoon — he was supposed to have arrived at noon.

They were to be married at seven thirty, September 14, 1835, in a small ceremony in the Winslow Mansion. Lidian's second vision came true. Downstairs, before she was fully ready, she talked to her cousins, aunts, uncles, and friends including George Bradford (Emerson's best man).* When the minister arrived, she dashed upstairs to dress.

---

*George Bradford was younger brother of Sarah Bradford Ripley. She'd helped to raise and educate him since their mother had died while he was small.

When Waldo finally went up to see what kept her so long, he met her on the landing and, as in her second vision, they descended the staircase and together came to the fireplace and stood before the minister.

Scholar Rusk reports that someone remarked of Lidian as having on the eve of her wedding day, the appearance of "one of the vestals, who in a fit of forgetfulness had let her lamp go out and was preparing herself for the living burial...."

There was no formal honeymoon. They went straight to Concord the next day. Waldo's mother and Charles had readied the house for them. Lidian's married life began with the acceptance of her new home as her mother-in-law had prepared it. Waldo's mother left to visit William in New York, but she was to return to live with them. Emerson was to have two "saints" in his house to share the management.

Lidian brought her furniture, her clothes, her prized Holland bulbs, her old-fashioned rosebushes, and had made arrangements for a later arrival for her chickens.

Within two days a married Quaker couple from New Bedford paid a visit, and Waldo was enthusiastic about being a new homeowner and he suggested they stay overnight. This was quite an annoyance to Lidian because her furniture had not been properly placed. Her sister, Lucy, also arrived, tired and overwrought from travelling. With endurance and patience, Lidian survived the first onslaught of many visitors which would come through their door.

Until November Waldo did not preach or work at his desk. He didn't report in his journal that on October 21 Bronson Alcott visited Concord for the first time, nor about the William Lloyd Garrison trouble at Scollay Square in Boston which had landed him in jail, nor that Alcott had visited Garrison and renewed his pledge to the cause of abolition. Neither Lidian nor Waldo paid much attention to some controversial books that were being circulated in support of Garrison's anti-slavery protests, written by a Southern woman whose family had owned slaves — Angelina Grimke. Nor did The Rev. William Ellery's Channing's small book, *Slavery* concern them.

In Concord life was idyllic and Emerson paid every attention to Lidian. She was supremely happy. Emerson did take time to write a letter to Harvard President Quincy asking that a small monetary dispensation be given to young Concord resident Henry David Thoreau so that he could attend the college. Also Emerson found time to preach in Lexington; Lidian went with him. She especially enjoyed his sermon.

As to money, the newlyweds could manage with economy. There was the income from Ellen's estate. Then there was Lidian's income, small, but substantial. A good portion of her money, though, they agreed, would help to support Lidian's sister and her children, since Lucy's inheritance had been used entirely to help pay her husband's debts.* He had failed in business and had deserted.

Thus Lidian, with marriage — though she brought her own money — became economically dependant.

Emerson, with marriage, commented about his new-found economic security: "I please myself with the thought that my accidental freedom by means of a permanent income is nowise essential to my habits."[47]

How would he have fared with no financial basis? He would probably not have written the books that brought him lasting fame.

Some Concordians thought the Emerson's well off. Daughter Ellen tells the story that a gardener once spitted out to Lidian, "Mr. Emerson has seventy thousand dollars with his first wife and twenty thousand with you! I guess he's got enough!"[48]

In the eyes of Concordians, Emerson seemed rich and indeed he did feel well off. What the Emersons had, though, was never enough to cover expenses.

Recently, sociologists have shown that men need and want marriage — they profit from it. Research evidence has shown that in marriage a man's health, both physical and mental, is better, and that marriage is an asset to a man's profession or career, including earning power. Men who become widows suffer psychological distress. The deathrate for widowers is twice as great as for married women. There is evidence that for men a married life is more comfortable than

---

*Emerson's daughter, Ellen, points out that Emerson made a remark that Lucy could live with them in Concord and "they would still have the use of Lidian's money."[49]

bachelorhood because love, friendship, companionship are offered, sex is always available, and responsibility is a rewarding experience. The "costs" of marriage for men are the imposition of sexual restrictiveness and the demands of economic responsibilities.

Says sociologist Dr. Jesse Bernard: "At the present time, at least… if not in the future, there is no better guarantor of long life, health, and happiness for men than a wife well socialized to perform the 'duties of a wife,' willing to devote her life to taking care of him, providing, even enforcing the regularity and security of a well-ordered home."[50]

Within two months of his marriage, Emerson was again writing about Ellen Tucker in his journal: "…the charming beauty which a few years ago shed on me its tender & immortal light. She needed not a historical name nor earthly rank or wealth. She was complete in her own perfections. She took up all things into her & in her single self sufficed the soul."[51] Thus, he indicates that he married Lidian for her historical Cotton name and for her money.

It should be noted that both of Emerson's wives who gave him economic and emotional support, have been largely obliterated from history.

The cold, snow-laden winter set in, and Emerson travelled and lectured, all the while carrying out his plans for re-modeling the L-shaped house so that his brother Charles and Elizabeth Hoar could settle in. Charles measured the space for Elizabeth's piano and they chose furniture.

Then, Lidian became pregnant and suffered from dyspepsia. She'd had dyspepsia before. She attributed it to overeating and said, "The food you don't eat does you more good than the food you do." She tried to leave the table hungry. Her mother had been an invalid and she'd read many of her uncle's medical books. She believed in hydropathy, cold water baths — both she and Emerson took one every morning. They kept doors open by day and windows open by night even in the cold New England winters.

Straightaway Emerson involved himself in community affairs, regularly attended Town Meeting, preached nearby in Lexington, lectured at the Masonic Temple in Boston, was elected a member of the School Board and found that one of his responsibilities as a young married was as village "hog reeve." This meant that he must assess fines to owners of stray pigs — in actuality he probably never assessed one fine. This was more of a tradition rather than a responsibility. He became a member of the Volunteer Fire Association and a member of the Concord School Library. Emerson's family, especially Aunt Mary, expressed alarm that he was turning further away from religion.

Then Charles was ill again. Emerson cancelled lectures and took Charles to New York to stay in a slightly warmer climate with his brother William who was now successfully practicing law, where his mother was staying now. Away from home, Emerson wrote Lidian long letters and implored her to write long ones to him, and to "love your Waldo E." He ended one with "And so farewell & happily my kind wife & time and the Lord of Time shall bring roses & sunshine for even you & me."

Lidian did have a beauty of her own, and he surely recognized it, at least in the early years. There's a story that she once made Emerson a bit jealous when she attracted a new church organist whereupon Emerson joked that "he guessed he would have to get his pistol out."

Emerson returned to Concord, but soon learned that Charles had worsened. He and Elizabeth Hoar immediately travelled to New York and arrived in time for the funeral. Charles had blacked out the day before, after taking a ride with his mother. Though he'd been plagued so long with lung problems, his death came as a shock. He was only twenty-eight years old.

Emerson wrote to Lidian: "A soul is gone so costly & so rare...." He was glad Lidian had known him. "I should not have known how to forgive you an ignorance of him, had he been out of your sight....And you must be content henceforth with only a piece of your husband; for the best of his strength lay in the soul with which he must no more on earth take counsel. How much I saw through his eyes. I feel as if my own were very dim."

Of Emerson's brothers, only William was left — and Bulkeley who was now confined to the McLean Asylum in Charleston.

Elizabeth Hoar took the death stoically. She spent two weeks at the Emerson home reading and sorting through Charles' letters and papers. She and Waldo considered compiling a memoirs, but the personal writings were heavy with melancholy and depression. Under Charles' outgoing exterior was another personality that wished for the sleep of death. In his papers he praised the dead Ellen Tucker, claimed that Elizabeth's letters gave him strength, and asked to be taken by God.*

Elizabeth Hoar felt a vast void in her life. Though she had opportunities for marriage, she chose to be celibate, true to the memory of Charles — even though Charles's letters encouraged her to be independent: "You will not depend on me for happiness."

She lived with her mother in the white homestead near the Emersons, became "sister" to Emerson and Lidian, "daughter" to his mother, "niece" to his Aunt Mary Moody Emerson, and "Aunt Lizzy" to his (and William's) children. She was the well educated, scholarly maiden aunt whose health was considered frail yet who had an enduring strength, who never ceased to read and learn, never ceased to write sensitive, thoughtful letters, who helped with the births, who read stories to the Emerson children (including Homer in the original Greek), who brought bundles of presents, ran errands, kept various members of the family connected. Thus, she typified the nineteenth century middle to upper class spinster who buried her emotions and spent her life caring about a family other than her own. Emerson wrote of her, "She makes scholars and civilizes by coming into a room."

Emerson may have been shy and self-conscious around women; yet as a sun has satellites, he was cultivating a well selected group, most of whom were single.

He was stimulated and stabilized by them, depended on their response, absorbed and/or borrowed their ideas, often quietly tried to control or influence them, and protected his own creative strength and energy through the use of their services and "covers."

There were many men and women who came in and out of their doors — "Waldo's menagerie," Elizabeth Hoar called them. Some were welcomed for lengths of time, and some who paid short calls. In fact, the cook finally posted a sign at the gate: "This House is not a Hotel."

But if we look closely at those who were most influential, those

---

*McAleer claims that surviving writings of Charles do not indicate that he could have surpassed Emerson in achievement.

who were most truly confidants, those who relieved him of daily burdens in order to free his time for work, we see that there were more women who benefited him than there were men. He needed his "maintenance-supports."

Emerson would not be the first or last man to accustom himself to this method of coping.* Clergymen, educators, writers, and others have often had a need (or vanity) to be paragons of excellence — and to establish an agreeable and enthusiastic female audience to validate their truth to themselves and the world.

In his lecture on "Woman," Emerson wrote that women have an "oracular nature." He discussed their "religious height which men do not attain." Civilization, he wrote, was "the power of good women." "...all wisdom Woman knows."

At the same time, Emerson was resistant towards women. Psychologists will tell us that the male ambivalence stems from the complex developmental relationships from childhood when the boy unconsciously must repress the feeling of a continuing relationship with mother. Though the adult male wants to connect closely with a woman, the fear of being again betrayed and abandoned moves in and draws him away.

What *was* Emerson's attitude towards women?

When it came to women, Emerson was not radical, not innovative, not sensitive. He was conformist. In fact, he had double-vision, just as many men have in the twentieth century.

In his essays Emerson mostly ignored the woman question, which Margaret Fuller and others in the country were triggering. He recognized the rights of women as one of the reforms of the day in his 1839 lecture series, "The Present Age," but he did not expound in any way. He did not again mention the rights of women in this series, nor in his essay, "Reform."

At the end of his essay, "Manners," he tagged mention of the issues. He viewed woman's sphere as being whatever was left over after defining man's sphere: "The open air and the fields, the street and public chambers, are the places where Man executes his will; let

---

* William Ellery Channing and Theodore Parker also were dependent on the support of their feminine disciples.

him yield or divide the sceptre at the door of the house." In other words, in the world the man holds all the power, but in the home man should release up to half of the power to women.

In this essay he ensured his listeners that "our American institutions have been friendly" to women. He felt that chivalrous men would always create whatever reform women wanted.

In his opinion there needed to be little reform in the realm of women's rights because women did not "wish this equal share in public affairs." (See his statement in Chapter VI.)

He was light years behind his radical male contemporaries William Henry Channing, Wendell Phillips, William Lloyd Garrison, Frederick Douglass and Horace Greeley.

Emerson's son, Edward, and other biographers have asserted that Emerson stood up for women's issues, but his writings prove differently. After Margaret Fuller gave validity to the importance of women's causes and after the early feminists had exerted pressure on public and press, then he relented somewhat, but he always appeased and exhaulted. (See Chapter V.)

Emerson believed that "each thing is a half, and suggests another thing to make it whole, as spirit/matter, and man/woman." But, though he encouraged and helped Margaret Fuller locate publishers, he did not largely support women, or their causes. At the same time he did expect and did receive large support from women for his work.

It seems hard to excuse him because he was a radical who led the revolution in thought for the day. He wrote and preached the doctrine of the individual and of the soul. He preached endless growth. He believed in ever-widening circles. (Just as Fuller did.)

Emerson was so humanist that he wrote in his journal in 1832: "There is water enough, we are only to shape aqueducts as to bring it to our door. There is air enough, we must only so build as that it shall ventilate our house. So with man's education. There is truth enough; only open the mind's door, & straighten the passages." [52] It seems he believed in water, air, and education for men only.

One way to understand Emerson's views on women is simply to read his journals. Since he considered these books to be a private resource for his own use, in these we find his gut feelings:

I wish to be a true & free man, & therefore would not be a woman, or a king, or a clergyman, each of which classes in the present order of things is a slave.

July 15, 1834 [53]

Women generally have weak wills.

January 21, 1834 [54]

Women have less accurate measure of time than men.
There is a clock in Adam; none in Eve.

February 8?/1836 [55]

A highly endowed man with good intellect and good conscience is a Man-woman & does not so much need the complement of Woman to his being <of Woman> as another. Hence his relations to the sex are somewhat dislocated & unsatisfactory. [56]

Women see better than men. Men see lazily if they do not expect to act. Women see quite without any wish to act.

November 1839 [57]

A hen without chickens was but half a hen. (NOTE: This has been excised from a paragraph. He means: A woman without children is but half a woman.)

Spring 1844 [58]

It is curious that intellectual men should be most attractive to women. But women are magnetic; intellectual men are unmagnetic; therefore as soon as they meet, communication is found difficult or impossible. Various devices are tried in the villages to wont them, such as candy parties, nut-crackings, picnics, sleighrides, charades, but with slender success.

March-April 1844 [59]

A woman's strength is not masculine, but is the unresistible might of weakness. [60]

Eve softly with her womb
Bit him to death
Lightly was woman snared, herself a snare.
Jan-March 1844 or 45 [61]

(Women) have the drawback of the perplexities of sex. [62]

Love is necessary to the righting the estate of woman in this world. Otherwise nature itself seems to be in conspiracy against her dignity & welfare; for the cultivated, high thoughted, beauty, loving, saintly woman finds herself unconsciously desired for her sex, and even enhancing the appetite of her savage pursuers by these fine ornaments she has piously laid on herself. She finds with indignation that she is herself a snare, & was made such. I do not wonder at her occasional protest, violent protest against nature, in fleeing to nunneries, & taking black veils. Love rights all this deep wrong, but who ever knew in real life a genuine instance of seasonable love? [63]

Women should not be expected to write, or fight, or build, or compose scores; she does all by inspiring man to do all. The poet finds her eyes anticipating all his ode, the sculptor his god, the architect his house. She looks at it. She is the requiring genius. [64]

Women's role in life was as "a docile daughter of God with her face heavenward endeavoring to hear the divine word and to convey it to me." [65]

Is not affluence or at least easy circumstances essential to the finish of the female character — not to its depth & resources perhaps but to the beauty of mind & manners? Is it not because woman is not yet treated properly but some taint of Indian barbarity marks yet our civilization? She was made not to serve but to be served & only wealth admits among us of that condition. — Or is it that an eye to interest is a fatal blot to the female character & the poor scarce can help it? [66]

Did one ever see a beautiful woman, & not wish to look again? Could one ever see enough of a beautiful woman?

March-April 1850 [67]

I scarse ever see young women who are not remarkably attractive without a wish an impulse to preach to them the doctrine of character. I have sad foresight of the mortifications that await them when I see what they look on. Could once their eye be turned on the beauty of being as it outshines the beauty of seeming, they would be saved. [68]

The female sex is another kind of men, more occult and fraudulent than we are through the imbecility of its nature. [69]

Quoted from Plato's *The Laws*,
translated by Thomas Taylor EPP/E Thurin/79

In every woman's conversation and total influence, mild or acid, lurks the *conventional devil.* They look at your carpet, they look at your cap, at your salt-cellar, at your cook and waiting-maid conventionally — to see how close they square with the customary cut in Boston and Salem and New Bedford.

May 2, 1843 [70]

Erasmus or More said it (marriage) was putting the hand into a bag having 99 snakes & one eel. Byron saith the process of love to marriage is like that of wine to vinegar. [71]

"Women," Plato says, "are the same as men in faculty, only less." I find them all victims of their temperament. "I never saw a woman who did not cry," said E. (Elizabeth Hoar) Nature's end of maternity — maternity for twenty years — was of so supreme importance, that it was to be secured at all events, even to the sacrifice of the highest beauty. Bernhard told Margaret that every woman (whatever she says, reads, or writes) is thinking of a husband. And this excess of temperament remains not less in Marriage. Few women are sane. They emit a coloured atmosphere, one would say, floods upon floods of coloured light, in which they walk evermore, & see all objects through this warm tinted mist which envelopes them. Men are not, to the same degree, temperamented; for there are multitudes of men who live to objects quite out of them, as to politics, to trade, to letters, or an art, unhindered by any influence of constitution.

October 14, 1851 [72]

Woman. It is the worst of her condition that its advantages are permissive. Society lives on the system of money and woman comes at money & money's worth through compliment. I should not dare to be woman. Plainly they are created for that better system which supersedes money. But today — In our civilization her position is often pathetic. What is she not expected to do & suffer for some invitation to strawberries & cream. Mercifully their eyes are holden that they cannot see. [73]

"Reigns of women always good, for then, men are sure to rule." [74]

Kindness redeems the condition of women which (in the) most favored excites sometimes profound pity from pity. [75]

A man pities a woman, but his wife does not excite pity any more than himself. He reckons her fortunate in being his. In the whole then no woman is pitiable. [76]

The heart of Woman is the temple of Sorrow. [77]

A man wants a wife to be silly unto. [78]

"See," said Mme de Maintenon, standing by the fishpond at Marly, "how languid the carp are; like me, they regret their mud!" [79]

My prayer to women would be, when the bell rings, when visitors arrive, sit like statues. [80]

Women carry sail, & men rudders. Women look very grave sometimes, & affect to steer, but their pretended rudder is only a masked sail. The rudder of the rudder is not there. [81]

Women are relative in their nature. They exist to take care of men, & when they take up bookmaking, or painting, or shopkeeping, with good earnest, it is only as a resourse or substitute, & is not with them a legitimate primary object, as it is with men. [82]

I am thankful that I am a man. 1833 [83]

Scholars of Emerson usually omit or pass over his views of women in whatever they write. Either they fail to see this issue themselves, or they surmise that Emerson can be forgiven because he had so many other worthwhile things to say and because his views on women were only typical of what all men and women were brainwashed with in early nineteenth century America.

But it is precisely because his views were typical that they need to be published today.

These views were the views of our most revered radical leaders of enlightened thought and intellect.

These views are hostile towards women.

These views promote the distancing between women and men, and sexual politics and/or power plays on the part of both sexes. They promote segregated sex or gender worlds.

These unfortunate views persist.

Throughout the winter of 1835-6 the English abolitionist Harriet Martineau stayed one week at the Emerson's. Time and again she praised Margaret Fuller to Emerson. She thought it would be worth his while to meet her. He promised that he was willing. He had admired Fuller's translation of Goethe's *Tasso.*

During the spring and summer of 1836 Emerson preached at his step-grandfather's Concord Unitarian Church, but found greatest regeneration by hoeing in his garden, writing poetry, swimming in Walden Pond, walking, twirling his walking stick along paths, pausing at Sleepy Hollow Cemetary, or Baker Farm or Peter's Field, or Columbine Rock on the Cliffs.

He was often criticized "for somewhat slovenly attire," as Theodore Parker expressed it. Generally he wore gray suits with a soft felt hat, except on the lecture circuit where his color was black. He had a slight stoop; invariably one shoulder was higher than another. Even so, his stance was majestic, eagle-like, and his deep blue eyes pierced deeply into each person.

Emerson's step-grandfather — the clergyman who told his hired hands to "Put the cow in the battlefield!" — was donating part of his land to the village to memorialize the Concord day that launched the American Revolution. A monument was to be erected and the official committee had asked Emerson to supply a poem. The stirring last two lines of the first stanza are remembered today:

> Here once the embattled farmers stood
> And fired the shot heard round the world.

The poem was to have been read at the unveiling celebration of the Battle Monument on April 29, 1836 but, because of a delay with the stone work, it was postponed.

Emerson had also been working on his book, a prose poem, *Nature,* ninety-five pages that were to launch a revolution in religion. His ideas were distilled from his vast reading.

Nature was a prophetic, idealistic, metaphysical, panthestic doctrine that argued that the past was past, that man had an original relation to the Universe, that there existed a relation of oneness between man and God or the divine. He proposed that communion of divinity is approached through nature directly, without an intermediary (not Jesus whom Emerson doubted was divine).

He felt that man had a responsibility to the Universe which was his property, and that divinity was everywhere around and within a being, within a soul, that religion should come from the depths of the heart, from intuition. "I become a transparent eyeball; I am nothing; I see all; the currents of the Universal Being circulate through me; I am part and particle of God..." he wrote in *Nature*.

Emerson paid one hundred dollars for one thousand copies to be printed by James Munroe & Company of Boston. He deliberately left his name off the book. The publishing date was delayed.

Lidian was feeling deathly ill. She was suffering from her first pregnancy. Years later Lidian told daughter that during her first pregnancy she had been so ill no one thought she would live.

Emerson consulted a doctor who said she was to be repaid for her suffering. She was to have the pleasures of lactation.

Emerson's attraction for Lidian had ebbed.

To him, love became more impersonal with every day. "Affections are but tents of a night." Passions are "deciduous." They end by merging into "the purification of the intellect and the heart." Love, like a pebble thrown into the pond, enlarged in circles as time goes on, and moves towards higher and more interior laws. The first feelings of love are succeeded and supplanted by what is more beautiful.

Likewise, the objects of the affections change.

He was at the height of his creative powers.

He complained in his journal that he lacked animal spirits.

Reserved, aloof, passive, he seemed to have developed an elusive defense, a cover for pain experienced by the deaths of Ellen and Charles.

The manuscripts of *Nature* and *Tasso* were on his library table when Margaret Fuller came face to face with him in July 1836.

S.M.F./R.W.E.
L.J.E./E.T.E.
Z./J./A.B./B.A.
E.H./H.D.T./J.F.C.
N.H./W.E.C.
E.R./W.H.C./C.K.N.
E.P.P./H.G.

AND A FEW OTHERS

Just how it came about that S.M.F. and R.W.E. met face to face at the "mansion of peace" in Concord is not entirely clear.

Emerson emphatically pointed out in *Memoirs* that Lidian issued the invitation.

But Lidian had never been introduced to Margaret Fuller.

Perhaps husband prodded wife because he was curious to see this "sneering, scoffing, critical, disdainful" translator of Goethe's *Tasso*.

He had heard rumors that Fuller "had a dangerous reputation for satire." He was not deaf to those who said she "made a disagreeable first impression on most persons" so that "they did not wish to be in the same room with her." He was aware "the men thought she carried too many guns, and the women did not like one who despised them."

Lidian had heard "from the best authority that she was sound at heart." She "could imagine no peculiarities of intellect or character, that could revolt me or repel my regard.... "

Evidently the advocate-of-all-new-ideas Elizabeth Peabody had also tried to persuade Emerson to "know Margaret better," to go beyond the barrier of first impression.

Or it may have been that Eliza Farrar and Harriet Martineau maneuvered a brief encounter at one of Farrar's parties. Emerson is not sure but he seemed to vaguely remember something like this. Possibly Fuller had indicated to these two women friends her intense desire to make his acquaintance.

Or it might have been that Farrar and Martineau felt so badly for Fuller because she couldn't accompany them to Europe that they tried to think of an alternative for her and sent messages to Lidian or to Elizabeth Hoar to summon Fuller to Concord. There exists a note, apparently from Elizabeth to Charles, that Mrs. Farrar wanted Miss Fuller "cared for spiritually" while she was away and that he should invite her to Concord "so as to draw that lady within the potent circle of the enchantments of Criticism & the First Philosophy."

However it happened, Farrar, Martineau, and the handsome Sam Ward went to Europe, with the beautiful Anna Barker sailing from New Orleans to join the party, and Margaret Fuller accepted the solicitation to Concord.

Lidian was always hospitable. A smoothly run home was one of her chief concerns. She was seven months pregnant, but this did not interfere with readying a room and planning generous meals, prepared by a cook and one of two or three servants. Her mother-in-law was also on hand to help.

When Emerson first laid eyes on Fuller, he saw:

> ...a face and frame that would indicate fulness and tenacity of life. She was rather under the middle height; her complexion was fair, with strong fair hair. She was then, as always, carefully and becomingly dressed and of lady-like self-possession. For the rest, her appearance had nothing prepossessing. Her extreme plainness, a trick of incessantly opening and shutting her eyelids, the nasal tone of her voice, all repelled; and I said to myself, we shall never get far. [1]

Fuller was equally excited. She saw at once Emerson's "high tendency," his "absolute purity," and "the freedom and infinite graces" of a cultivated intellect "much beyond any I had known."

By traditional accounts Margaret laid siege to Waldo. She observed his manners and remarks and agreed with his opinions.

Emerson wrote she "at first astonished and repelled us by a complacency that seemed the most assured since the days of Scalinger."

> She spoke, in the quietest manner, of the girls she had formed, the young men who owed everything to her, the fine companions she had long ago exhausted. [2]

> Margaret, who had stuffed me out as a philosopher, in her own fancy, was too intent on establishing a good footing between us, to omit any art of winning. She studied my tastes, piqued and amused me, challenged frankness by frankness, and did not conceal the good opinion of me she brought with her, nor her wish to please. She was curious to know my opinions and experiences. Of course, it was impossible long to hold out against such urgent assault. She had an incredible variety of anecdotes, the readiest wit to give an absurd turn to whatever passed; and the eyes, which were so plain at first, swam with fun and drolleries, and the very tides of joy and superabundant life.

> I believe I fancied her too much interested in personal history; and her talk was a comedy in which dramatic justice was done to everybody's foibles. I remember that she made me laugh more than I liked; for I was, at that time, an eager scholar of ethics, and had tasted the sweets of solitude and stoicism, and I found something profane in the hours of amusing gossip into which she drew me.[3]

As to her famous satire, he saw that she had been judged superficially, that it was only "the pastime and necessity of her talent, the play of superabundant animal spirits. And it will be seen, in the sequel, that her mind presently disclosed many moods and powers, in successive platforms or terraces, each above each."

He attributed her disagreeable reputation due to "partly the effect of her manners, which expressed an overweening sense of power, and slight esteem of others, and partly the prejudice of her fame."

The first meeting ended with Emerson returning to his library, where he "had much to think of the crackling of thorns under a pot."

Mornings at Concord were for working, reading and writing. After Emerson's ritual of rising at six o'clock and breakfasting on pie and coffee, he would isolate himself in his study, sitting in a favorite rocking chair next to a round center table surrounded by cozy bookcases (on which might be ripening a few pears), backed by a fireplace with mantel topped with a statuette of Goethe and a bust of Plato, both of whom faced a picture of the Fates by Michelangelo. No one was to distract or disturb R.W.E. while in his study.

S.M.F. would usually stay, at work, in the guest room across the hall, the only downstairs chamber, which would alternately be used as Lidian's "birthing room," a medium sized, light, airy room, with a front view of Lexington road and a side view of the orchard. It was nicely furnished with a double-sized bed, washstand and chair.

Emerson was editing Thomas Carlyle's *Sarter Resartus* for U.S.A. publication. Fuller was in the beginning stages of translating the recently published two volumes, *Conversations with Goethe*, written by Goethe's companion/secretary, Johann Peter Eckermann. Also, she was trying to pull together pages for her biography on Goethe.

Lidian and her mother-in-law, Ruth, would busy themselves about the house and garden, manage the servants and worry about the dinner, and read.

At one or two o'clock R.W.E. and the three women had dinner. Lidian had a sharp mind, but probably the two intellects dominated. In the afternoons the four went walking, visiting, or they read aloud to one another. This was followed by tea, after which neighbors and friends often came to socialize. Elizabeth Hoar and grandfather Ezra Ripley would frequently be there. Then there would be the evening meal during which, if there were guests, Emerson permitted the serving of wine. Bedtime was at ten unless special visitors invited delay.

After a few days Fuller's highly favorable first impression of Emerson took on the nuances of what she called "the questioning season."

> I was greatly disappointed in my relation to him. I was, indeed always called on to be worthy – this benefit was sure in our friendship. But I found no intelligence of my best self; far less was it revealed to

> me in new modes; for not only did he seem to want the living faith which enables one to discharge this holiest office of a friend, but he absolutely distrusted me in every region of my life with which he was unacquainted. The same trait I detected in his relations with others. He had faith in the Universal, but not in the Individual Man; he met men, not as a brother, but as a critic. Philosophy appeared to chill instead of exalting the poet.... His "accept" is true; the "I shall learn," with which he answers every accusation, is no less true. No one can feel his limitations, in fact, more than he, though he always speaks confidently from his present knowledge as all he has yet, and never qualifies or explains. He feels himself "shut up in a crystal cell," from which only "a great love or a great task could release me" and hardly expects either from what remains in this life. But I already see so well how these limitations have fitted him for his peculiar work, that I can no longer quarrel with them; while from his eyes looks out the angel that must sooner or later break every chain.... [4]

Emerson noticed Fuller's "rather mountainous ME:.... She could say, as if she were stating a scientific fact, in enumerating the merits of somebody, 'He appreciates me.'"

> In the first days of our acquaintance, I felt her to be a foreigner – that, with her, one would always be sensible of some barrier, as if in making up a friendship with a cultivated Spaniard or Turk. She had a strong constitution, and of course its reactions were strong.... She was in jubilant spirits in the morning, and ended the day with nervous headache, whose spasms, my wife told me, produced total prostration. She had great energy of speech and action, and seemed formed for high emergencies. [5]

Unexpectedly, Fuller's visit was extended to three weeks, July 21 to August 11, 1836.

As the days spanned, Emerson found himself fascinated – "talent, memory, wit, stern introspection, poetic play, religion, the finest personal feeling, the aspects of the future...." He was left "enriched and sometimes astonished by the gifts of my guest. Her topics were numerous, but the cardinal points of poetry, love, and religion, were never far off."

> When I found she lived at a rate so much faster than mine, and which was violent compared with mine, I foreboded rash and painful crises, and had a feeling as if a voice cried, Stand from under! – as if, a little further on, this destiny was threatened with jars and reverses, which no friendship could avert or console. This feeling partly wore off, on better acquaintance, but remained latent; and I had always an impression that her energy was too much a force of blood, and therefore never felt the security for her peace which belongs to more purely intellectual natures. She seemed more vulnerable. For the same reason, she remained inscrutable to me; her strength was not my strength – her powers were a surprise. She passed into new states of great advance, but I understood these no better. It were long to tell her peculiarities....When she turned her head on one side, she alleged she had second sight, like St. Francis. [6]

He gave her an autograph of Jeremy Bentham, philosopher of utilitarianism.

When Emerson heard that Fuller had to become a breadwinner, he summoned his neighbor, educator Bronson Alcott, over to the house. He had a teaching position available – his assistant, Elizabeth Peabody, had walked out over a disagreement. His innovative Masonic Temple School was located in the same Boston building Emerson lectured.

Bronson Alcott was the type of educator who had told an administrator at the American Institute at Worcester that "man is a God on earth." This was a remark which had roused the administrator to express his regret that the expression had been used.

Bronson Alcott was a blue-eyed idealist with corn colored locks and a courtly, simplistic manner who could not understand why people should concern themselves with food and shelter when they could discuss Absolutes. He was married to a woman who said, "Neither the butcher nor tailor will take pay in aphorisms or hypotheses."

His poem, "The Seer's Rations," contains these lines:

> Bowls of sunrise for breakfast,
> Brimful of the East.

People claimed that the sunrise was the food upon which the family feasted.

Bronson Alcott's priority was the pursuit of self-truth and the mystery of life relationships. Largely self-educated, he was an ex-peddler who had travelled through many states selling his wares, an experience which led to his ingenious idea of going off on conversational excursions, the purpose of which was to gather individuals who would pay to converse with him.

Wife Abby May was raised in an intellectual and advantaged atmosphere more prestigious than her husband's. She was a descendent of the May, Sewall and Quincy families, famed in Massachusetts, the men having been judges, scholars, and reformers. She was large, warm, open, volatile, captivating, not beautiful. She could have directed herself towards a scholarly or activist life similar to Margaret Fuller's, as her husband would comment, but she was more interested in the present and temporary. Defensive of her husband's hopes and philosophy, she preferred not to tangle in his "sphere" which did not seem as useful as household and children, Anna, five years old, Louisa May ("Louy"), four years old, and baby Elizabeth ("Lizzy"), named after Elizabeth Peabody, Alcott's assistant.*

Elizabeth Peabody was the exuberant kind that sought out reformers. With her key connections, she'd found some students for a school of her own, but when she met Alcott, she handed them to him and promoted his school until there totalled eighteen five to ten year-olds, including Dr. William Ellery Channing's daughter and the grandson of the president of Harvard. She found furniture and volunteered her assistance for two and a half hours per day for whatever payment could be afforded. She was also teaching in private homes seven hours per day, helping to support her own family – the Peabody name in earlier generations had wealth, now it commanded respect.

By the end of August, Emerson was receiving "like a new coat, full of vexations," the first proof sheets of *Nature*. Fuller, back in the depressing situation of Groton, was querying Bronson Alcott.

---

*Louisa May Alcott became the famed author of *Little Women*. In her fictional story her mother, Abby May, was characterized as "Marmee," Anna as "Meg," Louisa May as "Jo," Elizabeth as "Beth." In 1840 the Alcotts were to birth their fourth daughter, named Abbie May, who would be portrayed as "Amy."

Salary would be low, but Fuller could send most of it to her mother by staying in Boston at her Uncle Henry's. She could also teach privately. Her brother Arthur could be sent to Leicester Academy, where their father had taught thirty-five years earlier. Eugene, now back from tutoring, could stay at home as well as Ellen who could go to school in Cambridge, and Richard's education could resume later on.

Meanwhile, the male ministers were talking of initiating a group support system, a club or symposium. Emerson, Frederic Henry Hedge, George Ripley and George Putnam met at Willard's Hotel in Cambridge and a second meeting at Ripley's house in Boston included Bronson Alcott, Channing, James Freeman Clarke, and others. All concurred that these meetings were worthy to continue.

These men were among the forty-four persons Emerson selected to send copies of his book, *Nature*, fresh off the presses September 9th – and included was the name of Margaret Fuller.

Fuller sent off her thank you note for her three-week visit and Emerson sent Lidian's love, and hoped she'd visit again "as soon as you can." He'd signed off "Your friend, R. W. Emerson."

Fuller invited Emerson to Boston to visit her at Anna Barker's.

Emerson was sorry he couldn't, but why couldn't they ride up to Concord. This would work a cure for Lidian who was ill but who loved her very much. He was going to exchange pulpits with Fuller's Groton paster but since she wasn't to be there he wouldn't see her. He signed off, "Your friend, R. W. Emerson."

Fuller's note opened "My Dear Friend" because "you have subscribed yourself my friend." She detested her Groton pastor because he had twice invited Emerson to preach when she couldn't attend. Wouldn't Emerson postpone? She'd "do twenty times as much" for him. "I would like to baffle the malice of my pastor, and hear better preaching than his own if I could."

She had already read *Nature*, and had passed a copy to Anna Barker whom he should meet since she was going to Concord. She closed: "Mrs. Emerson does not love me more than I love her; but I am not sure how successfully our visit might have ministered to her well-being....Mrs. Emerson's and your friend, S. M. Fuller." Capriciously, she added: "It is a great gain to be able to address yourself directly, instead of intriguing as I did last year."

Emerson dashed off a note. It was too late to alter his Groton preaching date, but he would "be very glad to see you here (at his house in Concord) & to carry you up to Groton & to bring you back with me." He would propose another pulpit exchange when she could be in Groton. He grieved "to have lost sight of your beautiful friend." (Anna Barker) Lidian was better and hoped to see her.

Lidian liked her. Lidian wrote Elizabeth Peabody: "We like her – she likes us. I speak in this way – because you know we came together almost strangers – all to one another and the result of the experiment...was doubtful – the tendencies of all three being strong & decided – and possibly not such as could harmonize."

Fuller was entering the Temple School just as Elizabeth Peabody was walking out and as Bronson Alcott was enveloped in a vitriolic attack against his radical methods of teaching.

Alcott based his Temple School on his own view of education and on the work of the Swiss reformer Pestalozzi. Teaching was simulating the work of Jesus. He believed in the inherent goodness of children, that thinking could be awakened through a conversational deductive system, such as Socrates had used. Openness, self-expression, imagination, the soul and spirit were the intangibles he tried to foster.

He had started his experiments with the birth of his children, he being the first American to keep extensive infant records, the first entitled, *History of an Infant: Observations on the Phenomena of Life as developed in the Progressive History of an Infant During the First Year of its Existence.* He continued his notetaking with the births of his second and third daughters. (The third [Elizabeth] was a birth he insisted on watching, an act considered totally uncouth.)

At the Cheshire School in Walcott, Connecticut, he designed individual desks and equipment that afforded space to the classroom. He introduced blackboards and slates. He advocated light, air and cleanliness, mutual cheerful spirit, mutual kindness. Learning developed with the affections first, then with understanding, memory, the senses, and the heart. He bought books with his own money.

Over the door of The Temple School he hung a sign that read "Universal Unity." In the room he set up pictures and plaster busts of Jesus, Shakespeare, Plato, Milton, a statue of Silence, a small library map, globes. His curriculum included reading, writing, arithmetic, spelling, composition, literature, biology, drawing, speech, geography and Latin. During conversations, he arranged the students' chairs in a semi-circle. He made sure every child kept a journal. He insisted on a playground.

Few were the rules. Punishment was psychological rather than corporal. Rejection and abandonment were his tools. A deviant would be excluded from the daily lesson. Or a child would have to stand in the hall. He would ask a dissenter to turn his face away from him. When someone was noisy, Alcott was apt to comment, "The greatest and most powerful things are not noisy. Did you ever hear the sun make a noise?" Sometimes Alcott would ask a naughty child to walk to an obedient one and touch him. Or, he would shake a good child for the misbehavior of another child. If he could no longer reason with a child, somewhere out of sight of the other children, he would take a ruler to the child's hand only once, or he might ask the child to strike the teacher on the hand. Or Alcott might hit himself. Such actions would show the culprit that wrongdoing had hurt others. Lasting remorse, shame and guilt would be felt.

The controversy that was the eventual ruination of the school started after Alcott decided to publish books describing his methods. Elizabeth Peabody had taken notes which became *Record of A School.* Authorities were attracted. Educators visited, observed. Children's psyches, their mental and physical growth had not before been considered. Alcott began to experience an increase in enrollment.

With almost forty students, Alcott opened the second year with a new series of conversations on the Gospels. He again instructed Elizabeth Peabody to take notes. Dissension developed. She thought the thoughts he elicited from the children resembled his own. He was also unable to take criticism or suggestion.

Alcott directed the new conversations towards what he called Spirit Soul or Spiritual Culturism. After talking about the life of Jesus and the meaning of the spirit, he started reading from the Bible on the births of John the Baptist and Jesus. He asked leading questions, using such words and phrases as "conceived," "deliver," "seed," "flesh," "circumcision," "conjugal relations," "mothers have signs," "she gives up her body to God, and he works upon it," "origin of the body," "the seed of a human being is placed in the midst of matter which nourishes it."

His lessons may have been the first on sex education, but it was an age when babies came from angels.

Peabody had missed these fateful sessions and had arranged as substitute her sister, Sophia, who admired Alcott and recorded his words verbatim. She didn't know her notes were to be published.

Alcott refused Elizabeth's suggestion to "black pencil" the manuscript, so she insisted on writing a forward in which she stated that though his teaching was superlative, she was opposed to some of his ideas. Then she resigned.

Margaret Fuller found Boston dynamic. People saved pennies to buy books and tickets to concerts and exhibits. Many of the new books challenged the stern theology of the past, among which was *Nature* whose author's name appeared nowhere on it. Anyone who was anyone knew who wrote it. If the question was asked "Who is the author?", the reply would be "God and Ralph Waldo Emerson."

Nature was not causing great agitation, but was getting a few mixed critical reviews. There were such statements as "beautiful writing and sound philosophy," but there were many phrases such as "occasional vagueness of expression,".... "a spice of affectation,".... "coarse and blunt," "bathos with malice pretense," "the effect of perusal is often painful, the thoughts excited are frequently bewildering, and the results to which they lead us uncertain and obscure."

Bronson Alcott called it "a gem," "a transparent emblem of the soul."

Thomas Carlyle wrote Emerson, "Your little azure colored Nature gave me true satisfaction."

As Emerson and Fuller were exchanging letters, books, art prints, and witty remarks, Lidian was decorating her magnificent fourposter bed and bedroom windows with matching fringed white curtains. She was anticipating her first-born. Emerson looked on in astonishment: "Too much parade." She dismantled and packed curtains away. Years later, in retrospect, she said: "Husband knows best was my creed in those days, and I really thought he did."

By the end of September, with the baby due any day, Emerson mused in his journal that love in marriage dissipates quickly: "... all love is mathematical."

The next day (probably), September 29, was the anniversary of his first marriage to Ellen, and Emerson doodled the word "Ellen" around his one line entry:

Ellen
I am glad of a day when I know what I am to do in it.
Ellen Ellen [7]

On October 31, a day after the baby was born, Emerson wrote in his journal: "Last night, at 11 o'clock a son was born to me!"

He took full credit for this event.

"Blessed child! A lovely wonder to me, and which makes the Universe look friendly to me. How remote from my knowledge, how alien, yet how kind, does it make the Cause of Causes appear!"

He did add that mother and babe looked beautiful and perfect together. "Every child presents a new aspect," he quoted Lidian as saying, "as the face of the sky is different every hour, so that we never get tired."

As Elizabeth Hoar moved into the Emerson household to help, Emerson named the baby Waldo Jr. He said, "the oldest son should always be named for his father."

Lidian, who had not chosen the name her husband called her, now had no part in the naming of her baby.

In the journals of him whom she most loved, her labor or her recovery was not acknowledged, though her illness was mentioned in a letter to "My dear Miss Fuller."

In Boston at The Temple School "Miss Fuller" spent her days teaching literature, Latin, French and German and, in spare time, was galvanizing private students to read Goethe, Schiller, Lessing and Richter, Petrarch, Ariosto, Alfieri, and Dante. She taught Latin orally to a blind boy and read him the history of England and Shakespeare's historical plays in ten weeks. She also attended concerts and lectures, and worked on her projected book on Goethe, often from her bed at Uncle Henry's. She agreed with Carlyle: "It is wicked to be sick."

One evening per week she went to the home of her "reproving angel," the revolutionary Unitarian reverend, Dr. William Ellery Channing. But instead of copying his manuscripts as Elizabeth Peabody had once done, Fuller alleviated his weak eyes by translating aloud the German writers, De Wette and Herder.

Their sessions would invariably be interrupted with visits by various luminaries...George Ripley, Lydia Maria Child, Jonathan Phillips, Richard Henry Dana, as well as Channing's nephews, William Ellery and William Henry. Her "reproving angel" had radical ideas about equality for women and that God, not men, should protect women.

Hard times hit America in 1837. One of the worst economic depressions our country has experienced was to last about half a decade. Because of expansion and prosperity in manufacturing, transportation, and other businesses, and because of the boom in Western land, there had been an overextension of credit, and now banks were suspending payments. Creditors suddenly couldn't collect. Many merchants were ruined. Three cotton firms failed. Unemployment was rampant. Factory workers returned to farms. Farmers couldn't pay mortgages. An estimated 300,000 trade unionists could not pay their dues. Families were evicted from their homes. Students cried for reform. There were riots in the streets. Debtor's prisons became overcrowded. There was no government assistance.

The Rev. George Ripley was so shaken by the inequalities between the poor and the rich that he introduced revolutionary reform within his church. Contributions were to be voluntary and he eliminated assignment of pews by social rank.

Emerson was one of those living comfortably. The year of the Panic of 1837 was the year he received the second half of his inheritance from Ellen Tucker's estate.

Whether or not Margaret Fuller would receive her salary from Bronson Alcott was a question which conceivably infuriated her headaches.

When Emerson needed extra money he found a hall, rented it, advertised a series of lectures, and put tickets on sale at a central outlet. As soon as enough tickets had sold to cover costs, he would set the dates. Profits were risky, usually moderate. He was now launching a series of ten lectures on the subject of "The Nature and Ends of History" which he delivered in the Masonic Hall.

Persons of all ages came to hear him, but biographer Cooke tells us that the belittling views of John Quincy Adams represented the majority: "...after failing the everyday vocations of a Unitarian preacher and schoolmaster, Emerson starts a new doctrine of Transcendentalism, declares all the old revelations superannuated and worn out, and announces the approach of new relations."

Generally, Emerson read from his manuscript, often misplacing his pages and stumbling. He began in a low tone, calm, sincere, modest, without much spirit, but as he progressed, he became earnest and magnetic. He had many mannerisms, such as rising up on his toes. He had one gesture. Clenching his hand, he would sweep his right arm downward.

His voice was musical, silvery, rich. One description of his style read: "Occasionally at the end of a sentence he would suddenly stop, for what seemed a long time, and with his eyes uplifted upon his audience, looking like one inspired. Everyone in the audience stopped breathing, as if afraid to mar the solemn impression produced. Then another sentence would be commenced on another key; and rising higher and higher, his voice would again drop to lower tones, like the solemn peals of an organ."

Wednesdays Margaret Fuller transcribed Alcott's "Conversations." His first subject was "The Sermon on the Mount," and Alcott admonished: "Nothing, I hope, is to be said here without thought. Nothing is to be expressed, no hand is to go up, without thought."

These encounters were unique even inspiring, but Fuller wrote to Henry Hedge, she was "as ill-placed, as regards a chance to think as a haberdasher's prentice or the President of Harvard University." The very young mind was not challenging, and Alcott was abstract and often dogmatic.

Public bombardment against Alcott climaxed as copies of Peabody's version of *Conversations On The Gospels* were being snatched up. A hundred sold within four days.

Clergymen called the book "filthy." A writer in the *Courier* suggested that Mr. Alcott be prosecuted for blasphemy. Alcott was labelled insane, half-witted, an ignorant charlatan. The most revered sage in Harvard and Boston circles, Andrews Norton claimed that "one third of the book was absurd, one third was blasphemous, and one third was obscene."

Emerson explained Alcott's methods in a letter to the *Courier.* James Freeman Clarke wrote publically that Alcott was a Socrates.

Elizabeth Peabody was sure her reputation would be hurt, but her published argument was ignored. Fuller defended Alcott in letters to Harriet Martineau and Henry Hedge.*

Student enrollment at The Temple School dropped to ten.

Into her fifth pregnancy, Abby May Alcott changed her third daughter's name from Elizabeth Peabody to Elizabeth Sewell Peabody. (The name Sewell came from her side of the family.)

The book on which Margaret Fuller worked, *Conversations II*, was not really read by anyone.

By April Fuller summed up her experiences as having "learned much and thought little."

Instead of paying her, Alcott praised Fuller to an admiring educator who was starting a similar school in Providence, Rhode Island.

Alcott valiantly struggled with his school, but then admitted a negro child. His enrollment decreased to four, the negro and his own three daughters.**

Meanwhile, because there was a void in America when it came to European literature and philosophy, George Ripley planned to publish fifteen volumes of representative European writing and thus one of his editors, a young minister fresh out of Harvard Divinity School, John Sullivan Dwight, pressed Fuller for German translations.

She sent along her translation of Eckermann's *Conversations with Goethe.* Her capable friend Reverend Henry Hedge had refused to translate on the ground that it was "impossible to English" Goethe without "degrading" him. But she defended the process: "Translations are no better at best than an asylum for the destitute, but that asylum must be provided."

Emerson sent Fuller two Thomas Carlyle essays, "The Diamond Neckless" and "Memoirs of Mirabeau," as well as a proof sheet of a

---

* Fuller wrote Harriet Martineau that Alcott was "a true and noble man...whose disinterested and resolute efforts for the redemption of poor humanity all independent and faithful minds should sustain, since the 'broadcloth' vulgar will be sure to assail them...A man the worldlings of Boston hold in such honor as the worldlings of ancient Athens did Socrates." To Henry Hedge: "Why is it that I hear you are writing a piece to 'cut up' Mr. Alcott?...There are plenty of fish in the sea..."

** In 1839 Alcott joined the ranks of the unemployed, picking up part time work digging and hammering for farmers.

new work, *French Revolution*, and Fuller sent him three books, one written by Goethe's literary colleague, Johann Heinrich Merck, plus two volumes of composer Karl Friedrich Zelter. She'd been so busy with petty tasks that she looked "to Concord as my Lethe and Eunoe...I am sure you will purify and strengthen me to enter the Paradise of thought once more."

Probably Fuller met Theodore Parker, a man impossible to dismiss, for the first time at a party. He'd been so poor that he'd never received an education comparable to his contemporaries, but he'd been admitted to Harvard because he'd passed the examinations with superlative scores. Half the time though, he didn't attend classes because he was also earning his living by teaching school in Watertown.

Youngest of eleven children of a Lexington, Massachusetts farmer, he'd latched onto every book in sight from early childhood on, and when he came out of Divinity School he was master of twenty languages. He chose as wife a quiet, intuitive, understanding woman named Lydia Cabot, and after they were married and he was ordained, he accepted the call to the small, rural, unsophisticated Unitarian Society Church in West Roxbury – because it was near Boston libraries. It suited his down-to-earth square-toed Yankee personality which charmed and delighted just about anyone he wished to charm and delight. He began to carve the reputation of a factual truth-seeking affectionate Savonarola, and he proceeded to fill his house with books and bears. In one room there was nothing but books and throughout the house were porcelain and wooden miniature bears, gold shirt studs imprinted with bears, a breakfast cup painted with a bear, and a silver candlestick in the shape of a bear, all in honor of his wife whom he affectionally called "Bear."

Emerson may not have admitted it, but he was feeling the jealousy of the new-father dilemma which psychologists explain encompasses fears of loss, competition and abandonment.

> In life all finding is not that thing we sought, but something else. The lover on being accepted, misses the wildest charm of the maid he dared not hope to call his own. The husband loses the wife in the cares of the household. Later, he cannot rejoice with her in the babe for by

> becoming a mother she ceases yet more to be a wife. With the growth of children the relation of the pair becomes yet feebler from the demands the children make, until at last nothing remains of the original passion out of which all these parricidal fruits proceeded; and they die because they are superfluous. [8]

Emerson's poem "Holidays" is explicit:

> Whither went the lovely hoyden?
> Disappeared in blessed wife,
> Servant to a wooden cradle,
> Living in a baby's life.

At the end of April Fuller and the author of *Nature* met (probably in Boston) and rode together in a carriage to Concord. Fuller had been so excited that she couldn't sleep. But she had "schooled" her "heart not to expect too much."

Presumably this second visit proceeded much as the first, except Lidian was busy with the baby who looked like his father and smiled sweetly. Fuller attempted to correct Emerson's German pronunciation. He seemed not particularly interested in perfecting his German pronunciation.

On Sunday she and the author took a beautiful drive to Watertown. The trees were not in leaf but the birds revelled and talked wildly of their hopes. "Care and routine fled...." She left several of her texts for him.

By the end of the month Fuller was getting ready to become Lady Superior at Hiram Fuller's Greene Street School in Providence, Rhode Island. (The administrator was not a relative.) She was to join a staff of two other teachers and was to teach elocution, composition, history, Latin, natural philosophy and ethics to teenagers, receiving an excellent salary of a thousand dollars a year for four hours of classes per day which would ease life for her mother and younger brothers and sister.

Conceivably, she would have time for her own projects.

Fuller mailed Emerson more books, prints, letters of friends.

He reciprocated thanks and books and Lidian wondered if Fuller wouldn't pitch her tent in Concord a day or two?

On the supposed day of her arrival, the stagecoach stopped and Emerson "left my corn, threw down my Admiral Vernon's hoe & hastened to receive you – and was much dissatisfied to find it was only some books."

He hadn't received her note that she couldn't come. The books were by Goethe and Scougal and there was a letter: "What do you suppose Goethe and Scougal will say to one another as they are journeying side by side?"

Could she stop overnight in Concord on her way to Providence next week?

Emerson responded: "Stop on Thursday and Friday too if you can," but later scrawled across the top of this letter: "What shocking familiarity."

She took the mail stage. Without realizing it, she crossed paths with the Grimke sisters from South Carolina. Sarah and Angelina were abolitionists on their way to Boston to begin their first speaking tour. People who listened to women orators could be expelled as members of their churches. Such had been the consequences to listeners of one Abby Kelley who'd lectured against slavery wherever she could command groups in churches, school-houses, barns, depots, public halls.

Still, many took the risk. Crowds flocked into parlors to hear the Grimke sisters and the meetings were moved to large public halls. Promiscuous audiences (men as well as women) trekked distances to hear Angelina's gentle voice proclaim: "Whatever it is morally right for a man to do, it is morally right for a woman to do. I recognize no rights but human rights."

New York newspapers were lambasting the first National Woman's Anti-Slavery Convention held in May. Many delegates were Margaret Fuller's friends, Lydia Maria Child, Rebecca Spring, Mary Gove, Henrietta Sargent, Sarah Pugh, Abby Kelley, Mary S. Parker, Anne Webster, Deborah Shaw, Martha Storrs, Mrs. A. L. Cox, and Abigail Hopper Gibbons. As a result of the Convention, Angelina Grimke wrote an appeal to the Christian women of the South, urging them to use their influence against slavery. Her sister, Sarah, wrote a similar appeal to the clergy.

Fuller had her own path to tread. Providence was small but The

Greene Street School was impressive with tall Greek columns, arched ceilings, a large central hallway with two dressing rooms, white and pink walls, a piano topped with a French scarf, a sofa for visitors, flowers in vases. There was a prominent card suspended with the motto, "Order is Heaven's First Law," and underneath this was another card with the words, "Study Hours." There were carpets, velvet covered tables, pictures and maps on the walls, all reminiscent of Alcott's Temple School except all was larger, more luxurious. The neatly dressed students were healthy, happy, and mannerly. What more could be wanted, except more books, a few casts of notable persons and a picture or two.

Fuller began a search for private students, planned to work on her Goethe translations, plus continue with her projected *Life of Goethe*, which George Ripley also wanted for his European series. Sam Ward and Eliza Farrar had sent some needed books from Europe but her headaches returned. "It is but a bad head," she complained, "as bad as if I were a great man!" Pain, she echoed Goethe, was a means of growth.

A week in Providence and she was pining for Concord. "Every day I have mentally addressed Concord, dear Concord, haven of repose where headache – vertigo – other sins that flesh is heir to cannot long pursue...."

Emerson was coming to Providence! – to deliver the dedication speech at the opening of The Greene Street School on June 10. Hiram Fuller had first asked Alcott who'd declined because he felt Providence would not welcome a controversial character like himself.

Fuller was ecstatic: "I look forward to your presence as the weary traveller does to the Diamond of the Desert – Flowers will, I trust, spring up.... " She sent "dear love to Lidian, and your Mother....and to little Waldo that I have thought since I came away of a hundred witty things I forgot to say to him: so he must want to see me again..."

If Providence was not ready for Alcott, Providence was not ready for Emerson. His discourse fell on "stony soil" as Fuller later wrote Alcott,* and a "bad" review appeared in the *Providence Journal.*

---

*The speech, now lost, is to have been incorporated later into Emerson's essay, "Education."

Emerson would have been better welcomed by his hometown Concordians for they were set for a festive unveiling of the Revolutionary Battle Monument. Yet he could not attend. His duty was to keep a promised visit to Lidian's relatives and friends in Plymouth even though the immortal Plymouth rock "looked hostile." So while he was walking the Plymouth woodlands on July 4, 1837, the Concord church choir sang Emerson's "Concord Hymn" to the tune of "Old Hundred." Among these celebrants stood a young man who had earned the reputation of attending Chapel at Harvard in a green coat when a black coat was prescribed by the rules. His name was David Henry Thoreau.

Never could Fuller find the time to translate as many Goethe poems as she hoped. English words were inadequate and her collection was "a sorry sight." With apologies she sent John Sullivan Dwight what she had, "To a Golden Heart" and "Eagles and Doves."

Every day the Lady Superior got up at five in the morning and took an hour to dress. Then she studied until seven-thirty, then breakfasted. School was from eight-thirty until twelve-thirty. She returned home, lunched, rested until three. She wrote or studied until six o'clock or tea-time. Saturdays and Sundays she had to herself.

Depression and illness were prone to hit, and she found it within herself to confess to Emerson that she was only kept up by the conviction that "till it was time for me to die, I ought to act as if I hoped to live."

The one drawback at The Greene Street School was "the hostile element of money-getting." She saw great need for reform, for "a great move in the cause of education." Many of the students' minds were "absolutely torpid." She sarcastically referred to her administrator as being "suited for his business."

Her teaching style was unorthodox. Truth held priority. A teacher's best qualities were gentleness, patience, sincere modesty combined with firmness, superiority in tact, quickness in sympathy, an animated manner, liberal views, and habits of exactness, accuracy in processes, principles, and search after the good and beautiful.

Her girls tried to please; she had one group who became worshipfully attached. She didn't try to be popular or beloved; her aim was to draw admiration and trust. She abstained from punishment as much as possible and used encouragement without flattery. "Life is severe," she noted. "An education which in any degree excites vanity is the very worst preparation." Her most important maxim was "If they are imperfect persons, they are immortal souls."

Years later she summarized her views: "Give clear views of the aims of this life, show them (students) where the magazines of knowledge lie, and leave the rest to themselves and the Spirit who must teach and help them to self-impulse."

On weekends she slipped into Boston to see her friends, especially free-spirited Carolyn Sturgis who alternately suffered highs of exhilaration and lows of disillusionment.

Cary was the kind of person who was to ask Henry James, Sr. why he did not raise his "barbaric yawp over the roofs of all the houses," like Walt Whitman.

She was to defiantly sit Sunday mornings at her window, sewing, while passersby went to church.

She was to talk about Henry Adams (who was on a future day to marry her sister's daughter) as a man who "sets himself before himself as the universe."

Sturgis was Fuller's young self, only with wealth and strong formal education, but with less purpose in life and less self-worth. What bothered Fuller was that Sturgis talked about death offering benefits. "You must not die, my Cary – you must keep on bearing noble."

The black cloud of mental insecurity hung over Cary's head. Cary's mother was a free-spirited idealist. To achieve her spiritual nirvana, she had secluded herself, away from her husband, on Cape Cod, stricken most of her married life. Both Cary and her sister Ellen always encouraged her to continue learning, to study German, astronomy, whatever. Cary confided: "Could I but see how she might have escaped her fate, how there was more than a bare chance for her, I should be glad...I believe life is a struggle with powers of darkness, and he who stands at last forth to the light, stands there pale and worn and scarred."

Cary was gifted, charming, capable, vital, imaginative, sensitive with depths of feeling. Growing up, she spent hours at the port of Boston where her father worked. She came to know the sailors, to absorb life aboard ship, to love the sea in all its changes. Her greatest joy was to launch a rowboat and take it far out into the harbor. The sailors watched nervously as she fearlessly plunged the oars back and forth, her hair flying in the wind.

Her "merchant prince" father, at the early age of nineteen, had made a fortune as captain of a China trade vessel. His sparse education never hindered him from becoming commissioner of the Sandwich Islands. Vigorous and powerful, his witticisms fascinated. He scorned pretense, and could speak the language and dance the dances of the Northwest Indians. His dynamic independence brushed onto his two daughters.

Fuller wanted to leave Providence in order to finish her biography of Goethe. She implored Henry Hedge, since he'd lived in Germany, to tell her about Goethe's personal life. No one would talk truthfully to her about this.

She shocked her employer/administrator by attending the Whig Caucus – respectable women, teachers of children especially, did not attend public meetings. She heard Tristam Burgess, whose baldness, she said "increases the fine effect of his appearance." The lawyer Whipple, she said, was not of the Webster class, but was first among men of the class immediately below.

Among visitors to her class she invited James Freeman Clarke who read poetry. And there was Yankee novelist and advocate of women's rights, John Neal. His genius was magnetic but at an evening party they disagreed about Richard III: "Mr. Neal does not argue quite fairly, for he uses reason while it lasts, and then helps himself out with wit, sentiment, and assertion."

She attended a course of readings of the English dramatists, given by the poet, Richard H. Dana: "When he has told you what he likes, the pleasure of intercourse is over.... "

Twice she saw the famous actress Fanny Kemble in *Much Ado About Nothing*, and *The Stranger*. After the first performance she went home, drank her milk, and "dreamed not of Miss Kemble." However, Kemble's second performance evoked tears.

She toured the French man-of-war, *Hercules*, anchored in Narragansett Bay. She should like to command such a vessel.

One letter only went to friend Emerson. She apologized for not writing because: "I have been in an irreligious state of mind, a little misanthropic and skeptical about the existence of any real communication between human beings."

Friendship was becoming a point of contention between the two. Emerson copied into his "Encyclopedia" or quotation book, "O my friends, there is no friend, said Aristotle."[9]

In his journal:

> Is it not pathetic that the action of men on men is so partial? We never touch but at points. The most that I can have of my fellow-man or be to him, is it the reading of his book, or the hearing of his project in conversation? I approach some Carlyle, with desire and joy. I am led on from month to month with an expectation of some total embrace and oneness with a noble mind; and learn at last that it is only so feeble and remote and hiant action as reading a Mirabeau or a Diderot paper. This is all that can be looked for; more we shall not be to each other. Balked soul! It is not that the sea and poverty and pursuit separate us. Here is Alcott by my door – yet is the union more profound? No; the sea, vocation, poverty, are seeming fences, but man is insular and cannot be touched. Every man is an infinitely repellent orb, and holds his individual being on that condition.[10]

Emerson maintained that people wished to communicate but there was always a wall of separation which prevented understanding and intimacy.

Fuller thought his conviction "paralyzing...However, I must say I feel a desire, now that my vacation really is coming, to see my dear no friends, Mr. and Mrs. Emerson.... " She closed: "I hope the baby has not grown too large for me to hold for my heart is much set upon that pleasure."

Her no-friend was working on a speech. He had been invited to give the Phi Beta Kappa address at Harvard commencement. Rev. Dr. Wainwright had turned the invitation down; Emerson was second choice.

Emerson suggested Fuller attend the ceremonies and then ride with him and Lidian in their carriage to his house for the Transcendental Club meeting on the following day. Women had never been admitted to the Club meetings, and he did not want to break rules but "what can you not mould the Transcendental members into in an hour!"

Thus, on the morning of the last day of August 1837, following a fanfare of band music and a promenade of gowned undergraduates across Harvard Yard to The First Parish, Fuller sat in the plain wooden meeting house* with the Phi Beta Kappa Society audience along with President Josiah Quincy, James Russell Lowell, Bronson Alcott, Frederic Henry Hedge (on visit from Bangour, Maine), James Freeman Clarke (on visit from Louisville, Kentucky), Lidian Emerson, Julia Ward Howe, Elizabeth Hoar, Elizabeth Peabody, Jane Tuckerman, Cary Sturgis, Fuller's brother and two hundred students, alumni and community residents.**

Emerson's American Scholar Address was an event James Russel Lowell described thirty-seven years later as being "an event without any former parallel in our literary annals." All writers have since similarly described the speech – except contemporary biographer John J. McAleer who found that Emerson's speech was received by many as "Transcendental nonsense."***

"What crowded and breathless aisles," Lowell wrote, "what windows clustering with eager heads, what enthusiasm of approval, what grim silence of foregone dissent!"

But McAleer points out that the opportunity to speak on this occasion was not considered especially exciting, and Emerson's remarks were not original.

Emerson's voice has been described by Nathaniel Parker Willis, editor of *The Evening Mirror*: "It is a voice with shoulders in it, which he has not; with lungs in it far larger than his; with a walk which the public never see; with a fist in it which his own hand never gave him the model for; and with a gentleman in it which his parochial and 'bare-necessities-of-life' sort of exterior gives no other betrayal of."

Fuller thought Emerson's elocution charming. "The tone of the

---

* Built in 1834, this meeting house succeeded the log meeting house where, in 1637, Anne Hutchinson had been brought to trial and exiled from the state of Massachusettes.

**At least one biographer claims that Dr. Oliver Wendell Holmes was among those seated, another has doubts, and perhaps David Henry Thoreau was there, though historical reference seems lacking; however, this was the year he graduated from Harvard and at Commencement exercises he had participated in a debate on the Commerical Spirit.

***This speech marked the end of Emerson's preaching, for only four more times was he invited to fill pulpits.

voice was a grave body tone, full and sweet rather than sonorous, yet flexible, and haunted by many modulations, as even instruments of wood and brass seem to become after they have been long played on with skill and taste...."

In the famous speech, Emerson called for an original American literature, independent of European culture. He attacked the materialism of the day, emphasized the importance of nature, the value of one's own thinking, working out of the living present instead of the past. "If the single man plant himself indomitably on his instincts, and there abide, the huge world will come round to him."

Dr. Oliver Wendell Holmes called his words, "Our Intellectual Declaration of Independence," proof that "the Transcendental nose was one that stretches outward and upward to attain a foresmell of the Infinite."

Conservatives and liberals felt Emerson was "burning the books," slapping them in the face. Hadn't they broken with traditional Calvinist beliefs.

Edward Everett Hale wrote in his diary that Emerson was "half-crazy" which seems to have also been the opinion of many.

In the *Boston Quarterly Review* Emerson was hailed by Orestes Brownson as one of the "youthful expectants of a coming brighter hour of social life...yet would we see him more fully warmed with the great social idea of our era...of human brotherhood, of sonship to God."

From across the seas in England, Thomas Carlyle praised: "...you have a fearful work to do! Fearful I call it, and yet it is great and the greatest."

A clever young Bostonian jack-of-all-arts, Christopher Cranch, sketched some satirical pictures. One showed a tower built of books by Homer, Virgil and Shakespeare, on top of which was a building that looked like Harvard. A giant caricature of the tall, thin Emerson, burdened with the gravity of books, says, "They pin me down." In another area small men complacently float in the River of Time on a raft in the form of a book labelled Cicero. One man yells, "He's talking against Cicero!!!"

Another amusing Cranch portrait is a profile of a long legged, thin, barefooted figure (Emerson) stepping ahead briskly in a formal dinner coat with tails flying. The head is abnormally large and round and out of it protrudes a large round eye. This signified the transparent eyeball Emerson had described in *Nature.**

The day after The American Scholar Address, September 1, Emerson gathered together his coterie at his house in Concord for the Transcendental Club meeting. The four brilliant women never before admitted were Margaret Fuller, Elizabeth Hoar, Sarah Alden Ripley, and Lidian Emerson. Lidian had the honor to hostess the eighteen who sat at her dining table for beef, boiled mutton with caper sauce, ham, tongue, corn, beans, tomatoes, macaroni, cucumbers, lettuce, applesauce, puddings, custards, fruit, and nuts.

Sympathies go out to Lidian. Even though she was quick, keen, and aware of current thought, even though leading intellectuals came in and out of her door every day, even though she was "a personality once seen never to be forgotten,"** she nevertheless was relegated to the backstage position of setting a lavish table, of feeding guests. The domestic life for which she was not paid closed in on her and consumed her, overshadowing any hope of her receiving recognition for her other abilities, overshadowing the possibility of her developing any identity other than Emerson's wife which in the end gave her no recognition at all.

The circle around Emerson's table was called "The Transcendental Club," or "Hedge's Club" because it met when Frederic Henry Hedge made the trip down from Bangor, Maine, or it was called "The Symposium Club," or "The Club of the Like-Minded" because, as Thoreau suggested, it was a group of individuals who could see all thought different.

These Unitarian reverend members have been adroitly described:

> Hedge supplied the trained philosophic mind; Convers Francis, the ominous mental appetite; James Freeman Clarke, the philanthropic comprehensiveness; Theodore Parker, the robust energy; Orestes A. Brownson, the gladiatorial vigor; Caleb Stetson, the wit;

---

* Cranch soon left for adventures in the West and in Louisville James Freeman Clarke snapped him up as staff member on *The Western Messenger.*

** A phrase used in her *Boston Herald* obituary.

> William Henry Channing, the lofty enthusiasm; (George) Ripley, the active understanding, (Cyrus) Bartol, the flame of aspiration; (Bronson) Alcott, the pure-idealism; Emerson, the *lumen siccum,* or dry light.[11]

Gradually, others were admitted such as John Sullivan Dwight, Rev. N. L. Frothingham, James Walker, Jonathan Phillips, Dr. William Ellery Channing, Jones Very, George P. Bradford, H. D. Thoreau, Dr. Le Baron Russell, and once George Bancroft.

Transcendentalism was a new word, a new growth, as Julia Ward Howe described it, "hard, dry, and thorny...like the blossoming of a century plant, beautiful and inconvenient," which, "if society would not give it room, it was determined to go outside of society, and to assert, at all hazards, the freedom of inspiration."

No one was really able to explain what this new growth meant; each Transcendentalist seemed to speak a different language. The ultimate was to achieve human perfectability. Transcendentalists were truth-seekers. They wanted to explore, to go beyond established custom, to feel, to perceive anew.

But it was just as permissible to stand and wait, to receive the self and truth from the faithful infinity. Being alone was given the glad-hand. Institutions, rituals, organizational structures were contraband unless rooted in individuality.

"The only guest not tolerated was intolerance," wrote The Rev. William Henry Channing who also summed up: "Trust, dare and be; infinite good is ready for your asking; seek and find. All that your fellow can claim or need is that you should become, in fact, your highest self; fulfill, then, your ideal."

Emerson was saying that divinity was within every human soul. Individuals could empower within themselves inward goodness and genius. His stance incorporated a spontaneous, intuitive sense, above and beyond the five senses, that would lead to the achievement of the ultimate of truth, harmony and beauty. God existed. God was within Man, within the Soul, and in Nature. You could commune with God through nature. There was no intermediary. Divine wisdom, absolute love, and joy could be found in all of life. Evil could change into good, wrong could change into right, pain would change to peace. Justice would prevail. Faith in God would make right. Truth was in the Soul.

Emerson's theories were not based on scientific fact, but on intuition and conscience. In his essay, "The Transcendentalist," he wrote: "The Transcendentalist adopts the whole connection of spiritual doctrine. He believes in miracles, in the perpetual openness of the human mind to new influx of light and power; he believes in inspiration, and in ecstasy...."

These concepts stemmed from the eighteenth century philosopher Immanuel Kant who had built upon the philosophy of seventeenth century Englishman John Locke who concluded that all ideas and knowledge came from sensory experience. Locke also advocated freedom and individuality. Kant worked out concepts on sensations and perceptions and showed that reason was man's greatest intellectual asset, with moral duty as an individual responsibility. He claimed that there were intangibles that could not be comprehended, due to the limitations of the mind, which transcended experience and this system he called Transcendental philosophy.

Two other eighteenth century German philosophers added their ideas. Frederick Henry Jacobi was a proponent of intellectual intuition and sense experience and his system came to be known as the philosophy of feeling. Johann Gottlieb Fichte, disciple of Kant, advanced mystical religious views that the soul mirrors God. Also, there was the German philosopher/disciple Fredrich Schelling who offered insight that within man there are irrational impulses; his metaphysical theory was known as the system of identity. And there was his friend, George Wilhelm Fredrich Hegel, who championed the Absolute Ideal and attempted to explain the universe as a systematic whole, that man's intuitive knowledge was the highest form of truth and experience, but Hegel was so ambiguous that many could not understand. He is quoted to have said, "One man has understood me, and he has not."

Schleiermacher was another contributing influence, positing that feeling exists, that God lives and works from within.

From England came the two poet friends, the dreamy sensual Samuel Taylor Coleridge and the metaphysical William Wordsworth whose joint publication of *Lyrical Ballads* launched what was considered as the Romantic Movement.

Then Thomas Carlyle, in an effort to promote German ideals to the English, wrote out translations and interpretations. The word of these great thinkers spread to America where all was latched onto, within the context and needs of the American mind, and thus all was Americanized to fit the inalienable rights of our own individualities.

All was quite radical to even the liberal Unitarians of 1837 who now rejected the Trinity, now asserted that Jesus was supreme and that he had lived, and was the mediator between God and man. To them, the miracles were literal truth.

So Transcendentalists gathered together.

Not at Lidian's lavish table after the American Scholar Address was David Henry Thoreau, native-born Concordian who considered it unfortunate that anyone was birthed in London, Paris or Rome. He may very well have been in Lincoln at Flint's Pond sharing a hut he and Charles Stearns Wheeler had built for loafing, reading, and sleeping.

After graduating from Harvard, Thoreau decided that teaching was a more apt profession than working in his father's pencil-factory where he was eventually to develop the perfect lead pencil. (Reportedly, when asked to market this worthy item, he said, "Why should I do this? I have shown that I am able to produce the best pencil that can be made. This was all that I cared to do.")

He accepted a teaching position at the Town School in Concord – the same school he'd attended as a boy. Emerson had networked to obtain the engagement. It was a real coup because jobs were impossible to find, the country still in a depression.

Thoreau's teaching career lasted a fortnight. He refused to flog the students. When the school committee Deacon informed him he must use corporal punishment, he accordingly whipped six students who apparently had done nothing wrong, but afterwards he felt so badly about it that he quit, an action which astonished the town elders.*

---

*Emerson tried to get Thoreau another position in New England – no one would take him on. Thoreau said: "Am I not made of Concord dust? I carry Concord ground in my boots and in my hat."

At about this same time, David Henry Thoreau decided to change his name. Probably he felt Henry David Thoreau sounded better.

Thoreau was brought to Emerson's attention by Lidian's sister, Lucy Brown. The hard-pressed Thoreaus were living at the Parkman House at Sudbury Corner and Henry's mother took in boarders, one of whom was Lucy. She was twenty years older than Henry and probably represented to him the idealization of womanhood. One day, on a short visit home from college, Henry cornered Lucy's attention by throwing through her window a bunch of violets which he'd picked during his day's walk. Tied around the stems was his poem, "Sic Vita," which begins:

> I am a parcel of vain strivings tied
> By a chance bond together,
> Dangling this way and that, their links
> Were made so loose and wise,
> Methinks,
> For milder weather.

One of Henry's two sisters, Helen, a Concord music teacher, showed Lucy a passage of Thoreau's 1837 journal. Both saw parallels with Emerson's thought. Lucy read some of the pages to Emerson who admired. Thus, the support of the women launched the friendship.

Thoreau was so influenced by Emerson that he took on his tone, voice, manners, gestures, methods of expression, style of writing – even brushed his hair, walked like him and copied his handwriting. Emerson wrote, "I am very familiar with all his thoughts – they are my own quite originally drest." Theodore Parker called Thoreau a small beer imitation of Emerson. Nathaniel Hawthorne thought he was ugly as sin, but "of an honest and agreeable fashion, and becomes him much better than beauty." He had a long crow's beak nose and a strange mouth, was sometimes uncouth and rustic, according to Hawthorne, but always courteous, and "a healthy and wholesome man to know."

Henry David Thoreau was the sharp-eyed, bright third child of four who was supposed to have brought the family fame and fortune by entering a profession or becoming a businessman. His father had gone bankrupt with a Concord general store, and the rest of his family, mother, brother, sister, struggled to combine their earnings to send Henry David through Harvard.

But Henry, who enrolled at the age of sixteen, hardly found the hallowed halls pleasant. He much preferred the library or walks by himself. One professor called him an "odd stick." There's a myth that he refused his Harvard diploma. It is recorded that upon learning that a science school was to be structured at Harvard he wrote Emerson: "They have been foolish enough to put at the end of all this earnest the old joke of a diploma. Let every sheep keep but his own skin, I say." Once, when Emerson asserted that Harvard offered all branches of knowledge, Thoreau parried with, "Yes, indeed, all the branches and none of the roots." He was later to write: "To my astonishment I was informed on leaving college that I had studied navigation! Why, if I had taken one turn down the harbor I should have known more about it."

History records that his gray-blue eyes were always down, either on the ground or on a book. He walked on the grass so as not to hear the sound of his footsteps. One sound that he liked to hear was an echo.

His mother had developed in him a love of nature lore by taking her children on walks in the woods at sunset, defining the joys of listening and seeing. She took her youngsters to lectures at the Concord Lyceum, gave them music and dance lessons, saw that Henry was schooled at Concord Academy. As a boy, he and his brother, John, shared hunting and tracking expeditions and fishing in the wilds of Concord, canoeing on the *Musketaquid*, the Indian name for the Concord River. They fantasized about building their own boat and gliding off to unknown regions – Henry built his first boat, a rowboat, *The Rover*, when he was sixteen. Three years later, while awaiting to re-enter Harvard after dropping out briefly with the first of his tubercular attacks, he nailed together another boat, "a kind of oblong bread-trough," with sails, which he called the *Red Jacket*.

When he and his brother John went to work in their father's pencil factory, John – who was considered by everyone gifted for the better future – developed symptoms of tuberculosis. Immediately John switched to tutoring, which was how Helen, the sister, earned sustenance, and the family turned to Henry David for financial solvency. But Henry David perceived the values of the world turned wrong side up, with money the goal and thinking for oneself mistrusted. Though it was torturous to decide to disappoint his family, he couldn't help but think that he was rich when he had little. His flute, his spyglass, his microscope and walking half of every day in the woods contented him. It was happiness to hike eight or ten miles "to keep an appointment with a beech-tree or a yellow-birch, or an old acquaintance among the pines."

In Providence teaching kept Fuller busy and depressed but not so busy and depressed that she couldn't mix in with the social scene of Sarah Helen Whitman and bluestocking, Rhoda Mardenbrough Newcomb, whose son, just graduating from Brown, was Charles King Newcomb. She visited phrenologists and mesmerists. Providence was the center of this "cult" that was sweeping the country. And Fuller visited a blind somnambulist, Loraina Brackett, who seemed to temporarily relieve pains in her head, but whom Fuller decided was "good for nothing" after Brackett told her she'd never be better if she continued to read.

Fuller worried about her family in Groton. "Sordid" Uncle Abraham dished out such heavy-handed dominance and "vulgar insults" to her mother that Fuller considered finding another lawyer. She counciled her mother "to act as we agreed when I was with you...You must not let his vulgar insults make you waver as to giving the children advantages to which they would be well entitled if the property were only a third of what it now is...Fit out the children for school, and let not Lloyd (who was mentally retarded) be forgotten...Ellen shall not be treated in this shameful way, bereft of proper advantages and plagued and cramped in the May of life...we will see if she is not to have a year's schooling from twelve to eighteen..." Fuller had to take additional private students to provide the dollars for her sister's education.

Also, she counselled Cary Sturgis, Jane Tuckerman and other friends. She was so sure she could help Cary find a sense of worth that she wrote to William Sturgis to permit Cary to temporarily stay with her so they could study and socialize, perhaps the entire winter. To Fuller's great happiness, he consented and she began to search for a proper boarding house.

By fall Fuller's headaches nagged her into submitting to that standard medical treatment of being bled by leeches. This seemed to relieve. She consoled herself by phrasing quips to Emerson – "Who would be a goody that could be a genius?"

How could she refrain from comparing her single lifestyle in boarding houses and classrooms with that of her female contemporaries? For instance, word now came that the wife of William Henry Channing had given birth to a daughter. He was resigning his church among the New York poor and was set to resume itinerant preaching in Boston.

Fuller pinned hopes on Cary's arrival. She planned a reading schedule for her beginning with Carlyle's *French Revolution* – which Emerson had just arranged to be published on this side of the Atlantic. But Fuller's sister Ellen visited for a round of social activities including seeing the English touring actress, Ellen Tree, and meeting with the leading phrenologist, Orson Fowler, for head examinations. Cary never came.

Another disappointment came with Harriet Martineau's new book, *Society in America.* It was not a book Americans could adore. Bostonians veered off since Martineau had damned Boston as the "headquarters of Cant." Most considered the book full of errors and generalizations. To Fuller it didn't matter that the press reviewed it unfairly. What mattered was that there was "a degree of presumptuousness, irreverence, inaccuracy, hasty generalization, and ultraism...."

Fuller had a theory about truth. If you told your friends the truth, the air would be cleared of social shams and hypocrisies. Friendship could deepen with genuine sincerity and respect on both sides.

So when Martineau filled page after page with the cant of abolitionism, Fuller felt compelled to offer the truth: "Why leaven the whole book with it?...It is a great subject, but your book had other purposes to fulfill."

Fuller sensed her criticism might be too strong: "if your heart turns from me, I shall still love you, still think you noble.... "

Martineau's heart did turn from Fuller. Their close friendship ended.

In Concord, everything was running the way Emerson wanted it to run.

> The ultra benevolence of mine Asia (Lidian) reminds me of the pretty fable of the seven cedar birds sitting on the bough who passed the morsel which one had taken from bird to bird with courtesy until it returned again to the first. None cared for the morsel. All are fed with love. Asia makes my gods hers. [12]

Lidian had become superb in making Emerson's gods her gods.

Lidian implored "Mr. Emerson" to express his love for her. There is an anecdote that she tiptoed into his study, took his pen and inscribed three names on a blank page: Ralph Waldo Emerson, Lidian Emerson, Waldo Emerson. Then she tiptoed away. Another time she left a maxim in his notebook that he would be sure to find: "If you wish men to love you, love them."

She slept with him, she adjusted to his life-style, she commemorated the memory of his first wife, she listened, and was there when he came home, had a baby by him, managed the household and fed and entertained his friends. Much of her money went to pay the bills. Was it too much to ask him to say I love you.

On his part, "Mr. Emerson" begged Lidian to love him. "You must love your affectionate husband." He wrote similar appeals time and time again. But he had little love to give her. Or he withheld his love. The underlying effective sexual politics were, "If you love me, you will do what I want." Or, "I will love you if..."

Biographers have described Emerson as a detached individual. He was pitiably incapable of establishing warm sensitive give-and-take relationships with those he needed most. His was an isolating reserve which closed off a part of himself to others, as well as to himself.

On February 9, 1838 he registered in his journal – and what is fascinating is that he copied and inserted these words into his major essay, "Self Reliance":

> You must love me as I am. Do not tell me how much I should love you. I am content. I find my satisfactions in a calm considerate reverence measured by the virtues which provoke it. So love me as I am. When I am virtuous, love me; when I am vicious, hate me; when I am lukewarm, neither good nor bad, care not for me.
>
> But do not by your sorrow or your affection solicit me to be somewhat else than I by nature am. [13]

The partner or other person must exert the flexibility if any unity is to occur. No allowance is made for difference. There is love only when two people agree with each other. Otherwise, there is divorce, separation or distancing.

His ideas generated from Swedenborg who thought love and marriage was a temporary form. Emerson expressed it in his essay:

> ...all loves and friendships are momentary. Do you love me? means, Do you see the same truth? If you do, we are happy with the same happiness: but presently one of us passes into the perception of new truth; – we are divorced, and no tension in nature can hold us to each other....Heaven is not the pairing of two, but the communion of all souls. We meet, and dwell an instant under the temple of one thought and part, as though we parted not, to join another thought in other fellowships of joy. So far from there being anything divine in the low and proprietary sense of Do you love me? it is only when you leave and lose me by casting yourself on a sentiment which is higher than both of us, that I draw near and find myself at your side; and I am repelled if you fix your eye on me and demand love. In fact, in the spiritual world we change sexes every moment. You love the worth in me; then I am your husband: but it is not me, but the worth, that fixes the love; and that worth is a drop of the ocean of worth that is beyond me. Meantime I adore the greater worth in another, and so become his wife. He aspires to a higher worth in another spirit, and is wife or receiver of that influence. [14]

Did Lidian clam up, or did she take a trip?

She did go on a trip to Plymouth about a week later. When he wrote her, he did an unprecedented thing. He signed the letter "Your loving husband." Generally he signed, "Yours affectionately. R.W.E." When she didn't write back, he wrote another letter. This time he admonished her and treated her like a little girl: "Who is a naughty girl? All the household inquires What news from Mrs. E.?"

The day before he had resigned from preaching at the church in East Lexington; therefore, he cut off a portion of income. Evidently he had not consulted Lidian on this decision. He was sensitive that she might not be pleased:

> ...But does not the Eastern Lidian, my Palestine, mourn to see the froward man cutting the last threads that bind him to that prized gown and band, the symbols black and white of old and distant Judah? [15]

That night he entered in his journal:

> Solitude is fearsome & heavy hearted. I have never known a man who had so much good accumulated upon him as I have. Reason, health, wife, child, friends, competence, reputation, the power to inspire, & the power to please. Yet leave me alone a few days, & I creep about as if in expectation of a calamity...my gentle wife has an angel's heart. [16]

The next day he wrote Lidian again. No longer was she naughty: "Why yes you are a good Lidian." His next letter he signed off, "You must nevertheless love your affectionate husband R.W.E." In his next letter she was addressed as "Excellent Lidian."

But within two weeks after Lidian had returned, Emerson so had his first wife Ellen on his mind that he spent an entire evening telling his second wife about his first wife's virtues. He reproached himself for his lack of warmth to Ellen:

> Last night a remembering & remembering talk with Lidian. I went back to the first smile of Ellen on the door stone at Concord. I went back to all that delicious relation to feel as ever how many shades, how much reproach...Ah could I have felt in the presence of (Ellen) as now I feel my own power and hope & so have offered her in every word & look the heart of a man humble & wise, but resolved to be true & perfect with God...I might haply have made her days longer & certainly sweeter & at least have recalled her seraph smile without a pang...This is the thorn in the flesh. [17]

Lidian must have been a solid support to him during that "remembering" night talk. He was sharing his thoughts and feelings. She wanted him to care about her own feelings. By confiding in each other, she hoped they could attain a closeness.

But when opportunity arose for him to listen sympathetically to a woman, he could show no heart. Elizabeth Hoar spoke to him about her troubling conflicts, which paralleled his since both of their first loves had died.

> Last night E. H. described the apathy from which she suffers. I own I was at a loss to prescribe as I did not sufficiently understand the state of mind she paints. [18]

His style of public lecture and performance conformed with his limitation. He stated his truths as he perceived them, implied they were experiments, and then closed the matter. His audience was expected to "take it or leave it." Within two years his first volume of *Essays* would be published with these revealing words from "Circles:"

> I am not careful to justify myself....But lest I should mislead any when I have my own head and obey my whims, let me remind the reader that I am only an experimenter. Do not set the least value on what I do, or the least discredit on what I do not, as if I pretended to settle anything as true or false. I unsettle all things. No facts are to me sacred; none are profane; I simply experiment, an endless seeker, with no Past at my back.

His audience accepted his statements as new, exciting, creative, open-ended, innovative.

Lidian, Margaret Fuller, Elizabeth Hoar, and Cary Sturgis attempted to understand, accept, and adapt. They admired. Loved.

To find time to write seemed impossible to Fuller. She had to inspire her proteges at The Greene Street School and also tutor German to a Baptist minister, a Brown professor and a graduate, a daughter of a member of congress, a poet. The conflict brought on despair.

Barely had she begun work on her Goethe article when George Ripley announced to the world in the first-volume preface of *Specimens of Foreign Standard Literature* that *A Life of Goethe* would soon be included in the series.

"Flat, stale and unprofitable," she moaned to friend Emerson about her life, yet to sustain his friendship she must hold to a light tone that captured his fascination.

> Many a Zelterian epistle have I mentally addressed to you full of sprightly scraps about the books I have read, the spectacles I have seen, and the attempts at men and women with whom I have come in

> contact. But I have not been able to put them on paper, for even when I have attempted it, you have seemed so busy and noble and I so poor and dissipated that I have not felt worthy to address you.
>
> At present I am not at all Zelterian in my mood but very sombre and sullen. I have shut the door for a few days, and tried to do something; you have really been doing something. And that is why I write. I want to see you, and still more to hear you. I must kindle my torch again. Why have I not heard from you this winter? I feel very humble just now, yet I have to say that being lives not who would have received from your lectures as much as I should. There are noble books, but one wants the breath of life sometimes. And I see no divine person. I myself am more divine than any I see – I think that is enough to say about them ... I hate everything that is reasonable just now, "wise limitations" and all. I have behaved much too well for some time past; it has spoiled my peace. What grieves me too is to find or fear my theory a cheat – I cannot serve two masters and I fear all the hope of being a worldling and a literary existence also must be resigned – Isolation is necessary to me as to others. Yet I keep on "fulfilling all my duties" as the technical phrase is except to myself.– But why do I write thus to you who like nothing but what is good i. e. cheerfulness and fortitude? It is partly because yours is an image of my oratory. I suppose you will not know what this means, and if I do not jest when I write to you I must pray....Devoutly if not worthily yours, S. M. Fuller.[19]

Depression and sullenness in women were emotions for which Emerson had no real sympathy. He had seen far too much in Lidian, Elizabeth Hoar and his Aunt Mary, and he was not pleased to see it in Margaret Fuller. Within the past few months he'd written in his private journals:

> .... to women my paths are shut up and the fine women I think of who have had genius & cultivation who have not been wives but muses have something tragic in their lot & I shun to name them. Then I say Despondency bears no fruit.... It is ignoble (to owe) our success to the coaxing & clapping of Society.... That only is great that is thoroughly so and from the egg, a god.
>
> Therefore I think a woman does herself injustice who likens herself to any historical woman, who thinks because Corinna or de Staël or M. M. E. (Mary Moody Emerson) do not satisfy the imagination and the serene Themis, none can, certainly not she.... let the maiden with erect soul walk serenely on her way, accept the hint of each new

> pleasure she finds, try in turn all the known resources, experiments, pleasures that she may learn from what she cannot as well as what she can do, the power & the charm that – like a new dawn radiating out of the Deep of Space – her new born being is.*
>
> Tears are never far from a woman's eye. The loveliest maiden on whom every grace sits, who is followed by all eyes, & never knew anything but admiration weeps much and if unexpected changes should blast her hopes then the tears fall so naturally as nothing but grief seems her native element. [20]

Emerson felt women should take hold of themselves, control their lives, stand on their own two feet rather than weep.

How could Fuller not agree, for she daily fought the battles. But she felt he was not sensitized to the laws which checked woman.

In Providence the banalities of the pseudo-intellects increased her headaches. To Lidian she mentioned her problems, but it was to Cary alone that she could talk about the dæmons that afflict women who desired to achieve: "We shall be in this life mutilated beings, but there is in my bosom a faith that I shall sometime see the reason...."

Undoubtedly, Fuller hailed the latest about the fiery Angelina Grimke. "Devil-ina," as the press labelled Grimke, had spoken out against slavery amidst yells of defiance, stones thrown against windows, shouts of "Fire!" She had broken established procedure by addressing a Committee of the Massachusetts Legislature at the State House and her reward had been press that inferred a woman who so exposed herself would never find a husband.

Fuller hadn't met the Grimkes. Sister Sarah had opened the first session of the National Convention of American Anti-Slavery Women in one of the most luxurious buildings in any city, the $40,000 Pennsylvania Hall. While outside crowds surged against walls and blocked the streets, she had cooled the abolitionists. Her followers had walked bravely through rioters, who were so angered that in the cover of night Pennsylvania Hall was burnt to the ground.

Undoubtedly, Fuller heard about Dorothea Dix who was touring the country making the public aware of conditions in asylums and prisons.

---

*This paragraph is included almost verbatim in Emerson's essay, "Heroism." He changed the names Corinna and M. M. E. to read Sappho and Sevigne.

Undoubtedly, Fuller heard pacifist sentiments of the American Peace Society, and about the energetic work of the female anti-alcohol crusaders led by The Rev. Lyman Beecher.

There was also the New York writer/lecturer, Mary Gove, whose women audience members fainted when she unveiled a nude female model. It was Gove's way of introducing the science of anatomy.

But public exposes, riots, demonstrations, burnings were not appealing to Fuller whose background and talent were literary. In Providence she was missing Emerson's newest lecture series, "Human Culture," but she managed a short trip to Boston, staying with the Sturgis family, and was able to attend his "War," sponsored by the American Peace Society. His words, praised highly by men such as William Lloyd Garrison, were directed to men:

> ...a man should be himself responsible, with goods, health, and life, for his behavior...should ask nothing of the State...because in himself reside infinite resources; because he is sure of himself, and never needs to ask another what in any crisis it behooves him to do.

She met him the next day in Boston and evidently asked if he would be her confidant and soul confessor. He hedged. By May he wrote that he "dreamed even of being the Auricular confessor you spake of in Boston to whom every day's fancies & results were to be dotted down & transmitted."

Rather than Goethe or Tennyson, he should talk to Fuller of his garden, his pig, his forty pine trees, and taxes because, as Kant ascribed, "'detestable was the society of mere literary men.'" He had just been to another Transcendental Club meeting. Being in the company of literary men "must be tasted sparingly to keep its gusto. If you do not quit the high chair, lie quite down, & roll on the ground a good deal, you become nervous & heavyhearted. The poverty of topics the very names of Carlyle Cambridge Dr Channing & The Reviews become presently insupportable. The dog that was fed on sugar died."

His son, Waldo Jr. was as handsome as Walden pond at sunrise. He invited Fuller to visit again. "Lidian, though not present, loves you." Onto his letter Lidian tagged her own note of welcome to Fuller and Sturgis, and she included some examples of Waldo Jr.'s babytalk.

So in June Fuller and Sturgis went to Concord. They took along a portfolio of several hundred engravings that Samuel Gray Ward had brought back from Italy.

Fuller and Ward had been sharing good moments. They'd meet in the Boston Athenæum, a favorite stamping ground for friends, because it contained fine exhibits of antique and contemporary sculptures, engravings and drawings of the French and Italian museums.

Ward was a bit older, a bit more sophisticated, and more knowledgeable about art and art history. Fuller was avid to hear his every word, not only about the Italian museums, but about all his European experiences. He shared pictures of Raphael, Michelangelo, Da Vinci, Guercino, of the architecture of the Greeks, the books of Palladio, the Ruins, and Prisons of Piranesi. His conflict of whether to become a banker or an artist kept gnawing; Fuller encouraged his artistic nature.

When Fuller and Sturgis left Concord, Emerson thought, "For a hermit I begin to think I know several very fine people." Then he turned his attention to his tomatoes and rhubarb and potatoes which were doing excellently despite bugs.

Back teaching in Providence, Fuller was fighting ninety three degree weather and a mile and a half walk to and from school plus homesickness.

Undoubtedly she was cheered to hear how members of the Massachusetts legislature had created the country's first Board of Education and how Horace Mann, as secretary, worked for free schools, compulsory teacher training and school attendance.

The two Thoreau brothers, Henry and John, had just opened the Thoreau School for boys at the abandoned Concord Academy and were establishing their own theories for learning which excluded flogging and included boat building, log floating, tree measuring, and half-hour recesses. Classes included a weekly walk in the woods to discover birds or Indian arrowheads or plants ready to bloom, or a sail on the river or a swim in a pond.

If only Cary were with Fuller. She felt "so much the need of somebody to bring me strengthening drinks, or to bathe my head.... I wish I could lean on some friendly arm for a while."

She took her August vacation, stopping a day or two at Concord with more Sam Ward European engravings. Emerson looked at them "with profit," but nerves were edgy in the household. "Dirt was being thrown" on Emerson, she wrote to a friend, though he "shown out through all this fog."

Emerson had stirred up new waves of controversy with his July 15 address delivered to the Harvard Divinity School senior class. The graduating class had numbered seven students, but the audience numbered about a hundred and the most prestigious scholars in the country had been in full force in the little Divinity Hall chapel, including Dean John Gorham Palfrey, Professors of Divinity Henry Ware and his son, and Rev. Andrews Norton, retired and working on his masterpiece. From the more radical contingent there was Frederic Hedge, Theodore Parker, George Ripley and Elizabeth Peabody. The "bridge" between the two opposing forces, The Rev. William Ellery Channing, might have been there.

Actually, Emerson was not saying anything new; it was his poetic style that made the thoughts sound fresh.

In a glorious rich baritone, which James Russell Lowell later described as "so charged with subtle meaning and music, as shipwrecked men on a raft to the hail of a ship that came with unhoped for food and rescue," Emerson challenged religious tradition, questioned the value of the scriptures, criticized the worship of the person of Jesus, denied that Christ was God, and advocated, not worshiping, but following the teachings of Jesus. To Unitarians, who believed that God could be reached through Jesus as mediator, Emerson said: "Dare to love God without mediator or veil." He challenged the graduates "to go alone...cast behind you all conformity, and acquaint men at first hand with Diety." Truth, good and reason was within the soul.

Emerson was surprised that some had thought he was trying to belittle the character of Jesus. On the contrary, he was trying to place reverence for Jesus upon its true ground.

The day after his Address, Emerson, silent in Concord, wrote in his journal, "Little Waldo cheers the whole house by his mooing calls to the cat, to the birds, to the flies – 'Pussy-cat, come see Waddow! Liddle Birdy, come see Waddow! Fies! Fies! come see Waddow!'"

No sooner had The Rev. Theodore Parker declared that ink would be spilled on both sides than the highly prominent Rev. Henry Ware wrote Emerson a letter advising him not to continue with his line of thought.

Emerson answered: "It strikes me very oddly that good and wise men at Cambridge and Boston should think of raising me into an object of criticism. I have always been.... a 'chartered libertine,' free to worship and free to rail'.... I could not possibly give you one of the 'arguments' you cruelly hint at, on which any doctrine of mine stands; for I do not know what arguments are in reference to any expression of a thought. I delight in telling what I think; but if you ask me how I dare say so, or why it is so, I am the most helpless of mortal men...."

Soon began a whispering word-of-mouth campaign: "folly"... "nonsense"... "disgraceful"... "impiety"... "misguided"... "dangerous."

Emerson was atheist, a heretic, a devote of Pantheism. His phraseology was lampooned: "Ever the sun shines." "Myrrh and rosemary."

His typical reaction was to withdraw – to remain silent. He left Concord briefly to give an address at Dartmouth, then quickly returned.

Ware preached a sermon against Emerson's view.

An anonymous article in the *Boston Daily Advertiser* made waves into the East: "The evil is becoming...disastrous and alarming... religion has been insulted...." The anonymous writer blamed the graduating class for having invited Emerson. Then the anonymous writer was recognized as Andrews Norton.

Cheering, of course, was the Transcendental faction, as well as wife Lidian, brother William and step-uncle Samuel Ripley.

Aunt Mary, who'd, because of a previous disagreement vowed never to return to the Emerson household except on a litter, was now so enraged that she demanded his address be thrown "to oblivion."

Harvard's doors slammed against him.*

---

* It was not until 1867 that Harvard finally honored Emerson with a Doctor of Laws and Overseer and asked him to again deliver the Phi Beta Kappa address. President Charles W. Eliot, nepthew of Andrews Norton, arranged to have the Emerson Hall built in Harvard Yard.

Emerson and Lidian began to worry that lecture dates would dissolve into thin air.

Emerson decided to print his Address at his own expense, after the Divinity School class had made an offer, and the public snapped up his pamphlet for twelve and a half cents each.

Some sort of friction developed between Fuller and Lidian. Fuller was worrying about her projected break from the Providence school and probably didn't know that Lidian was three months pregnant. Whatever the problem, back in Groton Fuller apologized for her "evil doing." Two days later Emerson mailed her a copy of his Address.

Fuller retreated for a part of the summer to Newport and spent time with Charles King Newcomb: " a character of monastic beauty," she wrote Jane Tuckerman. He had fine perceptions and could talk about Homer and Dante and Goethe.

The Divinity School Address saga continued for more than two years. Andrews Norton published his masterpiece, *The Evidence of the Genuineness of the Four Gospels.* A year later, as the invited lecturer, his stance was: "There can be no intuition, no direct perception, no metaphysical certainty." He damned the new thinking in his Address, "A Discourse on the Latest Form of Infidelity."

He published this sermon in a pamphlet, to which the brilliant Rev. George Ripley answered in "The Latest Form of Infidelity Examined: A First, Second and Third Letter Addressed to Mr. Andrews Norton."

In turn, Norton ridiculed and accused Ripley of scholarly incompetence.

Ripley attacked Norton's logic, stating that his tone and ideas were outdated.

Norton and others replied.

In retaliation, Ripley wrote over four hundred printed pages.

The whole incident was seen as "dirty" theology because the unwritten code of conduct upheld by Unitarian ministers was to refrain from attacking each other publicly.

George Ripley had been in his youth the "good boy" who'd followed directions and learned everything. Warm, cheerful, scholarly and studious, he'd come from a wealthy family living in the Berkshires. At Harvard he'd been called "Ripley the pious," and had graduated with top ranking. Within a year, after being installed in the Purchase Street Church, across from the site of the Boston Tea Party, he feared the preacher's soul "falling into a dead palsy and performing his sacred functions with little more emotion than he would tend the boiler of a steam engine or turn the wheel of a grindstone." Arguing that "the wandering sheep in the wilderness excited more interest than the ninety and nine which were safe in the fold," he used his learned scholarship in lectures outside the milieu of his church.

In 1840 Theodore Parker got out a pamphlet, "The Previous Question between Mr. Andrews Norton and His Alumni Moved and Handled in a Letter to all Those Gentlemen." Signing his name "Levi Blodgett," Parker argued: "You make our religion depend entirely on something outside, on strange events which happened, it is said, two thousand years ago, of which we can never be certain...."

In the July 1840 *Boston Quarterly Review* Orestes Brownson honed his knife: Mr. Andrews Norton "usually sits in a room with the shutters closed which has the double effect of keeping the light out and the darkness in."

James Freeman Clarke defended Emerson in his newspaper *The Western Messenger*, and Christopher Cranch was well fueled for a series of cartoons. He passed these along to friends and James Freeman Clarke collected them in a scrapbook called "Illustrations of the New Philosophy." One landed into the hands of enemy Andrews Norton who advocated publishing them since he thought they ridiculed Emerson.

Almira Barlow made the remark that Transcendentalism was "a little beyond."

One man described the new philosophy as something "which has risen maintaining that nothing is everything in general, and everything is nothing in particular."

Feelings of vulnerability and insecurity surfaced within Emerson:

> The censure...does not hit me; and the praise is very good.
>
> I know too well my own dark spots, not having attained, not satisfied myself, far from a holy obedience, how can I expect to satisfy others, to command their love? A few sour faces, a few biting paragraphs – is but a cheap expiation for all these shortcomings of mine.[21]

In the end Emerson wrote a poem about the controversy, "Uriel" – himself against the establishment.

One reason Transcendentalism seemed so eccentric was because each adherent promoted differently. Alcott, for instance, hiked through backwoods areas to hand out his and Emerson's writings.

The fact that each adherent considered it was his right to pursue whatever method seemed best to accomplish goals seemed divisive to traditionalists, but to Transcendentalists diversity – and freedom – represented strength. Transcendentalism could be identified as dissent. Dissent was noble.

That summer of 1838, Emerson was making two new friends. Since Fuller urged, he invited Sam Ward to Concord for the weekend. Concord was hardly Ward's upper crust social sphere. He went because of his long standing friendship with Fuller. There was also an age difference – Ward was years younger. But the idealism of Ward and Emerson turned out to be simpatico and long lasting.

Emerson was also striking up a kinship with one of Ward's Harvard classmates, Jones Very , who had twice won the Bowdoin Prize. Elizabeth Peabody had brought this meeting about. She had been so taken by Very's lecture on epic poetry that she wrote Emerson to invite him to speak at the Concord Lyceum. Emerson's reaction was: "Such a mind cannot be lost."

This eccentric was thought by many to be insane. He beheld visions from the Holy Ghost who spoke to him and dictated what he should write. He had just been released from a month's stay at MacLean Asylum in Charlestown. He had been committed after being dropped as freshman tutor in Greek at Harvard because he'd cried out to his class, "Flee to the mountains, for the end of all things is at hand!"

After visiting with Very for a week, Emerson wished "the whole world were as mad as he." Very "charmed us all by telling us he hated us all."

John Sullivan Dwight queried Fuller as to how she wanted her name signed under her German translations. All contributors to his European series were men – except for her. Some were signing their full names, George Bancroft, James Freeman Clarke, William Henry Channing, Charles T. Brooks, Frederic Hedge, but some used initials:

N. L. Frothingham, C. P. Cranch, G. W. Haven. Fuller requested her initials: "S. M. Fuller."

Fuller's translations were received favorably by the Transcendentals, including Thomas Carlyle who claimed that no Englishman had "uttered as much sense about Goethe and German things."

In December Fuller missed Emerson's new lecture series, "Human Life," which opened at the Masonic Temple in Boston with "The Doctrine of the Soul," which contained the embryo of his philosophy, that within the temple of man is the Oversoul...that man is wiser than he knows and can accomplish and enter the highest sphere.*

Fuller also missed his lectures, "Home," "The School," and "Love." His fifth, "Genius," was set for January 2,1839. Fuller was ecstatic. She could be there. But as she arrived, the audience was leaving. The lecture had been postponed because Emerson had felt sickly.

"How could you omit your lecture?" Fuller berated in a letter. "Could you not have taken some other time for your 'slight indisposition.' I fancied L. (Lidian) was worse and had passed from diet on ricewater to nothing at all. I sent a maiden to inquire at Mrs. A.'s (Alcott's) and she returned all smiles to tell me that Mrs. E. (Emerson) was quite well, that Mr. E. (Emerson) had lost a night's rest!! but had since rode to Waltham, walked five miles, sawed wood, and by use of these mild remedies was now perfectly restored. Imagine my indignation: lost a night's rest! as if an intellectual person ever had a night's rest...."

Friend was apologetic and defensive: "As Night preceded the first Day, so always wise men have slept upon their problems, and an insomnolent counsellor is as good as none."

Fuller could always read his lectures at leisure. He lent them to her whenever she requested. In the one entitled "Love," there would be little with which she could agree.

Emerson always wrote from the standpoint of universality but, like most writers, he wrote from his own perspective, basing his premises on his own private experience. No woman can identify with or benefit from his premise.

---

*Later to be published with the title, "The Over-Soul."

Emerson was saying that love is a beautiful illusion. Though there are moments when the affections rule, as time goes on, as lovers discover faults in one another, love becomes more impersonal.

Sexual love is a degradation; affections are "but tents in a night." It is only bodies touching – not souls. Lovers give gifts, but never give of themselves.

People cannot love each other. A person always loves himself.

Love is an imprisonment. A wise person will see through the illusion. "In the procession of the soul from within outward it enlarges its circles ever, like the pebble thrown into the pond, or the light proceeding from an orb."

Love cannot last, though the original attraction will reappear from time to time, and at last other strengths will be found.

Love and affection will be lost but will be supplanted by what is more beautiful, the intellect and soul. "The real marriage is the purification of the intellect and the heart.... That which is so beautiful and attractive as these relations, must be succeeded and supplanted only by what is more beautiful, and so on forever." When two persons achieve impersonal relations, they have achieved the highest sphere.

Fuller's conclusions were entirely different. She could agree that the first passionate love cannot last, but she insisted she would love in faith that could not change. She advocated a search for the ideal great love which is ennobling and pure. "Pure love, inspired by a worthy object, must ennoble and bless, whether mutual or not." She quoted: "Steep the soul in one pure love, and it will last thee long."

Emerson considered that the law of love and friendship was ebb and flow – change – and each person should leave attachments when necessary.

Fuller could not totally disagree with these laws of change, but in no way could she support the advocacy of less intimate, impersonal relationships. She envisioned new understandings, new ways of being, sharing and caring that bring new levels of satisfaction. She wanted men and women to aim towards balanced structures, which permitted couples to live together with considerably more ease than was so far known, to "live in perfect harmony, where they would correspond to and fulfill one another, like hemispheres, or the tenor and bass in music."

Man must see that woman was half himself, that her interests were identical with his.

She awaited the day when the sexes would meet as equals, when they would meet mind to mind, and a mutual trust was produced "which can buckle them against a million," when they would become partners in work and in life, "the pillars of one porch, the priests of one worship."

The subject was one they'd discuss eternally.

When Emerson heard that the Fullers were selling the Groton Farm, he suggested they move to Concord. He said Lidian also urged the move. He suggested Fuller rent the Thoreau house or one next to the Hoar's, or another that he thought would be available. Lidian was now seven months pregnant, often ill, and Elizabeth Hoar had come back into the household, again to smooth and soothe. Then Emerson caught cold and had to stop househunting for "O Excellent Lady," but she should come to Concord and look for houses herself. He said Lidian begged her to take the first coach.

Nothing could make Fuller happier than to sell the farm and resign her teaching position in Providence. As to a permanent move, she was considering Cincinnati where her family would be near William Henry Channing's church. But she thought it best to stay on the farm until April, for an "Elysian peace" – the first free time she'd had in seven years. She could continue with her Goethe book, and give Ellen lessons in German and her brother Latin and composition. Later perhaps her mother, Ellen and she would board somewhere while the boys would be off in school.

Isolating herself by spreading the word that she needed to work, she began to arrange her books, clothes, papers, accounts, letters. After this she felt so depleted that she dropped into bed. Then Ellen and her mother became sick and she in turn nursed them.

Removing herself again, she studied, read Goethe, Plato, Coleridge, Jones Very's sonnets and his Shakespearean essay sent by Emerson. (It was "inferior"; he did not grasp his subject. Emerson was concerned about Very; he was dying or becoming hopelessly mad.)

Her mother made her some loose fitting robes and she wore these when she had severe pain, plus she applied friction to her head, when necessary. When the torment prevented her from working at a table, she would work from her bed. When she couldn't write, she would dictate to Ellen or her mother.

She read Ben Jonson, her father's debates in Congress, and she revised her translation of Eckermann's *Conversations with Goethe* for the George Ripley series. To lull herself to sleep she read Vivian Grey and Maryatt's novels.

She examined more than a thousand of her father's letters accumulated over forty years. She packed her father's books in preparation for the upcoming family auction, and left her room only to take mile-long walks and to play the piano.

Meanwhile, what could bring Cary Sturgis to a "high"? Cary was entering another bleak depression. "The mountain and the valley express it exactly – We do not soar up direct like the lark! but our advance is always in the undulating line....You must expect a season of dimness and grey discontent.... Do thou build high and strong the ladder before thou dost try to climb –" She sent Cary books, pictures and various letters of friends, including Emerson's.

By the end of January Fuller "banqueted" with Plato's *Phaedrus* and was "delighted as ever in anything really Greek." More words of cheer to Cary – one learns to appreciate the good life only by experiencing trauma.

> I love the stern Titanic part, I love the crag, even the Drachenfels of life – I love its roaring sea that dashes against the crag – I love its sounding cataract, its lava rush, its whirlwind, its rivers generating the lotus and the crocodile, its hot sands with their white bones, patient camels, and majestic columns toppling to the sky in all the might of dust. I love its dens and silvery gleaming caverns, its gnomes, its serpents, and the tigers sudden spring. Nay! I would not be without what I know better, its ghostly northern firs, haggard with ice, its solitary tarns, tearful eyes of the lone forest, its trembling lizards and its wounded snakes dragging to secretest recesses their slow length along.
>
> Who can know these and other myriad other children of Chaos and old night, who can know the awe the horror and the majesty of earth, yet be content with the blue sky alone. Not I for one. I love the love lit dome above I cannot live without mine own particular star; but my foot is on the earth and I wish to walk over it until my wings be grown....Tell me your secret, tell me mine. To be human is also something?... [22]

Fuller sent Cary her translation of *Tasso,* adding: "I have great faith in you – And I do not wish to urge myself on you as a heroic or a holy friend. I believe it is best to receive me principally through the intellect, yet love me as much as you can."

Cary sent a letter box she'd decorated and lined. It was not pretty enough to house Sam Ward's letters. Ward was an Ariel that deserved every creature's best.

Wouldn't Cary "tax her genius" to illustrate a portfolio of Fuller poetry – even though it was "All 'rhetorical and impassioned' as Goethe had said of Madame de Staël…."

She labored over the proof sheets of Eckermann's *Conversations with Goethe* and finally sent them off to Ripley.

In Concord, Lidian was due any day to give birth to her second child. She told husband that she'd dreamed they'd been together in Heaven with Ellen, his first wife, and after talking, Ellen had released Emerson to her, and then had disappeared.

Emerson commented: "None but the noble dream such dreams."

On February 25, 1839, Waldo wrote in his journals: "… (yesterday) a daughter was born to me."

This time he did mention Lidian: "Lidian who magnanimously makes my gods her gods, calls the babe Ellen."

Not only did Lidian insist on the name Ellen, but she added Louisa and Tucker as middle names, so that her daughter carried the entire name of Emerson's dead first wife.

He wrote in his journal: "I can hardly ask for more for thee, my babe, than that name implies. Be that vision and remain with us, and after us."

Emerson may or may not have been blind to Lidian's motivation. It seemed to be an attempt to break down Emerson's distancing, to gain his approval and love.

Mrs. Thoreau (Henry David's mother) and two neighbors came to the home to help out.

The Emersons ran a comparatively large-sized household with servants and their doors were always open to visitors, most of them Emerson's acquaintances or admirers.

The E's seemed always to need money during these years and lecturing in the winter and spring was how he closed the gap between inherited income and expenses. Travelling involved long hours of being jostled on stage coaches and buggies or canal boats or ferries or trains in all kinds of weather, getting up and going to bed in unheated rooms in hotels or boarding houses, eating irregular meals cooked differently by unknown cooks, and Emerson claimed he did not relish or look forward to it.

On tours Emerson often accepted small compensation, sometimes nothing, especially in small communities. He received small renumeration from *Nature*, as it was not what you'd call a best-seller. He paid advances on Thomas Carlyle's books and arranged for them to be published in America. There was giving to needy idealists – he'd help the Alcotts by leaving twenty dollar bills behind sugar bowls for his wife to "discover." Sometimes he paid Alcott and William Ellery Channing for labor such as wood chopping.

Some people thought he was the dupe of the reformers but his rebuttal appeared in his 1841 journal:

> Rich say you? Are you rich? how rich? rich enough to succor the friendless, the unfashionable, the eccentric? rich enough to make the Canadian in his wagon, the travelling beggar with his written paper which recommends him to the charitable, the Italian foreigner with his few broken words of English, the ugly lame pauper hunted by overseers from town to town, even the poor insane or half-insane wreck of man or woman, feel the noble exception of your presence and your house from the general bleakness and stoniness; to make such feel that they were greeted with a voice that made them both remember and hope? What is vulgar but to refuse the claim? What is gentle but to allow it? [23]

In the pattern of spending a large portion of projects were those that benefited or interested or furthered Emerson and his friends, not Lidian or her friends or interests.* The exception was that Lidian's

* He paid a few final bills of *The Dial Magazine*. He paid for publishing *Poems* in 1847. He paid for Alcott's trip to England. He once paid Alcott $50 to build a study or retreat or summer house for himself. He gave money towards William Ellery Channing's trip to Europe and paid him to write a book. Cabot tells us his friends thought he paid more than a fair proportion of town taxes. In October 1844 he bought fourteen acres adjoining his property on the shores of Walden Pond in order to save the woods from being cut down by speculators, an act sickening to Henry David Thoreau: "Thank God, they cannot cut down the clouds!" Son Edward tells us there was a problem with fraud on real-estate and book interests by a trusted agent which Emerson's son-in-law eventually rescued. In 1870 Emerson gave money towards the construction of Memorial Hall at Harvard and in late years gave money towards a public playground in Concord.

inheritance was shared with her impoverished sister. Also, Lidian's life was eased by servants, but these persons were usually inexperienced and needed supervision, thus they could be seen as burdens. Lidian's horizon was limited. Beyond a few trips to Plymouth and perhaps once to Philadelphia and Maine, Lidian stayed home.

In Boston that winter Fuller and Emerson met and attended the season's cultural highlight, the Washington Allston exhibit at the Anthenæum.*

Fuller loved Allston's romantic brown-toned landscapes. His pictures were "a bath of roses, potent enough to perfume one's earth for days and years of after life."

Talking with the artist, she found he was "as beautiful as the towncriers have said....I was so fascinated, that I forgot to make myself interesting."

It was rumored that while Fuller was at the exhibition she fainted. Probably she had another attack of headache, but she wrote to her Providence friend, Sarah Helen Whitman, not to contradict the story "as I think it makes me appear very interesting, something like the Chevalier Mozart."

Cambridge's "saint," Washington Allston, made a prestigious fragile figure walking the streets with his snowy white curls capping a fine face centered with starry idealistic eyes. Invariably he wore a quaint old fashioned coat and hat, yet there was a worldly manner about him. A graduate of Harvard, his advantage over other artists was that he'd studied at the Louvre, had been a part of the European art scene. Now he lived alone in Cambridgeport where he had a large studio. He'd begun one great painting, "Belshazzar's Feast," in 1820, with the support of ten patrons who'd each contributed a thousand dollars, but eight years later he'd ceased work on it. He was to start it again but never finish it. He'd composed a series of female heads which portrayed ideal women. He also created marble busts of Byron and Napoleon, a head of poet Ennius, and busts of Edward Everett and Daniel Webster.

---

* Emerson visited several exhibitions with Fuller, and at first "listened reverently to her opinions, and endeavored to see what she saw." After a time he criticized: "I came to suspect my guide, and to believe at last that her taste in works of art, though honest, was not on universal, but on idiosyncratic grounds."

With the auction and move to a Jamaica Plain house, Fuller found little time to write Cary the letters she needed. Could "equal friend" be content with this relationship?

She sent a copy of Hermann Puckler-Muskau's *Tutti-Frutti: Aus den Papeiren des Verstorbene.* If Cary did not want to read him, "only let him lie in your room till I come, he is too refined to be an intruder any where, though his coat is not in the best condition."

The Concord house was crowded with William Emerson and wife but Fuller squeezed into an upstairs room with Elizabeth Hoar and this afforded opportunity for both to cultivate their lifelong friendship.

Sam Ward visited. For a book-mark Fuller tucked a sprig of basil in *The Life of Raphael.* Then there was tea with Sarah Bradford Ripley who'd been tutoring Arthur for Harvard examinations. The shy introvert mystic Charles King Newcomb called briefly. Then Fuller spent a week of repose at Dr. William Ellery Channing's.

Concentration on the Goethe book was impossible because the spring intoxicated. "Willow Brook," the new Jamaica Plain house, was elevated amidst willow and apple trees, wild columbine, cardinals, waterfalls and ponds and rocks, where they could delight in a garden, a cow, a pig, a horse, hens and ducks, and walk about five miles to Boston. Richard was attending school and Ellen and Lloyd were still at home. Two pupils from Providence stayed in the house; Fuller tutored. Best days were when she did "nothing but go to the rocks to gather the wild columbines, or lie down by the gay little brook."

Emerson offered the encouragement she needed. He asked to see the draft of her chapter: "A great undertaking we allow ourselves to magnify, until it daunts & chills us and the child kills the father.... I know that not possibly can you write a bad book a dull page, if you only indulge yourself and take up your work somewhat proudly."

On her twenty-ninth birthday she put the finishing touches on her preface for Eckermann's *Conversations with Goethe.* The familiar conflicts churned. To Elizabeth Hoar: "It is all one earth, all under one heaven – but the moment – the moment."

"The moment" was when two persons communed intimately, both mentally and physically.

Sam Ward who had the soul to bring beauty to the world, was one man who could understand and appreciate Fuller, and vice versa. Fuller could imagine Ward in a studio painting lovely Raphael-like angels, or breathtaking landscapes.

There were also shared letters, books, poems, occasional walks into woods and sunsets with delicate, sensitive Charles King Newcomb. Together they not only saw, but felt nature. She wrote: "All with him leads rather to glimpses and insights, than to broad, comprehensive views. Till he needs the public, the public does not need him. The lonely lamp, the niche, the dark cathedral grove, befit him best."

Emerson was now experiencing depression – not to be labelled postpartum blues. The bite from his July 15 Divinity School Address was relentless. He was trying to edit Jones Very's essays and poems, and Lidian kept reminding him that these precious baby days were too beautiful to be ignored. But there was still another problem. "How can I hope for a friend to me who have never been one?"

Yet there was one Spanish proverb that he thought significant: "a wall between both, best preserves friendship." He wrote it in his journal. "I chide society; I embrace solitude," he had written to Fuller a year earlier.*

Visitors trouped to Emerson's lectures and doorstep – not only provocative persons from his inner circle, but also strangers. He was certainly amiable to all these people, cognizant of their strengths and needs, aware that they looked to him for guidance. He called them, "devastators of his day."

Fuller's greatest pleasure was mixing with a wide variety of persons. She once wrote, "My voice excites, my pen never!" Instead of writing her book, she'd be writing to friends.

Transcendentalists looked upon eloquence and discourse as a noble art. Good talk attested to power and influence. So popular was the lyceum platform that it was burgeoning into big business – there had opened over a hundred lyceums in Massachusetts alone. Transcendentalism was once defined as "Operations on the Teeth."

Bronson Alcott, with his periodic backwoods Conversational tours, had insisted on good talk. He noted in his diary:

---

* Emerson inserted these words into his essay, "Friendship."

Garrison made the Convention
Greeley made the Newspaper
Emerson made the Lecture
And Alcott is making the Conversation.

Fuller's name should have been included in this ditty.

Elizabeth Peabody had opened a cozy bookstore where the like-minded could converse. In the front downstairs room of her West Street house you could meet friends, buy books, read the current newspapers, subscribe to foreign reviews and periodicals, you could even pick up the latest German and French works. Selling was one objective – Peabody was trying to secure income for her family – but good rapport was considered just as primary.

Emerson admired Fuller's "larger lungs, inhaling this universal element...." Her conversation was "surprising and cheerful as a poem, and communicating its own civility and elevation like a charm to all hearers...."

Emerson attracted people out of awe and respect. His audiences were fascinated and stimulated, but he never created an intimacy. He rarely looked directly at his audience, though often he looked upward. He never extemporized; he read from his paper. He hesitated at periods and between paragraphs – "as if he was sorting his keys for opening his cabinets," wrote Henry David Thoreau. He was usually motionless on the platform. Usually his voice, though musical and compelling, was on an even keel with little varied intonation. He never ventured to argue his theories, he stated them. If people were enlightened, well and good; if not, so be it.

Fuller sized up her listeners, saw at once into motives and wishes, then directed her thoughts accordingly, while at the same time brought them to a plane higher than could be imagined. Julia Ward Howe described her gift: "She divines what each most purely wishes, most deeply hopes; and so her words reveal to those present not only their own unuttered thoughts, but also the higher significance and completeness which she is able to give to these thoughts under the seal of her own conviction."

Few people, Emerson felt, were worth his time – with the exception of certain friends like Fuller.

No one, she felt, shared her literary hopes as well as friend Emerson.

Provocatively she invited him to visit her:

> Will you not come to see me. If you will come this week I will crown you with something prettier than willow, or any sallow. Wild geranium stars all the banks and rock clefts, the hawthorn every hedge. You can have a garland of what fashion you will Do but come....[24]

Emerson passed up the invitation, but he sent her a rave review for her translation of Eckermann's *Conversations with Goethe*, which had just come off the presses:

> My dear friend...The translating this book seems to me a beneficent action for which America will long thank you. The book might be called – Short way to Goethe's character – so effectually does it scatter all the popular nonsense about him, & show the breadth of common sense which he had in common with every majestic poet....The Preface is a brilliant statement.... That you can write on Goethe, seems very certain....So speed the pen.... [25]

Most welcome words – nourishment from the person she most respected; this would sustain. Fuller valued this letter "more than I should a voucher from any other quarter."

He was "sorry that you have sat down in a place so inaccessible." Wouldn't "Excellent Lady" introduce him "to your Récamier." He facetiously meant Anna Hazard Barker.

Fuller let a few days in mid-June steal away by vacationing at a favorite beach, Nahant, Massachusetts, with Cary Sturgis and other friends. They thoroughly enjoyed the tides and sands, rocks, sunsets, clouds, stars, moon. Still headaches put her to bed with wet towels. Fuller asked Sturgis if she loved her and Sturgis "could not at once say yes."

Sam Ward had led Fuller to believe that he was serious, and Sturgis had male admirers, one of whom was the charming poet William Ellery Channing who was writing her love poetry.

Yet Fuller and Sturgis were becoming attracted to one another in a way that made both of them pull away from each other, wary of a new feeling that may have been frightening to Sturgis at least.

The developing tenseness elicited this letter from Fuller:

> Caroline, I feel that you have character enough to claim that I should think about you and judge you by your own nature. In order to do this I must put time and other objects between you and me. You, too, will know the state of your own mind better by and by. Let us wait, and meanwhile why should we avoid seeing one another?... We cannot be more estranged than we were at Nahant...We need not be false, nor need we be cold, and it is not desirable to attract the attention of others to any misunderstanding. [26]

Soon she clearly took the lead:

> If Fate has in store for my Caroline a friend of soul and mind like mine of mine equal age and fortunes, as true and noble, mine beautiful and pure, I should accept what I have known of her as an equivalent for the little one situated like me can give. Otherwise I shall be faithful to you in my own way. One word more lest my letter seem cold and rigid. Your letters move so unspeakably and, if I wrote what I feel from one, my words would flow as balmy soft as tears. But I feel it is best to drag the heart from the present I might - no matter what now. Let it be so. [27]

"Black Friday" descended. Gnawing was the worry that Sam Ward seemed to be avoiding her. Her heart ached with imaginings. Finally, she wrote to her Rafaello:

> The kernel of affection is the same, no doubt, but it lies dormant in the husk. Will ever a second Spring bid it forth leaf and flower?... The bitterness of checked affections, the sickness of hope deferred, the dreariness of aspirations broken from their anchorage. I know them all....if you love me as I deserve to be loved, you cannot dispense with seeing me...We knew long ago that age, position and pursuits being so different, nothing but love bound us together, and it must not be my love alone that binds us. [28]

She tried to fend off the fact of Ward's coolness by work and exercise and lovely memories.

Henry David Thoreau fell in love with Ellen Sewall, a lovely seventeen year-old, on the first day of her two-week visit to her grandmother who boarded in the Thoreau household. She was from Scituate. Immediately, he wrote poetry to her, took her on walks, for a sail on the river. The problem was his brother. John was also in love with her.

Depression folded in on "The spirit of Love, as well as of Intellect," as Fuller liked to term Elizabeth Hoar. Fuller steered Jane Tuckerman to Concord and advised a vacation location where "the plash of the waves and the fanning of the sea-breeze" would heal and cheer. In August Fuller visited friends in Rhode Island.

In Concord Henry David Thoreau and his brother had taken a week in the spring to build the *Musketaquid*, a boat fifteen feet long and three and a half feet wide, like a flat-bottomed fishing boat, the fastest boat on the river.

The brothers fitted the *Musketaquid* with two small masts and a sail and they equipped it with wheels so it could take the falls. Poles helped through shallow spots. They made sure it was seaworthy by taking their sister out for a ride on it as well as some members of the Transcendental Club. Then they outfitted it with tents, blankets, food, etc. for an open-air nature study-excursion as far as the Concord and Merrimack Rivers would take them and on into the White Mountains of New Hampshire and back.

It rained the day Henry and John Thoreau pushed off in the *Musketaquid*; nevertheless, they were given a bon voyage by family and friends. They stood on the banks at different points, waving goodbye. The journey was all that they could have hoped for. When they returned, Thoreau gave a melon party in celebration. By now he had the reputation of growing the biggest and best melons in Concord. He had planted sixty hills with a hundred seeds each and the results produced a grand feast. John had another trip to take, but this time he went alone: to Scituate to visit Ellen Sewall. That year Ellen was the recipient of opals from John and poetry from Henry.

The Transcendentalist Club members were talking of starting a new magazine or review that would serve as their platform, and Fuller was brewing an idea of starting discussion groups for women. The men had various opportunities to develop skills and a support system that would promote growth but there was nothing for women beyond sewing circles or parties. Change in women's condition could only occur if consciousness were changed. One had only to look at Elizabeth Hoar, Cary Sturgis or Lidian or herself to realize that even well-educated women lacked self-esteem and a broadened awareness of the world's knowledge.

She would explore the great questions: "What were we born to do? How shall we do it?" It was a plan that would generate some income.

By the end of August she outlined her idea to friend Sophia Ripley:* "To pass in review the departments of thought and knowledge," to "systematize thought and give a precision in which our sex are so deficient." She would ascertain what pursuits were best for women and how women could make best use of their means.

It would be hard for the women "to lay aside the shelter of vague generalities, the cant of coterie criticism and the delicate disdains of good society." But the process must be started.

Emerson was vying again to meet Anna Barker – after he'd returned from the White Mountains with the quiet eccentric procrastinator, minister-turned-teacher, George Bradford. He'd taken along Fuller's private journals to read and he'd also seen Sam Ward, who led "the life of a blade of grass in mere wind & sun...."

The distancing between herself and him who called her the sacred name of "mother" was on his part purposeful. "You love me no more," she wrote her "Raphael" (Sam Ward).

> ...You call me your best of friends, your dearest friend, you say that you always find yourself with me.... But the confiding sweetness, the natural and prompt expression of attachment are gone – are they gone forever?
>
> ...You come here to go away again.... You write to me – to say you could not write before and ask me why I do not write. – You invited me to go and see Michel's work – by myself! You send me your books and pictures – to ask me what I think of them! Thus far at least we have walked no step together and my heart deceives me widely if this be love, or if we live as friends should live....
>
> You say you love me as ever, forever. I will, if I can, rely upon your word....[29]

---

*Scholars have conjectured that it was Sophia Ripley to whom Fuller wrote.

She vowed to never wound his heart.

October brought the terrible, anticipated blow. The "divine" Anna Barker came to visit her in Jamaica Plain, and the story unfolded.

It was delightful to see her again, and Fuller took her to Concord to introduce her to Emerson.

He was obviously entranced by the golden-curled New Orleans woman, "a vision of grace and beauty...a natural queen...the very heroine of your dreamed romance."*

But he found fault with the Barker mind. "She is not an intellectual beauty~~....the predominating character of her nature is not~~ thought but emotion ~~or sympathy, and of course she is not~~ of my class, does not resemble the women whom I have most admired and loved...."

The women he most admired and loved were his wives, his mother, his Aunt Mary, Sarah Bradford Ripley, Elizabeth Hoar, Cary Sturgis, and Margaret Fuller.

Emerson had discussed man's ideal definition of beauty in his book *Nature*. Beauty is enjoyed first as natural form. The second higher form is the spiritual aspect. The third, absolute highest form, is "an object of the intellect."

Put to this test, Margaret Fuller would soar to the top, as well as Sarah Bradford Ripley.

Both wives, Ellen and Lidian, would make the second level as well as his mother.

Elizabeth Hoar and Aunt Mary would waver between the second and third levels, and Carolyn Sturgis, skipping the second rung, would adroitly verge between the first and third.

Anna would measure on the lowest.

If Emerson had subscribed to his own system he would have written of the glory of Fuller's magnificent beauty, of the unique, elegant, resplendent strength and stunning power of her intellect, of the nobility of her crystalline genius, of the shapliness of her values which would take your breath away, of her sublimely divine remarks

---

*A year later Emerson wrote of Anna, "The moment she fastens her eyes on you, her unique gentleness unbars all doors, and with such easy and frolic sway she advances & advances & advances on you, with that one look...."

coming straight from heaven which set her off always to good advantage, of the unadorned elegance of her neck movements, of the knockout way she had of squinting her eyes.

Such a declaration would have caused a revolution, fired a shot heard round the world. Women everywhere would have changed their lives to emulate Fuller's intellectual excellence. Her face would have launched a thousand ships.

But make no mistake. Emerson's notes on woman's beauty are stereotypically male:

> *Gratior est veniens inpulschro corpore virtus.* (Worth .... shows more winsome in a fair form.) Virgil, *Aeneid*, V, 344
>
> *Formosa facies muta commendatio est.* (A handsome appearance is an unspoken testimonial.) *Publilius Syrus*, 199.
>
> A beautiful woman is universal. How she takes all things up into herself. R.W.E.

When beautiful Anna Barker left Jamaica Plain, Fuller collapsed into bed.

Tides of feeling overwhelmed. In journals she poured forth prayers and passionate calls for strength in such sentimental emotion that a reader is tempted to turn away with a laugh but instead feels such a sinking of heart that the response is a silent cry of woe.

Anna Barker had told Fuller that she and Sam Ward were in love.

Too depleted at first to open a letter from Cary Sturgis, Fuller finally turned to this most compatible woman friend for the needed sustenance:

> I loved you, Caroline, with truth and nobleness. I counted to love you much more. I thought there was a firm foundation for future years. In this hour when my being is more filled and answered than ever before, when my beloved has returned to transcend in every way not only my hope, but my imagination, I will tell you that I once looked forward to the time when you might hold as high a place in my life as she. I thought of all women but you two as my children, my pupils, my play things or my acquaintance. You two alone I would have

> held by the hand. And with Mr. E for the representative of religious aspiration and one other of Earth's beauty I thought my circle would be as complete as friendship could make it.
>
> How this hope was turned sickly, how deeply it was wounded you know not yet, you do not fully understand what you did or what passed in my mind. – I will own that in no sacred solitary wood walk, in no hour of moonlight love had I been able to feel that that hope could recover from its wound. My feelings had not changed since you went away. I had not been able, much as I desired it, to take a different view of the past or future. But your letter has changed it. Your vow is registered in heaven.– I know not yet whether I can avail myself of it, but, oh, my Caroline, for mine you must ever be in memory of your first hours of real youth, blessed the Great Spirit, that it has been offered, that you have not been permitted to quench a flame upon so lonely, so ill-sustained an altar.
>
> Whatever is done shall be noble, be true. Only for a moment did I cease to love you. I wept at the loss you were to sustain in me. I would have given all but self-respect to save you. I said, Worldwise, at least I can always be her friend in the spirit realm I will wait for her. O may it be that on earth I can walk with you. [30]

In the nineteenth century female bonding was "above the bestial nature of man," out of the mainstream of the marketplace. In fact, sociologists have pointed out that intimate female relationships verify the unfortunate inequality and distancing that exists between men and women. Such female friendships often "saved" marriages, for they were considered innocent. They served women's needs, especially for those who were boxed into a separate world, relegated as less important than men.

Fuller once expressed the dilemma superbly: "'Tis an evil lot to have a man's ambition and a woman's heart."

On October 15 Sam Ward wrote Fuller, confirming his engagement to Anna Barker.

The story circulated that Barker had told Ward that there was little probability of marriage unless he'd give up his life in art and literature and find a suitable financially solvent profession. Considering his upbringing in the cream of Boston society, it was not surprising that Ward chose entry into her father's banking firm.

His decision could not be a greater mistake, Fuller was convinced. To the outside world she hid her wrenching heart.

She wrote Sam Ward, affirming friendship forever:

> ...believe me, I understand all perfectly...though I might grieve that you should put me from you in your highest hour and find yourself unable to meet me on the very ground where you had taught me most to expect it, I would not complain or feel that the past had in any way bound either of us as to the present...I had thought too, that in ceasing to be intimates we might cease to be friends. I think so no longer. The knowledge I have of your nature has become a part of mine, the love it has excited will accompany me through eternity. My attachment was never so deep as now, it is quite unstained by pride or passion, it is sufficiently disinterested for me to be sure of it.
>
> Time, distance, different pursuits may hide you from me, yet will I never forget to be your friend nor to visit your life with a daily benediction...O I could weep with joy that real life is lived....Live without me now. Do not bid yourself remember me, but should an hour come...and you have any need of me, you will find me in my place and find me faithful to you.... [31]

It must have been another twist of the screw to receive a message from friend Emerson that Anna Barker was "that very human piece of divinity in whom grace goodness & wit have so constitutional a blending that she quite defies all taking to pieces." He wanted "more time & more opportunities to arrive at any steady vision of a person so excellent & so remote too from my usual experiences."

When Fuller went to Concord the next Sunday she announced the engagement. But Emerson, aware that she was experiencing an emotional conflict, seemed to have no desire to sensitize himself to whatever her problem was. Perhaps it was an unhealthy religious experience.

Back in Jamaica Plain Fuller succumbed to her scorpions, a three-week headache.

Emerson again felt the need of a friend. With a few select sincere friends, he could "face with more courage the battle of every day –

and these friends, it is a part of my creed, we always find; the spirit provides for itself."

Striking up a warm correspondence with Sam Ward, he wrote that he conceived of him "as allied on every side to what is beautiful and inspiring, with noblest purposes...."

He came to decide Margaret Fuller needed "more exercise in the Concord coach" – that is, she should visit him more often.

Fuller retreated to her earlier vow of living a life of intellect and celibacy. She would "write constantly...life would ripen into genius."

Her Conversations were about to start. She arranged to hold them at Elizabeth Peabody's West Street Bookstore.

Then, unexpectedly, Emerson and the other male literati voted her editor of their projected Transcendental magazine.

If there were no outlets for women's expression, neither did the men feel there was media open to their voices. Orestes Brownson, who produced the best current journal, *The Boston Quarterly Review*, offered space to the Transcendentalists, but they considered his paper too narrow, and circulation was limited. *The Liberator* was the only journal which had root in the soul and flourished, as Alcott expressed it, but it was an abolitionist tabloid. And Emerson called the conservative *The North American Review*," the snore of the Muses." Andrews Norton said he would resign if articles were printed by the enemy camp in the newspaper he co-edited, *The Christian Examiner*. In England there was Heraud's *New Monthly Magazine*, which all admired, but that was in England.

Needed was a periodical, but Alcott took a realist stance in his diary: "We...lack the ability to make it worthy of our position."

Emerson figured that if twenty thousand copies of Addison & Steel's *Spectator* were sold in a day, and if four persons read each copy, then "each of those moral lessons" was read by "more than fifty thousand persons."

Surely hungry New Englanders would buy an eminent quarterly. Lecture halls were always filling up. The soul and the moral life had always predominated New England thought and habit, and people were searching for intellectual stimulation as never before. Magazines in general were on an upward climb. Most were mediocre, jammed with love tales and light reading. Their new magazine would serve as a literary hope for free thought and social progress. Transcendental words could impact on society.

The Dial, which was Bronson Alcott's title for his diary, would reflect "the Garden itself, in whose leaves and flowers and fruits the suddenly awakened sleeper is instantly apprised not what part of dead time, but what state of life and growth is now arrived and arriving."

All were enthused. But if the truth were known, none of the men wanted to expend the time and effort to launch and edit a magazine of major significance. Theodore Parker thought it would "go" and voted Emerson as editor, but Emerson told his brother, "I will never be editor."

The man whose original idea it was to have a journal, Henry Hedge, was too far away, in his post as minister in Bangor, Maine, though he would send manuscripts when he could.

Emerson put forward the name of the keen minded George Ripley who was dedicated, but he was too busy with his church and his project of editing foreign literary works. However, since he preached that the age needed not words, but deeds, he agreed to handle the financial, subscription, printing and distribution function.

No editor could be paid, though payment was to come. Spinster Fuller, all concurred, was the best qualified, even though appointing her would be a radical move. She could pull together the varying "isms" of the Transcendentalist factions.... George Ripley's associationism, William Henry Channing's socialism, Emerson's pantheism. Besides, women had more compassion when it came to giving of their time and talents for little or no money.

For money-making, Fuller had advertised her Conversations in Peabody's bookstore for a steep twenty dollars for ten sessions, but she needed the income – like any male head of household.

Fuller and Peabody were not the greatest of friends, though their paths seemed often to touch. Fuller was respectful. Peabody was one of the most forward thinking and generously activated of women in Boston. It was her method and temperament that turned Fuller off.

Peabody was the type James Freeman Clarke described as "always engaged in supplying some want that had first to be created."

She seemed always to be launching into causes, going off on lost tangents. She seemed to throw herself at a person, or to attach herself too readily so as to generate the other person to recoil in defence.* Fuller held herself at arms length, yet didn't mind offering to pay $0.00 for the use of her bookstore. On the other hand, Peabody would keep profits on books sold due to the interest Fuller created.

Twenty-five women, some friends, some strangers, sat in a semicircle in the bookstore on November 6, 1839 at 11 o'clock in the morning.

Fuller, in lovely unostentatious dress, a flower in her hair, the usual lorgnette looped about her neck, opened with a brief statement. "Women are now taught, at school, all that men are. They run over, superficially, even more studies, without being really taught anything. But with this difference: men are called on, from a very early period, to reproduce all that they learn. Their college exercises, their political duties, their professional studies, the first actions of life in any direction, call on them to put to use what they have learned. But women learn without any attempt to reproduce. Their only reproduction is for purposes of display. It is to supply this defect that these conversations have been planned."

Her first subject was Greek Mythology because, "It is quite separated from all exciting local subjects. It is serious without being solemn, and without excluding any mode of intellectual action; it is playful as well as deep. It is sufficiently wide, for it is a complete expression of the cultivation of a nation. It is also generally known, and associated with all our ideas of the arts."

She began by extemporizing. She generalized broadly, gave facts, anecdotes, quotations, described differences and commonalities. Her power of voice and articulate choice of language commanded

---

*Years later, in Fuller-like honesty, she wrote Peabody the penetrating truth: "Your tendency to extremes.... is so strong, I am afraid you will not wholly rise above it... A little, only a little less of this in you would give your powers the degree of fresh air they need.... I admit that I have never done you justice.... Yet where I have looked at you, truly, I have also looked steadily, and always feel myself in your debt that you cordially pardon all that must be to you repressing – and unpleasant in me." This anecdote told by Emerson in *Memoirs* must concern Peabody, though her name has been deleted: At his house, Dr. William Ellery Channing said, "Miss Fuller, when I consider that you are and have all that Miss ______ has so long wished for, and that you scorn her, and that she still admires you – I think her place in heaven will be very high."

attention. Her extensive reading, powers of memory, keen grasp of thought sustained interest and provided imagery and illustration.

By "fanning the coals" of the women, she opened discussion. She listened intensely and appreciatively to all comments, sensing the needs and moods of each individual, while channelling the conversation to afford unity and substance. At the end she succinctly and meaningfully summed up the results, and then would unfold her own view.

Emerson asked how the Conversations went…"though I can really entertain no doubts."

Fuller responded: "…from the very first I took my proper place, and never had the feeling I dreaded, of display, of a paid Corinne. I feel as I would, truly a teacher and a guide. All are intelligent; five or six have talent. But I am never driven home for ammunition; never put to any expense; never truly called out. What I have is always enough; though I feel how superficially I am treating my subject."

Emerson felt badly because these Conversations took time away from her book on Goethe "whose pinnacle is waited for by the States and by the nations."

One session covered the subject of Beauty: "I could not make those ladies talk about Beauty: they would not ascend to principles, but kept clinging to details."

Emerson wanted her to write to him whenever she could. At the bookstore he couldn't find the book she'd recommended, George Sand's *Mauprat*, therefore he'd bought *Andre, Leone Leoni,* and *Indiana.* Though he liked some of Sand, he objected to her "sickness of the French intellect." Sand was a "Parisian Corinna."

Fuller's response: "I am sorry you read the wrong Sands first." *Mauprat* was now available; he should rent it because it was "worth your reading, but not your buying." And she promised to find for him *Les Sept Cordes de la Lyre.*

A private nagging surfaced. Into Emerson's journal went a line he'd written six months earlier: "I dare not look for a friend to me who have never been one."

There is this cryptic note: "Why should they call me good natured? I too like puss have a rectractile claw."

Elizabeth Hoar was "a sovereign woman." Emerson wrote Fuller that he did not wish "to know the opinions of celebrate[illegible] celebrated conservers, or indeed of celebrated leaders [illegible] They are all officers & through their lips I hear always [illegible] million speak. But you are queen of yourself & in your privacy & detachment possess a superiority to which we must all defer."

Fuller, who had not felt a headache for a week, tendered to her friend: "I feel both happy and wise, and could bring the Finite much more resolutely in face of the Infinite..." She commended into Emerson's safe keeping a poem she'd written, the canto in one of Cary's poems, Cary's letter, two passages in her own "poetical journal," apologizing for her last winter's work since she had been so sick. "Now I am a perfect Phoenix compared with what I was then and it all seems Past to me."

Depression hit again. "I do never expect to blossom forth on earth, and all postponements come naturally."

One night she sat on the sofa, and "saw how the flame shot up from beneath, through the mass of coal that has been piled above. It shot up in wild beautiful jets, and then unexpectedly sank again, and all was black, unsightly and forlorn. And thus, I thought, is it with my life at present. Yet if the fire beneath persists and conquers, that black dead mass will become all radiant, life-giving, fit for the altar or the domestic hearth."

She watched a sunset that made her wish Charles King Newcomb were there to share it with her.

Fuller's letters afforded Emerson "a rich hour." He wrote her: "They make me a little impatient of my honorable prison – my quarantine of temperament where from I deal courteously with all comers, but through cold water...I joy in your studies & success. Continue to befriend me...I delight much in what I dreamed not of in my first acquaintance with you – my new relations to your friends."

They saw each other at a Boston social gathering early December where they tangled again on the subject of friendship. He later apologized and told her to forget what he'd said: "It may be of little import what becomes of our personal webs, but we will be equal to an Idea so divine as Friendship."

Then he turned to the subject of persuading her to become the editor of the new journal: "For the sake of the brilliant possibility I would promise honest labor of some sort for a year, but I should wish to leave myself the latitude of supreme indifference, nay abhorrence of such modes of working forever after. But if your labors shall introduce a new age, they will also mould our opinions, and we shall think what you think."

Fuller did not want to be diverted again from her Goethe biography, but being editor had advantages: mainly, it would give her a foothold in the literary world and it might eventually pay cash.

Emerson thanked her for another packet she sent, and he wished she could find him his subject for his upcoming sermon. "It must be politics I believe.... I should indeed be happy tonight to be excited by your eloquence & sympathy up to the point of vision – and what more can friendship avail?"

On the day after Christmas, Fuller imparted: "I am on the Drachenfels,* and can't get off; it is one of my naughtiest moods.... I remember you say, that forlorn seasons often turn out the most profitable. Perhaps I shall find it so. I have been reading Plato all the week, because I could not write. I hoped to be tuned up thereby.... "

Friendship was the most attractive of all topics, Emerson wrote Sam Ward that month. "Because the subject is so high and sacred, we cannot walk straight up to it; we must saunter if we would find the secret. Nature's roads are not turnpikes but circles, and the instincts are the only sure guides.... If men are fit for friendship I think they must see their mutual sympathy across the unlikeness and even apathy of to-day." He felt Ward's views would concur with his own.

Fuller was discovering the Conversations a vehicle for "real society, which I have not before looked for out of the pale of intimacy. We have time, patience, mutual reverence and fearlessness eno' to get at one another's thoughts...."

Emerson was discovering that intelligent friendships reminded him of his weaknesses: "Then once & again the regard & friendship of the nobleminded is offered me, I am made sensible of my disunion with myself. The head is of gold, the feet are of clay. In my worthiness I have such confidence, that I can court solitude...of my unworthiness, the first person I meet shall apprize me.... "

---

*The home of the dragon slain by Siegfried in the German epic poem, *TheNibelungenlied.*

He was thirty-seven years old. In his lectures he was telling his audiences: "It is said the great geniuses have done their best things before thirty....After thirty a man begins to feel the walls of his condition."

Despite feelings of ageism, insecurity and inability to relate to humankind, he kept vigil over the tight-knit group of friends, Fuller, Ward, Barker, Sturgis, and he continued work on his essay, "Friendship."

Despite familiar pains of frustration, Fuller held to her pressurized schedule of writing letters, writing her book "to what purpose time will show!", seeing to her mother who was sick with stomach complaints, managing household accounts, helping with emotionally disturbed brother Lloyd, tutoring three young ladies (who boarded with them) "to be carved into roses," continuing reading Goethe, Lessing, etc., seeing "some good people," counselling those who sought her out, conducting her Conversations with the women in Boston which "breaks up my time a good deal...," struggling with the January cold, "my thoughts have a frostbitten meanness," and launching the three-dollars-a-year quarterly, the hundred thirty-six page *Dial.*

With what she thought was the solid support of the men, she set April 1840 as the date for the first issue. Since George Ripley was "too busy fighting the battles of Spinoza and other infidels,"* she wrote the men to submit articles. She was proceeding "to tune the instruments" and what part would William Henry Channing play in "the grand symphony?" She emphasized with a postscript: "At Newport you prophesied a new literature; shall it dawn in 1840."

Channing's response was that he'd send a religious novelette piecemeal, but he intended being "a listener only" to the "grand concert."

To Henry Hedge: "I have counted on you for the first number because you seemed so really in earnest.... for it is the best way to be heard from your sentry-box there in Bangor.... "

---

*Ripley had just written his pamphlet-attact on Andrews Norton: *A Reply to Norton's Remarks on Spinoza: A Second Letter.*

Hedge responded: "You frighten me with your sudden announcement.... I should like now, if possible to have no other part in it than that of reader & subscriber.... my whole heart is with you.... "

Sam Ward sent Emerson some poetry by the unknown young William Ellery Channing (who'd written love poetry to Cary Sturgis). Emerson tried to get in touch with him by knocking on Dr. William Ellery Channing's door – the young man's uncle – only to learn that the poet had cut out of Harvard and was off to Illinois to live by himself in a hut.

Wouldn't Emerson give something on Shakespeare?

Her weekly Conversations were developing to be "singularly prosperous." The subjects ranged from Mythology to Beauty, to Life, covering such topics as Fine Arts, Education, Ethics. "Mrs. Bancroft came out in a way that surprized me. Mrs. Josiah Quincy keeps us in good order....I assure you there is more Greek than Bostonian spoken at these meetings, and we may have pure honey of Hymettus to give you yet."

The most cultivated, prominent and politically activated women in Boston flocked to join: Sarah Alden Ripley, Sophia Ripley (niece of Richard Dana), Lydia Maria Child, Louisa Loring, Ruth Channing and her daughter Mary, Ednah Littlehale (later Dow Cheney), Elizabeth Davis Bancroft, Sarah Freeman Clarke, Caroline Sturgis, Ellen Sturgis (Hooper – Cary's sister), Elizabeth Hoar, Lidian Emerson, Elizabeth Peabody, Mary Peabody, Sophia Peabody, Mrs. Josiah Quincy, Mrs. Russell, Rhoda Newcomb, Anna Shaw, Maria White (fiance to James Russell Lowell), Mary Greeley (Mrs. Horace Greeley), Lydia Parker (Mrs. Theodore Parker), Caroline Dall, Almira Barlow, Jane Tuckerman, Marianne Jackson (sister-in-law to Oliver Wendell Holmes). The number totalled over forty persons.

Julia Ward Howe, who also attended, reported: "The value of what she had to impart was felt by her class from the first."

Another participant commented: "All was said with the most captivating address and grace, and with beautiful modesty."

"The charm of a Platonic dialogue," another claimed.

Her adherence to truth struck Sarah Freeman Clarke: "She broke her lance upon your shield. Encountering her glance, something like an electric shock was felt. Her eye pierced through your disguises.

Your outworks fell before her first assault, and you were at her mercy. And then began the delight of true intercourse. Though she spoke rudely searching words, and told you startling truths, though she broke down your little shams and defences, you felt exhilarated by the compliment of being found out, and even that she had cared to find you out. I think this was what attracted or bound us to her."

Elizabeth Hoar said Fuller had no mercy for stubbornly opinionated people. "And so her enemies were made."

Excruciating headache would wash in on Fuller after each session. Sometimes the tormentor would last two weeks, and there appeared frantic outpourings in her diary.

> I am weary of thinking. I suffer great fatigue from living. Oh God, take me! take me wholly!...In the depth of my prayer I suffer much.... No fellow-being will receive me.... It is not that I repine, my Father, but I sink from want of rest, and none will shelter me. Thou knowest it all. Bathe me in the living waters of Thy Love. [32]

Biographers have continually labelled these outcries a religious passion, but these calls seem a desperate search for love.

Emerson also searched.

> Some people are born public souls, and live with all their doors open to the street. Close beside them we find in contrast the lonely man, with all his doors shut, reticent, thoughtful, shrinking from crowds, afraid to take hold of hands; thankful for the existence of the other, but incapable of such performance, wondering at its possibility; full of thoughts, but paralyzed and silenced instantly by these boisterous masters; and though loving his race, discovering at last that he has no proper sympathy with persons, but only with their genius and aims.... Heaven 'betrayed me to a book, and wrapped me in a gown.'

Fuller felt wonded by men, but she would strive to forgive and never wound:

> Does any man wound thee? not only forgive, but work into thy thought intelligence of the kind of pain, that thou mayest never inflict it on another spirit. [33]

Driven from home to home, she would try to content herself with watching the lives of others.

In his journal he built his defence:

> Do not be afraid of cold water nor cold weather, nor cold countenances. Frost is wholesome. It hardens the constitution. [34]

But without a home and without love of her own, life was empty: "Keys of gold, silver, iron, and lead are in my casket....No one loves me."

Because he was of one mold, why should he also be forced to be someone that he was not?

> She (Margaret Fuller) says truly...that I 'always seemed to be on stilts.' It is even so. Most of the persons whom I see in my own house I see across a gulf. I cannot go to them, nor they come to me.... I see the judiciousness of the plight as well as they. But having never found any remedy I am very patient with this folly or shame, patient of my churl's mask.... I make rockets: Must I therefore be a good senator? [35]

She prayed not to become embittered. In better moments she held out hope that love would come. "I am myself growing better, and shall by and by be a worthy object of love."

Being single enabled certain advantages. "Can I fail to feel this a great privilege? I have no way tied my hands or feet."

A double dilemma was the fact that people and family sponged time from his work. On the Fourth of July he wrote:

> I hate father and mother and wife & brother when my muse calls me. I say to these relatives that if they wish my love they must respect my hatred. I would write on the lentils of the doorpost: Whim. Expect me not to show cause why I see or why I shun company.* [36]

For instance, he was selecting a third of some two hundred Jones Very poems so they could be published in a volume. It was a project

* These words, which he called his "doctrine of hate," are repeated in his famous essay, "Self-Reliance."

he initiated and believed in, yet it did take time from his work. Then Very refused to make changes, since the Spirit had dictated to him, not even spelling corrections. Emerson had to pressurize: "Cannot the Spirit parce and spell?"

To Fuller, Emerson's path was constantly cleared and smoothed by females who took care of all bothersome details. If her time could be so ordered, she could accomplish miracles.

There was no mistaking that the men at the Transcendentalist meetings looked to their near equal to initiate *The Dial.**

The editor of the second sex wrote an introduction for the first number and sent it on to her assistant editor of the superior sex. He was busy collecting his essays for a volume. He concluded it were better *The Dial* be stillborn than to occupy his primary time. He admonished that Fuller should regard *The Dial's* progress in the same vein...not to ruin her health.

She postponed the publication date for the first issue to July.

He thought *The Dial* should "give expression to that spirit which lifts men to a higher platform, restores to them the religious sentiment, brings them worthy aims and pure pleasures... not to multiply books, but to report life...."**

She thought *The Dial* should be "a perfectly free organ" for individual expression. There should be no particular standard, nor dogmatism, nor compromise. They couldn't show high culture or lead public opinion, but they could stimulate each reader to judge and think more deeply.

Both concurred that it be universal and poetic.

---

*William Henry Channing reported: "Men – her superiors in years, fame and social position, – treated her more with the frankness due from equal to equal, than the half-condescending deference with which scholars are wont to adapt themselves to women. They did not talk down to her standard, nor translate their dialect into popular phrase, but trusted to her power of interpretation. It was evident that they prized her verdict, respected her criticism, feared her rebuke, and looked to her as an umpire. Very observable was it, also, how, in side-talks with her, they became confidential, seemed to glow and brighten into their best mood, and poured out in full measure what they but scantily hinted in the circle at large."

**This is what he eventually advocated in the introduction. Also, he wanted his own view reflected, as proven when he eventually became editor.

By the turn of the new year an intense shy introvert had made a daring move to Boston. Ten years earlier, in Salem, he'd paid to have his first novel published, but because it didn't sell he'd burned his copies, along with some rejected short stories, and secluded himself to the point of morbidity. As soon as he confessed to his neighbor Elizabeth Peabody that he wanted "to have something to do with this material world," she'd praised him to George Bancroft, husband of a friend and Collector of the Port of Boston.

The Peabodys had lived for years across the street from him and his family and had barely seen them. Nobody visited this "Castle Dismal," as the house was known. Finally, Elizabeth knocked on the door. Slowly she came to know them – he was the most friendly. His two sisters lived there and his mother stayed upstairs, but never showed herself.

The three Peabody sisters thought him extremely handsome and interesting. They thought he came to their house to visit Elizabeth, but it was the beautiful and sickly Sophia with the mischievous smile who magnetically attracted.

In Boston, true to her character, Elizabeth took him under her wing. She warned that Sophia would never marry because she was ill. He should drop his interest, learn German and continue writing for children.

The job George Bancroft offered him was weighing cargoes of coal and salt at the Boston Custom House. As "Weigher and Gauger," he thought he'd have time to work on his novel but, exhausted and dirty with coal dust at the end of the day, he only had energy to write love letters to Sophia who began to be mutually attracted. His real name was Hathorne; he had changed it after college graduation to Nathaniel Hawthorne.

While Nathaniel Hawthorne was coming out of his shell in Boston, the assistant editor, R.W.E., got in touch with Henry David Thoreau who had just been appointed Secretary of the Concord Lyceum. Thoreau complied by sending a poem to Fuller, "Sympathy," about an eleven year-old who would be enrolling in the Thoreau School, who was brother of the pure gentle Ellen Sewall with whom he'd fallen in love.

The editor passed "Sympathy," to her assistant editor, suggesting revision. Thoreau balked. Emerson returned the piece to Fuller. The editor observed that her assistant editor had limitations:

> Mr. E. scarce knows the instincts. And uses them rather for rejection than reception where he uses them at all. In friendship with R.W.E., I cannot hope to feel that I am his or he mine. He has nothing peculiar, nothing sacred for his friend. He is not to his friend a climate, an atmosphere, neither is his friend a being organized especially for him, born for his star. He speaks of a deed, of a thought to any commoner as much as to his peer. His creed is, show thyself, let them take as much as they can.... His friendship is only strong preference and he weighs and balances, buys and sells you and himself all the time.[37]

In February Thoreau sent Emerson an essay about the Roman poet, Aulus Persius Flaccus. Emerson pressured Fuller to print it. Fuller thought it badly written and needed revision.

She confessed to her mentor/minister her dilemma: "I am like some poor traveller of the desert, who saw, at early morning, a distant palm, and toiled all day to reach it...but when he reached it, alas! it had grown too high to shade the weary man at its foot."

As a troubled child attempting to elicit attention to herself, she cut her problem short: "Why do I write thus to one who must ever regard the deepest tones of my nature as those of childish fancy or worldly discontent?"

Though still February, Emerson was feeling the youthful pangs of soft spring winds when Literature took second place to love:

> These are the days of passion when the air is full of Cupids & devils for eyes that are still young; and every pool of water & every dry leaf & refuse straw seems to flatter, provoke, mock, or pique us. I who am not young have not yet forgot the enchantment, & still occasionally see dead leaves & wizards that peep & mutter. Let us surrender ourselves for fifteen minutes to the slightest of these nameless influences – these nymphs or imps of wood & flood of pasture & roadside, and we shall quickly find out what an ignorant pretending old Dummy is Literature who has quite omitted all that we care to know – all that we have not said ourselves.... R.W.E.[38]

Fuller could succumb to his wooing words, but Dummy Literature must take priority.

She again asked the men for promised articles. To Frederic Hedge, for a second time: "Henry, I adjure you, in the name of all the Genii, Muses, Pegasus, Apollo, Pollio, Apollyon...to send me something good for this journal before the 1st of May. All mortals, my friend, are slack and bare; they wait to see whether Hotspur wins, before they levy aid for as good a plan as ever was laid."*

Emerson failed her: "I whose name is Unit am tormented & impoverished by the dins & combinations which enrich you whose name is Polyanthos." He sent only two poems written by his most recent fan, Christopher Pearse Cranch, who was now back in the Boston area under Theodore Parker's wing.

From Louisville James Freeman Clarke said he'd send something later. She wished to become acquainted with Henry Channing's article, "Ernest the Seeker," but, if not ready, please to send her something shorter.

She liked Cary Sturgis' poems so she asked her to copy all of them for her.

The energetic Theodore Parker sent a long piece, "The Divine Presence in Nature and in the Soul."

Emerson and Ripley found a publisher, Weeks, Jordan & Co., not without some trouble.

Emerson announced the publication of the first issue, then informed not to expect much from his pen. He would be busy with a new lecture series, "The Present Age." He would mail off his advice to her as he travelled from city to city.

In desperation Fuller began to write copy herself. The press had largely ignored Washington Allston's 1839 summer art exhibition, so she'd write a critique, suggesting the painter go beyond his perfection.

Cary finished copying her poems. Her success in poetry surprised. Fuller sent the needed nourishment: "The most irregular pulses beat with the mighty heart."

---

*"By the Lord, our plot is a good plot as ever was laid, our friends true and constant." Shakespeare

She felt their friendship growing and they shared a commonality – neither could find reciprocal love with a man. "Believe me worthy to know your nature as I believe you worthy to know mine. Believe as I do that our stars will culminate at the same point."

It chilled Fuller that Cary reacted with passivity and ambivalence – even repulsiveness. Fuller vowed to wait for a change of heart, for she felt that in time Cary would attain more liberality.

> I am rejoiced to meet a nature that makes it worth my while to wait, to watch, to study....
>
> W. also at times resists or leaves me, though in a different way from you. He always returns, and so I think will you....
>
> With you, I would have no pedantry of nobleness or justice. I would be spontaneous and free, but I would also feel that my years more of life command me not to be rash, and sometimes to be silent till I can be sure you know and I know what is in your mind.... [39]

Weddings always prompted a reminder of her perpetual state of being single. Her younger brother William Henry was united in marriage and he and his wife were settling in New Orleans to start a mercantile business, and her other younger brother, Eugene, was to join them.

She hoped James Freeman Clarke, newly married and living in Pennsylvania, would soon send to *The Dial* some sound rough fruit of American growth, but he continued to send all of nothing.

From Emerson, on his lecture tour, she had hoped for literary criticism. Instead, he "tacked" together an old poem, "Woodnotes," and he promised he would revise two lectures.

He grudged lecturing in Providence, he wrote Lidian, because he missed being at home.

On the first day of spring Fuller went into the woods and read a little book called *Nature* through for the first time. "'Tis strange," she wrote Emerson, "that it should be the first, but you read it to me originally, and so since whenever I have opened it I missed the voice and laid it aside....Then I caught the melody now I recognize the harmony. The years do not pass in vain."

Henry David Thoreau refused to revise his pieces, but said he'd allow Emerson or Fuller to revise.

She wrote William Henry Channing she didn't expect to be of much use on the *Dial* "except to urge on the laggards, and scold the lukewarm, and act Helen Mac Gregor to those who love compromise, by doing my little best to sink them in the waters of Oblivion!!..." Readers would be disappointed, for they were "looking for the gospel of Transcendentalism."

The assistant editor penned changes in the editor's article, "A Short Essay on Critics," even though he thought it had the rare merit of being readable. In her Allston critique he suggested she use "I" instead of "the writer." He signed off, "I am still your friend R. W. Emerson." He re-wrote Thoreau's Persius piece.

By April 25 Emerson had done nothing about Fuller's introduction except to mention that some of it was too fierce. Then Ripley read it and told her it lacked strength. So she wrote Emerson:

> It is no wish of mine to have an introduction or to write it...I never can tell what you will like, so that sometimes it seems I was not born to be your friend, but then again the flowers spring up and I am sure I was.[40]

In a "P. S." she promised that Thoreau's "Persius" would go into the first issue.

Emerson reacted by writing a new introduction which was not to be modified without his knowledge and it must be printed anonymously. The new American literature could not be found in books and the country needed fresh expression and standards for literary criticism.

Fuller didn't argue.

He thanked his editor for remembering him to the beautiful Anna Barker "whose words still vibrate on my ear out of the distance of last September, yet I should need a serene & select hour to write anything for her eye."

He also sent along a roll of Alcott's "Orphic Sayings." "They are better than I feared...but...labor with his inveterate faults."

Fuller thought Alcott's "Sayings" were "quite grand, though ofttimes too grandiloquent."

There were a few more corrections on Thoreau's "Persius." Otherwise Emerson thought it excellent.

During these months, April and May, another essay, "Man In the Ages," written by a Calvinist minister from Maine, passed back and forth between the editors. Emerson wound up revising it.

May 8th, Emerson invited Fuller not to fail to stay over at his house and settle *Dial* affairs at the Transcendental meeting.

During May, Emerson to Fuller: "I have come to think it a piece of extreme good nature to read twenty pages in any volume and do think weeding onions a better employment."

May 31, Fuller to Emerson: "I don't think that 'weeding onions' would be the way I should take of linking myself to Nature in this her *liebersvollste Tag.**– ...I don't wonder you economize your time if you are to have your house full of company all the beautiful, solitary summer. I will try not to wish to see you...."

That spring in upstate New York a Scottish clergyman omitted the word "obey" from a wedding ceremony because the bride insisted. Her marriage was to be one between equals. The groom agreed. Moreover, the bride refused to take the name Mrs. Henry Stanton, because changing her name to her husband's signified being under his dominion, as a slave. The bride would be called Elizabeth Cady Stanton. After the wedding ceremony, the couple left for London on a honeymoon, highlighted by the World Anti-Slavery Convention; her husband was one of four delegates.

Henry Stanton had belonged to the American Anti-Slavery Society where arguments arose against women participating in a man's organization, against women speaking and becoming officers, against women working with men on committees. Therefore, Henry Stanton, William Lloyd Garrison, and Theodore Weld formed a new organization which supported women's activity, the American and Foreign Anti-Slavery Society.

Meanwhile, Emerson, uninvolved with abolitionists, sent "Excellent Friend" sixty-three pages blasting Goethe for leaving the world as he found it. Needed was a new redeemer of the Human Mind. The

---

*Most charming day.

editor could use "Thoughts On Modern Literature," in one or two *Dial* issues, or she could "damn the piece to silence." If she printed it in one issue, he would not be a large contributor to the next issue because he would "sink the boat." He wished she would write him concerning her friends. "Are they not my friends?"

He finished making a few corrections on his lecture, "Love." He could see its transparencies, but would not go deeper into the subject. "I – cold because I am hot – cold at the surface only as a sort of guard and compensation for the blind tenderness of the core – have much more experience than I have written there, more than I will, more than I can write. In silence we must wrap much of our life, because it is too fine for speech, because also we cannot explain it to others, and because somewhat we cannot understand."

On June 21 the assistant editor thought to praise Anna Barker again. "A woman in every part beautiful is a practical poet, is she not? awakening tenderness & hope & poetry in all whom she approaches.* Write me all you can of Anna."

With another wedding impending – Anna and Sam's – these words must have struck like a knife in Fuller's heart.

The next day, Emerson asked Sam Ward to comment on his new essay. "Friendship" was indebted to Ward, Sturgis and Fuller. He had culled their conversations and letters and had defended his perception of friendship against what they said.

The assistant editor, who did not want that job title, complained: "*The Dial* brings me papers to read and judge, which, as I am not editor but only a contributor, I like not."

When the editor targeted the criticism she was receiving, he told her: "Don't cry before you are hurt."

The assistant editor also provided two poems he'd written, one about a fair stately maid he admired (perhaps Elizabeth Hoar), and an essay and poem from journals of his brothers, Charles and Edward, both dead, and a verse by his dead first wife, all unsigned.**

---

*This sentence appears in Emerson's essay, "Beauty."

** These would also be included in his 1847 publication of *Poems* with additional poems written to Ellen.

The assistant editor never submitted anything by Lidian. Their daughter years later informed that her mother, who wanted to be read to even while she was gardening, had a desire to write.

"I don't do it for a few good reasons," Lidian is to have said, "chief of which is that I am a nobody. The editors would not publish anything I wrote. Another, that I don't know well enough how to write English not to make myself ridiculous. If I published in my language ask how Papa (Emerson) would like that?"

Lidian did write a short "Transcendental Bible," a satire on the actions and non-actions of intellectuals who, in her opinion, did not soar high enough. She attacked the sin of pride, selfishness, the individual who emphasized the intellect over the heart. "Queenie's Bible" Emerson called it, and it gave her family good laughs for years to come and was proof of a fine potential talent that required an encouragement that was never offered.

Never encouraged, never believed in, never taken seriously, never exhibited, never developed. Thus, Lidian, like so many women throughout the centuries, was psyched to talk herself out of writing, thus not permitted to know her own strengths. Thus she never thought of herself as able to accomplish equal to her husband or to other writers of her time. Denigrating oneself is a skill many women cultivate and thus they perpetuate their own dependent position. Thereby, those in the power positions are alleviated the task of stamping out competition and retain their power. Fuller often asked the question, Why do we not have any female Michelangelos? She knew why.

She merged the closing lines of her article on Allston's art exhibit with a sonnet by Sam Ward, signed with the letter "J," and followed it with another poem signed "O," which may or may not have been her own poem. And this was followed by another unsigned Sam Ward poem, which in turn was followed by Emerson's poem of the fair stately maid.

She signed her substantive article, "A Short Essay on Critics," with the letter "F."

Theodore Parker's learned article was signed "P," and William Henry Channing had finally sent a chapter of "Ernest the Seeker," a satirical fictional account of a young idealist encountering the realities of world and church. (Wasn't this autobiographical?) This was printed unsigned.

Alcott's "Orphic Sayings" was the only article which appeared with byline under the title. Composed of fifty short pithy maxims numbered with Roman numerals, each represented ideal law. The first justified the title of the journal:

> I
>
> Thou art, my heart, a soul-flour, facing ever and following the motions of thy sun, opening thyself to her vivifying ray, and pleading thy affinity with the celestial orbs, thou dost the livelong day Dial on time thine own eternity.

Both of Thoreau's pieces were signed "T." He never saw the proofs; there were innumerable printer's errors.

"Brownson's Writings" was signed "R" for the author, George Ripley.

John Sullivan Dwight offered "The Religion of Beauty" which ended with a poem, "Sweet is the Pleasure," and he also wrote an overview of "The Concerts of the Past Winter." All were signed "D."

The two Christopher Cranch poems were signed "C." There was a beautiful Ellen Hooper poem, unsigned, which came to be oft quoted:

> I slept, and dreamed that life was Beauty;
> I woke, and found that life was Duty.
> Was thy dream then a shadowy lie?
> Toil on, sad heart, courageously,
> And thou shalt find thy dream to be
> A noonday light and truth to thee.

Another piece was about William Ellery Channing's translation of Jouffroy, by W. D. Wilson, signed "W."

Most of R.W.E.'s "Thoughts on Modern Literature" was set into type before Fuller realized there was not enough space for it, even with some deletions suggested by Emerson, so she postponed its publication. Therefore, Emerson figured he was relieved from working on another article for the next issue.

Having pulled Emerson's article, the editor found she was then slightly short. So she inserted one of Sarah Clark's poems, "Dante," signing it "S," and two more of her own, unsigned.

Dahlia
My cup already doth with light o'errun
Descend, fair sun;
I am all crimsoned for the bridal hour,
Come to thy flower.

The Sun
Ah, if I pause, my work will not be done,
On I must run,
The mountain wait. – I love thee, lustrous flower
But give to love no hour.

In total she had inserted, of her own work, two major articles, seven poems and one filler.*

Her assistant editor was angry and advised to: "Omit to count pages," for "Every dull sentence vulgarizes the book," and "The sincere and the sensible will not ask, are there a hundred ten or a hundred fifty pages? but is there one page?"

The editor was the first to be aware that the quality of the magazine was uneven but she hoped to make a beginning and let it evolve into something with its own identity. She wanted it to reflect the thoughts of the Dialists as they worked through their search for truth. The contents would have to have strong appeal, for there were no illustrations and it was distributed in a plain brown wrapper.

Reaction to the first issue was divided. The editor was disappointed. The assistant editor was disappointed.

Ripley called it "quite unworthy of its pretensions." He'd wanted something more radical: "They had expected hoofs and horns while it proved as gentle as any sucking dove."

Alcott wrote, "It is but a twilight *Dial.*"

Carlyle wrote, "...pure, ethereal...All spirit-like, and yet...it is too

*Scholars have conjectured that Fuller wrote them.

ethereal, speculative, theoretic: all theory becomes aeriform, aurora-borealis-like...."

Much of the press ignored the "coming out." Those that responded were not exactly ecstatic:

> *BOSTON TIMES:* "...one of the most Transcendentally (we like big words) ridiculous publications....Duck tracks in the mud convey a more intelligible meaning...."
>
> *RECORDER: The Dial* "reflects only the rays of a mock sun...its religion, if not all moonshine, is something worse."
>
> *PHILADELPHIA GAZETTE: The Dial's* writers are "considerably madder than the Mormonites."
>
> *NEW WORLD:* Transcendentalism is "clear as mud."
>
> *KNICKERBOCKER:* "...good thoughts, but they are smothered in words...or, as the plainspoken Yankee told the Paris chef, 'If your meats are good, what is the use of disguising them?'"
>
> *BOSTON COURIER:* "When the fog shall have expanded and vanished, light may appear."
>
> W. J. PARODIE IN A PROVIDENCE NEWSPAPER: The "absurdities of the magazines are 'so absurd' that they need but to be clearly perceived to be immediately rejected."
>
> EMERSON'S REACTION TO PARBODIE'S REVIEW: "The piece seems to be written by a woman. It begins with round sentences but ends with Oh's & Ah's."

Alcott's "Orphic Sayings" were ridiculed. Schoolboys parodied them. They were like "a train of fifteen coaches going by, with only one passenger."

Fuller told Emerson: "The next issue will be better."

Emerson told Fuller: "Change the pale face lily liver lettering on the title page...Print the word DIAL in strong black letters that can be seen in the sunshine....Print the poetry in a large and glorious type.... It is a good book & the wise public ought to accept it as such."

The editor bewailed the printing errors. She had been away when it had gone to press.

She would not be away again when it went to press. She was irritated that the printer had put all the fillers together instead of spreading them throughout. It was "like inviting people to a stately feast with regular courses and ending with a dish of minced meat."

The editor would have liked the poetry better in small type. She would defer to the assistant editor's taste, but thought it undesirable to make changes until the next year, so that the issues in the first year's volume would be uniform. She wished she had consulted with the assistant editor, but did not know he attached great importance to externals, as he did so little in others. It was far "from that eaglet motion" she wanted.

Alcott wrote Charles Lane in England, "It does not content the public, nor even ourselves." To Heraud he wrote: "*The Dial* partakes of our vices....It satisfies me not, nor Emerson. It measures not the meridian but the morning ray; the nations wait for the gnomon that shall mark the broad noon."

Theodore Parker, in his journals, compared the younger writers to "awkward and lurching dancing school pupils." He complained of the "uncouth & barbarous" words that they used, some of which were "virginal in respect to English language still." Later he complained that what *The Dial* needed was a beard.*

From Louisville, Kentucky, James Freeman Clarke – who'd now submitted some poetry which he admitted wasn't polished and which Fuller returned for polishing – wrote that it promised to be good.

Elizabeth Peabody said it was "domestic."

Sophia Ripley said it was "a charming book."

People started asking who were the writers. Who was "J" for instance?

The editors did not divulge identities. Those who were acquainted with the Transcendental circle knew.

Now the "Queen of the American Parnassus," as the assistant editor called her, faced the clamor of those who would receive free copies. The assistant editor wanted free copies for Thoreau, Aclott (so he could send them to his friends in England), and to Christopher Cranch and others so they'd be inspired to contribute articles.

---

*Later Theodore Parker started his own magazine, *Massachusetts Quarterly Review* which, wrote Thomas Wentworth Higginson, "was to be the *Dial* with a beard, but which turned out to be the beard without the *Dial*." [41]

The editor said he could have as many free copies as he wished for the first number only. Mr. R (Ripley) would get twelve to pass along to contributors, out of which she would receive two. Mr. Thoreau, who sent for a subscription with cash which Emerson bounced back to him, would get a free copy because they counted on his help, but she could not send free copies to all the authors. Her friends Cary Sturgis, Ellen Hooper and Charles King Newcomb subscribed to it.

No sooner was the first issue off the presses than the editor began the second.

Did Emerson wish to make alterations in "Thoughts on Modern Literature" which would open the next issue? The first part was already in type. She'd allot him an "E" at the end of his piece.

She had the eleven poems by Cary Sturgis, many about her love of the sea, which she could scatter throughout the magazine, all to be signed "Z."*

And Fuller started working on a review of another art exhibit at the Boston Athenæum and planned articles on Romaic ballads and Honoré de Balzac.

Sturgis' sister, Ellen Hooper, sent along four poems and none were printed with signature or initial.

The editor searched for women's writing; she found nothing beyond Hooper, Sturgis and herself.

Emerson asked Thoreau for more poetry. He sent "Nature doth have her dawn each day" and "When winter fringes every bough." Emerson asked for revisions. Thoreau delayed, finally withdrew the second poem. Therefore, "Nature" did not dawn into *The Dial* until the third issue, and "Winter" never did spring forth under Fuller's thumb.** She had to also consider a Thoreau essay on bravery, "The Service."

James Freeman Clarke returned his poetry, now polished, and she would sign both "First Crossing the Alleghenies" and "Nature and Art of the Three Landscapes" with "F.C."

---

*Some are conjectured to be Sturgis poems.

**It would wait for Emerson to become editor and make its appearance in the October 1843 issue. Thoreau cleverly included it in his essay, "A Winter Walk."

Henry Hedge submitted a rather marvelous article, "The Art of Life – The Scholar's Calling," that was to be printed unsigned, which pointed out that the only inherent worth of life was self-culture of the mind.

George Ripley submitted "Letter to a Theological Student." It was signed "R."

"P" or Theodore Parker filled many fat pages with "A Lesson for Today," about ideal man, and he also offered a shorter piece, "Truth Against the World."

Chapter II of "Ernest the Seeker," the fictional young man who continued to seek the elixir of life through truth and religion, came in from William Henry Channing.

There was also a Christopher Cranch review of a pamphlet written by a free -thinking Calvinist divine from the West, as well as his "Musings of A Recluse," unsigned, which consisted of bits of thoughts. The editor found that more often than not she would receive second-best work since some of the writers sent their best articles to periodicals that paid.

Emerson told Fuller it was of no importance that the subscription list had only thirty names. He thought the magazine would sell.

A young woman reader made this comment: "The Transcendentalists soar into the illimitable, dive into the infinite, and never pay cash!"

The assistant editor worked so busily on it that he had to forego letter-writing.

Fuller felt that in all honesty she would have to reject more of Alcott's "Orphic Sayings." In her diary she wrote of him: "I wish I could overcome my distrust of Mr. Alcott's mind." Nothing of his appeared in the October issue.

About Theodore Parker who had by now amassed a nice-sized following called "Parkerites" and who never withheld his opinions, Fuller asserted: "He cannot be the leader of my journal…." But she acknowledged that he could be "a very valuable aid." Parker's reaction to this specific is unknown.

After putting *The Dial* to bed, she'd take to her own bed, sometimes for days. Her Goethe biography would await another day.

Fuller was unaware through the summer that, across the ocean in

London, prominent American women delegates were barred from participating in the World Anti-Slavery Convention. The delegate honeymooners Elizabeth Cady and Henry Stanton were there. Others were Lucretia Mott, a distinguished Quaker who represented the Philadelphia Female Anti-Slavery Society, Abby Kelley, Sarah Pugh, Abby Kimber, Elizabeth Neal, Anne Green Phillips, Emily Winslow and Abby Southwick. These women, some of whom wore modest Quaker outfits, were charged with being disturbers of the peace. They had dared to speak at promiscuous assemblies. They had gathered petitions against slavery which brought on mob violence and press ridicule. They had been denounced by the pulpit.

There had been agitation as soon as these women stepped onto English shores. American clergy, who had arrived earlier, clamored loudly. At the opening session, the American politician/abolitionist Wendell Phillips proclaimed that "friends of the slave" were invited and this meant women as well as men.

The English Reverend J. Burnet suggested that the ladies withdraw. Rather than to include the women, it were better to dissolve the Convention.

Discussion followed which took up the entire first day. One American speaker asked: "Will you take away the rights of one-half of creation?"

An English Reverend rebutted: "If I were to give a vote in favor of females...I should be acting in opposition to the plain teaching of the Word of God."

The clergy waved and shook their Bibles vehemently, until at last an American delegate demanded: "Prove to me, gentlemen, that your Bible sanctions the slavery of women...and I should feel that the best work I could do for humanity would be to make a grand bonfire of every Bible in the universe."

Another Englishman said: "I tremble at the thought of discussing the question in the presence of these ladies...it would be impossible for the shrinking nature of woman to subject itself to the infliction of such a discussion."

A vote was held and the overwhelming majority voted to exclude women as delegates.

Wendell Phillips said, in order to ease and unify the heated situation: "There is no unpleasant feeling in our minds. I have no doubt the women will sit with as much interest behind the bar...."

The women accordingly climbed to the gallery and took their seats behind a bar and curtain, such as was used in a church to separate choir from the worshipers.

William Lloyd Garrison arrived on the scene, along with two other men from New England. They were so angry that they joined the women behind the bar, in protest.

That night Lucretia Mott and Elizabeth Cady Stanton walked down Great Queen Street and came to the conclusion that they must hold a woman's rights convention in the United States.

Back in New England John Thoreau proposed to Ellen Sewall while they strolled on a beach in Scituate. She accepted. Later she realized it was the other brother she best liked, and she broke the engagement.

Emerson revealed to Fuller that Anna Barker had so trusted him as to personally confide in him. Fuller told him that Anna must have put her trust in him because he "gave her the feeling of the holy man, the confessor...that she...spoke as she would in the confessional."

Soul mate Charles King Newcomb was in desperate need of help. Metaphysical doubts and fears had propelled him into illness. Creative talent was there, but how could it be brought forward. He stayed at Fuller's house during the July 4 holidays.

Anna Barker came to the forefront again on July 8 when Emerson wrote Fuller that the Ward/Barker engagement was broken.

William Henry Channing came in from Cincinnati and visited Fuller one sunny morning at Willow Brook. She had come in from gathering wildflowers, and she described the symbols she saw in them as she arranged them, and then conversed at length about the engravings hanging on the wall, which led to Greek subjects. Soon both were out walking, climbing up a rocky path to her favorite moss-cushioned ledge in Bussey's wood. For the first time he penetrated the surface of what he'd always perceived as the arrogant temperament of Margaret Fuller.

The Rev. William Henry Channing was a lofty, inspired idealist with gentlemanly, elegant manners. His membership was in the Church Universal; truth was his maxim. Biographers have described him as "a flame," "a breath of mountain air," "a pure breeze from the north," "a knightly soldier," "a fervent apostle," "a radiant presence." "He lifted up drooping hearts." "He flung his banner to the breeze."

He envisioned a superhuman world, declared war on evil and suffering. In religion lay the hope for mankind. He was inspired to awaken souls, to transform character. His message was joy and hope, and he delivered it with all the gifts of the fluent speaker.

On July 19 proof of Emerson's essay, "Modern Literature," was ready. George Ripley and Fuller criticized. "Mr. Ripley is much distressed at what he thinks a falling off in the end of your paragraph about the Majestic Artist, and I think when you look again you will think you have not said what you meant to say."

The editor commenced. "The 'eloquence' and 'wealth,' thus grouped, have rather l'air bourgeoisie–"

Emerson cut the word "eloquence" and left in the word "wealth."*

She continued: "'Saddens and gladdens' is good. Mr. R. hates prettiness, as the mistress of a boarding house hates flower vases."**

Emerson did not adhere to her suggestion.

She continued: "'Dreadful melody' does not suit me. The dreadful has become vulgarized since its natal day."

The sentence reads today as Emerson originally wrote it.***

"So much for impertinence!" If her remarks cut, Fuller apologized.

But she was not finished. His statement about Goethe's genius was

---

* The sentence reads: "Such was his (Goethe's) capacity, that the magazines of the world's ancient or modern wealth, which arts and intercourse and skepticism could command he wanted it all."

**The sentence reads: "And this is the insatiable craving which alternately saddens and gladdens men at this day."

*** The sentence reads: "Poetry is with Goethe thus external, the gilding of the chain, the mitigation of his fate; but the Muse never assays those thunder-tones which cause to vibrate the sun and the moon, which dissipate by dreadful melody all this iron network of circumstance, and abolish the old heavens and the old earth before the free will or Godhead of man."

"too imperfect to be true."* Fuller felt Goethe required "to be minutely painted in his own style of hard finish. As he never gave his soul in a glance, so he cannot be painted at a glance."

She had two other specifics: "I cannot like that illustration of the humors of the eye."**

Emerson made no attempt to change.

"I wish," Fuller continued, "the word 'whipped' was never used at all and here it is twice in nearest neighborhood."

Emerson cut one "whipped."***

Fuller deferred her criticism to headache. Wouldn't he send some promised verses to fill gaps in *The Dial*? She post scripted: "Be good to me, by and by I will be good so as to deserve it."

Emerson was "obliged" for the criticism. He deplored her headaches. "Cannot you say, Out vile Larva!"

He sent his editor some poems, one, "Silence," and selected four poems out of several written by Ellen Hooper. These and his three page poem, "Woodnotes," were printed unsigned.

He suggested *The Dial* discuss issues and events of the day rather than adhering to the limitations of "a mere literary journal."

On July 27, he brought up Anna again: "I have no coldness no commonness when any tidings or thoughts of the fair Anna come, no apathy about these. You need never fear my desecration of such demands."

He found fault with four lines of Cary Sturgis' poetry, and in Henry Thoreau's verse, "Stanzas," he changed "climb to see" to "climb and see."

---

* The statement reads: "That Goethe had not a moral perception to his other powers, is not then merely a circumstance, as we might relate of a man that he had or had not the sense of tune or an eye for colors; but it is the cardinal fact of health or disease; since, lacking this, he failed in the high sense to be a creator, and with divine endowments drops by irreversible decree into the common history of genius. He was content to fall into the track of vulgar poets, and spend on common aims his splendid endowments, and has declined the office proffered to now and then a man in many centuries in the power of his genius of a Redeemer of the human mind."

** The sentence reads: "An interchangeable Truth, Beauty, and Goodness, each wholly interfused in the other, must make the humors of the eye, which would see causes reaching to their last effect and reproducing the world forever."

*** His final phrasing stands: "Are we not evermore whipped by thoughts.... "

Fuller arranged that printing for the October issue of *The Dial* go forward. Amazingly, she was three or four weeks ahead of schedule.

Fuller tried several times to receive the same ministering advice from Emerson as Anna had. But she could not break through.

Friend had his own perception of these moments:

> She made many attempts to describe her frame of mind to me, but did not inspire me with confidence that she had now come to any experiences that were profound or permanent. She was vexed at the want of sympathy on my part, and I again felt that this craving for sympathy did not prove the inspiration.... [42]

By August 6 the Ward/Barker engagement was "on" again.

Ten days later sparks flew between Fuller and Emerson.

Barker was visiting Fuller in Jamaica Plain. On the 16th Emerson invited his three women friends, Fuller, Barker and Sturgis, to Concord for an afternoon's visit. The hours went well – until Emerson decided to join them in the ride back to Jamaica Plain.

In the stage coach S.M.F. lashed out at R.W.E. for having "inhospitably of soul." She claimed that both Cary and herself offered him full and sacred friendship, but he remained apart, critical, a stranger. Their friendship was commercial, that was to say, she was a friend only as long as she kept bringing him new thoughts, new pictures, new facts. When show-and-tell was over, the relationship disintegrated.

Emerson retaliated by saying he could not converse with the divinest person longer than a week.

She responded that "no friendship could be so soon exhausted."

If he were to fault-find, their friendship consisted too often of mere literary gossip.

She admonished that he should know how to "prize a silence as much as a discourse."

This surprised Emerson. She "would have him say and do what surprised him."

Her accusation burrowed deeply. He confessed to her charge "with humility unfeigned."

Years later he claimed he "did not understand" her: "In the summer of 1840 she passed into certain religious states, which did not impress me as quite healthy, or likely to be permanent; and I said, 'I do not understand your tone; it seems exaggerated. You are one who can afford to speak the truth. Let us hold hard to the commonsense, and let us speak in the positive degree.'"

Into his journal, he inserted a fragment of her letter to him: "Does water meet water? – no need of wine, sugar, spice, or even a soupcon of lemon to remind of a tropical climate? I fear me not. Yet, dear positives, believe me superlatively yours, Margaret."

His relationship with "faithful sister" Elizabeth Hoar was beautiful and less conflicted, "not however free from the same hardness and fences...."

The easiest person to talk to, he decided, would be the scholarly-minded, quiet, shy George Bradford.

Happiness would be, Emerson reflected, to melt his icy barriers. But, on further consideration, not one of his friends exalted him. "How joyfully would I form permanent relations with the three or four wise and beautiful whom I hold so dear, and dwell under the same roof or in a strict neighborhood. That would at once ennoble life. It is easier than things which others do. It is easier than to go to Europe or to subdue a forest farm in Illinois...."

This same day he asked Fuller in a note if he could see her in Boston. He had the idea of launching a university in Concord. Students would pay whatever they could afford. Fuller, Alcott, Hedge, Parker, Ripley, and others could lecture and live in Concord: "Elizabeth Hoar said very truly when I talked with her one day about friendship – 'I do not wish my friend to visit me or I him, but I wish to live with him.'"

Within a few days he wrote Cary Sturgis that they "should be friends on imperial terms" because "we are both too proud to be found & too true to fain." He could not "make" "sister Cary" a friend "necessary" to himself because she was sure, "in some heaven foreign to me," to find another mate and then his "beautiful castle" would be "exploded to shivers." On second thought, her new mate would be a new gain in friendship for himself. "When she gives herself away it will be only to an equal virtue, then will I gain a new friend without utter loss of that which now is."

As to the accusation that he was "inhospitable of soul," he defended: "I confess to the fact of cold & imperfect intercourse, but not to the impeachment of my will, and not to the deficiency of my affection. If I count & weight, I love also. I cannot tell you how warm & glad the naming of your names makes my solitude. You give me more joy than I could trust my tongue to tell you."

He reasoned that the law of friendship ruled it better to be silent than to express love (or warmth) to benefactors. "Perhaps it is ungrateful never to testify by word to those whom we love, how much they are our benefactors. But to my thought this is better to remain a secret from the lips to soften only the behavior."

Was it really his fault their relationship was distant? Nothing would make him happier were Cary to move to Concord. "Come & live near me whenever it suits your pleasure & if you will confide in me so far I will engage to be as true a brother to you as ever blood made...."

"Sister" Cary, who assuredly responded warmly to this divine articulation, did not take Emerson up on his invitation.

A few days later, Emerson continued the debate, defining a true friend to be only the extension of our own selves. He affirmed his love for Cary while affirming her search for another lover whose love would make his love seem cold, which it was not. They were nearest when they were farthest apart.

> I hate everything frugal and cowardly in friendship. That, at least should be brave and generous. When we fear the withdrawal of love from ourselves by the new relations which our companions must form, it is mere infidelity. We believe in our eyes and not in the Creator. We do not see any equal pretender in the field, and we conclude that Beauty and Virtue must vail their high top, and buy their Eden by the loss of that which makes them ours. But we are wiser with the next sun, and know that a true and native friend is only the extension of our own being and perceiving into other skies and societies, there learning wisdom, there discerning spirits, and attracting our own for us, as truly as we had done hitherto in our strait enclosure. I wish you to go out an adventurous missionary, into all the nations of happy souls, and by all whom you can greatly, and by any whom you can wholly love, I see that I too must be immeasurably enriched.

> Not I, not thou, shall put on the God such an affront, as to fancy we know the best – have already seen the flower of his angels. This little colored world, these few homely gossips we have chatted with, are not all of nature, nay not even the first scene of the first Act, but the poor prologue only. The rent and revenues of character, we have not yet computed: great spiritual lords walk among us hourly as benefactors, but how can we see them, we who look down and not up, who appropriate and not give? As we, dear sister, are naturally friends, we shall not need to have respect unto each other. We can carry life after its own great way, without lagging for the dull convoy, without bending to please or to explain, sure that we are then nearest when we are farthest on our own road. I feel how clearly the law of friendship requires the grandest interpretation, when I glance from the dearest lover to the vast spirit impatient of bounds, impatient of persons, foreseeing the fall of every fondness, of every specialty. Only that which is related, can weather His sky or grow with the growing world. It gives me great joy to write over again to you the old creed of the heart, which is always new. So, dear child, I give you up to all your Gods - to your wildest love and pursuit of beauty, to the boldest effort of your Imagination to express it to the most original choices of tasks and influences and the rashest exclusion of all you deem alien or malign; - and you shall not give me so great a joy as by the finding for yourself a love which shall make mine show cold and feeble - which certainly is not cold or feeble.... [43]

Lidian had to have read this letter because it exists copied in her handwriting.

What conflicts Lidian must have silently maintained, as her husband claimed to maintain love for her in silence. Never did Emerson write to his wife as eloquently and seductively as he wrote to Sturgis and Fuller.

Having lovingly held Sturgis at arm's length – yet at not so far a distance as to dispel her rays of admiration – Emerson again focused his attention on Fuller.

He wrote straightaway that Anna Barker was "the Framer & inspirer of all beauty & love." Fuller was "the holiest nun" whose "rays" shine from a "house of heaven."

He would "never go back to his old arctic habits." Had he not been "raised out of society of mere mortals, by being chosen the friend of the holiest nun?"

But the privilege of noble friendships was ended. However, he had lived one day in friendship, and now he was ready "to fresh pastures." He would not lose Sam Ward as a friend because he was to marry Anna Barker. But Fuller, whose heart was a sea that hates an ebb, would lose both Sam and Anna as friends. She must be generous in rejection.

Fuller should bury her yearnings of the heart and retreat to and accept Celestial Love,* that is heavenly or divine, or spiritual love – that is, celibacy – and be replenished or empowered to make new "things."

He intimated that she was his teacher, he the truant pupil, "behind in my class." He was glad to be her debtor, but his solitude was necessary to himself. He invited her to write to him "from any mood." He wanted the "ray" from her "particular house of heaven."

> Thanks, my dear Margaret, for the good letter of Wednesday & thanks ever more to you & to our friends & to the Framer & inspirer of all beauty & love, for the joy I have drawn & do still draw from these flying days – I shall never go quite back to my old arctic habits – I shall believe that nobleness is loving, & delights in sharing itself. But what shall I say to you of this my sudden dejection from the sunlit heights of my felicity to which I had been as suddenly uplifted. Was I not raised out of the society of mere mortals by being chosen the friend of the holiest nun & began instantly to dream of pure confidences & "prayers of preserved maids in bodies delicate," when a flash of lightning shivers my castle in the air. The confessions the hope of being often & often shined on & rained on by these influences of being steeped in this light & so ripened to power whereof I yet dreamed not, are ended, the fragment of confidence that a wife can give to an old friend is not worth picking up after this invitation to elysian tables. What of that? I have lived one day. "Tomorrow to fresh fields & pastures new." Ward I shall not lose. My joy for him is very great. I have never had occasion to congratulate any person so truly. What an event to him! Its consequences to the history of his genius who can foresee? But ah! my friend, you must be generous beyond even the strain of heroism to

*Celestial Love is a title of one of Emerson's poems.

> bear your part in this scene & resign without a sign two Friends; - you whose heart unceasingly demands all, & is a sea that hates an ebb. I know there will be an ardent will & endeavor on their parts to prevent if it were indeed possible & in all ways to relieve & conceal this bereavement but I doubt they must deal with too keen a seer and a heart too thoroughly alive in its affections to cover up the whole fact with roses & myrrh.
>
> P.M.
>
> Well, & I too, it seems have done you injustice and can never speak to you in the current day but always to the ghost of your yesterday. That must be snow in summer & a wound in the house of a friend. But how is it that you can leave me in this ignorance, with such a will on your part to teach & on my part to learn? I will not vex these vain questions but instead rejoice with you that from each other & from all these tormenting lovers we can retreat always upon the Invisible Heart upon the Celestial Love, and that not to be soothed merely but to be replenished, - not to be compensated but to receive power to make all things new. I am very happy & greatly your debtor in these days and yet I find my solitude necessary & more than ever welcome to me. Austerely kind, nature calms my pleasant fevers, flatters me never, tells me still what a truant pupil I have been, & how far I am behind my class. Nay my solitary river is not solitary enough; it interrupts, it puts me out, and I cannot be alone with the Alone. From these thoughts I would gladly write to these sons & daughters of time in this culminating hour of love & joy which I also have so gladly shared. Write to me from any mood: I would not lose any ray from this particular house of heaven. [44]

Qualms and insecurities about his communication skills Emerson revealed again in his journal:

> I, conscious all the time of the short coming of my hands, haunted ever with a sense of beauty which makes all I do & say pitiful to me, & the occasion of perpetual apologies, assure myself to digest those whom I admire, and now suddenly it comes out that they have been loving me all this time, not at all thinking of my hands or my words, but only of that love of something more beautiful than the world, which, it seems being in my heart, overflowed through my eyes or the tones of my speech. [45]

His friends were "sacred," he wrote, using explicit sexual verbiage, to "sister" Elizabeth Hoar on September 12.

> Have I been always a hermit, and unable to approach my fellow men, & do the Social Divinities suddenly offer me a roomful of friends? Please God, I will not be wanting to my fortune but will eat this pomegranate – seeds stems & leaves – with all thankfulness. So consider me as now quite friendsick & lovesick....What I think & feel, you think & feel also – Why should I sit down to write it out? Are you not the true sister of
>
> Your affectionate brother
> W. [46]

Elizabeth Hoar assuredly responded warmly to this divine confidence.

The next day, September 13, he confided to Fuller that he was writing often to Caroline, "with whom I have agreed that we are brother & sister by divine invisible parentage, and she has sent me golden epistles." He also dreamed of our radiant pair of lovers" (Sam Ward and Anna Barker), and continued his sexual metaphor. He wanted to test if friendship could actually exist:

> Since I have been an exile so long from the social world and a social world is now suddenly thrust upon me I am determined by the help of heaven to suck this orange dry – no that cannot be – the expression is profane – the oranges of Olympus renew themselves as fast as the eater eats. But I will study to deserve my friends – I abandon myself to deserve my friends – I abandon myself to what is best in you all....We are likely, my dear friend, soon to prove among us whether more than two can speak together. [47]

On this same day he wrote even more intimately to Sturgis. She had been sent to him from Heaven so that there would be someone to whom he could speak the truth; he could love her with an eternal heart. She would always be present as an angel was present, even in absence she would never be absent from him:

> (Heaven has sent you) to make me feel that in speaking to you I may dismiss the consideration of you, may forget all persons, may speak the truth, & may love with the primary eternal heart.... Always men, if they have talent, though they be tolerably simple, have a little lawyer in them who argues & suspects & provides, & would construct bridges for the Impassable, & is no match for the Oracle in Woman, wh. conveys her without hands & without stairs to the heights of sentiment. Now I will identify you with the Ideal Friend, & live with you on imperial terms. Present, you shall be present only as an angel might be, & absent you shall not be absent from me. So let these tides of the Infinite wherein love, truth & power blend & are one, roll unchecked for me, for thee, their everlasting circles. Let them, only make us happy on the way to Peace on earth & good will to all beings & not in a solitary & sheltered benefit.... [48]

The divine verbal sexual foreplay is obvious.

Late September Fuller's love must have exploded. No letter of hers exists today of any such declaration, but Emerson mentioned a letter from her in which he quoted her as saying, "I am yours & yours shall be." He also mentioned a last interview, a "last Wednesday" when he found her "the meekest & most loving of the lovers of mankind."

A love encounter/appeal must have occured; various journal passages lead to this same conclusion. According to Emerson, Fuller surprised him by speaking in the softest, most modest manner.

Emerson rejected her. It must have taken at least half a day for him to compose his wooing words which would hold her off. The two of them were different; they met "like foreign states." A true friendship could only be based on like opinions and like fate.

He had always been afraid she was so "eccentric" that one day she might reach a crisis and he would not be able to help.

Theirs was a "temporary relation." So it would be best to part, immediately.

But he was the first to recognize there could be a change in their relationship. Barriers of difference could dissolve. He would open his doors to her sunshine. He sent her his honor and love, by crowning her with a wreath of laurel or, better, olive and palm. He reminded her that he had a family. He assured her that his wife sent her love and was happy Fuller had her "Bible in hand."

My dear friend,

The day is so fine that I must try to draw out of its azure magazines some ray to celebrate our friendship, and yet nature does rarely say her best words to us out of serene and splendid weather. Twilight, night, winter, & storm, the muses love, & not the halcyon hours. You must always awaken my wonder: our understanding is never perfect: so was it in this last interview, so is it ever. And yet there is progress. Ever friendly your star beams now more friendly & benign on me. I once fancied your nature & aims so eccentric that I had a foreboding that certain crises must impend in your history that would be painful to me to witness in the conviction that I could not aid even by sympathy. I said, it is so long before we can quite meet that perhaps it is better to part now, & leave our return to the Power that orders the periods of the planets. But you have your own methods of equipoise & recovery, without event, without convulsion, and I understand now your language better, I hear my native tongue, though still I see not into you & have not arrived at your law. Absent from you I am very likely to deny you, and say that you lack this & that. The next time we meet you say with emphasis that very word. I pray you to astonish me still, & I will learn to make no rash sentences upon you. – Now in your last letter, you, O divine mermaid or fisher of men, to whom all gods have given the witch-hazel-wand, or caduceus, or spirit-discerner which detects an Immortal under every disguise in every lurking place, (and with this you have already unearthed & associated to yourself a whole college of such,) do say, (for I am willing & resolute for the sake of an instance to fix one quarrel on you,) that I am yours & yours shall be, let me dally how long soever in this or that other temporary relation. I on the contrary do constantly aver that you & I are not inhabitants of one thought of the Divine Mind, but of two thoughts, that we meet and treat like foreign states, one maritime, one inland, whose trade & laws are essentially unlike. I find or fancy in your theory a certain willfulness and not pure acquiescence which seems to me the only authentic mode. Our friend is part of our fate; those who dwell in the same truth are friends; those who are exercised on different thoughts are not, & must puzzle each other, for the time. For the time! But who dare say how quickly the old eternity shall swallow up the Time, or how ripe is already in either soul the augury of the dissolution of the barriers of difference in the glimpse of ultimate unity? – I am willing to see how unskillfully I make out a case of difference & will open all my doors to your sunshine & morning air. Nothing is to me more welcome nor to my recent speculation more familiar than the Protean energy by which the brute horns of Io become the crescent moon of Isis, and nature lifts itself through everlasting transition to the higher & the highest. Whoever lives must rise & grow. Life like the nimble Tartar still overleaps the Chinese wall of distinctions that had made an eternal boundary in our geography – and I who have taxed your exclusion in friendship, find you – last Wednesday, the meekest & most loving of the lovers of mankind. I thought you a great court lady with a Louis Quatorze taste for diamonds & splendor, and I find you with a "Bible in your hand," faithful to the new Ideas, beholding undaunted their tendency, & making ready your friend "to die a beggar." Honor & love to you ever from all gentle hearts – a wreath of laurel, &, far better, the wreath of olive & of palm. My little boy for whom you promised good fortune was dressed & on his feet when I came home & is recovering his good health. All things go smoothly with me in these days but myself who am much of the time but a fat weed on the lazy wharf. Lidian sends her love to you & is overjoyed to hear of "the Bible."

Your affectionately,
R.W.E. [49]

If Emerson was attempting to hold Margaret Fuller's ardent nature at arms' length (but not too far) by defining their differences, he was on this same September 25 day, defining to his other "sister of Fate," Cary Sturgis, the similarities and the bonding nature of their alliance:

What can be trusted if that pure complacency cannot w. gives us joy in the existence of others who live in the light of the same truth with ourselves, nay are for the moment beads of ether strung on the same ray?...Can I not – I believe that I can – carry this office of dear love to its sacred height by simple following the law of the soul, so that there shall be no jar, friction or impediment in it, for there shall be nothing of me in it, but it shall be all somewhat better than me, or, the joy of God in God.... If you, dear Caroline, are not my sister of Fate, you are not mine at all. If you could depart from yourself I could not follow you. Nay, to speak out straight to the end the hating love of this law. If you, if all, depart from yourselves & from me I cannot be a loser. In whatsoever thought of God I live, I must find the inhabitant of that

> thought. I see not how any alliance can have any security on any other foundation. Is not this the secret of our league? I discern very well the degrees of stability in my relations to my friends I can behold with great security the play of time & chance, the faults of the past, the decays of mortality, the interruptions of intercourse, whilst I know that highest nature binds to me my friends nor can we get away from each other whilst we keep the commandments.... [50]

Since the Emerson/Sturgis relationship does not seem to have ever progressed beyond this heated phase, we can surmise that she accepted his words in the spirit of the highest plane of sacred friendship which bound him to her.

On the very next day, September 26, Emerson noted in his journal:

> You would have me love you. What shall I love? Your body? The supposition disgusts you. What you have thought and said? Well, whilst you were thinking and saying them, but not now. I see no possibility of loving anything but what now is and is becoming; your courage, your enterprise, your budding affection, your opening thought, your prayer, I can love, - but what else? [51]

There is no indication to whom Emerson was referring but in view of letters and circumstances, it seems reasonable to conclude that he was referring to Margaret Fuller. She came too near. She should have stood off, like Cary Sturgis, so that he could then "turn on."

There is no evidence that Fuller collapsed into her sick bed. She did undergo a change. Emerson claimed it was "spiritual" – and Fuller used the same label.

He disliked this "sort of ecstatic solitude."

On this same eventful day Margaret Fuller wrote Cary of the cold winds that blew through her home:

> Of the mighty changes in my spiritual life I do not wish to speak, yet surely you cannot be ignorant of them. All has been revealed, all foreshown yet I know it not. Experiment has given place to certainty, pride to obedience, thought to love, and truth is lost in beauty "I am no more below" – I have no words, nor can I now perceive that I shall be able to paint for any one the scenery, nor place in order the history

> of these great events. Yet I have no wish to exclude any one, and of you I almost daily think with love. When we meet you may probably perceive all in me. When we meet you will find me home. Into that home cold winds may blow, keen lightnings dart their bolts, but I cannot be driven from it more. From that home I look forth and address you sweetly as my friend. Is it not enough?–[52]

During these September days, Fuller suggested to the bride-and-groom-to-be, Sam Ward and Anna Barker, that she hoped an excellent, truthful, "brotherly" communication between them could ripen. The three of them could cultivate a new type of friendship that would be better than any they'd yet known.

A few days later, Fuller made a second plea to Emerson. He must understand. She made "no claim" on him. She was "dictated by a feeling of truth." She was "prompted by true love." She was not a "usurper." She only asked "mine own inheritance." If she was mistaken, if he did not truly feel the same as she did, she would give up "the choicest vineyard."

Certainly both of them knew "the path" she was taking. If he had not seen her feelings and her motives, then he had been "wholly ignorant" of her. Hadn't he wanted "a 'foe in your friend?'"* She knew she never would be "a beautiful foe," yet within her "sweetest harmonies are momently breathing." Did not these make her beautiful?

She was one of life's waves of gentlest force. She would not recede like a wave, but would with gentlest momentum continue "to pierce and rend asunder."

She would no longer "claim," but would be "claimed."

Lidian was a saintly soul. Fuller was "no saint," only "a great soul born to know all."

She gave herself and him up to the Central Power, to fate.

> I have felt the impossibility of meeting far more than you; so much, that if you ever know me well, you will feel that the fact of my abiding by you thus far, affords a strong proof that we are to be much to one

---

*Fuller must have seen draft copies of Emerson's essay on friendship or he must have allowed her to read his journal for these statements are included in both.

another. How often have I left you despairing & forlorn. How often have I said, This light will never understand my fire; this clear eye will never discern the law by which I am filling my circle; this simple force will never interpret my need of manifold being.

Dear friend on one point misunderstand me less. I do not love power other than every vigorous nature delights to feel itself living. To violate the sanctity of relations - I am as far from it as you can be. I make no claim. I have no wish which is not dictated by a feeling of truth. Could I lead the highest angel captive by a look, that look I would not give, unless prompted by true love.

I am no usurper. I ask only mine own inheritance. If it be found that I have mistaken its boundaries, I will give up the choicest vineyard, the fairest flower garden, to its lawful owner.

In me I did not think you saw the purity, the singleness, into which, I have faith that all this darting motion & restless flame shall yet be attempered & subdued. I felt that you did not for me the highest office of friendship, by offering me the clue of the labyrinth of my own being. Yet I thought you appreciated the fearlessness which shrinks from no truth in myself & others, & trusted me, believing that I knew the path for myself. O it must be that you have felt the worth of that truth which has never hesitated to infringe our relation, or aught else, rather than not vindicate itself. If you have not seen this stair on which God has been so untiringly leading me to himself, you have indeed been wholly ignorant of me. Then indeed, when my soul, in its childish agony of prayer, stretched out its arms to you as a father – did you not see what was meant by this crying for the moon; this sullen rejection of playthings which had become unmeaning? Did you then say, 'I know not what this means; perhaps this will trouble me; the time will come when I shall hide my eyes from this mood': – then you are not the friend I seek.

But did you not ask for a 'foe' in your friend? Did not you ask for a 'large formidable nature'? But a beautiful foe, I am not yet, to you. Shall I ever be? I know not. My life is now prayer. Through me sweetest harmonies are momently breathing. Shall they not make me beautiful,- Nay, beauty? Shall not all vehemence, all eccentricity, be purged by these streams of divine light? I have, in these hours, but one pain;

the sense of the infinite exhausts & exalts; it cannot therefore possess me wholly; else, were I also one wave of gentlest force.

Again I shall cease to melt & flow; again I shall seek & pierce & rend asunder.

But oh, I am now full of such sweet certainty, never never more can it be utterly shaken. All things have I given up to the Central Power, myself, you also; yet, I cannot forbear adding, dear friend. I am now so at home, I know not how again to wander & grope, seeking my place in another soul. I need to be recognized. After this, I shall be claimed, rather than claim, yet if I speak of facts, it must be as I see them.

To L. (Lidian) my love. In her, I have always recognized the saintly element. That, better than a bible in my hand, shows that it cannot be to me wholly alien. Yet am I no saint, no anything, but a great soul born to know all, before it can return to the creative fount. [53]

Emerson could conjure no immediate reply.

He absented himself from the late September Transcendental Club meeting. So he did not see Fuller.

At the meeting the men discussed possibilities of starting a new church with a universal creed. Henry Hedge claimed the church on its own ground had and did accomplish much. George Ripley claimed that the Social Principle had "yet to be educated," and the "Church of Humanity" had "yet to grow."

On October 1 came Emerson's reply in which he stated he was not ready to reply:

Today I think I shall not reply to your seven chords of melody which came to me last night. I do not know how I have ever deserved any friends. I behold them as they approach, with wonder. If they depart from me I shall not wonder more. And yet now & then we say things to our mates or hear things from them which seem to put it out of the power of the parties to be strangers again. Especially if any one show me a stroke of courage, a piece of inventive wit, a trait of character, or a pure delight in character when shown by others, always I must be that man's or that woman's debtor....

Farewell, benine friend. R.W.E. [54]

Emerson's final reject was written the next day – it was the day before the society wedding of Anna Barker and Sam Ward – just when Fuller's emotional conflicts were most intense.

> You are very gentle & tender in your questions. If you should rate me soundly it would be juster. You have a right to expect great activity great demonstration & large intellectual contributions from your friends, & tho' you do not say it you receive nothing. You may as well be related to mutes as to uncommunicating egoists. Yet I plead not guilty to the malice prepense. Tis imbecility not contumacy, tho' perhaps somewhat more odious. It seems very just the irony with wh you ask whether you may not be trusted, & promise such docility. Alas! We will all promise, but the prophet loiters. Strange disproportion betwixt our apprehension & our power to embody & affirm! Sometimes I think that those who love the law, & have once discerned glimpses of the characters of fire, should not eat or sleep nor buy, nor sell, nor possess, until they caught new sights of the inscription & spelled out a sentence for the world. And whether they should not brake all conventions & leave all so called duties undone for an end so universal? Heaven walks among us ordinarily muffled in such triple or tenfold disguises that the wisest are deceived & no one suspects the days to be gods. Yet we are often impressed with a conviction that if we were elsewhere in other company or employment or in no company, in turrets near the stars, or in caves underground, enlarged by science, or melted by music, or kindled by poetry, we should come into the conditions of sight & the universal cloud would roll up & disappear. The morning & evening cannot touch us with their delicate fingers, the finer hints of all beneficent spirits are lost on the flannel & buckram customs in which we wrap ourselves warm, & wherein we cheaply earn the praises of all aunts & uncles. Certainly the votary of the true God will see that his most commended virtues are snares to his feet, fatal barriers to his progress. He must be divorced & childless & houseless & friendless a churl & a fool if he would accompany with the Cherubim & have the Alone to his friend. I think nothing is more monotonous narrow & clannish than our education & ways of thought. As soon as we are more catholicly instructed we shall be helped by all vices & shall see what indispensable elements of character men of pride libertinism & violence conceal. I have no immediate thought either of burglary or arson, & am much more likely to keep a safe distance from all the instructive extremes of life & condition. Yet I would gladly dare to ask for wisdom & deserve it. [55]

The rejection, from the radical who had not hesitated to break with religious convention, seemed firm.

She probably did not attend the wedding of Anna Barker and Sam Ward at her good friend's house in Cambridge, Professor John and Eliza Farrar. Emerson was there for the ceremony and to watch the bride and groom take off on their honeymoon to Franconia. A few weeks later Elizabeth Hoar's brother was married.

The Dial appeared in bookstores late because Emerson's article introducing William Ellery Channing's poems had been late to the printer.

Since Emerson had never even been able to locate the young Channing, he felt he could not tamper with his unfinished work. So he wrote an introduction claiming Channing was a genius incapable of perfection. This poet sought the Ideal rather than the secondary aim of polish.

It was a better issue. Greeley reprinted articles. Most friendly newspapers like Greeley's and *The Knickerbocker* praised. *The Boston Morning Post* praised for not "cutting such antic tricks" as had been done in the first issue. Orestes Brownson in *The Boston Quarterly Review* said it was "a truly remarkable work," but it was "somewhat injured by its puerile conceits, and childish expressions."

The writer at *The Western Messenger* said the Transcendentalists "have not shewn the power they possess." John A. Heraud, the English editor of the *Monthly Magazine* claimed that the ideas presented were the same as his own.

The writers in the *Philadelphia National Gazette* and *Literary Register* ridiculed and the *Providence Daily Journal* called it "the organ of the incomprehensible."

The man at the *Boston Daily Advertiser* did not like Emerson's article on Channing and chided his maxim, "the failures of genius are better than victories of talent."

Said the reporter at the *Boston Courier*: "We were petrified, we were confounded, we were taken not un-aback...by these stupendously stupid 'ejaculations.'...Are the editors of the *Dial* ready to receive into their columns any amount of un profitable, un savory, un harmonious, un connected, hopeless jargon."

Friends far and wide said they'd distribute *The Dial* and contribute to it.

Friendship offered only a "momentary glow & nobility," Emerson wrote Fuller a few days later. When he reached his own hearth, Emerson was no more than when he left it. Nevertheless, that "magnanimity walks & works around us we need: it is the best of all external experiences, we pray toward it as to the holy city...."

The Lidian/Emerson marriage had been going on five years and Lidian claimed that she and Waldo were getting more and more married all the time. But she had one consternation. Mr. E. had given up family prayers. Lidian and Emerson's mother mourned. They had to hold their own private Bible reading and hymn-singing sessions. Lidian's husband was not the Christian she'd believed him to be. To realize that spiritual support came from her mother-in-law, rather than her husband, was a bitter pill.

Lidian's health became worse.

Daughter Ellen reports that "old griefs and anxieties about animals returned...."

Lidian projected human feelings onto animals and when they suffered she suffered. There's one story of how rats had gotten into the chimney and she fed them doughnuts and toast because she was interested "in all their concerns.... and in their little families."

There's another story about how her chickens had dug up all the seeds and roots in her garden, so Mr. Emerson shut them up in the roost. But thinking of them without fresh air so oppressed her that Henry David Thoreau made some neat little cowhide boots for them, which he tied neatly about their ankles, so at least they could promenade about the yard.

Lidian kept to her bed with fevers sometimes for a week or two. She'd call the doctor whose diagnoses was, "If 'twas anyone else I should say you wouldn't live a week, but as it's you I guess you'll pull through this time."

Gradually, she became skilled in homeopathic remedies. When Emerson or the children became sick, she nursed them back to strength. She saved blankets and other useful items and donated them to the sick in Concord.

Lidian's daughter Ellen wrote years later that her mother's "heaviest cloud" and "dungeon" was the "natural result of her character":

> It was her character to desire actual solid truth, her temper was combative....Her principles were that she ought to forgive. Every injustice, every slight, every wrong to her that anyone was guilty of lived before her mind and caused her permanently the same resentment that she felt at the first moment (unless the sinner had expressed a sense of his misconduct's being misconduct, which inevitably blotted it out. Now unhappily most of the offenders held the view that begging pardon was unnecessary, and others didn't know that their speeches had been reported to her.) She ought to treat these false friends well, but it wasn't true to do so. She ought to forgive. How could she forgive, for they considered wrong right, and wrong that hurt her so terribly? She read the Bible, she read every work on forgiving that she could find. She consulted Father, and he said no one should be forgiven while he persisted in his wrong course. But as Father said of himself, "his vials of wrath were soon emptied" and troubled him very little; he never could have any guess of what Mother's were to her. She asked him whether she couldn't set forth her views of their actions to those who had so troubled her, but he said "No indeed." She studied this question year in and year out, her poor mind was all worn to deep & hopeless ruts, the deepest ones of course in her natural sensibility now morbid and exaggerated, those in the intellectual part, which had never yet led anywhere, only a little less deep. Through sleepless nights, in church, at work in her garden, even in company she laboured at this problem in her heart. It was made worse by a natural trait, uncorrected by education or experience, inability to see both sides. [56]

That month Mr. Emerson gave his first wife's letters to Elizabeth Hoar to read.

Both Emerson and Fuller showed up at the next Transcendental Club meeting. The infidel George Ripley had been West and had seen how different it was from Eastern "filtered Conservatives and Conventionalists."

Ripley's inspiration was to create a utopia – a Phalanx or commune, modelled after the doctrine of the Frenchman, Charles Fourier, and Swedenborg, open to souls unhappy with the hypocrisy and materialism of conventional life. All necessities of life, housing, food, equipment, books, recreation, labor and wages were to be provided equally. Members would have direct contact with nature. Intellectual work would take priority over muscular. Shares would be sold to members at five hundred dollars – Elizabeth Peabody would sell them at her bookstore – and nothing was to be accepted from supporters of the capitalistic system.

Communes were not new in America. Many had cropped up since the seventeenth century on various principles such as free love and religious fanaticism, but Ripley's New Eden would offer freedom of soul. Ripley found one hundred and seventy-nine rocky acres in West Roxbury, not the greatest for cultivation but good enough, and it could be had for ten thousand five hundred dollars. Within nine miles of Boston, members would have easy access to concerts, lectures, and other cultural events.

Should Emerson raise the siege of his hencoop "and march baffled away to a pretended siege of Babylon?"

He reacted in his journal the next day: "I wished to be convinced, to be thawed, to be made nobly mad by the kindlings before my eye of a new dawn of human piety. But this scheme was arithmetic and comfort, a hut borrowed from Tremont House and United States Hotel; a rage in our poverty and politics to live rich and gentleman-like; an anchor to leeward against a change of weather...and not once could I be inflamed, but sat aloof and thoughtless; my voice faltered and fell.... I do not wish to remove from my present prison to a prison a little larger. I wish to break all prisons."

Emerson remembered the boarding houses he'd lived in as a boy. He was not a joiner nor a political activist. Organizing diverse personalities was not his talent. Hoeing in his own garden was sometimes a chore. He preferred the unity of being alone. He believed the perfectibility of the individual was to be achieved internally, not externally, certainly not through regimentation. He was perfectly happy in his mansion of peace where his wife and mother and hired help paved his freedom.

Fuller had her own doubts. Groton Farm experiences had taught her that thinking persons could not devote time and energy to all-consuming farm chores. Change in environment was not reform. "Why bind oneself to a central or any doctrine? How much nobler stands a man entirely unpledged, unbound!"

She cried out, "It is a constellation, not a phalanx, to which I would belong."

So the benign, no-longer-young George Ripley was the first to activate the dawn. His wife Sophia was enthused – she had once expressed her fear of losing humanity in abstractions. Despite criticism that branded him as vulgar and visionary, Ripley resigned his Purchase Street Church – sold his possessions at auction, and moved his valuable library of books to West Roxbury, thereby launching the Brook Farm Institute of Agriculture and Education.

Emerson commented to Fuller: "His step cannot be without an important sequel."

Fuller stated that the reformers could not feel themselves ready for the task until they could say that they were willing to fail.

Now came word of a change of heart in Cary. She was forgiving herself, bringing an end to her doubts and distrust in life.

At the same time Emerson began again to express his wish "to float through the great heavens a while longer" with Fuller.

There had been another confrontation. They had had an intimate conversation "in some cold room" at some "stolen moment." He had cut her off. But now, he apologized. There was wide irreconcilability, but he advocated they continue their relationship for the sake of the moments they could totally agree:

> I should gladly have talked with you another day that we might have brought things to speech somewhat more reverently than in a cold room at abrupt & stolen moments. Yet what would another day have done to reconcile our wide sights? Much time much comparison habitual intercourse with an advancing private experience interposed, would do, will do the work of interpretation. A strong passion, or the opportunity of a great work accurately adapted to one's latent faculties, – these are the sudden schoolmasters who have short methods & teach the art of life in "six lessons." Nothing less than such as these could give me a look through your telescope or you one through mine; – an all explaining look. Let us float along through the great heavens a while longer and whenever we come to a point whence our observations agree, the time when they did not will seem but a moment. With you I do not quarrel when we do not understand; for, what degree of difference there is in any thought, there is the same in every faculty & act throughout our constitution. But I wrote Caroline a good scolding letter for presuming to differ from me & siding with you &

> pretending to see your lights which I know to her as to me must be stark naught. – A strong passion or a fit work, I said, were the abridged methods. The first will never come to such as I am; the second I do not absolutely despair of, especially in these days of Phalanx, though phalanx is not it. I delight to find that I have not quite done learning, nor have I absolutely cut off my hands, though my life for so many years might lead one to think so. But if new thoughts & new emerging facts should not renovate me as a better seer, let us not fail to practice still the sure old methods, for it is not divine to be in a hurry.... [57]

He signed off "Your friend yet, Waldo E."

Fuller, in a divine hurry, appears to have plunged forward and written a letter(s) to Emerson of such passion that Emerson did not want posterity (nor Lidian) to know about it. Her letter(s) to him at this point in time do not now exist. Fortunately, all can be gleaned from her October 22 communication to Cary Sturgis who had been writing that she saw the way clear for a life renewal.

Fuller, was in euphoria at Cary's change of heart.

> Love goes forth towards you as I read your truest words. I would fain bless you for your recognition. You will go forth, you will leave your heaven, you will not only make the lights, the night, the day, and the great sea but in the least creeping thing will harmonize love and express faith in the revolutions of being. Amen....
>
> Oh Caroline, my soul swells with the future. The past, I know it not. I have just written a letter to our dear Waldo which gives me pain. It was all into the past. His call bids me return, I know not how, yet full of tender renunciation, know not how to refuse. All the souls I ever loved are holy to me, their voices sound more and more sweet yet oh for an hour of absolute silence, dedicated, enshrined in the bosom of the One.... [58]

Fuller considered the possibility of accepting the spiritual world of death which Cary had chosen as the answer which would quiet the tumult within her. But Fuller was too full of exuberance. It were better to live out her life as Fated, if Fated. The time for a life change had come.

> Yet the cross, the symbol you have chosen seems indeed the one. Daily, hourly it is laid upon me. Tremulously I feel that a wound is yet to be given. Separation!.... My Caroline, I am not yet purified. Let the lonely Vestal watch the fire till it draws her to itself and consumes this mortal part. Truly you say I have not been what I am now yet it is only transformation, not alteration. The leaf became a stem, a bud, is now in flower. Winds of heaven, dews of night, circles of time, already ye make haste to convert this flower into dead-seeming seed–yet Caroline far fairer shall it bloom again. [59]

In discursive brilliance, utilizing many comparisons, that leave interpretation open to more than one meaning, Fuller unleashed her emotions.

Using the powers of her intellect could be of service to human-kind.

She had felt compelled to rush "like a great sea" into the world, to burst forth with unending energy, fearing no rebuffs or scandalous publicity, full of expectation, undefended against all odds and barriers to carry out this work with nun-like dedication, yet underneath the stern, even angry, exterior she was soft and tender, pure and, above all, humble.

She, from the depths of darkness and chaos, wanted to walk where no one had tread, to follow a light no one else had dreamed existed.

She rejoiced in the blight of winter because spring would come.

She understood that such an aim might eventuate an "ascetic life" and since no one had answered her call for love, though she had long been ready – could not Cary read what she could not write? – she had the strength to wait forever, and asked no more now from her friends.

Only to like-minded Cary could Fuller pour forth such deeply felt soul.

On this very same day Emerson penned an unsigned letter to Fuller, reaffirming his "inside of stone."*

He was made of ice. His defense was, "ice has its uses."

---

*Scholars conjecture the date of his letter as Oct. 22.

If he acknowledged his friendships, they would be apt to disappear.

He wished to be treated as "a mute" – as one who did not communicate:

> None knows better than I – more's the pity – the gloomy inhospitably of the man, the want of power to meet and unite with even those whom he loves in his "flinty way." What amends can he make to his guests, he asked himself long since. Only to anticipate and thus if possible mitigate their disgust & suspicion at the discovery, by apprising them beforehand that this outside of wax covered an inside of stone. Ice has its uses when deception is not thought of and we are not looking for bread. Being made by chemistry & not by cooks its composition is unerring, and it has a universal value as ice, not as glass or gelatine. Would you know more of his history? – Diffident, shy, proud having settled it long ago in his mind that he & society must always be nothing to each other – he received with astonishment the kind regards of such as coming from the opposite quarter of the heavens he now calls his friends – with surprise and when he dared to believe them, with delight. Can one be glad of an affection which he knows not how to return? I am. Humbly grateful for every expression of tenderness – which makes the day sweet and inspires unlimited hopes. I say this not to you only, but to the four persons who seemed to offer me love at the same time and draw to me & draw me to them. Yet I did not deceive myself with thinking that the old bars would suddenly fall. No, I knew that if I would cherish my dear romance, I must treat it gently, forbear it long, – worship, not use it, – and so at last by piety I might be tempered & annealed to bear contact & conversation as well mixed natures should. Therefore, my friend, treat me always as a mute, not ungrateful though now incommunicable. [60]

Whereupon Fuller must have dashed off, in her truth-telling style, another revelatory letter wherein she described her inner feelings, charged him with being cold and unkind, and asked him what he thought of their mutuality. This letter no longer exists, but two days later Emerson made it bluntly clear he should never have allowed her to draw him into a discussion of their relationship. (Author's emphasis: he assumed he had nothing to do with beginning or maintaining this discussion.)

He no longer wanted to "bring the relation to speech" because it brought about quarrels. It brought home how solitary he was, not only in friendships but in his personal life. Why should she try to change or interfere with what they had. The stars in Orion shined peacefully in the old society.

In essence, he continued to say, Don't keep probing....Don't get near me.

> My dear Margaret,
>
> I have your frank & noble & affecting letter, and yet I think I could wish it unwritten. I ought never to have suffered you to lead me into any conversation or writing on our relation, a topic from which with all persons my Genius ever sternly warns me away. I was content & happy to meet on a human footing a woman of sense & sentiment with whom one could exchange reasonable words & go away assured that wherever she went there was light & force & honor. That is to me a solid good; it gives value to thought & the day; it redeems society from that foggy & misty aspect it wears so often seen from our retirements; it is the foundation of everlasting friendship. Touch it not – speak not of it – and this most welcome natural alliance becomes from month to month – & the slower & with the more intervals the better – our air & diet. A robust & total understanding grows up resembling nothing so much as the relation of brothers who are intimate & perfect friends without having ever spoken of the fact. But tell me that I am cold or unkind, and in my most flowing state I become a cake of ice. I can feel the crystals shoot & the drops solidify. It may do for others but it is not for me to bring the relation to speech. Instantly I find myself a solitary unrelated person, destitute not only of all social faculty but of all private substance. I see precisely the double of my state in my little Waldo when in the midst of his dialogue with his hobby horse in the full tide of his eloquence I should ask him if he loves me? – he is mute & stupid. I too have never yet lived a moment, have never done a deed – am the youngest child of nature – I take it for granted that everybody will show me kindness & wit, and am too happy in the observation of all the abundant particulars of the show to feel the slightest obligation resting on me to do any thing or say any thing for the company. I talk to my hobby horse & will join you in harnessing & driving him, & recite to you his virtues all day – but ask me what I think of you & me – & I am put to confusion.

Up to this hour our relation has been progressive. I have never regarded you with so much kindness as now. Sometimes you appeal to sympathies I have not and sometimes you inquire into the state of this growth. – that for the moment puts me back, but you presently return to my daylight & we get on admirably.

There is a difference in our constitution. We use a different rehetoric. It seems as if we had been born & bred in different nations. You say you understand me wholly. You cannot communicate yourself to me. I hear the words sometimes but remain a stranger to your state of mind.

Yet are we all the time a little nearer. I honor you for a brave & beneficent woman and mark with gladness your steadfast good will to me. I see not how we can bear each other anything else than good will though we had sworn to the contrary.

And now what will you? Why should you interfere? See you not that I cannot spare you? that you cannot be spared? that a vast & beautiful Power to whose counsels our will was never party, has thrown us into strict neighborhood for best & happiest ends? The stars in Orion do not quarrel this night, but shine in peace in their old society. Are we not much better than they? Let us live as we have always done, only even better, I hope, & richer. Speak to me of every thing but myself & I will endeavor to make an intelligible reply. Allow me to serve you & you will do me a kindness; come & see me & you will recommend my house to me; let me visit you and I shall be cheered as ever by the spectacle of so much genius & character as you have always the gift to draw around you.

I see very dimly in writing on this topic. It will not prosper with me. Perhaps all my words are wrong. Do not expect it of me again for a very long time....

Yours affectionately,
R. W. Emerson. [61]

Emerson sealed the wall.

It was about ten days before he wrote again, totally on *Dial* business. Then there was another space of about twenty days, again on *Dial* business.

Even less frequent were his letters to Cary.

He critically discussed Margaret Fuller's psyche with Elizabeth Hoar.* Evidently, both agreed she had a problem.

On October 25 Fuller renewed overtures to shift the entire torch of her friendship to Cary:

> Waldo is still only a small and secluded part of Nature, secluded by a doubt, secluded by a sneer. I am ashamed of him for the letter he wrote about our meeting.–It is equally unworthy of him and of what he professes for you. He calls you his sister and his saint yet cannot trust your sight. There are many beings who have reached a height of generosity and freedom far above him.
>
> But none is truer, purer, and he is already profound....
>
> I cannot read these (Emerson's) letters without a great renewal of my desire to teach this sage all he wants to make him the full-formed Angel. But that task is not for me. The gulf which separates us is too wide. May thou be his friend, it would be a glorious office. But you are not so yet. [62]

Fuller and Cary took a three-day boat cruise together during which they read over all the letters they'd received from Emerson over the past summer.

Then Fuller returned to the "world of dust and fuss and conflicting claims," that is, Willow Brook in Jamaica Plain, to bid goodbye to her mother who was sailing to New Orleans to visit her son Eugene's family. Ellen, her sister, was off to Louisville to improve her health, which left Fuller and brother Lloyd at Willow Brook.

Fuller knew that Emerson had come from humble beginnings, was basically a simple, modest person, who revered the ordinary, abhored affectation, wore plain clothes, respected hard labor, carried his own valise, yet his view of friendship confirmed an image of him standing

---

*This is revealed by Hoar's letter of March 20, 1841 to Emerson, in which Hoar confesses she has judged mistakenly in their discussions of Fuller, has found growth in her and praise for her: "'Out of the strong come forth sweetness.' The Mephistophilic vein which used to trouble me had wholly disappeared – & with it the restlessness."

aloof, arrogant, righteous, not wasting his time and energies on people who did not serve his purpose.

His reasoning led to the sceptical position that friendship is disillusioning, not worth the time consumed. People reached the highest level of friendship when they did without friendship...when friendship is spiritualized or eternalized...when human contact is lofty.

Fuller felt abiding connections brought about a balanced sense of well being, gave value to life.

To Emerson, friendship was an egotism.

To Fuller, friends were "sharers of our very existence."

Emerson could agree to an extent but, to him, friendship represented a need to rid oneself of burdensome thoughts and to gain a better understanding of oneself. To commit to another in friendship or in love was to ask for betrayal.

Fuller would counter that friends ministered to one another; revealed themselves to the other, guided, inspired. "Friends should be our incentives to Right, yet not only our guiding but our prophetic stars."

Emerson would proffer that true friendship/love was a transcendence, a going beyond the person or love object. True love dwelt on the eternal. Every man or woman is alone in the world. Each must follow his own path.

She, who in one letter said, "I could live for my friends," felt people were more for having met. She wanted tangible friends, face to face, living and breathing in the here and now.

He claimed he did not seek friends; they always came to him. He did not find them but "the Deity in him chose them."

She deliberately cultivated an inmost circle of relations. She listened instinctively on acquaintance and when she and another seemed to "rise at a glance" she would "yield to an impression." She said such meetings were fated.

Emerson felt people seek friends that will help them to grander self-acquaintance. People liked people who are like themselves. "I shall not like him, unless he is at last a poor Greek like me."

She looked for equal give-and-take. "I want habitual intercourse, cheer, inspiration, tenderness. I want these for myself; I want to impart them...I have loved to give."

Emerson maintained that as friends meet, both parties find out the other is not what he/she was thought to be. Apathies develop; friends must compromise or part in solitude.

> We are armed all over with subtle antagonisms, which, as soon as we meet, begin to play, and translate all poetry into stale prose. Almost all people descend to meet. All association must be a compromise, and, what is worse, the very flower and aroma of the flower of each of the beautiful natures disappears as they approach each other. What a perpetual disappointment is actual society, even of the virtuous and gifted! [63]

To him, communication offered a threat. "Though I prize my friends, I cannot afford to talk with them and study their visions, lest I lose my own. It would indeed give me a certain household joy to quit this lofty seeking this spiritual astronomy or search of stars, and come down to warm sympathies with you; but then I know well I shall mourn always the vanishing of my mighty gods."

Fuller was ready to receive. "There were no traditionary notions in my mind; I believed in nothing merely because others believed in it; I had taken no feelings on trust. Thus my mind was open to their sway."

He felt that the laws of friendship are of one web with the laws of nature – ebb and flow forevermore. "Is it not that the soul puts forth friends as the tree puts forth leaves, and presently, by the germination of new buds, extrudes the old leaf?"

Fuller believed in the law of ebb and flow, but her perspective was that the germination of friendship could never be lost. It was true that as time progressed, the path could not usually be re-trod; for neither party would be again what the other wanted or needed. Still, past friends were "intelligible thoughts of the divine mind. We like to see how they unfold; we like to meet them and part from them; we like their action upon us and the pause that succeeds and enables us to appreciate its quality....We bear them in our memory, tales which have been told, and whose meaning has been felt." Past attachments opened regions of being which burst into leaf and bloomed, "which would else have laid sealed in cold obstruction."

Emerson perceived that there were two elements of friendship. One was truth. But truth in society is practically unattainable. "Every man alone is sincere. At the entrance of a second person, hypocrisy begins....We can seldom go erect."

The other element was tenderness, which "is fit for serene days and graceful gifts and country rambles, but also for rough roads and hard fare, shipwreck, poverty and persecution."

For her, the interchange of mutual influence allowed for imperfection as well as perfection. "Why am I to love my friend the less for any obstruction in his life? Is not the very time for me to love most tenderly, when I must see his life in spite of seeming? When he shows it to me I can only admire.... I am taken captive."

For her, it was not weakness to be emotionally dependant on friends. Dependency allowed the development of nurturing and sustaining relationships.

Emerson's attitude was that his friends must serve him. "I do then with my friends as I do with my books. I would have them where I can find them, but I seldom use them.... I cannot afford to speak much with my friend. If he is great he makes me so great that I cannot descend to converse."

In illustration of her idea, Fuller told this story: "'He raised me,' said a woman inspired by love, 'upon the pedestal of his own high thoughts, and wings came at once, but I did not fly away. I stood there with downcast eyes worthy of his love, for he had made me so.'"

Fuller's stance was that if we expect the impossible, we will find it.

To Emerson, friendship encompassed power and consent.

> Better be a nettle in the side of your friend than his echo.... Let it be an alliance of two large, formidable natures, mutually beheld, mutually feared, before yet they recognize the deep identity which, beneath these disparities, unites them.... Leave to the diamond its ages to grow....Let him be to thee for ever a sort of beautiful enemy, untamable, devoutly revered, and not a trivial conveniency to be soon outgrown and cast aside.

She felt the greatest friendship was sustained by faith. She wrote: "To love by sight is much, to love by faith is more; together they make up the entire love without which heart, mind, and soul cannot be alike satisfied."

He argued that the greatest friendship treats its object like a god and deifies both parties.*

Fuller argued that friends "are not merely one another's priests or gods, but ministering angels, exercising in their part the same function as the Great Soul does in the whole."

To her, a person who lived in this world without friends was "a stranger to its real life, deluded like the maniac who fancies he has attained his throne, while in reality he is on a bed of musty straw."

Margaret Fuller's friends reached so far and wide that Elizabeth Hoar said, "Margaret Fuller wore her friends as a necklace of diamonds about her neck." William Henry Channing wrote that Margaret Fuller was The Friend.

Emerson liked people in theory but in reality it was more comforting to take a walk in Concord woods.

One can imagine Lidian's loneliness as she tried to adjust to Emerson's separate Olympic throne.

Fuller was now finding it more rewarding to confide in William Henry Channing.

> Men disappoint me so, I disappoint myself so, yet courage, patience, shuffle the cards, Durindarte....
>
> I wish I were a man, and then there would be one. I weary in this play-ground of boys, proud and happy in their balls and marbles. Give me heroes, poets, lawgivers, Men.

---

*These ideas and experiences are again reflected in Emerson's essay "Manners": "I like that every chair should be a throne, and hold a king. I prefer a tendency to stateliness to an excess of fellowship. Let the incommunicable objects of nature and the metaphysical isolation of man teach us independence. Let us not be too much acquainted....We should meet each morning as from foreign countries, and, spending the day together, should depart at night, as into foreign countries. In all things I would have the island of a man inviolate. Let us sit apart as the gods, talking from peak to peak all round Olympus. No degree of affection need invade this religion....Lovers should guard their strangeness....coolness and absence of heat and haste indicate fine qualities. A gentleman makes no noise; a lady is serene.... Not less I dislike a low sympathy of each with his neighbor's needs. Must we have a good understanding with one another's palates?.... Every natural function can be dignified by deliberation and privacy."

> There are women much less unworthy to live than you, Men; the best are so unripe, the wisest so ignoble, the truest so cold!* [64]

As for the Fuller/Emerson friendship, it did continue – after all, she was his most vital connection to humanity.

Their work resumed on the January *Dial.* The letters that passed back and forth were written in the spirit that was comfortable for Emerson – warm, business-like.

Fuller had a log of material that had been left out of the first two issues, but she would decline to print more of Emerson's dead brother's, though she would insert an unsigned well written poem by his dead first wife, "The Violet." It compared the beauty of human life and death to the flower.

Emerson rejected Elizabeth Peabody's paper on "Patriarchal Traditions."

Fuller would do nothing about the left-over William Ellery Channing poems.

Alcott expressed his disappointment in having more of his "Orphic Sayings" rejected, and Theodore Parker complained that Fuller was full of "petty jealousies," with "a contemptible lust of power, & falling into freaks of passion."

"Man in the Ages," would become the lead article, signed "S" for T.T. Stone. She would include Sam Ward's long "Letters from Italy," about the famous author of the *DeCameron*, Boccaccio, eulogizing perpetual youth. But not a "J" would appear at the end.

Five new poems by Cary Sturgis, in praise of seascapes, winds and waves, would be linked in. All but one would be signed with the "Z." Emerson sent along some James Russell Lowell sonnets which the editor felt were too imitative of Alfred Lord Tennyson, but she would print one, signed "M.L.O."

The editors passed back and forth William Wetmore Story's article on art until Fuller decided to hold it for April revision, but never was there a re-submission.

---

* Perhaps "the best" referred to Sam Ward, "the wisest" was Goethe, and "the truest" was Emerson.

Back from Louisville with wife and son was James Freeman Clarke ready to start a liberal-conservative new church to bridge new theology with the old. No longer could he totally share the radical views of the Transcendentalists.

Back from their honeymoon were the newlyweds, Sam and Anna Ward. Fuller faced them one evening in their new home located in the fashionable Louisberg Square. William Henry Channing heard about the occasion: "Anna's strongest expression of pleasure and which she repeated again and again was 'I feel as if I had been married twenty years.'"

A proposal of marriage went forward to Ellen Sewall in Scituate. She turned to her father for advice; he was not in favor of Transcendentalists. A short note was advanced to Henry David Thoreau; she was seeing another young man.

Fuller told Emerson that she was beginning to be more interested in *The Dial.* It brought "meat and drink to sundry famishing men and women." His poem "Woodnotes," in the October *Dial,* had been read with delight.

She would include some "Orphic Sayings" in the January issue and would Emerson "prithee woo thereto, as you know how."

Emerson "wooed," and Fuller received fifty. Again the byline "by A. Bronson Alcott" was inserted under the title.

She left unsigned Sturgis' sister's poem, "To the Ideal," about courage in living despite the thwart of dreams.

Thoreau's essay on bravery had been on her desk five months. It was "rich in thoughts...But...I seem to hear the grating of tools on the mosaic...." She asked for a re-write.

She accepted Thoreau's poem which Emerson had passed along to her, "Nature relumes her dawn each day."

Emerson had not informed Fuller, but he had changed Thoreau's verb to "relumes" because in Othello he liked, "that can thy light relume." Thoreau preferred his own choice, "doth have."

Emerson told Thoreau that actually it was Fuller's re-write.

Thoreau became stubborn.

Finally, Emerson wrote Fuller: "Our tough Yankee must have his tough verse."

Emerson suggested Fuller supply a title.

She called it "Stanzas," and signed it "D. H. T."
The poem appeared:

> Nature doth have her dawn each day
> But mine are far between;
> Content, I cry, for sooth to say,
> Mine brightest are, I ween.

Thoreau did not re-submit his essay on bravery.*

The word "relume" appeared in Emerson's journal and then in his essay, "Friendship."**

Digging into her 1833 notebooks Fuller brought out her piece on "Meta," and she also was working on an article about the yuca filamentosa plant, but gave it up temporarily to write "The Magnolia of Lake Pontchartrain." She wrote some reviews for the Record of the Months section, praising Hawthorne's *Grandfather's Chair.* These articles were left unsigned.

It was dear to her heart to have an article by Sophia Ripley on "Woman," her place and role in society. It was signed "W. N." – probably short for "woman."

For some future *Dial,* Fuller was translating Bettina Brentano von Arnim's *Günderode* and had sent the author her Goethe translation in Ripley's volume, a copy of *The Dial,* and Emerson's *Nature.*

Still Fuller lacked copy. "Where is George Bradford's promised essay? – with last year's snow?" About abolition, it was never freed from the author's desk.

Dwight had sent a short piece from a projected series about work which would be signed "D."

---

*Thoreau later submitted it to Emerson when he became editor, but it was never published in *The Dial.* Thoreau's vindication was to write in his book, *A Week on the Concord and Merrimack:* "I know a woman who possesses a restless and intelligent mind, interested in her own culture, and earnest to enjoy the highest possible advantages, and I meet her with pleasure as a natural person who not a little provokes me, and I suppose is stimulated in turn by myself. Yet our acquaintance plainly does not attain to that degree of confidence and sentiment which women, which all, in fact, covet. I am glad to help her, as I am helped by her; I like very well to know her with a sort of stranger's privilege."

** Emerson's sentence in his journal and in his essay, "Friendship," reads: "Pleasant are these jets of affection which relume a young world for me again."

Emerson sent in the poem he'd struggled with, "The Sphinx." He asked to see the proof as he might change two words.

And Theodore Parker had sent in "German Literature," a vigorous attack on the German critic, Wolfgang Menzel, who had downgraded Goethe. According to Menzel, Goethe was an ape…"a woman in a manly age." Goethe was the weak-hearted, pleasure-loving vain child of fortune whose ideal was himself. He represented luxury, soft effeminate vices, sentimental spirit and foppish mannerisms.

Parker called Menzel an incompetent critic, and Fuller signed his article "P."

Then, fully aware of the criticism she would create because she was a woman, she wrote her own defense of Goethe, "Menzel's View of Goethe." She signed it "F."

How can a nature so rich as Goethe's be neglected, she argued. To call him an Epicurean sage and a debauchee was only a partial view. Goethe was prophet of his age. No one was his peer. If he valued the present too much, it was not for pleasure but for use. She did not ask if he lived up to other people's standards, but did he live up to his own. He'd written sixty volumes which attested to a life of serious work. If he failed to reach the highest level of achievement, he was at least a worthy guide.

Fuller opened her second series of Conversations with the touching announcement that she had undergone a great change. She could only give her new thinking partial expression because it was of so deep and sacred a character.

Encircling her were the familiar faces, plus many new women. Fine Arts was the subject for the year. Sessions covered sculpture, music, painting, and a most interesting one was "What is Life?"

After each Conversation the inevitable attack of headache swept in. Eliza Farrar sat with her after one session and asked if she thought the headaches would reoccur all winter. Fuller said she subscribed to Goethe's belief: "The growth of genius in its relations to men around must always be attended with daily pain." To William Henry Channing: "Pain has no effect except to steal some of my time. "

Weekly, Fuller prodded *Dial* writers for better materials while she tried to weigh, balance, conform to space requirements, and correct sloppy grammar.

Emerson had hoped he'd need only submit a sonnet, but now he was offering an article on art because he could derive it from a Concord Lyceum lecture. When the editor saw his draft, she believed something better could be achieved.

How do you criticize the work of a friend whom you know wants and needs your love, but who has made it clear you are not to express your love and who has criticized your actions and doubted over half the tenets of your beliefs – yet whom you still admire and value and want desperately to keep as a trusted friend?

> I wrote to you last night, and today the lines about your Essay seem so dull, so cold, and so impertinent withal that I have a mind to burn the paper – Yet let them go – I should have said the same, and the office of our best sentiments is to make us altogether better not to induce us to suppress the worst or select the best of ourselves.
>
> Yet there is something obviously wrong in this attempt to measure one another, or one another's act. It seems as if we could not help it in this our present stage, as if we should jostle and bruise one another, if we had not some idea of our respective paths and places. But surely there will come a purer mode of being even in the world of Form. We shall move with an unerring gentleness, we shall read in an eye beam whether other beings have any thing for us; on those who have not our only criticism will be to turn our eyes another way. Then there will be no more negations, we shall learn to be ourselves by the achievements of other natures and not by their failures.
>
> Then our actions will not be hieroglyphics any more but perfect symbols. Then parting and meeting will both be equally beautiful, for both will be in faith. Then there will be no more explanations but with every instant revelations. Then will be no more intercourse, but perfect communion with full-eyed love. – But then – we shall write essays on Art, more than cavils at them.
>
> Adieu–*en Dieu* [65]

With him she seemed always to suppress her greatest most human of passions.

S.M.F. returned R.W.E.'s "Thoughts On Art" for re-writes, after which she published it, unsigned.

R.W.E. sent major poetry, "The Snow Storm," and a six-line filler, "Suum Cuique." Neither was awarded an ending initial.

Henry Hedge sent in a good poem, but it was far from the "solid gold bullion" she had expected. James Freeman Clarke sent two poems, one a hymn and prayer and one about broken young love.

Cranch sent seven poems, with an introduction, and Fuller awarded him three "C's" at the end of three poems.

The Dial came out on January 1, 1841. Emerson said the public should humbly thank Fuller for holding it together.

Again, *The New-York Daily Tribune* subscribed it far above other American magazines.

The public had their own mixed opinions: "grand," "pretentious," "inspiring," "cant and humbug," etc. One Boston paper thought it "the quintessence of folly and extravagance." Alcott's "Orphic Sayings" were attacked as representing "the step from the sublime to the ridiculous." Another reviewer parodied: "Ever the true Putty faststicketh." Fanny Appleton (who would later become Longfellow's wife) thought Emerson's "The Sphinx" could only have been written in Bedlam.

Emerson praised Fuller's article, "The Magnolia."

By the end of January Fuller was in for another bloodletting. Weakened, she wrote metaphor after metaphor to Sturgis.

The next day Emerson read "Man the Reformer" before the Mechanics' Apprentices' Library Association at the Masonic Temple. It covered the dignity of work and the inequalities of labor systems. Should he allow this Association to publish it? He preferred that it be printed in *The Dial* because then he wouldn't have to write anything this month. He had the proofs of his book *Essays* to read. The genius of reading and of gardening were antagonistic: "The writer ought not to be married, ought not to have a (house) family. I think the Roman Church with its celibate clergy & its monastic cells was right. If he must marry, perhaps he should be regarded happiest who has a shrew for a wife, a sharp-tongued notable dame who can & will assume the total economy of the house, and having some sense that her philosopher is best in his study suffers him not to intermeddle with her thrift.

He shall be master but not mistress, as Elizabeth Hoar said."

Fuller continued to find that she could better confide in William Henry Channing: "Once I was all intellect; now I am almost all feeling. Nature vindicates her rights.... I shall burn to ashes if all this smoulders here much longer. I must die if I do not burst forth in genius or heroism."

Like a child, *The Dial* demanded constant attention. For April there was Emerson's "Man the Reformer," which he'd not given to the Mechanics' Apprentices' Library Association. The prolific Theodore Parker readied "Thoughts on Labor," and John Sullivan Dwight offered "Ideals of Every-Day Life, II." The editor had finished an autobiographical piece, "Leila," and was working on a "Dialogue" on art.

She had William Ellery Channing poems, which would be unsigned, one about a false fool world in which the poet could not wear a smiling face, and the other about a lover/poet who finds inspiration in a beautiful maiden. (Could this be Cary Sturgis?)

There were three of Ellen Hooper's delicate poems, to be unsigned, a to-be-unsigned poem from James Freeman Clarke, "The Dream," in which he vividly described a binding love union, and "Sic Vita" from Thoreau, though she finally decided against this one in favor of verses from Cary Sturgis – and without the "Z" – one entitled "The Wind" comparing the poet-speaker to the woeful wind which goes on forever "I know not where, I've no toil or care, yet rest I never." And she had three new writers.

Beginning in March Fuller tried the experiment of inviting men to her winter series of ten Conversations devoted to the subject of Greek Mythology, all held at George Ripley's house. She thought the men would lend added dimension with their objective viewpoints, greater experience and educations. Thus Emerson, Frederic Henry Hedge, James Freeman Clarke, Willliam Wetmore Story, Bronson Alcott, Charles Stearns Wheeler, and Jones Very intermingled with Elizabeth Hoar, Caroline Sturgis, Anna Barker, Sophia Dana Ripley, Eliza Farrar, Elizabeth Peabody, Sophia Peabody, Carolyn Healy Dall.

The plan did not work. Carolyn Healy Dall who took notes claimed "Emerson pursued his own train of thought. He seemed to forget that we had come together to pursue Margaret's."

March 15 Emerson was writing to Cary Sturgis: "Who is fit for friendship? Not one."*

Emerson thought the April *Dial* was a "Morgue." It was a few days late to the bookstores because the printer was having economic problems. This time it was not even ridiculed in the news media.

On April Fools Day, 1841, George Ripley, his wife, Sophia, his sister, Marianne, his church newspaper printer, Minot Pratt with wife and three children, another young friend, and a domestic sat down for the first time at the Brook Farm table.

In Concord Emerson invited his servants to eat at his family table. He convinced Lidian that this was the thing to be done, and he convinced her to do the asking.

But this was not the servants' idea of equality. When dinner was ready they claimed they'd already eaten.

Next, was Emerson's commitment to bread and water for breakfast, later to meatless meals. These reforms were soon dropped.

Since the air was full of communitarism, Emerson was issuing invitations to needy like-minded intellectuals to live at his mansion of peace: Henry David Thoreau accepted. Mary Russell, a friend of Lidian's from Plymouth, accepted – she stayed as school teacher to Waldo Jr. and other neighborhood children including the two Alcott girls, Lizzie and Louisa May.

The Bronson Alcotts turned down an offer of "half our house and storeroom free" with separate dining tables "save one oven to bake our potatoes, and the same pot for our potatoes; but not the same cradle for our babies." Mr. Alcott was to have shared garden duties, while Mrs. Alcott was to have shared household duties. All had been discussed thoroughly with Lidian and mother. But wife Abby May

---

*Friendship was to be a much-written about subject for Henry David Thoreau also. His words were to echo Emerson's: "November, 1851: I love my friends very much, but I find it is no use to go and see them. I hate them commonly when I am near them. They belie themselves and deny me continually.... That which we love is so mixed and entangled with what we hate in one another, that we are more grieved and disappointed – aye, and estranged from one another – by meeting than by absence.... Nothing makes me so dejected as to have met my friends; for they make me doubt if it is possible to have any friends...."

reneged. Why become more indebted to Mr. Emerson? – he was already paying their rent at Hosmer's Dove Cottage.

Henry David Thoreau stayed in the tiny upstairs room at the top of the stairs, called "The Prophet's Chamber" because of a text that read: "Let us make a little chamber, I pray thee, on the wall, and let us sit there a bed and a table and a stool and a candlestick and it shall be when he cometh to us that he shall turn in thither."

Thoreau received his board by painting, planting, and grafting trees, repairing locks, putting up shelves, cleaning out the chimney, caring for children and chickens. He delighted in giving Waldo Jr. rides on his back. For Lidian he built a little drawer under the seat of a dining room chair so she could safe-keep her gloves. He often also did small repairs for Lucy Brown who lived in her own house near the Emersons.

It seemed an excellent arrangement. Thoreau was often ill, but he did not smoke, drink coffee, tea, alcohol. He was courteous though brusque. He could read Greek better than almost any Concord author and also was well versed in Latin, French, German, Italian and Spanish. He knew Virgil by heart. He had a wide knowledge of the English classics, knew both the English and Latin names of flowers. The only time off he wanted was the afternoons when he would take three-hour walks into the Concord woods. "I go out to see what I have caught in my traps, which I set for facts," he said.

He did not own more than one decent suit, would not ride if he could walk; would not vote, pay taxes, nor go to church, and when in the woods adopted the survival skills of the Indian. One of his greatest cultivated skills was in asking questions. "No" was a word in his vocabulary he readily used.

Many Concordians stigmatized the Henry David Thoreau thinking as "tomfoolery." He was a ne'er do well...a loafer who refused to help his family. After all, he wanted to live without following any profession, to live for the sake of living, to watch the sun and moon rise and set, to pick every berry he passed. His Aunt Maria said she wished he "could find something better to do than always walking off somewhere." Emerson was to eventually write: "It was not the Ship of State Henry was aching to captain, but only a huckleberry party or a search for chestnuts or grapes." His mother and sisters defended him staunchly.

Stories are recorded about Thoreau's infatuation with Lidian, with her sister Lucy, and with Mary Russell. Lidian, it is said, confided in Henry and offered him encouragement in a sisterly or motherly fashion. In the fall, when Mary Russell left the Emerson household, Thoreau wrote a poem to her, "To the Maiden in the East."

In Boston James Freeman Clarke was being called a thief, a robber, a disturber. He carried "a piratical flag." His Church of the Disciples was attracting about three hundred worshipers each Sunday, many of whom travelled long distances to sit in quite an unattractive Williams Hall, about which one woman said "bonnets seen there were of so singular a description, as constantly to distract attention from the minister's sermon."

There was nothing new in Clarke's ideas; it was just that they were not popular with traditionalists. He took whatever was good, as he saw it, from traditional Christian doctrine. His was belief in the existence of God, Jesus as the son of God, the truth of the Bible, the worth of human nature and the importance of the church as a place where people could unite and work together. This latter notion was quite revolutionary.

He did the unheard by organizing evening discussion groups at the church. He wanted his congregation to participate, to become family. He introduced voluntary contributions, that is, a free pew system,* lay preaching, singing of hymns by all with accompaniment, and he allowed anyone to partake of communion, member or not. These ideas earned a following which included Dr. Nathaniel Peabody and daughters, Elizabeth, Sophia, and Mary, Dr. Walter Channing, Dr. Samuel Cabot, Julia Ward Howe, and John and Eliza Farrar.

Brook Farm, which carried that name because a clear brook ran past the front of the main building, attracted courteous and moral radicals, farmers, scholars, seamstresses, preachers, teachers, of varying ages, with varying motives and skills, some needing education, all enthusiastic about change, though none could agree on methods. One felt meditating in the woods in a wigwam was divinity.

---

*Clarke's wife was independently wealthy and income from investments afforded them a comfortable living; therefore, Clarke was enabled to start his voluntary church.

Members wore flowing blouses of varying colors and little vizorless caps that caused one observer to comment they were "exquisitely unfitted for horny-handed tillers of the soil."

Most conformed to house themselves in the web of buildings being built, which included The Hive (the main building featuring the kitchen and the large dining hall where everything was white, the walls, tables, chairs, and dishes), The Eyrie (a wooden building with French windows on the highest point overlooking the Charles River, where consociates or married persons stayed including the Ripleys – where Ripley's prized library was shelved), The Nest (the school), The Pilgrim House (a man from Plymouth had gifted it), and the Margaret Fuller Cottage (donated by a woman who lived in part of it, built in the form of a Maltese cross, with four gables, a stairway in the center – supposedly the prettiest and the best furnished house on the place, but it's contact with nature was admirably close – at all seasons it's external and internal temperatures corresponded).*

In the surrounding forest amidst birch, pine, wild columbine, and mosses, stood Pulpit Rock where years earlier the "Apostle to the Indians," John Eliot had assembled a red-skinned congregation and where William Henry Channing would assemble the Brook Farmers for services which would end with all joining hands in a circle, the symbol of Universal Unity.

Labor was scheduled during morning hours. (Always there was more labor than laborers.) Besides potatoes, the Brook Farmers produced for sale Britannia ware, oil lamps, window sashes and blinds, shoes and boots. (It turned out that few public spirited persons wanted to buy Britannia ware, oil lamps, window sashes and blinds, shoes and boots.) Milk and vegetables sold. The Brook Farmers also made teapots, doors, and nature books. They ran their own printing press and eventually published a newspaper, *The Harbinger*, whose editor was "Pun King" – as George Ripley was called because he once made so many puns while harvesting pumpkins.

Afternoons were for greater growth. Classes were set up on the classics, mathematics, literature, aesthetics, and other subjects.

---

*The Margaret Fuller Cottage stood almost a hundred fifty years; it burned down in 1985.

Sophia Ripley sat on the Council and served as Director of Education and taught History and Modern Languages; also she knelt on floors while scrubbing them, and spent long hours in the laundry and muslin rooms. She was also in charge of the "Household Corps," a group who prepared and cleaned up after meals. (Always a "Graham table" was set, that is, a table where service conformed to the vegetarian standards of the Graham Diet.) The clean-up crew would invariably accompany washing dishes with singing " O Canaan, bright Canaan." At tea time "brewis" was served, a mush of baked corn meal and molasses.

The school turned out to be Brook Farm's best source of income. It was so esteemed that parents living in the area enrolled their children. It was run by "Her Perpendicular Majesty," or tall and angular Marianne Ripley.

George Bradford taught literature, science and astronomy, and had chief care of the clothesline. Bradford also milked cows, cleaned their stalls, and worked in the fields.

Discussion was even more important than other activities that included walks in the woods, picnics, dances, musicals, masquerades, tableaux, theatricals, poetry readings, and any kind of created fun the Amusement Group or any one person could think of. Evenings were for recreation.

Orestes Brownson is best remembered for his pounding on the table to get his points across. Albert Brisbane talked on Fourierism, as well as Horace Greeley. Christopher Cranch came to play the flute with John Sullivan Dwight who had given up the ministry. Cranch and Dwight energetically organized the Brook Farmers into choir-singers.

Visitors came, even from afar. One year there were more than four thousand. Discipline was Ripley's weightiest problem.

Among the hundred and fifty aesthetic and cultivated members who actually lived and worked at Brook Farm for more than one season, there was Charles A. Dana (later journalist and manager of *The New-York Daily Tribune* and *The Sun*) who was chief of the "Waiter Corps," griddle master, teacher of Greek and German, and Director of Finance. There was Minot Pratt, treasurer and Ripley's right arm, and his wife, Maria. There was George William Curtis, (later of *Harper's*) who trimmed the lamps, Isaac Hecker (later founder of the Paulist Fathers) whose bread was said to be better baked than his ideas, and Francis Channing Barlow (later New York secretary of state and attorney general). And there was Nathaniel Hawthorne.

"I have milked a cow!" Hawthorne exclaimed proudly his first week after arriving in a freak April snowstorm.

Because the political winds of change had turned him out of his position as weigher and gauger in the Boston Custom House, he had invested his savings of one thousand dollars into Brook Farm, hoping he could work for his and Sophia Peabody's room and board and write during the evenings.

Brook Farm was a bold step for Hawthorne who had lived so reclusively in Salem that he later wrote: "I doubt whether so much as twenty people in the town were aware of my existence." He saw his mother and sisters only at tea when they sat together in the little parlor in their seventeenth century house built by his grandfather. During one period he did not see his sister Elizabeth for three months. He and his mother never spoke confidingly to each other, though it is recorded there was enduring love between them.

His chamber had been under the eaves where he had sat writing or gazing out the curtained window at the church. At dusk or dawn, depending on his mood, he would take long walks to Endicott's Orchard Farm, or over witchcraft ground and Gallows Hills, or along the coast. He felt, as he was to write to his beloved fiance later "as if I had only life enough to know that I was not alive...."

He was hamstrung with an upbringing by a mother who had, at the age of twenty-eight, waited in vain for the return of her thirty-three year-old captain husband, who'd died of yellow fever in Surinam while on a sea voyage. Thus she secluded herself from the world; this was considered highly acceptable behavior in the Puritan tradition.

Hawthorne was four. He was watched over by his aunts, but because he was a boy, he'd been allowed freedoms which his two sisters were denied. It was quite permissible for him to play, fight, wander around the wharf, watch the merchant ships, listen to sea and weather tales, and make friends with other youngsters.

He was keenly aware of his heritage. In 1630 his town Magistrate ancestor, William Hathorne, had sentenced women who did not adhere to Puritan code. He commanded they be lashed by horse's tails. He had hung men for killing Indians. His son, John, as magistrate, accused women of being witches, one of whom was Rebekah Nurse who retaliated by inflicting a curse upon the family, not only upon them but upon "their children's children."

Nathaniel Hawthorne graduated from Bowdoin College in Maine. A well-to-do uncle had paid his way. His family had wanted him to be a lawyer or doctor. But he'd always figured ways to avoid responsibility. In Maine, as a young boy, he'd wander the woods, gun in hand. He used to skate, fish, and follow bear tracks. Only when he felt like it did he attend school – or when forced. At Bowdoin drinking and gambling took up a good part of his time as well as catching trout, shooting pigeons and squirrels.

After graduating, he returned to Salem, for twelve years to sit at his window, smoking silently. After dark he'd start out on his long lonely ambles to Marblehead, Swampscott, North Adams, or the White Mountains.

Externally, he was handsome – there was a story bandied about that a Gypsy met him in a woods and exclaimed, "Are you a man or an angel?" He had thick dark wavy hair, piercing, striking blue eyes, was five-feet ten, broad shouldered with a light athletic frame. Internally, he was gnawed by the sins in his family legacy.

He destroyed his first novel. When *Fanshaw* failed – which he'd paid to have published anonymously – he got rid of all unsold copies. In 1837 at the age of thirty-three he published, under his own name, *Twice-Told Tales*, and became a local celebrity. Then the-girl-next-door Elizabeth Peabody, knocked on his door. She eventually introduced him to her sister, Sophia, who thought he was "handsomer than Lord Byron."

His theory that he'd have leisure at Brook Farm to work on his writing was dashed as George Ripley introduced him to a four-pronged dung-fork and manure pile or "gold mine," as it was called. This, along with hoeing potatoes and raking hay was his reality. Working with the cows his first week, he wrote in his daily journal: "The number is now increased by a Transcendental heifer belonging to Miss Margaret Fuller. She is very fractious, I believe, and apt to kick over the milk pail...." And the next day he observed: "Miss Fuller's cow hooks other cows, and has made herself ruler of the herd, and behaves in a very tyrannical manner." Obviously, Hawthorne did not like strong, articulate women.

Fuller visited Brook Farm frequently, sometimes for a week or two, and held her Conversations. She had little hope that the Brook Farmers would free themselves of the evils of society, but she did love the beauty of the place, and the woods "full of perfume."

She found herself saying, "I have found myself here in the amusing position of being a conservative."

Her first Conversation was on Education, but the free-thinkers showed "a good deal of the *sans-culotte* tendency in their manners, – throwing themselves on the floor, yawning, and going out when they had heard enough."

Her next Conversation was held after a "picturesque" husking party, and she chose the subject deliberately: Impulse. "None yawned, for none came, this time, from mere curiosity."

One young woman, Georgiana Bruce, admired her so much that she brought her coffee every morning in the one and only china cup.

If she'd stay, the Brook Farmers promised to excuse her from hard labor; her labor would be her Conversations. But Fuller considered these terms unequal. "It would be the same position the clergyman is in or the wandering beggar with his harp. Each day you must prove yourself anew."

Phalanxes were not for Henry David Thoreau either. He consistently stated that he resigned from all societies he had never joined: "I think I had rather keep bachelor's hall in hell than go to board in heaven.... In heaven I hope to bake my own bread and clean my own linen."

Bronson Alcott claimed he was going to build his own utopia. But he did visit Brook Farm and parlayed brilliant conversation. After he left, everyone mimicked the question he always asked at the long dinner table: "Is the butter within the sphere of your influence?"

Several times per week Theodore Parker, from his church in West Roxbury, would walk to utopia, talk for hours. Supportive of Ripley, he wasn't willing to slam the door on his own platform. If he couldn't preach in Boston, he knew how to make his words resound into Boston. Reform could best be accomplished by remaining in the church. In a letter to his brother, he wrote, "I preach abundant heresies and they all go down, for the listeners do not know how heretical they are...."

William Henry Channing would have signed up for permanent membership in Brook Farm, but his commitment was to his congregation in Cincinnati. He visited whenever possible, lectured on how to rescue humanity from pauperism and crime. (A day would come when he'd become an active part of the experiment.)

Twenty-one year-old Charles King Newcomb did join and he was the happiest he'd ever been. In this environment his eccentricities were accepted as normal.

"Are you not ready to come up hither to Concord and make the bright days brighter?" Emerson wrote. A visit from Fuller would make Lidian well. "Do I not need music and enchantments?" Lidian sent her love.

> Will you not bring me your charitable aid? If my tongue will wag again, I will read you some verses, which, if you like them, you shall have for the *Dial.* At all events I will lend you the most capacious ears, I will listen as the Bedoween listens for running water, as Night listens for the earliest bird, as the Ocean bed for the coming Rivers, as the Believer for the Prophet.... If we could play at dice as Hermes did with the moon for intercalary lunations, if instead of this shuttle or rocket speed, we could vegetate along like a good Dragontree to some twelve or fourteen hundreds....think how life would gain in invention & diversity....We could live alone & if that did not serve, we could associate. We could enjoy and abstain, and read and burn our books and labor and dream. But fie on this Half this Untried, this take-it-or-leave-it, this flash-of-lightning-life. In my next migration, O Indra! I bespeak an ampler circle....Come, o my friend, with your earliest convenience, I pray you, & let us seize the void betwixt two atoms of air the vacation between two moments of time to decide how we will steer on this torrent which is called Today....Instantaneously yours, Waldo E. [66]

Who could resist such ardent words?

When she arrived Emerson was struggling to finish the second part of his poem, "Woodnotes." She was on the verge of finishing her apology of Goethe. Lidian was in a melancholy mood. Her Plymouth friend, Mary Russell, was bustling about, busy with the children's school.

Right away the editors scheduled "Dialese" conferences as well as walks to Sleepy Hollow Cemetary and to other favorite stamping grounds. George Ripley's situation as *Dial* publisher needed pondering...he had less time for business matters. There were decisions to be made as to content. No longer could the editors respond to every manuscript received; they agreed to print a "To the Contributors" page explaining why criticism could not be given to unpublished authors.

Fuller was careful to avoid argument with Emerson over "Woodnotes;" in fact, she declined all comment. She persuaded him to help write an upcoming review column.

Emerson pressured for more Thoreau verse. Fuller firmly gave the negative to "With frontier strength ye stand your ground" but she tapped the one she'd earlier rejected "Sic Vita," the poem Thoreau had thrown through Lucy Brown's window. This time his initials would appear reversed: "H. D. T."

Her article on Goethe would take one-third of the issue – and she would sign it "F."

From Dorchester came verses by Eliza Clapp – held for revision since last October and inserted unsigned. A. J. Saxton had a long piece entitled, "Prophecy – Transcendentalism – Progress."

She was delighted to have two pieces by Sophia Ripley, "Painting and Sculpture," which veered on man's freedom. (It would be inserted unsigned.) "Letter" was about an interesting visit the Ripleys had made to a German commune in Zoar, Ohio.

Cary Sturgis offered a short poem, "Bettina," which would serve as a convenient prelude to the translation Fuller planned.

One night, late, Henry David Thoreau rowed Margaret Fuller out on Walden Pond, probably in *Musketaquid.* They "staid till the moon was almost gone," she wrote her brother Richard, "...heard the whip-poor-will for the first time this year. There was a sweet breeze full of apple blossom fragrance which made the pond swell almost into waves. I had great pleasure."

Once Thoreau was cornered and asked if he and Fuller were going to be married. "No, in the first place Margaret Fuller is not fool enough to marry me; and second, I am not fool enough to marry her."

On May 28 Emerson wrote this solitary item in his journal:

> I gave you enough to eat & I never beat you;
> what more can the woman ask? said the Good Husband. [67]

If this was occasioned by a fight with Lidian, now that Fuller was again under the same roof, it is not known, but Emerson did write these lines in his journal and obviously intended to save and possibly refer to them at some future time. It is known that he was frustrated because "Woodnotes" was not taking shape.

And it is known that he started to manipulate an absence for Lidian. A trip to Plymouth with her sister was his idea, but Elizabeth Hoar arrived one morning, threw her arms around Lidian and suggested that they visit Emerson's brother, William and his gracious wife, Susan, on Staten Island. Hoar had money for both fares.

He saw his "invalid" off at the same time he welcomed his mother who would take hold during Lidian's absence. When Fuller left, probably to visit her brother Lloyd who lived at Brook Farm, who but Caroline Sturgis arrived. It was a good visit though she made it vehemently clear he should forget "Woodnotes."

He was glad when Cary left, at least this is what he wrote Lidian, "else I shall not have Margaret Fuller's matters ready." He could not join Lidian because he "must go once to the sea & once to Maine this summer."

With Fuller went her work. She stopped at the Farrar's in Cambridge. For the July *Dial* William Henry Channing had sent a fictional piece on Michelangelo, a protest against the age. She signed "U." Another piece, "Wheat Seed and Bolted Flour," by Channing, signed "T. T.", consisted of maxims similar to Bronson Alcott's "Orphic Sayings," except that Channing's made sense. There were two charming poems about nature and life by Cary Sturgis, one about death's release by James Russell Lowell, signed "Hugh Peters," and one by Christopher Cranch about inner life and the glorious All, signed "C."

There were two love songs, unsigned, by William Ellery Channing, and another short allegory, unsigned, (author unknown to this day).

Fuller favorably reviewed Carlyle's *On Heores, Hero-Worship and the Heroic in History*: "This book is somewhat less objectionable than the French Revolution to those not absolutely unjust critics, who said they would sooner 'dine for a week on pepper, than read through the two volumes.... '"

She confessed her disappointment in James Russell Lowell's *A Year's Life:* "...superficial, full of obvious cadences and obvious thoughts; but sweet, fluent, in a large style, and breathing the life of religious love."

Fuller continued to publish every Theodore Parker article even though their personalities constantly tugged. He offered a hammering piece, "The Pharisees," about the hypocrisy and hollowness of persons, such as husbands, fathers, journalists, merchants, politicians, preachers and worshipers. This she signed with the customary "P." Also, he apologetically sent along his first poem entitled "Protean Wishes." "I don't think myself made for a poet, least of all for an amatory poet. So if you throw the lines under the grate, in your critical wisdom, I shall not be grieved, vexed, or ruffled.... " His poem seemed a love offering to his wife, and would remain unsigned.

Parker, exposing sham in Christianity, had created a bigger scandal than any of the Transcendentalists. He'd delivered a sermon so radical that Unitarian ministers stopped exchanging pulpits with him. He'd delivered it in a voice described by Julia Ward Howe as "like the archangel's trump, summoning the wicked to repentance and bidding the just take heart." What is more, the truth leaked out that he was "Levi Blodgett," the writer who'd blasted Andrews Norton. Parker was branded "impious." A spokesman for the *Boston Courier* stated that it would be better to have every Unitarian church razed to the ground than to have one man like Parker. Even his friend, Convers Francis, shunned him. But Parker was a fighter. "I will go eastward and westward, and northward and southward, and make the land ring."

His radicalism was not what irritated Fuller. It was his hypocritical attitude towards women. He rated masculine and feminine qualities – and even set the feminine above the masculine. But his actions conformed to the stereotypical male behavior of the day. To command *The Dial* and receive equal treatment from him, Fuller had to foist a determined will.

At the end of June Emerson made a special trip to Jamaica Plain and Brookline to elicit the opinions of Margaret Fuller and Cary Sturgis on his newly revised "Woodnotes II." For inspiration he'd searched the fields and woods of Concord, the Boston Athenæum, the wharfs and salt water of Boston, and had increased his poem to eight pages, but had now reached a stalemate.

Fuller was in a depression which she "would not wish on any foe." Angrily, she took Emerson's work to task. He argued. After he'd gone, she apologized and twisted the blame onto herself:

> Dearest Waldo:
>
> By the light of this new moon I see very clearly that you were in the right and I was in the wrong. I don't know how I could persist so in my own way of viewing the matter.... I think I was very ill-natured, perverse, and unreasonable, but I am punished when I think of you riding home alone and thinking it all over as I know you must for I have been able to get in to your way of viewing it now. Whatever I may have said in my pet this afternoon be sure I can never be long ignorant what is due to you and that I am more happy to find you right than to be so myself because in many respects I value you more than I do myself. In truth today there was a background to my thoughts which you could not see, and I might have known you could not but which altered the color and position of every object. Now will you not as soon as you sincerely can write to say that you will bear no thought of this unless I behave again in this ungracious way and then you must tell me what I said this time and check my impetuous ways. I wanted this afternoon, as soon as you were really out of the house, to run after you and call as little children do, kiss and be friends; that would not be decorous really for two editors....[68]

Emerson melted. "I shall never dare quarrel with you, if you are so just, mitigable, & bounteous. I see not how I can avoid sending you my verses to read, whilst the white wand is extended.... In sunshine and in frost, yes, even in my native glaciers, am I ever your affectionate.... Waldo."

The next day he rushed "Woodnotes II" to the printer for the July issue. But he missed the deadline by two days, so he sent it to Fuller who placed it in her portfolio for October.

The July *Dial*, miraculously on sale on time, was not generally reviewed by the press. "About our poor little *Dial*," bemoaned Fuller, "it irks me to think."

Hedge loved Fuller's Goethe article. All of the Transcendentalists, as well as Emerson, regarded it as the best ever written on Goethe in America.

Fuller rejected work turned in by William Henry Orne, a Harvard graduate, and Anthony White whom her assistant editor favored. Her assistant editor had turned down a manuscript of a Miss. A. D. Woodbridge, and a Daniel Parker.

Her assistant editor, who had avoided the water ever since his father had tried to teach him to swim by throwing him into a river, went to Nantasket Beach alone, without Lidian. Watching lovers on the beach, he wondered if Cary Sturgis couldn't "protect" him from the sickness of love: "Never let me be with lovers again, those capricious, unstable ridiculous fanatics, groping after they know not what.... Study how you can protect me...."

To Margaret Fuller, would the sea air brace him, would it add more hours to the day? If he could find rhymes, he would send them to her. "Write thou," he implored.

To Elizabeth Hoar, he'd like to walk along the beach with her: "I should like to come out here with the little company of my friends, and spend July & August in tents or cabins at the high water mark. We would worship in the morn, we would work all the forenoon, we would sit or sail or walk in pairs or alone in the afternoon & evening...."

Though he missed his friends, he did not particularly like to be with them. "I know not what to say to them, except in rare halcyon hours."

To Lidian, do not bring him a coat. Though he'd promised to meet her in Plymouth, he now was indefinite. He wished to be at home again. Would she deliver two books to Elizabeth Peabody in Boston, one to pass along to Margaret Fuller? Would she send a few wafers, a piece of sealing wax from his table, and a pocket inkstand borrowed from his mother? He wanted her to get well & strong. He would save a beach pebble for Waldo Jr.

In his July journal this entry appears:

> I value my welfare too much to pay you any longer the compliment of attentions. I shall not draw the thinnest veil over my defects, but if you are here, you shall see me as I am. You will then see that though I am full of tenderness, and born with as large hunger to love & to be loved as any man can be, yet its demonstrations are not active & bold, but are passive & tenacious. My love has no flood & no ebb, but is always there under my silence, under displeasure, under cold, arid, and even weak behavior. [69]

There is no proof that this passage was directed towards Lidian, but it correlates with the pattern of his demonstration towards her.

In his July 20 letter to Lidian who had evidently quoted some rave reviews about him from the newspapers, he wrote, "I think it is high time to drop all compliments to me. Your kindness must not be cheated by a newspaper: they always shame me. It may yet please God that I should arrive at worth; but whilst I slumber & sleep in this mire of idleness you should be too much my friend ever to repeat their flourishes.–W."

Lidian expressed so much wit and insight at times that Emerson, who generally did not bother to mention her in his journals, was forced to quote her:

> Queenie (Lidian) (who has a gift to curse & swear) will every now & then in spite of all manners & Christianity rip out on Saints, reformers, & Divine Providence with the most edifying zeal. When Burrill Curtis asks whether trade will not check the free course of love, she insists "it shall be said that there is no love to restrain the course of, & never was, that poor God did all he could, but selfishness fairly carried the day. [70]

"Queenie" came to realize there was no such thing as love.

Feelings of inadequacy and idleness still haunted Emerson at the age of thirty-eight.

> If I should or could record the true experience of my late years, I should have to say that I skulk & play a mean, shiftless, subaltern part much the largest part of the time. Things are to be done which I have no skill to do, or are to be said which others can say better, and I lie by, or occupy my hands with something which is only an apology for idleness until my hour comes again.[71]

At the end of 1841:

> I am awkward, sour, saturnine, lumpish, pedantic, & thoroughly disagreeable & oppressive to the people around me. Yet if I am born to write a few good sentences or verses, these shall endure & my disgraces utterly perish out of memory. [72]

An August vacation at Newport Beach was open air Fuller needed. Her mother was temporarily staying with the Canton relatives, but seemed always ill with bilious colic, or ague, or stomach problems. Eugene, the eldest, a businessman in New Orleans, was moderately successful, while the next eldest brother, William Henry, was obviously failing in business. Richard was finding work in a Boston dry goods store not to his taste and was clamoring to attend Harvard, and Arthur, now in Harvard, seemed to be holding his own.

Ellen had consumption problems; after Louisville she'd gone to Cincinnati and had remained, sick and feverish, until February when her brother William Henry was able to take her to New Orleans where it was hoped she'd recover at Eugene's home.

Then she received an offer to teach music and French in Louisville. James Perkins, partner with James Freeman Clarke and *The Western Messenger* group, had helped to network. By August, the heat of the school room proved too much for her, so she had headed back home to Cambridge, first stopping in Cincinnati to see old friends. There, she'd met James Perkins's nephew – who happened to be the poet Emerson couldn't find (Dr. William Ellery Channing's nephew), whose poems of genius Emerson had published in *The Dial*, (Cary Sturgis's ex-boyfriend). The young William Ellery Channing's purpose in Cincinnati was to study law but he was discovering that he was not fit for the study of law.

At Newport Fuller could wander freely about the high rocks, pick berries, watch the break of the surf, the violet sunsets and the rose red moon. She enjoyed watching the horsemen careen on the beach and plough the deep for seaweed. Dr. Channing's daughter, Mary, had arranged for her to stay near the beach, opposite the gate of Channing's Paradise Farm, where she visited every day. William Henry Channing came for a time. He had decided not to return West, and was now considering a farm in Stockbridge.

A letter from Emerson arrived: "Dear Margaret, ever to me a friendly angel with a cornucopia of gifts." He had received her pacquet and was reading her letter "as a piece of my life." Though he was an "awkward lover" of friends, he'd just discovered his friends were so important that he even wished to die because he had friends:

> Yet is it not strange that our love & our labor should ever be so disunited streams.... Among other things I have discovered that the cause of that barrier some time talked of between us two, is that I have no barrier, but am all boundless conceding & willowy: and many other such like wisdoms have I, too numerous to be sounded by any trumpet. Friends are luxuries, are they not? things that honest poor people can do without but indispensable as serenades & ice to all fanciful persons. [73]

When Fuller returned to Cambridge, she met the dissolver of barriers and together they attended Henry Hedge's Phi Beta Kappa address at Harvard.*

Then she heard of her sister's engagement to William Ellery Channing.

William Ellery Channing was capable of saying "I am universal, I have nothing to do with the particular and definite."

He was also capable of ending a poem with this line:

> If my bark sink 'tis to another sea.

Here was a poet who admitted "I will not sing for gain, nor yet for fame."

> I had rather be,
> The meanest worm that haunts our berry-fields,
> than wear the purple on those distant thrones,
> And live far more the breath of Liberty
> Across our poor, uncultured, sandy soils,
> Than all the crumbling empires in their shrouds.

---

*Fuller criticized Hedge's address: "It was high ground on middle ground," – meaning she would have preferred him to have taken firmer positions on current issues.

Channing wrote about "ragged independence" and the "wealth of Penury." "Earth Spirit" reveals his sensibility:

I have woven shrouds of air
In a loom of hurrying light,
For the trees which blossoms bear,
and guided them with sheets of bright;
I fall upon the grass like love's first kiss,
I make the golden flies and their fine bliss.

Emerson found him to be one of his best walking companions. With him you "always see what was never before shown to the eye of man." Once in his journals Emerson commented: "If I could write as well as you, I would write a great deal better." Thoreau claimed that one of Ellery's lectures was "all genius, no talent." Nathaniel Hawthorne thought Channing had "some originality and self-inspiration in his character, but none, or very little, in his intellect." And Margaret Fuller called him "a great Genius with a little wretched boy trotting beside him."

His flaw was an erratic impulse. Her sister's flaw was a fiery temper. Fuller foresaw nothing but trouble.

It wasn't hard to see why Ellery loved Ellen. She had a rare beauty, white skin, deep blue eyes, blond ringlets around her face – "an expression of unbroken purity," as Sam Ward had said. Hers was a sensitive poetic idealistic nature, living every day with beauty and elegance.

Ellery's father was Dr. Walter Channing, a leading obstetrician at Harvard Medical School. His mother, from the wealthy merchant family of Perkins, had died when Ellery was five, and he had been farmed out to various relatives. He never heeded discipline, wouldn't shoulder responsibility. He'd read everything he could find when he was young, having at hand the libraries of George Ticknor and the Boston Athenæum. He attended the Round Hill School and other academies and Harvard, but had left the hallowed halls where scholars "were wearing out the elbows of their coats, in getting by heart some set lessons of some little text-books"...where professors "loved wine and puddings better than literature and art."

After five years at his father's house reading and writing, he'd travelled and tried life in an Illinois log cabin but switched back to big city life in Cincinnati near his uncle.

He was the kind of person who answered Fuller's question as to how his affairs were going: "Affairs – I have none of them. I am not a person of affairs. I may wake up myself some day, & find I have been doing something, but no one will ever tell me of it. I have never yet had any one tell me I was doing anything, either for myself, or others."

The day after Anna Barker Ward gave birth to her first child, Ellen and Ellery were married in Cincinnati. Mrs. Fuller joined them in the spring. Ellery didn't mind helping with domestic chores and he became a journalist on the *Cincinnati Daily Gazette* for nine hundred dollars a year, plus there was money from his father.

He wrote Fuller: "We are not rich in the world's goods, but I considered myself better off in the love of Ellen, than were I master of $10,000 a year.... Now may the floods beat, now may the winds rave, & the great sun himself be eclipsed, for I have found what I wished."

Meanwhile, because promises for *Dial* articles had dissolved into procrastinations, Fuller's hand was forced to write eighty-five pages for the October issue. Her "Lives of the Great Composers" was over fifty pages. Signing it "F," she despaired it was hurried and wordy. But it did bring forward new and interesting material on the great composers, Hayden, Mozart, Handel, Bach, and Beethoven.

Her other article, a dialogue-review discussing differing opinions on Philip James Bailey's *Festus*, a long poem on the legend of Faust, was thirty pages, also signed "F."

"E" had thought of editing Henry Hedge's Phi Beta Kappa Address but this did not materialize. However, "Woodnotes II" was set and the editor had coaxed from the assistant editor an article in praise of Walter Savage Landor. ("E" had coaxed Elizabeth Hoar to help him.) He'd also offered two other poems, "Painting and Sculpture," and "Fate," but was unhappy with them. These she printed unsigned.

She had a good solid piece, which she used unsigned, by Elizabeth Peabody, "A Glimpse of Christ's Idea of Society," a search for the ideal man and a discussion of idealistic communities in Europe and

America. Fuller tacked on a note that the article would continue in the next issue.

Bronson Alcott sent in more "Orphic Sayings" which she rejected, but she accepted his selections from Dr. Henry More's "Cupid's Conflict," a long poem which she used as her lead piece, again with full byline under title. There were two poems by Cary Sturgis, "Light and Shade," a searching cry for soul in life, and "Windmill," which contrasted vast nature with midget man, both of which Fuller printed unsigned. There were also two "Poems on Life," signed "W." It is not today clear who "W" was.

Thoreau offered three poems. One, "The Fisher's Son," she immediately rejected. Another was a re-write of "With frontier strength ye stand your ground." She asked for another re-write. (Emerson had written that Thoreau said he would try to scrape or pare them down or cover the peaks with a more presentable greensward.) The third poem, "Friendship," with the subtitle "Friends, Romans, Countrymen, and Lovers," she printed, signing it "H.D.T." Emerson had read it a year before, had suggested revisions, and Thoreau had finally made them.

At the last moment Fuller whizzed Christopher Cranch's poems to the printer. Cranch had left Brook Farm to become minister of a small Unitarian society in Fishkill-on-the-Hudson, New York. But because of mailing and editorial problems, only the first half of his two-part poem was printed; "C" appeared at the end.

There were misprints in Thoreau's poem.

What was surprising was that there weren't more misprints.

The press delighted again to make *The Dial* the butt of jokes. *The Christian Advocate and Journal* offered up the definition of Transcendentalism as "the spiritual cognoscente of psychological irrefragability, connected with concutient ademption of incoluminent spirituality and etherealized contention of subsoltory concretion."

The Weeks publishers went bankrupt. Clarke and Peabody had made a thorough examination of *The Dial* accounts and learned the awful truth.

George Ripley had to quit as business manager because of responsibilities at Brook Farm.

Dial troubles had to be addressed. Emerson broke a long silence by addressing his editor, "O silent & secret friend, where hidest thou?"

Fuller swung up to Concord in October. The hot/cold game was resumed with force.

Lidian was eight months pregnant. But her condition only served as background and apparently she did remain in the background.

The two editors criticized, analyzed and complimented each other's work and psyche. When Emerson tired or when he had no more to say, he simply withdrew. He ducked into his library and shut the door. This action set off a train of confusion, guilt and remorse in Fuller.

For long periods S.M.F. and R.W.E. stayed in their respective rooms across the narrow hall. They could not face or speak to each other. Communication took the form of notes which they handed to Emerson's five year-old son, Waldo Jr. The obedient little boy, whom they both dearly loved, alternately carried messages to Fuller's bedroom and then to Emerson's library.

Probably more times than once, late at night, when she was sleepless, Fuller quietly stepped across the narrow hall to Emerson's sacred space, to find a book. How strongly she felt his soul in his room at midnight when he was not there. How powerfully she was drawn to him, yet how unprofitable were their encounters. His life was beautiful, but there seemed no hope they could reconcile their differences. She could only express her feelings in written notes:

> Dear Waldo, I know you do not regard our foolish critiques, except in the true way to see whether you have yet got the best form of expression. What do we know of when you should stop writing or how you should live? In these pages I seem to hear the music rising I so long have wished to hear, and am made sensible to the truth of the passage in one of your letters, "Life like the nimble Tartar &c."

> I like to be in your library when you are out of it. It seems a sacred place. I came here to find a book, that I might feel more life and be worthy to sleep, but there is so much soul here I do not need a book. When I come to yourself, I cannot receive you, and you cannot give yourself; it does not profit. But when I cannot find you the beauty and permanence of your life come to me.

"She (Poesie) has ascended from the depths of a nature, and only by a similar depth, shall she be apprehended!" – I want to say while I am feeling it, what I have often (not always) great pleasure in feeling – how long it must be, before I am able to meet you. – I see you – and fancied it nearer than it was, you were right in knowing the contrary.

How much, much more I would fain say and cannot. I am too powerfully drawn while with you, and cannot advance a step, but when away I have learned something. Not yet to be patient and faithful and holy however, but only have taken off the shoes to tread the holy ground. I shall often depart through the ranges of manifold being, but as often return to where I am tonight.[74]

They agreed to visit Brook Farm together, for the purpose of inspiring more contributions to *The Dial*. Lidian remained at home.

A costume picnic party in honor of the six year-old Frank Dana was held in the woods, and all adults and children cavorted amongst the trees as Indian chiefs, Gipsy fortune tellers, foresters, etc. There were games, dances, cakes and fruit.

A goddess Diana shot an arrow and hit Nathaniel Hawthorne's hand.

Fuller and Emerson discussed ballads – the subject of Fuller's article – but she admitted she could not intellectualize in the atmosphere of the woods, where she found herself expressed.

Unfortunately, none of the Brook Farmers seemed inspired to create stories or poetry for *The Dial*.

The never-ending subjects of love, friendship, marriage, beauty were resumed as the two editors settled back into the "mansion of peace" at Concord.

Emerson felt himself greying, losing his fire and force, too aged for love. Love was an illusion. Love faded and repelled with time – this is what he told Fuller, for she answered him in another room-to-room note:

My dear friend, We shall never meet on these subjects while one atom of our proper individualities remains. Yet let me say a few words more on my side. The true love has no need of illusion: it is too deeply prophetic in its nature to be baffled or chilled, much less changed by the accidents of time. We are sure that what we love is living, though the ruins of old age have fallen upon the shrine. The "blank gray" upon the hallowed locks, the dimmed eye, the wasted cheek cannot deceive us. Neither can the diminution of vital fire and force, the scantiness of thought, the loss of grace, wit, fancy and springing enthusiasm, for it was none of these we loved, but the true self, that particular emanation from God which was made to correspond with that which we are, to teach it, to learn from it, to torture it, to enchant it, to deepen and at last to satisfy our wants. You go upon the idea that we must love most the most beauteous, but this is not so. We love most that which by working most powerfully on our peculiar nature awakens most deeply and constantly in us the idea of beauty. Where we have once seen clearly what is fit for us, if only in a glance of the eye we cannot forget it, nor can any change in the form where we have seen it deceive us. We know that it will appear again and clothe the scene with new and greater beauty.

For the past year or two I begin to see a change in the forms of these my contemporaries who have filled my eye. It is a sight that makes me pensive, but awakens, I think, a deeper tenderness and even a higher hope than did these forms in the greatest perfection they ever attained. For they still only promised beauty not gave it, and now seeing the swift changes of time I feel what an illusion all is, all imperfection is. As they fail to justify my expectation, it only rises the higher and they become dearer as the heralds of a great fulfillment. The princely crest is lowered, the proud glow of youth, its haughty smile and gleaming sweetness are fled, every languid motion assures me that this life will not complete the picture I had sketched, but I only postpone it for ages, and expect it on the same canvass yet.

The fact you repel of the mother and the child as seen in other nature does not repel, why should it in human Nature? It is beautiful to see the red berry, the just blown rose and the rose bud on the same stalk as we sometimes do; nor are we displeased with the young blossoming scion that it grows up beside the aged tree; it borrows rather a charm from the neighborhood of that which it must sometimes resemble. But I might write a volume, and then should not have done. I seem to myself to say all when I say that the chivalric idea of love through disease, dungeons and death, mutilation on the battle field, and the odious changes effected by the enchanter's hate answers my idea far better than the stoical appreciation of the object beloved for what it positively presents. I would love in faith that could not

> change and face the inevitable shadows of old age happy in some occasion for fidelity....

It was all right if he wanted to withdraw. She also wanted to be alone at times.

She compared both of them to the picture that Cary had drawn of a rock and a wave. Like a rock she was bold, noble, steady, but, like a wave, would flow with flexibility, could be depended upon to return.

He, like a rock, was "deeply rooted," waiting. Like the wave, he persisted in the recede of change.

Her impatience could only be a momentary fragment within the entire span of life emotions. If there were a shadow of a doubt, it would be he who doubted, not she. His doubt could only bring her closer insight into his character:

> Do not fancy I complain or grieve. I understand matters now, and always want you to withdraw when you feel like it; indeed, there is nothing I wish more than to be able to live with you, without disturbing you. This is the main stream of my feeling. I am satisfied and also feel that our friendship will grow. But I am of a more lively and affectionate temper or rather more household and daily in my affection than you and have a thousand evanescent feelings and ebullitions like that in the letter. Cary has made a picture of the rock and the wave; if she had made the rock a noble enough figure it might stand for frontispiece to the chapter of my deepest life. For the moment the rock dashes back with a murmur, but it always returns. It is not now a murmur of sorrow but only the voice of a more flexible life. I would not have it otherwise. The genial flow of my desire may be checked for the moment, but it cannot long. I shall always burst out soon and burn up all the rubbish between you and me, and I shall always find you there true to yourself deeply rooted as ever.
>
> My impatience is but the bubble on the stream; you know I want to be alone myself – It is all right. As to the shadow I do not know myself what it is, but it rests on your aspect, and brings me near the second-sight as I look on you. Perhaps if we have Scotch trists enough I shall really see the tapestry of the coming time start into life, but, if I do, I shall not tell you, but with wise economy keep it for a poem which shall make ever sacred and illustrious the name of yours
>
> Margaret[75]

Emerson responded by noting in his journal that Fuller was unsettled and lived for long periods in a religious trance:

> Margaret is "a being of unsettled rank in the Universe." So proud & presumptuous yet so meek; so worldly and artificial & with keenest sense & taste for all pleasure of luxurious society, yet living more than any other for long periods in a trance of religious sentiment; a person who according to her own account of herself, expects everything for herself in the Universe. [76]

At the end of October S.M.F. left the R.W.E. household to vacation at Newbury with Cary. Afterwards, she went to Boston to stay at her Uncle Henry's where she received an apology from R.W.E. who found himself very pleased that she should love him, for her love made him feel better and look on the world in a better spirit.

> After you went away from the cold house, I read with pleasure & pride the paper on the composers, and wondered after you – I say to myself, it is surely very generous in such a rich & great minded woman to throw her steady light on me also, and to love me so well. I think better of the whole Universe, and resolve never to be mean. So now do not withdraw your rays: but still forgive all my incapacities; and it shall be counted to you for righteousness with all the angels.
>
> Waldo E. [77]

He enclosed tickets to his upcoming Boston series of lectures, which he hoped she'd help to distribute.

Lidian gave birth, on November 22, to a daughter, "a meek dear little drowsy creature who will not open her eyes for me & Waldo to pry into any more than enough to show us now & then that she has eyes."

At the moment of birth Waldo dashed off a note to Elizabeth Hoar who was again living in the upstair room at the "mansion of peace" in order to help out. She was to come downstairs. Hoar wrote an affirmative answer. Waldo E. managed to break the news to Excellent Friend without mentioning the mother.

He did want to call the baby "Lidian." But after some time, the husband and wife settled on "Edith."

After the first harvest at Brook Farm Nathaniel Hawthorne questioned: "Is it a praiseworthy matter that I have spent five golden months in providing food for cows and horses?" First person to leave, he had to sue Ripley to get back his share of money.

Fuller feared there could be no January publication of *The Dial.* Weeks and Jordan insisted on being paid to release the subscription list – which the editors learned for the first time numbered not five hundred persons, but three hundred. George Ripley took time off from Brook Farm to negotiate. Finally Emerson hired a Boston lawyer. He commanded Fuller to end the journal "by Proclamation as Victoria does her Parliament!"

A decision was made to change the name and to turn the printing over to Elizabeth Peabody, even without the subscription list. Then Weeks and Jordan hurried to end the crisis and Elizabeth Peabody became Boston's first lady publisher.

The I-really-ought-to-be-out-in-the-open-air-all-the-time Fuller resumed weekly tutoring with eight or nine students plus she continued her Conversations. Fuller kept the house in Cambridge for her mother but stayed in Boston with her Uncle Henry. Her brother Richard was in Concord preparing for Harvard examinations under the tutorship of Henry David Thoreau and Elizabeth Hoar who steered in Greek. Richard lived on milk, crackers and applesauce pies baked by the goodness of Lidian and Thoreau's mother. Lloyd remained at Brook Farm. Fuller was trying to figure a way for Ellen and Ellery to move to a Cambridge or Concord farm.

For the January *Dial* Fuller had the two Cranch poems, that were supposed to have appeared in the October issue, "Inworld" and "Outworld." She would continue Peabody's excellent two-part piece on the Ideal society, focusing on Brook Farm. Peabody had also written some reviews. The leading spot would go to Peabody's friend, William Green for an article, "First Principles," an explanation of the laws of the universe and the relationship between the mind to "what is without." "P" (Theodore Parker) had contributed another masterly article, "Primitive Christianity," from which he boiled two maxims, "Love Man," and "Love God." James Freeman Clarke submitted "Plan of Salvation."

Poems were collected by B.F. Presbury, signed "B.F.P.", which

Emerson had sent to her along with three of his own poems and a short piece quoting Calvinist and Quaker beliefs on Transcendentalism. She also had a poem from Ellen Hooper, unsigned, three sonnets by Lowell, signed "J.R.L." She had abridgements from Alcott's diary which Emerson approved, but as soon as Fuller decided to cut, Alcott refused permission.

For a third time she received Thoreau's revised poem, "With frontier strength ye stand your ground." She returned it: "I do not find the poem on the mountain improved by mere compression, though it might be by fusion and glow."*

Herself contributed "Yuca Filamentosa," a companion piece to "The Magnolia of Lake Pontchartrain," about two rare flowers that bloomed only by the light of the moon with the premise that love occurred to those who trustfully waited. She prefaced it with a sonnet by William Ellery Channing.

Her article, "The Epilogue to the Tragedy of Essex," was a translation from Goethe, wherein Queen Elizabeth affirmed privately that she would live a death if Essex died. She also wrote six book reviews which included a translation of Goethe's "Egmont, A Tragedy in Five Acts" and a book on Goethe's *Tasso.* These pieces Fuller left unsigned.

By far the biggest stir she created was with her translation of an 1805-06 correspondence between Bettina Brentano and Caroline von Günderode, two dreamy teen-age German girls. Fuller's article, "Bettine Brentano and Her Friend Günderode," excited intellectual circles because it offered insights into Goethe and concepts of friendship.** And through the lips of the girls, Fuller could express her own ideal of friendship – perhaps she was really speaking to Emerson.

---

*Thoreau finally saw this poem in print when he inserted it in the opening of his essay, "A Walk to Wachusett," (the trip taken with Fuller's brother, Richard), printed in the *Boston Miscellany* in January 1843.

**In 1842 some of the letters were published by Elizabeth Peabody in a pamphlet without Fuller's name. After Bettina Brentano von Arnim died, Elizabeth Peabody convinced Mrs. Minna Wesselhoeft to finish the translation and it was printed with Fuller's work and preface by a Boston bookseller (Burnham) in 1860. Later, it came to be known that the correspondence was fictional – spurious. Fuller had not been aware of this.

Young Brentano had idealized Goethe. He was aware of her feelings, and made a puppet show of them for his own amusement.

She personified nature's fresh, vigorous, brilliant youth, and was from a cultured wealthy family who had literary connections.

Günderode represented the Ideal, the spiritual angel with the delicate Madona-like beauty. She was eight or nine years older, and experienced a narrowed lifestyle. She lived in an order as a Canoness, though she still had opportunities to mix with worldly society.

The two girls needed not "descend to meet," Fuller quoted Emerson's phrase in her preface.

Readers could glean that friendship could be defined as generosity, modesty, unwearied sympathy, revelation of thoughts, mutual stimulus, reciprocal balm, faith in one another, infinite promise, stern demand of excellence on either side, love, patience, confidence, joy and pride in each other, mind in mind, two souls prophesying to one another, two human hearts sustaining and pardoning one another.

Fuller found Brentano "only interesting." Günderode was "dear and admirable." She wrote, "Günderode throws herself into the river because the world is all too narrow. Bettina lives, and follows out every freakish fancy, till the enchanting child degenerates into an eccentric and undignified old woman."

Fuller, "quite unfit to hold a pen," barely made her deadlines by Christmas Eve. She revived by hearing the Messiah, by perusing the booths of the Anti-Slavery fair, and by going to a Beethoven concert with the Wards.

People would not read the January *Dial*, jeered one reporter from the *Boston Advertiser.* Fuller's article on Bettina was "defaced" by the "broken English."

A writer from *Graham's Magazine* spilled out "Orphicism, or Dialism, or Emersonianism, or any other pregnant compound indicative of confusion worse confounded."

The Boston Morning Post was complimentary.

Horace Greeley reprinted some of the poems in his *Tribune.*

Emerson said it was "more witty" than George Sand or Madame de Staël.

Carlyle said he found it "a decided weariness."

January 1842 brought two terrible tragedies. John Thoreau suffered a cut on his little finger which became infected, and he died from lockjaw. It was such a shock for Henry David that for awhile he succumbed to all the signs of lockjaw.

The second tragedy occurred when the boy who kissed violets in the woods rather than picking them, Waldo Jr., suddenly contracted scarlet fever and "nature's heir" was gone within four days.

Numb with grief, Emerson conveyed the news to Margaret Fuller: "Shall I ever dare to love any thing again. Farewell and Farewell, O my Boy!"

Fuller had loved Waldo Jr. more than any child she had known. He was an angel, a beautiful thought, fresh, original. To friend William Henry Channing, "...why he, why just he," who "bore within himself the golden future..." Even her brother Richard mourned and wrote a poem about the boy.

Emerson, Lidian, and Elizabeth Hoar grieved by reciting stories about "our fair boy...The Star of Hope." Biographers write at length of Emerson's sense of loss, but not of Lidian's feelings which assumably were just as inconsolable. Her illnesses increased.

In his anguish Emerson plaintively composed a long poem. In "Threnody" the father remembers the sunny face of the boy during a school march, looks at the painted sled standing "where it stood," gazes at the hole he dug in the sand, visits the "daily haunts," sees the "innocence that matched the sky." "O richest fortune sourly crossed!/ Born for the future, to the future lost!"

Emerson, in an oblivion of work, left for lecture engagements in Providence, Boston and New York. "Thy true sister" – as Elizabeth Hoar signed letters to her "dear brother" – came to stay with Lidian at the "mansion of peace."

From Staten Island Emerson complained to Fuller. "I was born to stay at home, not to ramble." He'd dined with Horace Greeley and Albert Brisbane at their Graham boarding house. Both of the men were egoists. Greeley was "no scholar but such a one as journals & newspapers make.... I should never content him." Brisbane wanted him to convert to Fourierism. Emerson cried to Fuller: "Pity me & conform me, O my friend, in this city of magnificence & of steam.... "

Ill and pressured by *The Dial,* Fuller sent her "Dearest Waldo" comforting words: "I have thought of you many times, indeed in all my walks, and in the night, with unspeakable tenderness...." But quickly she changed her tact to newsy reportage.

Two days later Emerson responded: "You know best of all living how to flatter your friend, both directly & by finest indirections. A warm friendly odorous air always breathes from your region....Your friend, W."

Five days later from the Wave:

> It is to be hoped, my best one, that the experiences of life will yet correct your vocabulary, and, that you will not always answer the burst of frank affection by the use of such a word as "flattery." Thou knowest, oh all-seeing Truth, whether that hour is base or unworthy thee, in which the heart turns tenderly towards some beloved object, whether stirred by an apprehension of its needs, or of its present beauty, or of its great promise, when it would lay before it, all the flowers of hope and love, would soothe its weariness, as gently as might the sweet South, and flatter it by as fond an outbreak of pride and devotion, as is seen on the sunset clouds.
>
> Thou knowest whether these promptings, whether these longings, be not truer than intellectual scrutiny of the details of character; than cold distrust of the exaggerations even of heart. What we hope, what we think of those we love, is true, true as the fondest dream of love and friendship that ever shone upon the childish heart. The faithful shall yet meet a full eyed love, ready as profound – that never needs turn the key on its retirement, or arrest the stammering of an overweening trust. [78]

About three days later from the Rock:

> Your eloquent expostulations bring to my lips the ancient ejaculation "I believe. Thou, Lord, help my unbelief!" Truly I never doubted that you befriend & cherish me always with that great generosity of love which is native to you.... I feel much as Ellery when he asks you, "Why did they not praise me for keeping the peace, & not committing homicide?" Yet blotted be every word written of mine & oblivion fall on every spoken word if any such have ever been which doubted your sincerity....Good news it is always that comes from you and my quarrel must always be with myself that I do not more richly deserve your love.... [79]

Surfacing feelings were set aside as they faced the finances of *The Dial.* There was no hope that Fuller would ever receive renumeration. Subscription moneys barely covered costs. Because she belonged "to the bread-winning tribe," she resigned her editorship, sending off an "I grieve to disappoint you" letter to Emerson. "It has been a sad business."

Emerson praised her time and effort; everyone was her debtor. Would Parker be editor? Or even co-editor? Emerson could easily edit and fill "one Number. Two look formidable, & Four incredible."

Fuller promised to continue help by contributing articles. Elizabeth Peabody volunteered to act as assistant editor.

Within a few days Emerson decided he would be editor, rather than have it go into "hands that know not Joseph...let there be rotation in martyrdom!"

He decided there would be no co-editor because he had little skill in partnership. "Send me word that your head aches less.... "

Within a few days he "& Lidian my wife entreat you to consider that this house is one of your homes, and that we account ourselves both gladdened & honored whenever you will come & stay with us."

Fuller drafted a suspension notice for the April issue.

Emerson quelched the suspension notice. Time might bring a remedy. An announcement could be made at the last minute.

April's lead was Alcott's "Days from a Diary," in type since December. Lifted from his diary, Alcott stated that his thoughts were "of too little value to waste words upon."

Emerson, having been busy lecturing, offered nothing.

There was another splendid article from "P," in despair because America had "the poorest of all poor philosophies." The best theologians were in Germany where "a new East out of which the star of Hope is to arise." Parker also contributed several book reviews.

There was a lengthy poem by "C" (Christopher Cranch), and another from Charles Dana of Brook Farm, unsigned.

Fuller had translated from the French, "Marie Van Oosterwich," signed "A." Perhaps her choice of material was another subtle message to Emerson. It was the story of a young woman's love for a talented artist whose feelings were insincere and selfish. It pointed out that women were capable of loyal and enduring love even though based on delusion.

The Dial came off the printer's table four days early. Inside each copy was an errata slip apologizing for mistakes in Alcott's manuscript.

On the back wrapper was a "To the Friends of *The Dial*" notice written by Elizabeth Peabody stating that because expenses were out of proportion to profits subscribers should pay on time or in advance.

Emerson sent out a circular announcing his editorship.

He asked Fuller and Parker for opinion and advice.

Parker, who thought that now *The Dial* would "grow up to vigorous manhood," suggested Emerson "write a great deal for it himself."

Fuller, keeping her head from aching by wrapping it with cold towels, dispensed her advice: "Since it is now understood that you are Pilot...The work cannot but change its character.... I think you will sometimes reject pieces that I should not. For you have always had in view to make a good periodical and represent your own tastes, while I have had in view to let all kinds of people have freedom to say their say, for better, for worse."

Fuller continued her Conversations – but this season no men were invited. And she was able to buy a house on Ellery Street in Cambridge, not far from where she'd lived at the Dana mansion. Lloyd had become dissatisfied with Brook Farm because, he said, he had been pressured to work when he was not willing. He would try six weeks with a Cambridge printer. Richard, at Harvard, was making the discovery that he didn't have the brilliance of his father or sister. Fuller took another needed rest – solitude in Canton where she boarded for a month with her aunt in a house with "plain kindness" and "unbroken silence except by the sounds from the poultry or wind." Then to Providence a few days, then to New Bedford for a week with Aunt Mary Rotch.

There was a change in her relationship with Cary Sturgis: "It is somewhat sad that two friends must become uninteresting to one another, because they have arrived at a mutual good understanding, yet this very thing makes the beauty as well as the sadness of life."

Emerson began "clucking and caring for the little *Dial*," first deliberately deciding to do nothing until May so he could work on his own projects – except he did arrange for Elizabeth Hoar to do some of the menial editorial work.

He collected poetry, one by E. T. Clapp about autumn leaves and eternity, a sonnet by C. A. Dana, signed "D," two by Jones Very, unsigned, one by Cary Sturgis, unsigned, a translation by Henry Hedge of a German poem signed "H." Fuller sent along seven poems by Ellery Channing, half of which were excellent.

There seemed no question as to whether Thoreau's work would be printed. Emerson persuaded Thoreau to take up an article about a scientific survey being done by the state of Massachusetts. He also inserted his poem, "My Prayer."

Emerson began to work on his own contributions. He had completed three poems which he would print, unsigned. He'd edit his December 2 Masonic Temple lecture, entitled, "Lectures on the Times," wherein he disclosed his view that there was a perfect chain of reform in the world which was beautiful, but he blasted the reformers' harsh methods and principles which were based on fear, wrath and pride rather than on love and inward truth and soul. Reform, he reasoned, is best accomplished by inaction.

He scoured his journals and based another article on his conversation with his neighbor-farmer Edmund Hosmer about a research project on the agriculture of Massachusetts. He showed that Hosmer knew better than any researcher how to bring the best from poor soil.

He decided to emphasize great ancient expression and he made selections from *The Heetopades of Veeshnoo-Sarma* for a monthly column. Thoreau lent a helping hand.

He searched through letters and newspapers for bits of information for a feature called "Intelligence." He would continue Fuller's book review column. Parker offered reviews and Fuller contributed a notice in praise of Hawthorne's *Twice-Told Tales.* In him she saw and demanded greatness and originality.

Emerson reviewed George Borrow's *The Zincali*, since Fuller refused. She also refused to critique Longfellow's poems: "...if you have toleration for them, it would be well to have a short notice written by some one (not me) ...."*

He wrote introductory notes to – and edited a bit – Albert Brisbane's revised by-lined article on Fourier and socialism.

---

*Probably *Ballads and Other Poems* (Cambridge, Mass., 1841) *Ballads* was never reviewed in *The Dial.*

He reported on the 1840 Chardon Street Convention, since he was on the organization committee. This event had caused particular excitement in theological circles because participants questioned the divine origin of the Scriptures and championed truth through free discussion.

Emerson included "The Two Dolons," signed "N" (Charles King Newcomb), which he'd nurtured for months probably because it was an original, cursive, vague, poetical story of feelings describing growth in a child – a child similar to Emerson's dead son. Even though he polished Newcomb's bad grammar, "Dolons" was to be as ridiculed as Alcott's "Orphic Sayings."

As for Alcott, he had sailed to England, with the help of Emerson who'd raised money by giving an additional lecture. Alcott's educational methods had been so admired in England by some radical reformers that a school named Alcott House had been established in Ham, Surrey. His ego was bolstered as he was received with honor by founders Charles Lane and Henry G. Wright. Alcott gave out copies of *The Dial*, obtained a few subscriptions, advocated the editors advertise in England for more subscriptions, and sent Emerson articles written by the English contributors.

Emerson now had to prod Fuller for more contributions. "For me who have leaned on you so long for so much good & fair, it will not do to be forsaken now...."

So Fuller in "Entertainments of the Past Winter," unsigned, covered opera, ballet, concerts, exhibits, lectures, and defended the drama against the prevailing opinion that it was indecent. She praised Fanny Elssler's dancing which she'd seen with Emerson. Alledgedly, after the performance he had commented: "Margaret, this is poetry." And she had said, "Waldo, this is religion."

At the printer's, he discovered too much copy. So he cut Parker's reviews. *The Dial* had its coming out only one day late.

Sometime during June Fuller styled two emotional letters to Emerson; they are lost now, but his response begins: "Wonderful sleepless working loving child, with such aspiration! and with all this doubt & self-reproach! Whether to admire or chide or soothe you?"

He thanked her for her *Dial* work and said her article was a "fine manly...deliberate criticism" which was "so flowing too & so readable." He said he was afraid for her health and life. "I hoped you were going to sleep – to sleep a solid month or trimester, and then wake newborn." He wanted her to finish her article on ballads, "but I had rather continue to want it, than that you should thus overstrain yourself always.... I often suppose myself quite incompetent to do you any justice in these years & think I shall in some hour of power roll up all your letters in cloth of asbestos & shooting across this lunar & solar sphere alight on the star of Lyra or the shoulder of Orion and there in some grotto of light meditate your genius until I have computed its orbit & parallax, its influence, its friend & its enemy." He closed by adding that he was a "dear valuer of your genius & virtues, & wish to know when you shall be in Cambridge...." [80]

His words would affect most women, and they must have affected Fuller.

Parker thought Emerson's *Dial* a "rich number," not without faults. William Henry Channing liked it. Alcott turned each page with the "truest delight." From England Thomas Carlyle wrote he loved the *Dial* but with "a kind of shudder."

Fuller liked that she did not have to proof-read, post-office or printer ink. The magazine was a "common ground of friendship."

Except for Newcomb's "Dolons," the reviewers were generally favorable. Horace Greeley again praised in his columns. He reprinted, in a series of four, Emerson's lecture on "The Times." Carlyle said: "Perge, Perge."

July, Emerson decided, would be a month for the progress of his own work.

Fuller considered again the possibility of living in Concord, perhaps on a small farm which would yield frugal subsistence for her mother, Ellen and Ellery.

Early July Fuller renewed acquaintance with her Providence friends; the next week she spent at Brook Farm, and followed this with a trip to the commanding White Mountains, and heard that her brother Richard and Henry David Thoreau had set off for a four day walking trip to Wachusett mountain on top of which they pitched a tent amongst swallows and robins, and where they feasted on blueberries.*

*Thoreau later described the expedition in "A Walk to Wachusett." [81] (*The Writings of Henry Daivd Thoreau*, Vol. IX, "Excursions," Houghton Mifflin & Co., Boston, 1893)

Cary needed sympathetic understanding. "Why will they not let me develop myself in my own way.... I wish some one in the world would have real faith in me...."

Fuller, per usual, tried to offer consolation, and she tried to give nourishment to Charles King Newcomb who was too ill to continue work on his "Dolon."

At the Peabody house in Boston – where Fuller still held her "Conversations" – a small, quiet ceremony took place on July 9. The Rev. James Freeman Clarke united in marriage the thirty-eight year-old introvert, Nathaniel Hawthorne, and the thirty-two year-old child-like Sophia Peabody who knew French, Greek, Latin, Italian, Hebrew, and whose perfect drawings not only sold every now and then at good prices but had so impressed Washington Allston that he sought her out and suggested she study art in Europe. But Sophia's every day was made difficult with chronic pain and headache.* During the long three-year engagement to Hawthorne, she insisted: "If God intends us to marry, He will let me be cured; if not, it will be a sign that it is not best."

But there was an even more insurmountable obstacle to this union. Hawthorne's older sister, Ebe, told him his mother would be so traumatized with his marrying an invalid that she would die.

So Hawthorne delayed. One day he risked breaking the news. To his delighted surprise, his mother received the news happily. Ebe had fabricated the story in order to keep her brother close to her. This marked the end of communication between brother and sister. Later, Ebe moved to a farmhouse in Beverly, isolated herself in her room, read, took walks alone on the shore.

---

* Her illness is ascribed to teething difficulties when, as a baby and as she was growing up, Salem and Boston doctors had proscribed all manner of drugs such as mercury, arsenic, opium, hyoscyamus, which her sister Elizabeth described as "poisons of the *materia medica.*" The side effects subjected her to "acute nervous headache which lasted uninterruptedly from her twelfth to her thirty-first year." Sophia described the pain as being "various corkscrews, borers, pinchers, daggers, squibs, and bombs." Noise such as the rattle of knives and forks, doors slamming, loud yelling, was unbearable to her and she spent a good part of her childhood upstairs in her room. The last doctor proscribed no drugs; she was to fight the pain herself.

The love Sophia and Nathaniel Hawthorne held for each other compared with that of Adam and Eve...so they facetiously called themselves. They moved into "Paradise," the homey, large, dark Old Manse, where Ralph Waldo Emerson had written *Nature*. The rooms welcomed them with fresh flowers brought by their first visitor, Elizabeth Hoar, who was ecstatic – she'd been influential in their move; she'd so wanted her good friends to live near. Henry David Thoreau and a black gardener had plowed and planted a garden.

Hawthorne married an adoring woman and in turn, he adored her and kept her, his doll-angel, on the pedestal.

> Dearest, I never think you to blame; for you positively have no faults. Not that you always act wisely, or judge wisely, or feel precisely what it would be wise to feel, in relation to this present world and state of being; but it is because you are too delicately and exquisitely wrought in heart, mind, and frame, to dwell in such a world – because, in short, you are fitter to be in Paradise than here....Were an angel, however holy and wise, to come and dwell with mortals, he would need the guidance and instruction of some mortal; and so will you, my Dove, need mine – and precisely the same sort of guidance that the angel would. [82]

Manuscripts piled upon Emerson's desk because, since he was editor, many writers wanted their names in *The Dial*. Thoreau soon commanded the title of "private secretary to the President of the *Dial*," because in the October issue Emerson printed eight of his poems which Fuller liked and Hawthorne said were "true as bird notes," though "very careless and imperfect." Thus, suddenly, Thoreau was anxious to solicit new subscribers. Also, he wouldn't mind helping proofread.

Five of the eight Thoreau poems would be signed "H.D.T." while two would be signed "T" and one would remain unsigned. There were two from Ellery Channing, "The Poet," short and insignificant, and the other one was untitled, so Emerson wrote across the top, "Dirge." It was a three-page poem describing the coming of autumn and the loss of love. (Who did he have in mind, his wife Ellen, or Cary Sturgis?) Both were left unsigned.

Emerson had a Cranch poem on hand, signed "C. P. C." He would print his December 9 Masonic Temple lecture on "The Conservative" from "The Times" series, with his by-line under the title. Sam Ward had sent in some notes on art. To give emphases to Oriental scriptures, he ran selections from the Bibles of the world. He also included an article on "Prayers," throughout the world and ages. He rejected Henry Hedge's "Conservatism and Reform;" he thought his style outdistanced his content. Because Horace Greeley had printed in his newspaper a criticism that *The Dial* editor should activate the real issues of the day, he began a search for articles on abolition, government and trade.

Fuller agreed to review Tennyson's poems.

Emerson began to tell Fuller that she should "protect" him from weaknesses. She should "make him noble," in order that he could find the strength to make her noble: "I know but one solution to my nature and relations. You instead of wondering at my cloistered manners, should protect me - from friendship, from my weaknesses. You should make me noble and the encourager of your nobility. Our friendship should be one incompatible with the vicious order of existing society."

Fuller's response is not known.

Fuller's next overnight was at the Ward's. Seeing Anna, Fuller's old emotions churned. Sam was off on a trip but Anna was as welcoming as ever. They slept in the same bed. With Fuller's head on Sam's pillow, sleep brought on a powerfully fateful, terrifying nightmare.

> I had a frightful dream of being imprisoned in a ship at sea, the waves all dashing round, and knowing that the crew had resolved to throw me in. While in horrible suspense, many persons that I knew came on board. At first they seemed delighted to see me and wished to talk but when I let them know my danger, and intimated a hope that they might save me, with cold courtliness glided away. Oh it was horrible these averted faces and well dressed figures turning from me, from captive, with the cold wave washing up into which I was to be thrown.... [83]

Her next stop was at the Farrar's. Since they were off on another trip, and she was to have the solitude of their home to work on her article on the old German and Greek ballads. Then the plans of the Farrars changed, so Fuller turned to the solitude of Concord:

> I should like to come to you next week, if you please.... I have no inspiration now, but hope it might come, if I were once fixed in some congenial situation. Should you like...that I should come and really live in your house a month, instead of making a visit....Would it entirely suit Lidian's convenience?....I must feel that I shall not be in any one's way....I am always sensitive about encamping on your territories.... [84]

Emerson was now under pressure with the second *Dial* deadline. Furthermore, the Emersons were still distraught from the death of Waldo Jr. Lidian was being extremely careful with the new baby, Edith, and with Ellen. Also, she was not feeling up to par because she'd just had dental surgery. And the household was crowded. Henry David Thoreau was living there again, and Ellery Channing was visiting from Cincinnati while looking for a permanent homesite in Concord. He might stay the entire winter and write, and Ellen was to arrive from Cincinnati within a few weeks. They were auctioning their furniture – and he hoped to find a publisher for his poems – even though he'd repeatedly said his poetry was too sacred to be sold.

Despite these problems, Emerson gave Fuller a welcome:

> Well, now please to come, for this I have always desired that you will make my house in some way useful to your occasions and not a mere hotel for a sleighing or summering party. I admire the conditions of the treaty, that you shall put on sulkiness as a surtout, and speech shall be contraband and the exception not the rule.... [85]

Fuller arrived late on a foggy August 17 evening, as Channing was enchanting the household with witty remarks.

The fog settled in and Fuller felt that everything seemed sad. She and Waldo walked down to the river in the misty moonlight "of fairy effect." They talked about what they had done the past few months, but the talk seemed "an interchange of facts." There was no conversation, "yet it was pleasant to be with him again." That night she began a new journal and determined to take extra pains with it because she thought "it would be as significant of the highest New England life, similar to Plato's marvellous Dialogues."

The next day Waldo brought her an inkhorn and pen – he had

'like a beaver" – but Fuller remained uninspired. Her
t its charm.

Lidian ie into Fuller's room, now called the red room. Together they told stories and cried for the lost child. Waldo showed her everything he had written of the boy, as well as what others had written.

Late afternoon Fuller and Emerson walked to Walden Pond, staying "till near sunset on the water's brink beneath the pines. It was a lovely afternoon, great happy clouds floating, a light breeze rippling the water to our feet...."

They talked about:

"...the subject of his late letter...."

"...the threatenings of the time...."

"...of some individual cases where Sorrow is still the word...."

"...of those who began with such high resolve...." They both agreed that this resolve was too high.

"We spoke of the prayer of a friend, Lord use me only for high purposes, no mean ones.... "

But their conversation was "just touch & taste and leave the cup not visibly shallower."

She felt there was a change between the two. "I feel more at home with him constantly, but we do not act powerfully on one another. He is a much better companion than formerly, for once he would talk obstinately through the walk, but now we can be silent and see things together."

That evening Ellery called her to a hill top overlooking a meadow. Amidst the moonlight he talked eloquently and excitedly about his life constantly changing. He felt he was urged on by a fate. He "disappointed everyone," he disappointed Margaret Fuller, "there was no hope of its ever being otherwise." She began to think of him as her brother in the spirit.

The next day Margaret Fuller resumed writing, but was again interrupted when Elizabeth Hoar arrived. It was alarming to see her frail, drained. Nevertheless, a strength and faith shown through. Hoar had said, "I am not a failed experiment, for in the bad hours I do not forget what I thought in the better."

Waldo and Fuller took another walk that evening, and watched the moonlight shimmer on the Concord river, but each saw in it different reflections which triggered good talk. "He said the same thing as in his letter, how each twinkling light breaking there summons to demand the whole secret, and how 'promising, promising nature never fulfils what she thus gives us a right to expect.' I said I never could meet him here, the beauty does not stimulate me to ask why? .... I was satisfied for the moment, full as if my existence was filled out, for nature had said the very word that was lying in my heart. Then we had an excellent talk: We agreed that my god was love, his truth. W. said that these statements alternate, of course, in every mind, the only difference was in which you were most at home, that he liked the pure mathematics of the thing."

The evening of the 20th Margaret Fuller visited the Hawthornes at the Old Manse. Adam and Eve were supremely happy in their Garden of Eden situated through "a Balm of Gilead trees" which lined a long avenue leading from the road. There they raced and took long walks into the hayfield, played and danced to the tune of a music box at night. There they saw only a milkman, a butcher, Mr. Hosmer with a cistern – for Paradise had no fitting water and Hawthorne claimed he prayed for the rain to fill their washtubs. When he got the cistern, he claimed it was bewitched "for while the spout pours into it like a cataract, it still remains almost empty...like the drinking cup in Hades, it has the property of filling itself forever, and never being full."

Mr. Emerson once broke their blissful recessiveness. He was feasted. "Mr. Thorow" – (Hawthorne constantly misspelled Thoreau's name) – visited twice to listen "to the music of the spheres" as well as Elizabeth Hoar whom Hawthorne commented "was more at home among spirits than among fleshly bodies."

Hawthorne and Sophia had cleaned and painted the house; it had never been painted. They wallpapered. They found and left a great chest of Dr. Ripley's sermons in the garret. They put in carpet, hung pictures and they rearranged the now antique furniture, on which Sophia painted gay little designs. She added vases full of graceful ferns and flowers. In all, they changed it "as completely as the scenery of a theatre," as Hawthorne stated. The ghosts of former occupants, Hawthorne surmised, "gave one peep into it, uttered a groan, and vanished forever." They became absorbed in the ancestry of the place, and they kept a lookout for apparitions, but they never saw one, though they did hear poundings and thumpings and paper crumpling. Telling ghost stores became a favorite pastime, especially to guests.

Fuller liked the house, "the poplars whisper so suddenly their pleasant tale."

Hawthorne walked her home that evening: "we stopped some time to look at the moon; she was struggling with clouds. Hawthorne said he should be much more willing to die than two months ago, for he had had some real possession in life, but still he never wished to leave this earth: it was beautiful enough."

She left a book at the Hawthorne's.

That day Ellery had shared with Fuller his poem, "Dirge:"

> I dress thee in the withered leaves &c
> I bear thee as the wain its sheaves
> Which crisply rustle in the sun....
> But fate who metes a different way
> To me, since I was falsely sold,
> Has gray haired turned the sunny day
> Bent its high form and made it old.

Fuller thought this poem "of exquisite music and of noble aims." The last four lines were her favorite.

Sunday, August 21, was "a happy, happy day, all clear light. I cannot write about it."

But Hawthorne wrote about it on Monday. Hawthorne had walked through the woods to return Fuller's book. He missed the turnoff and wandered into a secluded portion that was shaded with oaks and pines, overgrown with bushes and underbrush. Entering an open space, he stood surrounded by tall trees and sensed he was the only human being to have visited this spot the entire summer. Coming into a clearing, a group of cawing crows in the tops of trees took flight. Somehow he regained his direction and found his way to the Emerson's. After dropping off Fuller's book, he turned homewards, tracking first through Sleepy Hollow:

> I perceived a lady reclining near the path which bends along its verge.... It was Margaret Fuller herself. She had been there the whole afternoon, meditating or reading; for she had a book in her hand.... Nobody had broken her solitude....Then we talked about Autumn – and about the pleasures of getting lost in the woods – and about the crows, whose voices Margaret had heard – and about the experiences of early childhood...about the sight of mountains from a distance, and the view from their summits – and about other matters of high and low philosophy....We heard footsteps above us, on the high bank; and while the intruder was still hidden among the trees, he called to Margaret, of whom he had gotten a glimpse. Then he emerged from the green shade; and, behold, it was Mr. Emerson, who, in spite of his clerical consecration, had found no better way of spending the Sabbath than to ramble among the woods....He said that there were Muses in the woods to-day, and whispers to be heard in the breezes. It being now nearly 6 o'clock, we separated, Mr. Emerson and Margaret towards his house, and I towards mine, where my little wife was very busy getting tea. By the bye, Mr. Emerson gave me an invitation to dinner to-day, to be complied with or not, as might suit my convenience at the time; and it happens not to suit. [86]

That happy Sunday Ellery gave Fuller another sonnet he'd written which she copied into her journal along with "Dirge," then handed both to Emerson for inclusion in *The Dial.*

Next, she penned a letter to her Rafaello (Sam Ward):

> I shall never pay off even the interest of this large debt I owe you, of fine thoughts, of noble deeds, now running on so many years, but if there is any God who meets men face to face, and knows their merits, I believe your goodness to me will not go unbalanced.

She told him how she had longed to see him a painter of the time, "even starving in some garret until with five hundred failures of your pencil until his life ran out a rich wine of beauty." She quoted:

> Who paints not here,
> Paints in that other sphere,
> And bends his line
> With forms divine.

The days glided by with good conversation; Fuller could not record it all.

On the 24th she admitted that she and Waldo had "good meetings." They walked and stopped at the lovely spots they always had.... "But my expectations are moderate now...." She prized "his beautiful presence" rather than their talks.

He had been reading her his drafts of new poems, "Saadi" and "The Poet," and asked if she didn't like the "little subjective twinkle all through." Fuller thought he had "indeed hit off the picture lively," and she acquiesced in Saadi's resolves.

Emerson had also been reading Ellery's poems aloud, but Fuller thought he did not read them as well as he read his own. "The Elysian sweetness of his tones don't suit them." She noted that Emerson did not understand Ellery, "though he likes him much, & keeps him before him as an object of smiling contemplation."

Evenings Ellery had been "painting the cruel process of life." He had talked about "the past experiences frozen down in the soul & the impossibility of being penetrated." He claimed all might have been different had he met Fuller in his youth. He talked about William Henry Channing, and of Sam Ward. He objected to Ward's marrying Anna Barker, a fashionable woman, older, who had first rejected him.

Beneath this "roof of peace, beneficence, and intellectual activity" was the balance of rest and satisfying pleasure that Fuller needed. "Do not find fault with the hermits and scholars." She could not help but quote Tennyson since she was reviewing his poems: "The true text is:–

> Mine own Telemachus
> He does his work – I mine.*

"All do the work," she wrote in a letter, "whether they will or no; but he is 'mine own Telemachus' who does it in the spirit of religion,

---

*From Tennyson's "Ulysses":

> "Most blameless is he, centered in the sphere
> Of common duties, decent not to fail
> In offices of tenderness, and pay
> Meet adoration to my household gods
> When I am gone. He works his work, I mine."

never believing that the last results can be arrested in any one measure or set of measures, listening always to the voice of the Spirit – and who does this more than Waldo?"

Thunder showers and a rain that turned the lake an inky black began to descend on Concord on the 27th. Richard came to visit; they gathered flowers together at Walden Pond, and Fuller found his common sense and homely affection a relief "after these fine people with whom I live at swords points, though for the present turned downwards." A thunder-shower gloomed up but no rain came till sunset.

Emerson gave her Bronson Alcott's letters to read. Alcott was still in England with the English Transcendentalists. Remainders of his book, *Conversations with Children on the Gospels,* for which she'd taken notes while teaching in his Temple School, had been sold as wastepaper. "It is miserable," she wrote, "to see his boyish infatuation and his swelling vanity already worse than ever."

It was pouring down rain and Emerson "had on his blue cloak falling in large straight folds; in that he looks as if he had come to his immortality as a statue."

She spent time with Emerson in his study; he had been gone for two or three days, spending one day at a party at Sarah Ripley's in Waltham. He had been working on a portrait of Alcott and read it to her and she thought it "masterly, and suppresses nothing," though she wrote she would "throw things into very different relations." Then they talked about "God and the world. W. hates Fate as much as I do though in a different way."

In her journal she included a letter from Hawthorne – his answer to her bold request that Ellery and Ellen board with them at the Old Manse. Hawthorne had worded his refusal cleverly and kindly: "Had it been proposed to Adam and Eve to receive two angels into their Paradise, as boarders, I doubt whether they would have been altogether pleased to consent."

The weather continued cold and rainy. Sarah Ripley visited, and Emerson read parts of his journal to her and, on Sunday, Fuller was able to finish her article, "Romaic and Rhine Ballads," though it seemed "a patchwork thing."

Ellery came to visit her in the red room. He berated her for being artificial and disciplined. "You will always be wanting to grow forward, now I like to grow backward too."

Fuller pleaded guilty. In her journal:

> We need great energy, and self-reliance to endure today....What despair must he feel who after a whole life passed in trying to build up himself, resolves that it would have been far better, if he had kept still as the clod of the valley, or yielded easily as the leaf to every breeze. A path has been appointed me. I have walked in it as steadily as I could. "I am what I am."...I will bear the pain of imperfection, but not of doubt. Waldo must not shake me in my worldliness...nor this child of genius, make me lay aside the armour without which I had lain bleeding on the field long since, but if they can keep closer to Nature, and learn to interpret her as souls, also – let me learn from them what I have not....It was no accident that the serpent entered Eden, that the regular order of things was destroyed, that a painful throe accompanies every precious truth. When the soul has mastered it all, when it has learnt the secret in all its series, then there shall be no more breaks, no sluggishness, no premature fruits, but every thought be unfolded in its due order. Till then let us stand where our feet are placed and learn bit by bit, secure that it must be the destiny of each man to fill the whole circle. [87]

The rain ended the next day. The sun, warm breezes and floating clouds unfolded. Fuller made "a holy day of it out in the woods," but she could get "no steady light."

The following "golden afternoon" she and Waldo walked to the hemlocks and stayed until sunset. He read verses and then:

> We got to talking, as we almost always do, on Man and Woman, and Marriage.–W. took his usual ground. Love is only phenomenal, a contrivance of nature, in her circular motion. Man, in proportion as he is completely unfolded is man and woman by turns. The soul knows nothing of marriage, in the sense of a permanent union between two personal existences. The soul is married to each new thought as it enters into it. If this thought puts on the form of man or woman, if it last you seventy years, what then? There is but one love, that for the Soul of all Souls, let it put on what cunning disguises it will, still at last you find yourself lonely – the Soul.

> There seem to be no end to these conversations: they always leave us both where they found us, but we enjoy them, for we often get a good expression. Waldo said 'Ask any woman whether her aim in this union is to further the genius of her husband; and she will say yes, but her conduct will always be to claim a devotion day by day that will be injurious to him, if he yields.'...I made no reply, for it is not worthwhile to, in such cases, by words. [88]

On September 1 Hawthorne bought "Thorow's" boat, probably the same boat in which Thoreau had rowed Margaret Fuller in the moonlight of Walden Pond. The day of the sale "Thorow" had dined with the Hawthornes, feasting on the first ripened water-melon and musk melons. The Concord River was swollen from the rains. Thorow and Hawthorne walked up to the bank and Thoreau shouted for a young man across the river to bring him his boat. With Thoreau rowing skillfully, they started up stream. The trees were standing up to their knees in water. When Thorow said he needed money and wanted to sell the boat, Hawthorne gave him seven dollars.

September 2 was a brilliant day, in sharp contrast to the rain, and Thorow rowed and floated his boat to the foot of Hawthorne's orchard to deliver it to him. The river had risen above the stone wall, beyond which Nathaniel Hawthorne and his "sunny wife" Sophia, as Hawthorne called her, and his visiting sister Louisa were gathering apples. Thoreau gave Hawthorne a lesson in rowing, but alas, Hawthorne noted, the boat was "bewitched." It "turned its head to every point of the compass except the right one."

Hawthorne later changed the name of *Musketaquid* to *Pond Lily* because the boat "will bring home pond lilies along the river's weedy shore."

Another storm suddenly erupted. Lidian had been in her upstairs room for two days, feverish. Fuller, who'd been concentrating on her work downstairs, vaguely assumed Lidian would come downstairs whenever she felt ready. When Fuller realized Lidian had been absent an inordinate length of time, she climbed the stairs to her room:

> She burst into tears, at sight of me, but laid the blame on her nerves, having taken opium &c. I felt embarrassed, & did not know whether I ought to stay or go. Presently she said something which

made me suppose she thought W. passed the evenings in talking with me, & a painful feeling flashed across me, such as I have not had, all has seemed so perfectly understood between us. I said that I was with Ellery or H(enry) T(horeau), both of the evegs & that W. was writing in the study.

I thought it all over a little, whether I was considerate enough. As to W. I never keep him from any such duties, any more than a book would. – He lives in his own way, & he don't soothe the illness, or morbid feelings of a friend, because he would not wish anyone to do it for him.... L. knows perfectly well, that he has no regard for me or any one that would make him wish to be with me, a minute longer than I could fill up the time with thoughts.

As to my being more his companion that cannot be helped, his life is in the intellect not the affections. He has affection for me, but it is because I quicken his intellect. – I dismissed it all, as a mere sick moment of L's. Yesterday she said to me, at dinner, I have not yet been out, will you be my guide for a little walk this afternoon. I said 'I am engaged to walk with Mr. E. but' – (I was going to say, I will walk with you first,) when L. burst into tears. The family were all present, they looked at their plates. Waldo looked on the ground, but soft & serene as ever. I said "My dear Lidian, certainly I will go with you." No!" she said "I do not want you to make any sacrifice, but I do feel perfectly desolate, and forlorn, and I thought if I once got out, the fresh air would do me good, and that with you, I should have courage, but go with Mr. E. I will not go."

I hardly knew what to say, but I insisted on going with her, & then she insisted on going so that I might return in time for my other walk. Waldo said not a word: he retained his sweetness of look, but never offered to do the least thing. I can never admire him enough at such times; he is so true to himself. In our walk and during our ride this morning L. talked so fully that I felt reassured except that I think she will always have these pains, because she has always a lurking hope that Waldo's character will alter, and that he will be capable of intimate union; now I feel convinced that it will never be more perfect between them....And where he loved her first, he loves her always....Yet in reply...I would...take him for what he is, as he wishes to be taken.... I don't know that I could have fortitude for it in a more intimate

> relation. Yet nothing could be nobler, nor more consoling than to be his wife, if one's mind were only thoroughly made up to the truth. – As for myself, if I have not done as much as I ought for L. it is that her magnanimity has led her to deceive me. I have really thought that she was happy to have me in the house...and she is, I know, in the long account, but there are pains of every day....
>
> I suppose the whole amount of the feeling is that women...don't see the whole truth about one like me....They have so much that I have not, I cant conceive of their wishing for what I have....But when Waldo's wife, & the mother of that child that is gone thinks me the most privileged of women, & that E(lizabeth) H(oar) was happy because her love was snatched away for a life long separation, & thus she can know none but ideal love, it does seem a little too insulting at first blush. – And yet they are not altogether wrong. [89]

A few days passed with no incidents except visits by Elizabeth Hoar. Ellery was "in a pet" about what Fuller did not fathom, and once during a walk at Waldon Pond Emerson suddenly appeared through the trees, a "lovely apparition;" then Emerson left for Cambridge.

One small scene caused them all consternation. Ellery received a letter from Caroline Sturgis, his former girl friend, asking him to visit her at Naushon. Should he see her? The flower of his life, wife Ellen, was expected to arrive on Wednesday. Fuller supported him in his decision to see Cary. He left the next morning.

Then Sam Ward arrived. Fuller and he strolled to Sleepy Hollow Cemetery and shared the best confidences they'd had since his marriage. He described the "pitched battle" he'd fought over the conflicts between his inheritance and his temperament, though he seemed to have achieved peace in his decision. "He seemed all lovely, a glancing bird, a sunbeam...." They walked to the Old Manse, and learned that Hawthorne was now steering the *Musketaguid* or *Pond Lily* like a pro, was making solitary excursions into remote parts of the Concord River, and was catching fish for his meals.

The black rain began to pour again. In her red room Fuller sat by a fire. She finished her rave review of Tennyson's *Poems.* She'd used such phrases as "more simply the songster than any poet of one time." She especially admired his melody and picturesque power. She took time out from work only for a walk with Elizabeth Hoar, to pass through luxuriant ferns and tall asters to Ellery's dell.

Once Waldo visited her in her room for another talk about marriage. He read from his journal and "we had a long talk. He listens with a soft wistful look to what I say, but is nowise convinced as late in a dark afternoon, the fine light in that red room always so rich, cast a beautiful light upon him, as he read and talked. Since I have found in his journal two sentences that represent the two sides of his thought:

> In time
> Marriage should be a covenant to secure to either party the sweetness and the handsomeness of being a calm continuing inevitable benefactor to the other
>
> In eternity
> Is it not enough that souls should meet in a law, in a thought, obey the same love demonstrate the same idea. These alone are the nuptials of minds. I marry you for better, not for worse, I marry impersonally." [90]

Fuller's comment,"I shall write to him about it."

Wednesday dawned – the day Ellen was expected to arrive on a stage from Cincinnati. Ellery had not yet returned from his Naushon visit to see Cary. Fuller dashed off a note to Cary. Lidian and Mamma joined Emerson and Fuller in the red room. It was an anxious moment when Ellen walked in. Her first question was of Ellery; Fuller did not "let her know where Ellery was gone." Ellen was clearly disappointed though she reacted sweetly.

Waldo immediately offered to take a stage for Boston to find out whatever he could of Ellery, but Fuller objected.

It was "a wretched night.":

> Ellen awoke, "M are you asleep," "No" – "I hope you will like Ellery so that he may enjoy being with you: he needs the stimulus of such minds. He values Cary's very much: he reads her letters a great deal: Do you know whether he has seen her?" "I believe, he has," said I, & I thought 'poor deluded innocent' – Then I thought over all these

> relations once more, but I still came to the same result that I always do. If I were Waldo's wife, or Ellery's wife, I should acquiesce in all these relations, since they needed them. I should expect the same feeling from my husband, & I should think it little in him not to have it. I felt I should never repent of advising Ellery to go whatever happened.
>
> Well, he came back next day, and All's Well that Ends Well.... Ellery told Ellen at once how it was, and she took it just as she ought.

Henry Hedge arrived, having travelled from Bangour, Maine, on his way to preach at Brookline and Fuller joined him on the stage to Cambridge. Fuller approved of his sermon, saw her Cambridge friends, and returned to Concord.

With Lidan the conversation always turned to Christ and religion. Fuller found it irritating. She wrote, "Nothing makes me so anti-Christian, & so anti-marriage as these talks with L. She lays such undue stress on the office of Jesus, & the demands of the heart."

One Wednesday:

> Waldo had got through with his tedious prose, & to day he got into the mood to finish his poem. Just at night he came into the red room to read the passage he had inserted. This is to me the loveliest way to live that we have. I wish it would be so always that I could live in the red room, & Waldo be stimulated by the fine days to write poems & come the rainy days to read them to me. My time to go to him is late in the evening. Then I go knock at the library door, & we have our long word walk through the growths of things with glimmers of light from the causes of things. Afterward, W. goes out & walks beneath the stars to compose himself for his pillow, & I open the window, & sit in the great red chair to watch them. The only thing I hate is our dining together. It is never pleasant and some days I dislike it so that I go out just before dinner & stay till night in the woods, just to break the routine. I do not think a person of more complete character would feel or make the dinner bell such a vulgarity as W. does, but with him these feelings are inevitable.
>
> He has put more of himself into Saadi and the other poem Masque than in anything he has written before....Late in the evening, he came in again, to read me some lines he had been adding.... [91]

Emerson decided to print "Saadi," unsigned, in the October issue of *The Dial.*

He'd also received a long article from Theodore Parker which presented a problem because Emerson had asked for a short piece.

Parker had been angered because Unitarian ministers at a Hollis Street council had upheld the decision of a congregation to dismiss their minister, Reverend John Pierpont, because he'd rebuked his parishioners as being hypocritical – they'd downgraded the use of liquor while profiting from its sale. As Pierpont saw it, this was just one of many incidents.

Emerson was totally against the magazine serving as platform for such dispute. When Parker's twenty-page article came in, he was grieved but closed his eyes and carried "Hollis Street Council" to the printer without reading it. The Pierpont article, then, and Fuller's article, "Romaic and Rhine Ballads," filled half the magazine.

Also, Emerson sketched out an overview of the English reformers from papers Alcott brought from England.

On the front wrapper he wrote an apology, "To Correspondents," for his omissions of submitted poetry.

As the magazine went to press, an article calling forth a new Cromwell came in from Charles Lane, and he somehow found space for it.

When the proofs came in he gave them to Thoreau while he and Hawthorne escaped for a day's walk to the Shaker community at Harvard, Massachusetts.

P. S. The October *Dial* was a few days late in coming off the presses, and Thoreau's proofing led to Margaret Fuller's complaint that in her Tennyson review the word "infamy" turned out to be "infancy," and "abstraction" was "obstruction." She was irritated because she had wanted Tennyson to see the review.

Emerson said that since Thoreau had corrected errors in the magazine, he must have overlooked these or thought they were "good Dialese."

Emerson was anxious that she translate Dante's *La Vita Nuova,* but would rather she write nothing for a year, than to put too much stress on her health.

Fuller had one more dinner with Nathaniel and "My Dove," and a

Musketaquid ride with them in their boat up the North Branch. One evening she accompanied a black-veiled Lidian to the churchyard for prayer at the tomb of Waldo Jr. One afternoon there was tea with Sophia Hawthorne, her mother, Sarah Clarke, Richard, her brother, her sister Ellen, and Ellery, and Ellen Sturgis Hooper and her daughter Clover, (who was to become Mrs. Henry Adams). After walking Sophia and her mother to the Old Manse, Fuller and Emerson shared the return walk in the moonlight walk. "We were more truly together than usual."

There were more good talks with Emerson in his library. Fuller spent time reading and also perused Emerson's journals, since he'd given permission. And she delighted in little Edith: "She likes me, & leans her head against me in the most sweet relying way."

She realized: "I ought to go away now these last days. I have been fairly intoxicated with his mind....I feel faint in the presence of too strong a fragrance. I think, too, he will be glad to get rid of me."

They had a farewell breakfast with Elizabeth Hoar, then Mamma and Lidian accompanied Fuller on the same stage to Boston. She closed her journal description of her visit with these words:

> Farewell, dearest friend, there has been dissonance between us, & may be again, for we do not fully meet, and to me you are too much & too little by turns, yet thanks be to the Parent of Souls, that gave us to be born into the same age and the same country and to meet with so much of nobleness and sweetness as we do...
>
> Going down I had a thorough talk with Lidian. I shall never trouble myself any more: it is not just to her. But I will do more in attending to her, for I see I could be of real use. She says she feels I am always just to her, but I might be more. [92]

A month later Fuller wrote her farewell to Emerson, the kind which maintains a friendship:

> I have not felt separated from you yet. – It is not yet time for me to have my dwelling near you. I get, after a while, even intoxicated with your mind, and do not live enough in myself. Now don't screw up your lip to an ungracious pettiness, but hear the words of frank affection as

> they deserve "*mente cordis.*" Let no cold breath paralyze my hope that there will yet be a noble and profound understanding between us. We have gone so far, and yet so little way. I understand the leadings of your thought better and better, and I feel a conviction that I shall be worthy of this friendship, that I shall be led day by day to purify, to harmonize my being, to enlarge my experiences, and clear the eye of intelligence till after long long patience waiting yourself shall claim a thousand years interview at least. You need not be terrified at this prophecy nor look about for the keys of your cell. - I shall never claim an hour. I begin to understand where I am, and feel more and more unfit to be with any body. I shall no more be so ruled by the affectionate expansions of my heart but hope is great, though my daily life must be pallid and narrow. [93]

Within a month, she was expressing hope to her other confidant, William Henry Channing, to see direct, honest communication between the sexes:

> When souls meet direct and all secret thoughts are laid open, we shall need no forbearance, no prevention, no care-taking of any kind. Love will be pure light, and each action simple – too simple to be noble. But there will not be always so much to pardon in ourselves and others....To speak with open heart and "tongue affectionate and true," – to enjoy real repose and the consciousness of a thorough mutual understanding in the presence of friends when we do meet, is what is needed. That being granted, I do believe I should not wish any surrender of time or thought from a human being. But I have always a sense that I cannot meet or be met in haste; as ______ said he could not look at the works of art in a chance half-hour, so cannot I thus rudely and hastily turn over the leaves of any mind. In peace, in stillness that permits the soul to flow, beneath the open sky, I would see those I love. [94]

Fuller reached towards Lidian. At moments they may have felt a rivalry, but when they searched into each other, they could see that they had the commonality of being women in nineteenth century America. It was only their background and station in life that created a difference.

Except for the two or three brief confrontations described, for which Fuller apologized, there is no indication that she and Lidian were not compatible. Fuller seemed always sensitive to Lidian's convenience in hospitality. Both were always sending their love via letters. Emerson claimed in *Memoirs* that they got along very well. If these women had not been friendly, at least on the surface, Margaret would not have been invited back.

Lidian probably had a certain admiration for Fuller mixed with a certain pity since she was not married. Fuller probably recognized Lidian's positive qualities and enjoyed her sense of humor. Probably, Lidian seemed uninteresting to Fuller. Fuller's interests encompassed a larger span than domesticity and religion, which is where Lidian fixed her mind. Lidian did seem to stay in the background. Fuller could not help but prefer the challenge of Emerson. But Fuller understood the binders in which women were entrapped. She was all too familiar with her own binders. She sought solutions and envisioned a new day for women.

If Lidian was aware of the ongoing attraction between Fuller and Emerson, there is no indication other than the story above. There is no evidence that she ever interfered or made an effort to terminate it. There is no evidence that Fuller did not leave Concord on good terms with both her host and hostess. As she settled into her house in Cambridge with her mother and her sister and Ellery, she continued to write for *The Dial*, continued communication with Emerson.

That Lidian felt left out, slighted and jealous is another piece that biographers and scholars consistently overlook. It is a shock to realize the space not given to Lidian, wife of forty-seven years who outlived Emerson and surely wielded some influence while he was achieving fame. There are two books on Ellen Tucker, first wife of barely over one year, but in biography after biography on Emerson, Lidian is given slight mention. Rusk entitled one of his chapters "Lidian," but subtly manages to slight and even denigrate her as he did Fuller. She is hardly "fleshed out."

There is no evidence that Emerson was ever conscious of a triangle situation. Radical in the lofty philosophy he proscribed for mankind, he was not sensitive to the dilemmas of womankind. However, he – always the articulator of divine life – had the solution for single intellectual females. In brotherly kindness, he advised. In a poem,

"To Rhea," which he published in the July 1843 issue of *The Dial*, he advocated that Fuller raise her unrequited love for him up to the celestial, that is, the divine or spiritual, and thereby improve the universe.

Emerson chose to equate Fuller with the earth-goddess figure of Rhea because Fuller had opened her 1841 Conversations, to which Emerson and other men attended, with a discussion of Greek Mythology in which she explained that Rhea was one of the children of Heaven and Earth.

In Greek legend Rhea personified Productive Energy. She was the mother of Zeus, and saved him in infancy from death. Rhea's husband had devoured each son born to them because his mother had told him a son would someday usurp his throne. So Rhea gave birth the third time in secret and she handed her baby, Zeus, to Ge (Earth) who took him to Crete and brought him up to manhood. Rhea influenced the development of Indomitable Will in Zeus who came to rule the Olympian Throne as Father of the Gods.

Thus, Rhea was looked upon as the innovator of a new age of humanism.

To Rhea

Thee, dear friend, a brother soothes,
Not with flatteries, but truths,
Which tarnish not, but purify
To light which dims the morning's eye.
I have come from the spring-woods,
From the fragrant solitudes;–
Listen what the poplar-tree
And murmuring waters counselled me.

If with love thy heart has burned;
If thy love is unreturned;
Hide thy grief within thy breast,
Though it tear thee unexpressed;
For when love has once departed
From the eyes of the false-hearted,
And one by one has torn off quite

The bandages of purple light;
Though thou wert the loveliest
Form the soul had ever dressed,
Thou shalt seem, in each reply,
A vixen to his altered eye;
Thy softest pleadings seem too bold,
Thy praying lute will seem to scold:
Though thou kept the straightest road,
Yet thou errest far and broad.
But thou shalt do as do the gods
In their cloudless periods;
For of this lore be thou sure,–
Though thou forget, the gods, secure,
Forget never their command,
But make the statute of this land.
As they lead, so follow all,
Ever have done, ever shall.
Warning to the blind and deaf'
Tis written on the iron leaf,
Who drinks of Cupid's nectar cup
Loveth downward, and not up;
He who loves, of gods or men,
Shall not by the same be loved again;
His sweetheart's idolatry
Falls, in turn, a new degree.
When a god is once beguiled
By beauty of a mortal child
And by her radiant youth delighted,
He is not fooled, but warily knoweth
His love shall never be requited.
And thus the wise Immortal doeth,–
'Tis his study and delight
To bless that creature day and night;
From all evils to defend her;
In her lap to pour all splendor;
To ransack earth for riches rare,
And fetch her stars to deck her hair:
He mixes music with her thoughts,
And saddens her with heavenly doubts:
All grace, all good his great heart knows

Profuse in love, the king bestows,
Saying, 'Hearken! Earth, Sea, Air!
This monument of my despair
Build I to the All-Good, All-Fair.
Not for a private good,
But I, from my beatitude.

Albeit scorned as none was scorned,
Adorn her as was none adorned.
I make this maiden an ensample
To Nature, through her kingdoms ample,
Whereby to model newer races,
Statelier forms and fairer faces;
To carry man to new degrees
Of power and of comeliness.
These presents be the hostages
Which I pawn for my release.
See to thyself, O Universe!
Thou art better, and not worse.'–
And the god, having given all,
Is freed forever from his thrall.

Fuller was not interested in raising men or gods into a new era, or freeing or modelling new races or faces to carry man to new degrees of power and of comeliness.

Neither was sexual denial the alternative Fuller wanted at this point in her thirty-four year life span. Had Emerson been celebate?

She was ready to drop this playground and go on to fresh horizons.

She wanted more out of life than a Puritan game or a Platonic game of mind over body.

The story of the hot/cold relationship does not end with Fuller's disillusionment.

But the balance of the game was changed. There was less intimacy, less frequency.

Both mailed off "My Dear Friend" letters. Both had superlative phrases to mete to the other.

Emerson called her "O daughter of Gallio!" a "saint," a "proven friend."

She let him know she "owed to the protection of your roof...the gentle beauty of the Concord wood."

Both were "Yours ever affectionately."

Once Waldo was "Your warm cold friend.

On a lecture tour, Emerson began "Dear Margaret, born for my benefactress, your letters are benefits."

Fuller would argue against being born to benefit Emerson.

Emerson continued, "Whatever comes to me from a friend looks unpayable. It ought not. If the earth draws an apple, the apple draws the earth, and they meet their middle point."

He'd sent along, for sharing, a letter from a new friend, William Tappan, "...lonely beautiful brooding youth who sits at a desk six hours of the day in some brokerage or other but carries no desk in his head or heart."

Fuller could not determine from the distance of a letter if Tappan were "the nucleus or the train of a comet that lightened afar." Goethe's dæmons "are not busy enough at the birth of most men.

They do not give them individuality deep enough for truth to take root in."

Tappan was the most tranquil and wise of all the Round Table but Emerson hesitated to make new friends because the best friendships had to be selective and limited to a few in number: "Not less than twelve Paladins* can we have nor less than twelve holy & magical women, finders all of the Sangreal." **

Fuller disagreed. "We need not economize, we need not hoard these immortal treasures. Love and thought are not diminished by diffusion. In the widow's cruse is oil enough to furnish light for all the world!"

Fuller had let her Waldo down for the January 1843 *Dial.* She had promised reviews and a memorial piece on her mentor, Dr. William Ellery Channing who'd died. Her admiration for the eminent man and friend did not match her sentences. Finally, Emerson wrote a commemoration. Thoreau had turned out some selections of Indian scriptures, and he'd translated Aeschylus' "Prometheus Bound." She felt honor bound to contribute something that would take up more than a third of the next issue.

"A third!" Emerson ejaculated. "Great is thy love & power, and I know I shall know thy star across the universe by the energy of its fires, whose spending the Universe shall gladly repair...." He signed off, "Farewell dear Margaret friend & benefactress of Waldo E."

Even so, the contents of Emerson's letters became more similar to those he wrote his wife – interesting long, objective recitals of external daily happenings.

The nuances of Fuller's letters are not known because her correspondence during this period does not survive. She did write because Emerson made reference to her letters.

In the house on Ellery Street in Cambridge, Fuller's life, inward and outward, continued with her daily dose of dæmons and family duty. But her desire was to move forward in life.

In the house on the Pike in Concord, Emerson's life flowed constant as the river. New experiences reinforced his belief that all places, all people, were the same: "The average of wit seldom varies."

---

*Twelve peers of Charlemagne's court; knight champions.

**The Holy Grail.

Lidian's external circumstances remained the same. When Waldo, off on another lecture tour, asked her to carry a letter to Margaret Fuller or to take messages about *Dial* printers and proof sheets to Thoreau, she complied. When he asked for an accounting "reciting all the depths & straits of your beggary & the methods by which you have kept the regiment of creditors at bay," she sent along a financial analysis. She tried to absorb Emerson's advice: "The Good Spirit is always nearest – do not hearken to that Sad brother." He told her he so hated travelling that he was going to quit and she must learn to starve gracefully.

When she asked him for a love letter, he answered: "My friend at Washington writes what you call love letters.... But consider that he is a great deal younger than I; else, should I, no doubt, write a sheet a day, to assure you of my dear regard, and that I am the same aspiring all-loving person whom you have known so long...."

Inwardly she dispaired: "I wish I had never been born." She saw no narrowing of the communication gap between her husband and herself. Nothing filled the emptiness she felt due to the loss of Waldo Jr.

So affected was Emerson by her mourning that he copied her words into his journal: "Queenie's epitaph: Do not wake me." Soon appeared: "I do not see how God can compensate me for the sorrow of existence."

Lidian was to be forty-one, a turning point for most women. At this time, psychologists tell us, women are ready to come into independence and self-hood. Women at mid-life are released from psychological bonds with mothers, from domination by fathers, husbands or mentors, and from childbearing rigors.

Eight years into marriage, Lidian saw no other change than the increase of her supply of medicine on her bureau.

Elizabeth Hoar, forty-one years old, was independent and seemed to have achieved a certain amount of self-hood. Yet her circumstances and choices in life caused her to fill her time with idleness: "I have no thoughts, & am like one waiting – weather-bound at a way-side inn, where I busy myself with what comes to hand that the time may not be too tedious."

Fuller, turning thirty-three, was independent, untied, yet she felt the void of an enduring love relationship. She could not earn a decent living from work of her choice. She yearned for change, but how could it occur?

Emerson, thirty-nine years of age, going on forty, had love, family, an assured income and preferred work. He had books and poems to write, *The Dial* to edit, Carlyle's *Past and Present* to handle, and another lecture tour, this year to Baltimore, Philadelphia and New York. His complaint concerned his diminished energy.

The Dial, Emerson sensed, was slipping into its death shroud. The "Ungrateful *Dial*...must be dashed in pieces." He would keep it going for Fuller's personal interest and use – "which you will never consider, O godlike friend..."

Writers kept supplying material – though Charles King Newcomb declined sending Part II of "The Two Dolons" – and much of the press was favorable. Still, the subscription list decreased from three hundred to two hundred twenty.

"Who reads *The Dial*, " said one reviewer from *New Englander*, "for any other purpose but to laugh at its baby poetry or at the solemn fooleries of its misty prose."

Hawthorne used *The Dial* as a soporific.

Carlyle wouldn't pay postage on one issue mistakenly addressed. While there was "not indeed anything except the Emersonian papers," which Carlyle liked, there was much that he did not dislike.

Ripley and Peabody discovered that costs were greater than monies received. Peabody didn't always meet printing deadlines, and distribution to booksellers was always a problem. Sometimes she never got it off to England.

Peabody now claimed that people were buying single issues of magazines, and she convinced Emerson that *The Dial* would sell singly.

The reason *The Dial* held onto last breaths for another year was because Emerson compassionately nursed it. He changed the publisher to his own James Munroe & Co., and he paid some bills out of his and Lidian's pocket.

He appointed Thoreau as editor when he left for his January and February 1843 lectures on "New England." He counted on Elizabeth Hoar's secretarial help too – she'd helped the previous month with his poem "To Eva at the South," written to his first wife Ellen.

Fuller offered a long piece on the sculptor Antonio Canova, and reviews. Lydia Maria Child came forth for the first time with "What Is Beauty?" Thoreau worked on poems and essays, one on a Greek poet, and he elicited pieces from Charles Lane, Alcott, and Wheeler. Emerson couldn't finish a review of Parker's *Miscellanies*, and it turned out that Wheeler's piece had already been printed. Other promised work never materialized. But Thoreau had enough material with reviews and a poem by Emerson's dead brother.

There was one two-day visit between Emerson and Fuller wherein she told him that no man invited her mind to full expression, that she felt she could enrich her own thoughts herself with great wealth and variety of materials which others would find tedious.

After the visit Emerson concentrated for pages in his journal, giving her the highest of praise: "a pure and purifying mind, self-purifying also, full of faith in men, & inspiring it." She was "far more excellent than we had thought. All natures seem poor beside one so rich." His life was lifeless besides hers. "Besides her friendship, other friendships seem trade....The wonderful generosity of her sentiments pours a contempt on books & writing." She was "an inspirer of courage, the secret friend of all nobleness...forgiver of injuries..." Margaret Fuller "rose before me at times into heroical & godlike regions, and I could remember no superior women, but thought of Ceres, Minerva, Proserpine, and the august ideal forms of the Foreworld." She was sincere, had energy, judgment, character, wisdom; she never talked narrowly or with hostility, was always rich of experience and "fast as Olympus to her principle." She was ready "to plunge into the sea of Buddhism & mystic trances," but "with a boundless fun & drollery" and she had "the most entertaining conversation in America." He summed up: "Whilst Dante's *Nuova Vita* is almost unique in the literature of sentiment, I have called the imperfect record she gave me of two of her days, *Nuovissima Vita.*"

Others of the Transcendental circle attempted to fulfill their quests. Sophia Hawthorne, "happy as a queen" at the Manse, took her diamond ring one evening at sunset – she was in her husband's study (the same room in which Emerson had written *Nature*) – carving words into the tiny glass window pane: "Man's accidents are God's purposes." She was pregnant. Then she wrote, "Sophia to Hawthorne, 1843."

Hawthorne clasped her diamond. After his name, he wrote: "This is his study, 1843." Leaving a space, he added in smaller penmanship: "The smallest twig leans clear against the sky.... Composed by my wife and written with her diamond."

It was Sophia's turn again: "Inscribed by my husband at sunset, April 3, 1843. On the gold light. S.A.H."

Ellen and Ellery Channing moved to Concord into a little house called Red Lodge. He chopped wood for Emerson; he and wife roasted apples, and were happy in the domesticity that Ellen created. Once Cary Sturgis visited overnight. Passions between her and Ellery had cooled into friendship. Then it was rumored that two of Ellery's poems in the April *Dial* had been written to Elizabeth Hoar. He'd sent off many impassioned letters to her, but she hadn't responded. Sam Ward paid a bill so that Ellery's verse could be published in a volume entitled *Poems*, which did not cause a public clamor.

Elizabeth Hoar was lamenting the fact that Emerson did not respond to her in the way she wished him to respond to her: "Why, O sun of your sister's heart, did you not draw into yourself the vapors that pressed toward you? but you withdrew to let them sink cold again into the dark earth."

She told herself before she went to sleep that love could not die in the heart...that clouds and chilling mists were but earthborn and would pass.

James Freeman Clarke and his sister Sarah – ("the perpetual peace offering," so mild and pure she was) – sent Margaret Fuller a poem and fifty dollars, and asked her to go on a trip West with them. Desperately, Fuller fought her dæmons to finish an article equivalent to two contributions to *The Dial*. Every morning, she told Emerson, she rose "happy as birds" and would proceed "to write as hard as these odious east winds will let me," then "about eleven comes one of these tormentors, and makes my head ache and spoils the day."

She entitled her long article "The Great Lawsuit: Man versus Men; Woman versus Women." It explored women's role in society.

The great need for this article was affirmed when her mentor/friend commented on Anna and Sam Ward's second baby: "Though no son, yet a sacred event."

The student thought it worthwhile to broaden her mentor's views:

"Why is not the advent of a daughter as 'sacred' a fact as that of a son. I do believe, O Waldo, most unteachable of men, that you are at heart a sinner on this point. I entreat you to seek light in prayer upon it."

Tension developed between Emerson and Thoreau. Thoreau left the Concord "mansion of peace" to live and tutor the children of the William Emersons on Staten Island.

In a year when many families were crossing the rocky mountains in covered wagons, the forty-three year-old Bronson Alcott put his family and his bust of Socrates into an open wagon, along with Charles Lane and his ten year old son, and about a thousand books on mystical philosophy. They moved fourteen miles out of Concord to establish their New Eden (Lane paid for it with his life savings), which included a two-story red farmhouse set amidst ninety acres of rolling hills and streams just outside the town of Harvard, which they named "Fruitlands," even though it boasted only ten apple trees. Louisa May Alcott (ten years old at the time) was to later quip that the "plenteous orchards were soon to be evoked from their inner consciousness."

Straight away Alcott and Lane announced that chickens had "the same right to life as human babies," and "the cow should not be robbed of her milk." Abby had to fight for the baby's right to milk.

Insisted on was plain housing, diet, linen clothing (because cotton came from slave labor), "pure bathing, unsullied dwellings, open conduct, gentle behavior, kindly sympathies, serene minds."

Emerson was dubious about the success of the venture, but he helped to promote with an article by Charles Lane and Bronson Alcott in the July *Dial*.

In time about fifteen men joined the Fruitlanders all of whom used hand spades instead of beasts of burden and insisted on growing only those vegetables that grew toward heaven, such as corn. Carrots and potatoes were vetoed because their roots grew downward.

When a woman showed up to help out, she asked Abby if there were any beasts of burden on the place. Abby replied: "Only one woman."

This new woman enjoyed poetry better than housekeeping and, after quarreling with Abby, she left. Finally, the farmers had to compromise with an ox and a cow, and somehow potatoes became acceptable.

On the day of Emerson's birthday, May 25 – two days after Fuller's birthday – Fuller boarded a train with James Freeman Clarke, his sister Sarah, and Cary Sturgis, and headed first to Niagara Falls. Emerson envied her "this large dose of America," yet he disparaged travelling. "If only we knew where for us the Spirit lurks today and were saved the despondency of groping for it in the vast Elsewhere."

Dismayed because she'd missed Jane Tuckerman's wedding, Fuller was lulled by the motion of the train and read one of fifteen hundred copies Emerson had managed to have published of Carlyle's *Past and Present.* It was Emerson's birthday present to her. He was reviewing it for *The Dial.* Fuller found it witty but Carlyle "sees scarce a step before him...He ends as he began...everything is very bad."

At Niagara Falls Fuller sent Emerson a birthday present, a tiny purse made by a Seneca squaw. "If you use it for a watch-pocket, hang it, when you travel, at the head of your bed, and you may dream of Niagara. If you use it for a purse, you can put in it alms for poets and artists, and the subscription-money you receive for Mr. Carlyle's book."

Fuller excitedly breathed in the atmosphere and kept a journal. Sarah Clarke sketched. After a tour of Lake Erie, Cary Sturgis turned back home; the others continued to Cleveland and boarded a steamer to the St. Clair River where they saw for the first time Indians camping on the banks.

How strange, Fuller wrote, at Chicago "to walk and walk but never climb!" In these flat lands they met Clarke's brother, William, a settler and an assistant engineer for the Chicago Board of Public Works. Fuller, carefully supplying Emerson with her forwarding addresses, wrote: "The men are all at work for money and to develop the resources of the soil, the women belong to the men. They do not ape fashions, talk jargon or burn out life as a tallow candle for a tawdry show. Their energy is real...."

She despaired the rough manners and selfish attitudes of the immigrants who poured off the steamboats, "so wholly for what they could get."* It was discouraging to think that the nation was to be

*Her statement was strikingly echoed by John F. Kennedy's, "Ask not what your country can do for you; ask what you can do for your country." Inaugural Address, January 20, 1961.

built by uncouth people. On one landing she selected from the tobacco chewing crowd, one man that looked clean and intellectual, and was told he was a famous Land-Shark.

William Clarke was an excellent Thoreau-like guide who told the legends of the country in a poetical manner. Their three-week excursion took them into an untracked Eden of "heavenly sweetness" in a strong "lumber wagon drawn by horses which defied all the jolts and wrenches incident to woodpaths, mudholes, and the fording of creeks." They went through Rock River valley near the site where Chief Black Hawk and his band were killed in the 1832 white-man's invasion, where one of Fuller's uncles had settled amid rich land, river and smooth bluffs three hundred feet high, and where she suggested to her brother Richard, who had failed to win the Bowdoin prize at Harvard, that they might have a farm and live "with a twentieth part the labor of a N England farm."

They pushed on to Belvidere, where her brother Arthur planned to open a school; then to the Territory of Wisconsin where they toured a chain of crystal clear lakes and stayed on a farm which had once been the site of a large Indian village.

At Milwaukee there was an encampment of Indians, some poor, some noble as Romans, and more immigrant Germans, Norwegians, Swedes, Danes, Dutch, Swiss.

Back in Chicago, she opened a copy of the latest *Dial* which Emerson had forwarded. It was one of the best issues, he wrote. Her article, "The Great Lawsuit: Man versus Men; Woman versus Women," dominated forty-seven opening pages, and Emerson's two-page poem to Fuller, "To Rhea," appeared fifty-seven pages later. He'd received so many contributions that he'd had to turn down pieces from Thomas Wentworth Higginson and the radical feminist Mary Gove.

The total circle, he wrote, felt "The Great Lawsuit" was "a piece of life. H. D. Thoreau, who will never like anything, writes, 'Miss F's is a noble piece, rich extempore writing, talking with pen in hand.' Mrs. Sophia Ripley writes that 'Margaret's article is the cream of herself, a little rambling, but rich in all good things' and Ellery testifies his approbation very distinctly & without qualification. I think the piece very proper & noble and itself quite an important fact in the history of Woman: good for its wit, excellent for its character – it wants an introduction; the subject is not quite distinctly & adequately propounded. It will teach us all to revise our habits of thinking on this head. But does it not seem as if only in the poetic form could this right & wrong be portrayed? – If there were fewer people and the vital force concentrated on those few, as in my garden five old fashioned strawberries now go to make one giant strawberry, we might yet have a good tragedy or a new & better Parliament of Love, that should describe this thing with sunbeams."

Fuller did not comment. She was happy the verses in "To Rhea" were "in so high a state of preservation." Emerson's other poem, "Gifts," was charming, and she enjoyed Ellery's poem, "The Earth." Charles Lane's article about the Fruitlands farmers "made me laugh till I cried it contrasted so whimsically with all I had been seeing and feeling in this region, where strong instincts and imperative necessities come upon you like the swoop of the hawk."

Emerson had included his review of Carlyle's *Past and Present.* His conclusions almost met Fuller's: "mountains of panegyric," but Carlyle "must write thus or nohow, like a drunken man who can run, but cannot walk."*

To Emerson Fuller described her observations of women who tried to adapt to the rugged pioneer life. The "foreign women...do not suffer as our Eastern women do; they have, for the most part, been brought up to work in the open air and have better constitutions." The Eastern women, who were afraid to walk on wild-wood paths because of dangerous rattlesnakes, retained the fashions of Eastern life, taught their daughters European values, and sent them to Eastern schools, all of which made them dissatisfied with Western life. This clinging to European tradition would blight original growth – a point she'd amplify in a book.

Travelling gave Fuller "a feeling of luxury and repose," yet homesickness was a constant. But where was her home? She didn't like the petty intellectualities and bloodless theory in New England, she wrote Emerson, but the Western instinctive existence pleased her no better.

Late in August Fuller mingled with the Chippewa and Ottawa

---

*Carlyle responded that the review was the "most dangerous thing" because he could recognize the likeness of himself in it.

Indians; some were painted and some danced in front of the stores and taverns. She spent nine days by herself on the island of Mackinaw when the tribes came to collect their annual government pension. Every day she watched them set up their morning household.

She deplored the White attitude. White men forgot that the Red men were the rightful owners of the land. White men abhorred the Indian dirt and could only breathe "Get you gone, you Indian dog!"

Perhaps Indians couldn't be civilized, but at least the French Catholics did not harm or corrupt. "The stern Presbyterian, with his dogmas and his task-work, the city circle and the college, with their niggard conceptions and unfeeling stare" had never given love or intelligence.

She studied the Indian women because "The observations of women upon the position of women are always more valuable than those of men." She used sign language. They crowded around her "to inspect little things I had to show them, but never press near; on the contrary, would reprove and keep off the children. Anything they took from my hand was held with care, then shut or folded, and returned with an air of lady-like precision."

They were coarse and ugly, except for their eyes, and they walked with an awkward gait, and their forms were bent by burdens. "This gait, so different from the steady and noble step of the men, marks the inferior position....It is impossible to look upon the Indian women without feeling that they do occupy a lower place than women among the nations of European civilization...."

She would make a strong plea in her book: "Let every man look to himself how far this blood shall be required at his hands. Let the missionary, instead of preaching to the Indian, preach to the trader who ruins him. Let every legislator take the subject to heart, and, if he cannot undo the effects of past sin, try for that clear view and right sense that may save us from sinning still more deeply."

Sault Ste. Marie was next on the agenda, and St. Joseph, then back to Mackinaw where she joined her friends, and where Sarah Clarke displayed a bulging portfolio of drawings. Together they returned to Buffalo; thence to Staten Island where she saw Emerson's brother and family, and Thoreau who, she learned, had been warmly corresponding with Lidian.

Back in Cambridge by mid-September, Fuller was too late to help with *The Dial*, copy all set.

She settled into the new house on Prospect Street which Richard had bought after selling the Ellery Street house. With her mother comfortable and with Richard in Harvard, she resumed her private tutoring and Conversations. This season her subject was health and she made a special point of inviting Lidian who'd had dyspepsia all summer. She tried to find students for her sister, Ellen, who was now pregnant and who was opening an elementary school in order to earn money. (Emerson enrolled his daughter, Ellen.) Fuller did her best to promote William Henry Channing's new magazine, *Present*, by praising it to her friends.* Then to Concord, for two days, bringing with her, as Emerson wrote to Sturgis, "potions of divine scorn."

They thrashed over again their favorite subject, man and woman. Emerson inserted his views into his journal: "It is folly to imagine that there can be anything very bad in the position of woman compared with that of man, at any time; for since every woman is a man's daughter, and every man is a woman's son, every woman is too near to man, was too recently a man, than that possibly any wide disparity can be. As is the man will be the woman; and as is the woman, the man."

There could be little agreement between the two.

Concord was in flux. Now when you walked the wooded paths you'd come face-to-face with one of the laborers who worked the railroad. You'd see their tumble-down shanties that dotted the edges of Walden Pond. Commonly it was thought the railroad would make Boston Massachusetts.

Thoreau was also back in Concord; the experiment with the William Emerson's hadn't worked out. He was proofing the October *Dial*, complaining of mistakes.

Emerson – like the editor before him – had to fill in many empty spaces himself. Parker was leaving for Europe and couldn't be counted on. Thoreau couldn't "finish an account of a winter's walk in Concord in the midst of a Staten Island summer." His poem, "A Winter Walk," formerly unsatisfactory, was still unsatisfactory.

---

* *Present*, filled with reviews, essays, poems, etc., had less than a year of life, until April 1844.

Emerson faulted Thoreau's constant trick of using the opposite word and he revised. Thoreau helped with "Ethnical Scriptures."

Emerson was considering how to quit *The Dial.* His expenditures added up to more than his time and energy, since he paid Thoreau and Channing himself. Ellery Channing would be a good editor, if there could be a salary.

Fuller volunteered to cover drama for the January issue. She liked "O Best Waldo's poem, 'Ode To Beauty,'" but Thoreau was disappointed in poor rhyme and stereotyped lines. He complained because "A Winter's Walk," had been printed with errors.

Fuller sent the editor her translation of a French piece. The editor didn't like it. He asked Thoreau and Ellery Channing to offer opinions. Their opinions coincided with the editor's. Therefore, the editor rejected the article.

This jousting jarred the former editor. She thought it worthwhile to protest:

> I must scold you about that little translation on these grounds. When I had the care of the *Dial,* I put in what those connected with me liked, even when it did not well please myself, on this principle that I considered a magazine was meant to suit more than one class of minds....
>
> You go on a different principle; you would have everything in it good according to your taste, which is in my opinion, though admirable as far as it goes, far too narrow in its range. This is your principle; very well! I acquiesce, just as in our intercourse I do not expect you to do what I consider justice to many things I prize. So if I offered you anything for your *Dial* and you yourself did not like it, I am willing you should reject it.
>
> But if you are going to take any other person's judgment, beside your own, why should you not take mine? Why do you set some other person to read and judge that which pleases me...? [1]

The two editors again locked horns on the subject of friendship. Emerson criticized Fuller and Henry Hedge for not being exclusive enough in their friendships. He'd emphasized his point a year earlier in his journal, and had shown it to Fuller: "They (Fuller and Hedge) must have talent in their associates & so they find that, they forgive many defects. They do not require simplicity. I require genius &, if I find that, I do not need talent: and talent without genius gives me no pleasure."

Fuller retaliated: "I wish my tastes and sympathies still more expansive than they are, instead of more severe. Here we differ."

To appease she composed and sent a poem which ended:

> Send from thy skies some mild and genial breeze
> So warm the post-bound ride on my poor tree
> Their bloom though scanty, yet might chance to please
> Eyes less fastidious than thine must be: -
> I ask for alm on this December day -
> A debt will owe it should I e'er see May.

Emerson revealed the same nagging insecurities: "Every person of worth, man or woman, whom I see, gives me a pain as if I injured them, because of my incapacity to do them justice in the intercourse that passes between us. Two or more persons together deoxygenate the air, apathize and paralyze me."

In order to write her book about her summer travels, Fuller needed to read about adventurous souls who'd earlier risked Western expeditions. The materials could be found in a nearby institution whose doors had never been opened to women.

Years later biographer T. W. Higginson evoked the image: "I can well remember to have seen Miss Fuller sitting, day after day, under the covert gaze of the undergraduates who had never before looked upon a woman reading within those sacred precincts."

Fuller had invaded the newly built, gothic-style Gore Hall, Harvard's library, the pride and joy of all Cantabridgians because it had the best scholarly collection of any university in the U.S.A.* Visitors came from afar to use its superb resources. Fuller's breakthrough into these premises was a giant step for women.

The Dial, however, absorbed most of her time. Her article, "The

---

*Today Widener Library takes the place of Gore Hall.

Modern Drama," which was to dominate a third of the magazine, was not up to par. She was missing the deadline because her headaches and pains plagued. To her editor, she paraphrased Goethe: "'Every man has a dæmon, who is busy to confuse and limit his life'....With me, for weeks and months, the dæmon works his will."

The editor confirmed to her that her article was "an infinite refreshment," but apologized to John Sterling, the English poet whose work she was reviewing, that allowance had be made for a pen that was inadequate and rambled a little.

But without the pens of Fuller and Thoreau the editor would have been in dire trouble. Their scatching took up over half of the issue. Thoreau supplied selections from the religious books of the Buddhists of Nepal, "The Preaching of Buddha," per Emerson's suggestion, and extracts from the old English translation of the *Divine Pymander of Hermes Trisnegistus.* He translated the difficult Greek poet Pindar (a work he was supposed to have finished for the previous issue). He also handed over his November 29 Concord Lyceum lecture which was on poets Homer, Ossian, and Chaucer.

Otherwise Emerson had an article by Sam Ward on Dante and a poem by Cary Sturgis which had been too late for the previous issue, and pieces by Dana and Lane. To fill out the magazine Emerson inserted short pieces of his own, two poems, an essay, and almost no one noticed that the January *Dial* was published eight days late.

Horace Greeley re-printed from the *Dial* in his newspaper, per usual, but the *Boston Post* reporter wrote that "Mr. Dial" was "more ardent than ever in the cause of the elevation of the masses, being himself elevated on high-heeled boots." Also, Oliver Wendell Holmes' poem in *Graham's Magazine* satirized Emerson and the Transcendentalists as "deluded infants."

The new year, 1844, brought excitement with celebrations and the opening of the new railroad. (The Concord stagecoach went out of business.) In Boston William Henry Channing and friends organized the Convention of the Friends of Social Reform, and Elizabeth Peabody covered it for *The Dial.*

Fuller spent January alternately ill with headaches – one lasted four days – and attended concerts and parties. She wrote one long letter to Emerson, commemorating the demise of Waldo Jr. She copied a poem her brother Richard had written in memory of the boy. Wouldn't her friend send a copy of his poem, "Threnody."

Within two days Emerson responded: "Thou steadfast loving wise & dear friend, I am always astonished at thy faith & truth – I cannot tell whether thy be more divine or human. How have you adopted the life of your poor friend and the lives that are dear to him, so easily & with a love at once connote & prophetic, which delights & admonishes me at the same time. I am glad of guardian angels, but life is a treasure of soberer worth under the fanning of their wings." Along with a copy of "Threnody," he sent tickets to his next lecture, "The Young American."

She'd had a session with the clairvoyant, Anna Parsons. Would Emerson experience a night of mesmerism with her? She had given Anna Parsons one of his letters, and in a trance, Parsons had said: "If he could sympathize with himself, he could with every one." Fuller felt this was "a most refined expression of the truth."

Emerson declined the invitation.

Fuller attended Emerson's lecture.

What would his "Tutelar Genius" contribute to the last number of *The Dial*. He accepted her "Dialogue" and some poems she'd collected from Sam Ward.

To his "O much performing friend," he confessed that he would be "the spoiled child of luxury" when liberated from the *Dial*.

There were poems from Channing. Thoreau did more translations from Pindar and reviewed the *Herald of Freedom*, an abolitionist newspaper. Channing offered "The Youth of the Poet and the Painter." An essay on Kant came in from James Elliot Cabot, a Harvard law student. Emerson contributed his lectures, "The Tragic," and "The Young American," a book review, a poem, and supplied more "Ethnical Scriptures." He rejected Lydia Maria Child's poem, "Childhood." Charles Lane gave "Life in the Woods," and "Millennial Church," and Elizabeth Peabody gave "Fourierism."

Brook Farm was bending to Fourierism, thanks to Albert Brisbane, who was introducing the more socialistic concepts under the name of Association and promoting with a column in Horace Greeley's *New-York Daily Tribune*.

Charles Lane left Fruitlands because Bronson Alcott and wife would not live up to ideals of total sexual abstinence. Lane claimed marriage obstructed a wider humanity. Lane and his son joined the Shakers, the nearby community wherein sexes were separated and intercourse was ruled out.*

The Alcotts gave up on Fruitlands in January. When harvest time came round, Alcott and Lane had left to tour the country by foot in order to meet like-minded spirits and spread the faith of Transcendentalism. Abby, the daughters, and Lane's son did their best to bring in what harvest they could, but by the time cold January swung around the Alcotts (the only remaining members) had almost nothing to eat except barley. Alcott succumbed to depression, refused to eat, and became desperately sick. Abby nursed him back to health and they moved, temporarily, to share housing with friends.

It was the season for babies. On February 25 Horace Mann Jr. was born to Elizabeth Peabody's sister, Mary; on March 3 Nathaniel Hawthorne wrote on his dining room window: "On this day my daughter Una was born, while the trees are all glass chandeliers." The little one was named after the heroine in Spenser's *Faerie Queene.* Jane Tuckerman was happy with a pretty baby. And Ellen was still expecting.

Fuller laid plans for six Conversations in Providence, and she reviewed favorably Lydia Maria Child's *Letters from New York* which had been serialized in the *Boston Courier* and in Horace Greeley's *New-York Tribune.* Child was trying to "untie her Pegassus" from "the black ox" of abolitionism. No one bought her books since she'd committed the crime of publishing *An Appeal to that Class of Americans called Africans.* So in *Letters from New York* she cut out most of the abolition testimony and, since publishers refused to distribute her work, issued it emblazoned with her own name, at her own expense. It was an immediate success. The first edition sold out and there was a demand for ten more editions over the next seven years.

The warm-hearted, ever frugal Lydia Maria Child who used envelopes twice and never used a whole sheet of paper when she could fare with half, who typically said "What do I care whether you live in

---

*After returning to England in 1846, Lane later got married. (It was his second marriage). He had five more children and converted to Catholicism.

one room or six? – I want to know what your spirit is doing," had been in New York for two years as editor of the *National Anti-Slavery Standard*, with offices near *The Tribune*. Needing money, she and her husband had tried sugar beet farming in Northampton, Mass., without the use of slave labor, but had not profited. Editorial work would bring her financial solvency, she thought, and she had been determined to turn out an anti-slavery paper that even the most cultured would approve and read. She'd taken over the helm single-handedly, and by steering clear of conflict and by reporting hard news, she'd built a fine following and had doubled the readership Garrison had with *The Liberator*. But in time, leading abolitionists became disenchanted with her straight reporting and, also, she'd never really received her full salary. Furthermore, within two years her husband had gone bankrupt with the sugar beet farm. Within a short time Lydia Maria Child had eased her husband into the assistant editors' position, then into editor. She took the revolutionary step of separating from him and disentangling her financial accounts since all her earnings were going to pay off his debts, and she was devoting her time to free lancing.

Word came that the second distribution of the Fuller estate was to be made – each child received a small amount. Fuller spun into depression "of almost unbearable anguish." She wrote into her journal:

> Love, hope and self-esteem are to depart,
> Since the two first must never bless my heart.
> Oh God! at least the barren third restore
> Without that one gift I can bare no more.

Emerson dispensed advice in his journal. He could not sympathize with fine women who wanted marriage:

> Shall a virgin descend & marry below her? Does she not see that Nature may be trusted for completing her own circle? The true Virgin will raise herself by just degrees into a goddess admirable & helpful to all beholders. [2]

Emerson, who had served a "Presidential term" of four years with *The Dial*, read his last proof sheets.

In April every able-bodied Concordian helped to put out raging hot flames that flared up in the woods. Henry David Thoreau and Edward Hoar, brother of Elizabeth Hoar, had gone on a camping and boating trip up Concord River. They had stopped on banks with dry grass and kindled a fire to cook some fish they'd caught. The accident blackened one hundred acres.*

Emerson, who was now being called "The Old Squire" in Concord, told Thoreau that Thoreau's poetry did not live up to expectations. So Thoreau destroyed his remaining manuscripts.**

Sam Ward left business. He and Anna moved to a lovely country home in the Berkshires near Lenox, Mass.

Horace Greeley had planned a good review of the last *Dial,* but the one and only copy in the office was stolen. So he wrote a review hoping he remembered most of the issue.

The *Knickerbocker* reviewer typified public feeling when he said Transcendentalism could be called "Incomprehensibilityosityivityalityationmentnessism."

Probably none of the Transcendentalists realized that Emerson and Fuller had sent messages to each other in the pages of *The Dial.* If Lidian was aware, she remained quiet. His poem, "The Visit," – especially the last two lines – was directed to Margaret Fuller.

> If Love his moment overstay
> Hatred's swift repulsions play.[3]
> (See Appendix for complete poem.)

Posterity has no indication of Emerson's response when he read Fuller's farewell to him which he printed. In "Dialogue" Fuller wrote about two close friends who see each other for the first time after a period of years. Their conversation is about the death of friendship and love. She quoted the lines Emerson had spoken when first they

---

*Thoreau afterward wrote that he felt badly but pointed out that "the locomotive engine has since burned over all the same ground....I was no better employed than my townsmen." Sanborn wrote that fifty years later he saw the Concord woods destroyed by a fire sparked by the railroad.

** Later Thoreau repented his action. The Thoreau poetry we read today dates from his earlier years.

met: "O my friends, there are no friends!" (See Appendix for full account of this article.)

After the April *Dial* was published, Emerson rushed off to Boston. He hoped to meet Fuller. He wanted to make arrangements with a publisher for her travel book, *Summer on the Lakes*. But he searched for her in vain.

Fuller was in New York seeing, among other people, editor Horace Greeley, who suggested she expand her *Dial* article, "The Great Lawsuit," into book length. His wife, Mary, who'd attended some of Fuller's Conversations, brainstormed the idea that Fuller be employed as literary editor and critic on *The Tribune*. Though Greeley didn't always agree with Transcendentalists, he did like their ennobling spirit. He made a firm offer of five hundred dollars a year, including room and board at their farm at Turtle Bay.

Fuller knew full well that New Englanders would think a woman of her stature should never deign work in the vulgarity of New York, a citadel of iniquity.

First, she must finish *Summer on the Lakes*. Every day she worked in her room in Cambridge in front of a window which displayed a show of a blossoming cherry tree and an apple tree full of yellow birds. "Opposite me was Del Sarto's Madonna; behind me Silenus, holding in his arms the infant Pan."

On April 28 she held her last Conversation. The women presented her with lovely gifts along with her favorite flower, the heliotrope. Afterwards she spent a serene afternoon with Cary.

On her birthday, May 23, 1844, she finished the last line and celebrated by walking, as she'd often done, along the familiar calm green garden of groves at Mt. Auburn Cemetery.

That same day Ellen gave birth to a daughter. What more fitting name could be given to the newborn than Margaret Fuller Channing. Fuller wrote the new godmother, Cary Sturgis: "Girls are to have a better chance now I think."

The new father couldn't stand the baby's crying. He took off for the White Mountains in New Hampshire, after which he and his best friend began a walking sojourn through the Catskills.*

---

*William Ellery Channing and Henry David Thoreau.

The childless spinster continued correcting proof sheets that arrived "like crabbed old guardians, coming to tea every night." She sent her creation to Emerson who passed it along to Henry David Thoreau, who claimed not to like it.*

The old maid thought the ending was not right. "I ought to rewrite the Indian chapter, were there but time." There were problems with the printer's plates, and Sarah Clarke's etchings, which she wanted to include, could not be used.**

Fuller did not record her headaches in her private journal. What she recorded was when they did not occur. "I am not fitted to be loved and it pains me to have close dealings with those who do not love."

She wrote to Emerson – or to someone else; it is unclear – "What I want, the word I crave, I do not expect to hear from the lips of man.... I cannot help wishing, when I am with you, that some tones of the longed-for music could be vibrating in the air around us. But I will not be impatient again; for, though I am but as I am, I like not to feel the eyes I have loved averted."

Emerson had just returned from a second trip to the Shaker community. Their philosophy of celibacy was in direct opposition to Swedenborg and Fourier. Swedenborg delighted in "horrid cavernous regions where imps & dragons delighted themselves in all bestialities." Fourier said man exists to gratify his twelve passions.

Fourier had three levels of sexual order, the highest being Chastity, Virgins & bachelors; a lower order of husband & wife; a lower of free companions & harlots.

Loneliness enveloped Fuller, but reviews were out for *Summer on the Lakes* and the word "entertaining!" was used by the press more than once. Horace Greeley thought it "One of the clearest and most graphic delineations, ever given...unequalled, especially in its pictures of the Prairies and of the sunnier aspects of Pioneer Life."

Yet the publisher wound up with an overstock of copies.***

---

*Perhaps Fuller's travelogue, *Summer on the Lakes,* inspired Thoreau's *A Week on the Concord and Merrimack Rivers.*

**Sarah Clarke's etchings appeared in the second edition.

***Over seven hundred copies were finally sold. Fuller felt it had done better than she expected. Greeley later said, "It was too good to be widely and instantly popular."

July 4 was cold, hostile and painful. "I need a full, a godlike embrace from some sufficient love."

Fuller composed a poem and had someone draw an illustration. The ending lines were:

Patient serpent, circle round
Till in death my life is found,
Double form of godly prime
Holding the whole thought of time,
When the perfect two embrace,
Male and female, black and white
Soul is justified in space,
Dark made fruitful by the light,
And centered in the diamond Sun
Time, eternity, are one. [4]

(See Appendix for entire poem.)

In this state of being Fuller started expansion of "The Great Lawsuit: Man versus Men; Woman versus Women."

She took her manuscript to Concord. She wanted to walk the Sleepy Hollow paths again with her Waldo and Elizabeth Hoar, and be near her sister and infant niece, nicknamed "Greta." She arranged to stay with the Hawthornes at the Old Manse, the "old old house with its avenue of whispering trees."

Sophia Hawthorne was giving Greta one feeding each day because Ellen couldn't adequately nurse. Greta was adorable with soul eyes, but Una, (the Hawthorne child) now four months old, was the most beautiful, next to Waldo Jr.

On July 10, 1844 – as she was writing Emerson at the "White House" to please find her glasses, if he ventured a walk to the exact spot where they'd been sitting in Sleepy Hollow, as well as her shoes which she'd left under their entry table – Lidian gave birth to a son. Again the name Waldo was chosen, but preceded by Edward.

Fuller spent the next day at the Emersons and was touched to see little Edith kneeling by the baby's bed. Emerson seemed especially happy and read aloud his essay on Life. That night she wrote in her journal, "How beautiful, and full and grand. But oh, how cold. Nothing but Truth in the Universe, no love, and no various realities. Yet how foolish with me to be grieved at him for showing towards me what exists towards all."

He shared a page from his journal "which made me rather ashamed of ever expecting more. But lure me not again too near thee, fair Greek, I must keep steadily in mind what you really are."

He walked her to the Old Manse and they passed an hour there, after which she composed another poem:

> Last year the curtain rose to show
>   A scene of grandeur, hope, and joy
> Kindred with the deep heart glow
>   Of Ganymede, ambitious boy!
> This year, the drop-scene hides
>   The tender glories of the past
> Those dolphin-bearing, moondrawn tide,
>   Swelled along too full to last.
> Meantime the bard, with various skill
>   Tries its power to make us wait
> Patient though against our will,
>   The next act of dramatic Fate. [5]

Two afternoons later, while Ellen was visiting Sophia Hawthorne for Greta's daily nursing, S.M.F. gave her poem, along with a letter, to Henry David Thoreau (who'd been visiting) to deliver to R.W.E. She also enclosed the front page of *The New-York Daily Tribune* because the lead article was an excerpt of *Summer on the Lakes.* It could hardly compare to the excellence of his essays, but it was her own felt voice.

> Your excellence never shames me, nor chills my next effort, because it is of a kind wholly unattainable to me, in a walk where I shall never take a step. You are intellect, I am life. My flowers and stones however shabby interest me, because they stand for a great deal to me and would, I feel, have a hieroglyphical interest for those of like nature with me. Were I a Greek and an artist I would polish my marbles as you do, as it is, I shall be content whenever I am in a state of unimpeded energy and can sing at the top of my voice, I don't care what. Whatever is truly felt has some precious meaning. I derive a benefit from hearing your pieces as I should from walking in the portico of a temple, amid whose fair columns the air plays freely. From it I look out upon an azure sea. I accept the benignant influence. It will be eight years next week since I first came to stay in your house. How much of that influence have I there received! Disappointments have come but from a youthful ignorance in me which asked of you what was not in your nature to give. There will be little of this, if any, in future. Surely! these essays should be a sufficient protest against such illusions....
>
> Farewell, O Grecian Sage, though not my Oedipus....
>
> The Egyptians embodied the Sphinx as in body a lion, in countenance of calm human virgin beauty. It was reserved for the Greek to endow her with wings.... [6]

Leaving the Old Manse Fuller and Ellen walked to the Red Cottage where Ellery was in a disagreeable and churlish mood. Fuller left their abode in the evening for the "White House," where The Grecian Sage read her his essays, "The Nominalist" and "The Realist," and then walked The Winged Sphinx through the whispering trees, back to the Old Manse. He said he'd thought her book on women needed an introduction and he would write it.

The Winged Sphinx could marvel at his work, could benefit from it, but her own path was as valid.

The Grecian Sage passed along pages from the speech he was

preparing for a celebration at the Concord Lyceum of the anniversary of the emancipation of Negroes in the British West Indies.*

It was easy, he pointed out, to remain silent regarding the subject of slavery (as he had largely done). But "...The civility of no race can be perfect whilst another race is degraded....Man is one, and you cannot injure any member without a sympathetic injury to all the members."

Were The Winged Sphinx writing the paper, she would have enlarged these ideas to include women as an enslaved group whose wasted talents injured civilization...."for a society beats with one great heart."

She spent the next few days lazily at the Hawthorne's "hearing the wind blow through the old trees," and playing with Una who charmed Fuller by leaning her forehead on hers. She sewed, wrote letters, went on afternoon and moonlit boat rides and walks with Thoreau and Hawthorne whom she loved "in this sweet tender homely scene." In the cold and damp sleepy evenings the three sat, talked and read by a hanging lamp in the study.

On the 16th, she spent the day at the "White House," and Emerson read to her his essays, "The Poet," and "Manners." Fuller jotted in her journal: "So fine a tissue full of splendid things, yet a few burning simple words would better please."

Elizabeth Hoar came to the Old Manse to visit, and Richard arrived the next day, a sultry morning, ready to leave with Henry David Thoreau for the Berkshires.

Then, one cloudy day, The Greek declined to take a walk with The Sphinx because, he told her, he was mentally dispirited. The silver clouds blackened, and Fuller perceived her Waldo's encircling barriers as dark as the sky above, worse than those surrounding the British West Indian negroes, or queens who could not bring forth male heirs. Unmercifully, she charged him in prose and poetry with the most pitiable of plights:**

---

* This lecture had been arranged by Henry David Thoreau, now Curator of the Concord Lyceum, and also encouraged by Lidian and her sister, Lucy Brown.

** For the poem Fuller wrote to Emerson, "Gentle River," see Appendix.

> I always thought the saddest position in the world must be that of some regal dame to whom husband, court, kingdom, world, look in vain for an heir! She is only supposed to eat, breathe, move, think, nay! love, for the sake of this future blessing. The book of her life is only permitted for the sake of its appendix. Meanwhile she, perhaps, persists in living on as if her life by itself were of any consequence, is the mother of no Prince or has even the impertinence to encumber the kingdom with a parcel of Princesses, girls who must be "weel-tochered" to make them of any value.
>
> But what is this pathos compared to that perceptible in the situation of a Jove, under the masculine obligations of all-sufficinness, who rubs his forehead in vain to induce the Minerva-bearing head-ache! Alas! his brain remains tranquil, his fancy daughterless! Nature keeps on feeding him and putting him to sleep as if she thought the oak was of consequence, whether it bear the mistletoe or not!
>
> Heaven help thee, my Druid! if this blessed, brooding rainy day do not. It is a fine day for composition were it not in Concord. But I trow the fates which gave this place Concord took away the animating influences of Discord. Life here slumbers and steals on like the river. A very good place for a sage, but not for the lyrist or the orator.
>
> But, Waldo, how can you expect the Muse to come to you. She hovers near, I have seen her several times, especially near night. Sometimes she looks in at your study windows when she can get a chance, for they are almost always shut... [7]

How superlative if her words could jolt her excellent, slumbering friend. Only by encountering the tumult of life, could he be expected to create inspiring work of originality.

She stayed longer in Concord because Ellen wanted her to babysit while she visited their mother in Cambridge. This afforded Fuller quiet time to write and to attend Elizabeth Hoar's thirtieth birthday tea party at the Hawthornes.

One day Waldo visited her at the Red Cottage. He talked his "Transcendental fatalism," and Fuller noted in her journal: "I had as lief he would sit here and not say a word, but it would be impossible to make him understand that."

While applying heat and pressure to her head to alleviate headaches, she read books on Confucius, who had been alone amidst his disciples, had continued to learn, had claimed that only heaven understood him. Her curse of being alone was "nothing compared with that of those who have entered into those relations but not made them real. Who only seem husbands, wives and friends."

From Cary Sturgis came a note confessing she could not wear the ring Fuller had given her: "That we are to meet very deeply I am sure, if it were only for that hour's sleep, about which I have always felt as you do.... I am too homeless to be adorned with jewels...."

Another day she saw Waldo for a few minutes, a visit which precipitated these remarks in her journal: "Sweet Child – Great Sage – Undeveloped Man! I made some foolish critiques on his writings. What is the use?...He has his own powers."

More time with the Hawthornes, including boat rides and visits with Elizabeth Hoar, a ride with Lidian and another ride with Emerson's mother, periodic playing with radiant Una, and moments walking through the temples of Sleepy Hollow, lazing on a favorite rock "looking up to the sky through the old twisted broken trees."

Cary Sturgis arrived in a drenching rain to stay in the little room at the top of the Emerson's stairs. More black rainy days followed, the kind that Fuller loved because they turned the sod to violets.

Henry David Thoreau and Ellery Channing returned from the Catskills in time for Thoreau to ring the village bell to announce Emerson's lecture on the emancipation of negroes in the West Indies. Fuller and Sturgis attended it together, and Fuller later wrote: "Waldo's oration, O that was great, calm, sweet, fair. All aspects melted and rendered into one. So beautifully spoken too! It was a true happiness to hear him, tears came to my eyes....Yes, it is deeply tragic on the one side, my relation to him, but on the other, how noble how dear! If not an immortal relation, it makes me more immortal. Let me keep both sides duly balanced in my mind. Let me once know him and I shall not be disappointed. But he is hard to know, the subtle Greek!"

There were more good talks and walks, and rides; then Fuller returned to Cambridge where she received two notes from the Rock.

"O wise & kindest friend," he began. He was pressured with corrections on his second series of *Essays* and he'd no time to write the promised introduction for her book on Woman. "So wait for me a little."

As best as headaches would allow and despite noble sunsets, Fuller continued with the book and suggested to Sturgis that they vacation in harmony in September.

Then she heard from the young woman who had brought her morning coffee at Brook Farm. Georgiana Bruce was now a matron at Sing Sing in New York, and was working under the direction of a woman who was trying to maintain decent prison conditions for women inmates, most of whom were prostitutes. Fuller advised Bruce to take notes and to encourage the women to write journals.

September brought a steady pain between the eyebrows.

Cohasset beach with Sturgis for two or three days brought a change but, despite a worthy sea and a delightful room with a view, Fuller's thoughts centered on Sam Ward and she leafed through his papers while she weighed her decision to accept Greeley's offer in New York. Emerson took a negative attitude: "The muses have feet, to be sure, but it is an odd arrangement that selects them for the treadmill."

She had dreams of falling off rocks, of great spiders running over her, of Cary drowning, of the death of her mother – a dream she'd had since childhood.

Literary criticism was treacherous and insecure work. There'd been libel suits by the literary lion James Fenimore Cooper. Horace Greeley had lost one case. A critic had to be wary of expressing the absolute truth. There were no professional standards.

Yet here was new challenge. She'd reach a wider readership, and the money was good. Greeley would give her a free hand and he published the work of Catherine Sedgwick and Lydia Maria Child on the front page.

The Prospect Street house was sold and she moved her frail mother into a comfortable boarding house. Richard had received his Harvard degree and was in Greenfield, studying law with George Davis. She settled Lloyd in the Andover institution; it was the best arrangement. Arthur was fine in Illinois, Eugene in New Orleans working as a newspaperman, and William Henry was still struggling in business, but well with wife and children in Cincinnati.

She helped her sister by persuading Greeley to hire William Ellery Channing as assistant. Ellery left for New York where he found a roommate in Emerson's newest friend, William Tappan. Fuller took some flowers to Lidian in Concord. She saw Ellen, had tea at the Hawthorne's and talked long with Waldo. Now he and Hawthorne agreed that her New York plan showed promise.

"Farewell, Waldo!" she wrote in her journal.

> How sweet and sunny you looked.
> Winding hence afar.
> O mild and steady star
> The oft deserted stream
> Will ne'er forget thy silver beam! [8]

She dreamed how Cary was lost on the seashore, how her feet were rooted to one spot, how her red silk cloak kept falling off when she tried to save Cary, how Cary's dead body finally washed up on the beach. The next night she dreamed again of her mother's death. She woke up sobbing.

She scheduled another vacation with Cary, this time in the North River country, Fishkill Landing.

She felt positively rejuvenated. It was a golden Indian summer. She was encircled by majestic mountains that compelled her to quote Tennyson: "'From the brain of the purple mountain' flows forth cheer to my somewhat weary mind.... How I wish my birth had been cast among the sources of the streams, where the voice of hidden torrents is heard by night, and the eagle soars, and the thunder resounds in prolonged peals, and wise blue shadows fall like brooding wings across the valleys! Amid such scenes, I expand and feel at home."

She had a quiet house to live in, "with nobody's humor, but my own to consult." From her windows she could see the gorgeous hues of autumn over the tops of trees. Within a few minutes she could walk to the river shore. She delighted in watching "two thousand" sail boats, "each moving softly as an angel's thought," and the great steamers proceeding forward "like some noble discovery breaking in upon the habitual course of human events to inform and extend it." She delighted in the mountain paths, the lonely glens, the gurgling streams, the many-voiced water-falls, the fallen trees. She spent her days, sometimes harmoniously with Cary, sometimes alone, boating, swimming, walking, communing "with this fair grandeur."

On the days that it rained, she worked on the book. The nights, too, were for writing and reading in front of wood fires in her room. Both she and Cary dreamed that Waldo was there with them. She counted on and awaited his introduction. There were no headaches, no interruptions. She felt like a "free nun."

She must have been boating with Cary one fine day on the stately river amongst the sailboats and steamers or sitting on the river bank under a blue sky with fluffy white clouds watching the hearty captains command the movements of the boats when she thought of a few simple words to include in her book which would inspire women for centuries to come: "Let Them Be Sea Captains If They Will!"

For a time Christopher Cranch and William Henry Channing visited, and for three days William Ellery Channing came, declaring he was through working on *The Tribune* because as soon as he'd arrived at the office, Greeley had been called off on an assignment and had left Channing with such vague instructions that he was completely baffled. Fuller consoled until he vowed he'd return for another try.

Then the four of them each received similar packages in the mail. Together, in the same room at the same time, each opened a box to find a copy of Emerson's newly published second series of *Essays.* They "sat solemnly each with a copy in hand drawing our fates.... Suddenly we saw the comic of the scene and laughter was full if not loud."

Critics and the reading public were latching adjectives onto Emerson's book, such as "unintelligible," "mannered," "obscure," "contradictory," and "illogical." Thomas Carlyle was an exception. He admired "this solitary under the stars...who wrote a beautiful square bag of duck-shot."

In another postal delivery Georgiana Bruce sent the journals written by the women prisoners at Sing Sing. Fuller couldn't help but admire the sustaining faith that shown through the hard lives of these prostitutes. One, Satira, idealized herself "in the face of cruellest facts." Another, Eliza, told a story which revealed her fine instincts and ability to grow.

Fuller wanted to know what prostitutes thought about "that part of the sex who are reputed chaste?" Georgiana Bruce proffered the truth that the women inmates did not value chastity.

One weekend towards the end of October, Fuller and William Henry Channing arranged a short jaunt to Sing Sing. They took a boat across in a resplendent moonlight that magically transformed the prison buildings into a palace. Channing spent Saturday night at the chaplain's, and Fuller bedded down in a room at the prison.

Sunday morning Fuller talked with a group allowed out of their cells. "They were among the so called worst, but nothing could be more decorous than their conduct, and frank too. All passed much as in one of my Boston Classes. I told them I was writing about Woman and as my path had been a favoured one I wanted to ask some information....They seemed to reply in the same spirit in which I asked. Several however expressed a wish to see me alone, as they could then say all, and they could not bear to before one another."

William Henry Channing talked with the male convicts. Fuller attended his service at the prison chapel, and watched the men as they intently listened to his words: "Many were moved to tears, some I doubt not, to better life."

As they left Sing Sing in a storm that was beginning to clear, Fuller understood clearly the hypocrisy of the social structure. Both classes, respectable women and prostitutes, were dependent on men. Both groups used sex for economic well-being. The difference was that the so-called lower class was given realistic sexual information while the so-called higher class women were denied sexual information as they made life decisions. The higher class were geared towards fairytale-like conceptions of courtship and marriage, while prostitutes learned to be tough realists. This was a view traditionalists, including the radical Emerson, never saw, never absorbed.

Emerson's views followed the typical male mentality. Public brothels were "safety-valves" to defend "virtuous women from the occasional extravagances of desire in violent persons & to yield a resort of less danger to young men in the fury of passion."

Fuller, aware that her perspective would shock, determined to bring these issues into public view through her book.

The autumn leaves were floating to the ground when they returned to Fishkill Landing and Fuller dashed off persuasive notes to her wealthy Boston women friends to send books to Sing Sing. She began to formulate the idea that a half-way house was vital, a place where women could live after being discharged from prison, where training for new skills and opportunities could be developed.

On a fine November morning Fuller went for her customary walk with Emerson's second series of *Essays* under her arm. "I read it one day high up in the mountain side amid a bed of large loose stones that seemed only held together by the vines; wings rustled near.... The mice tuned their slender pipes beneath my pillow." Concentration was difficult. "Even Confuscious is too civic and limitary for out-door reading." So one morning she tried indoor reading: "The *Essays* did not chime with in-door life either."

Another morning, on November 10, Fuller took her customary exhilarating walk, then returned to her room, sat down and wrote continuously until nine in the evening. "Then I felt a delightful glow as if I had put a good deal of my true life in it, as if, suppose I went away now, the measure of my foot-print would be left on the earth."

She had finished the first final draft of her book, *Woman in the Nineteenth Century*.

Another revision would be required before it reached editors, but she needed time away from the material. To William Henry Channing in New York she wrote that she hoped the book would be in print by Christmas. Would he see Mr. Greeley about publishing it, or perhaps she would pay costs if not over a hundred fifty dollars for a thousand copies which she expected would sell over two or three years. She wished to retain full rights since in upcoming editions she would "make it constantly better."

Because William Ellery Channing was leaving Fishkill Landing, she gave him some books to deliver to Emerson, plus a poem she'd written that he could add to his file of her material. Also, she scribbled a note that she'd finished "the-never-to-be-sufficiently-talked-of" pamphlet, and had finished reading *Essays*. "It will be a companion through my life. In expression it seems far more adequate than the former volume, has more glow, more fusion." More she would say after she'd examined further. Greely published one of the essays, "Manners," in serial form in *The New-York Daily Tribune.*

By the next week, the river had turned "from blue to lead, the mountains from purple to gray" and all was "corpse-like cold."

Was it failure that awaited her in New York? The emptiness and the interminable loneliness.

The city of iniquity had a population of 370,000 and was considered by many to be a cultural and intellectual center, technologically advanced beyond the rest of the country. Only Bostonians thought Boston to be superior. The energy of the New York planners could be seen and felt. The street arrangement was simple and logical. There were handsome new buildings designed by distinguished architects, an admirable system of public transportation, Croton waterworks that supplied enough needed water, ferry service from Staten Island, a block long John Jacob Astor mansion that had running water above the first floor. A telegraph pole was coming to Broadway and Wall Street, and people talked about the possibly of a bridge to connect Brooklyn. There were philanthropic institutions encircled with flower beds – all of which connotated big money and power. But still the city boasted the unrest of poverty, the noisiness of riots and demonstrations. Irish and German immigrants flooded in. Omnibus drivers raced and swore. Newsboys gambled and fought. Cows, pigs, goats and vagrant dogs roamed the streets.

Horace Greeley's office symbolized the heart of Yankee political radicalism. Located across from City Hall on Nassau Street, The Tribune Building was a square five stories. The first floor was devoted to the general publication, and the editorial office comprised the third floor. The basement contained the press room with a steam-driven press (type setting and folding were by hand). There was a ware room at the rear of the second story with sleeping apartments for clerks.

Before launching *The New-York Daily Tribune* (named after the Roman tribunes) Greeley had had ten years of work credits in New York on several small newspapers, including a one-penny venture which failed within a month, and a quality literary and political weekly that achieved good circulation and fame but went under due to poor financial practices. In 1841 Greeley invested two thousand dollars to start another one-cent Whig political, reform and human interest paper. He competed with thirty established papers, the most threatening being the popular *The New-York Herald.* Almost overnight *The New-York Daily Tribune* was a success, however not without difficulties including a news carrier fight during which he had to bribe the boys, but after that he lucked out in finding partner Mr. Thomas McElrath, a wealthy lawyer with publishing background and good connections. Now, at two cents – Greeley had known from the beginning he couldn't produce a decent paper for one penny – with new type style and other enlargements, with fifty thousand readers, the paper turned out a solid daily account of social, political and cultural events.

Competition was so fierce that Greeley called the man over at the *Courier and Enquirer* an "escaped State Prison bird," and claimed William Cullen Bryant's *Evening Post* "would like to be an honest journal, if it could afford it." *The New York Express* was the "basest and paltriest of all possible journals."

An admitted work-acholic, Greeley bearishly dominated the *Tribune* office with his warm-hearted personality. Standing at his paper-cluttered pine desk, he wrote an average of four columns per day – sometimes his right arm would break out into boils. He peppered his front pages with a wide variety of progressive articles written by prominent persons, including some spectacular accounts of seduction, rape, crime and violence.

He advocated a great Reform. He promoted and raised funds for improvement of conditions for the poor, unemployed, ignorant and, of course, he took the abolitionist stance. He championed the able-bodied who would take initiative to work to rise above their inferior position.

These ideas were controversial because prevailing arguments claimed that poverty and destitution were caused by indolence and drunknenness. In his opinion, free discussion and open acknowledgement were avenues to progress, justice and equality. To this end he was interested in socialist experiments like Fourierism.

Greeley had the services of one indefatigable, black-bearded Henry Jarvis Raymond, a young Vermont college graduate who at first volunteered, but was so indispensable that when he was offered a paying job on another paper Greely assigned him eight dollars per week. In a couple of years time the *Courier and Enquirer* offered Raymond even more which left crusader Greeley with a position open.*

Margaret Fuller arrived on the first day of December to live with Greeley, his wife, and eight month-old son, Pickie, in the "entirely charming" country, about two miles out of the city.** (Cary returned to Massachusetts.)

To reach the farm you commuted about an hour on the Harlem omnibus through a winding road and three large swing-gates. The old-fashioned wooden house, the former country residence of a New York banker, had a wide piazza which faced the East River. Greeley called it "Castle Doleful," while Fuller was to quip that Mary kept it "in Castle Rankrent-style," meaning in as messy disarray as the descriptions of the disorganized castle in Maria Edgeworth's famous novel of the same name.

Petite, vivacious, strong-minded, Mary Greeley – or Molly as she was often called – a former school teacher, was grateful to open her doors to so stimulating a female companion.

She led Fuller to a delightful, peaceful room with windows that faced a box-bordered flower garden and shade and fruit trees. One could look down at gravel lanes which curved amidst brook, moss-covered rocks and overgrown shrubs and led to a steep bank and bay, where "the sails glide sidelong, seeming to greet the house as they sweep by." Beyond was Blackwell's Island.***

An acre of the property was devoted to the farm. Greeley hired a neighbor to work it. Greeley came to be known as a "dictionary farmer." A story circulated that he'd bought for six dollars a dozen Shanghai eggs which he'd deposited under a hen who hatched snapping turtles.

At first, as on Brook Farm, Fuller felt like a conservative. The Greeleys delighted in not having curtains, rugs or pictures. They were Grahamites, that is followers of the health reformer, Sylvester

---

*Henry Jarvis Raymod established *The New York Daily Times* seven years later.

**The Greeley farm was located on land that is today approximately 49-50th and 1st Avenue in New York City in the section known as Turtle Bay.

***Today it is Roosevelt Island, a community unto itself with high rise apartments, with access to Manhattan via overhead tram.

Graham; in fact, the Greeleys had met each other in a Graham boarding house where Greeley had gravitated after discovering his hand trembled after drinking coffee. Thus, they did not drink coffee, tea, cider, beer, or liquor. Fuller was a devotee of strong tea.

Greeley told this story: "Once, while we were still barely acquainted, when Margaret Fuller came to the breakfast-table with a very severe headache, I was tempted to attribute it to her strong potations of the Chinese leaf the night before. She told me quite frankly that she 'declined being lectured on the food or beverage she saw fit to take;' which was but reasonable in one who had arrived at her maturity of intellect and fixedness of habits....Though words were suppressed, looks and involuntary gestures could not so well be; and an utter divergency of views on this and kindred themes created a perceptible distance between us."

Nor did the Greeleys eat meat or use spice. Their diet consisted of beans, potatoes, boiled rice, puddings, bread made of unbolted flour, and butter. Only a bit of salt was used. Tobacco and opium were forbidden. Mary was (though seemingly frail) an iron-willed believer in hydropathy and she gave Pickie two baths a day and was extremely careful and proud to brush his golden locks. Medicine was disdained; Pickie was not vaccinated. As he was to grow, she would not permit haircuts or trousers, and she forbade him to see other children or adults who might use improper language or corrupt his mind.

There's a story regarding Fuller and Molly who was so against the killing of animals that, one day, when she saw Fuller wearing kid gloves, she shrieked out, "Skin of a beast, skin of a beast!" Margaret queried, "What do you wear?" Molly said, "Silk." Retalliated Margaret: "Entrails of a worm."

Greeley (according to biographers) succumbed with uncomplaining patience and endurance to all Molly's disagreeable temper, habits and opinions, her disinterest in her husband's greatest interest, politics. Married eight years, she had had two miscarriages and two stillbirths and this supposedly accounted for much irritability (according to biographers), and she'd shared the risks of his lean years. Greeley spent less and less time at home; divorce was out of consideration because Greeley believed that once married, always married. Still the two of them now possessed one wonderfully beautiful golden-haired, blue eyed son and his welfare was their aim of existence.

Fuller liked both the Greeley's and she loved Pickie even if he seemed to cry a great deal. She found she could quiet him as no one else could, and she became "Aunty Margaret," much to her delight.

Greeley was a man without leisure, nor did he want any. Greeley and Fuller met at breakfast; otherwise he was off for the day. His usual routine was to arrive at his New York office about noon and to return late at night. His was a pace Fuller could not hope to keep up with.

Greeley had been a child who grew up struggling during the country's economic depressions. Not caring how he looked, always shabby in the same suit, with a spectacled moon-face fringed with whiskers, frequently awkward and ill-mannered, child-like with his tow-colored hair and pale blue eyes, nor caring what he said or how he said it or that his voice grated so high pitched it was, so long as what he said was honest. He identified with the homespun, hard working, independent, farmers and wage-earners who were intelligent and often exploited.

Fuller recognized his abilities: "Outwardly unrefined, he has the refinement of true goodness." She felt they reached a mutual understanding. "He is, in his habits, a plebeian; in his heart, a noble man."

He thought her writing was fresh and vigorous, but it lacked clarity. More importantly, why couldn't she write faster? He could write ten columns to her one. Why did she succumb to headaches? He was always in his office, even when ill. "That the writer should wait for the flow of inspiration, or at least the recurrence of elasticity of spirits and relative health of body, will not seem unreasonable to the general reader; but to the inveterate hack-horse of the daily press, accustomed to write at any time, on any subject, and with a rapidity limited only by the physical ability to form the requisite pen-strokes, the notion of waiting for a brighter day, or a happier frame of mind, appears fantastic and absurd. He would as soon think of waiting for a change in the moon."

Fuller wrote her friends not to expect letters from her because she must now write articles with a speed to which she'd never been accustomed.

Her first article, printed a week after her arrival, was a review of Emerson's second series of *Essays*. It dominated two and a half left columns on the front page – considered the top placement. This was to be Fuller's accustomed spot.

If a writer were well known, Greeley would print the writers' full name or initials at the end of an article. But Fuller received special treatment. At the end of her article he set a large black ✳. All readers soon learned that this black ✳ which looked like a large star or asterisk signified the writing of Margaret Fuller. It was a technique that set her apart from all other writers.

Fuller did not hold back her opinion on Emerson's book. She charged that Emerson was "a father of the country," but a "shepherd" to which the people do not listen. "These essays, it has been justly said, tire like a string of mosaics or a house built of medals....Here is undoubtedly the man of ideas, but we want the ideal man also; want the heart and genius of human life to interpret it, and here our satisfaction is not so perfect. We doubt this friend raised himself too early to the perpendicular and did not lie along the ground long enough to hear the secret whispers of our parent life."

Right away Greeley challenged her with the assignment of covering the city institutions on Blackwell's Island which included an almshouse, an insane asylum, a hospital, an orphanage, and a penitentiary. William Henry Channing agreed to accompany her, one visit per week, and she began to made arrangements, while turning out some trifles, on "Thanksgiving," "Christmas," and "New Year's Day."

Meanwhile, she found it amusing that when she went into the *Tribune* office her brother-in-law, William Ellery Channing, began to offer her fatherly advice concerning her new career in journalism. Luckily, she could avoid most such conversations with him since she managed to do most of her writing at the farm.

The farm turned out to be a stimulating environment because people of all walks of life breezed in and out. Most were new types but, as she wrote Sam and Anna Ward, she began "to find the level here."

During Christmas holiday, while word came from Boston that Maria White married James Russel Lowell, *Woman in the Nineteenth Century* went into printer's ink – without Emerson's promised introduction since it had never materialized.

On Christmas Day Fuller returned to Sing Sing to wish a happy Christmas to the women prisoners in the chapel. In a speech she articulated the strengths she knew to be in each of them and councilled them to be true to themselves and to prepare to take a better direction when released. She saw the prisoners "As women like myself, save that they are victims of wrong and misfortune."

Greeley expected one or two critical reviews to come from her pen per week plus one on social concerns, and she alternately praised and faulted the poetry of Elizabeth Barrett in *A Drama of Exile: And Other Poems.* She could not "hesitate to rank her, in vigor and nobleness of conception, depth of spiritual experience, and command of classic allusion, above any female writer the world has yet known." But Miss Barrett was "deficient in plastic energy," was "diffuse." Forced. "There is often a want of pliant and glowing life."

At the same time proofing of *Woman in the Nineteenth Century* commanded her attention despite influenza. Cary's letter reported sleigh rides, concerts, and good weeks, but her emotional level remained low: "I do not know what the Powers above or below have in store for me, but certainly not to walk on Terra Firma." Fuller suggested New York. Cary declined.

Everyone began to talk about a haunting poem which had appeared in the *Evening Mirror* on January 29, 1845 and re-appeared in the February *American Whig Review.* Entitled "The Raven," it was written by the author of the popular short stories, "The Murders in the Rue Morgue" and "The Gold Bug" (which had won a prize). This writer was going to be co-editor, with Charles Briggs, of the *Broadway Journal,* a weekly review of the arts. He had been in New York less than a year, had previously been mixed up in literary feuds in Philadelphia, had significantly increased the circulations of the journals for which he'd written, had lectured on poetry, and was now working fourteen or fifteen hours per day in his office just down the street from the *Tribune.* He was happily married and lived with both wife and mother-in-law. He didn't drink, because he would suffer terrifying bouts of meanness and anger. In him Fuller recognized a mind she could respect. His name was Edgar Allen Poe.

Americans were so horrified by the actions of a scandalous French woman writer that many felt contaminated if they even touched a cover of her novels. This woman had separated from husband and children. She lived with men, including the composer Chopin. She wore men's clothing.

But Fuller told her shocked American readers in her front page article that George Sand was a woman who faced the truth.

George Sand had fallen into an unfair situation. "She found herself impatient of deception and loudly called by passion....She protested; she examined; she assailed. She hacked into the roots of things."

Sand's stories "all promise far more than they perform....Sometimes she plies the oar; sometimes she drifts. But what greatness she has is genuine; there is no tinsel of any kind, no drapery carefully adjusted or chosen gesture about her."

Some nights, to avoid the late night commute after concerts and theatre, Fuller stayed in the city with Lydia Maria Child, who lived with her husband David Lee Child on East Third St. Child was not particularly sympathetic to Transcendentalists, but Fuller was a remarkable mind and she was sorry they lived so far apart. These two top journalists, considered eccentrics by "good" society, could talk social reform and religion for hours.

Child was intensely interested in *Woman in the Nineteenth Century* and Fuller gave her the proof sheets to read. Instantly, Child wrote a pre-publication review for the *Boston Courier*, lauding the book as one of the prophetic signs of the age. Fuller was "a woman of more vigorous intellect and comprehensive thought than any other" in the country, though her writing was deficient in clarity and her mind "is like a room too much crowded with furniture" because she had too great profusion of materials.

The radical Child called Fuller a bold heroine because she dared to speak plainly "on subjects which men generally do not wish to have spoken of and of which women dare not speak." She would not have had such courage.

During a heavy snowstorm hot red flames licked up the Tribune building and its contents in February 1845. A clerk had kindled a fire in a stove in the basement press room. Two assistants asleep in the ware room on the second floor barely saved themselves by jumping out of the windows. Insurance covered about ten thousand dollars; the loss added up to about eighteen thousand dollars. It was enough to dishearten the staunchest person, but Horace Greeley arranged to borrow the presses of other city papers. He temporarily moved to his old offices on Ann Street, and turned out a paper the very next day, inserting the story of the fire on a quiet inside page. He promised his readers the building would be rebuilt and the *Tribune* would suffer only new type and many improvements.*

The black star appeared regularly. In "Children's Books," Fuller pointed out the need for challenging children's minds rather than merely offering them "baby-talk with malice prepence." She reviewed a book on Animal Magnetism or mesmerism and admitted to her belief in the methodology. "Cheap Postage Bill" was a plea for the individual to retain soul and vitality despite commercial pressures. "The Excellence of Goodness," was a defence of Theodore Parker, who was mixed in a controversy over minister's rights.

After a Valentine's Day dancing party at Bloomingdale Asylum for the Insane, Fuller cried out on the front page, "Let no one dare to call another mad who is not himself willing to rank in the same class for every perversion and fault of judgment."

The next month she attacked George B. Cheever's views in *A Defence of Capital Punishment.* She challenged a readership response and got it in the form of a March 7 *Morning Courier and New-York Enquirer* article signed by one "T.L." This "T.L." supposed the *Tribune's* "fair correspondent" had written the article but he would credit the editor because a "fair correspondent," foolish and vain, could not possibly be his proper and legitimate adversary.

Retaliated Fuller: "We had always supposed that, in the field of literature, the meeting was not between man and woman, but between mind and mind."

Fuller's expose on city institutions dominated the front page on March 19, entitled: "Our City Charities: Visit to Bellevue Alms House, to the Farm School, the Asylum for the Insane, and Penitentiary on Blackwell's Island."

At the Almshouse Fuller found more kindness and cleanliness than she'd expected, but there were no activities and the poor had "the most vagrant, degraded air." At the Farm School, the orphans were given care and basic reading and writing, but there was a void

---

*The Tribune building was rebuilt.

when it came to character development and skills preparatory to earning a livelihood. There were twice as many inmates at the Asylum for the Insane as accommodations and the mentally disturbed crouched in corners, with "no heart for hope." The Penitentiary was "one of the gloomiest scenes that deforms the great metropolis." Administrators had no compassion. They slanted regulations to their own advantage. The turn-over in personnel, even on the top level, was enormous. The inmates were provided with only the barest of physical necessities. There was no attempt to meet emotional needs. Over half the prisoners were women, but guards were male. The women's hospital was little better. Fuller advocated furnishing books, giving instruction, opening eyes to self-respect and offering new hope. The practices at Bloomingdale Asylum in Harlem with its lectures, amusements, and light work could serve as model.

Fuller, Lydia Maria Child, William Henry Channing toured the labyrinthine alleys and streets of the Five Points district, which were frightening even to the police, and she structured articles calling for rehabilitative houses. She never felt she was a social activator, but hoped her pen would pressure awareness and stimulate public authorities to do something. Greeley cheered her on.

Increasingly, the doors of the New York social scene were opening. She received invitations to attend the literary salons of Anna Lynch, a lovely dark-eyed woman who'd edited an anthology and whose critiques and poetry were occasionally published in various newspapers. At Lynch's home on Waverly Place the best of New York authors, artists, critics, wits were seen, including Edgar Allen Poe who recited "The Raven" and other eloquent monologues by reading from long slips of blue paper. There was also Frances Sargent Osgood who fascinated Poe, N. P. Willis, Charles F. Briggs, Evert Duyckinck, editor at Wiley & Putnam, Anna Cora Mowatt, who wrote, staged and produced her own play, *Fashion*, Fenno Hoffman, Elizabeth Oakes Smith, novelist and poet, Catherine Sedgwick, writer, Horace Greeley, Christopher Cranch, Parke Godwin.

Fuller liked Anna Lynch but found her salon full of literary gossip not especially enjoyable. Generally, she kept close to Turtle Bay and visited only long-time established friends, such as Marcus Spring and wife, Rebecca, in Brooklyn, Sam and Anna Ward who now lived in

New York, William Henry and Lucy Channing, and Christopher Cranch and his wife.

Then many of her Boston friends came to the farm, Elizabeth Hoar, Charles Newcomb, and Eliza Farrar. Among new acquaintances was a Danish novelist and revolutionary, Harro Harring, to whom she lent five hundred dollars to publish his novel. (Emerson claimed this was a mistake; Harring was a half author whom no charity could relieve. It turned out Emerson was right, but Fuller's response was: "It will not do to calculate too closely with the affectionate human impulse....We must consent to make many mistakes, or we should move too slow to help our brothers much.") Greeley was amazed that so many people came to see her and that they would with "almost oriental adoration" confide in her. Her marvellous talent for impersonation and mimicry gave cause for his facetious comment that, if she had wanted, she could have been the first actress of the century.

Fuller's migraines continued, as well as the pains in her back. Mary Greeley recommended a French mesmerist/hypnotist, Dr. Theodore Leger, to whom Fuller often went.* Like Cary, she still felt "no real hold on life...I seem a wandering Intelligence, driven from spot to spot, that I may learn all secrets, and fulfill a circle of knowledge."

Woman in the Nineteenth Century was off the presses and selling out during the same month that Thoreau began to whack a protest against civilization in Concord. Thoreau borrowed an axe from Bronson Alcott to cut down some white pine on Emerson's land to build a hut along the shores of Walden Pond. "I must walk toward Oregon, and not to Europe," he wrote in an essay. As one biographer pointed out, he walked two miles East of Concord.

Fuller's protest in *Woman in the Nineteenth Century* was the same heartfelt cry for self-reliance that the Transcendentalists were advocating – except Fuller spoke to the totality of the human race, a human race that included women. Self-reliance in men was looked upon with admiration, but in women it was a trait seen as a fault.

---

*Dr. Theodore Leger authored *Animal Magnetism; or, Psychodunamy* (New York, 1846), which Fuller reviewed.

"Let every arbitrary barrier be thrown down!" she called out. Women should be as free and equal as are men in all their privileges.

Her premise is that all souls are equal before God. Women, as well as men, have the right as persons to grow, as intellects to discern. All people have the right to an equal education, to legal and political equality which implied the right to vote.

She opened with the words: "Frailty, thy name is woman." Too long had the sex been restricted. In order to break out, women needed to say "Nay" to their subjugation to the wills of men, "Nay" to their "second place." Women needed to learn to love themselves in order to absorb the full ramifications of this principle. "They are taught to learn their rule from without, not to unfold it from within....The difficulty is to get them to the point from which they shall naturally develop self-respect, and learn self-help."

Women ought to learn from each other; schools and institutions for women should be run by women because women best perceived women's perspectives. "Ascertain the true destiny of Woman; give her legitimate hopes and a standard within herself; marriage and all other relations will by degrees be harmonized with these....What women needs is not as a woman to act or rule, but as a nature to grow, as an intellect to discern, as a soul to live freely and unimpeded, to unfold such powers as were given her when we left our common home."

Fuller analyzed relationships and roles of both sexes throughout the centuries in mythology, literature and history. She quoted from contemporary thinkers. She showed that early on every man had grown up under woman's power. Then he had educated her more as a servant than a daughter and eventually found himself a king without a queen. She proclaimed that choice and control of life were within women's god-given rights. Women should not be defined by their relationships – or their lack of relationships – to men.

Women did not want power over men, she pointed out. Women wanted "the birthright of every being capable of receiving it – the freedom, the religious, the intelligent freedom of the universe to use its means, to learn its secret, as far as Nature has enabled them, with God alone for their guide and their judge."

Women did not wish to be men or to take men's place. "The

intellect, no more than the sense of hearing, is to be cultivated merely not that Woman may be a more valuable companion to Man, but because the Power who gave a power, by its mere existence signifies that it must be brought out toward perfection."

Marriage should not presume to lead to a trap of servitude for women. Marriage could be an equal sharing and caring partnership between two persons, a pilgrimage towards a common shrine.

Unmarried women need not be social parasites or socially stigmatized. Unmarried persons, unfettered, could give their time and talents to the broad scale of humanity.

Men would benefit as well as women, she wrote. She called for legal protection so that women could own and inherit property, could keep their own earnings, could claim rights over shiftless and abusive husbands. She advocated equal employment opportunities and made a plea for women to seek and develop their own innate gifts and strengths.

Fuller recognized that there were masculine qualities in women and feminine qualities in men.

> It is so true that a woman may be in love with a woman and a man with a man....Male and female represent the two sides of the great radical dualism. But, in fact, they are perpetually passing into one another. Fluid hardens to solid, solid rushes to fluid. There is no wholly masculine man, no purely feminine woman.
>
> History jeers at the attempts of physiologists to bind great original laws by the forms which flow from them. They make a rule; they say from observation what can and cannot be. In vain! Nature provides exceptions to every rule. She sends women to battle, and sets Hercules spinning; she enables women to bear immense burdens, cold, and frost; she enables the man, who feels maternal love, to nourish his infant like a mother....
>
> Man partakes of the feminine in the Apollo, Woman of the masculine as Minerva. [9]

In a day when unmarried women in polite circles were not supposed to know that sex or prostitution existed, Fuller attacked the myth that men had uncontrollable sexual natures. She denounced the double standard. While many men, including legislators, argued that prostitution was a necessary ingredient in the world, Fuller denounced the practice. Neither were the systems of polygamy, the harem, or mistresses acceptable. Envisioning a great moral law, Fuller challenged men to live up to the same high standards asked of women.

She chastised the social tradition that concealed vice and sexual facts from women.

> "You," say the men (to women), "must frown upon vice; you must decline the attentions of the corrupt; you must not submit to the will of your husband when it seems to you unworthy, but give the laws in marriage, and redeem it from its present sensual and mental pollutions."
>
> This seems to us hard. Men have, indeed, been, for more than a hundred years, rating women for countenancing vice. But, at the same time, they have carefully hid from them its nature, so that the preference often shown by women for bad men arises rather from a confused idea that they are bold and adventurous, acquainted with regions which women are forbidden to explore, and the curiosity that ensue, than a corrupt heart in the woman. As to marriage, it has been inculcated on women, for centuries, that men have not only stronger passions than they, but of a sort that it would be shameful for them to share or even understand; that, therefore, they must "confide in their husbands," that is, submit implicitly to their will; that the least appearance of coldness or withdrawal, from whatever cause, in the wife is wicked, because liable to turn her husband's thoughts to illicit indulgence; for a man is so constituted that he must indulge his passions or die! [10]

Women of intellect, like Mary Wolstonecraft and George Sand, were caught in unfair vices. Fuller argued that such women should never be so trapped.

Aligning her view with Emerson's thought, Fuller hailed celibacy as a possible temporary solution to the conflicts involved in attempting to achieve self-reliance, for only by becoming a Unit – she even picked up on Emerson's terms – could one achieve Union:

> If any individual live too much in relations, so that he becomes a stranger to the resources of his own nature, he falls, after a while, into a distraction, or imbecility, from which he can only be cured by a time of isolation, which gives the renovating fountains time to rise up. With a society it is the same. Many minds, deprived of the traditionary or instinctive means of passing a cheerful existence, must find help in self-impulse, or perish. It is therefore that, while any elevation, in the view of union, is to be hailed with joy, we shall not decline celibacy as the great fact of the time. It is one from which no vow, no arrangement, can at present save a thinking mind. For now the rowers are pausing on their oars; they wait a change before they can pull together. All tends to illustrate the thought of a wise contemporary.* Union is only possible to those who are units. To be fit for relations in time, souls, whether of Man or Woman, must be able to do without them in the spirit.[11]

Fuller declared that human beings, both men and women, needed to pause, to restructure, to commence a learning process, in order to maturate true worthy relationships.

Thus, Fuller blazoned the taboo subject of sex into public limelight. She gave validity and credibility to women's position and problems. She wrapped the issues into a philosophy or theory that people could speak to.

Hers was the first American book length treatise on feminism in America. The edition of a thousand copies sold out within a week to the booksellers, and she received an eighty-five dollar profit when she had not expected a penny.

Acclaimed by some as the Great Book of the Age, it was "hot," a "must" for newspapers and magazines to snap up and review.

Immediately, Fuller was attacked as an old maid who couldn't know anything about sex – and if she did, her words as well as her person could hardly be respected.

An anonymous reviewer for the *Broadway Journal* wrote: "Her most direct writing is on a subject no virtuous woman can treat justly. No woman is a true woman who is not wife and mother."

Lydia Maria Child, who knew that this reviewer was editor Charles

---

*Fuller here refers to wise contemporary Ralph Waldo Emerson.

Briggs, responded: "Briggs, though a man of considerable smartness, knows no more how to judge of Margaret Fuller, than I do of Goethe's theory of colors, which I never read. His ideas of women are at least a century behind the age." These things needed to be said, "and she is brave to do it....she is a great woman and no mistake."

Another reviewer suggested that "Women cannot command." He emphasized that "The privilege of voting is one which they (women) could not exercise if it were taken for granted."

Other opinions surfaced, most expected.

"It is natural law that man is the head of the woman."

"To make sailors of women and milliners of men is to have imperfect sailors and imperfect milliners."

In short, woman's role was so high that to make her equal would be a demotion.

Two editors praised. Horace Greeley: "I think this can hardly have failed to make a deep impression on the mind of every thoughtful reader, as the production of an original, virorous, and earnest mind."

William Cullen Bryant, editor of *The Evening Post*, wrote: "Although its language is pretty strong, the thoughts it puts forth are so important that we should rejoice to know it read by every man and woman in America."

Some of Fuller's friends had mixed opinions and reservations. Cary Sturgis admired but was troubled: "It makes me sad that it is necessary such a book should be written but since it is so it cannot but do good to lift the veil as you have done!"

Henry David Thoreau was now able to retaliate for Fuller's rejection of his work: "It is too good not to be better even."

Ellery Channing recommended it "without qualification."

Sophia Ripley found it "rich in all good things."

The Sophia Hawthorne types disagreed. Sophia to her mother: "If she were married truly she would no longer be puzzled about the rights of woman.... Home, I think, is the great arena for women, and there, I am sure, she can wield a power which no king or conqueror can cope with."

Sophia's mother responded: "Seems to me I could have written on the very same subjects, and set forth as strongly what rights yet belonged to woman which were not granted her, and yet have used language less offensive to delicacy. A consistent Christian woman will be exactly what Margaret would have woman to be; and a consistently religious man would readily award to her every rightful advantage. I believe that woman must wait till the lion shall lie down with the lamb, before she can hope to be the friend and companion of man.... The book has great faults....yet it is full of noble thoughts and high aspirations."

John Neal wrote to Fuller that she had not been radical enough. "You go for thought – I for action.... I go for the whip and spur – I go for making people get up and take care of themselves....You might as well educate slaves – and still keep them in bondage."

Copies of Fuller's book circulated overseas and into the Western frontier. She felt complimented that it was quickly pirated in London.*

While Greeley was enthusiastic, he thought there was one flaw: "So long as a lady shall deem herself in need of some gentleman's arm to conduct her properly out of a dining or ball-room – so long as she shall consider it dangerous or unbecoming to walk half a mile alone by night – I cannot see how the 'Woman's Rights' theory is ever to be anything more than a logically defensible abstraction."

Whenever she waited for him to open a door for her, he would exclaim, "Let Them Be Sea Captains If They Will!"

At a party Fuller met a blue-eyed blond Jew from Hamburg, Germany, James Nathan. He was immediately attracted to a woman who commanded everyone's attention. Fuller was magnetized to a gentle, sensitive literary man whose family heritage encompassed two nationalities she admired.

He'd come to the United States in 1830 and had alternately been a commission agent and a banker. Currently, he was employed on Wall Street, not far from *The Tribune* office, in an import house, but wanted to be a writer. He asked her to visit an exhibit of a diorama of Jerusalem. Fuller had a poem she wanted to read to him; then she invited him to Handel's *Messiah*. Then they attended operas together.

---

*It was pirated that year, 1845, and again in 1850. During the year prior to the publication of *Woman in the Nineteenth Century*, 1844, Horace Greeley had been promoting the establishment of international copyright law as vital to the growth of national literature.

Fuller gave him a copy of *Woman in the Nineteenth Century*, which he asked to keep. He admired her retelling of the story of married love in Xenophon's *Cyropaedia*. Soon they were walking the paths and shoreline of the Greeley farm with his Newfoundland puppy bounding alongside.

He spoke to her on a personal, intimate level as no one else had. Not an intellect, he was poetic, admiring of Fuller's vast knowledge. He told her about his youth, about immigrating to the United States, how he hoped to travel and write. He played the guitar and sang German songs, and enjoyed gathering spring flowers. He told her he could read her thoughts; he knew her mind, could even control her thoughts by his will. She willingly listened.

Soon it became clear that Greeley did not approve, perhaps because he suspected Nathan of using Fuller or because he thought Fuller was seeing in Nathan more than he had to offer.

Fuller advocated an open relationship, but she wanted to keep their meetings quiet, even secret, since she did not particularly want to irritate Greeley. Nathan, too, preferred no gossip. From his Wall Street office Nathan began to send a messenger with notes to Fuller's *Tribune* office. Then Fuller responded with notes. They saw each other in out-of-the-way coffee shops, bookstores, parks, at Lydia Maria Child's apartment – often after Fuller had her spinal visits at Dr. Leger's, after church. Few people knew the extent of the relationship.* Fuller managed to write Nathan many flowerly, confiding, counselling, intimate, soul-searching notes, some of which seem embarrassing to twentieth century readers.**

She was melodramatically passionate and femininely dependent – she probably decided not to use her intellect. Experience had proven that intellect did not inflame romance.

She addressed some letters *Mein Liebster*. He egged her on.

Once he likened himself to the cherry tree by her window. He also cautioned that she did not fully understand him. Once he responded: "You must be a fool, little girl." She'd been called names, but never had she been called "foolish" or a "little girl."

---

* Clark and Channing published the *Memoirs* with no mention of Nathan.

** Julia Ward Howe saw to their publication: *The Love-Letters of Margaret Fuller, 1845-1846.)*

Eventually, he was prevented from writing as many notes as he liked because of office interruptions. It was just as difficult at his place of residence because often someone was around.

Within a short time, Fuller discovered there was another woman. He explained; then he told her he had a lower and a higher instinct that she was not aware of.

She reacted with unbelief. Hurt, she continued the relationship as before, fully trusting he now reciprocated her strong feelings.

One night, having misread her meaning in an especially emotionally charged letter, he made sexual advances. Fuller was repulsed. She wrote that this effected "as violent a change as the famous three days of Paris." (She referred to the July Revolution of 1830 when the citizen king, Louis-Phillipe, came into power.) Fuller could not reconcile herself "to your having such thoughts, and just when you had induced me to trust you so absolutely." She was so striken that she walked the streets, grief piercing her eyes. "It was all not right between me and one I had chosen"..."Nature was stript of her charms."

The next morning she woke with a headache but, as she was walking through the city, a change of feeling overcame her and she saw "a gleam of hope that the earth-stain might be washed quite away." It was suicide, she wrote him, to do otherwise. "I felt the force of kindred draw me and that things could not be other than they were and are. Since they could be so let them; I cannot do other than love and most deeply trust you, and will drink the bitter part of the cup with patience."

She pleaded for him to rise above "lower" natures and "in that faith" to "kill" her with truth, "if it be needed, but never give me less...but if you cannot tell me all the truth, always, at least tell me absolute truth. The child, even when its nurse has herself given it a blow, comes to throw itself into her arms for consolation, for it only the more feels the nearness of the relation."

She asked him to destroy her letters.

He asked that she not "grieve or be weary" – or too sensitive. She should not let disappointments over-affect her.

She wrote that his hand had removed "at last the veil from my eyes." It was "herself who had caused all the ill." She had flattered herself, had let self-love, pride, and distrust creep upon her. She would "not say forget these days; we cannot and we need not," but they would recede in the distance.

They would be "Gods good children."

He had been sick, so had she. She had been *ueberspannt*, the German word for strained, but now she was *seligkeit*, in bliss. He had sent a letter which gave her repose, "the power of sleep," which she'd not lately had.

She told him she spent much time where they had been together on the rocks by the East River.

He left his guitar in her keeping at the Greeley Farm. He wrote of some clouds in his daily life.

She would "have no time to blame myself. Yet forgive if I have done amiss, forgive when I shall do amiss. And I too 'do not understand'!!...Am I to repel thee? O no! it will not be so; I shall understand yet; have patience." The relationship was deep and "we cannot get out of the labyrinth."

He failed to come when she most wished to see him.

Yet still she felt he "read her so deeply." Once she wrote, "I long to be human, but divinely human....Are you my guardian to domesticate me in the body, and attach it more firmly to the earth?"

He told her he was going to Europe, but he would return.

He continued long recitations, which caused her torment. She retaliated with "I wish much I were strong that I might be a fit companion for you and not weigh upon your motions."

He retaliated that she must rest.

She desired to rest, but could not since he roused in her so many thoughts and feelings. She twice repeated that she wanted to burn or destroy her letters to him.

He needed a travel fund; he needed letters of introduction. Fuller wrote Boston friends for contributions, and obtained a letter of introduction from her and Emerson's friend, George Bancroft, who was now secretary of the Navy under President Polk. She promised to encourage Greeley to print his travel articles which she would personally edit.

They had a farewell parting on Sunday, June 1. They walked down through the woodsy paths of the Greeley Farm and sat on the rocks next to the waves that gently tapped at their feet.

He told her she should "become related from within."

She told him she wished to do all she could for him. She wished to trust him. He was the only one she'd ever found who could feel the minute shades of her life.

He gave her a gift of a white veil and told her she must promise not to guess why he had given it to her. He gave her his dog, Josey, and would leave his guitar. She could take care of them while he was gone. And he gave her a memorandum book. He apologized again for not writing notes to her more often, but promised he would write fully to her from Europe, if she would write to him.

So in her first letter she sent him a pen and hoped "it will pen down some fine thoughts and passages of life during your journeyings."

She felt "alone among the multitude of men."

Once she saw Elizabeth Hoar and Cary Sturgis who were visiting William and Susan Emerson on Staten Island, but most of her time was spent in reading and reviewing, turning out pieces advocating better treatment and conditions for the underprivileged, asking for donations of furniture, books and clothes for a refuge home for women.

Frederick Douglass in his autobiography was "simple, true, coherent, and warm with genuine feeling."* William Lloyd Garrison, who had written the introduction, was "Like a man who has been in the habit of screaming himself hoarse to make the deaf hear."

Irish immigrants, commonly seen by Americans as problems, should be welcomed into the country as a valuable element. She continued to encourage Americans to broaden their outlook by reading European writers, such as George Sand, Honoré de Balzac, Alfred Tennyson, Elizabeth Barrett and Robert Browning.

The days passed.

In Boston James Freeman Clarke was appointed Secretary of the American Unitarian Association. The ungainly independent Theodore Parker was moving into a rented, plain four-story building, the old Melodeon on Washington St. where his Twenty-Eighth Congregational Society, the largest in the city, flocked to hear him preach what some called irreligion.

---

* Narrative of the *Life of Frederick Douglass, an American Slave.*

In Concord Lidian suggested in June that Cary Sturgis board at the Emerson home, but Sturgis turned the offer down because "Lidian would find me more trouble than she anticipates; for I am always unpunctual & at meal-times & so unsocial at all times."

William Ellery Channing bought twenty acres on the slope of Punkawtasset Hill, a mile from the village, and started building a permanent cottage for his family. He'd helped Thoreau with his Walden Pond hut, but it was not finished when Thoreau moved in on July 4, 1845, a date carefully chosen because Concordians were dually celebrating Independence Day and the U. S. support of the Mexican War. It was also the day Texas voted annexation to the United States. Thoreau's move was an act of non-violent dissent.

The loafer's isolation signified "holy living." He would "Do what nobody else can do for you," and "Omit to do anything else." He could spend his days recording the movements of birds, weather, sun and moon, studying ferns, toads, and beavers.

The non-conformist non-violent female wage earner moved into a wider political arena with her "Fourth of July" article, a protest. She called for one or a few geniuses of independent thought who would lead the country away from violence and falsehood. America had talent, energy, and achievement, but her beloved country consented to extend slavery, had an insatiate love of wealth and power. "No heart we think, can beat to-day with one pulse of genuine, noble joy." Her solution lay in the restorative power of the individual who led a deeply private life, from whose integrity and faith would spring a rebirth of the nation:

> If nations go astray, the narrow path may always be found and followed by the individual man. It is hard, hard indeed, when politics and trade are mixed up with evils so mighty that he scarcely dares touch them for fear of being defiled....It is not easy, it is very hard just now to realize the blessings of Independence. For what is Independence if it does not lead to Freedom?...Things are still in that state where ten just men may save the city....The safety of the country must lie in a few such men – men who have achieved the genuine independence, independence of wrong, of violence, of falsehood.

> We want individuals to whom all eyes may turn as an example of the practicability of virtue....We want deeply rooted characters, who cannot be moved by flattery, by fear, even by hope, for they work in faith. The opportunity for such men is great, they will not be burnt at the stake in their prime for bearing witness to the truth, yet they will be tested most severely in their adherence to it. There is nothing to hinder them from learning what is true and best, no physical tortures will be inflicted on them for expressing it. Let men feel that in private lives, more than in public measures must the salvation of the country lie....The private lives from which the public must spring, as the verdure of the plain from the fountains of the hills....The Country needs to be born again; she is polluted with the lust of power, the lust of gain. She needs Fathers good enough to be God-fathers – men who will stand sponsors at the baptism with all they possess, with all the goodness they can cherish and all the wisdom they can win, to lead this child the way she should go....Let (men)....take the narrow, thorny path where Integrity leads, though with no prouder emblem than the dove. He may there find the needed remedy which...shall have power to restore.... [12]

The nation's leading critic had a brief and enjoyable literary tangle with the nation's other leading critic, Edgar Allen Poe. These two saw little of each other except at Anna Lynch's parties. But as soon as one offered a new book, the other served the witty, honest review.

Poe, who called Transcendentalists "Frogpondians" because they lived in foggy, misty Boston, had lambasted Fuller's grammar and use of words in *Woman in the Nineteenth Century*, so when his *Tales* appeared, Fuller returned the compliment: "Even the failures are those of an intellect of strong fibre and well-chosen aims."

Letters from Nathan were few and far between, though she sent across the seas long, frequent and intimate pages. When he did respond she found his words tender and elevated.

She found a new delightful place on the East River, near where they'd been together, where forty feet of rocks made a wall and where the water came up to her feet, and she swam there and watched sailboats glide by, and wrote Nathan that it was a pity he would never see it.

She swayed back and forth on the hammock with the endearing

and affectionate Pickie, telling him stories and teaching him words, and she walked along the river with Nathan's dog, Josey, tossing sticks into the water for him to run after. Sometimes she and the Greeleys would take Pickie to Rockaway Beach to dip into the ocean and play in the sand until moonlight.

The Greeleys talked about selling the Farm and moving into the city. Perhaps this would appease Molly whose erratic moods made life difficult even for Fuller.

The sunlit days and the moonlit nights on the beautiful acreage passed "in the most tranquil sweetness," but to her beloved Cary alone did she confide her ceaseless frustration: "I believe this true life will never with me take form in art or literature."

She had moments when she felt her constant striving to achieve was useless. She envisioned that instead of being a genius, she would be a mother of a genius – a son. Cary would understand: "Do you remember that night last summer when we fell asleep on the bed and we were like Elizabeth and Mary.* I have often wanted to express what appeared to me that night but could not, only every day I understand it better. I feel profoundly bound with you and hope you wear my ring."

To her readers, Fuller underscored the womanly lot by choosing to review two books, *The Duty of American Women,* written by either Lucy Stone or Catherine Beecher – no one seemed to know who the author was since both disclaimed the honor – and *The Wrongs of American Women,* written by Charles Burdett. On the front page: "Hundreds and thousands must step out of that hallowed domestic sphere, with no choice but to work or steal, or belong to men, not as wives, but as the wretched slaves of sensuality."

Fuller foresaw a nobler day when the work of both men and women, of whatever occupation, "may be done with a wisdom, a mutual understanding and respect unknown at present."

---

*Scholow Robert Hudspeth explains this passage: Elisabeth, mother of John the Baptist, and her cousin Mary, mother of Jesus: "And Mary arose in those days, and went into the hill country with haste, into a city of Juda; And entered into the house of Zacharias, and saluted Elisabeth. And it came to pass, that, when Elisabeth heard the salutation of Mary, the babe leaped in her womb; and Elisabeth was filled with the Holy Ghost" (Luke I:39-41) Fuller also observed the names of the two queens Mary Stuart and Elizabeth I.

By August she had praised, edited and seen to it that Nathan's travel articles were printed in the *Tribune.* She sent the printed copies, urged him to write more, and asked for his picture. Then she did not hear from him for five weeks. His next letter was "cold and scanty." She answered by praising his articles, by advising him to add his personal observations, and to write from Paris and Rome. He sent her a book about Petrarch which she'd already read, and a new batch of articles which she eased into print during the balmy days of September. She sent protestations of her love. She told her "brother of the soul" that her head ached, she faulted herself for being too sensitive, for not having enough noble faith. She'd received an invitation to go to Europe, but it might never work out. She "kept her promise and never thought why you gave me that token," the white veil, but she often looked at it and felt, "I am with thee, my brother, and repeat the holy vows I made when thy generous soul was most made known to mine...and thy voice in its rich persuasive tones answers to the vow." She would never, now without him, go to the spot on the rocks where they had parted.

In mid-October Fuller went to Concord, but Waldo "was with Plato, I was with the instincts." He was working on a lecture series, "The Uses of Great Men."

"Of the Hawthorne tree, I saw the blossom, lovely still, but not so much so as in first bud."

The Hawthornes were leaving Paradise. Dr. Samuel Ripley and his wife, Sarah Alden Bradford Ripley, were retiring from Waltham and they wanted to return to the Old Manse, the house where he'd been born and raised. Thus, Adam and Eve were forced to drink a farewell cup of tea. With daughter, Una, and a newly written *Mosses From An Old Manse,* they reluctantly travelled to Salem where Hawthorne had a new job as Surveyor at the Custom House.

Ellen and Ellery were settled into a new house which was pretty and convenient, though a distance from Concord. Ellen, pregnant again, was without help and lonely much of the time. Ellery seemed unhappy.

Cary spent Thanksgiving days with the Emersons. Sending Fuller a gift of tea, she expressed her great love of life, yet the purposelessness of a life devoid of love: "I wish I could dance the Tarantualla - dance myself to death. I stretch forth my arms for life & large-winged psyches fly into them & flutter away over my head...."

Waldo called Cary his comrade, but he worked every day and she roamed the surrounding areas and sketched. They smiled at each other over basins of sand & soup. She sat by the blazing fire with Elizabeth Hoar who was troubled because Cary had "quit the course of Providence." Cary thought that Elizabeth should not judge. "The bird, who is abandoned in its nest, has a right to fly away."

Charles Newcomb and Ellery came to dine. "Would it not be funny to see all these fine spiritualists eating plum pudding together, with a lady abbess preciding?" Cary felt like an aged grandmother beside Newcomb: "He seems only a wild child who likes to see tops whirl round & chase fairies in a dark wood."

Because the dilapidated Greeley Farmhouse was impossible to heat and because the situation between husband and wife strained, Fuller thought it best to move into the heart of New York City to a boarding house on Warren Street.* Within walking distance to the *Tribune* office, she could also better enjoy the artistic life – picture galleries, theatres, Philharmonic concerts, German operas, violin concerts, lectures. Still, the people in her social circle did not touch her deeply, and the image of James Nathan was always with her.

Though Nathan said he'd write and wanted letters from her as he arrived in every city, he now claimed he "would not be able to keep up a real correspondence" with her while absent.

Fuller reminded him that he no longer was interrupted by office duties, so when would he find time to write.

Would he return to the States in the spring. She wanted to think he needed her, as she needed him, yet his letter puzzled her. She inclined not to write again unless they could have a full correspondence. Her head ached and she felt sick. Would he promise not to tell his family when he saw them in Hamburg of their personal alliance because, if they were to part, it should be a private matter between the two of them. Did he wish copies of the *Tribune* with his published articles.

---

*Interestingly, a short while later Edgar Allen Poe moved into Turtle Bay to the farmhouse of Mrs. John C. Miller.

Word came that Emerson had refused an invitation to speak at the New Bedford lyceum because the group had voted against accepting colored people as members. In a *Tribune* article Fuller lauded him.

Edgar Allen Poe had now realized his dream and was sole editor of the *Broadway Journal.* He had borrowed from everyone he knew, including Horace Greeley. He worked night and day.

In *The Raven and Other Poems* Poe made introductory statements about his failings and limitations. So when Fuller reviewed the book, she parried that she could hardly injure her rival. Fragmentary, his work did leave "something to desire or demand." His poem, "The Raven" (to which she gave less than a dozen words), was a "rare and finished specimen," but "the productions in this volume indicate a power to do something far better."

Greeley handed Fuller Longfellows' *Poems* to review. She tried to graciously bow out. "The Raven" (as Poe was now known) had fanned Longfellow's popularity by charging in the *Mirror* that "Midnight Mass for the Dying Year" was outrageously similar to Tennyson's "The Death of the Old Year" – in other words Poe accused Tennyson of plagiarism.

Poe and Charles Briggs (then editor of the *Broadway Journal*) fired their heavy artillery over weeks, probably to stir publicity and circulation. Other journalists had jumped into the foray. A rift ensued in the friendship of Poe and Longfellow's friend, James Russell Lowell.

Fuller thoroughly agreed with Poe, but she had no interest in adding to the wounds, especially since Longfellow was now an American institution. But Greeley could never find time to write a critique, and handed the assignment back to her. Reluctantly and cautiously, she loaded her gun:

> We must confess to a coolness toward Mr. Longfellow, in consequence of the exaggerated praises that have been bestowed upon him. When we see a person of moderate powers receive honors which should be reserved for the highest, we feel somewhat like assailing him and taking from him the crown which should be reserved for grander brows....
>
> Mr. Longfellow has been accused of plagiarism. We have been surprised that any one should have been anxious to fasten special charges

> of this kind upon him, when we had supposed it so obvious that the greater part of his mental stores were derived from the work of others. He has no style of his own growing out of his own experiences and observation of nature. Nature with him, whether human or external, is always seen through the windows of literature. [13]

Public reaction to this review was loud.

Poe lauded it as one of the best in America.

Suddenly, Fuller became one of Poe's lead subjects.

Not being able to pay his sixty-day notes, he'd lost the *Broadway Journal* and was free lancing. He was doing a series of sketches of the New York literati – most of whom he met at Anna Lynch's salon – for America's most popular women's magazine, *Godey's Lady's Book*.

Straight off he did a piece on Fuller. He publicly disavowed being the anonymous *Broadway Journal* author who'd criticized *Woman in the Nineteenth Century*. The villain had been his associate, Charles Briggs. Fuller's writing was "the very best with which I am acquainted... singularly piquant, vivid, terse, bold, luminous..." in spite of "frequent unjustifiable Carlyleisms, such as that of writing sentences which are no sentences...."

How could "The Raven" not resist other vitriolic qualifications: "...her personal character and her printed book are merely one and the same thing....Her acts are bookish, and her books are less thoughts than acts."

About *Woman in the Nineteenth Century*: "...a book few women in the country could have written, and no woman in the country would have published with the exception of Margaret Fuller....The essay is nervous, forcible, thoughtful, suggestive, brilliant, and to a certain extent scholarlike...but I must say that the conclusions reached are only in part my own. Not that they are too bold, by any means – too novel, too startling, or too dangerous in their consequences, but that in their attainment too many premises have been distorted, and too many analogical inferences left altogether out of sight....Miss Fuller has erred, too, through her own excessive subjectiveness. She judges woman by the heart and intellect of Miss Fuller, but there are not more than one or two dozen Miss Fullers on the whole face of the earth."

New York was expensive for "a poor scribe." Aunt Mary Rotch sent Fuller an 1846 New Year's gift of money for wine in the belief that it would help headache, but Fuller turned a portion of it into a new dress. It was a disadvantage not to pay calls or attend parties because the white gloves, the visiting cards, and carriage hire couldn't be afforded – which is why Lydia Maria Child stayed home.

In Concord carpet mending was an absorbing occupation that kept Lidian at home. Emerson laughed at her, but she was fastidious. She was happy because she thought she was saving Emerson money.

Emerson kept busy with Plato and his representative men for his Boston Lyceum lecture series. His selections included Swedenborg (the mystic), Montaigne (the skeptic), Shakespeare (the poet), Napoleon (the man of the world), Goethe (the writer). The qualities and ideas of these men represented traits to be emulated – and some not to be emulated. He also had his volume of poems, and was trying to negotiate with the New York editor at Wiley and Putnam, Evert A. Duyckinck, who was offering unsatisfactory terms.

In New York, Duyckninck saw Fuller at Lynch's salons and asked her to collect her best *Dial* and *Tribune* articles for a book. Fuller reminded him that Emerson was disenchanted with his offer for his volume of poems.

She was also considering how she could improve *Woman in the Nineteenth Century* for a second edition. In the *Tribune* she was giving high praise to Kentucky abolitionist/editor Cassius M. Clay, writing sketches on the rich and the poor, reviewing books, some with "monstrous" premises.

Her liberal Quaker philanthropist friends, Marcus and Rebecca Spring, kept talking about their trip to Europe to survey political and social conditions.

Then, unexpectedly, Ellery Channing asked Fuller to raise money for him to go to Europe. Would Horace Greeley assign him the position of foreign correspondent?

Fuller was jolted. It was obvious Ellery was going to Europe because Ellen was having another baby. Apparently, Ellen agreed to this trip. Fuller wrote her brother Richard that it was "a little too much for my nerves."

Fuller could understand Channing's frustration, but what "cuts me," she wrote Cary, "is Ellen's being thrown on the sympathies of my poor mother. She is to be the one sacrificed & after so many years of steady effort I find my poor little schemes for her peace all baffled."

It was another obstacle to her own trip to Europe. She was making arrangements with Horace Greeley to become a free-lance foreign correspondent herself.

She did nothing to help Channing, but he raised money from Emerson, Sturgis, Ward and others; however, he was not hired as Greeley's foreign correspondent.

A rose from Shelly's grave came in the mail from Nathan and Fuller responded that she would probably be going to Europe in August. What should she do with his dog Josey – the Greeleys were moving into the city. Did he plan to return to the States before she left for Europe. She continued with proofing her collection of articles and turning out critical reviews, including one on Michel Angelo Titmarsh, the pseudonym Thackeray used for *Notes of a Journey from Cornhill to Grand Cairo.*

There was no response from Nathan.

Fuller's mother, frail and weak, insisted on living with and helping Ellen. Arthur had only one year left in Harvard Divinity School. Fuller was dispensing advice to Richard on his love life; he was well launched as a lawyer. William was settled, Eugene settled, to be married during the summer.

If Fuller returned to the States in debt, what did it matter. She would earn her fare by serving as ward to the Spring's son. Horace Greeley would pay one hundred and twenty dollars for fifteen travel articles.

Meanwhile, Brook Farm, turning Fourierist, was in financial straits. Marcus Spring generously donated money. George Ripley tried to whip up interest with his newspaper, *The Harbinger.* Visitors and applicants increased, but others lost interest. Enrollment at the school dropped. Debt remained.

To top off the difficulties in March a devastating fire broke out in the wooden Phalanstery, three quarters built and paid for, almost two years under construction. It was to have been three stories high, over one hundred rooms, a dining room seating three hundred persons, parlors, reading rooms, reception rooms, assembly hall, kitchen, bakery, and suites for about one hundred fifty persons. The fire, noticed during a dance at the Hive, was caused by a faulty basement chimney. Farmers and neighbors fought in vain to extinguish. There was no insurance because the building had not yet been in use.

Alcott made an effort to sell Fruitlands, and Thoreau spent a night in jail. Thoreau had refused to pay his poll tax, which indirectly supported the Mexican War, the annexation of Texas, and the extension of slavery.*

There is a story that Emerson visited Thoreau in jail and questioned, "Why are you here, Henry?"

Thoreau replied, "Why are you not here?"**

An anonymous donor paid the bill and Thoreau was released.

Freed from jail, Thoreau went huckleberrying.

Europe did not stimulate William Ellery Channing. He came home to behold a new daughter named Carolyn Sturgis Channing. What he gave birth to was a new volume, *Conversations in Rome.*

Herman Melville's *Typee* came across Fuller's desk. She reviewed the novel as entertaining; the author had a power "to make pretty and spirited pictures."

At the end of April Fuller had given up her relatively expensive boarding house in order to save money for her European trip. She spent a few days at the Greeley Farm and walked over the ground where she and Nathan had walked. She felt a desire for him that amounted to anguish. She wrote him she was moving to a boarding

---

*Thoreau wrote, "For my own part, I should not like to think that I ever rely on the protection of the State. But, if I deny the authority of the State when it presents its tax-bill, it will soon take and waste all my property, and so harass me and my children without end. This is hard. This makes it impossible for a man to live honestly and at the same time comfortably in outward respects. It will not be worth the while to accumulate property that would be sure to go again. You must hire or squat somewhere, and raise but a small crop, and eat that soon. You must live within yourself, and depend upon yourself, always tucked up and ready for a start, and not have many affairs."

** Emerson paid taxes without protest. He once wrote: "A man cannot free himself by any self-denying ordinances, neither by water nor potatoes, nor by violent passivities, by refusing to swear, refusing to pay taxes, by going to jail, or by taking another's crop or squatting on his land – By none of these ways can he free himself; no, nor by paying his debts with money; only by obedience to his own genius; only by the freest activity in the way constitutional to him, does an angel seem to rise & lead him by the hand out of all wards of the prison."

house in Brooklyn Heights until the first of August when she would sail for England, Scotland, and Hamburg – she hoped to see him. The Greeleys could not keep his dog, Josey, and what should be done.

Hawthorne's *Mosses from an Old Manse* was published and Fuller opened her review by admitting that she had sat for ten minutes, "pen in hand, thinking what we can possibly say about this book that will not be either superfluous or impertinent." His stories had charm but "still brood over his page the genius of revery and the nonchalance of Nature, rather than the ardent earnestness of the human soul.... Hawthorne does not lay bare the mysteries of our being...."

Throughout the summer she continued collecting her best articles for the permanent book form. She realized while selecting her pages on "Modern British Poets," "The Modern Drama," "Lives of the Great Composers," plus her criticisms on Elizabeth Barrett, Robert Browning, Milton, James MacIntosh, and Washington Allston, that what was lacking was an evaluation of the contemporary American literary scene. Her effort was one of her greatest successes.

Many people would object to her subject, she conceded in "American Literature; Its Position in the Present Time, and Prospects for the Future,"* because no American literature existed. Imitations or reflections of European works or thoughts could not be identified as American literature. What suited Great Britain "does not suit a mixed race that has abundant opportunity to develop a genius, wide and full as our rivers, flowery, luxuriant and impassioned as our vast prairies, rooted in strength as the rocks on which the Puritan fathers landed. That such a genius is to rise and work in this hemisphere we are confident."

The birth of a truly original American literature could not occur until "this nation shall attain sufficient moral and intellectual dignity to prize moral and intellectual, no less highly than political, freedom, not till the physical resources of the country being explored, all its regions studded with towns, broken by the plow, netted together by railways and telegraph lines...." Without these ideals "a national

---

*Her brother Arthur later reprinted it, without alteration, in *Art, Literature, and the Drama.*

literature must end in abortions like the monster of Frankenstein...soulless...revolting..."

Progress could occur only if individuals felt the need to be sternly sincere:

> Truth is the nursing mother of genius. No man can be absolutely true to himself, eschewing cant, compromise, servile imitation, and complaisance, without becoming original, for there is in every creature a fountain of life which, if not choked back by stones and other dead rubbish, will create a fresh atmosphere, and bring to life fresh beauty. And it is the same with the nation as with the individual man. [14]

Nothing was needed but preparation of the soil, and freedom in the atmosphere, for the ripening of a new and golden harvest.

It was impossible for ninety-nine out of a hundred people to use the pen because they could not afford the time they needed to prepare themselves. "No man of genius writes for money; but it is essential to the free use of his powers, that he should be able to disembarrass his life from care and perplexity....The state of things gets worse and worse, as less and less is offered in pecuniary meed for works demanding great devotion of time and labour."

The publisher was enforced to view writing as a business. "This will not do!" Fuller cried. "The public must learn how to cherish the nobler and rarer plants, and to plant the aloe, able to wait a hundred years for its bloom."

Fuller suggested a convention of authors examine the problem and seek solutions.

Boldly surveying the contemporary American literary scene, she covered the historians, William Hickling Prescott, George Bancroft, and the philosophers, Dr. William Ellery Channing, and Ralph Waldo Emerson, who "has a very different mind....He is a man of ideas, and deals with causes rather than effects....His influence does not yet extend over a wide space; he is too far beyond his place and time, to be felt at once or in full, but it searches deep, and yearly widens its circles. He is a harbinger of the better day."

The novelist Washington Irving "has drawn the scenes amid which his youth was spent in their primitive lineaments, with all the charms of his graceful jocund humor." No one could occupy his niche.

As to James Fennimore Cooper, the first enthusiasm "having subsided, we remember more his faults than his merits. Neither...the baldness of his plots, shallowness of thought, and poverty in the presentation of character, should make us forget the grandeur and originality of his sea-sketches, nor the redemption from oblivion of our forest-scenery, and the noble romance of the hunter-pioneer's life."

Hawthorne was the best writer of the day, in a similar range with Irving, but touching more points and discerning more deeply.

William Cullen Bryant stood alone on the list of poets, however "His range is not great, nor his genius fertile....But his poetry is purely the language of his inmost nature...and the atmosphere of his verse refreshes and composes the mind, like leaving the highway to enter some green, lovely, fragrant wood."

Longfellow was "artificial and imitative...The ethical part of his writing has a hollow, second-hand sound. He has, however, elegance, a love of the beautiful....His verse breathes at times much sweetness...."

She could not "say as much for James Russell Lowell, who...is absolutely wanting in the true spirit and tone of poesy....His great facility at versification has enabled him to fill the ear with a copious stream of pleasant sound. But his verse is stereotyped; his thought sounds no depth, and posterity will not remember him."

Emerson she ranked as a poet highest "in melody, in subtle beauty of thought and expression," but his poems were "mostly philosophical, which is not the truest kind of poetry. They want the simple force of nature and passion, and, while they charm the ear and interest the mind, fail to wake far-off echoes in the heart. The imagery wears a symbolical air, and serves rather as illustration, than to delight us by fresh and glowing forms of life."

A rave review went to William Ellery Channing: "Some of the purest tones of the lyre are his, the finest inspiration as to the feelings and passions of men, deep spiritual insight, and an entire originality..." Unfortunately he was frequently unfinished and obscure and had a habit of forcing words.

The country's journals, she thought, breathed the day's life force, "rich, bold, various," which had basically been her vision for *The Dial.*

"Newspaper writing is next door to conversation, and should be conducted on the same principles...."

Truth was the standard for the professional journalist. "Writers have nothing to do but to love truth fervently, seek justice according to their ability, and then express what is in the mind; they have nothing to do with consequences, God will take care of those. The want of such noble courage, such faith in the power of truth and good desire, paralyze mind greatly in this country. Publishers are afraid; authors are afraid; and if a worthy resistance is not made by religious souls, there is danger that all the light will soon be put under bushels, lest some wind should waft from it a spark that may kindle dangerous fire."

Among those who faulted her essay was, not surprisingly, James Russell Lowell.

Edgar Allen Poe was also angry. She'd not mentioned him. Therefore, Poe called Fuller "grossly dishonest," and wrote to a friend: "...she is an ill-tempered and very inconsistent old maid – avoid her."

She contacted the award-winning photographer, John Plumbe, who had developed a new process for the daguerreotype and had galleries in Boston and New York. She had her picture processed and presented to family and friends.

From Hamburg James Nathan answered. Wouldn't she help with the publication of a collection of his *Tribune* articles? His London agent, Mr. Delf, might have one of his manuscripts to give to her. Perhaps he'd be in London himself. Maybe they could meet in Hamburg.

She talked with Greeley, then wrote Nathan it would be best if his book were published in London before he tried the United States. She packed up his articles and promised to send them to Delf as soon as she arrived in Liverpool.

She left for Boston from where she would sail. She spent a few days with her family. She invited Cary to visit her in Europe, and she visited the Emersons in Concord.

Emerson was receiving reaction to his *Poems.** Friendly critics were

---

*Published at his own expense, with Monroe & Co. as printers. Three-fourths of all American poetry was published at the expense of the poet.

anointing the book with such compliments as superior, original and exceeding refined...one of the finest poets of the time. Unfriendly reviewers used such phraseology as, "more height than breadth," "hymns to the devil," and "fantastic nonsense."

Emerson gave Fuller a letter of introduction to Thomas Carlyle – she was "an exotic from New England, a foreigner from some more sultry and expansive clime." And she carried letters of introduction to Elizabeth Barrett and Robert Browning, and Eckermann.

America's first female foreign correspondent set sail for Europe aboard a modern ship, *The Cambria*, on August 1, 1846.

In order to meet anticipated costs, the thirty-six year-old world figure borrowed from Anna and Sam Ward, the Springs and other friends.

The day she sailed, her page one "Farewell to New York" informed Americans that she went to Europe to "behold the wonders of art, and the temples of old religion. But I shall see no forms of beauty and majesty beyond what my Country is capable of producing..." Two great stages of progress were ahead for America: education for the cultivation of individual minds, and the improvement of conditions for women.

Lidian had gone to Plymouth. Her husband could not join her in Plymouth. He had hoped Plymouth air, freedom and friends "would scatter every cloud for three weeks at least." He still found "black" in the letters of "O sincere, true, high-principled one!"

To her communication, his response opened: "I do not hear that there is any reply to be made today to your bandbox letter of last evening, unless it be a suggestion from myself, that you will sharpen your pencil-point a very little...."

The Cambria, equipped with both sail and steam, crossed the Atlantic in record time, ten days and sixteen hours.

On September 23 an excerpt from "American Literature" dominated the left front page columns of *The Tribune* – and Greeley inserted Fuller's name under the title.

A week later Fuller's new series, "Things and Thoughts in Europe" dominated four and a half of the six front page columns. She had the title of Foreign Correspondent. Her familiar ✳ re-appeared at the end of her article.

Europe was ripening for revolution. Napoleon was dead and the French Revolution was a war of the past. Now ruthless aristocratic powers had taken hold. The industrial revolution had created a new class, a working class. The overproduction of factories had given rise to unemployment and economic depression. Moreover, there had been two years of ruined crops, plus a widespread potato disease that was causing famine. Anger was fermenting in England, France, Italy.

Fuller and the Springs travelled through England via coach, canal boat and railroad. They were at once struck by the poverty and destitution. In the industrialized textile manufacturing cities, wages were low. People crowded into cellars and tenements. Garbage cluttered the streets. The air was foul with coal smoke. The travellers walked through neighborhoods where there were problems of malnutrition, drunkenness, prostitution and disease. In Liverpool Fuller was mobbed by squalid and shameless beggars. She talked to Manchester mill girls, dulled, hopeless of a better future. "One has to grow insensible or die daily," she wrote to her readers.

In Ambleside she visited Harriet Martineau for over a week, but there seemed no way to resume their former close relationship. She called on William Wordsworth at Rydal Mount but was disappointed. He was seventy-six, an elderly Tory. They travelled in stages to Edinburgh where Fuller had a good talk with Thomas de Quincy, the famed opium eater. Here she contacted Nathan's London agent, Mr. Delf, as to Nathan's whereabouts and soon received a letter from Nathan which she excitedly tore open to read that he planned to marry a Hamburg woman.

A forgery, she thought at first; then a headache forced her to bed. Later she addressed her reply in care of Delf. Yes, she'd received his letter but she was too busy with travelling and social engagements to give it more than a moment's thought.

They toured the highlands in a coach and Fuller got lost overnight atop the mountain Ben Lomond which she'd climbed on foot with Marcus Spring. At dawn shephards found her, exhausted and distraught.

On to Glasgow; there was even worse poverty. "Help must be sought by other means than words," she told Americans.

They stopped at Sir Walter Scott's home in Abbotsford where

Fuller was to note that the grass grew green everywhere except on Scott's grave.

York and its cathedral was ruined by Protestantism, and Warwick Castle and Stratford, overtaken by tourists. At Birmingham and Sheffield she saw soot and furnaces. At Newcastle the party descended, like miners, into the coal mine – in a bucket tied to a rope.

Back in London she was given the celebrity treatment. Positive reviews for *Papers on Literature and Art* had appeared in the English journals. She hardly had time to dress or sleep.

She called on Nathan's agent, Mr. Delf. Would he ask Nathan to return her letters. Nathan responded through Delf that he could not immediately return her letters, but would sometime in the future. Their relationship had always been based on friendship, and he would always be manly and honorable, but by requesting her letters she was condemning and insulting him without a hearing. These words caused Fuller another collapse.

She involved herself in a round of social activity and sightseeing. The prison at Pentonville was much like New York's. She met William and Mary Howitt, co-editors of *The People's Journal*, a workingman's publication. She was asked to write for some English journals. Then she met an activist, Giuseppe Mazzini. He was the exiled leader of the Italian republican movement. Mutual attraction was immediate.

Mazzini behaved like a man touched with a special destiny. Condemned by the Italian government for sixteen years for activating uprisings – all of which had been harshly suppressed – Mazzini wore black, in mourning for his country. Constantly he was trailed by spies. He had organized the underground group Young Italy, and conducted an evening school for Italian workingmen and street boys. Politically skilled, noble and idealistic, he made speeches, wrote and smuggled pamphlets via seamen into Italy where they were passed from hand to hand.

He was ascetically handsome, with a saintly, fragile intensity. He was infinitely patient, energetic, and spiritual. He'd abandoned Catholicism. His maxim which appeared on his banner was, "God and the People." Unmarried, he remained true to his former mistress, it was said, who was a widow living in Italy. Actually, he had no leisure for love. His one-and-only was the Italian unification.

Was there anything an American journalist could do to help? She could give a talk to students at his school.

Jane Carlyle was wearing black velvet as she opened the door to Fuller who stepped into the gold, red, and black drawing room. After first greetings Fuller uttered barely a word because Thomas Carlyle harangued the entire evening. He wrote Emerson that Fuller was "a strange lilting lean old maid, not nearly such a bore as I expected."

Fuller wrote Emerson: "He was in a very sweet humor, full of wit and pathos....I was quite carried away with the rich flow of his discourse....I admired his Scotch, his way of singing his great full sentences....He let me talk a little now and then, enough to free my lungs, and change my position, so that I did not get tired."

He talked of politics and told stories of the Scotch peasantry.

She thought Carlyle was worth a thousand Emersons, because he was not ashamed to laugh when amused.

At another dinner Carlyle, in a more acid mood, railed against poetry and became wearisome. She wrote Emerson, "You are a perfect prisoner when he has once got hold of you." Afterwards, she was able to talk to Jane, who "hitherto I had only seen, for who can speak while her husband is there?" Fuller found her full of grace, sweetness, and talent, but her eyes were sad.

Once, around Fuller's dinner table with Jane and Mazzini, Carlyle railed against "rose-water imbecilities," and suggested that tormenters should have collars noosed around their necks. Such talk unnerved the exiled Mazzini whose daily life challenged imprisonment and hanging for himself and his followers.

In November Fuller and the Springs left for Paris. They'd thought of taking Mazzini with them, smuggling him into Italy with a disguise and a false American passport. But the more they discussed the idea, the more dangerous it seemed. Instead, they carried his letter to one of his agents.

In Paris the weather was "mud and mist," as Fuller wrote her *Tribune* readers. The French were "slippery." In an attempt to improve her French, she spent three or four hours per day with a teacher and she saw the traditional tourist sights, and attended lectures, operas, plays, one of which starred the famous actress Rachel who "surpassed my hopes" in *Phedre*. She attended a royal ball at the

Tuileries and was presented at court. She visited weavers in their cottages and was saddened to see children hard at work at the looms. The winter had brought famine and unemployment, but news of it had been suppressed. The poor suffered miserably. The price of bread was astronomical. Secret revolutionary societies were being organized.

Once she went to hear the astronomer Leverrier speak at the Sorbonne, but a guard stopped her from entering the auditorium because women were never admitted.

Fuller's essay, "American Literature," had been translated, and she was encouraged to translate *Woman in the Nineteenth Century,* and to become a correspondent for *La Revue Independent,* a journal George Sand had helped to found. Also, she met the ex-priest, republican Félicité-Robert de Lamennais, and the poet Béranger.

By far her most interesting meeting was with George Sand. Fuller would be considered a hussy for reminding Americans of the existence of this outrageous woman who wore men's clothes and who lived openly with men without marrying them. "She needs no defence, but only to be understood, for she has bravely acted out her nature, and always with good intentions. She might have loved one man permanently, if she could have found one contemporary who could interest and command her throughout her range; but there was hardly a possibility of that, for such a person. Thus, she has naturally changed the objects of her affection, and several times. But she was never coarse, never gross, and I am sure her generous heart has not failed to draw some rich drops from every kind of wine-press."

Fuller also saw Chopin, no longer Sand's lover, though he still lived with her. "Ill and frail as a snowdrop," she wrote, "but an exquisite genius." He played the piano for her.

There is an account that after talking for twenty minutes to the national poet of Poland, Adam Mickiewicz, Fuller fainted. Since Mickiewicz had promoted Emerson's *Essays* amongst his Parisian friends, Fuller sent him Emerson's *Poems* and invited him to visit.

Mickiewicz turned out to be a highly sensitive fifty year-old, broad-shouldered, blue eyed blond who immediately connected with Fuller's consciousness. She wrote Emerson, "I found in him the man I had long wished to see, with the intellect and passions in due proportion for a full and healthy human being, with a soul constantly inspiring...How much time had I wasted on others which I might have given to this real and important relation."

He affected Fuller "like music, or the richest landscape," she wrote the Springs. "My heart beat with joy that he at once felt beauty in me also. When I was with him I was happy...."

Mickiewicz was the practical idealist, the genius with faith. He had been exiled by the Russian Tsar since his youth because he had written the epic poem *Pan Tadeusz* which celebrated the heroism of his people during the 1830 resurrection. In Paris he held the chair in Slavonic Languages and Literature at the College de France and he was the center of the revolutionary group of Polish exiles. It was his dream that Europe be freed through a series of revolutions. A Catholic who detested Puritanism, he believed in democracy, land reform, political equality for women, freedom for his country and all oppressed groups. He had an unhappy marriage.

He and Fuller must have discussed her celibacy because via letter he encouraged her to believe she was beautiful, to fall in love: "For you the first step of your deliverance...is to know whether you are to be permitted to remain a virgin...I would like you to learn to love not only Italy, but the Italians."

From Concord Ralph Waldo Emerson sent word that he was ready for new experience, new society. He might soon be in England on a lecture tour. John Ireland, his English guide during his 1833 lecture tour, had invitations for him, and his essays had been read by the English, plus there had been an English edition of his *Poems*, thanks to Thomas Carlyle. Though Emerson felt "fastened down by wife and children, by books and studies, by pear trees and apple trees," Lidian was encouraging him to go, and his work load had eased.

This was the same year Susan B. Anthony made her first speech at a public meeting of the Daughters of Temperance in Canajoharie, N.Y., the same year an Oberlin College student by the name of Antoinette L. Brown delivered the first of several speeches on temperance in Ohio, and the same year that Lucy Stone gave her first speech on woman's rights in her brother's church at Brookfield, Mass.

In March 1847 Fuller reached Naples: "I have at last found my Italy."

She arrived in Rome before Easter: "Italy is beautiful, worthy to be loved and embraced, not talked about."

Fuller and the Springs took rooms on the Corso, the "Fifth Avenue" of Rome. Immediately, Fuller went sightseeing and gave her readers eye-witness accounts. Once she visited the Colosseum by moonlight; her companions were the owls. She ran into George W. Curtis, also sightseeing. Many Americans lived in Rome – there was an American artists' colony – and there she found Christopher Cranch and family.

From Paris Mickiewicz mailed advice to seek "the society of Italians, conversations with Italians, the music of Italians....Enjoy what surrounds you. Breathe life through all your pores.... Learn to appreciate yourself as a beauty, and, after having admired the women of Rome, say, 'And as for me, why, I am beautiful!'"

It was advice she took to heart.

On Easter Sunday she attended services at St. Peter's with the Springs. Afterwards, she decided to wander independently about the tall columns and chapels and told the Springs to wait for her. But when she tried to rejoin them, they seemed to have dissolved into thin air.

Momentarily panicking, she glanced up to see a decidedly handsome young man standing before her, cane in hand, asking if he could be of help. Together they searched the adjoining doorways, but in vain. Evidently the Springs had misunderstood. By this time all carriages had vanished and Fuller, still unfamiliar with the streets, was faced with finding her way back to her lodgings. The young gentleman offered to be her guide.

His name was Giovanni Angelo Ossoli. He was about ten years younger than Fuller. He believed in a united Italy, even though this was opposed to his family's traditional stance. He was impressed and excited to learn that Fuller was a friend of Mazzini, whom he'd long admired.

About this same time Fuller met in the bohemian district along the Via Margutta the twenty-three year-old American painter, Thomas Hicks. Attracted, Fuller made an attempt to know him better. She wrote two unsigned letters, one to a Dear Youth: "...to love you and to have you love me.... I wish this for both our sakes, for mine, because I have so lately been severed from congenial companionship, that I am suffering for want of it, for yours because I feel as if I had something precious to leave in your charge."*

Hicks' gentle and sensitive reply states that she "would find but a few embers on the hearth of a lonely ambitious man – one whose life has been as solitary as it is unknown.... I am the child of autumn.... Do you not see that I cannot make you happy?..."

There was no rejection from the other young man. Tall and handsome he stood on the street, below her window, beckoning her to join him. He took her sightseeing, to political meetings, to cafes.

His full family name, recorded in the Golden Book of Italian Nobility, was Ossoli della Torre. Since 1685 his family had been associated with the Papal court. They had a castle in the Sabine country and a family chapel in the Church of the Maddalena, near the Pantheon. His eldest brother, twenty-one years older than himself, held a position in the papal court, and his two other older brothers were officers in the *Guardia Nobile*, the Pope's guarde. He had one sister who was married, and a younger sister in Ireland whom the family rarely saw. He lived with and cared for his father, Marchese Filippo, who was over seventy and unwell, in a palazzo on Via Tor di Specchi.

There was a little scar on his face. "It was made by a jealous dog when my mother was caressing me as an infant," he told her with pride; it confirmed how much his mother had loved him. She had died when he was small. Whatever formal education he'd received had been from an elderly priest whose priority had not been this boy's education. To Transcendentalists, he would seem positively illiterate, but to Italians it was enough that he was a gentleman who knew the practical details of running a large estate. He was an excellent horseman and cognizant in the use of arms.

Increasingly, Fuller and Ossoli attended the political meetings and

---

*Scholar/biographer Bell Gale Chevigny recently unearthed the unsigned letters at Houghton Library at Harvard University. Previous scholars who read them evidentially attributed Fuller's letter to Ossoli; however, Fuller and Ossoli spoke and wrote to each other in Italian since Ossoli did not speak or read English. Chevigny matched Hicks' handwriting with other letters he'd written. Her analysis and the letters are published for the first time in her book, *The Woman and The Myth.*

mixed with revolutionaries working for the freedom and unification of Italy. They drank wine with artists and writers at the Caffe Greco and the Caffe delle Belle Arti, favorite spots where the underground felt safe from the threat of police.

Ossoli did not introduce Fuller to his family who disproved radical activities. In no way would they approve of his serious interest in an older republican American woman, who was not Catholic. With what woman Ossoli spent his leisure hours was really of no concern to them – until he considered marriage. It was not long before Ossoli proposed marriage.

Fuller said No. She loved him, of that she knew, but differences were too great.

He expressed disappointment and declared he'd wait.

The Spring's tour plans were to leave Rome in June and travel to northern Italy, and then to Germany through Switzerland.

Adam Mickiewicz wrote again warning her not to be "too hasty about leaving places where you feel well," and not to "leave lightly those who would like to remain near you. This is in reference to that little Italian you met in the Church."

By the end of April, Fuller was thinking of staying in Rome for a year.

Italy was divided into nine separate states, each with its own power. The Pope had temporal power over central Italy which included Rome. The Austrians occupied Lombardy and Venetia as well as the states of Tuscany, Parma, and Modena. Spanish Bourbons corruptly and brutally held the throne in Naples and Sicily. In Piedmont there was the Italian King Charles Albert who'd exiled Mazzini, who'd tortured and executed members of Mazzini's organization, Young Italy.

In Rome the relatively young Pope Pius IX, just elected, granted a general amnesty to political prisoners. He took other measures to which the Romans responded with joy. The way seemed paved for a constitutional government. The Romans loved Pio Nono.

News arrived from Emerson. He was pleased Fuller had such an interesting meeting with George Sand. He was helping Thoreau with publishing arrangements for his book, *A Week on the Concord and Merrimack.* Parker, Channing, Cabot, Dwight, and others were "filled with rage" to start a new journal, *The Massachusetts Quarterly Review.* James Elliot Cabot was to be editor. "I suppose you are not one of those sleepers who dream the same dream over many times....It seems I am."

He wanted to renew his relationship with his greatest ego support. "I set out pears & apples in these April days, and I hope you shall find our no-landscape a little positive, when you come home again."

In May the Pope promised the Italian people a representative council. Shouting vivas, the Romans formed a long torchlight procession to the Quirinal which passed under Fuller's windows on the Corso. But though the Italians had high hopes, Mazzini and Fuller could only have doubts that he could achieve a new day.

"The famine in Europe only affects potatoes," Emerson wrote in his next June 4 letter, while "the sterility in America continues in the men...." He'd heard that her Uncle Abraham had died and he hoped she'd be in for some money. He wished he could help her out monetarily, but his "unskillful economics" had "brought me latterly into increasing debt," what with their "sprawling style of housekeeping which sometimes threatens to get unmanageable."

Fuller decided to continue touring with the Springs. They left Rome for the picturesque city of Florence where she could not help but feel at home. She met American artists who had come to be a part of the world art scene, Horatio Greenough, Joseph Mozier, and Hiram Powers, whose statue of John C. Calhoun she viewed. She made contact with the politically active Marchioness Costanza Arconati Visconti, whom she'd met briefly in Rome and who had been, along with her husband, exiled by the Austrian authorities.

Visconti was one of the most distinguished names in Europe; their ancestral roots went back to the respected Dukes of Milan. The family had a palace in Milan, had entertained lavishly. Now they were committed to the common goal of a unified Italy. The Marchioness introduced Fuller into the Florentine intellectual community. And Fuller wrote her brother to send any money from Uncle Abraham's estate in care of the American sculptor/businessman, Joseph Mozier.

The travellers moved on to Bologna, Ravenna, Ferarra, Padua, and finally Venice where Fuller, fixated on returning to Rome, broke the news to the Springs that she would stay on alone with a servant while they travelled on to Switzerland. Thus, Fuller eliminated her trip to Germany and her lifelong hopes of researching for her book on Goethe.

She stayed two weeks in Venice, the highlight of which was meeting the aged romantic revolutionary poet/novelist Alessandro Manzoni who made a strong impression on her; then she toured the northern cities, landing at Lake Como at the end of August for a visit with Mme. Arconati, after which she went to Lake Lugano and then back to Milan where she mixed with some young radicals and the Polish Princess Radziwill.

From New York she heard that Ellery Channing's book on Rome was considered by the intellectual community more readable than anything he'd written. Former Brook Farmer Charles A. Dana was now employed as journalist and manager at the *Tribune.* He was expert at handling foreign news.

In another letter Adam Mickiewicz warned: "You ought not to confine your life to books and reveries. You have pleaded the liberty of women in a masculine and frank style. Live and act as you write.... I have seen you, with all your learning, and all your imagination, and all your literary reputation, living in a bondage harder than that of a servant....The relationships which suit you are those which develop and free your spirit, responding to the legitimate needs of your body and leaving you free at all times. You are the sole judge of these needs."

Greeley was asking for more articles; he would give her a slight raise, ten dollars each, and he encouraged her to draw advances.

Lidian was taking a rest-cure in the mountains and lakes of Maine. Emerson's mother was taking care of the Concord house and children.

To Elizabeth Hoar Fuller wrote: "Italy receives me as a long-lost child."

To Cary: "Rome... must be inhaled wholly, with the yielding of the whole heart. It is really something transcendental, both spirit and body...its genius triumphed...."

And Fuller returned to Rome on October 13th.

That same month Emerson left Concord for Europe, launching his European lectures. Lidian, back from Maine, had spent a good deal of time on his wardrobe, making sure it was appropriate, clean, mended, properly folded, and that his trunk and valise were in perfect order. Once abroad, Emerson complained he had too many clothes. He sent some back.

While Emerson was gone, Thoreau and Lidian took charge of the "mansion of peace." Alcott was busy in the Emerson cornfield choosing branches and special pieces of wood in order to build a fantastic open air structure with arched rafters and gables which he called Emerson's summerhouse.*

As Emerson travelled through Scotland, Liverpool, Manchester, Glasgow, Edinburgh, and London, he tried to achieve variety by alternating lectures from his series, "The Uses of Great Men," with ones he'd earlier delivered. His reception was not quite as successful as anticipated.

Lidian wrote asking Emerson again to write a love letter. He answered: "I fear that I shall not be able at this time to write you yet, those full and 'private' letters, which you so rightfully demand. I am a wanderer on the face of this island, and am so harried by this necessity of reading Lectures...."

Lidian was trying to make up her mind as to whether or not to return to Plymouth. Emerson wrote her: "Pray do not ask me for advice or liberty on the Plymouth visit.... Do as you find it best...."

At the same time, Elizabeth Hoar was suggesting via letter that Emerson could turn to her, could tell her "all those things which if modesty forbids you write in your grand letter to Lidian, you can communicate, under cover, to me."

In Rome Fuller and Ossoli were lovers. Even though tension was smoldering and thousands of young men were volunteering to join the Civic Guard organized by the Pope, there were entertainments galore. It was a lovely warm autumn and the flowers continued to bloom. Fuller and Ossoli went to fiesta, races, fireworks, masses at churches, concerts, balls, walks in gardens, excursions into the country with wine and baskets of lunch – besides the political meetings.

---

*Emerson eventually called it Tumbledown Hall and Lidian referred to it as The Ruin. It stood for fifteen years. Emerson never used it.

It seemed an unlikely alliance – Fuller acted on a strong impulse. Still, the relationship answered deep-felt needs in both. Ossoli had grown up an orphan to a mother's nurturing warmth. He could respond to Fuller's sympathetic understanding regarding his family problems and politics. He admired her mature attitude and knowledge, her intense interest in Italy and its problems, her friendships with the leaders of the revolutionary cause.

On Fuller's part, long had she longed to fill a maternal role. It was joyous to accept the attention, the love, the sexuality of this handsome, quiet, ardent, mannerly young gentleman who never ceased to press his suit. What could she have cared about his intellect.

Fuller committed every Monday night to interacting with the intellectuals. She received guests in her brightly lit, neatly furnished room on the Corso overlooking the Pincian Mount, the Piazza del Popolo and the Villa Borghese. She did not serve refreshments, but she did decorate it with fresh flowers. There were the Cranches, Princess Radziwill, the American painters, Thomas Hicks and Jaspar Cropsey, the very witty and exhuberant William Wetmore Story and his cultivated, open-hearted wife, Emelyn, and their baby son. Story, the son of Supreme Court justice Joseph Story, had been a Boston lawyer, but preferred literary and artistic endeavors. Wealthy enough not to have to pursue law, he'd come to Florence to become a sculptor and with his long flowing moustache and whiskers he adapted to the scene.

In November Ossoli joined the Civic Guard. Immediately he was made sergeant and he wore a dark blue and red-corded uniform and a *kepi* for a cap.

In December Fuller and Ossoli were allegedly married, secretly, though no records remain to verify the fact. One biographer speculates that if there were records, the building in which they were kept was bombed during World War II. There is reason to doubt that the marriage occurred because of the conflict in religion. A Catholic wedding would require special dispensation. If that were obtained Ossoli's family would learn of it and the consequences would be his disinheritance. As for a Protestant ceremony, Ossoli could not have taken it seriously.

To Emerson she wrote that she lived, ate, and walked alone in

Rome and enjoyed the stillness. She was out one morning to see the manoeuvres of the Civic Guard, but she made no mention of Ossoli.

From England, on December 5, Emerson stated he was glad Fuller was happy in Italy but that she must not stay long alone. In his plea he used sexual imagery:

> Shall we not yet...you, you, also...as we used to talk, build up a reasonable society in that naked unatmospheric land, and effectually serve one another? 'tis the worse for me - but, I believe, all the persons who have been important to my - imagination - shall I say? personal imagination (is there no such thing in just psychology?) retain all their importance for me. I am their victim, and ready to be their victim, to the same extent as heretofore. [15]

On December 12, 1847 Caroline Sturgis and William A. Tappan were married.* Cary had told no one, not even her mother, though she'd allowed a small newspaper announcement to appear. True to her eccentricities, she'd casually asked her mother to meet her at her sister's house where she'd arranged for William Henry Channing to minister the small and informal ceremony, after which they'd taken a coach to Brookline and then to New York where they were to live.

Tappan went into business and Cary took up drawing and studied at the School of Art and Design. She'd just had a book of fairy tales published, *Rainbows for Children.* She'd written it for her friends, but Lydia Maria Child had been so taken with it that she channeled it for publication.

On December 16 Fuller wrote to her mother how well and happy she had been for the past six weeks.

Four days later her mood was completely reversed. She wrote Emerson:

> Nothing less than two or three years, free from care and forced labor, would heal all my hurts and renew my life-blood at its source. Since Destiny will not grant me that I hope she will not leave me long in the world, for I am tired of keeping myself up in the water without

---

* Emerson had introduced Tappan to Sturgis.

> corks, and without strength to swim. I should like to go to sleep, and be born again into a state where my young life should not be permanently taxed.[16]

Fuller suspected she was pregnant.

About a week later Emerson bewailed to Elizabeth Hoar his lack of friends. He asked Hoar to remain faithful in friendship to himself and his wife who was "that cloud of mine at home," but he had not energy enough to sustain a close confiding relationship.

> The hour will come & the world, wherein we shall quite easily render that account of ourselves which now we never render, and shall be very real brothers & sisters. I sometimes think how glad I should be if I had a friend to whom I could tell things. Alas & alas, I have not health or constitution enough to bear so dear demanding a relation. So do not soar another pitch in your bounty, & say, you will be my abbestt, & hear my shrift. I have not music enough to modulate the egotism which would grate intolerably without music, and I must mope awhile longer.[17]

America was reading some of Fuller's finest work. Her 1848 New Year's article in the *Tribune* attacked the unthinking, conceited, shallow American who came to Europe to spend money without making the effort to understand the people and the culture.

Americans must "stammer and blush" when we speak of "this cancer of slavery and the Mexican War.... I find the cause of tyranny and wrong everywhere the same – and lo! my country! the darkest offender...." Hope was in the youth "who I trust will yet expand, and help to give soul to the huge, over-fed, too hastily grown-up body."

Under normal circumstances pregnancy would have made Fuller ecstatically joyful. But there was nothing normal about her circumstances. Every day she felt ill. She no longer took wine, coffee, or meat. She hated the horrible cabbage the Romans loved and was irritated with noises, smells, and sounds of daily life. The steady bone-chilling rain depressed her. Her headaches returned.

To Cary alone her despair surfaced. She did not divulge her secret:

> I have known some happy hours but they all lead to sorrow; and not only the cups of wine, but of milk, seem drugged with poison for me. It does not seem to be my fault, this Destiny; I do not court these things – they come. I am a poor magnet, with power to be wounded by the bodies I attract....With this year, I enter upon a sphere of my destiny so difficult, that I, at present, see no way out, except through the gate of death....The beautiful forms of art charm no more, and a love, in which there is all fondness, but no help, flatters in vain. [18]

In Rome there were constant street demonstrations. In Milan there had been riots against the Austrian boycott of tobacco. In Tuscany and Piedmont the people had forced significant concessions from their King Carlo Alberto. In Hungary there had been a revolt against the Austrians. In Prussia there'd been a revolt against Friedrich Wilhelm IV. News of the same revolutionary ferment came from Genoa, Leghorn, Sicily, Naples.

This year the Emerson's would be celebrating their thirteenth wedding anniversary. From Manchester Emerson chastised Lidian for being self-accusatory:

> I pray you to omit all the compunctions & apologies which begin & end your letters; for the letters have no need of them, but are full of good matter & rightly disposed. They are too welcome to me to allow me to see any fitness in these accusations. [19]

In February Lidian needed additional money for household bills. She'd desperately drawn an advance on an account from Emerson's brother William – an action they'd taken before, albeit unwillingly. However, Emerson had had to borrow eight hundred dollars for his trip and his English lectures had not grossed much beyond paying his own expenses. He had nothing to send Lidian:

> If you cannot manage to live, you must draw again on William, which, to be sure, is a ruinous way. I might send thirty pounds home just now, but do not wish to prejudice my freedom in London....We must yet learn, late as it is, to mend our economy.... [20]

Emerson was economizing by residing in hotels, visiting castles, attending meetings of Parliament, receptions and dinner in his honor at Lord Ashburton's, at Lady Palmerston's, at Lady Morgan's, at Lady Molesworth's, at Lord Lovelace's, at Lady Baring's and other celebrities, such as Charles Dickens, Tennyson, Thackery.

Lidian told Elizabeth Hoar she was glad her husband couldn't see her so gauntly yellow, feverish. Twelve days later Lidian, who'd written her husband that she was worn with her own illness plus the children's illnesses, received another chiding letter from Perth. Her "self-accusing spirit" benefited him:

> The kind letters you send me loaded with so many benedictions from that strange self-accusing spirit of yours, (afflicting you, benefitting me,) and with all these touching anecdotes & now drawings & letters of my darlings - duly come to my great joy and ought to draw answers to every letter & almost to every piece of information. But I cannot yet answer but with most ungrateful brevity. I live in these days in a whirl from town to town & in strange houses and can ill command the short hour that is needed to write a letter. But you shall have a short chronicle of my late journeys.... [21]

In page after page Emerson described the stimulating people he was meeting and the experiences he was having. Among a host of names, he mentions de Quincy, Combe, the Thomas Carlyles, Harriet Martineau, William Wordsworth.

He trusted Lidian was quite well of her illness and he never forgot the children and he was "often tempted to run ignominiously away from Britain & France" to see them. He closed the letter with "Love to all who love - the truth! And continue you to be merciful & good to me...Your affectionate...W."

He did not send his love to Lidian, but asked her to continue to be merciful and good to him.

It is ironic to read Emerson's essay, "Compensation:"

> You cannot do wrong without suffering wrong....The exclusionist in religion does not see that he shuts the door of heaven on himself, in striving to shut out others. Treat men as pawns and ninepins and you shall suffer as well as they. If you leave out their heart, you shall lose your own....All infractions of love and equity in our social relations are speedily punished.

"Every act rewards itself" was Emerson's maxim but, it does not seem that Emerson suffered punishment because he shut out Lidian.*

In Rome in February Ossoli's father died. Ossoli's hopes for an inheritance lessened, for the eldest brother, who had long disproved Ossoli's actions, took control of the estate.

Fuller did not write *Tribune* articles that month. The couple planned that she would give birth in the mountains – their liaison still must be kept a secret. Ossoli would not jeopardize the possibility of receiving his share of the family fortune.

Meanwhile, Henry Hedge came to Rome; Fuller saw him briefly. Princess Cristina Trivulzio Belgioioso, an Italian political activist, stopped during her tour of Italy to drum up interest in supporting the republican cause – Marchesa Arconati Visconti had arranged that Fuller meet her.

Belgioioso personified the dazzling beautiful, wealthy, aristocratic intellectual that Fuller had dreamed of being during her imaginative childhood. Belgioioso moved in the most cultivated and politically powerful circles in Italy. In Paris she had entertained a salon for artists which included, among others, George Sand, Victor Hugo, and Stendhal. Because of her revolutionary anti-Austrian activities, she was followed by spies and her every movement accounted for. She and her husband, also of aristocratic and honored heritage, had chosen to live and take separate paths; however, both had been exiled, and once he, a Carbonaro, had barely escaped the death penalty. Belgioioso lost friends when she radically lent her support to the republican cause of Mazzini.

Next, Adam Mickiewicz appeared in Rome to organize Polish exiles to fight with the Italians. He stayed with Fuller; she talked to him about her immediate problem, but talk was only a temporary

---

*Greeley confessed to a similar problem concerning his wife, Mary. On January 27, 1848 he wrote Fuller: "I have never known anyone but you whose influence upon her was not irritating but if I could be alone with her and household cares did not interpose to drive her crazy, she would steadily improve…" But Greeley did not cut back on his long working hours to allow more time with his wife and child. As he admitted, he was usually away from home, busy with politics and events.

relief. For all his compassion and emotional support, he could offer no practical solution.

On March 2, 1848, Emerson, still in Manchester, wrote Fuller a witty letter about an hour and a half's visit with Wordsworth, "bitter old Englishman he is" but "a fine healthy old man with weather-beaten face." He mentioned how ill Lidian and the children had been, then said he would change his plans if Fuller would meet him in Paris.

> But my plans would easily change with inviting or forbidding circumstances. I shall be very glad to see you in Paris....How much your letter made me wish to say, come live with me at Concord! Then instantly came the poor exhausted Lidian's tragic letters – but I mean yet to coax you into Mrs. Brown's little house opposite to my gate....*[22]

Lidian rebuffed the idea of Fuller's living with them. So Emerson speedily retracted in his March 8 letter to "poor invalid:"

> I do not wonder that in these late afflictions, my plans for Margaret looked calamitous enough to the poor invalid. Be comforted; for I withheld my letter to her...carried it in my pocket for weeks; it became too old to send, and I had literally no time to write another, and then I waited for your reply. Now I have written her only my regrets that I am not a prince, with good hope, too, that she may yet be a tenant of Mrs. Brown's house, if that remains open.... [23]

There was possibility of more lectures in London, which would help their financial situation, but money was uncertain, "but I shall not probably accept any of the dozen invitations I have had from Societies here, though I should go home to poverty.... So if I have no money to go to France, I shall not go."

He wrote his brother William that he would regret it if he didn't go to France, though he'd like to go home "to relieve that poor child – Lidian, I mean – by my presence, since my absence has been no relief, as I hoped it might prove, to her cares."

---

* Mrs. Brown was Lucy Brown, Lidian's sister, for whom Emerson was having a house built on his Walden Pond acreage.

Lidian must have again implored Emerson to write her special words of love, in the style she knew he could write. Such a letter does not seem to exist; however, in this same March 8 letter Emerson finally answered his wife of thirteen years whom he had not taken to Europe:*

> As you still ask me for that unwritten letter always due, it seems, always unwritten, from year to year, by me to you, dear Lidian – I fear too more widely true than you mean – always due & unwritten by me to every sister & brother of the human race. I have only to say that I also bemoan myself daily for the same cause - that I cannot write this letter, that I have not stamina & constitution enough to mind the two functions of seraph & cherub, oh no, let me not use such great words - rather say that a photometer cannot be a stove. It must content you for the time, that I truly acknowledge a poverty of nature, & have really no proud defence at all to set up, but ill-health, puniness, and Stygian limitation. Is not the wife too always the complement of the man's imperfections, and mainly of those half men the clerks? Besides am I not, O best Lidian, a most foolish affectionate good man & papa, with a weak side toward apples & sugar and all domesticities, when I am once in Concord? Answer me that....

Then Emerson proceeded to write about all the dinners and soirees he was attending, mentioning the Carlyles, Harriet Martineau, and the Belgian Ambassador, how he went to the House of Lords, to the Commons, and the British Museum, the French Theatre, the Opera, and he described the conditions in London and Glasgow. He excused himself from not writing to the children and acknowledged the serious illness of daughter Ellen. But Lidian could do something for him:

> My chief errand only is this that if it can be done without much expense I should be glad to have the one apple tree which Mr. Alcott shall elect removed from the old orchard & set down near the gate of

*Years later in 1872 Emerson would travel a third and last time to Europe and also to Egypt, but not with Lidian – he took his daughter Ellen who had, by this time, acquiesced in the position of secretary/care-taker.

> the cowyard. I think the post of the gate seemed the right spot. But he must use a large discretion. Also I wish as many of the pear trees in the heater piece as good places can be found for in the yard set out.[24]

Whether or not "poor invalid" directed Bronson Alcott to move the one apple tree is not known, but we can surmise that she must have been disappointed not to find the emotional warmth she sought from her husband who then wrote that he should "not soon go roving again" because it brought on "a crop of annoyances & pains." Seeing "good men & good things" and having fine privileges was "thrown away" on him because people threw him out of spirits and he only forgot his experiences anyway. He told her about meeting Harriet Martineau, the novelist Mrs. Jameson, Lady Byron and innumerable women of distinction. "There are in England the usual sprinkling of enthusiastic young ladies."

In Rome Carnival week was underway despite drenching rains which failed to stop street parades of merry-making and nightly masked balls. News broke that the Paris revolutionaries had dethroned Louis Philippe. In Vienna Metternich had been compelled to flee the country. In northern Italy, Modena and Parma, the people had secured freedom of Austrian dominance.

Romans wept and embraced in the streets, crying "*Miracolo! Providenza!*" The Carnival celebrators lit the *moccoletti*, long candles, and marched through the streets in candlelight processions. Demonstrators dragged Austrian arms through the streets and burned them in the Piazza de Popolo. Enthused as never before, many men rushed to join the regiments, eager to fight at the frontier. Those who couldn't join helped to mobilize equipment and supplies.

Fuller, caught up in the jubilance, considered it her privilege to record the events in the *Tribune*.

"It is a time such as I always dreamed of," she wrote to William Henry Channing. "Perhaps I shall be called on to act....War is everywhere. I cannot leave Rome, and the men of Rome are marching every day into Lombardy....A glorious flame burns higher and higher in the heart of the nation."

Mickiewicz, hailed as "the Dante of Poland," had gone off to Florence and Milan with his squadron of exiles.

Meanwhile, in Concord, Lidian must have read through a file of correspondence from Emerson's dead first wife. She must have praised her highly because Emerson's return letter stated that Ellen's letters:

> ...deserved all you have said. For they came out of a heart which nature & destiny conspired to keep as inviolate, as are still those three children of whom you send me such happy accounts...But you should have seen Ellen. When she left this world, I valued everybody who had seen her, and disliked to meet those who had not. [25]

We do not have Lidian's reaction. The average wife would be deeply wounded to hear her husband praise his first wife when he avoided and refused to speak of his love for his present wife.

In Rome the rains ended, and as the flowers began to bloom, Fuller began to feel physically better, and she and Ossoli joined once again for outdoor excursions. "Gods themselves walk on earth, here in the Italian spring," she wrote Cary Sturgis. "My character is not in what may be called the heroic phase, now. I have done, and may still do, things that may invoke censure; but in the foundation of my character, in my aims, I am always the same: and I believe you will always have confidence that I act as I ought and must – and will always value my sympathy."

On April 25, from London, Emerson reiterated to Fuller (now four months pregnant) to take the first steamer to Marseilles, to meet him in Paris and return to the United States with him.

Greeley sent payment for articles and pressured Fuller to return: "Why should you live in Europe in such miserable health?...Europe is too troubled and apprehensive just now to be either safe or pleasant travelling ground for a lonely invalid especially a woman."

Count Rossi, the Roman prime minister, was imposing strict measures on the people. The news broke that the Austrians at Ferrara had executed a member of the civic guard, an artist of renown. Crowds rushed to the Quirinal, the Pope's quarters, to demand that war be declared. The Pope stated that the war should be hushed up, differences should be smoothed over. Losing faith in their Pope, the Italians determined to take matters into their own hands.

Fuller sent an eloquent message to Americans: "To you, people of

America, it may perhaps be given to look on and learn in time for a preventive wisdom. You may learn the real meaning of the words FRATERNITY, EQUALITY: you may, despite the apes of the past who strive to tutor you, learn the needs of a true democracy. You may in time learn to reverence, learn to guard, the true aristocracy of a nation, the only real nobles – the laboring classes...."

Emerson thought that since he was feeling well in Paris he should stay in the "best bower anchor."

To Lidian: "I am promised introduction to some French ladies.... But you do not want me in Concord; and I shall learn French fast, perhaps you will send me commands to stay or to return hither where I am so well?"

Fuller's brother Richard now had a plan to collect a five hundred dollar pool from all brothers so she could return to America.

But Fuller activated her own plan. She sent a letter to Greeley stating that her health required her to stop sending him despatches. She secured a passport with her name listed as Margherita Ossoli, her birthplace as Rome, and her age as twenty-nine. To the painter Thomas Hicks, Fuller handed a bundle of letters that he was to send to her family in case of her death.

She packed a daguerreotype of Ossoli along with her papers and clippings – the beginnings of her new book, a history of the Revolution. She sent small gifts to her family. She arranged that letters from America be sent to her bank's office where Ossoli could pick them up and forward them to her. She ended her *Tribune* article with these words: "...the nightingales sing; every tree and plant is in flower, and the sun and moon shine as if paradise were already re-established on earth. I go to one of the villas to dream it is so, beneath the pale light of the stars."

Ossoli and she took a last brief trip into the hills near Rome, then on May 29 they travelled with two servants to a lodging house in Aquila on the slope of a hill, on which stood farm houses, churches, and a ruined baronial residence, in the midst of olive and almond groves and vineyards and beautiful snow-capped mountains.

Two days later from Paris, Emerson commanded his "sister": "But you will not wait but will come to London immediately and sail home with me!"

Her answer contained only partial truth: "I should like to return with you, but I have much to do and learn in Europe yet. I am deeply interested in this public drama, and wish to see it played out. Methinks I have my part therein, either as actor or historian."

Emerson, finding it impossible to extend his tour,* returned to the United States to find his wife miserably ill with jaundice or hepatitis. Then illness spread to his son and mother.

No American knew where Margaret Fuller was or what she was doing, not her mother, nor none of her Italian friends other than Ossoli. As she strolled along the Aquilla county roads, the peasants murmured, *Povera, sola, soletta,* poor one, alone, all alone!

Meanwhile, in America, five women were stirring up their own revolution. In Waterloo, upstate New York, Elizabeth Cady Stanton, Lucretia Mott, the Quaker preacher, Martha Wright, her sister, Jane Hunt and Mary Ann McClintock, sent out an announcement to the *Seneca County Courier* that "A Convention would be held to discuss the social, civil, and religious condition and rights of women" in the Wesleyan Chapel at Seneca Falls on the 19th and 20th of July, 1848. This was the event envisioned eight years earlier because Stanton and Mott had been excluded as delegates to the World Anti-Slavery Society in London.

As the five women sat in Mary Ann McClintock's parlor to write their declaration and resolutions – three days before the Convention – they suddenly realized they did not know how to frame a resolution. In desperation they reviewed the declarations of the Peace, Temperance and Anti-Slavery organizations, but nothing seemed to germinate. Finally one woman read aloud the Declaration of Independence. All of them immediately realized that this document could serve as pattern. The group wrote eighteen resolutions.

The Wesleyan Chapel door was locked when three hundred women and men arrived on the morning of the Convention. Nothing could be started until a young man climbed through an open window to unlock it from the inside.

---

*Emerson's tour had been financially unprofitable. Many audiences had been unexpectably small, tickets had been priced high, and his lectures did not take into account the revolutionary ferment which was topmost on people's minds.

Men had not been invited to the Convention, but there they were. The women did not bar their presence.

How should the meeting start?

Suddenly, it dawned on the women that they'd no experience in running a Convention. So, the leaders gathered at the altar. After brief discussion they agreed that the more experienced men could help. Lucretia Mott's husband, James, (in Quaker costume) took the chair. Lucretia Mott, who'd spoken at Friends meetings, stated the objects of the Convention. Stanton, McClintock and others made speeches, and Martha Wright read satirical articles published in the press. A Declaration of Sentiments listed the wrongs to women that existed in society, all of which passed by unanimous vote except the ninth resolution, the right to the elective franchise. Henry Stanton, who'd so actively supported everything was now insensed. His wife, Elizabeth Cady Stanton, was so insistent that this resolution be voted on that he walked out of the church and left town. Frederick Douglass remained to give Elizabeth Cady Stanton moral support.

One hundred men and women signed the Declaration of Sentiments.*

The Convention was adjourned after scheduling another meeting, two weeks following, on August 2 at the Unitarian Church in Rochester.

The press called the women "Amazons" and love-starred spinsters.

Many ministers were loud in their denunciation.

Then, many of the signers of the Declaration of Sentiments withdrew their names.

On July 28 Frederick Douglass pointed out in his newspaper, *The North Star*, that many good persons would look with favor on a discussion on the rights of animals but not so on a discussion about woman's rights. Many people had discovered at last that the negroes had rights but "have yet to be convinced that women are entitled to any.... In the judgment of such persons the American slave system, with all its concomitant horrors, is less to be deplored that this wicked idea."

---

*One signer was Charlotte Woodward who seventy two years later also signed the nineteenth amendment to the Constitution which granted women the right to vote. She was the only one of the early suffragists alive (1920).

In Aquila, Italy, arrests were being made. Neopolitan soldiers crowded the streets and sat drinking at night in Fuller's lodging house. Mail deliveries were often delayed. Letters were censored. Fuller suffered from headaches, toothaches, chestaches, and the heat. She had a bloodletting. She felt decidedly lonely though Ossoli visited when he could, and she desperately needed money. Ossoli sent what he could, as did her brother Richard, and she received loans from her bank.

She decided Riete, nestled amongst hills and snowy mountain peaks amid farms, cypress plantations, ancient villas, and old baronial castles, was a safer town. It was closer to Rome, inside the papal frontier, there were no soldiers, and no foreign tourists. Here, Ossoli could more often visit.

Fuller moved, along with her servant from Rome, at the end of July, in the heat of threshing season, into quiet, simply furnished, upstairs rooms of a Riete house amidst vineyard and whispering willows, and with a loggia, or wooden terrace on the river Nera whose ceaseless sounds charmed. She could buy figs, grapes and peaches for five or six cents, and salads for two persons for one cent a day.

No one here spoke English; now she thought in Italian. Mail was unbelievably slow; it took four months to hear from her family. Money due from Horace Greeley never arrived and she remained ill with headaches, nosebleeds and boredom, and was bled again. From Rome all news was bad.

In Concord Emerson, relaxing and seeing to his garden, had no idea that Fuller was in hiding, awaiting birth. He wrote in his journal:

> None ever heard of a good marriage from Mesopotamia to Missouri and yet right marriage is as possible tomorrow as sunshine....We are not very much to blame for our bad marriages. We live amid hallucinations & illusions, & this especial trap is laid for us to trip up our feet with & all are tripped up, first or last. But the Mighty Mother who had been so sly with us, feels that she owes us some indemnity, & insinuates into the Pandora-box of marriage amidist dysepsia, nervousness, screams, Christianity, "help," poverty, & all kinds of music, some deep & serious benefits & some great joys. We find sometimes a delight in the beauty & the happiness of our children that makes the heart too big for the body. And in these ill assorted connections there is ever some mixture of true marriage. [26]

The Austrians attacked in Bologna and it was thought the Pope would send the Civic Guard. This meant that Ossoli might depart for Bologna immediately. Fuller wrote him that he must go if his honor was at stake, but she thought the Pope would do nothing. She was right. Ossoli arrived in Riete in time for the birth of his son on September 5. The child was named Angelo Philip Eugene, after his father, his grandfather on Ossoli's side, and Fuller's brother. Shortly thereafter, Ossoli had to return to Rome, and Fuller was left alone with recovery and care of her newborn.

Nestling the baby's head in her arms, she felt every care fade away: "I thought the mother's heart lived in me before, but it did not – I knew nothing about it. Yet before his birth I dreaded it. I thought I should not survive; but if I did and my child did, was I not cruel to bring another into this terrible world?...When he was born, that deep melancholy changed at once into rapture, but did not last long. Then came the prudential motherhood.... I became a coward...."

Within days Fuller had to fire the nurse who threatened to reveal the secret of the baby's birth. Fuller reacted to these worries with fitful, sleepless nights and a fever which soured her milk and then she had to find a wetnurse.

But this was only the first anxiety. A smallpox epidemic had broken out. The doctor promised vaccine, but never delivered it. Also, the dear, beautiful baby cried so often, and she needed money. She slowly realized that the Italians were overcharging her. Most took advantage of her, including the doctor. She could trust no one. It would be too cold in the rooms for the baby in the winter, but she kept delaying a move until Angelino was vaccinated.

She dared not take her son outside for a walk for fear of his contracting the dreaded small pox. She tried to convince Ossoli that mother, son and wetnurse should go to Rome so mother could resume work for the *Tribune*, but Ossoli felt it too dangerous. Their presence in Rome, so near his friends and brothers, would surely be discovered; news would leak to his family and that would be the end of obtaining any portion of his inheritance.

Finally, Fuller learned that there was no vaccine left in Riete. That was why the doctor had not supplied it. Somehow Ossoli, from Rome, rushed the medicine through armed lines and Angelino was vaccinated. Then Ossoli insisted on choosing a godfather and on a Catholic baptism. He wanted to give his son his name, title and inheritance. In Italy without baptismal papers, a person was considered stateless. He had to accomplish this without his brothers' knowledge, without leak of information. Fuller opted for Adam Mickiewicz. He was Catholic and would feel honored to serve in this capacity, but she didn't know where he was. Ossoli finally selected a trusted relative.

That Ossoli's religion differed from Fuller's had never mattered. Ossoli was devout, yet remained a radical anti-clerical republican. She would never try to change him. She gave her son to the ritual of baptism because it seemed to be important to Ossoli.

With the baptism accomplished and arrangements made with a wetnurse, mother separated from son in order to earn money. Through rain, mud, and a flooded Tiber River, Ossoli and Fuller journeyed to Rome in a diligence.

Her new room was on the Piazza Barberini, located between the Quirinal Palace, the quarters of Pope Pius IX and the Palace Barberini, the home of an Italian family whose wealth had been protected by the Church through centuries. From her sunny high window she could look down on the passersby – most of whom could be described as the Italian working class. As an American, she was an anomaly – most Americans had fled Rome.

Mid-November crowds were marching on the Quirinal demanding to see the Pope. From her ringside window seat, Fuller could see Sergeant Ossoli standing guard outside the Pope's palace. The Pope refused to recognize a delegation from the people. The people burned his doors. Then the Pope agreed to demands. Days later, on November 24, the Pope put on a pair of large glasses. Disguised as an ordinary priest, he escaped in a carriage with the Bavarian envoy and his wife. They drove to the lands of the Bourbon king of Naples, where the Pope received protection in the fortress of Gaeta.

This astounded the Italians. Mazzini commented: "Pius IX has fled: the flight is an abdication."

Fuller was unforgiving. She thought he should have resigned.

Her words appeared in *The Tribune*: "Well, who would have thought it? The Pope, the Cardinals, the Princes are gone, and Rome is perfectly tranquil, and one does not miss anything, except that there are not so many rich carriages and liveries."

She called upon America to send an ambassador: "...one that has experience of foreign life, that he may act with good judgment.... Another century, and I might ask to be made Ambassador myself...but woman's day has not come yet...."

An election was held, the first universal suffrage to occur in Italy. All those over the age of twenty-one could vote by secret ballad, and on November 29th the Constituente Romana was proclaimed. Expected to follow was a Constituente Italiana which would eventually lead to the unification of Italy, making it one republic – Mazzini's dream.

Fuller received word from Greeley that his wife Molly had given birth to a daughter. He was still worried that Fuller remained in Rome: she should stop writing and return to America "just when Italy and Europe were in the throes of a great Revolution."

With the change of political parties in the United States – Zachery Taylor was now in the White House – Nathaniel Hawthorne was dismissed from his position as surveyor of the Salem custom house. Sophia had been jubilant: "Oh, you can write your book!" Because Sophia had saved enough from her housekeeping money to sustain them for awhile, Hawthorne was freed to begin a work he'd long been thinking about – *The Scarlet Letter*.

Brook Farm was being rented out. Ripley had had to auction off his collection of books and the greenhouse plants; still not enough money had been raised to pay debts. George Bradford had migrated back to Plymouth where he earned a living tilling a patch of ground and selling its produce from door to door. It seemed a poor profession for one with such a fine mind.

Fuller's brother Arthur, now ordained as a Unitarian minister with a church in Manchester, New Hampshire, had to commit Lloyd to an insane asylum in Brattleborough, Vermont.

William Henry Channing had published a three-volume memoir of Dr. William Ellery Channing.

In lecturing on womanhood, Richard H. Dana ridiculed equality; he eulogized Desdemona, Ophelia and Juliet as ideal role models.

A woman by the name of Elizabeth Blackwell was the first to

graduate with honors, along with eighteen men, from Geneva Medical College in New York.

Men from the East were rushing to California, positive they would find gold.

Fuller spent Christmas, with a cold contracted from riding in the coach to Riete, in the cold upstairs room with Angelino. He had had chickenpox but seemed well now, though small, and seemed to keep warm enough, bundled in blankets as he was. He played delightfully with his toys.

New Year's, 1849, she returned to Rome. It steadily rained and the people's anger towards the Pope was at a high pitch. On January 5th the Pope, from Gaeta, sent a document which was posted on walls throughout the city. It proclaimed that all those involved in the November uprising and the establishment of the Constitutional Assembly would be excommunicated.

The people tore the Pope's printed warnings off the walls, tied these posters to the end of candles, and used them to light a procession through the Corso, while they loudly mocked imitations of priestly chants. Some threw the flyers into privies.

The Pope secretly appealed to France, Spain, Austria and even to the United States to use force and influence to help restore Papal power.

Fuller wrote in her daily journal: "The Romans go on as if nothing were pending. Yet it seems very probably that the French will soon be at Civita Vecchia and with hostile intentions."

She wrote Emerson that she was leading a lonely life in Rome, though her spirits were risen to concert pitch. She tried to think of nothing but the present.

In need of money, she wrote to Richard for a loan and sent off two good articles to Greeley. Greeley reiterated his plea that she return to the States. Rome was the "Eternal city but why stay there eternally?"

Greeley was causing a sensation on the floor of Congress and in the pages of *The Tribune* by exposing extravagant travel expenses of Congressmen, including an overpayment to a young man from Illinois, Abraham Lincoln. Greeley had temporarily turned politician and had been appointed to take over a brief unexpired term in Congress, representing the district of New York above Fourteenth Street. His wife was overworked and tired.

On February 5 the Romans paraded through the streets in celebration of the opening of the Constituent Assembly. They had elected as deputies Mazzini and Garibaldi, the atheist exiled guerilla leader, the hero of Montevideo, who had been leading his troops to Venice when the events of the revolution caused him to head to Rome.

From her balcony Fuller watched Garibaldi enter Rome. He was an imposing figure, of average height but powerfully built, with light chestnut hair flowing to his shoulders, blond moustache and beard. He wore a red tunic and a black broad-brimmed felt hat trimmed with an ostrich feather. People compared his expression of sublime serenity to the paintings of Christ the Savior.

Within four days Fuller stood amidst the crowds that heard the formal announcement of the formation of the Roman Republic. There were banners, bells, cannon blasts, and shouts of "*Viva la Repubblica! Viva l'Italia!*"

A few days later Roman walls were plastered with posters advocating that Mazzini be given Roman citizenship since he was now elected to the Assembly, and a call went out to him to return. Fuller wrote Mazzini her tribute: "For your sake I would wish that at this moment to be an Italian and a man of action. But though an American, I am not even a woman of action ; so the best I can do is to pray with the whole heart: Heaven bless dear Mazzini...."

On the night of March 5 Mazzini entered Rome, on foot to avoid crowds, through the Porta del Popolo. Within three days he was knocking on Fuller's door. They talked for two hours. Dearly, she loved Mazzini. His soft, radiant look made music to her soul.

To her American readers: "He enters to defend Italy, if any man can, against her foes...Can any? – I fear the entrance into Jerusalem may be followed by the sacrifice."

Fuller quoted Mazzini's stirring first address to the Assembly. "After the Rome of the Emperors, after the Rome of the Popes, will come the Rome of the People. The Rome of the People is arisen; do not salute with applause, but let us rejoice together!"

Fuller thought Mazzini looked exhausted and melancholy when he finished his speech. Sustained by the fire of his soul, he said, "We will conquer." Fuller said, "Such men as Mazzini conquer always – conquer in defeat."

The fervor did not postpone Carnival season. This year Fuller could join the merrymakers, but it seemed less splendid because the rich coaches of the dukes and princes were nowhere to be seen, and there were no foreign visitors. Still, the costumes and flowers were colorful. To her *Tribune* readers: "The Roman still plays amid his serious affairs...." She was gathering materials and keeping notes on the revolution for her new book.

Mail from the United States was months late; some was lost. Finally she received the needed money from Richard. One check he'd sent had been intercepted and forged. Her rent would be paid with her *Tribune* articles. Richard had been married to a women she had never met. The baby son of her brother Eugene had died. Ellen and William Ellery Channing had separated. Cary's sister, Ellen Hooper, had died at the age of thirty-six. Mary Rotch had died and had left no legacy for Fuller from all her weath. Cary was expecting a baby – she would be in the mountains (as Fuller had been) for the birth. Lidian had been too enfeebled to do her housework so she hired a former Brook Farm housekeeper. Copies of James Russell Lowell's book, *A Fable For Critics,* were filtering into Italy. It hurt to read his sharp attack on her.*

She no longer could withhold her secret from Cary Sturgis: "All the solid happiness I have known has been at times when he went to sleep in my arms.... I do not look forward to his career and his manly life: it is now I want to be with him, before care and bafflings begin. If I had a little money I should go with him into strict retirement for a year or two and live for him alone. This I cannot do; all life that has been or could be natural to me is invariably denied. God knows why, I suppose."

But the sun shone and she and Ossoli went out of the city on picnics, carrying roast chestnuts and bread and wine. The Storys returned to Rome since Fuller had advised all was calm. They enjoyed breakfasts, walks, evenings at the opera.

That Garlibaldi's legion was stationed at Rieti caused constant worry. These men had reputations for being desperadoes; there was

---

* For an account of Lowell's attack, see Vol. II in this series, *Why Margaret Fuller Ossoli Is Forgotten,* by Laurie James.

fear of looting, raping, killing. But Fuller could work out no other arrangement for Angelino.

Cary Sturgis promised to take the dear one if anything happened to her and Ossoli, a promise which touched Fuller deeply.

The dear one seemed in excellent health when she visited Rieti at the end of March, but a violent fight involving knives broke out in the household. She was so apprehensive that she sent for Ossoli.

In Rome by the end of April the threat of war came from all sides. The Bourbon king of Naples was to the south; the Austrian emperor to the north and east. The King of Spain was sending troops from the west, by sea.

The French regiment landed at Civita Vecchia, about forty miles northwest of the city, and General Charles Oudinot announced that his several thousand men had come, not to attack, but to stabilize. In actuality, Louis Napoleon wanted to achieve military power in the Italian peninsula and to become emperor. He needed the Pope to consecrate his rule.

The French envoy told Mazzini that he would block Austrian and Bourbon intervention and appease the Pope and the people. Mazzini took the message back to the Constitutional Assembly who voted to resist the French. Garibaldi brought his forces out of the mountains, and the Romans began building supports for cannons and wooden barricades to strengthen the Roman Walls.

Princess Belgioioso came to Rome and, without money since her lands had been confiscated, organized some ecclesiastical facilities into hospitals. She raised funds by begging from door to door, and called upon women to serve as nurses. Fuller received a note from her to take charge of the hospital of the Fate Bene Fratelli which was on the island in the Tiber river, close to what might become the front lines of the attack.

"Italians never fight" was the precept in the mind of the French General Oudinot as he marched his disciplined, well trained, well equipped army towards Rome. The priests at Gaeta had led him to believe that the Romans were sympathetic to the Pope and that there would not be much resistance.

The general had no idea that he faced a resolute army made up of Garibaldi's men and Lombard sharp shooters, supported by the national guard, papal regulars who had deserted, and numbers of hastily recruited men, volunteers and university students. Still, the Romans were disadvantaged in that many were untrained. Their equipment and arms were inferior and out-of-date.

Fuller took her place in the hospital on the Tiber Island. The handful of Americans still in Rome moved to the relatively safe Casa Diez, a house which displayed the American Flag. (It was to be within sight of the gunfire.)

The Roman troops, which included Citizen Captain Ossoli – his skills had been recognized and he had been promoted – were stationed nearby atop the walls above the Vatican gardens and gate, near the Porta Pertusa.

Outside the walls Garibaldi and his men were waiting at the Villa Corsini. This is where the French army attacked at eleven o'clock in the morning. Garibaldi sent out his untrained university students, who fought with spirit, then he brought out his reserves.

By five o'clock Fuller had seventy wounded in her hospital. The French were forced to retreat to about four hours march out of Rome. They had five hundred dead and three hundred sixty-five prisoners. The Italians were jubilant with their win.

That night Fuller "saw the terrible agonies of those dying or who needed amputation, felt their mental pains and longed for their loved ones...."

Meanwhile, other enemies appeared on the horizon: a force of Neopolitans were marching towards Rome, and Bourbons and Austrians threatened as well. Garibaldi led his troops out of Rome and was successful in various surprise assaults which temporarily halted.

In Rome all was quiet the next month as the French sent an envoy to negotiate.

Most of the time Fuller was busy in the hospital, but whenever possible she and the Storys took provisions to Ossoli, stationed on the Vatican Wall. He shared whatever they brought with the other men. Fuller and Ossoli could only speak impersonally since he was always surrounded by fellow soldiers. They expressed their love and concern for each other in short and quickly written notes.

It was almost impossible to receive word from Rieti. One messenger who managed to break through the French lines brought a threatening letter from the wetnurse, demanding more money. Fuller finally got the money to her by sending it through Angelino's physician.

She had terrible images of what might happen if she and Ossoli were killed, and decided she must tell someone in Italy of their situation. She chose her compassionate friend Emelyn Story who promised to see that if anything happened Angelino would be sent to America to her mother and Cary Sturgis. But soon, and it was not totally surprising, the Storys decided to exit under the white flag for Germany.

Fuller turned to the American envoy, Lewis Cass, Jr., who had recently become a friend, who'd seen that she'd moved to the Casa Diez. He'd been keeping her informed of negotiations between the Triumvirs and Ferdinand de Lesseps, the French envoy, and had been giving her various documents which she translated and published with her articles in the *Tribune*. Cass promised he'd see to all particulars.

In odd moments Fuller went to the bohemian district along the Via Margutta where painter Thomas Hicks remained in his studio. (Two other American artists had joined the fight.) She sat, probably talking English to him, while he, a kindred spirit, painted her portrait.* It seems natural that she would arrange for a picture, as she had arranged for a daguerreotype when she'd left the United States. A portrait would be a worthy parting gift to her son, her son's father, her mother and family.

In her *Tribune* article Fuller called the next involvement the "Second Act of the French farce." It seemed the Triumvirate and de Lesseps had reached an agreement, but Oudinot refused his signature, and announced his troops would attack on Monday, June 4. De Lesseps had left for Paris. Evidentially, Oudinot had been using the month of negotiation to gather heavy reinforcements.

Most Roman troops had been stationed inside the city walls, but there was one small regiment outside the walls in two villas which was in direct line to the Porta San Pancrazio and the Janiculum Hill.

---

*The Hicks portrait appears on the cover of this book. It is owned by Constance Fuller Threinen.

Oudinot launched a surprise attack while these soldiers slept, before dawn, on Sunday, June 3. By dawn the French had taken these villas and were shelling the Porta San Pancrazio.

From her window Fuller saw "the smoke of every discharge, the flash of bayonets; with a glass could see the men." On the walls a band of Roman musicians diligently played the Marseillaise in hopes of psyching the French into remorse; Fuller heard the strong rhythms through the noise of the gunshots.

In her *Tribune* article: "The attack began before sunrise, and lasted all day.... The French fought with great bravery, and this time it is said with beautiful skill and order, sheltering themselves in their advance by movable barricades. The Italians fought like lions, and no inch of ground was gained by the assailants. The loss of the French is said to be very great; it could not be otherwise. Six or seven hundred Italians are dead or wounded. Among them are many officers, those of Garibaldi especially, who are much exposed by their daring bravery, and whose red tunic makes them the natural mark of the enemy."

The Italians rushed into the streets, shouting "*Roma o Morte!*" Bells were ringing, drums were beating. Mazzini sent out a proclamation: "Romans, arise! To the walls, to the gates, to the barricades! Let us show that not even treachery can vanquish Rome..."

Fuller described: "The musket-fire was almost unintermitted; the roll of the cannon, especially from St. Angelo, almost majestic...."

Stretchers and carts brought a continual stream of wounded into the hospital. Fuller feared that at any moment she would face a wounded Captain Ossoli. She had seen blood stream down a wall next to where he had stood. She had picked up a fragment of a bomb that had burst close to him.

One rocket exploded in the hospital courtyard just as Fuller was arriving. In the streets the Roman civilians daily extinguished live bombs with wet clay. They kept stones piled high and oil boiling in their homes in case the enemy invaded. The cannonade and bayonet sieges were continuous during that hot June month.

"Should I never return – and sometimes I despair of doing so," Fuller wrote in response to a letter from Emerson who complained about wasted time and mumps sweeping through his household just as he was trying to reprint *Nature* and revise his "Great Men" lectures.

"...I am caught in such a net of ties here – if ever you know of my life here, I think you will only wonder at the constancy with which I have sustained myself; the degree of profit to which, .amid great difficulties, I have put the time, at least in the way of observation. Meanwhile, love me all you can; let me feel, that, amid the fearful agitations of the world, there are pure hands, with healthful, even pulse, stretched out toward me, if I claim their grasp....Rome is being destroyed, her glorious oaks – her villas, haunts of sacred beauty, that seemed the possession of the world for ever – the villa of Raphael, the villa of Albani, home of Winckelmann and the best expression of the ideal of modern Rome, and so many other sanctuaries of beauty – all must perish, lest a foe should level a musket from their shelter. I could not, could not!

"I know not, dear friend, whether I shall ever get home across that great ocean, but here in Rome I shall no longer wish to live. O Rome, my country! could I imagine that the triumph of what I held dear was to heap such desolation on thy head!"

How she suffered to see the wounded and amputated...yet how noble the young men were. As they recovered, she took them books and flowers, and she read and talked with them in the gardens of the Pope's palace, now committed to the use of convalescents.

A letter came from her sister Ellen. She had just given birth to a baby boy. Ellery was off on another expedition to Cape Cod with Henry David Thoreau. Fuller wrote back: "The world seems to go so strangely wrong! The bad side triumphs; the blood and tears of the generous flow in vain....A baleful star rose on my birth, and its hostility, I fear, will never be disarmed while I walk below."

On June 22 Fuller reported there was a tremendous cannonade. "That was the fatal hour for the city." But the Italians fought a second line of defence for eight days. "After the 22nd of June, the slaughter of the Romans became every day more fearful.... My heart bled daily more and more...now the balls and bombs began to fall round me also...."

Ossoli was stationed on Pincian Mount, the highest and most exposed position in Rome, directly in line of the expected final shelling. Fuller decided to share the last hours. Together they walked up the hill. It was a bright-starred night. From atop they could look down on the shadowed umbrella pines and Roman rooftops. Statues below reflected beauteous cream-white. All night they gazed at the gorgeous scene while they tensely waited for the first bolt of battle.

Then the dawn rose. All remained quiet. Word spread that the war was over. Garibaldi had made his last stand, had fought bare-handed with his sword; there was no more ammunition. The choices the Triumvir had were to fight as best they could in the streets, to surrender, or to move into the mountains and march to Venice to battle the Austrians. Garibaldi preferred the mountains and battle at Venice.

On July 2,1849 Garibaldi, on a white horse, stood in the center of a piazza, and gloriously called on those who wished to follow. He offered "hunger, thirst, forced marches, battles and death. Let him who loves his country in his heart and not with his lips only, follow me."

Several thousand men "put on the beautiful dress of the Garibaldi legion...." Fuller described the scene for her readers. "Their long hair was blown back from resolute faces; all looked full of courage.... I saw the wounded, all that could go, laden upon their baggage cars; some were already pale and fainting, still they wished to go. I saw many youths, born to rich inheritance, carrying in a handkerchief all their worldly goods. The women were ready; their eyes too were resolved, if sad.... Garibaldi went upon the parapet, and looked upon the road with a spy-glass, and, no obstruction being in sight, he turned his face for a moment back upon Rome, then led the way through the gate. Hard was the heart, stony and seared the eye, that had no tear for the moment."

On the 4th of July the French occupied Rome. "Yes–" Fuller wrote, "July 4th, the day so joyously celebrated in our land is that of the entrance of the French into Rome!"

Fuller and Ossoli did not go out into the streets that day. They sat by their window. Fuller worked on what was to be her last dispatch to the *Tribune*: "O men and women of America, spared these frightful sights – acknowledge as the legitimate leaders and rulers those men who represent the people, who understand their wants, who are ready to die or to live for their good....Friends, countrymen, lovers of virtue, lovers of freedom, lovers of truth! be on the alert. Rest not supine in your easier lives, but remember 'Mankind is one, and beats with one great heart.'"

For about eight days Fuller and the Principessa Belgioioso continued their care of those who remained in the hospital.

Clerical power in Rome was restored.

The French announced that all foreigners who had aided the Republic must leave or face punishment.

It was heartbreak to abandon the wounded men: "Could I have sold my hair or blood from my arm, I would have done it," Fuller wrote.

Mazzini walked the streets. Fuller went to see him where he stayed with a friend. "He had grown old; all the vital juices seemed exhausted; his eyes were all blood-shot; his skin orange; flesh he had none; his hair was mixed with white; his hand painful to the touch; but he had never flinched, never quailed; had protested in the last hour against surrender; sweet and calm, but full of a more fiery purpose than ever; in him I revered the hero and owned myself not of that mould."

He needed a passport, and Fuller approached Lewis Cass for arrangements. With this Mazzini went by sea to Marseille, then through Geneva, to London.

Then word came from Washington D.C. that Lewis Cass, as representative, was permitted to acknowledge United States recognition of the Roman Republic. The news, too late, could only add to the heaviness of Fuller's heart.

Ossoli made another attempt to secure his rightful inheritance – in vain.

A letter came from Horace Greeley: "Ah Margaret!" were his words, "the world grows dark with us. You grieve for Rome has fallen; I mourn for Pickie is dead!" Never having been vaccinated, his son Pickie had died fifteen hours after coming down with cholera. Fuller cried more tears.

Fuller and Ossoli made their way to Rieti, to their son.

An even greater shock. Angelino was a skeleton. The wetnurse, without money to buy milk, had fed Angelino on bread soaked with wine. He was near death.

For four weeks the mother and father nursed him day and night.

Fuller couldn't help but wonder if bringing him back to the cruel world were really an act of love. But "I could not let him go, unless I went with him; and I do hope that the cruel law of my life will, at least, not oblige us to be separated."

An incident involving Ossoli's being held overnight by the police reminded them again that they were not safe near Rome.

No longer was there reason to keep their liaison secret from U.S.A. family and friends. Fuller's mother was sympathetic and loving. She wrote that she looked forward to her daughter's return, to meeting Ossoli, and to seeing their child, as did most of Fuller's friends. Emerson heard the truth in mid-October. He did not acknowledge a word by letter.

Elizabeth Hoar remained silent.

Horace Greeley did not respond.

Fuller supposed that many of her friends simply didn't know what to say. She wrote her sister to tell them that they needn't say anything, but please write. "I am just the same for them as I was before."

Malicious rumors were spreading about her, according to letters from Cary Sturgis, Emelyn Story and William Henry Channing. Fuller's reaction: "I pity those who are inclined to think ill, when they might as well have inclined the other way. However, let them go; there are many in the world who stand the test, enough to keep us from shivering to death."

The three ventured through the Umbrian hills to Florence where they settled into small rooms in a house in the American community. People opened warm arms to them – after overcoming the initial amazement of seeing Fuller with a mate and a year-old son. Their money, Fuller and Ossoli hoped, would hold out for the winter.

Florence was occupied by Austrians. Again the police began to pressure. Fuller arranged clearance with a Lewis Cass contact. Suspicion quieted.

Soon there was an enjoyable social life of concerts and evening soirees. Robert and Elizabeth Barrett Browning were friendly. Since Elizabeth had a fat, laughing, violet-eyed baby and was again pregnant, the two women had a new commonality. The Marchesa Arconati Visconti was there, as was the sculptor, Horatio Greenough and his wife. The artist Joseph Mozier and daughter, Isabella, were there; he was helpful in trying to secure Fuller an opportunity to write a series of "Letters From Florence." There was also a former Brook Farmer Horace Sumner, who'd been travelling throughout the South of Europe for about a year for his health. He was the youngest son of Fuller's father's Boston friend, the Hon. Charles P. Sumner, well known for his legal and literary eminence. The young Sumner was totally admiring of Fuller, brought her flowers every day. And Isabella began to study with Fuller – the money helped Fuller to pay her wetnurse.

It was glorious to watch the child grow. While he slept in the mornings, the mother worked on her book and the father, often wearing his uniform jacket (in the house only), would sit and read. He also studied sculpture with Greenough. Fuller's Italian history was returned from a London editor because a recent copyright law made publishing foreign work difficult.

Even so, life in Florence was pleasant for the family. They were together and that, after having been separated so long, brought joy and peace, though they were quite aware that they were closely watched by the Austrian police. Lewis Cass helped Ossoli obtain a U.S.A. passport.

The eldest Ossoli brother had broken promises to his sister – she was retaliating by taking him to court for her part of the family inheritance. Thus, there seemed no hope that Ossoli would obtain his share.

Lewis Cass informed that in Rome the hunt was on for revolutionaries; they were being fined and imprisoned.

Fuller figured that Emerson would help with the publication of her Roman history which presumably would substantiate a means of income.

In America she could also write for other periodicals. Perhaps she could resume her position on the *Tribune*, though Greeley had not yet communicated.

At The Town and Country Club meetings in Boston Emerson vetoed women from becoming members. Elizabeth Hoar was serving as his copyist and secretary. Marcus Spring and Henry James helped Emerson by organizing some lecture dates in Brooklyn, Manhattan, and Newark, and so Emerson left on another lecture tour.

From the Astor House in New York where he stayed, Emerson wrote Lidian that nothing would keep him away from Concord except the necessity of earning money. Would she tell Mr. Thoreau to give a day of attention to set new posts for the vines?

Emerson's *Representative Men* appeared in the bookstores and was eliciting the usual mixed press. There were comparisons with Carlyle's *Heroes and Hero-Worship*. Some said the book had nothing original or vital to offer. The man was past his peak.

A Week on the Concord and Merrimack was also appearing in the bookstores. The author, Henry David Thoreau, paid for publication.

News came that Edgar Allen Poe had been found lying on a Baltimore street in a dazed stupor and had died, delirious, within a few days in a hospital. A numbing tragedy.

Fuller faced decisions in the spring of 1850. Ossoli, of course, would be warmly welcomed into the U.S.A. by the Fuller family, at least, but adjustment was sure to be difficult, and he would have to leave his sister whom he loved. He did not speak English, though he was trying to learn and, as an Italian nobleman, he did not have the education or intellect to mix well with Fuller's friends.

She might return to America without Ossoli. But what would he do? He had no money, and there was no career open to him. It would be heartbreaking to separate him from his son, not to mention her own sadness in separation from him.

Surely he would be able to find some happiness in America in his love for their child and his pleasure in woods and fields – until political and economic changes, perhaps a new revolution, enabled their return to Rome.

Suddenly Emerson was discouraging Fuller's crossing the ocean. He would keep to his promise to find her the best possible publisher, but her absence would be advantageous. It would promote "solidity to your testimony" and "new rays of reputation & wonder to you as a star – advantages which no bookseller can overlook for a moment. It is certainly an unexpected side for me to support – the advantages of your absenteeism – I, who had vainly imagined that one of these days, when tired of cities, our little Concord would draw you to itself, by the united claims of your family and of your friends – O but surprise is the woof you love to weave into all your web…"

Lidian, he added, was never well, but perhaps not much more invalid than when Fuller knew her.

Fuller guessed that this change of attitude in Emerson was due to the rumors being spread about her throughout the United States.

Fuller anticipated that Emerson would never understand how she could have life in common with Ossoli who knew nothing of the great ideas, who seemed externally inarticulate and passive. Emerson, as well as other friends, would not appreciate the practicality of his person, the purity and simple strength of his character. They would not see that for her his genuine affection and love was meaningful.

As for Ossoli, he was never concerned with the opinions of her intellectual friends. He was used to her circle, and when he could not respond he simply found other things to do.

He had always been there for her, soothing her through her weakest hours. True, he answered to only a part of her life, but there was no interference "with anything I ought to have or be," she wrote William Henry Channing. "I do not feel any way constrained or limited or that I have made any sacrifice." They harmonized well together. His steady companionship was comforting. There was no burden in this partnership of daily life.

Whether Ossoli's love for her could endure permanently, she was unsure, though she wrote her sister she had confidence in it. Their love in the present was what was relevant. She was the eldest, and this was a drawback. In time the difference would become readily apparent. She was prepared to face the problem whenever it evolved, and to allow him the freedom he might need. What was significant, she felt, was that they did love and, even for a moment in time, it was great.

She delayed the decision. Florence was joyous, the three of them together. She wrote Cary Sturgis: "It is very sad we have no money; we could have been so quietly happy awhile. I rejoice in all that Ossoli did but the results in this our earthly state, are disastrous, especially as my strength is now so much impaired. This much I do hope, in life or death to be no more separated from Angelino."

To buy steamer tickets Fuller borrowed money from Costanza Arconati and from a bank with the help of Marcus Spring's signature.

To Emelyn Story: "I go home prepared to expect everything that is painful...."

She read newspaper accounts of several shipwrecks. To Costanza Arconati: "Safety is not to be secured, then, by the wisest foresight. I shall embark...in my merchant ship; praying, indeed fervently, that it may not be my lot to lose my babe at sea, either by unsolaced sickness, or amid the howling waves. Or that, if I should, it may be brief anguish, and Ossoli, he and I go together."

As a child Ossoli had been told by a fortune teller, "Beware of the sea!" He'd never been on a ship.

Fuller remembered her nightmares of drowning.

She wrote: "I am absurdly fearful, and various omens have combined to give me a dark feeling. I am become indeed a miserable coward, for the sake of Angelino. I fear heat and cold, fear the voyage, fear biting poverty....I feel perfectly willing to stay my threescore years and ten, if it be thought I need so much tuition from this planet; but it seems to me that my future upon earth will soon close.... I have a vague expectation of some crisis – I know not what....My life proceeds so regularly, far more so than the fates of a Greek tragedy, that I can but accept all the pages as they turn."

The sun shown and there was a clear blue sky May 17,1850 when they embarked on the three-masted American merchant ship, the *Elizabeth*, which carried a cargo of old paintings, almonds, olive oil, silk, a hundred fifty tons of Carrara marble and Hiram Powers' statue of John Calhoun. Packed in Fuller's trunks were her Italian history, the love letters she and Ossoli had written, Mazzini's letters, and innumerable documents concerning the revolution. She was turning forty years.

Emerson, lecturing in Cincinnati, celebrated his forty-seventh birthday by taking the day off. He travelled thirty-five miles with a group of men to Fort Ancient, Ohio, where there was a commemoration of inhabitants who'd lived there three thousand years earlier.

He wrote Lidian that she could "very thankfully dispense with me." So he was going to take the long way home, that is, sightsee in Louisville, Nashville, Mississippi, Chicago. From St. Louis he wrote a long detailed letter to Lidian: "I long, of course, to be at home."

On board the *Elizabeth* there was a white nanny goat they'd bought to give the milk Angelino needed. There were a handful of passengers: the Ossolis, Celeste Paolini, a young Italian girl who would help with Angelino, Horace Sumner, and Catherine Hasty, the captain's wife.

The first calamity occured when Captain Hasty became ill with smallpox. They landed at Gibraltar to receive help, but he died, and they were quarantined for a week. When all seemed fine, the first mate took command, and they embarked again.

Soon Angelino came down with the deadly fever. Again the Ossolis nursed day and night. Miraculously, he survived.

On the evening of July 18 a sudden summer hurricane swept in with rain and winds of gale force. The first mate went to bed thinking they were off Cape May or Barnegat, New Jersey, but by 3:30 AM, now July 19, 1850, they had struck a sandbar off Fire Island, New York. The cargo of marble broke through, and water rushed into the ship. The life boats were swamped. The frightened passengers in their flimsy nightclothes made their way through the darkness to the forecastle and hoped the rain and winds would abate. One sailor took a life preserver and another took a spar and both managed to get to shore.

Another sailor made several dangerous trips back to the cabin to secure valuables for the passengers, but the waves finally forced him to desist before he had retrieved Fuller's manuscript of the Italian Revolution (and perhaps the official papers she'd earlier given to Lewis Cass). Soon thereafter the ship cracked in half and Fuller's hopes for an income sank to the bottom of the ocean.

The passengers waited to be rescued. They could see the shore, could see some of the silk and other pieces of cargo wash on to the shore, could see beach pirates gathering the cargo as souvenirs. A life boat appeared, but it was not launched. Men tried to throw a line with mortar shot, but the effort thwarted. The tide came in.

The sailors took planks of wood, tied ropes on them, and urged each passenger to hold tight and jump into the ocean, to be followed by a sailor who would swim alongside. The captain's wife attempted this maneuver. Hers was a life-and-death struggle, with the sailor rescuing her by grabbing her hair. But both made it to the sandy beach. Then Horace Sumner jumped in with a plank. He immediately drowned.

Fuller, seated at the foremast with Angelino in her arms, still in her white nightgown, her hair flowing, would not be separated from Angelino. She is reported to have said, "I see nothing but death before me. I shall never reach the shore." Ossoli took no action, seemed to be waiting for Fuller's lead.

Other sailors dove into the swirling waters. Some reached the beach. Finally, the last strong sailor clasped Angelino, wrapped him in a sack which he tied round his shoulders and neck, vowing his most superior effort. Then he jumped.

A wave next took Ossoli and Celeste. The following wave took Fuller. Shortly, the bodies of Angelino and the sailor washed onto shore. The bodies of Fuller and Ossoli were never found.

Emerson, who'd been in Concord about three weeks after his Mid-West lecture tour, did not immediately hear of the dreadful tragedy since the facts were slow in reaching *The Tribune* office and Greeley could publish only short fragments as they came in. On July 23 a full report was printed, which Emerson read.

Emerson considered going to Fire Island, then decided to advance money to Henry David Thoreau to investigate. Thoreau went off, as did William Ellery Channing and William Henry Channing. They met Arthur Fuller, Charles Sumner, and Marcus Spring there. Representing the *Tribune* was journalist Bayard Taylor, who'd done some excellent reporting on the California gold rush for Greeley. They talked with survivors, found a trunk, some love letters, a piece of Ossoli's clothing. Taylor wrote a heartrending account which Greeley published as well as Catherine Hasty's experience.

Americans had not known whether to scorn or to accept Fuller when she returned. Her friend, the poet/philosopher (whose second edition of *Nature* had just been printed), summed up Margaret Fuller's position in his private journal:

> The timorous said, What shall we do? how shall she be received, now that she brings a husband & child home? But she had only to open her mouth & a triumphant success awaited her.
>
> ...Her integrity was perfect. She was bent on truth. But she lost herself in sentimentalism. She made numerous mistakes. [27]

Then, in seven words, he subordinated her to himself: "I have lost in her my audience."

To Thomas Carlyle: "She died in happy hour for herself. Her health was much exhausted. Her marriage would have taken her away from us all & there was a subsistence yet to be secured, & diminished powers, & old age."

When Horace Greeley wanted to publish a memoir of Fuller, Emerson countered, "Is Margaret Fuller worth a Memoirs?" He commented in his journal that "Margaret Fuller & Her Friends" must be written, but not post haste.

The book on Fuller was an essential line of American history, he noted, but advised Greeley that in whatever articles to be printed of Margaret Fuller's to "let the notices of Longfellow and of Lowell be omitted....There is no need to repeat the wounds."

Two men who at first agreed to work on her *Memoirs,* Sam Ward and William Ellery Channing, eventually backed out.

Paulina Wright Davis, who'd earlier hoped that Margaret Fuller would return from Europe to help lead the woman's rights movement, was now working single handedly on the First National Woman's Rights Convention to be held in Worcester, Massachusetts on October 23-24, in Brinley Hall. She contacted many persons, among them Ralph Waldo Emerson who signed The Call but did not attend.

Among the thousand persons who attended were William Lloyd Garrison, Wendell Phillips, Frederick Douglass, Adin Ballou, Gerrit Smith, Elizabeth Cady Stanton, Angelina Grimke Weld, Sojourner Truth, Lucretia Mott, Lucy Stone, Antoinette L. Brown, Ernestine Rose, Abby Kelley, Elizabeth Blackwell, Dr. Harriot K. Hunt, Rebecca Spring, Elizabeth Oakes Smith, the future Mrs. John Stuart Mill, and William Henry Channing who was elected vice president. Davis was elected president.

The Call included words that Fuller could have written: "Men and women in their reciprocities of love and duty, are one flesh and one blood....The sexes should not, for any reason or by any chance, take hostile attitudes toward each other....they should harmonize in opinion and co-operate in effort, for the reason that they must unite in the ultimate achievement of the desired reformation."

Wendell Phillips presented the resolutions which included woman's right of suffrage and of eligibility to hold office. William Henry Channing outlined a plan for organization and a National Central Committee was formed.

The press had a heyday in reporting this event, as they had had during the Seneca Falls Conference. An Arabic saying was quoted: "When a hen crows like a cock it is time to cut her head off."

The New York Herald article lashed out at: "...that motley mingling of abolitionists, socialists, and infidels...this hybrid, mongrel, piebald, crackbrained, pitiful, disgusting and ridiculous assemblage...may God have mercy on their miserable souls."

Horace Greeley's *Tribune* was the only paper to treat the Convention seriously.

Emerson inserted his opinion in his journal:

> I do not think a woman's convention...can much avail. It is an attempt to manufacture public opinion, & of course repels all persons who love the simple & direct method. I find the Evils real & great. If I go from Hanover Street to Atkinson Street – as I did yesterday – what hundreds of extremely ordinary, paltry, hopeless women I see, whose plight is piteous to think of. If it were possible to repair the rottenness of human nature, to provide a rejuvenescence, all were well, & no specific reform, no legislation would be needed. For, as soon as you have a sound & beautiful woman, a figure in the style of the Antique, Juneo, Diana, Pallas, Venus, & the Graces, all falls into place, the men are magnetised, heavens open & no lawyer need be called in to prepare a clause, for women moulds the lawgiver. I should therefore advise that the Woman's Convention should be holden in the Sculpture Gallery, that this high remedy might be suggested.

In November, in preparation for Fuller's *Memoirs,* R.W.E. read S.M.F.'s letters to C.S.:

> Yesterday I read Margaret's letters to C S (Carolyn Sturgis) full of probity, full of talent & wit, full of friendship, ardent affections, full of noble aspiration. They are tainted with a female mysticism which to me appears so merely an affair of constitution that it claims no more respect or reliance than the charity or patriotism of a man who has just dined well & feels good....In our noble Margaret her personal feeling colours all her judgments of persons, of books, of pictures, & of the

> laws of the world. This is easily felt in common women & a large deduction is civilly made on the spot, by whosoever replies to their remark. But when the speaker has such brilliant talent & literature as Margaret, she gives so many fine names to these merely sensuous & subjective objects, that the hearer is long imposed upon, and thinks so precise & glittering nomenclature cannot be of mere *muscae volitantes*, but must be of some real ornithology hitherto unknown to him.
>
> This mere feeling exaggerates a host of trifles, as birthdays, seals, bracelets, ciphers, coincidences & contretemps, into a dazzling mythology; but when one goes to sift it, & find if there be a real meaning, it eludes all search. Whole sheets of warm fluent florid writing are here, in which the eye is caught by "carbuncle," "heliotrope," "dragon," "aloes," "Magna Dea," "limboes," "stars," & "purgatory," but can connect all this or any part of it with no universal experience.
>
> Yet Margaret had her own merits, & we shall not see her like. What a basis of earnest love & knowledge & love of character! Her decided selection so sagacious generally of her friends; in some instances, her election anticipates for some years any personal intercourse & her fidelity to them, & generous forgiving appreciation. – She estimates society & its opinion, very well – far better than so many people of talent. Her expensiveness creates tragic relations & feeling of it, and thence with ill health comes all the unworthy sentimentalism of Destiny, Dæmon, god & the cross. [28]

The problem Emerson faced was what portion of Fuller's letters and papers would go "to the press or to the flames."

He wrote Sam Ward that Cary Sturgis might help decide.

A year later, on October 7, 1851, Emerson wrote Conference conveners Paulina Wright Davis and Lucy Stone that he could not attend or speak at the Second National Woman's Rights Convention soon to be held in Worcester, Massachusetts, though he was in sympathy with their purposes, because he was busy editing a "Life" of Margaret Fuller.

William Henry Channing was working on the same "Life," but he attended, plus many others, who so crowded the rooms that hundreds could not enter and therefore they moved to the large auditorium at City Hall. Channing helped to draft the resolutions which called for equal rights, widening job opportunities, equality in education and earnings, in ownership of property, in the guardianship of children, in inequities in the law including all-male juries, the taxation of women without representation by their own sex, and he spoke against the supreme right of men to govern women without their consent.

By December 3 Emerson had backed off from Fuller's *Memoirs.* He "receded" from supervision and decided to make his own independent sketch, drawing on Fuller's correspondence with him and Cary Sturgis.

In the next year, looking through her papers, he seemed surprised to discover that Fuller had human sexual needs. In his journal:

> The unlooked for trait in all these journals to me is the woman, poor woman: they are all hysterical. She is bewailing her virginity and languishing for a husband. 'I need help. No, I need a full godlike embrace from some sufficient love.' [29]

Next, the friend, the perceptive poet/visionary, selected, censored, scissored, put into the flames or otherwise destroyed the Fuller letters and papers he had, and shaped the portrait/biography which he felt should be passed along to posterity.*

Never again did Ralph Waldo Emerson publicly help to promote the name of Margaret Fuller.

In December 1852 he wrote Richard Fuller that he could not help with a book of a collection of Margaret Fuller's writings: "My working time which weak eyes and other accidents make shorter is too little for my own tasks."

A year later he complained into his private journal of the bitter satire that the American public was relieved to hear of the deaths of persons such as Margaret Fuller who had attained "the highest & broadest culture that any American woman has possessed," for such persons could not support themselves financially or fit into society adequately. (See Appendix for the full text of Emerson statement.)

---

* For a detailed description on how he gathered and mutilated the material and put together the *Memoirs,* see Volume II of this series, *Why Margaret Fuller Ossoli Is Forgotten,* by Laurie James.

That same year, on September 7, 1853, Emerson again turned down Richard Fuller's request to write a introduction for a collection of Fuller's work: "My two tasks at present...will leave me no week before winter to write an introductory essay...."

Fuller was dead. Her claim to immortality was largely in the hands of her "Dear Wise One."

Lidian was right. She said that the only sin which people never forgive in each other is a difference of opinion.

P.S.

1850

The word-of-mouth that followed Margaret Fuller's tragic death by shipwreck was so noisy that the U. S. government began to allocate funds for better life saving methodology.

Government involvement had been practically non-existent. In 1848 Congress had appropriated some monies for hut-like life saving stations along the dangerous Long Island coast, and the following year some wealthy New Yorkers formed the Life Saving Benevolent Association. But the actual operation and maintenance systems were in a developmental stage, and equipment was inadequate and vandalized. Furthermore, volunteers were slow to appear at scenes of disaster.

After Margaret Fuller's tragedy, the general consensus was that more moneys were needed to launch studies, to build better structures, to equip stations with surfboats and apparatus, and to hire trained personnel. (See notes under headings 1854, 1858, 1878, 1918.)

❧ ❧ ❧

During July, the same month Margaret Fuller drowned, Florence Nightingale ignored family objections and resolved to train for a nursing profession at the Kaiserwerth Institute in Germany. She had met Fuller in Rome during the Italian Revolution when Fuller was directing a hospital for the war wounded. Nightingale was to lead a revolution in nursing practices and in hospital sanitation.

❧ ❧ ❧

November 11 - Powers' marble statue of John C. Calhoun, whose weight had helped to cause the sinking of the *Elizabeth*, was raised from the bottom of the Atlantic by deep sea divers and moved to its intended destination, the Capital Building in Washington D. C. Later, it was moved again, for safety purposes, to Columbia, South Carolina. It was destroyed during Sherman's capture of the city.

❧ ❧ ❧

Sam Ward succeeded his father as American agent for Baring Brothers, the English investment firm. He and Anna Barker lived on an elegant farm called "Highwood" in Lenox, Massachusetts, and Ward combined farming and intellect. The couple were gregarious social leaders and gave parties for fifty or sixty guests. The farm failed to be self-sustaining and Ward's father helped financially. Ward translated some Goethe, wrote a series of critical essays, and continued sketching landscapes. As Ward's fortune increased, he became a generous patron of the arts.

❧ ❧ ❧

After John Stuart Mill wrote his essay, "The Subjection of Women," Cary Sturgis made a statement that echoed Margaret Fuller: "I should like to thank John Stuart Mill for being just & understanding that women are slaves still politically – & therefore socially – & for so nobly protesting against the injustice shown them."

Sturgis developed her intuitive and psychic powers, loved the exotic, analyzed handwriting, and came to think of herself as a "mediocre female."

Sturgis and husband William Tappan named their daughter after Margaret Fuller's sister, Ellen. They involved themselves in the liberated Berkshire literary circle, dominated by writer/educator/prison reformer Catherine Sedgwick. Sturgis also devoted effort to the founding of Radcliffe College.

❧ ❧ ❧

Elizabeth Hoar translated the Italian correspondence which had washed ashore on Fire Island beach – the letters of Margaret Fuller and Giovanni Angelo Ossoli. Today the originals and the translations are in Houghton Library, Harvard University.

❧ ❧ ❧

William Henry Channing spent hours working on a new magazine, *The Spirit of the Age.*

❧ ❧ ❧

March 7 - Daniel Webster delivered a famous speech, "On The Constitution and the Union." Thereafter, the Fugitive Slave Law was enacted.

❧ ❧ ❧

Forty-six year-old Hawthorne completed *The Scarlet Letter.* Immediately it sold five thousand copies.

At the Custom House where Hawthorne worked, he'd come across some old documents affixed with the cutout of a velvet scarlet letter "A." The documents described the crime of Hester Prynne, a young colonial New England woman who had dared to break the moral code of her village. In Hawthorne's novel, some parallels can be drawn from Margaret Fuller's life-story.

❧ ❧ ❧

Amelia Bloomer designed the Bloomer dress. Among the women wearing and promoting it were Elizabeth Cady Stanton, Lucy Stone, and Susan Anthony.

❧ ❧ ❧

After Pickie died, the Horace Greeleys became involved in spiritualism and attended seances wherein they thought they received messages from their dead son. Finally, Greeley concluded that spiritualism was a hoax. He and wife Molly moved out of Turtle Bay into the city, but Greeley often stayed overnight in hotels rather than at his city home.

❧ ❧ ❧

On midwest lecture tours Emerson wrote more often to his daughters than his wife or Elizabeth Hoar or Cary Sturgis.

Lidian's illness worsened. Her daughter said she dwelt on slights real and fancied: "violently pacing her room, looking wild, and wringing her hands." It would bother her if a vase was out of place. Often when guests came she excused herself and went to her room - "Mother dreads household company."

She wore black silk, a white illusion cap with baby blue ribbons, had a beautiful carriage and walk, "like a lady abbess," Sophia Hawthorne declared. She adopted the current interest in clairvoyants and table tipping. Daughter Ellen tells the story of how "Mother had settled into the habit of thinking she couldn't go anywhere." Once she left for Seconnet to be with a friend but was back within two days, to the astonishment of Emerson and Ellen. When they questioned her, she said, "Why Ellen said in her letter her Father had caught a cold."

Lidian became a knowledgeable homeopathist, according to daughter Ellen: "...a little medicine chest appeared on her bureau. The squills and paregoic with which we (children) had formerly been dosed when we were sick disappeared forever. She had soon four or five medical books and for forty years was diligent in consulting them and selecting remedies for her own ailments and those of all her large clientele of dependants and semi-dependants."

❧ ❧ ❧

After the failure of Brook Farm George Ripley set up an editorial room in the *Tribune* building in order to continue publishing *The Harbinger*, but this paper faded into oblivion. Ripley took Margaret Fuller's chair at *The Tribune*. He became editorial director of the literary department. He wrote reviews and listed the new books, but he worked without byline. He also free lanced and tried to pay off Brook Farm debts. Both he and his wife grew tired of reform. Sophia passed through a religious crisis, converted to Catholicism, and found employment teaching in Flatbush, Brooklyn, New York.

❧ ❧ ❧

In order to earn money since her husband didn't, Abby May Alcott operated an employment agency out of her house. She placed poor immigrants as servants into wealthy homes. Essentially, an unrenumerative business, it had to be abandoned after a few years. Then, working for missionary groups, she became Boston's first social worker. She managed to find wealthy patrons who'd pay her salary to survey the needs of the poor and make recommendations such as job-training programs, higher wages, education, a national plan with home subsidy.

❧ ❧ ❧

When two women, Mary Upton Ferrin of Salem, Mass. and Mrs. Phebe King of Danvers, realized how unfair the married woman's property law was, they visited Senator Judge Benjamin C. Pitkin of Salem hoping he would use his influence to amend the law without petitioning the Legislature.

He told them: "The law is very well as it is regarding the property of married women. Women are not capable of taking care of their own property; they never ought to have control. There is already a law by which a woman can have her property secured to her."

The women protested: "But not one woman in fifty knows of the existence of such a law."

He answered: "They ought to know it; it is no fault of the law if they don't. I do not think the Legislature will alter the law regarding divorce. If they do, they will make it more stringent than it now is."

The women collected more signatures on petitions.

The law was to be passed in 1854.

❧ ❧ ❧

At the April 19-20 Woman's Rights Convention in Salem, Ohio, the women officers barred men from speaking on the platform.

❧ ❧ ❧

Lucretia Mott, William Lloyd Garrison and other abolitionists and women's rights activists began to study and quote Bible scripture in order to defend themselves against objections of the clergy.

1851

Hawthorne's *House of the Seven Gables* was written while he and Sophia were living in a little red house in Lenox, Mass. There, their last child, Rose, was born. Herman Melville was living nearby in Pittsfield, and he and Hawthorne enjoyed conversations.

❧ ❧ ❧

Moby Dick by Herman Melville was published.

❧ ❧ ❧

At the May 28-29 Akron Ohio Convention the uneducated eighty year-old "Lybian Statue" Sojourner Truth, a former-slave, spoke out so eloquently about the rights women did not have that many white observers were swayed to look on the cause with admiration.

❧ ❧ ❧

September 18 - *The New York Daily Times* rolled off the presses for the first time. It was an instant success, four pages, six columns, a penny paper which increased to two cents the second year. The editor was the Henry Jarvis Raymond – the man who had first worked on Greeley's *Tribune.*

❧ ❧ ❧

Molly Greeley gave birth to a second son; he lived to age six. Molly was to have nine pregnancies; only two daughters would live to adulthood. As the years progressed, Molly traveled for her "health," to the West Indies and Europe. She became "queer" and "irascible."

1852

Daniel Webster died.

❧ ❧ ❧

Hawthorne's *Blithedale Romance* was published. He claimed that his characters were not drawn from people he'd known on Brook Farm. But his leading character, Zenobia, is very like Margaret Fuller. (See notes Volume II of this series: *Why Margaret Fuller Has Been Forgotten*, by Laurie James.) Hawthorne's fame spread; he was no longer in debt. He bought the Alcott house in Concord and named it The Wayside.

❧ ❧ ❧

Everybody read *Uncle Tom's Cabin* by Harriet Beecher Stowe; thus the pitiful reality of slavery rose to the forefront of public consciousness. The Fugitive Slave Law became impossible to enforce.

❧ ❧ ❧

John Sullivan Dwight launched the *Journal of Music* which led to a decided improvement in the average American's taste in music.

❧ ❧ ❧

William Henry Channing settled and preached in Rochester, N. Y., which was the last stop on the underground railroad for fugitive slaves headed for Canada. Channing raised money for the cause, and also continued to promote woman's rights and temperance.

❧ ❧ ❧

The husband of Elizabeth Peabody's sister Mary, Horace Mann, as President of Antioch College, toured the country lecturing and criticizing the suffrage movement. Elizabeth Cady Stanton said "It was as if one in our own camp had suddenly turned traitor."

❧ ❧ ❧

June 2 – In West Chester, Pennsylvania, the first Woman's Rights Convention was called to order by Lucretia Mott, and a letter from Sarah Grimke was read which ended: "If we adopt as our watchword the language of Margaret Fuller, we can not but overcome all obstacles, outlive all opposition: "Give me Truth. Cheat me by no illusion. Oh, the granting of this prayer is sometimes terrible; I walk over the burning plowshares and they sear my feet– yet nothing but Truth will do."

1853

In the spring Susan B. Anthony and Amelia Bloomer, lecturing throughout New York State on temperance, became aware that woman's rights would have to be won before anything could be done about temperance.

When, in September at the World's Temperance Convention, the Rev. Antoinette Brown took the platform to speak, she faced ministers and public who shouted, "Shame on the woman!" "She shan't speak!" Then a resolution was presented by the Hon. Samuel Carey – and this resolution passed – that women would not be allowed to speak at the Convention.

Thus, delegate Susan B. Anthony decided to devote her life to working for woman's right to speak.

❧ ❧ ❧

The Greeleys bought a farm at Chappaqua, N. Y. Greeley spent most of his time on lecture tours and in his office.

❧ ❧ ❧

Elizabeth Cady Stanton echoed Margaret Fuller's words in a letter to Susan B. Anthony: "Women's degradation is in man's idea of his sexual rights. Our religions, laws and customs, are all founded on the belief that woman was made for man. It lies at the very foundation of all progress...." Stanton was first to advocate the vote for women and liberal divorce laws.

❧ ❧ ❧

July 6 - Sophia and Nathaniel Hawthorne set sail for Liverpool where he was to serve as consul, having received the appointment from President Franklin Pierce.

❧ ❧ ❧

June - In Concord Ellen and William Ellery Channing named their fourth child after Margaret Fuller's husband and brother, Giovanni Eugene.

William Ellery Channing lectured with no significant success. When *Poems* was published, he reportedly threw the book down on the floor and said: "I never thought a Channing would have been such a dam'd fool." He became embittered and destroyed as many copies as he could find.

To help their constant financial crisis, Emerson paid Channing to write a book, *Country Walking*. It was published twenty years later. Channing included a portion of it in his biography, the first on Henry David Thoreau.

The Channing marriage became increasingly traumatic. He succumbed to moods, often exploded and used abusive language, even threatened violence. She, frail and ill, coughed a good deal. He found life better near the river. She considered leaving him and in November she took her children to live in Worchester with Ellery's brother-in-law, Thomas Wentworth Higginson. Dr. Walter Channing sent money.

The family criticized Ellery Channing as the Thoreau family criticized Thoreau.

Ellen's cough persisted.

❧ ❧ ❧

Henry David Thoreau bought 706 copies of his book, *A Week on the Concord and Merrimack Rivers* (the remainders from his publishers). He carried them upstairs to his room. He later said: "They are something more substantial than fame, as my back knows, which has borne them up two flights of stairs.... I have now a library of nearly nine hundred volumes, over seven hundred of which I wrote myself."

Greely praised him in the *Tribune.* When Thoreau lectured, people fell asleep.

❧ ❧ ❧

Harriot K. Hunt received the degree of M. D. from The Woman's Medical College of Pennsylvania. She had started practicing medicine at the age of thirty in 1835, and twelve years after, was refused admission to Harvard Medical Lectures.

❧ ❧ ❧

Nov. 16 - Emerson's mother, Ruth Haskins Emerson, died unexpectedly, in the arms of Elizabeth Hoar. She was eighty-four years old. Hoar called her "Mama." Emerson wrote Sam Ward: "She was born to live."

1854

Congress, providing additional funding for life saving operations, selected Point o' Woods on Fire Island (where Margaret Fuller drowned) as one of several key spots for a life saving station.

❧ ❧ ❧

William Henry Channing left Concord for England, stayed for years.

❧ ❧ ❧

Thoreau published *Walden* and began to achieve recognition for his philosophy and preferred lifestyle. He said, "The law will never make men free, it is men who have got to make the law free." Women were not included in his statement.

❧ ❧ ❧

Oct. 18 - Ernestine Rose took the chair at the Fifth National Convention for woman's rights in Philadelphia, and said: "For is woman not included in that phrase, "all men are created free and equal"?...Tell us, ye men of the nation, ay, ye wise lawmakers and law-breakers of the nation, whether woman is not included in that great Declaration of Independence? And if she is, what right has man to deprive her of her natural and inalienable rights? It is natural, it is inherent, it is inborn, it is a thing of which no one can justly deprive her. Upon that just and eternal basis do we found our claims for our rights; political, civil, legal, social, religious, and every other...."

Among the audience was Lucretia Mott and Lucy Stone (dressed in bloomers), as well as William Lloyd Garrison and James Mott, Paulina Wright Davis, Thomas Wentworth Higginson, Susan B. Anthony, Elizabeth Cady Stanton, Dr. Ann Preston, Mary Channing Higginson, and Wendell Phillips.

The Rev. Henry Grew, of Philadelphia, said that his opinions on woman's rights were drawn from the Scriptures and he quoted texts to prove that it was God's will that man was superior to woman and that the Bible taught that women should be in subjection.

A Mrs. Cutler quoted Bible text to show that man and woman were a simultaneous creation and were equal in power and glory. Dominion over the creatures of air, sea, and earth had been given to women as well as to man. It was time for women to read and interpret Scripture for herself. It was a pity that the Bible would be quoted on the side of tyranny and oppression.

Lucretia Mott said that it was not Christianity but priestcraft that subjected woman.

1855

September 20 - Emerson stood on a Boston platform in front of a group of radical women reformers at the Woman's Convention and stated his truths:

Plato said, Women are the same as men in faculty, only less in degree. But the general voice of mankind has agreed that they have their own strength; that women are strong by sentiment; that the same mental height which their husbands attain by toil, they attain by sympathy with their husbands. Man is the will, and Woman the sentiment. In this ship of humanity, Will is the rudder, and Sentiment the sail: when Woman affects to steer, the rudder is only a masked sail: When women engage in any art or trade, it is usually as a resource, not as a primary object. The life of the affections is primary to them, so that there is usually no employment or career which they will not with their own applause and that of society quit for a suitable marriage. And they give entirely to their affections, set their whole fortune on the die, lose themselves eagerly in the glory of their husbands and children. Man stands astonished at a magnanimity he cannot pretend to....

As for Plato's opinion, it is true that, up to recent times, in no art or science, not in painting, poetry, or music, have they produced a master-piece...But, in general, no mastery in either of the fine arts – which should, one would say, be the arts of women – has yet been obtained by them, equal to the mastery of men in the same. The part they play in education, in the care of the young and the tuition of older children, is their organic office in the world....

Women are...the civilizers of mankind. What is civilization? I answer, the power of good women....

...(Women) finish society, manners, language. Form and ceremony are their realm. They embellish trifles....Their genius delights in ceremonies, in forms, in decorating life with manners, with proprieties, order and grace....(In the) department of taste and comliness...woman is the prime genius and ordainer....And I think they should magnify their ritual of manners. Society, conversation, decorum, flowers, dances, colors, forms, are their homes and attendants. They should be found in fit surroundings – with fair approaches, with agreeable architecture, and with all advantages which the means of man collect....More vulnerable, more infirm, more mortal than men, they could not be such excellent artists in this element of fancy if they did not lend and give themselves to it. They are poets who believe their own poetry. They emit from their pores a colored atmosphere, one would say, wave upon wave of rosy light in which they walk evermore, and see all objects through this warm-tinted mist that envelops them....

Women "are victims of the finer temperament. They have tears, and gaieties, and faintings, and glooms, and devotion to trifles. Nature's end, of maternity for twenty years, was of so supreme importance that it was to be secured at all events, even to the sacrifice of the highest beauty. They are more personal. Men taunt them that, whatever they do, say, read or write, they are thinking of themselves and their set. Men are not to the same degree temperamented, for there are multitudes of men who live to objects quite out of them, as to politics, to trade, to letters or an art, unhindered by any influence of constitution.

Though...justice is not to be denied, yet the best women do not wish these things; (equal rights in employment, education, marriage, property, the vote, etc.) ...if the laws and customs were modified in the manner proposed, it would embarrass and pain gentle and lovely persons with duties which they would find irksome and distasteful.... I can say, for one, that all my points would sooner be carried in the state if women voted. On the questions that are important; – whether the government shall be in one person, or whether representative, or whether democratic; whether men shall be holden in bondage, or shall be roasted alive and eaten, as in Typee, or shall be hunted with bloodhounds, as in this country; whether men shall be hanged for stealing, or hanged at all; whether the limited sale of cheap liquors shall be allowed; – they (women) would give, I suppose, as intelligent a vote as the voters of Boston or New York.

We may ask, to be sure – why need you vote? If new power is here, of a character which solves old tough questions, which puts me and all the rest in the wrong, tries and condemns our religion, customs, laws, and opens new careers to our young receptive men and women, you can well leave voting to the old dead people. Those whom you teach, and those whom you half teach, will fast enough make themselves considered and strong with their new insight, and votes will follow from all the dull...

I do not think it yet appears that women wish this equal share in public affairs. But it is they and not we that are to determine it....

> Let us have the true woman, the adorner, the hospitable, the religious heart, and no lawyer need be called in to write stipulations, the cunning clauses of provision, the strong investitures; – for woman moulds the lawgiver and writes the law. But I ought to say, I think it impossible to separate the interests and education of the sexes. Improve and refine the men, and you do the same by the women, whether you will or no. Every woman being the wife or the daughter of a man, – wife, daughter, sister, mother, of a man, she can never be very far from his ear, never not of his counsel, if she has really something to urge that is good in itself and agreeable to nature....
>
> For there are always a certain number of passionately loving fathers, brothers, husbands and sons who put their might into the endeavor to make a daughter, a wife, or a mother happy in the way that suits best. Woman should find in man her guardian. Silently she looks for that, and when she finds that he is not, as she instantly does, she betakes her to her own defences, and does the best she can. But when he is her guardian, fulfilled with all nobleness, knows and accepts his duties as her brother, all goes well for both.
>
> The new movement is only a tide shared by the spirits of man and woman; and you may proceed in the faith that whatever the woman's heart is prompted to desire, the man's mind is simultaneously prompted to accomplish.

❧ ❧ ❧

Lucy Stone, who was to be married to Henry Blackwell, omitted the word "obey" from the marriage ceremony. She kept her own name and identity, and she called herself Lucy Stone Blackwell. After a year she dropped "Blackwell" completely.

❧ ❧ ❧

Walt Whitman published *Leaves of Grass.*

❧ ❧ ❧

In March James Freeman Clarke bought Brook Farm from the city of Roxbury.

❧ ❧ ❧

Longfellow brought out his poem, "Hiawatha."

❧ ❧ ❧

James Russell Lowell succeeded Longfellow as professor of modern languages at Harvard.

❧ ❧ ❧

Ellen and Ellery Channing were reconciled, and Ellen became pregnant again. He took a job as assistant editor of the *New Bedford Mercury*.

❧ ❧ ❧

Horace Greeley employed eighteen foreign and twenty domestic correspondents on his *Tribune* and he had a long list of special correspondents. He hired two hundred people, half of whom worked full time, twelve editors and six partners. Charles A. Dana was Greeley's right arm, and George Ripley was still writing literary reviews for his paper.

1856

In June Ellen Fuller Channing gave birth to her fifth child; she was always ill with an internal inflammation.

❧ ❧ ❧

Sept. 22 - Ellen Fuller Channing died at Dr. Walter Channing's home at the age of thirty six. She was buried at Mt. Auburn Cemetery.

Ellery could not take care of the children. Dr. Walter Channing and other relatives divided the responsibility. Ellery quit his *Mercury* position and moved to Concord, alternating isolation and socialization with Emerson, Alcott, Thoreau. He tramped with Thoreau and others. He helped edit *The Maine Woods* and *Cape Cod*. He wrote a good poem, "The Wanderer," which Emerson published. His biography of Henry David Thoreau, *The Poet Naturalist,* was a success. He spent his last years living in biographer Frank Sanborn's house, reading at the Boston Public Library and the Athenæum, and writing poetry.

❧ ❧ ❧

Horace Greeley interrupted the serialization of Charles Dicken's *Little Dorrit* in *The Tribune* in order to run Lydia Maria's Child's story, *The Kansas Emigrants.*

1857

July/Aug. - Thoreau and Edward Hoar (brother of Elizabeth Hoar), accompanied by an Indian guide, Joe Polis, travelled to Maine, climbed mountains and canoed over three hundred miles. Edward Hoar, whose profession was the law, preferred being a naturalist and a botanist. Retiring and refined, he enjoyed books, appreciated and studied flowers, could recognize bird songs. He had the reputation of being able to hit a bird on the wing at two hundred yards.

❧ ❧ ❧

September - The Alcott family moved to the Orchard House in Concord.

1858

The U. S. government appropriated moneys to re-build and put into operation the Fire Island Lighthouse.

❧ ❧ ❧

Henry David Thoreau and Edward Hoar climbed New England's highest peak, Mt. Washington, New Hampshire.

❧ ❧ ❧

Dec. 28 - In Florence Edward Hoar married "the girl next door." He'd joined his sister Elizabeth in her furnished apartment in Rome.

The Nathaniel Hawthornes lived on the Piazza Poli. While Sophia and Elizabeth explored Rome, Hawthorne was writing *The Marble Faun.*

Sculptor William Wetmore Story and wife were living in the Palazzo Barberini. Anna Barker Ward lived with her daughter on the Corso.

Also in Rome were poets Robert and Elizabeth Barrett Browning, ex-President Franklin Pierce and his wife, Charles Sumner, and Samuel Joseph May, brother of Abby May Alcott.

1859

Caroline H. Dall, the young woman who'd taken notes at Margaret Fuller's Conversations and had compiled them into a book, gave a series of literary lectures in different parts of the country – her subject: "Woman's Claims to Education."

❧ ❧ ❧

Emerson jotted a note in his journal: "Shall I blame my mother, whitest of women, because she was not a Gypsy, & gave me no swarthy ferocity? or my father, because he came of a lettered race, & had no porter's shoulders?"

❧ ❧ ❧

George Ripley at last achieved esteem, fame, and riches when he and Charles A. Dana began to publish sixteen volumes of the *New American Cyclopaedia.*

❧ ❧ ❧

Henry Jarvis Raymond of *The New York Daily Times* went to Italy to cover the war of 1859.

❧ ❧ ❧

John Brown attacked Harper's Ferry. Lydia Maria Child was one of the persons who raised funds to help his family.

❧ ❧ ❧

Theodore Parker, who'd been preaching at the Melodeon and editing "The Dial without the beard," *The Massachusetts Quarterly Review*, suffered a hemorrhage of the lungs. His doctors advised West Indies, where he went, after which he travelled to Florence. There, his health worsened and he died at the age of fifty.

1860

Fifty-five year-old Elizabeth Peabody founded the first American kindergarten, based on the ideas of Frederic Froebel. She believed children should find goodness in themselves early, and she advocated teacher training. Her sister Mary worked with her. Elizabeth never married, wrote textbooks on grammar and history.

❧ ❧ ❧

Walt Whitman was in Boston printing a new edition of *Leaves of Grass*. Neither Sophia Thoreau, Abby May Alcott nor Lidian Emerson would invite him to visit; he was too radical. Twenty-one years later Whitman did dine with Emerson and F. B. Sanborn.

❧ ❧ ❧

The Nathaniel Hawthornes returned to the United States; they lived at Wayside.

❧ ❧ ❧

Most women abandoned bloomer outfits because the public ridicule seemed to damage the suffrage movement. Nevertheless, bloomers continued to be worn for skating and gymnastic exercises, and in seminaries and sanitariums.

1861

The first battle of the American Civil War occured at Bull Run, July 21.

❧ ❧ ❧

Sophia Ripley died. She had earlier undergone surgery for a lump in breast.

1862

Henry David Thoreau died in his room in Concord of tuberculosis. In his last days many people visited and brought flowers. He had some regrets for being an isolationist. He was, though, satisfied with his life. Forty-five bells were rung to signify the number of years he'd lived. He was buried in Sleepy Hollow. Emerson gave the eulogy, which he later edited and published. He suggested that Thoreau was deficient in qualities of friendship. (He did not draw on any of Lidian's reminiscences.) Most Concordians felt Thoreau would be forgotten; he was considered a misfit.

❧ ❧ ❧

Elizabeth Hoar helped to arrange some of Thoreau's manuscripts for publication. She read Greek aloud to Emerson's children, Ellen and Edward.

❧ ❧ ❧

Charles A. Dana and Greeley had a difference of opinion and Greeley asked Dana to resign from *The Tribune* which he did. Dana became an investigative agent for the War Department.

❧ ❧ ❧

James Freeman Clarke arranged that his Brook Farm land be used as a training camp for a Civil War regiment of volunteers. He said the Massachusetts Second was the best crop the land was to ever produce.

1863

President Abraham Lincoln issued the Proclamation of Emancipation, declaring the freedom of slaves.

❧ ❧ ❧

Mary Moody Emerson died, age eighty-nine.

❧ ❧ ❧

Louisa May Alcott had her first success with *Hospital Sketches*, letters which she, as a nurse, had written for soldiers at Georgetown Hospital during the Civil War.

1864

Ill, Nathaniel Hawthorne went to the White Mountains for a change of scene and died at Plymouth, New Hampshire, May 19. James Freeman Clarke, who had not seen the Hawthornes since he'd officiated at their marriage, officiated at the funeral at Concord church. Hawthorne was buried at Sleepy Hollow. Wife Sophia, later edited his *Notebooks*.

❧ ❧ ❧

Arthur Fuller (Margaret's brother), formerly pastor of the Unitarian Church at Manchester, New Hampshire, died at battle of Fredericksburg.

1865

The Civil War ended on April 9 when General Robert E. Lee

surrendered at Appomatax. The 13th Amendment to the Constitution was adopted, which gave freedom to slaves.

❧ ❧ ❧

October - Elizabeth Hoar assisted in the wedding at the "mansion of peace" of Edith Emerson (Emerson's daughter) and Col. William Hathaway Forbes, owner of yachts, who served in the Civil War and had been present at the surrender of General Lee. They lived lavishly in a house at Naushon and brought guests over to visit in their yacht. Once a year they staged a deer hunt.

They had eight children. The first was named Ralph. The sixth was named Waldo. The seventh was named Ellen, after R.W.E.'s first wife. Not one was named after Lidian.

In *The Ipswitch Emersons* Benjamin Kendall Emerson devotes six lines to Edith (page 370), and twenty-five lines to her husband, and informs the reader that a "masterful" article can be found on Col. Forbes' career.

❧ ❧ ❧

Sam Ward, along with other businessmen, laid the plans for the founding of the Metropolitan Museum of Art in New York City. Ward contributed towards the purchase of the first collection of paintings. He was elected first treasurer and a trustee. Though the paths of Ward and Emerson widened, their friendship continued.

❧ ❧ ❧

George Ripley remarried.

1866

Elizabeth Hoar's mother died. Elizabeth and Edward lived alone with servants at the homestead on Main Street in Concord.

1867

July - Sarah Bradford Ripley died, age seventy-four. She'd lived twenty years in the Old Manse after her husband Samuel Ripley had died. When they'd moved to Concord, she'd been freed from all domestic, parish, and teaching responsibilities, and spent the rest of her life studying, learning Spanish, pressing flowers, receiving visits from her children and grandchildren, watching birds, exchanging notes on nature with Henry David Thoreau, attending Emerson's lectures, etc. She had earlier written: "Death is an event as natural as birth, and faith makes it as full of promise...The Unknown, which lighted the morning of life, will hallow and make serene its evening. Conscious or unconscious, we shall rest in the lap of the Infinite."

1868

Lydia Maria Child published *An Appeal to the Indians*, which she hoped would bring public attention to the Indian cause.

❧ ❧ ❧

Charles A. Dana became editor and part owner of *The Sun*.

1869

May - Richard Fuller died.

❧ ❧ ❧

George Ripley helped to establish the National Institute of Literature, Art and Science.

❧ ❧ ❧

Louisa May Alcott achieved fame with the publication of her book, *Little Women*. With her earnings, the Alcott's experienced their first financial stability.

❧ ❧ ❧

May 26 - Emerson attended the meeting of the New England Woman's Suffrage Association and was elected a vice-president. He delivered a friendly speech which was printed in the *Boston Daily Advertiser.*

❧ ❧ ❧

In July Emerson was asked to participate in a convention sponsored by the Essex County Woman's Suffrage Association, but he declined because he could not take on anything that was not "imperative." He wished to convey to all members "that while I think their political claim founded in equity, and though perhaps it does not yet appear to any what precise form in practice it will and ought to take, yet the seriousness and thoughtfulness with which it is urged seem to me to mark an important step in civilization." His letter was printed in the *Boston Daily Advertiser,* July 29, 1869 and in *The New York Times,* July 30, p. 4.

In her address Julia Ward Howe "asked what the man of God taught woman." She thought that "in order to have true women in the congregation, we must occasionally have a true woman in the pulpit."

She said that the argument which pointed out that women did not want rights and suffrage was immoral. "Do all children cry for the slate and spelling book?"

She contested the stand that women, particularly wealthy women like herself, had everything. She challenged privileged women to broaden their outlooks.

Harriet Beecher Stowe, who said the woman's question was the question of the age, asked Emerson to contribute a few words about women's issues in *Hearth and Home* – she was associate editor – but his words never crossed her desk. She circumvented the difficulty – and gave Emerson the credit – by writing in her August 28 article: "At a convention recently...a letter also was read from Ralph Waldo Emerson, in which he says that the seriousness, earnestness, and perseverance with which this subject has been presented merits the attention of every thoughtful mind."

1870

January - Emerson, who'd used many of Elizabeth Hoar's quotes in his lectures without crediting her, wrote Hoar for permission to print her two-page ballad at the end of his essay "Courage" in his latest collection, *Society and Solitude.* Hoar gave her okay. But he omitted her name in one line of credit: "as narrated in a ballad to whom all the particulars of the fact are known..."

❧ ❧ ❧

Paulina Wright Davis gave a report on the 1851 Second National Woman's Rights Convention held in Worcester, Massachusetts – the Convention Emerson refused to attend. Davis expressed her great disappointment that Margaret Fuller had not been alive to serve as leader of the woman's rights movement. "To her, I, at least, had hoped to confide the leadership of this movement. It can never be known if she would have accepted it; the desire had been expressed to her by letter; but be that as it may, she was, and still is, a leader of thought; a position far more desirable than a leader of numbers."

❧ ❧ ❧

James Freeman Clark sold Brook Farm to Lauranna C. Munroe, wife of James W. Munroe. Later it was bought by G. P. Burkhardt who deeded it to the Association of the Evangelical Lutheran Church for Works of Mercy who subsequently built the Martin Luther Orphan Home for homeless children. Today the acreage is a cemetery.

❧ ❧ ❧

Edward Hoar moved to Palermo, Sicily, where he cultivated oranges, lemons, and figs. Elizabeth Hoar spent the winter with him.

1872

Emerson's house in Concord burned down; furniture and pictures were saved, but his wife's bedstead in the Red Room was lost. Emerson went to Europe and Egypt while all was re-built. He took daughter Ellen with him. Lidian remained in Concord.

1878

Elizabeth Hoar helped Ellen Emerson and James Elliot Cabot to compile Emerson's papers for publication. She took much to the printer for copying. After a prolonged illness, Elizabeth Hoar died.

❧ ❧ ❧

The United States government established the United States Life Saving Service to aid shipwreck victims and to protect property on the American coastline. The many daring rescues made folk heroes of the courageous surfmen.

1880

George Ripley died.

❧ ❧ ❧

Lydia Maria Child died. Her legacy was a published book every few years. A mammoth undertaking was *Progress of Religious Ideas in Successive Ages,* and another book dear to her heart was *The Freedman's Book.* Profits helped freed slaves. When she was buried, a magnificent rainbow spanned the eastern sky. She loved rainbows and often arranged prismatic glasses so that their colors would be reflected onto the walls of her room.

1882

Ralph Waldo Emerson died at the age of seventy-nine. For years he'd suffered loss of memory, and he'd contracted pneumonia. The bells in Concord's Unitarian church tolled seventy-nine times. James Freeman Clarke preached the funeral sermon and Bronson Alcott read a sonnet he'd written. Emerson was buried in Sleepy Hollow.

1888

Bronson Alcott and Louisa May Alcott died.

1892

November 13 - Lidian died, unwrinkled, at ninety years of age. Her memory and other faculties had given her difficulties. The scholar Delores Bird Carpenter writes: "Her contemporaries did not doubt Lidian's contribution to the forces that made Emerson the man he was." Daughter Ellen had this story:

> Mrs. Chamberlaine said, "Mr. Emerson doesn't quote. He thinks out all his thoughts himself – doesn't borrow them." "Yet you often hear the thoughts of others in what he says," said Mr. Sanborn. "Yes," said Lizzy, "don't you think sometimes he says things he learned from Mrs. Emerson?" "Often!" said Mr. Sanborn decidedly. When Lizzy said this I remembered Mrs. Nathan Brooks's remark, "Mr. Emerson wouldn't be the man he is if it weren't for Mrs. Emerson. People have no idea how much he owes to his wife." [1]

1893

Edward Hoar died of lung disease.

❧ ❧ ❧

Because the trees were getting old and dying at the tops, Sam Hoar started to cut down the thirty acres of pines and timber owned by the Emersons. Ellen and Edith were appalled, so Edith bought the tract of land.

1901

July 19 - To commemorate Margaret Fuller, Lillie Devereau Blake pulled the cord which unveiled a bronze tablet in a newly erected Colonial Pavilion on Fire Island beach opposite the site of the shipwreck. She, as president of the Improvement Society of Point o' Woods, sponsor of the event, made a speech in the community hall, followed by commentary from Charlotte B. Wilbur, the Rev. Robert W. Meredith of Brooklyn, and Rev. Howard Townsend of Orange, N. J. Letters were read from Julia Ward Howe, Ednah B. Cheney, Col. Thomas Wentworth Higginson, and Elizabeth Cady Stanton.

Julia Ward Howe wrote the inscription on the tablet which read: "To commemorate Margaret Fuller, Marchioness Ossoli, author, editor, poet, orator, who with her husband, Marquis Ossoli, and their child, Angelo, perished by shipwreck off this shore July 19, 1850, in the 40th year of her age. Noble in thought and in character, eloquent of tongue and of pen, she was an inspiration to many of her own time, and her uplifting influence abides with us."

1918

– or a short time after –

The Colonial Pavilion built to commemorate Margaret Fuller at Point o' Woods on Fire Island beach was undermined by the rapacious surf and disappeared out of sight, never to be re-built. The inscribed bronze tablet was removed by the Coast Guard on April 12. Forgotten over the years, the bronze tablet has not to this day been located.

1920

The Nineteenth Amendment to the Constitution was ratified, signed by Bainbridge Colby in the early morning of August 26, thereby giving women the right to vote.

1923

The Equal Rights Amendment to the Constitution was first introduced into the Congress and re-introduced at each Congress.

1953

Claire Booth Luce became the first woman U.S.A. Ambassador to Italy – one hundred and three years after Margaret Fuller first expressed the wish to serve in that position.

1970

The resurgence of the women's movement forced hearings on the Equal Rights Amendment.

1974

The Fire Island Lighthouse was in disrepair and it was closed.

1979

July 19 - Margaret Fuller Day was proclaimed by the City of Cambridge (Massachusetts). The day's events were sponsored by Cambridge Arts Council and The Margaret Fuller Network, co-founded by Ramona Barth and Laurie James. Radcliffe college sponsored a reception. The great grand nephew of Margaret Fuller, Buckminster Fuller, introduced Laurie James in her original solo drama on Margaret Fuller, *Still Beat Noble Hearts*, at Longfellow Hall, Harvard.

It had long been Buckminster Fuller's habit to begin his lectures with a line or two about his admired great aunt who had been an inspiration to him, and on this occasion he held up the portrait of Margaret Fuller painted by Thomas Hicks in Rome in 1848-9. Margaret Fuller Day at Cambridge launched Laurie James' tour throughout the United States, Mexico, Hong Kong and Scotland.

1981

October 18 - The Margaret Fuller Ossoli Square was dedicated at Garden & Mason Streets in Cambridge, Mass. This was followed by Laurie James' solo performance at the Congregational Church. Participants in the ceremony were Ramona Barth, co-founder of the Margaret Fuller Network, Frank Duehay, Mayor of Cambridge, Alfred Vellucchi, Councilman, and Pat King, Director, Schlesinger Library, Radcliffe college.

1982

Demise of the Equal Rights Amendment, which advocated equality of rights to women under the law.. (Exactly one hundred years after the death of Emerson.) In Maine, on national TV, Laurie James, in Margaret Fuller costume, quoted excerpts from *Woman in the Nineteenth Century*.

1985

Due to the work of The Margaret Fuller Network, Margaret Fuller was selected as one of America's unsung heros to be highlighted on "American Portrait," a one-minute CBS television segment celebrating the 100th anniversary of the Statue of Liberty. Actress/activist Jean Stapleton, narrated the commentary.

1986

May 25 - The Fire Island Lighthouse celebrated a re-lighting ceremony. Since lighthouses are being replaced with automated equipment, the Lighthouse Preservation Society raised over a million dollars to rescue it from oblivion and to restore the keeper's quarters into an information and visitors center. Margaret Fuller's picture is included in the exhibit of Fire Island's history.

1987

September 8 – Ellen Threinen Ittelson gave birth to a daughter which she proudly named Margaret Fuller.

❧ ❧ ❧

Oct. – The Margaret Fuller Network, Cambridge City Council and the Dante Alighieri Society in Cambridge, Massachusetts, planned and sponsored a second Margaret Fuller Day with a performance by Laurie James in *Still Beat Noble Hearts* at City Hall and a plaque commemorating Margaret Fuller was unveiled in the foyer.

Ramona Barth co-ordinated a week of events at the following locations:

(1) Widener Library, Harvard, where Gore Hall stood – the library Fuller stepped inside as first woman,

(2) Mt. Auburn Cemetery where Fuller's monument stands in the family plot, and where Angelino is buried,

(3) The Dante Alighieri Society where Ramona Barth started the Margaret Fuller Library,

(4) The Margaret Fuller birthhouse on Cherry Street in Cambridge,

(5) The Brattle Street House where Fuller lived as a young adult, which is an Adult Education Center today,

(6) The Marriott Hotel in Kendall Square Cambridge, where the presidential suite was named after Margaret Fuller Ossoli.

1988-89

Laurie James simultaneously published two books, *Why Margaret Fuller Ossoli Is Forgotten,* and *The Wit And Wisdom of Margaret Fuller Ossoli,* and opened her drama at The Thirteenth Street Repertory Theatre in New York City. The artistic director, Edith O'Hara (who'd written a college paper on Fuller), incorporated the play into the company's repertory, giving it an extended run.

In order that the name Margaret Fuller be better remembered, the title was changed to *Men, Women, and Margaret Fuller,* after Edgar Allen Poe's comment, "Humanity can be divided into three classes, Men, Women, and Margaret Fuller."

Thereafter, Laurie James toured her drama to the Edinburgh Fringe Festival in Scotland, and returned to The Thirteenth Street Repertory Theatre for another long-term run.

Appendix

Emerson's Poem to Margaret Fuller, "The Visit"

Askest, 'How long thou shalt stay?
Devastator of the day!
Know, each substance and relation,
Thorough nature's operation,
Hath its unit, bound and metre;
And every new compound
Is some product and repeater,—
Product of the earlier found.
But the unit of the visit,
The encounter of the wise,—
Say, what other metre is it
Than the meeting of the eyes?
Nature poureth into nature
Through the channels of that feature,
Riding on the ray of sight,
Fleeter far than whirlwinds go,
Or for service, or delight,
Hearts to hearts their meaning show,
Sum their long experience,
And import intelligence.
Single look has drained the breast;
Single moment years confessed.
The duration of a glance
Is the term of covenance,
And, though thy rede be church or state,
Frugal multiples of that.
Speeding Saturn cannot halt;
Linger, — thou shalt rue the fault:
If Love his moment overstay
Hatred's swift repulsions play.

(from *The Dial*, April 1844; also published in P/RWE)

of Fuller's Article to Emerson, "Dialogue"

s of "Laurie" closely parallel Fuller's views while those of "Agla resemble Emerson's. The scene is set late one moonlit night in a tastefully furnished room at a city boarding house. (Fuller had lived in city boarding houses.) Laurie knocks on the door, the two greet each other, and settle themselves cozily in front of a fire.

Laurie asks if Algauron sees a change in him.

Algauron says there is no change. It is just that Laurie has found other friends; therefore, their relationship is changed.

L says A speaks coldly. His friendship for A is the same as always.

A says L now has feelings which flow in another channel. No one is to blame that this has happened. A should have varied and expanded his nature to meet L's, and therefore the bonds of friendship would have been firmly knit.

L asks could they be friends again?

A responds that friendship can only be given once. Flowers once touched by a cold wind will not revive.

L points out that the seeds of their friendship remain the same.

A Yes, but only to seek a new spring. Seek elsewhere for another friend that will better meet you now.

L thinks there needed to be good understanding between them.

A agrees.

L says that A had been tempted to think him heartless.

A responds that in breaking up their friendship L had been heartless for a moment only.

L claims that A was both cold and friendly and L could not understand someone being both cold and friendly.

A says L would understand when he has lent as well as borrowed. It is an age difficult for immortal friends, equal friends who march with the same step. A recites a poem by Wordsworth:

> There *is* a change, and I am poor;
> Your Love hath been, nor long ago,
> A Fountain at my fond Heart's door,
> Whose only business was to flow;
> And flow it did, not taking heed
> Of its own bounty, or my need.

What happy moments did I count
Blest was I then all bliss above;
Now, for this consecrated Fount
Of murmuring, sparkling, living love,
What have I? shall I dare to tell?
A comfortless and hidden WELL.

A well of Love, it may be deep,
I trust it is, and never dry;
What matter? if the Waters sleep
In silence and obscurity,
Such change, and at the very door
Of my fond heart, hath made me poor.

Then A says he found a soliloquy by Coleridge that gave a more sufficient answer:

Unchanged within to see all changed without,
Is a blank lot and hard to bear, no doubt.
Yet why at other's wanings shouldst thou fret?
Then only might'st thou feel a just regret,
Hadst thou withheld thy love, or hid thy light
In selfish forethought of neglect and slight,
O wiselier, then, from feeble yearnings freed,

While, and *on whom,* thou mayst, shine on! nor heed
Whether the object by reflected light
Return thy radiance or absorb it quite;
And though thou notest from thy safe recess
Old Friends burn dim, like lamps in noisome air,
Love them for what they *are;* nor love them less,
Because to *thee* they are not what they *were.*

A says we will feel transient pangs when the chain of intercourse is broken, when confidence is dismayed, and thought driven back upon its source. The wave receding, leaves the stand for the moment forlorn and weed bestrown.

L wonders if there is no other way, no help for this losing of friends?

A. If you can show me one relationship that is not selfish forethought of neglect or slight, I would wear it and recommend it as the desired amulet. As yet, I know no pride, no prudence except love of truth....Let us drink the bitter with as good a grace as the sweet....No more talk of ourselves....

L. Talk of those other, better selves, the poets....about Coleridge....His nature was ardent, intense, variable in its workings, one of tides, crises, fermentations. His was the flint from which the spark must be struck by violent collision....His heart all ebb and flow, or like a bark, in some half-sheltered bay, above its anchor driving to and fro.

But Wordsworth whose wide and equable thought flows on like a river through the plain, whose verse seemed to come daily like the dew to rest upon the flowers of home affections....In him we should not find traces of the sort of wound, nor deep human melancholy....

A quotes a Wordsworth sonnet:

> Why art thou silent? Is thy love a plant
>   Of such weak fibre that the treacherous air
> Of absence withers what was once so fair?
>   Is there no debt to pay, no boon to grant?
> Yet have my thoughts for thee been vigilant,
>   (As would my deeds have been) with hourly care,
> The mind's least generous wish a mendicant
>   For nought but what thy happiness could spare.
> Speak, though this soft warm heart, once free to hold
>   A thousand tender pleasures, thine and mine,
> Be left more desolate, more dreary cold,
>   Than a forsaken bird's nest filled with snow,
> Mid its own bush of leafless eglantine;
>   Speak, that my torturing doubts their end may know.

A thinks that is the most pathetic description of the speechless palsy that precedes the death of love....Wordsworth would know the tempests of the ocean too as well as his peaceful lake....It needs not that one of deeply thoughtful mind be passionate, to divine all the secrets of passion.

They began to discuss Hamlet.

A thinks that man needs some shelter, both from wi

L. Could Hamlet not have found this in the love of O

A. Probably not....she was to him a flower to wear in his bosom, a child to play the lute at his feet....This love could have been only the ornament, not the food of his life. The moment Hamlet is left alone, his thoughts revert to universal topics.

It was becoming daylight.

L feels it is time to leave, to say good night.

A Good night, and farewell

L. You look as if it were for some time.

A. That rests with you. You will generally find me here and always I think like-minded, if not of the same mind.

An ancient sage had all things deeply tried
    And, as result, thus to his friends he cried,
"O friends, there are no friends." And to this day
    Thus twofold moves the strange magnetic sway,
Giving us love which love must take away
    Let not the soul for this distrust its right,
Knowing when changeful moons withdraw their light,
    Then myriad stars, with promise not less pure,
New loves, new lives to patient hopes assure,
    So long as laws that rule the spheres endure.

(from *The Dial*, April 1844)

Fuller's Poem to Emerson, "Gentle River"

    Gentle River
stealing on so slowly ever
from reeds that grow thy bank along
easy would flow the pastoral song

    But the shell
Which may be strong for lyric swell
    Or trumpet spire for oratory
    Seek these mid the Tritons hoary,

Where an incalculable wave
Wrecks the warship tall and brave,
Rushes up a mile-long strand
Hails the stars, and spurns the land
Pushes back the noblest River
Seeking in vain its love forever,
    There mightst thou find a shell
Fit to be strung for strains of Delphian swell
    Seeing seated pen in hand,
By a gentle dubious light,
    One whose eyebeam, purely bright,
Marks him of her chosen band,
    She thinks, "at last I may draw near
And harbor with a mortal find
In the wide temple of his mind
No jangling notes can rend my ear."
    So she furls her various wings,
Breathes a soft kiss on his brow,
    And her lark-like song she sings
As clear as Earth's dull laws airs allow;
    But why sudden stops the strain
Why backward starts that music-form
    Flutters up the heavens again
With backward wings that rouse the storm
    Rouse thunder-peal and lightening glare
In the repelled, earth-wooing air?

    In that temple so divine
She sought at once the inmost shrine
    And saw this thought there graven—
"Earth and fire, hell and heaven,
Hate and love, black and white,
Life and death, dark and bright,
        All are one
        One alone
    All else is seeming
    I who think am nought
    But the One a-dreaming
    To and fro its thought:
    All is well,
    For all is one;

The fluid spell
is the cold stone;
However voluble
All life is soluble
Into my thought
And that is nought,
But self-discovering
self recovering
Of the One
One Alone.

"Ciel!" cried the muse "what then is my music?"
"That" says the oracle "is soul fallen sick,
  To motion excessive
  And by curves successive
  Circling back again
  On the sea a drop of rain."

  "What" says she, "has my song,
My most creative, poised and long
  Genius-unfolding song
No existence of its own?—
Have I no eternal throne
  Deeper based than Fate?
  I thought mine a state
  Permanent as Truth,
  Self-renewing Youth!"
  "It *seemed* so," quoth he
"But there's no Eternity
  Except Identity."
"I dont know what you mean" she cries
"But this I feel
At your cool replies
On my just now so clear eyes
  Sad films steal;
  And in my dry throat
  Rises no clear note;
  And each wing
To my cold side begins to cling;
  I must away

Where the day
With many-colored ray
But now an aspect gave
To the worlds, more fair
Than they show in this cave,
Shut from the living air;
Don't lure me here again with your sweet smile
As the sweet herbs that on the mountain grow
Allure the chamois to the path of toil
And to the clefts beguile
Through which he falls into the caves below
Where in age-treasured snow buried!—
He yields his breath,
Quite unconvinced that life no better is than Death."

(ALCMH:bMS Am 1280 [2375]; also LMF/RH/III/215)

Emerson on Fuller After Her Death
From His 1853 Private Journals

"It is a bitter satire on our social order, just at present, the number of bad cases. Margaret Fuller having attained the highest & broadest culture that any American woman has possessed, came home with an Italian gentleman whom she had married, & their infant son, & perished by shipwreck on the rocks of Fire Island, off New York; and her friends said, 'Well, on the whole, it was not so lamentable, & perhaps it was the best thing that could happen to her. For, had she lived, what could she have done? How could she have supported herself, her husband, & child?' And, most persons, hearing this, acquiesced in this view, that, after the education has gone far, such is the expensiveness of America, that, the best use to put a fine woman to, is, to drown her to save her board!! Well, the like or the stronger plight is that of Mr. Alcott, the most refined & the most advanced soul we have had in New England, who makes all other souls appear slow & cheap & mechanical; (because he can) a man of such a courtesy & greatness, that, (in conversation) all others, even the intellectual, seem sharp & fighting for victory, & angry, — he has the unalterable sweetness of a muse, — yet because he cannot earn money by his pen or his talk, or by schoolkeeping or bookkeeping or editing or any kind of meanness, —nay, for this very cause, that he is ahead of his contemporaries, —is higher than they, —& keep himself out of the shop-condescensions & smug arts which they stoop to, or, unhappily, need not stoop to, but find themselves, as it were, born to....therefore, it is the unanimous opinion of New England judges that this man must die; we shall all hear of his death with pleasure, & feel relieved that his board & clothes also are saved! We do not adjudge him (indeed) to hemlock, or to garroting, we are much too hypocritical & cowardly for that; — but we not less surely doom him, by refusing to protest against this doom, or combin(ing) to save him, & to set employments fit for him & salutary to the state, or to the Senate of fine souls, which is the heart of the state."

(JMN/RWE/XIII/139-40)

Fuller's Poem "Leila"
From Her 1844 Journal

(Composed before she started writing *Woman in the Nineteenth Century,* as she realized she must put aside her youthful worship of Emerson and strike out for new horizons in New York.)

Leila in the Arabian zone
Dusky, languishing and lone
Yet full of light are her deep eyes
And her gales are lover's sighs.

So in Egyptian clime
Grows an Isis calm sublime
Blue black in her robe of night
The horns that Io's brow deform
With Isis take a crescent form
And as a holy moon inform
The magic Sistrum arms her hand

And at her deep eye's command
Brutes are raised to thinking men
Soul growing to her soul filled ken.

Dean of the lonely life
Hecate fed on gloom and strife.
Phoebe on her thrown of air
Only Leila's children aver.

Patient serpent, circle round
Till in death my life is found,
Double form of godly prime
Holding the whole thought of time,
When the perfect two embrace,
Male and female, black and white
Soul is justified in space,
Dark made fruitful by the light,
And centered in the diamond Sun
Time, eternity, are one.

(1844J/MF/25-27)

Footnotes

Initials and numbers indicate the source material as follows: the title/the author/the volume or article title/the page number.

Using this key, refer to the bibliography to locate the detailed information for each source.

Chapter 1

1. JMN/RWE/VIII/109
2. HRS/CS
3. E/RWE/"Self-Reliance"
4. PLA/MF/"American Literature; Its Position in the Present Time, and Prospects for the Future"
5. JMN/RWE/III/122
6. PLA/MF/"American Literature"
7. PLA/MF/"American Literature"
8. E/RWE/"Circles"
9. N/RWE
10. *The New-York Daily Tribune*/MF/ "Fourth of July"/July 4, 1854
11. E/RWE/"Man The Reformer"
12. M
13. W19C/MF
14. PLA/MF/"American Literature"
15. PLA/MF/"American Literature"
16. W19C/MF
17. W19C/MF
18. PLA/MF/"American Literature"
19. M/II/97
20. N/RWE
21. LMF/RH/I/348
22. W/RWE/"Divinity School Address"
23. M/II/85-6
24. RWE/JEC/I/306
25. M/II/95
26. N/RWE
27. W19C/MF
28. W19C/MF
29. M
30. M/I/288-9
31. PLA/MF/"American Literature"
32. JMN/RWE/VII/95
33. JMN/RWE/IX/115
34. M/II/38
35. M/I/100

Chapter 2

1. M/I/Appendix/374-5
2. M/I/Appendix/377-80
3. M/I/23-24
4. M/I/14-16
5. M/I/17-18
6. M/I/18-22
7. M/I/17
8. M/I/33
9. M/I/33
10. M/I/40-41
11. M/I/26-27
12. M/I/31-2
13. M/I/32
14. AM/OWH/Jan.'69/117
15. M/I/91-92
16. M/I/132-33
17. M/I/52-54
18. MF/PB/56
19. M/II/6-7
20. LMF/RH/I/162-3
21. MF/PB/57-8
22. M/I/69-70
23. MF/BGC/113
24. M/I/139-40
25. M/I/140-1
26. MF/JWH/38

27. LMF/RH/I/348
28. M/I/153
29. M/II/64-5
30. MFO/TWH/188
31. HWS/ECS/I/99
32. MFO/TWH/55

Chapter 3

1. RWE/GWA/8
2. RWE/JEC/I/35
3. RWE/JEC/I/33-4
4. RWE/OWH/ Introduction/10-13, 26-33
5. RWE/GWA/37
6. RWE/GWA/39
7. RWE/GWC/20
8. RWE/GEW/17
9. RWE/GWA/39
10. RWE/JEC/I/54-59-63
11. JMN/RWE/Oct. 24 & RWE/ GWA/53
12. RWE/GWA/53
13. JMN/RWE/I/134
14. RWE/JEC/I/64
15. RWE/JEC/I/64
16. JMN/RWE/I/133
17. RM/JP/289
18. RWE/GWA/62
19. RWE/GWA/74
20. FAF/SEW/4
21. RWE/GWA/75
22. JMN/RWE/II/240-41
23. RWE/GWA/76
24. RWE/GEW/30
25. ET/BP/37
26. JMN/RWE/III/72
27. FAF/SEW/18
28. RWE/GWA/112-13
29. E/RWE
30. LRWE/RLR/I/318
31. JMN/RWE/III/227
32. E/RWE/"Compensation"
33. LRWE/RLR/I/323
34. JMN/RWE/III/260-1
35. JMN/RWE/III/272
36. JMN/RWE/III/318-19
37. JMN/RWE/IV/47
38. RWE/GWA/239-40
39. LLJE/EET/48
40. LRWE/RLR/I/434-5
41. RWE/GWA/242-3
42. LRWE/RLR/I/438
43. JMN/RWE/V/19
44. JMN/RWE/V/22
45. JMN/RWE/V/24-25
46. JMN/RWE/V/77
47. JMN/RWE/VII/71
48. LLJE/ETE/71
49. LLJE/ETE/51
50. FM/JB/24-5
51. JMN/RWE/V/108
52. JMN/RWE/IV/47
53. EIHJ/JP/125
54. JMN/RWE/V/256-7
55. JMN/RWE/V/119
56. JMN/RWE/VIII/175
57. JMN/RWE/VII/310
58. JMN/RWE/IX/54
59. JMN/RWE/IX/82
60. JMN/RWE/V/505
61. JMN/RWE/IX/164
62. EIHJ/JP/396
63. JMN/RWE/XI/31
64. JMN/RWE/VII/149-50
65. JMN/RWE/VI/372
66. JMN/RWE/IV/16
67. EIHJ/JP/412
68. JMN/RWE/V/398
69. JN/IX/190
70. JMN/RWE/VI/391

71. JMN/VI/154/Encyclopedia
72. JMN/RWE/XI/444-445
73. EIHJ/JP/326
74. JMN/RWE/VI/186/Encyclopedia
75. JMN/RWE/VI/188/Encyclopedia
76. JMN/RWE/VI/188/Encyclopedia
77. JMN/RWE/VI/188/Encyclopedia
78. JMN/RWE/VI/188/Encyclopedia
79. JMN/RWE/VI/189/Encyclopedia
80. JMN/RWE/XI/275/1850
81. JMN/RWE/XI/338/1851
82. JMN/RWE/XI/234/1850
83. JMN/RWE/IV/81

Chapter 4

1. M/I/202
2. M/I/234
3. M/I/202-3
4. M/II/67-68
5. M/I/227
6. M/I/228-9
7. JMN/RWE/V/216
8. JMN/RWE/V/297
9. JMN/RWE/VI/161
10. EIHJ/JP/163
11. MFO/TWH/144
12. JMN/RWE/V/422
13. JMN/RWE/V/452
14. W/RWE/ "Representative Men"/ "Swedenborg"/128-29
15. RWE/JEC/I/324
16. JMN/RWE/V/454
17. JMN/RWE/V/456
18. JMN/RWE/V/489
19. LMF/RH/I/327-8
20. JMN/RWE/V/410
21. RWE/OWF/80-81
22. LMF/RH/II/39-41
23. EIC/EWE/201-2
24. LMF/RH/II/202-3
25. LRWE/RLR/II/201-3
26. LMF/RH/II/79-80
27. LMF/RH/II/81-2
28. LMF/RH/II/81
29. LMF/RH/II/90-1
30. LMF/RH/II/92-3
31. LMF/RH/II/95-6
32. M/II/38-9
33. M/II/107
34. JMN/RWE/VII/296
35. JMN/RWE/VII/301-2
36. JMN/RWE/VII/224
37. LMF/RH/II/161
38. LRWE/RLR/II/255
39. LMF/RH/II/105-6
40. LMF/RH/II/132-3
41. MFO/TWH/161
42. M/I/308-9
43. LRWE/RLR/II/326-7
44. LRWE/RLR/II/327-8
45. JMN/RWE/VII/512
46. LRWE/RLR/II/330
47. LRWE/RLR/II/332
48. LRWE/RLR/II/334
49. LRWE/RLR/II/336-7
50. LRWE/RLR/II/337-8
51. JMN/RWE/VII/400
52. LMF/RH/II/159
53. LMF/RH/II/159-60
54. LMF/RH/II/340-1
55. LRWE/RLR/II/342-3
56. LLJE/ETE/128-29
57. LRWE/RLR/II/349
58. LMF/RH/II/166-169
59. LMF/RH/II/166-169
60. LRWE/RLR/II/350-51
61. LRWE/RLR/II/352-3
62. LMF/RH/II/169-70
63. E/RWE/"Friendship"
64. MFO/TWH/112

65. LMF/RH/II/188
66. LRWE/RLR/II/398
67. JMN/RWE/VII/454
68. LMF/RH/II/212-13
69. JMN/RWE/VIII/6
70. JMN/RWE/VIII/88
71. JMN/RWE/VIII/10
72. JMN/RWE/VIII/149
73. LRWE/RLR/II/437-9
74. LMF/RH/233-4
75. LMF/RH/II/234-6
76. JMN/RWE/VIII/131
77. LRWE/RLR/II/464-5
78. LMF/RH/III/52
79. LRWE/RLR/III/32
80. LRWE/RLR/III/63
81. LRWE/RLR/III/75
82. MF/PB/190
83. 1842 J/MF
84. LMF/RH/III/79
85. LRWE/RLR/III/79-80
86. AN/NH/342-43
87. 1842J/MF/329-30
88. 1842J/MF/330-1
89. 1842J/MF/331-2
90. 1842J/MF/335
91. 1842J/MF/338
92. 1842J/MF/339-40
93. LMF/RH/III/96
94. M/II/71

Chapter 5

1. LMF/RH/III/60
2. JMN/RWE/IX/103
3. P/RWE
4. 1844C/MF/25-6-7
5. 1844C/MF/50-1
6. LMF/RH/III/209-10
7. LMF/RH/III/215
8. 1844C/MF/129
9. W19C/MF/115-116
10. W19C/MF/150
11. W19C/MF/119
12. *The New-York Daily Tribune/* "Fourth of July"
13. *The New-York Daily Tribune/* December 10, 1845
14. PLA/MF/"American Literature; Its Position in the Present Time, and Prospects for the Future."
15. LRWE/RLR/III/447-8
16. MF/JJD/96
17. LRWE/RLR/III/459
18. M/II/231-33
19. LRWE/RLR/IV/8
20. LRWE/RLR/IV/14
21. LRWE/RLR/IV/17-24
22. LRWE/RLR/IV/25-28
23. LRWE/RLR/IV/32-36
24. LRWE/RLR/IV/33, 35-6
25. LRWE/RLR/IV/54
26. JMN/RWE/X/351-2
27. JMN/RWE/XI/256-7
28. JMN/RWE/XI/293-4
29. EIHJ/JP/414

Chapter 6

1. LLJE/ETE/xiii-xiv

Key and Bibliography

References in the text have keys designated as follows:

Initials of title/
Initials of author or editor/
Volume or title of essay or magazine/
Page number

- Margaret Fuller's *Memoirs* is distinguished by the initial "M".
- The collections of letters of Margaret Fuller and Ralph Waldo Emerson are distinguised by the initials "LMF" and "LRWE" respectively.
- Books not listed in the Bibliograpy are written in full in the text references.
- When possible, the author has chosen to list source books which are currently and readily available to the general reader, rather than to list the original which is generally difficult to locate or found only in rare book libraries.

Key to References	Bibliography
RWE/ABA	Alcott, Amos B., *Ralph Waldo Emerson*, New York, Gordon Press, 1978.
RWE/GWA	Allen, Gay Wilson, *Waldo Emerson*, Penguin Books, The Viking Press, 1981.
MF/MA	Allen, Margaret Vanderhaar, *The Achievement of Margaret Fuller*, University Park and London, The Pennsylvania State University Press, 1979.
MF/KA	Anthony, Katharine, *Margaret Fuller, A Psychological Biography*, New York, Harcourt, Brace and Howe, 1920.
MC&MF/HB	Baer, Helene G., "Mrs. Child and Miss Fuller," *New England Quarterly*, June 26, 1953, pp. 249-55.
WF/NB	Baym, Nina, *Woman's Fiction, A Guide to Novels by and about Women in America, 1820-1870*, Ithaca and London, Cornell University Press, 1978.
AL/HAB	Beers, Henry A., *Initial Studies in American Letters*, Flood and Vincent, New York, The Chautauqua Reading Circle Press, 1895.

MF/MB Bell, Margaret, *Margaret Fuller,* New York, Charles Boni Paper Books, 1930.

FM/JB Bernard, Jessie, *Future of Marriage,* New Haven and London, Yale University Press, 1982.

FW/JB Bernard, Jessie, *The Female World,* New York, The Free Press, A Division of Macmillan Publishing Co., Inc. London, Collier Macmillan Publishers, 1981.

MF/PB Blanchard, Paula, *Margaret Fuller From Transcendentalism to Revolution,* New York, Delacorte Press/Seymour Lawrence, 1978.

RWE/CB Bode, Carl, *Ralph Waldo Emerson, A Profile,* New York, Hill and Wang, 1968.

JFC/AB Bolster, Jr., Arthur S., *James Freeman Clarke, Disciple to Advancing Truth,* Boston, The Beacon Press, 1954.

OM/PB Brooks, Paul, *The Old Manse and the People Who Lived There,* The Trustees of Reservations, 1983.

EAO/VWB Brooks, Van Wyck, *Emerson and Others,* New York, E. P. Dutton & Co., 1927.

LOE/VWB Brooks, Van Wyck, *The Life of Emerson,* New York, The Literary Guild, 1932.

MF/AB Brown, Arthur W., *Margaret Fuller, United States Authors Series,* New York, Twayne Publishers, 1964.

RWE/JEC Cabot, James Elliot, *A Memoir of Ralph Waldo Emerson,* 2 Vols., Boston, Houghton Mifflin Co., 1887. Also, AMS Press, New York, Second Printing, 1969. Reprinted from a copy in the collection of Northwestern University Library, From the edition of 1887, Cambridge.

ESQ Cameron, Kenneth Walter, "Emerson, Thoreau, and The Town and Country Club," *The Emerson Society Quarterly,* No. 8, III Quarter, 1957, p. 2.

ELE/WC Charvat, William, "A Chronological List of Emerson's American Lecture Engagements," *Bulletin of the New York Public Library,* 64 - Sept., 1960, p. 502.

MF/BGC Chevigny, Bell Gale, *The Woman and the Myth,* New York, The Feminist Press, 1976.

TP/EC Cheyfitz, Eric, *The Trans-Parent; Sexual Politics in the Language of Emerson,* Baltimore and London, John Hopkins University Press, 1981.

L/LMC Child, Lydia Maria, *Lydia Maria Child, Selected Letters, 1817-1880,* ed. Milton Meltzer and Patricia G. Holland, Francine Krasno, Amherst, University of Mass. Press, 1982.

MF/FC Chipperfield, Faith, *In Quest of Love,* New York, Coward McCann, 1957.

JFC/JFC Clarke, James Freeman, *James Freeman Clarke, Autobiography, Diary and Correspondence,* ed. Edward Everett Hale, New York. Reprinted by Negro Universities Press, A Division of Greenwood Publishing Corp., 1968.

TP/HSC Commager, Henry Steele, *Theodore Parker, Yankee Crusader,* Boston, Beacon Press, 1936.

EAHA/MDC Conway, Moncure Daniel, *Emerson At Home and Abroad,* New York, Haskell House Publishers, Ltd., 1968.

RWE/GWC Cooke, George Willis, *Ralph Waldo Emerson: His Life, Writings, and Philsophy,* Boston, James R. Osgood and Co., (Fifth Edition), 1882. Also, Norwood, 1975.

LHG/WMC Cornell, William M., L.L.D., *The Life and Public Career of Hon. Horace Greeley,* Boston, D. Lothrop & Co., No copyright date given.

CIBC *Stereotypes, Distortions and Omissions in U. S. History Textbooks,* New York, The Council on Interracial Books for Children, Racism and Sexism Resource Center for Educators, 1977.

RWE/SMC Crothers, Samuel McChord, *Ralph Waldo Emerson, How To Know Him,* New York, Bobbs Merrill, 1921.

M&HF/CHD Dall, Carolyn W. Healey, *Margaret and Her Friends or Ten Conversations with Margaret Fuller upon The Mythology of the Greeks and Its Expression in Art,* New York, Reprint, Arno Press, A New York Times Co., 1972; Boston: Roberts Brothers, 1895.

MF/JJD Deiss, Joseph Jay, *The Roman Years of Margaret Fuller,* New York, Thomas Y. Crowell Company, 1969.

EOC/AD Derleth, August, *Emerson, Our Contemporary,* London: Crowell-Collier Press-Collier-MacMillan Limited, 1970.

FAC/AD Douglas, Ann, *The Feminization of American Culture,* New York, Avon Books, 1977.

IE/BKE Emerson, Benjamin Kendall, *The Ipswich Emersons,* assisted by Capt. Geo. A. Gordon, Boston, Press of David Clapp & Son, 1900.

EIC/EWE Emerson, Edward W., *Emerson In Concord, A Memoir,* Boston and New York, Houghton, Mifflin and Co., 1889.

L/ELTE Emerson, Ellen Louise Tucker, *One First Love, The Letters of Ellen Louise Tucker Emerson to Ralph Waldo Emerson,* ed. Edith W. Gregg, Cambridge, Mass., Harvard University Press, 1962.

LLJE/ETE Emerson, Ellen Tucker, *The Life of Lidian Jackson Emerson,* ed. Dolores Bird Carpenter, Boston, Twayne Publishers, 1980.

EIHJ/JP Emerson, Ralph Waldo, *Emerson In His Journals*, ed. Joel Porte, Cambridge, Mass., Harvard University Press, 1982.

E/RWE Emerson, Ralph Waldo, *Essays, First and Second Series*, Boston and New York, Houghton Mifflin Co., 1865 and 1876.

JMN/RWE Emerson, Ralph Waldo, *The Journals and Miscellaneous Notebooks of Ralph Waldo Emerson*, ed. W. G. Gilman et al., 14 Vols., Cambridge, Mass., Belknap Press, 1960-1978.

J/RWE Emerson, Ralph Waldo, *The Journals of Ralph Waldo Emerson*, ed. E. W. Emerson and W. E. Forbes,10 Vols., Boston, Houghton Mifflin, 1909-1914.

LAF/RWE Emerson, Ralph Waldo, *Letters from Ralph Waldo Emerson To A Friend, 1838-1853*, ed. Charles Eliot Norton, Cambridge, Boston and New York, Houghton, Mifflin and Co., The Riverside Press, 1899.

LRWE/RLR Emerson, Ralph Waldo, *Letters of Ralph Waldo Emerson*, ed. Ralph L. Rusk, 6 Vols., New York, Columbia University Press, 1939.

N/RWE Emerson, Ralph Waldo, *Nature*, Boston, Beacon Press, 1985, 1986.

M Emerson, Ralph Waldo, William Henry Channing, and James Freeman Clarke, *Memoirs of Margaret Fuller Ossoli*, Boston, Phillips, Sampson, 1852. Reprinted by Burt Franklin, 1972.

P/RWE Emerson, Ralph Waldo, *Poems, 1847*, Boston, Ticknor and Fields, 1860, and Houghton Mifflin & Co., The Riverside Press, Cambridge, Mass. 1894.

W/RWE Emerson, Ralph Waldo, *The Works of Ralph Waldo Emerson*, ed. J. E. Cabot, 14 Vols., Boston, Houghton Mifflin, 1883-87.

RWE/OWF Firkins, Oscar W., *Ralph Waldo Emerson*, New York, Russell & Russell, 1965.

CS/EF Flexner, Eleanor, *Century of Struggle*, Cambridge, Mass., London, England, The Belknap Press of Harvard University Press, 1959, 1975.

BU/OBF Frothingham, Octavius Brooks, *Boston Unitarianism, 1820-1850, A Study of the Life and Work of Nathaniel Langdon Frothingham*, New York & London, G. P. Putnam's Sons, The Knickerbocker Press, 1890.

WHC/OBF Frothingham, Octavius Brooks, *Memoir of William Henry Channing*, Boston and New York, Houghton, Mifflin and Co., The Riverside Press, Cambridge, 1886.

TNE/OBF Frothingham, Octavius Brooks, *Transcendentalism in New England*, New York by G. P. Putnam's Sons, 1876. Reprinted, Harper & Row,1965.

AH&A/MF Fuller, Margaret (Ossoli), *At Home and Abroad*, ed. A. B. Fuller, Boston, Crosby, Nichols; London, Sampson Low, Son & Co., 1856. Reprinted by Kennikat Press.

Fms/HLH Fuller Manuscripts and Papers, Cambridge, Mass., Houghton Library, Harvard University.

LMF/RH Fuller, Margaret (Ossoli), *The Letters of Margaret Fuller*, ed. Robert N. Hudspeth, 5 Vols., Ithaca and London, Cornell University Press, 1983.

LWLW/MF Fuller, Margaret (Ossoli), *Life Within and Life Without*, ed. A. B. Fuller, Boston, Brown, Taggard, & Chase; New York, Sheldon; Philadelphia, J. B. Lippincott; London, Sampson Low, Son & Co., 1860. Reprinted by Gregg Press.

LL/MF Fuller, Margaret (Ossoli), *Love Letters of Margaret Fuller, 1845-1846*, ed. Julia Ward Howe, New York, D. Appleton, 1903. Reprinted by Greenwood Press.

1839J/MF Fuller, Margaret (Ossoli), "Margaret Fuller's 1839 Journal: Trip to Bristol," ed. Robert N. Hudsputh, Cambridge, Mass. *Harvard Library Bulletin*, October 27, 1979, pp. 445-70.

1842J/MF Fuller, Margaret (Ossoli), "Margaret Fuller's 1842 Journal, At Concord With The Emersons," ed. Joel Myerson, Cambridge, Mass., *Harvard Library Bulletin*, July 21, 1973.

1844C/MF Fuller, Margaret (Ossoli), *Commonplace Book, 1844*, Perry-Clarke Collection, on deposit at Massachusetts Historical Society.

EALL/MF Fuller, Margaret (Ossoli), *Margaret Fuller: Essays on American Life and Letters*, ed. Joel Myerson, New Haven, Conn., College & University Press, 1978.

PLA/MF Fuller, Margaret (Ossoli), *Papers and Literature on Art*, New York, Wiley & Putnam, 1846.

SOL/MF Fuller, Margaret (Ossoli), *Summer on the Lakes*, Boston, Charles C. Little & James Brown, 1843; New York, Charles C. Francis, 1844.

W19C/MF Fuller, Margaret (Ossoli), *Woman in the Nineteenth Century*, New York, Greeley & McElrath, 1845. Reprinted by W.W. Norton and Co., 1971.

WKP/MF Fuller, Margaret (Ossoli), *Woman in the Nineteenth Century and Kindred Papers*, ed. Arthur B. Fuller, Boston, John P. Jewett, 1855.

LE/RG Garnett, Richard, *Life of Emerson*, Folcroft, Pa., Folcroft Library Edition, 1974.

GR/HLG Golemba, Henry L., *George Ripley*, Boston, Twayne Publishers, A Division of G. K. Hall & Co., 1977.

RWE/EEH — Hale, Edward E., *Ralph Waldo Emerson,* Folcraft, Pa., Folcraft, 1972.

HAL/RPH — Halleck, Reuben Post, *History of American Literature,* New York, American Book Company, 1911.

DHT/WH — Harding, Walter, *The Days of Henry Thoreau,* New York, Alfred A. Knopf, 1967.

RWE/DGH — Haskins, David G., D. D., *Ralph Waldo Emerson, His Maternal Ancestors,* Boston, Cupples, Upham & Co., Assoc. Faculty Press, 1887.

NH&W/JH — Hawthorne, Julian, *Nathaniel Hawthorne and his Wife, A Biography,* Volume I & II, first published in 1884. Reprinted Hamden, Conn., Archon Books, 1968.

AN/NH — Hawthorne, Nathaniel, *American Notebooks,* ed. Claude M. Simpson, Columbus, Ohio State University Press, Modern Language Assn., 1932.

MFO/TWH — Higginson, Thomas Wentworth, *Margaret Fuller Ossoli,* Boston, Houghton, Mifflin and Co., 1884.

ST/HHH — Hoeltje, Hubert H., *Sheltering Tree: A Story of the Friendship of Ralph Waldo Emerson and Amos Bronson Alcott,* Durham, N. C., Duke University Press, 1943.

RWE/OWH — Holmes, Oliver Wendell, *Ralph Waldo Emerson,* Boston and New York, The Riverside Press, Cambridge, 1884. Republished Detroit, Gale Research Library, 1967.

AM/OW — Holmes, Oliver Wendell, *Atlantic Monthly Magazine,* January 1969, p.117.

MF/JWH — Howe, Julia Ward, *Margaret Fuller,* Boston, Roberts Bros., 1883.

R/JWH — Howe, Julia Ward, *Reminiscences 1819-1899,* Boston, Houghton Mifflin, 1899.

EC/RH — Hudspeth, Robert N., *Ellery Channing,* New York, Twayne Publishers, Inc., 1973.

RWE/AI — Ireland, Alexander, *Ralph Waldo Emerson, His Life, Genius, and Writings,* London, 1882. Reissued, Port Washington, New York, Kennikat Press, 1972.

TB/HJ — James, Henry, *The Bostonians,* London, Macmillan, 1886.

WWS/HJ — James, Henry, *William Wetmore Story and his Friends,* 2 vols., Boston, Houghton, Mifflin, 1903.

OEF/LJ — James, Laurie, *O Excellent Friend!,* dramatic play script, (unpublished), copyright 1982.

MW&MF/LJ James, Laurie, *Men, Women, and Margaret Fuller,* formerly entitled *Still Beat Noble Hearts,* dramatic play script, a solo portrait, (unpublished), copyright 1979.

W&WMF/LJ James, Laurie, *The Wit and Widsom of Margaret Fuller Ossoli,* Vol. I in a series, New York, Golden Heritage Press, Inc., 1988.

WMFF/LJ James, Laurie, *Why Margaret Fuller Ossoli Is Forgotten,* Vol. II in a series, New York, Golden Heritage Press, Inc., 1988.

PW/EJ Janeway, Elizabeth, *Powers of the Weak,* New York, Alfred A. Knopf, 1980.

HTH/SJ Johnson, Sonia, *From Housewife To Heretic,* New York, Anchor Press/Doubleday, 1983.

EMHA/EK Kaledin, Eugenia, *The Education of Mrs. Henry Adams,* Philadelphia, Temple University Press, 1981.

TP/RK Kluger, Richard, with the assistance of Phyllis Kluger, *The Paper, The Life and Death of The New York Herald Tribune,* New York, Alfred A. Knopf, 1986.

GS/GL Lerner, Gerda, *The Grimke Sisters from South Carolina,* New York, Schocken Books, 1971.

MFIP/GL Lerner, Gerda, *The Majority Finds Its Past, Placing Women in History,* Oxford, New York, Oxford University Press, 1981.

DOE/JMc McAleer, John J., *Days of Encounter,* Boston, Little Brown, 1984.

MFT/ARM Marble, Annie Russell, "Margaret Fuller as Teacher," *Critic 43,* October 1903, pp. 334-45.

STD/HEM Marshall, Helen E.,"The Story of the Dial, 1840-1844," *New Mexico Quarterly 1,* May 1931, pp. 147-65.

CPC/FDM Miller, F. DeWolfe, *Christopher Pearse Cranch And His Caricatures of New England Transcendentalism,* Cambridge, Mass., Harvard University Press, 1951.

EEC/EMM Maxfield-Miller, Elizabeth, "Emerson and Elizabeth of Concord," *Harvard Library Bulletin,* Cambridge, Mass., July 19, 1971, pp. 290-306.

EOC/EMM Maxfield-Miller, Elizabeth, "Elizabeth of Concord: Selected Letters of Elizabeth Sherman Hoar to the Emersons, Family, and The Emerson Circle," (Part One), ed. Joel Myerson, *Studies in the American Renaissance,* 1984, Charlottesville, The University Press of Virginia, pp. 229-279.

EHCT/EMM Maxfield-Miller, Elizabeth, "Elizabeth Hoar of Concord and Thoreau," *Thoreau Society Bulletin,* no. 106, Winter 1969, pp. 1-3.

CC/FTM	McGill, Frederick T., Jr., *Channing of Concord,* New Brunswick, N. J., Rutgers University Press, 1967.
ETEY/RM	Michaud, Regis, *Emerson, The Enraptured Yankee,* New York, AMS Press, 1930.
MF/PM	Miller, Perry, *Margaret Fuller, American Romantic,* New York, Doubleday & Co., Anchor Books, 1963.
TT/PM	Miller, Perry, *The Transcendentalists, An Anthology,* Cambridge, Mass., Harvard University Press, 1950.
AJ/FLM	Moll, Frank Luther, *American Journalism, A History of Newspapers in the United States through 250 years, 1690 to 1940,* New York, The MacMillan Co., 1941.
SB/HM	Moscow, Henry, *The Street Book, An Encyclopedia of Manhattan's Street Names and Their Origins,* New York, Hagsstrom Company, Inc., 1978.
CDR/JM	Myerson, Joel, "Caroline Dall's Reminiscences of Margaret Fuller," Cambridge, Mass., *Harvard Library Bulletin 22,* October 1974, pp. 414-28.
CRBD/JM	Myerson, Joel, "The Contemporary Reception of the Boston Dial," *Resources for American Literary Study 3,* Autumn 1973, pp. 203-20.
CEMF/JM	Myerson, Joel, *Critical Essays on Margaret Fuller,* Boston, G. K. Hall & Co., 1980.
EWF/JM	Myerson, Joel, "The Emerson-Ward Friendship: Ideals and Realities," *Studies in the American Renaissance, 1984,* Charlottesville, The University Press of Virginia, pp. 299-325.
MF/JM	Myerson, Joel, *Margaret Fuller, A Descriptive Bibliography,* Pittsburgh, University of Pittsburgh Press, 1978.
MDEMF/JM	Myerson, Joel, "Mrs. Dall Edits Miss Fuller: The Story of Margaret and Her Friends," Concord, Mass., Concord Library.
NETD/JM	Myerson, Joel, *The New England Transcendentalists and the Dial,* London and Toronto: Associated University Presses; Rutherford, Madison, Teaneck: Fairleigh Dickinson University Press, 1980.
HCM/LRP	Paige, Lucius R., *History of Cambridge, Mass.,* Boston, H.O. Houghton, 1877.
MCAT/VLP	Parrington, Vernon Louis, *Main Currents in American Thought, An Interpretation of American Literature from the Beginnings to 1920,* 3 vols., New York, Harcourt, Brace and Co., 1927.
RS/EP	Peabody, Elizabeth, *Record of a School,* Boston, 1836. Reprinted Arno Press, 1969.

ET/BP Perry, Bliss, *Emerson Today,* Hamden, Conn., Archon Books, 1969.

LNYC/EAP Poe, Edgar Allen, "The Literati of New York City," *Godey's Lady's Book 33,* No. III, July 1846, pp. 13-19.

RM/JP Porte, Joel, *Representative Man, Ralph Waldo Emerson in His Time,* New York, Oxford University Press, 1979.

EPTS/JER Roberts, Josephine E., "Elizabeth Peabody and the Temple School," *New England Quarterly,* 15, September 1942, pp. 497-508.

COE/TJR Rountree, Thomas, J., *Critics on Emerson,* Coral Gables, Florida, University of Miami Press, 1973.

RWE/RLR Rusk, Ralph L., *The Life of Ralph Waldo Emerson,* New York and London, Columbia University Press, 1939.

EWA/PR Russell, Phillips, *Emerson, The Wisest American,* New York, Bretanno's, 1929.

GCE/FBS Sanborn, Franklin B., *Genius and Character of Emerson - Lectures at the Concord School of Philosophy,* Cambridge, Mass., Houghton, Mifflin & Co., The Riverside Press, 1895.

LHDT/FBS Sanborn, Franklin B., *The Life of Henry David Thoreau,* Boston and New York, Gale Library of Lives and Letters, American Writers Series, Houghton Mifflin & Co., 1917.

PE/FBS Sanborn, Franklin B., *Personality of Emerson,* Boston, The Merrymount Press, 1903.

RSY/FBS Sanborn, Franklin B., *Recollections of Seventy Years,* Vol. I & II, Boston, The Gorham Press, 1909.

ELW/JS Searle, January, *Emerson, His Life & Writings,* Folcroft, Pa., Folcroft, 1973.

PP/OS Shepard, Odel, *Pedlar's Progress,* Boston, Little Brown & Co., 1937.

POD/AS Snitow, Ann, Stansell, Christine, and Thompson, Sharon, eds, *Powers of Desire, The Politics of Sexuality,* New York, Monthly Review Press,1983.

EW/BMS Solomon, Barbara Miller, *In The Company of Educated Women,* New Haven and London, Yale University Press, 1985.

WOI/DS Spender, Dale, *Women of Ideas And What Men Have Done to Them,* London, Boston, Melbourne and Henley, Routledge & Kegan Paul, 1982.

RWE/WS Staebler, Warren, *Ralph Waldo Emerson,* New York, Twayne Publishers, 1973.

HWS/ECS Stanton, Elizabeth Cady; Anthony, Susan B., and Gage, Matilda Joslyn, editors, *History of Woman Suffrage,* 2 Vols, New York, Fowler & Wells, 1881.

MF/MS — Stern, Madeleine B., *The Life of Margaret Fuller,* New York, E. P. Dutton, 1942.

MFPP/MS — Stern, Madeleine B., "Margaret Fuller and the Phrenologist-Publishers," *Studies in the American Renaissance,* 1980, pp. 290-306.

NSC/TS — Stoehr, Taylor, *Nay-Saying in Concord, Emerson/Alcott/ & Thoreau,* Folcroft, Pa., Folcroft, 1977.

HSR/CS — Strauch, Carl F., "Hatred's Swift Repulsions: Emerson, Margaret Fuller, and Others," *Studies in Romanticism,* The Graduate School, Boston University, Vol. VII, Winter 1958, Number 2.

EPP/ET — Thurin, Erik, *Emerson As Priest of Pan: A Study in the Metaphysics of Sex,* Lawrence, The Regents Press of Kansas, 1981.

WFL/JT — Todd, Janet, *Women's Friendship in Literature,* New York, Columbia University Press, 1980.

TJQ/MOU — Urbanski, Marie Olesen, "The Ambivalence of Ralph Waldo Emerson Towards Margaret Fuller," *Thoreau Journal Quarterly,* July 1978.

MF/MOU — Urbansky, Marie Mitchell Olesen, *Margaret Fuller's Woman in the Nineteenth Century,* Westport, Conn., Greenwood Press, 1980.

MF/MW — Wade, Mason, *Margaret Fuller, Whetstone of Genius,* New York, The Viking Press, 1940.

WMF/MW — Wade, Mason, *The Writings of Margaret Fuller,* New York, Viking Press, 1941.

RWE/EW — Wagenknecht, Edward, *Ralph Waldo Emerson, Portrait of a Balanced Soul,* New York, Oxford University Press, 1974.

MFRWE/HRW — Warfel, Harry R., "Margaret Fuller and Ralph Waldo Emerson," *PMLA 50,* June 1935, pp. 576-94.

HM/RKW — Webb, R. K., *Harriet Martineau, A Radical Victorian,* London, Columbia University Press,1960.

FMF/LW — Wellisz, Leopold, *The Friendship of Margaret Fuller D'Ossoli and Adam Mickiewicz,* Union Square, New York City, Polish Book Importing Co., 1947.

FAF/SEW — Whicher, Stephen E., *Freedom and Fate, An Inner Life of Ralph Waldo Emerson,* New York, A. S. Barnes & Co., Inc., University of Pennsylvania Press, 1953.

RWE/GEW — Woodberry, George Edward, *Ralph Waldo Emerson,* New York, Haskell House, 1968, first published 1907.

FN/CWS — Woodham-Smith, Cecil, *Florence Nightingale,* New York, London, Toronto, McGraw-Hill Book Co., Inc., 1951.

RWE/DY — Yanells, Donald, *Ralph Waldo Emerson,* Boston, G. K. Hall, 1982.

Index

Why Margaret Fuller Ossoli Shocked Americans

She:

- Did not conform to the accepted standard of womanhood. She was considered ugly, bright, arrogant, aggressive, outspoken. "Truth at all costs," was her maxim.
- Read, translated, wrote and spoke about the work of Goethe when intellectual men refused to touch his writings.
- Wrote the first book in America advocating equality for men and women.
- Dared to explode myths and hypocracy in friendship, love, marriage, celebacy, homosexuality and prostitution.
- Defended the character and actions of George Sand and Madame de Staël, both of whom had open love affairs.
- Sympathized with the poor and insane, and cited the need for halfway houses for jailed prostitutes when ladies held silence on these subjects.
- Challenged men to pattern their sexual lives after the same high ideals society held for women.
- Criticized stingingly the work of Longfellow, Poe, Emerson, Lowell and other contemporaries, and called for a new growth of American literary geniuses.
- Became a New York journalist when journalism was considered unfitting employment for a woman, especially for a single, and when New York was considered culturally disadvantaged.
- Pleaded the causes of slavery, the Indian and the immigrant when public opinion on these issues was controversial.
- Proclaimed herself a citizen of Italy, and gallently joined the Revolution of 1848.
- Ventured a love liasion with a Roman nobleman ten years younger than herself, who was not equally intellectual, not a Protestant, who could not speak English.
- Gave birth, it was scandously rumored, out of wedlock, secretly.

Literary Concord *Uncovered*

Concord Center (north side), before 1865. Courtesy of Concord Free Public Library.

Walden Pond, Summer. Taken by Joseph L. Andrews, 2008.

Literary Concord *Uncovered*

Revealing Emerson, Thoreau, Alcott, Hawthorne, and Fuller

by Joseph L. Andrews

Author of *Revolutionary Boston, Lexington, and Concord: The Shots Heard 'Round the World!*

Founding Director of Concord Guides Walking Tours "Revolution, Renaissance and Renewal"

Library of Congress Control Number: 2014911301

ISBN:	Hardcover	978-1-4990-3985-6
	Softcover	978-1-4990-3984-9
	eBook	978-1-4990-3986-3

This book was printed in the United States of America.

Rev. date: 07/10/2014

To order additional copies of this book, contact:
Xlibris LLC
1-888-795-4274
www.Xlibris.com
Orders@Xlibris.com
552590

For: Lesley, Joe, Michael and Garrett Andrews

Jennifer, Adam, Aaron and Pete Burke

Sara K. Andrews

*

For: The Paxton, Kotzen and Eldridge Families

*

For Elaine Inker

*

In Loving Memory of:

Margareta Langert Andrews

Katherine New Andrews & Joseph Lyon Andrews Sr.

Ann Andrews Paxton

Lynn Andrews Kotzen

*

Contents

Photos and Illustrations for *Literary Concord Uncovered*

Drawn by J.W. Barber, 1839; Engraved by J. Downes, Worcester.

CENTRAL PART OF CONCORD, MASS.

The above is a northern view in the central part of Concord village. Part of the Court – House is seen on the left. Burying – ground Hill (a post observation to the British officers in the invasion of 1775) is seen a short distance beyond. The Unitarian Church and Middlesex Hotel are seen on the right.

Central part of Concord village, 1839,after a wood engraving by John Barber.

Introduction

Why Concord?

The small inland farming village of Concord, Massachusetts, became the epicenter of a great creative surge in American literature in the mid-1800s, known widely as "the flowering of New England" and also as the American Renaissance.

Essayist and naturalist Henry Thoreau; lecturer, essayist, and poet Ralph Waldo Emerson; novelist and short story writer Louisa May Alcott; novelist Nathaniel Hawthorne; and essayist and journalist Margaret Fuller, all lived and wrote in Concord simultaneously. They lived side by side as neighbors, frequently met informally at each others' houses to discuss literary, religious, philosophical, and political ideas, tramped the woods together, played with each others' children, and sometimes even read each others' daily journal entries.

The Concord authors' creations were notable for their originality and their topical and stylistic departures from most of their European and American predecessors. Their best literary achievements include Thoreau's *Walden* and the lecture that he turned into his essay "Civil Disobedience," Emerson's essays "Nature" and "Self Reliance," Alcott's autobiographical novel *Little Women,* Hawthorne's novels *The Scarlet Letter* and *The House of Seven Gables,* and Fuller's *Women in the Nineteenth Century.* Today these master works are still held in great esteem by readers, teachers, and literary critics, both in America and around the world.

One contemporary author, Susan Cheever, hypothesizes in *American Bloomsbury* that this extraordinary nexus of creativity was due to the fact that in the nineteenth century, Concord was a village inhabited by "a cluster of geniuses." Although few readers and literary critics agree completely with this theory, the question still remains: why did so much literary creativity occur in this small New England farming village?

Why was the town of Concord the intellectual vortex of America in the mid nineteenth century? What were the characteristics of this community of roughly 2,000 souls (according to an 1830 census), twenty miles northwest of Boston, that encouraged some of America's most talented authors to live and to write there? There are numerous varied theories put forward by literary historians, but I have found no better explanation than that of Van Wyck Brooks's, who wrote this explanation in his book *The Flowering of New England*: "Plain, low, quiet, the village had no obvious distractions. The enterprising Yankee passed it by. It had no port, no trade, no water power, no gold, lead, coal, oil, or marble. As wood and grass were its only staples, Emerson advised his fellow townsmen to manufacture school teachers and make them the best in the world. The village air favored this, as it favored meditation and contemplation. The hills and woods, not too exciting, afforded a gentle stimulus to genial and uninterrupted studies. . . Emerson found it so in his woodland walks. Once he had left his study, only in the fields with the lowing cattle, the birds, the trees, the waters, the satisfying outlines of the hills and ponds, he seemed to come to his own and made friends with nature. He found health and affinity there—no petulance, no fret, but eternal resource, a long tomorrow, rich as yesterday."

Thoreau had expressed similar thoughts when he wrote in his Journal in 1841 at age twenty-four: "I think I could write a poem to be called 'Concord.' For argument I should have the river, the woods, the ponds, the hills, the fields, the swamps, and the meadows, the streets and the buildings and the villagers. Then morning, noon, and evening, spring, summer, autumn, and winter night, Indian summer, and the mountains in the horizon."

Contemporary author John Mitchell writes insightfully in *Walking Towards Walden:* "More than any other community in America, Concord, Massachusetts, evokes what the Hopi people call *tuwanasaapi,* the centering place, the place where you belong, the spiritual core of the universe. The town is among those fast-disappearing communities that actually have real main streets with shops and local gossip. . . Because of an accident of history, or geography, or some mystical, as yet unidentified force, things have happened in the place that is now called Concord. For five thousand years the local Native Americans would congregate in the area at the confluence of the Assabet and Sudbury rivers, which is located more or less in the present geographical center of the town. The tract was the first inland community to be settled by Europeans. It was the place where the world's first war of independence began; it was the place where American literature first flowered; and it is a place that to this day attracts writers of one species or another—some four hundred have lived or worked here in the town's short history."

Concord literary historian, Tom Blanding, summarizes how features of the town that Concord authors wrote about have become not just local but also universal symbols for both national and international visitors: "The Concord authors—Ralph Waldo Emerson, Henry D. Thoreau, Bronson and Louisa May Alcott, Nathaniel Hawthorne, and others—left a legacy not only in literature, but also in landscape. They intentionally transformed the features of the town, such as the North Bridge and Walden Pond, into universal symbols of cherished American values. It is this enduring symbolic identity that attracts ever-increasing numbers of pilgrims to Concord from all over the world."

After I moved to Concord in 1995, I discovered that these "classic" Concord authors' creations and lives are still very much alive in the hearts and minds of many of today's Concordians. I discovered an abundance of literary lectures, book signings, workshops, exhibits, courses, seminars, meetings of named author societies, visits to the authors' homes and the publication annually of a new crop of critical books about the Concord authors, all occurring over 170 years after these famous Concord sages ceased to write.

Why are the creations of these nineteenth century Concord authors still relevant to today's readers? As we will see, Thoreau was a pioneer in valuing and writing about nature. He presaged today's widespread environmental awareness. For example, his detailed observations and descriptions about seasonal changes among Concord's native plants and animals provide an important scientific observational baseline, which helps modern scientists chart the speed of climate changes today.

Thoreau also wrote eloquently and passionately about human rights and about nonviolent resistance to injustice. His words inspired Mahatma Ghandi, Martin Luther King, John F. Kennedy, and Nelson Mandela in their modern struggles for freedom, equality, and justice.

Emerson in his essays, poems, and lectures sparked an American intellectual revolution, which challenged Americans to think and write independently from their European predecessors. He urged his readers to think about religion and the relationship between man and the universe in nontraditional ways. He suggested that they take their inspiration from nature, rather than from ancient Biblical tests or from their ministers' dogmatic sermons.

Louisa May Alcott was one of America's first successful women authors. She described the intricacies of family life, especially among four very different sisters and their parents in her semi-autobiographical novel *Little Women.* While in *Work* she portrayed the formidable challenges women of her day faced as they first entered the workplace.

Novelist Nathaniel Hawthorne, with his multigenerational Salem background, looked backward at his Puritan New England ancestors and their overriding concerns with sin, guilt, anger, and punishment. In perhaps his best known novel, *The Scarlet Letter,* he explored the moral anguish and tragic consequences caused by adultery between a Puritan minister and one of his parishioners, who was a married woman.

Margaret Fuller was a pioneering feminist. Her best known book, *Women in the Nineteenth Century,* directed a spotlight on both women's limited role in mid-nineteenth century society and on what she identified as the pressing need to improve it. In her own life she demonstrated that women could be effective as editors, social critics, and foreign newspaper correspondents.

Among the Concord authors Thoreau was the only one who was actually born in Concord, although Emerson, who was born in Boston, had deep ancestral roots in Concord. Bronson Alcott, Louisa's father, was drawn to Concord in large part due to the pull of Emerson's personal and intellectual magnetism, as well as by his generosity. Both Thoreau and Emerson became fervent abolitionists, urging their readers and listeners at their lectures to abolish slavery well before the beginning of the Civil War.

Hundreds of books continue to be written today about the Concord authors, both nationally and internationally. New biographies, as well as critical and psychological studies appear annually. Many are written by academic experts who devote their lives to the study of particular Concord authors. Their career advancement is heavily dependent on the quality and success of their targeted literary critiques.

So why write yet another book about the Concord authors? Why should I write it? And why should you read it?

Over the past twenty years, I have had the pleasure of meeting and interacting with thousands of American visitors to Concord from many sections of the country, who have been participants in my Concord Guides Walking Tours: Revolution, Renaissance, and Renewal. I often asked visitors from all over America, as well as many from abroad, if they have read *any* books by a Concord author. While most visitors express real interest in learning more about major Concord authors, many of them admit that they have not yet had the opportunity to actually read any of their works.

My purpose in writing this "introductory overview" of major Concord authors, rather than a narrow critique limited to only one writer, is to pique the curiosity and interest of you, the contemporary reader, to get you to actually read and to really enjoy works by these American masters. I write not from the point of view of an academic specialist, but from that of a non-academic, non-specialist, an aficionado, a generalist, and an enthusiast.

Although I have been a practicing physician for my whole life, my earlier training was as an English major at Amherst College, writing my honors thesis about American literature. I could not decide between becoming a doctor or becoming a writer. So I decided to try to do both. Throughout my medical career I have also been an essayist, an author of a best-selling book about the American Revolution, *Revolutionary Boston, Lexington, and Concord: The Shots Heard 'Round the World!* and a freelance journalist for the *Boston Globe,* the *Concord Journal* and for many other newspapers and magazines. In connection with researching this book I decided to read many books by classic Concord authors for the first time and to re-read many others that I first encountered as a young student. (By way of perspective, Emerson's essays were the most popular among Concord's literary creations that teachers selected when I was in high school in the fifties. But after the turbulent mid-sixties, Thoreau's writings became—and remain—more popular.)

I hope to be able to share my enthusiasm, along with some intriguing, newly researched knowledge with my readers, enough to encourage many to pick up books (or electronic tablets) and to experience for themselves, perhaps for the first time or yet again, the pleasures of reading masterpieces by Concord's timeless sages.

For each of Concord's most famous writers, I will describe how their lives relate to their major creations. I will summarize some of the best essays, novels, and poems that each author wrote in order to familiarize modern readers with their scope, substance, and style. To make the relation between the authors' lives and creations clearer, I will include a separate biographical and creative timeline for each author. Also I will describe which Concord sites relevant to the authors' lives can be visited today, enabling visitors (and readers) to gain a better appreciation of the natural, social, and historical settings that each author wrote about. Photographs of the authors and their houses and other important sites will illuminate these descriptions.

Among the renowned nineteenth century Concord authors essayists Emerson, Thoreau, and Fuller were self-proclaimed Transcendentalists. Novelists Alcott and Hawthorne were not. What is Transcendentalism? Many historic and contemporary writers and literary critics answer this question in different ways. I will discuss this more fully in chapters on individual authors and in the Appendix chapter on Transcendentalism.

Today's Concord with its unique literary tradition still provides an engaging home to scores of well-known writers, from Presidential historian Doris Kearns Goodwin to Gregory McGuire, author of *Wicked*. I will discuss some of these contemporary Concord authors briefly, as well as their works and the influence of Concord's extraordinary literary legacy on their creativity in the concluding chapter of this book, "Postscript: Literary Concord Today."

Henry David Thoreau, 1854. Crayon Portrait by Samuel W. Rowse. Courtesy of Concord Free Public Library.

Chapter 1

Wild in Walden Woods: Henry David Thoreau

A twenty-seven year old naturalist, a native of Concord, Massachusetts, was out fishing with a friend on the Sudbury River on the last day of April in 1844. After the two friends came on shore they placed their fish on a tree stump and lit a fire to cook them.

Sparks and flames from the fire "suddenly caught the dry grass of the previous year which grew about the stump on which it kindled" and quickly "spread rapidly upward through the long, dry, wiry grass interspersed with bushes." The two men tried desperately to stomp out the flames "at first with our hands and feet" and then with a board. However, the fire spread to nearby trees along the river bank, "flashed up the pines to their tops, as if they were powder" and then traveled rapidly up a hill, where it became a roaring inferno.

Within minutes the whole forest was in flames. Before the night was over, 300 acres of prime Concord forest, valued at over $2000 according to the *Concord Freeman* of May 3, 1844, had "burned to the ground due to the thoughtlessness of two of our citizens." Smoldering ashes were all that remained. News of the fire spread rapidly to the towns people of Concord. The word was out. What is the name of this unintentional arsonist? Henry David Thoreau.

Six years later in his journal notes of May 31, 1850, Thoreau admits that, "I had felt like a guilty person—nothing but shame and regret." And even though he claims that he eventually came to believe that "I have done no wrong," it was to take many years for him to overcome his humiliation as the consequence of his unintended incendiary forest adventure, which still caused some townsmen to call him a "damned rascal" and others to shout "burnt woods" behind his back. (A 2009 novel, *Woodsburner* by John Pipkin, even implies that Thoreau's lingering guilt might have been what inspired him to build his cabin at Walden Pond just a year later.)

Two hundred years later that same Henry Thoreau has earned the admiration of people around the world as a pioneering naturalist and environmentalist. His almost total redemption has created the irony that he now has the widespread reputation as a great lover of forests and wildlife, a man who presaged the field of ecology and of today's environmental movement. Harvard biologist E. O. Wilson in his 2012 address to the Thoreau Society proclaimed that Thoreau "was the founding saint of the conservation movement."

Henry David Thoreau (1817–1862) was a pioneering naturalist whose insights and writings still inspire worldwide efforts for promoting natural ecology and land conservation. He described himself as "a mystic, a Transcendentalist and a natural philosopher to boot." His actions and writings on civil disobedience inspired such diverse leaders as Mahatma Gandhi, Martin Luther King Jr., and John F. Kennedy. Little known during his life time, he grew famous as later generations discovered the inspiring depths of *Walden; or, Life in the Woods*, "Civil Disobedience," *Cape Cod*, and *The Maine Woods.*

Thoreau's life was marked with fascinating contradictions. Famed for the original power of his words in both prose and poetry, a so called right brained activity, he is also known for his meticulous observations as a natural scientist, an activity powered by the left brain. Known as a pacifist who resisted the power of his government to conduct war, he later supported John Brown, the fanatical and violent abolition activist. Disciplined and productive in several fields, paradoxically Thoreau was called by Emerson "the only man of leisure in town."

The only one of Concord's famous writers to actually have been born in Concord, Thoreau lived in and wrote about his special world of Concord almost exclusively throughout his lifetime. "I never got over the surprise that I should have been born in the most estimable place in all the world, and in the very nick of time, too," he stated. "I have traveled a good deal in Concord," he observed in *Walden.*

Thoreau's life in Concord inspired him greatly. As he confided to his journal in 1856, "It would be a wretched bargain to accept the proudest Paris in exchange for my native village. I wish to live ever as to derive my satisfactions and inspirations from the commonest events, every day phenomena, so what my senses hourly perceive, my daily walks, the conversations of my neighbors may inspire me, and I may dream of a heaven, but not which lies about me. . . The sight of a marsh hawk in Concord meadows is worth more to me than the entry of allies into Paris...Only that traveling is good which reveals to me the value of home and enables me to enjoy it better. That man is the richest whose pleasures are the cheapest. . . I shall never find in the wilds of Labrador any greater wilderness than in some recess of Concord."

Thoreau spent four to six hours a day walking (which he called "sauntering") in the woods and meadows of Concord or floating in his handmade boat down its rivers or over its ponds. He observed nature closely and patiently, and experienced it sensually—the seasonal blooming of flowers and trees, the spring return of blue birds, the sound of crickets, the running of fish, the trails of foxes, the taste of huckleberries, the growth and spread of seeds from maple and oak trees, the bravery of a muskrat, the skill of a squirrel, the walk of a turtle, and the escape of a toad. Then he returned to his cabin and translated his notes into eloquent prose in his daily journal entries. During his life time he compiled fourteen volumes of his journal which dated from 1837 to 1861. These insightful observations later became the basis for his later essays, books, and lectures.

An 1837 Harvard graduate and well-read classics scholar, Thoreau supported himself variously during his life as a teacher, pencil maker (eventually running his family's pencil business), writer, land surveyor, lecturer, handyman, and a doer of odd jobs.

Thoreau sought to live simply and to minimize his material wants, so that he could live to live, not solely to work. "Simplify, simplify," he urged. "I found that by working six weeks a year I could meet all the expenses of living. The whole of my winters, as well as most of my summers, I had free and clear for study." (The fact that he never had a family to support and lived simply enabled him to follow this unusual life style.)

Perhaps the best way a Concord visitor can evoke Thoreau's life and legacy is to visit Walden Pond in Concord. For it was on Walden's shores that Thoreau decided to live for two years and two months and two days, from July 4, 1845 to September 6, 1847. He chose to live in the Walden Woods both to immerse himself in nature and write a book in tribute to his brother John, who had died tragically of lockjaw three years previously at the age of twenty-seven. His reminiscences about the boat trip that the brothers had experienced in 1839 became Henry's first published book, *A Week on the Concord and Merrimack Rivers (*1849).

Thoreau wrote famously in *Walden; or, Life in the Woods* (1854) that, "I went to the woods, because I wished to live deliberately, to front only the essential facts of life, and see if I could not learn what it had to teach, and not, when I came to die, discover that I had not lived." (A rustic sign with this declaration today marks the site of Thoreau's hut on a small hill overlooking Walden Pond.)

Thoreau built his cabin close to the northern shore of Walden Pond, overlooking the water. He constructed a simple, one room, ten-by fifteen-foot cabin for the total cost of $28 12 ½ cents. The hut was just big enough for a bed, a desk, a fireplace, and three chairs, "One for solitude, one for friendship and one for society." Behind his hut Henry planted a bean patch and later harvested his beans to eat and to sell.

After he left his Walden cabin in 1847 he visited and wrote about his visits to Maine, Cape Cod, Canada, New York, and to New Hampshire. Beyond descriptions of nature, his concerns and essays extended as well to abolition and civil disobedience. In 1846, he spent one night in jail for refusing to pay his poll tax, since he did not want to support the Federal government, which at the time was engaged in the Mexican-American War. He believed that if America triumphed, that Texas would enter the Union as a slave state. His fear later did come true.

"Government is best which governs the least;" he stated in a lecture at the Concord Lyceum in 1848 and in an essay which followed. He believed that government exists only to guarantee individual freedom, that if it unjustly opposed this principle, such as in its support of slavery, that the individual was free to take nonviolent action to resist it, such as by nonpayment of taxes,

Thoreau helped escaped slaves flee to Canada on the so called Underground Railway. After passage of the controversial Fugitive Slave Law of 1850, which mandated that citizens of northern states must help capture and return to their owners slaves who had escaped in the south and fled to the north.

. Thoreau's opposition to slavery was so strong that he even advocated for the use of violence against the spread of slavery, in direct conflict with his mostly pacific beliefs. In 1857 he met and was impressed by Captain John Brown during his visit to Concord. Despite Brown's use of violence in his active opposition to slavery in Kansas, Thoreau considered him a national hero, braver than heroes of the American Revolution, since Brown "had the courage to face his country herself when she was in the wrong."

Two years later, after Brown was captured following his raid against the Federal arsenal in Harper's Ferry, (West) Virginia, Thoreau delivered a speech, "A Plea for Captain John Brown" in Concord, Boston and Worcester. Although many in the audience considered Brown a fanatical violent traitor, Thoreau expressed "sympathy and admiration" for Brown. After Brown was hanged for leading an insurrection, both Emerson, Bronson Alcott and Thoreau participated in a memorial service and eulogy for him. Scholars today still debate the apparent contradiction between Thoreau's mainly pacifist beliefs and his later support of the violent strategies of the militant insurgent abolitionist activist John Brown.

Considering his important achievements in another area, Thoreau pioneered the new science of ecology. In the few years before his death he was intensely involved in recording his observations as a naturalist and scientist. In the words of Gary Naban, he integrated "his scientist's skill for detailed observation with a poet's command of language. Thoreau was someone who saw no polarity between poetry and nature's economy, but instead envisioned a vast ecology that spans both and enriches our senses, our hearts, and our minds."

Renowned Harvard biologist E. O. Wilson, the cofounder of Biodiversity Days, observed in an address to the Thoreau Society in 2012 that Thoreau's "devotion to observation" made him the first "scientific natural historian."

Thoreau's detailed observations and meticulous records of seasonal occurrences have assumed added importance recently. They help to document climate changes in nature now, presumably due to global warming, as is described by Boston University biologist Richard Primack. For example the flowering times for many plants occur on the average twelve days earlier now than they did when Thoreau recorded them over 150 years ago. This is believed due to the fact that springs are much warmer now than they were previously. Similarly, Thoreau's charting of ice-outs (melting times) for Walden Pond demonstrate that melting ice occurs two weeks earlier now, around March 17, than it did in the past, when it occurred around April 1. This conclusion is based on comparing Thoreau's observations (1845–1860) with recent observations (1995–2009). Bird arrival times and "leafing out" times are also weeks earlier now than in Thoreau's day.

Shortly before his death, Thoreau assembled lengthy manuscripts on *The Dispersion of Seeds, On the Succession of Forest Trees* and on *Wild Fruits.* He presented some of this material in lectures, but his manuscripts remained unpublished as books at the time of his death in 1862. One hundred and thirty-one years would pass before these works were edited by Bradley Dean and published as *Faith in a Seed* in 1993.

In these works Thoreau documents the natural habitats, interrelationships and yearly calendar appearances of plants, trees, fruits, animals, and birds that he observed in his daily saunters in the Concord woods. For example, he observes that in mid-September the sickle shaped green pine cones at the top of white pine trees "turn brown, open in the sun and wind and away go the seeds of future forests flying far and wide." He rejects the then current explanation of the start of plant life by spontaneous generation. Instead he declares that all plant growth is necessarily preceded by the dispersion of seeds by varied mechanisms. For example, silky milkweed seeds are spread widely by the wind and cherry seeds, ingested by birds, are discharged over land, which leads to the birth of new cherry trees.

The life work of Henry Thoreau is beautifully and succinctly summarized by critic Robert D. Richardson in his Introduction to *Faith in a Seed:* "The writer of *Dispersion of Seeds* has traveled a long road from *Walden,* although he has not yet gotten farther than Concord. *Walden* is a great—perhaps greatest—celebration of the sweet freedom of a life in nature that is single, unattached, and uncommitted. *The Dispersion of Seeds,* in contrast, celebrates fertility, fecundity, and interconnectedness. *Walden* is about the growth and cultivation of the self; *The Dispersion of Seeds* is about the growth of communities and the rise of new generations. *Walden* is the acknowledged masterpiece of Thoreau the poet-naturalist; *The Dispersion of seeds. . .* is the culminating work of Thoreau the writer-scientist."

Another area in which Thoreau maintained a lifelong interest was in the history and culture of Native Americans. He shared their respect for the land and in the mystical/ spiritual aspects of natural sites, like Mt. Katahdin in Maine. On his journeys to explore the untamed forests, rivers, and mountains of Maine, he treasured the character and wisdom of his guide, Joseph Polis, a Penobscot Indian. After his death, scholars discovered Thoreau's many fact filled notebooks about American Indians, which remain unpublished. They also found an extensive collection of Indian arrowheads, collected throughout Thoreau's life, many of them in Concord.

When Thoreau was bed ridden and close to death, he maintained his characteristic bluntness and sardonic humor. When Parker Pillsbury, a Quaker abolitionist, visited him a few days before his death, Pillsbury remarked, "You seem so near the brink of a dark river, that I almost wonder how the opposite shore may appear to you?" Thoreau replied pithily, "One world at a time."

When his aunt Louisa asked him if he had made his peace with God, he replied "I did not know we had ever quarreled, Aunt."

Henry Thoreau died of tuberculosis in 1862 at age forty-four.

Probably the fullest synopsis of Thoreau's life and writings are found in the eulogy by his mentor, colleague, friend, and sometimes nemesis, Ralph Waldo Emerson. Thoreau, Emerson eulogizes, "was bred to no profession; he never married; he lived alone; he never went to church; he never voted; he refused to pay a tax to the state; he ate no flesh, he drank no wine, he never knew the use of tobacco, and, though a naturalist, he used neither trap nor gun." Thoreau lived for the day, was highly organized and industrious, but as Emerson observed, Thoreau "was the only man of leisure in town."

Emerson remarked that Thoreau was a Transcendentalist, since he viewed "the material world as a means and a symbol." He was strongly American, since his aversion "from English and European manners and tastes almost reached contempt."

Emerson also observed that Thoreau was argumentative, that he only felt to be truly himself when he stood in opposition. "He wanted a fallacy to expose, a blunder to pillory, I may say it required a little sense of victory, a roll of the drum, to call his powers into full exercise," Emerson proclaimed.

As to his literary success Emerson felt that: "Mr. Thoreau dedicated his genius with such entire love to the fields, hills and waters of his native town that he made them known and interesting to all reading Americans and to people over the sea."

As to his only defect, Emerson believed that "I can't help counting it a fault in him that he had no ambition." However, this assessment remains controversial. Many Thoreauvians today challenge Emerson's opinion, by relegating Thoreau's lack of ambition, if this assessment is indeed true, to his literary career only. Otherwise, Thoreau lived as a truly energetic, hands-on naturalist and as a fearless prophet of individual freedom beyond the arbitrary constraints of restrictive and often incorrect social norms.

To summarize Thoreau's importance to America, Emerson concluded his eulogy by stating that "The country knows not yet, or at least in part, how great a son it has lost." Ironically, it would take more than a century for most Americans to realize Emerson's assessment, for them to appreciate Thoreau's originality, relevance and brilliance.

Thoreau Birth House on Virginia Road. Photo by Joseph L. Andrews

Walden;

on,

LIFE IN THE WOODS.

Title Page of Walden; or, Life in the Woods
by Henry D. Thoreau. Boston: Ticknor and Fields, 1854.
Courtesy of Concord Free Public Library.

A Thoreau Timeline (1817–1862)

1817 David Henry Thoreau is born to John and Cynthia (Dunbar) Thoreau in Concord, MA, on July 12.

1818 Family moves to Chelmsford, MA

1821 Family moves to Boston; **1824** Family moves back to Concord.

1828 Thoreau enters Concord Academy.

1833 Enters Harvard College;

1835 Teaches school in Canton, MA briefly

1837 Graduates from Harvard; begins *Journal;* teaches briefly in Concord; meets Ralph Waldo Emerson.

1838 First trip to Maine; opens private school with brother John; lectures at Concord Lyceum.

1839 Boat excursion on Concord and Merrimack Rivers with his brother John; falls in love with Ellen Sewall;

1840 Publishes his first essay and poem in *The Dial;* Ellen Sewall declines his (as well as his brother John's) marriage proposals.

1841 Lives at the Emerson house for two years; is attracted to Lidian Emerson.

1842 Brother John dies on January 11. Hawthorne moves to Concord into the Old Manse.

1843 Helps Emerson edit *The Dial;* tutors William Emerson's children on Staten Island

1844 Sets fire to the Concord woods accidentally; builds family "Texas house" with his father.

1845 Moves into his Walden Pond cabin on July 4; active at observing nature and writing.

1846 Jailed overnight for nonpayment of poll tax; travels to Maine, climbs Mt. Katahdin.

1847 Leaves Walden hut in September; lives at Emerson house while RWE in England;
Begins professional surveying; gathers natural specimens for Prof. Agassiz.

1848 "Kataadn" serialized. Talks at Concord Lyceum on "Civil Disobedience."

1849 Publishes first book, *A Week on The Concord and Merrimack Rivers;* Sister Helen dies. First visit to Cape Cod; "Resistance to Civil Disobedience" is published.

1850 Moves to Yellow House on Main St. with family. Visits Cape Cod, Fire Island and Canada.

1851 Helps fugitive slave escape to Canada.

1853 Second trip to Maine woods; Opening portions of *A Yankee in Canada* published.

1854 Speech "Slavery in MA" on July 4. *Walden; or, Life in the Woods* published on August 9.

1855 First episodes of *Cape Cod* appear in *Putnam's Magazine.*

1856 Surveys and lectures. Meets Walt Whitman in Brooklyn.

1857 Meets Captain John Brown in Concord and is deeply impressed by him.

1858 Publishes "Chesuncook" in *Atlantic Monthly.* Visits Mt. Monadnock in N.H.

1859 Father dies. Meets John Brown again. After Brown is captured delivers "A Plea for Captain John Brown."

1860 More essays, two on John Brown. Lectures on "Succession of Forest Trees," which was later published in *New York Weekly Tribune* by Editor, Horace Greeley.

1861 Travels to Minnesota in search of good health. Revises many manuscripts, including *Wild Fruits, **D**ispersion of Seeds, Walking* and *Life Without Principal.*

1862 Dies of tuberculosis on May 6, aged forty four years. Thoreau is buried at Sleepy Hollow cemetery on Authors' Ridge in Concord. Emerson delivers the eulogy.

Books published after his death: *The Maine Woods* in 1864 and *Cape Cod* in 1865;
A Yankee in Canada, with Ant-Slavery and Reform Papers in 1866;
Faith in a Seed in 1993; *October or Autumnal Tints,* 2012.

(**Sources:** Meltzer, M.and Harding W. *A Thoreau Profile, 1962*
Bode, C. *The Portable Thoreau,* 1947.
The Thoreau Society, *Thoreau Chronology,* 1998.
Thoreau, H., *Faith in a Seed;* Bradley Dean, Editor, 1993;)

Thoreau Cabin Replica at Walden Pond. Statue of Henry Thoreau. Taken by Joseph L. Andrews.

Thoreau Sites in Concord

Walden Pond - Thoreau spent two years from 1845 to 1847 living in a ten- by fifteen-foot one-room cabin that he built himself on the shores of Walden Pond on Emerson's wood lot. His experience became the basis for his best known book, *Walden; or, Life in the Woods* (1854).

The visitor today will find a beautiful "glacial kettle pond," set amid banks green with maples and pines. The parking lot requires a $5 entrance fee (free for seniors). Next to the parking lot is a **replica of Thoreau's cabin,** fronted by a life size **statue** of Henry, with an outstretched arm with cupped hand, perhaps welcoming the visitor as he contemplates the significance of a seed.

There is a beach for summer swimming or boating. A 1.7 mile unpaved footpath circles the pond, requiring about an hour to walk it. Midway on the path on the western shore is **Thoreau's cabin site**, marked by granite posts. It was rediscovered by Roland Robbins in 1945. Nearby stands a cairn, a rock pile, the signed rocks having been left as a tribute to Thoreau since 1875 by pilgrims who travel to Concord from around the world.

The Thoreau Society Shop at Walden Pond is across Route 126 from the Pond at 915 Walden St. The shop carries an extensive line of books by Thoreau as well by other Concord authors. Books are also available to purchase from their web site: *www.ShopWaldenPond.org.* Telephone: 978-287-5477.

Thoreau Birthplace and Farm—Henry Thoreau was born on July 12, 1817 in a plain farmhouse belonging to his maternal step-grandfather, Jonas Minot, on Virginia Road in Concord. Henry David (originally named David Henry) was the third child born to Cynthia Dunbar Thoreau and John Thoreau. The family lived in this house for only eight months after Henry's birth there. The house was moved about 300 yards east to its present site at 341 Virginia Road in 1878.

The house belonged to a local farmer as recently as 1995. It was very rundown and in danger of being torn down and the surrounding seventeen acres of land sold to developers, when in 1997 it was purchased by the town of Concord. In 2004, the **Thoreau Farm Trust**, bought the house, finished rehabilitating it in 2010 and currently manages it.

The house is 2.5 miles from Concord Center. Visitors can take either a free self-guided tour or a scheduled guided tour. Appointments are necessary. Call 978-369-3091. Information may be found at *www. info@thoreaufarm.org.*

The house also serves as the headquarters for the **Thoreau Society**. Founded in 1941, the society promotes Thoreau's literary legacy through annual meetings, which include academic scholars as well as amateur aficionados, educational programs, academic scholarship, an annual gathering in July, a journal, *The Concord Saunterer,* and the quarterly *Thoreau Society Bulletin*. Its website is *www.thoreausociety.org.*

Thoreau's Path on Brister's Hill is a one mile, self guided interpretive trail in Concord's historic Walden Woods. It leaves Walden Street just past the Concord-Carlisle High School just before Route 2 on the way to Walden Pond. It was created by the Walden Woods project. To walk the one mile path a minimum of one hour is suggested. For information call 781-259-4730.

The Thoreau-Alcott House at 255 Main Street is a short walk from Concord Center village. It is privately owned and hence can only be viewed from the street. It is an impressive yellow colonial house, which was first built around 1820 and was altered in succeeding years. Henry Thoreau's mother ran a boarding house here. Henry's room was in the attic. Here he wrote many of his works. The family's pencil factory was located in the south wing.

Henry died here in 1862. Later Louisa May Alcott helped purchase the house with her widowed sister, Anna, for their parents and for Anna's sons. It remained in the Alcott family until the early twentieth century.

Thoreau Institute of the Walden Woods Project is at 44 Baker Farm Road in Lincoln, a short distance from Walden Pond.

The organization promotes Thoreau's legacy through conservation, education, research, and advocacy. It has conserved hundreds of acres of forest land within the Walden Woods that otherwise would have been lost to development. Much of its fund-raising has been led by rock and roll singer Don Henley, for whom its library, with its large collection of original Thoreau books, is named. Scholars can use the library resources, but must call for an appointment first: 781-259-4700. The web site is *www.walden.org*.

Ralph Waldo Emerson

CHAPTER 2

Nature's Naked Eye: Ralph Waldo Emerson

A young former minister faced all seven of the future ministers who constituted the entire senior class of the Harvard Divinity School in 1838. What he said would cause tidal waves in American theological and intellectual circles, which reached way beyond Cambridge, MA and the small group of listeners who heard him that day.

Ralph Waldo Emerson, the speaker, was the fifth in the long line of ministers in his family. He had left the Divinity School nine years previously (without having actually graduated). Nonetheless he and been ordained junior pastor of the Second (Unitarian) Church of Boston in 1829. Then three years later he resigned his ministry due to his poor health and the fact that he was unhappy with church dogma concerning communion. He was disenchanted with religion in general and with the ministry in particular and believed that man could best understand God by studying himself.

Emerson, the invited speaker, startled the Divinity School graduates and their faculty that day by stating that "God is; not was; he speaketh, not spake." Thus, he asserted the "immediacy of God," who could be revealed not just in the distant past to Biblical characters, but directly to ordinary people of that day, who needed only to look at themselves and nature around them.

He implied that present revelations to current believers were more important than previous revelations, as related in the Bible. Emerson stated that the just and moral man "was God," since "the immortality of God, the majesty of God do enter into that man with justice."

Emerson's views shocked his listeners that day, both theology professors and their students, many of whom considered his assertions to be blasphemy and heresy. Emerson was critical of the Church—and organized religion as a whole—as it then existed. He claimed that it was disconnected from the moral needs of his time. "I believe in the universal decay and now almost death of faith in society. The soul is not preached. The Church seems to totter to its fall, almost all life extinct." All of these beliefs were counter to beliefs then prevailing among Protestant ministers in New England, most of whom were Congregational and Unitarian. Ironically, this was the group from which Emerson himself had descended.

Emerson also excoriated dull preachers he had listened to, who were uninspiring and removed from the realities of every day life. "Whenever the pulpit is usurped by a formalist, then is the worshipper defrauded and disconsolate." Outside of the Concord church where he once sat, "the snow storm was real; the preacher merely spectral. . . He had lived in vain. He had not one word intimated that he had laughed or wept, was married or in love, been commended, or cheated, or chagrined. If he had ever lived or acted, we were none the wiser for it. The capital secret of his profession, namely to convert life into truth, he had not learned. . . It seemed strange that people should come to church. It seemed that their houses were unentertaining that they should prefer this thoughtless clamor."

Vociferous critical protests of Emerson's Divinity School address followed. Professors Henry Ware and Andrews Norton were very critical of Emerson the critic. The latter attacked Emerson's views as "the latest form of infidelity." It was to be twenty-four more years before Emerson was invited back to Harvard to speak again.

Emerson's theological and genealogical origins can be traced back to one of Concord's first—and most prominent—settlers, who was also Concord's first minister. Rev. Peter Bulkeley had been forced to abandon his Anglican pulpit in England, because his Puritan beliefs and religious practices were no longer tolerated by the Anglican hierarchy. His only recourse was to ship out to begin anew in America. Bulkeley took the pulpit at Concord's First Parish Church at the village's founding in

1635 and many parishioners followed him to the new wilderness town of Concord.

Six generations of Rev. Peter Bulkeley's descendants became ministers, almost all of them in Concord. William Emerson, Ralph Waldo Emerson's grandfather was Concord's pastor when British Redcoats marched into Concord on April 19, 1775. When asked by his fellow townsmen and parishioners for counsel as the British troops approached, he famously stated: "Let us stand our ground. If we die, let us die here," as quoted in Shattuck's *History of Concord.* William Emerson probably witnessed the battle of the North Bridge, which began the American Revolution, from a window of the Old Manse, the house that he had built in 1770, which is adjacent to the North Bridge.

In 1776 Rev. William Emerson volunteered as chaplain to accompany the newly formed Continental Army in its quest to seize cannons at the British Fort Ticonderoga. Unfortunately Rev. Emerson died of camp fever on the return trip and is buried in Rutland, Vermont. Thus, he did not live to see the cannons hauled—by men and oxen—successfully over 300 miles back to Boston, dragged on rolling logs over ice and snow. He did not see them break the British siege of Boston and force all British forces to abandon Boston for good on March 17, 1776, (This date is still celebrated in Boston today as Evacuation Day—along with toasts of green beer to a certain saint from Ireland, whose birthday is on March 17 as well.)

The minister's widow, Phebe Bliss Emerson, then married her former boarder at the Old Manse, the Rev. Ezra Ripley. He took over William Emerson's pulpit at Concord's First Parish Church and thus became Ralph Waldo Emerson's step-grandfather. Remarkably Ripley remained as minister in Concord for the next sixty-three years. (Phebe therefore became the wife of two Concord ministers, mother of a third and the grandmother of a fourth, Ralph Waldo Emerson.)

Emerson's father, also the Rev. William Emerson, was minister of the First Church of Boston. Ralph Waldo was born there in 1803, the third of six sons. Like many middle children he was considered "the silly one" and his relatives judged him to be the least promising of the Emerson children. His father died in 1811, when Ralph Waldo was eight years old. The Emerson boys were then raised by their mother, Ruth Haskins Emerson. Although the Emerson family was often strapped financially, through hard work and ingenuity Ruth was able to put all her children through college. His father's sister, aunt Mary Moody Emerson, a brilliant but quirky auto-didact, also had a great influence on her nephews.

Emerson graduated from the Boston Latin School in 1817 and from Harvard College, where he had been an average student, in 1821. For the next four years he taught school at his brother William's school for girls.

However, he loathed his days as a teacher and decided that teaching was definitely not for him. He then decided that he would train for his family's profession, to become a minister; so he entered the Harvard Divinity School in 1825. Despite never graduating, he was ordained Junior Pastor at Boston's Second (Unitarian) Church in 1829. In December of that year he married Ellen Tucker, who was eighteen years old. He and his bride had very happy, but limited days together. Tragically, Ellen died of tuberculosis in 1831 at age nineteen.

Emerson was devastated by his young wife's death. He became morose and suffered from ill health, causing him to resign his post at Boston's Second Church in 1832. For the next two years he traveled in England, France, and Italy, where he met and befriended prominent European men of letters including Scottish essayist Thomas Carlyle and British poets Samuel Taylor Coleridge and William Wordsworth.

When he returned to America in 1835, he moved from Boston to Concord, where he lived for the next forty-seven years. He married Lydia Jackson from Plymouth, whom he called "Lidian." He also made a decisive mid-career correction in his life's work. Abandoning the ministry completely, he decided to earn his living as a lecturer and essayist. His sermons before church goers, which had served him as a preacher, now became lectures before the general public, whose themes and substance he often took from his conscientiously drafted daily journal entries. Thus, his journal notes morphed into lectures, which often then served as the basis for his essays and later on of his books.

Emerson began his journals in 1820, when he was a junior at Harvard. He conscientiously recorded his ideas daily for the next fifty-five years. He led a life of deliberate introspection. "After the fashion of his Puritan ancestors in England and New England," observed Austin Warren; "he was a self-analyst, a diarist—a self explorer." What follows are some excerpts from his journal:

(Age 17, January 25, 1820, when he was a junior at Harvard, he wrote his first entry.)

"The Wide World, NO. 1

Mixing with the thousand pursuits and passions and objects of the world as personified by Imagination is profitable and entertaining. These pages are intended at their commencement to contain a record of new thoughts (when they occur); for a receptacle of all the old ideas. . . under that comprehensive title *Common Place Book.*"

(Age 30, 1833)

"A man contains all that is needful to his government within himself. He is made a law unto himself—He only can do himself any good or any harm. . . The purpose of life seems to be to acquaint a man with himself. He is not to live to the future as described to him, but to live in the real future by living into the real present. The highest revelation is that God is in every man."

(Age 43, 1846)

"*The Superstitions of our Age:*
The fear of Catholicism:
The fear of pauperism;
The fear of immigration;
The fear of manufacturing interests;
The fear of radicalism or democracy;
The faith in the steam engine."

(Age 59, 1862)

"I like people who can do things. When Edward (his son) and I struggled in vain to drag our big calf into the barn, the Irish girl put her finger into the calf's mouth and led her in directly."

(Age 65, 1868)

"A man never gets acquainted with himself, but is always a surprise. . . A new thought is awaiting him every morning."

The next several years saw him completing four of his most influential essays, which he had delivered as lectures: "Nature' (1836),

"The American Scholar" (1837), "The Divinity School Address" (1838), and "Self-Reliance" (1841).

Emerson's essay "Nature" stated the Transcendentalist manifesto, which expressed the relationship between man's soul and nature: "Nature always wears the colors of the spirit; in the woods we return to reason and faith." In a famous, but still controversial passage he described his personal relationship with nature: "Standing on the bare ground—my head bathed by the blithe air and uplifted into infinite space—all mean egotism vanishes. I become a transparent eye-ball. I am nothing. I see all. The currents of the Universal Being circulate through me; I am part or particle of God."

His "American Scholar" address at Harvard has often been called America's Intellectual Declaration of Independence, because it initiated a renaissance in native American literature. Here Emerson states that expressions by writers in the new world are every bit as valuable as historic works by classical European writers in the past. He wrote: "He who has put forth his total strength in fact allows it as the richest return of wisdom," and "The day is always his who works it with serenity and great aims."

In "Self-Reliance," he urged each individual: "Trust thyself: every heart vibrates to that iron string," and to "believe your own thought, your private heart is true for all men,—that is genius." He also famously stated: "Whoso would be a man, must be a nonconformist."

Emerson was frequently asked to lecture in Concord at its Lyceum series. He also spoke at many town events, such as on the opening of its free library, on the death of Henry Thoreau, at the consecration of Sleepy Hollow Cemetery (where he and his family all rest today) and on the one hundredth anniversary of the start of the American Revolution in 1875.

According to *The Massachusetts Lyceum During the American Renaissance,* of 784 lectures presented at the Concord Lyceum between 1838 and 1881, 98 or 13 percent were given by Emerson. During the months of March, April, and May in 1839 Emerson, as the sole lecturer each week, delivered seven consecutive lectures on subjects as disparate as Love, Genius, Tragedy, and Demonology. A Mr. Frost commended Mr. Emerson for giving all his lectures in Concord gratuitously. Emerson's generosity to his fellow townsmen was duly recorded by Henry D. Thoreau, Secretary.

Since lecturing was his main source of income, he often lectured on the Lyceum circuit elsewhere as well, appearing before audiences in many small towns throughout the U.S. For example, he gave a lecture each year in Salem. Soon he "became his own lecture bureau. . . and placed notices in the papers, hired the hall and wrote out tickets of admission," according to literary critic Alfred Kazin. In the course of two weeks during the winter of 1855 he appeared in twelve towns in New England. Over one season alone, in 1865-1866, he lectured in Massachusetts, New York, Pennsylvania, Michigan, Indiana, Illinois, Wisconsin, and Iowa. To get to widely separated lecture sites, he spent much time traveling by train, boat, and carriage.

He addressed farmers in the Midwest as well as merchants in St. Louis on general subjects, which often then became essays. For example his lectures on Eloquence, Manners, Immortality, Woman, Shakespeare, and the Over-Soul eventually were transformed into essays, according to Kazin. Emerson was also often asked to lecture on the issues of the day such as the emancipation of slaves in the British West Indies, his opposition to the Fugitive Slave Act and the martyrdom of fanatical abolitionist John Brown

Emerson was a founder of the short-lived Transcendentalist journal *The Dial* in 1840. Margaret Fuller, a strong advocate for women's rights, was the journal's co-editor for its first two years. She was succeeded by Emerson for its last two years. They published essays of literary criticism, biography, and travel, as well as poetry.

Emerson considered himself a serious poet. "As in his relationship with the church, he struggled to break out of the rigid time–honored forms: the fourteen-line stanza of the sonnet, the monotony of heroic couplets. . . Out of his rebellion emerged a new freedom of style, one of discordant sounds like those in "Merlin," according to an analysis in the Dover book of Emerson's poetry. Emerson, himself expressed it, thusly:

> "The kingly bard
> Must smite the chords rudely and hard
> As with a hammer or mace."

The content of Emerson's poetry was a fusion of the everyday and what he considered to be universal truths. To quote from Emerson's journal: "When you assume the rhythm of verse and the analogy of

Nature, it is making proclamation, 'I am now freed from the trammels of the Apparent; I speak from the Mind.'"

His approach to free verse helped to blaze a trail for poets who followed him, such as Walt Whitman and Emily Dickenson, and for later Modernist poets like T.S. Elliot and Wallace Stevens.

Perhaps Emerson's most memorable lines are those of the "Concord Hymn," which were sung at the completion of the Concord Battle Monument in 1837. The monument, a granite obelisk, commemorates the Battle of the North Bridge on April 19, 1775, which had sparked the American Revolution. These words of the first verse are now engraved at the base of sculptor Daniel Chester French's Concord Minuteman statue, which stands on the opposite shore of the Concord River and looks over the North Bridge.

"By the rude bridge that arched the flood,
Their flag to April's breeze unfurled,
Here once the embattled farmer stood,
And fired the shot heard 'round the world.

The foe long since in silence slept.
Alike the Conqueror silent sleeps,
And Time the ruined bridge has swept
Down the dark stream which seaward creeps.

On this green bank, by this soft stream,
We set today a votive stone,
That memory may their deed redeem,
When like our sires our sons are gone.

Spirit! Who made those freemen dare
To die, or leave their children free.
Bid time and nature gently spare
The shaft we raise to them and thee."

In "Ode," inscribed to Rev. William H. Channing, Emerson critiques what he felt was the rampant materialism of his time:

"Things are in the saddle,
And ride mankind.

There are two laws discrete
Not reconciled,
Law for man, and law for thing,
The last builds town and fleet
But it runs wild,
And does man un-king."

Emerson was prominent in his day as an intellectual leader for a coterie of writers and eccentrics that he attracted to Concord like a powerful personal magnet, as is so vividly described in Carlos Baker's *Emerson Among the Eccentrics.* He was often called the "sage of Concord" as well as Concord's "oracle." Men and women in Emerson's circle included Henry Thoreau, Margaret Fuller, Bronson Alcott, Ellery Channing, Nathaniel Hawthorne, and Theodore Parker.

Perhaps the wide scope and seminal importance of Emerson's life was best summarized in his obituary printed in the *Concord Freeman,* dated May 4, 1882, as reprinted in *Obituaries of Concord:*

"Concord's Irreparable Loss!

The world mourns for the loss of genius, for the stilling of a mind that discovered and illumined so much of truth. . .

Concord mourns for all this, and more. Here, for half a century, he walked up and down among the people grandly, yet humbly; thinking and living at times in a realm far above and beyond the people, yet like all truly great men, in sympathy with his surroundings, and interested in commonest neighborly events. . .

(He was) the sympathizing neighbor, true friend, valued citizen, eminent philanthropist, scholar, and writer, and the venerable sage. . ."

An Emerson Timeline (1803–1882)

1803 RWE is born in Boston on May 25 to Ruth Haskins and Rev William Emerson

1811 William Emerson dies at age 42.

1812-17 RWE attends Boston Latin School

1817-21 Attends Harvard College

1821-25 Teaches at brother William's school for girls

1825 Admitted to Harvard Divinity School

1826 Travels to St. Augustine, Florida

1828 Engaged to Ellen Tucker; his brother Edward becomes deranged.

1829 Ordained Junior Pastor of Boston's Second Church; marries Ellen, Dec. 17.

1831 Ellen dies from tuberculosis at age 19.

1832 Resigns from Second Church due to ill health; sails for Europe.

1833-4 Travels in Italy, France and England; begins lecturing career.

1835 Marries Lydia ("Lidian") Jackson of Plymouth; moves to Concord, where he lives for the next 47 years.

1836 Brother Charles dies; "Nature" Published anonymously; first child, Waldo is born.

1837 Delivers "American Scholar," Phi Beta Kappa oration at Harvard;
Lectures on human culture.

1838 **Delivers controversial "Divinity School Address" at Harvard.**

1839 **Daughter Ellen is born; preaches last church sermon.**

1840-44 ***The Dial,*** **Transcendentalist journal, is published; Margaret Fuller is the first Editor.**

1841 ***Essays*** **published; daughter Edith born; Thoreau joins household.**

1842 **Son Waldo dies of scarlet fever; RWE succeeds Fuller as** ***The Dial*** **Editor.**

1844 **Son Edward is born; last issue of** ***The Dial; Essays, Second Series*** **published.**

1845-7 **Thoreau lives in hut on Emerson's Walden Pond wood lot.**

1846 ***Poems*** **published.**

1847-8 **Second trip to England and France.**

1849 **"Nature,"** ***Addresses and Lectures*** **published.**

1850 **"Representative Men" published; Margaret Fuller Osscoli dies in ship wreck.**

1849 **Delivers "Fugitive Slave Law" Address.**

1853 **Mother, Ruth Haskins Emerson, dies.**

1854-5 **Heavy lecture schedule.**

1856 **"English Traits" published.**

1859 **Brother, Bulkeley, dies.**

1860 **"The Conduct of Life" is published.**

1862 **Lectures on "American Civilization" and meets President Lincoln in Washington; Eulogizes Henry Thoreau.**

1864 **Attends Nathaniel Hawthorne's funeral.**

1866 **Lectures in the west; Harvard awards him its Doctor of Laws degree.**

1867 **Publishes *May Day and Other Pieces.***

1868 **Brother William dies.**

1870 ***Society and Solitude* published.**

1871 **Visits California by train.**

1872 **Concord house is damaged by fire; visits Europe and Egypt with daughter Ellen.**

1874 ***Parnassus* is published.**

1875 **Publishes *Letters* and *Social Aims.***

1882 **Emerson dies of pneumonia in Concord on April 27 at age 79.**
He is buried on Authors' Ridge at Sleepy Hollow Cemetery in Concord.

[Sources: Richardson, *Mind on Fire*
Baker, *Emerson Among the Eccentrics*
Porte, *Journal*
Emerson Society. *Timeline]*

Emerson Standing Portrait, Mens' Room, First Parish Church. Taken by Joseph L. Andrews, 2012.

Emerson's House, Cambridge Turnpike, Concord.
Taken by Joseph L. Andrews, 2011.

Emerson Sites

The Emerson House.

In 1835 Ralph Waldo Emerson moved into a house on the Cambridge Turnpike in Concord with his newly married second wife, Lydia ("Lidian") Jackson and with his mother. The white clapboard colonial house had been built in 1829 as a summer house. Emerson would live in this house for next forty-seven years, until his death in 1882. Here the Emerson's had their four children, Waldo Jr., Ellen, Edith, and Edward.

Here he wrote some of his most famous essays, such as "Self-Reliance" and "The American Scholar." Here Emerson often met with and discussed the political and cultural issues of the day with some of the most prominent literary lights of his era—including Henry Thoreau, Bronson and Louisa May Alcott, Margaret Fuller, Nathaniel Hawthorne and Walt Whitman

In 1872 there was a fire in the attic of the house, when a new domestic servant knocked over an oil lamp. The attic was destroyed and there was much smoke and water damage, but most of the house was intact. Neighbors saved most of the content of the house, including books and manuscripts, which they carried out wrapped in blankets.

After the fire Emerson and his daughter Ellen traveled to Europe. When they returned in the summer of 1873, they found that their friends and neighbors had made over the house, resulting in many improvements.

Following Emerson's death in 1882, Lidian's in 1892 and Ellen's in 1909, the house was cared for by two teachers, who had been boarders. Descendents formed the Ralph Waldo Emerson Memorial Association. Several members felt strongly that Emerson's original books and manuscripts were too much of a fire hazard to keep in the house. Therefore, in 1930 most books were transferred, along with the furniture and pictures in his study, to the Concord Antiquarian Society, now called the Concord Museum, across the street. The manuscripts and most valuable books were donated to the Houghton Library of Harvard University.

The Ralph Waldo Emerson Memorial House at 28 Cambridge Turnpike is open for guided individual and group tours, which last approximately thirty minutes, from mid-April to late October. Call 978-369-2236 for information.

The Concord Museum

The Museum houses Emerson's reconstructed study, including books, furniture and wall hangings, which were moved from his house across the street, because of a fire (see above). The Concord Museum is located at the intersection of Lexington Rd. and the Cambridge Turnpike. Telephone: 978-369-9763. Web: www.concordmuseum.org.

Louisa May Alcott c. 1858. Courtesy of the Louisa May Alcott Memorial Association.

Chapter 3

Running Girl; Working Woman: Louisa May Alcott

A young girl runs freely over hills and through forests of Concord, exulting in the youthful freedom of her mind and of her body. She remembered years later and confided in her journal:

"...running over the hills just at dawn one summer morning, and pausing to rest in the silent woods, (I) saw through an arch of trees the sun rise over river, hill and wide green meadows as I never saw it before.

I always thought I must have been a deer or a horse in some former state, because it was such a joy to run. No boy could be my friend till I had beaten him in a race and no girl if she refused to climb trees, leap fences, and be a tomboy.

My wise mother, anxious to give me a strong body to support a lively brain, turned me loose in the country and let me run wild, learning of nature what no books can teach..."

Louisa May Alcott (1832-1888) played many roles during her life time: obedient but often rebellious daughter, teacher, governess, servant, seamstress, author, actress, nurse, and companion, before she finally became a successful writer in 1868 at age thirty six as the author of *Little Women.* She was a prolific author, writing eight novels and over three hundred stories and publishing thirty books and a collection of short stories in her life time.

In her most famous work, *Little Women,* her heroine Jo, modeled on herself, led a life of family love and was surrounded by her beloved books. However, Louisa's real life was an arduous one. She was to face poverty, disappointment, depression, rejection, loneliness, and bodily pain. In the early days of her childhood, as she ran wildly and exuberantly through the fields and forests of Concord, she was able to build a spiritual foundation that enabled her to persevere as she grew older, while many others would have given up. As she told her journal:

"Something born of the lovely hour, a happy mood and the unfolding aspirations of a child's soul seemed to bring me very near to God; and in the hush of the morning hour I always felt that I 'got religion,' as the phrase goes. A new and vital sense of His presence, tender and sustaining as a father's arms came to me then, never to change through forty years of life's vicissitudes, but to grow stronger for the sharp discipline of poverty and pain, sorrow and success.

Those Concord days were the happiest of my life. . ."

Louisa's whole life was dedicated to supporting her birth family, both financially and morally. She called her family the "pathetic family," since for most of her early life the family was often plagued by disappointment, poverty, and frequent moves. Her relationship with her father, Amos Bronson Alcott, was ambivalent. Several recent books by John Mattison and Susan Cheever have detailed this intense, unusual father-daughter relationship.

On the one hand, Bronson Alcott's lofty idealism coupled with his frequent failing endeavors, impractical projects and his inability to ever earn enough money to support his wife and four daughters continually threw the family into turmoil and poverty. Louisa with her impulsive personality was frequently challenged by her father to control her temper and rebelliousness. On the other hand, she was usually a dutiful daughter and often backed her father both with encouraging words and later in her life with her hard-earned dollars.

Bronson Alcott was born on a farm in Connecticut in 1799 and was mostly self-educated. Although he lacked formal university studies, he thought of himself as an innovative teacher and philosopher. He started several progressive schools, but he had a pattern of soon disenchanting and maddening the parents of his students who then withdrew their children, so that the schools eventually were forced to close. His last endeavor, the Temple School in Boston closed in 1834 when he became under fire after publishing *Conversations With Children on the Gospels.* This account with its allusions to the ability of students to speak directly to God and with its frankness about sex and birth scandalized proper Bostonians. Because Bronson's economic status was so precarious, despite accepting gifts and loans from family and from friends, often from Ralph Waldo Emerson and later from Louisa herself, his family was forced to move frequently–twenty two times in thirty years. The Alcott family seldom knew solvency or security.

Louisa's mother, Abigail (Abby) May came from an established Boston family. She was wise, steadfast, patient, and loving and, as is shown in *Marmee and Louisa,* a recent book by Eve LaPlante, provided much support and encouragement for her four daughters. In *Little Women,* Abby was the model for the beloved mother, Marmee, who possessed many of Abby's admirable characteristics.

Bronson and Abby Alcott had four daughters: Anna, Louisa (born in 1832), Elizabeth and May, who later served as the models for Louisa's best known characters: Meg, Jo, Beth, and Amy, respectively, the four March sisters in *Little Women.*

"If the father had to give up his cherished projects of a school modeled after his ideas, he could at least conduct the education of his own children; and he did so with the most tender devotion," according to Louisa's earliest biographer, Ednah D. Cheney.

Bronson Alcott was a strict disciplinarian and practiced his educational theories on his own daughters. The hours of their days were rigidly delineated: three and a half hours for labor, four and a half hours for study, three and a half hours for play, nine hours for sleep, as is prescribed on the Order of Indoor Duties chart, made at the Wayside in 1846 by Bronson Alcott.

At 5:00 a.m. they arose, took a cold water bath and dressed. After breakfast at 6:00 a.m. they did housewifery, that is they washed the dishes and swept the floors. In the late morning they studied, often with their father. (Louisa was completely home schooled and never attended an outside school, although her easy access to the family's erudite neighbors, Ralph Waldo Emerson and Henry Thoreau, certainly compensated for her absence of formal schooling.) After lunch the Alcott girls had sewing, conversation, and reading with their mother.

In keeping with his educational philosophy, which stres innate, innocent wisdom of young children, Bronson set down s objectives of his educational activities for his four daughters. were to achieve "vigilance, punctuality, perseverance; prompt, ch unquestioning obedience; government of temper, hands and t gentle manners, motions and words." He insisted that work, s and play be distinct and that there be no interchange of labors.

He encouraged his children to constantly question their own a and motives and to record their thoughts in their own journals. L started her diary at least as early as age three with Bronson's hel continued it for the rest of her life. (It is of interest that members family were free to read and comment on each others' journals an so regularly.)

A frequent theme in Louisa's self analytical entries into her jo is that she feels that she is "cross" too much and should try hard control her temper. She believes that all her lessons and self-ana will produce the virtue of self control. She displays a generous s and is constantly putting the needs of other people, particularly family members, before her own. She is very demanding of herself, repeatedly accepts responsibility for the welfare of others. Bronson her "duty's faithful child."

In 1843, when Louisa was ten, Bronson decided to move his far twenty miles west to Harvard, MA to start a utopian community, wh they named Fruitlands. His co-leader was Charles Lane, a domineer British disciplinarian who had been teaching at a British school pattern after Bronson's teaching theories and named for him. Louisa dutifu kept a diary about the family's trying months at Fruitlands. In 18 with the hindsight of 30 years, she wrote a satirical story about t family's horrendous experiences there, called "Transcendental W Oats." Louisa was an astute observer of the foibles she later wrote abo

Here is her opening description of Fruitlands:

"The kingdom of peace is entered only through the gates of sel denial. . .

The prospective Eden at present consisted of an old red farm house, a dilapidated barn, many acres of meadow-land, and a grove. Te ancient apple trees were all the 'chaste supply' which the place offere as yet; but in the firm belief that plenteous orchards were soon to b r consciousness, these sanguine founders had ı Fruitlands."

ıembers of Fruitlands commune were forbidden heese; to wear leather or any clothes made out ıse money or to use animals or manure in their virtues were held to be reform, self-denial, and spent most of their time debating philosophy or utopian communities. This left all the household ›oking, and baking tasks, as well as much of the es like sowing and harvesting to an overworked, ı the help of her four daughters. One man "did the one by the brethren (Alcott and Lane), who were so l defining great duties that they forgot to perform cording to Louisa.

remarkable that only one woman (her mother) ever nity. Another lady, Ann Page, who lived at Fruitlands ;iven to writing poetry and shirking all tasks. When ıere any beasts of burden in this place?" Mrs. Alcott one woman! (herself)." Ann soon departed after being ıe supposed sin of sneaking a small piece of fish to g hunger.

nd of their experiment Lane insisted that Bronson adopt sake his marriage and children, since Lane believed that rom the pure utopian ideals that he thought they should ıne insisted that Bronson choose between his family and at Fruitlands. Louisa describes how her father then went pression. He was barely able to rise from his bed, where ay turning his face to the wall. Abby threatened to leave any days of grim deliberation, Bronson made the choice d family. Lane departed.

›wy day on January of 1844, only seven months after uitlands, the Alcott family placed all their possessions into ith the parents trudging besides the children in the wagon, itlands. Hungry and impoverished, but still together as a moved temporarily to a nearby village before returning to the end of the year.

Throughout her life Louisa felt a deep responsibility to work very hard to earn enough money to support her whole family, including her parents and her three sisters. Even when she was an unknown writer, often using a man's pseudonym to get published, she put in fourteen hour days, writing furiously. At first she churned out sensationalistic fictional pot boilers, often gothic thrillers, for a few dollars a story. Later, as an established author after writing *Little Women,* she still wrote late into the night to produce stories and books for the many hundreds of dollars that each would bring in, so that she could afford food and clothes for her family, pay for May's art education in Europe, help support her nephews after her brother in law's death, and in later years buy fashionable new duds for Bronson to replace his tattered old clothes.

Between working as a teacher in Concord and moving to Boston, when Abby started a social agency to help the poor, Louisa published her first poem, her first story and her first novel, *The Inheritance,* all before she was twenty. Her first two stories, "Rival Painters" and "Masked Marriage," published in 1852 are both set in romantic Italy. Both have stilted dialogue, archaic speech, and far-fetched, unbelievable plots.

In 1854 she brought her first and last memoir essay, to be read by the Boston publisher James T. Fields. The publisher's verdict was: "Stick to your teaching Miss.Alcott. You can't write." Her reaction, according to her memories of the encounter as recorded in her 1862 journal, was: "Being willful, I said, I won't teach and I can write and I'll prove it!" Which is just what she did.

The Civil War started in 1861. Louisa was working as a kindergarten teacher in Boston when Dorothea Dix was appointed as Superintendent of nurses for the Union Army. Louisa volunteered to be a Union nurse on November 29, 1862. She received a letter on December 11, 1862 ordering her to travel south to help staff the military hospital at the former Union Hotel in Washington, D.C.

On December 13 at Fredericksburg, Virginia soldiers from General Ambrose Burnside's Union Army of the Potomac's 115,000 men, who had been procrastinating nearby for two months, finally attacked the smaller Confederate Army of 78,000 men, led by General Robert E. Lee. The Confederates were dug in behind fortifications on the high ground above the city. Wave after wave of Union soldiers, sixteen altogether, tried to invade the Southern fortifications, but were mowed down. "The battle of Fredericksburg was one of the worst defeats in the history of the United States Army; 12, 700 men were killed that day, as Burnside ordered charges over and over again into death, as his soldiers obediently followed his orders. Fredericksburg quickly became a symbol of stubbornness in the face of unbeatable odds and the resulting almost incomprehensible horror," writes Susan Cheever in her biography of Louisa.

On December 13, 1862 the now thirty year old Louisa, having traveled by train and by ship, arrives in Georgetown, D.C. She describes her excitement with her first journey outside of New England in *Hospital Sketches.* This became her first widely read book in 1863, as readers were eager to learn firsthand news about the war. She is almost giddy as she begins her adventure, referring to herself as "Nurse Periwinkle." However, after her arrival at the Union Hotel Hospital her mood changes abruptly. "There they are!" she declares as hundreds of gravely wounded soldiers, piled in carts, arrive from the killing fields of Fredericksburg, and are carried into the sparsely staffed hospital.

Louisa, who had no formal training as a nurse, was immediately charged with washing and dressing gruesome wounds on terribly mangled bodies, with feeding and nursing and trying to comfort a floor full of severely wounded young soldiers, many of them either nearly dead or dying. As a night nurse she sits by the bedside of John, a gravely wounded Virginia blacksmith, and describes movingly their conversations. "Let me help you, dear John," she offers before he dies in front of her. In the midst of the gore that confronts her, she has the presence to wax both prophetic and poetic: "The Potomac can never wash away the red stain of the land," she proclaims.

Louisa works many hours, both day and night and has little time for herself. After less than six weeks working as a nurse, she becomes so debilitated that she cannot move from her bed. Hospital doctors diagnose typhoid and pneumonia. Daily they dose her with calomel, a mercury compound with disastrous side effects, such as bone pain, severe headaches, and hair loss, all of which she was to suffer for the rest of her life. Although friends advised her to return home, she was reluctant not to keep her three month commitment. However, "one fine morning, a grey-headed gentleman rose like a welcome ghost from my hearth; and, at the sight of him, my resolution melted away, my heart turned traitor to my boys, and when he said, 'Come home,' I answered, 'Yes, Father;' and so ended my career as an army nurse."

Although she only had "typhoid, ten dollars, and a wig" to show for her month as a Union Army nurse, she concludes that she has learned much: "A good fit of illness proves the value of health; real danger tries one's mettle; and self-sacrifice sweetens character." She opines that "though a hospital is a rough school, its lessons are both stern and salutary; and the humblest of pupils there, in proportion to his faithfulness learns a deeper faith in God and in herself."

Some years after her return, in 1867, Thomas Niles, Louisa's Boston publisher, requested that she write a book for girls. "I said I would try. But I didn't like it," she confided to her journal. Her diary note for May, 1868 reads: "Mr. N. wants a *girls' story*, and I begin *Little Women*. So I plod away, though I don't enjoy this sort of thing. Never liked girls or knew many, except my sisters; but our queer plays and experiences may prove interesting, though I doubt it." Years later she added a note to her journal: "Good joke—L.M.A."

However, she worked feverously on her new writing project, *Little Women,* which she started in May and finished only three months later in July, 1868. Part I was published in October, 1868. Her semi-autobiographical coming of age novel follows the lives of the four March sisters, Meg, Jo, Beth, and Amy, modeled closely on the four Alcott sisters, Anna, Louisa, Elizabeth, and May, respectively. It lovingly depicts her mother, here called Marmee. In the book the girls' father was absent, away at the Civil War, throughout most of the book. (Was this subtle evidence of Louisa's resentment of Bronson Alcott, her distant and improvident father, as some critics believe?)

Little Women received an enthusiastic reception from countless readers, including women and men as well as from the girls it first targeted. Because many readers demanded to learn more about the fates of the four March sisters, Niles asked Miss Alcott to write a sequel that would follow the March girls through their early womanhood and marriages. She began her sequel, the second part of *Little Women,* in November, 1868. Part II was published in May, 1869, when Louisa was thirty seven years old. The completed volume brought Louisa the wide readership, adulation, and financial success that had eluded her previously.

Why was *Little Women* received so well by readers of her day? Why does it continue to enthrall readers today? Not surprisingly, literary critics of different eras give different reasons for the novel's enthusiastic acceptance and universal appeal.

Ednah D. Cheney, Alcott's first biographer in 1889, quoted Louisa as remarking, "It reads better than I expected. . . We really lived most of it, and if it succeeds, that will be the reason of it." Cheney goes on to observe:

> "But that is not the whole secret of it its success. Through many trials and failures Louisa had learned her literary art. By her experience in melodrama she had proved the emptiness of sensational writing, and knew how to present the simple and true—seemingly without art. . . It still commands a steady sale; and the mothers who read it in their childhood renew their enjoyment as they watch the faces of their little girls brighten with smiles over the theatricals in the barn, or moisten with tears at the death of a beloved sister. One of the greatest charms of the book is its perfect truth to New England life. But it is not merely local; it touches the universal heart deeply."

Cornelia Meigs, the author of *Invincible Louisa* in 1933, concurs that, "It was almost the first book of its kind, a direct, natural, truthful tale, with no straining after emotion and effect. It was just what girls had been starving for, although scarcely anyone knew it. Louisa did, when she refused to give up, even in the face of Thomas Niles (initial) disappointment."

Other unique aspects of the book are noted by Ruth K. MacDonald in 1983: "*Little Women* was quite different from any other children's book of the time. . . At that period there were no books for adolescents, especially for those between the ages of fifteen and twenty. . . Alcott knew how to portray real children and so had her characters speak colloquially. She captured the real voices of children and young people in her writing, for the first time in the history of American children's literature."

Contemporary writer Susan Cheever paints a glowing tribute to Alcott in *American Bloomsbury* (2006). She credits Alcott not only with a revolutionary breakthrough in women's literature, but also with inspiring Cheever and other women authors both in their personal lives and in their literary creations:

> "Jo March offered me a different kind of image, a new definition of what it meant to be a girl. Instead of a graceful young lady who always minded her manners and knew that her future lay in loving the right man, she was an outspoken, clumsy girl who turned down the right man even though he loved her.
>
> *Little Women* gave my generation of women permission to write about our daily lives. . . Alcott's greatest work was so powerful because it was about ordinary things—I think that's why if felt ordinary even as she wrote it. She transformed the lives of women into something worthy of literature. Without even meaning to, Alcott exalted the everyday in women's lives and gave it greatness."

Cheever goes on to explain that "the huge success of *Little Women* changed the direction of Alcott's career, and for the remaining twenty years of her life she churned out best-selling sequels to the brilliant novel she wrote, almost by accident in the spring of 1868. Although the money enabled her family to live comfortably, Alcott was never really resigned to her role as the beloved and celebrated author of her books for girls. She worried that she had become 'a literary nursemaid providing moral pap for the young.'"

Some of the many works written by this now famous authoress during this era were *An Old Fashioned Girl (1870), Little Men (1871), Work ((1873), Eight Cousins (1875), Under the Lilacs (1878), Jack and Jill (1880), and Jo's Boys (1886).* Most of these books were well received by the reading public, which purchased them partly on the strength of Alcott's fame as the author of *Little Women.*

Alcott started her novel *Success* in 1861, changed its name to *Work: A Story of Experience,* and eventually published it in 1873. It was very different from her previous creations. Whereas, *Little Women* was a semi-autobiographical exploration of domestic relations of her New England family, *Work,* which detailed in fiction specific work which Alcott herself had pursued, gave "a sense of formation of women's consciousness in the nineteenth century" and was "an expression of Alcott's feminist principles," according to literary critic Monika Elbert. Appropriately, it was dedicated to her mother.

The heroine, Christie Devon, is an orphan, raised on a farm by her aunt and uncle. She states emphatically that she is "old enough to be independent. . . a new Declaration of Independence. . . I can take care of myself. I can't be happy until I do. . . I need to break loose from this narrow life." She sees her alternatives as marriage—which she rejects—, or being a drudge, a spinster, or a suicide victim. Her first job is as a servant to a haughty society lady. There she meets a humble black cook, who is a runaway slave, Hepsie, who becomes a life-long friend and inspiration.

Next she becomes a stage actress, portraying the Queen of the Amazons, whom she calls "a heroic spirit." She does well as an actress, but soon finds her life as humdrum as her old life. And she is wary of temptations to become "selfish, frivolous, and vain. . . to have no care for anyone but myself," transfixed by "admiration and fame."

Her next position is as a governess for the children of an upper crust Yankee lady, Mrs. Saltonstall. Here she is courted by Mrs. Saltonstall's dilettante brother, Phillip Fletcher. She was tempted to say yes to his marriage proposal, but dismissed her desire for a loveless marriage to women's foibles of vanity, ambition, and love of pleasure. She further justifies her refusal, because "It is what we *are,* not what we *have.*"

Next she becomes the companion to a crazed woman from a family characterized by insanity. She soon leaves this turbulent scene for the relative calm of being a seamstress. Here she keeps to herself, because the other girls are preoccupied only with "dress, gossip, and wages." Feeling very lonely, she reaches out to another girl, Rachel, who is expelled from the work place. Christie, feeling more lonely and despondent, considers suicide, but is rescued by a chance encounter with Rachel.

She next finds herself doing housework and childcare for the Wilkins family with their six brawling children. When she leaves them, a saintly Rev. Power, places her with Mrs. Sterling and her moody son, David, a greenhouse gardener (who is reputedly is modeled after Henry David Thoreau.) As she helps David with his ferns and flowers, she initially considers him a friend, not a lover, that is until she falls in love with him. Then they marry.

The Civil War begins. When David volunteers as a Union Soldier, Christie volunteers as a military nurse (a la L.M.A.). At the front David is killed, but Christie returns to Boston, where she has her baby, Pansie.

Christie, now forty, summarizes her (and Louisa's, as well) reverence for work: "I can teach, nurse, sew, write, cook. . . I am useful. I am happy. . . I have been and mean to be a working woman all my life. . . having found in labor the best teacher."

". . .I have found independence, education, happiness, and religion." At the end of the book she becomes a vocal a spokeswoman for disaffected women of all classes, ages, and races, and a leader of the new emancipation, where reform is needed to mold more active earnest lives. She concludes that the greatest of God's gifts to us is the privilege of sharing his great work.

Some contemporary critics of *Work* praised the extension of Alcott's social concerns into realistic depictions, often based on her own life, of women's often harsh mid-nineteenth century experiences in the work place. Others cautioned that New Englanders are already too work-obsessed.

Louisa's newfound financial success enabled her to better support her parents, to travel to Europe once again and to purchase the former Thoreau house on Main Street in Concord for her newly widowed sister Anna and her two sons (the models for her "Little Men"). Her independent spirit prompted her to lead a counter demonstration of women during Concord's 1875 Centennial Celebration of the Concord Fight and of American Independence, and in 1879 to become the first woman to register to vote in Concord. In 1880 she adopted Lulu, the infant daughter of her sister May, who died in Paris in 1879. Alcott's novel production came to a halt, when she then turned to short stories so that she could have enough time to care for Lulu.

In 1882 Bronson Alcott suffered a stroke. Louisa spent much time at her father's bedside. Both Bronson and Louisa were receiving medical care in Boston, when. Bronson died on March 4, 1888. Louisa died on March 6, two days later. As mourner (and later Louisa's first biographer) Ednah D. Cheney, remarked at Bronson's funeral about the fatefully closely timed deaths of father and daughter, "His faithful child could not be spared to stay after him."

Louisa's obituary in the *Concord Freeman* lamented, "Miss. Alcott's death causes a wide wave of sorrow to pass over our town. No person within our borders was more respected and loved than this gifted author." Both father and daughter, along with Abby and two other Alcott daughters, are buried in the Alcott family plot on Author's Ridge in Sleepy Hollow Cemetery in Concord.

Hillside 1846

Order of In-door Duties

for Children.

	Morning		Forenoon		Noon		Afternoon		Evening
5.	Rise, Bathe, Dress	9.	Studies with Mr Lane.			1.	Rest.	6.	Supper.
6.	Breakfast					2.	Sewing, Conversation, and Reading, with Mother and Miss Ford.		Recreation, Conversation, Music.
	Housewifery	10½	Recreations.	12	Dinner				
	Recreations. (Chores) in care of Miss Foord	11.	Studies with Father			4.	Errands and (Chores) Recreations.	8.	
								8½	Bed.

Bathing Hours		Labor Hours
5. 10½ 6.	Vigilance, Punctuality, Perseverance.	6½ to 8. 2 to 4.
Study Hours	Prompt, Cheerful, Unquestioning, Obedience.	Play Hours
9 t. 10½. 11 t. 12	Government of Temper, Hands, and Tongue.	8 to 9. 10 to 10½. 4 to 6
	Gentle Manners, Motions, and Words.	Eating Hours
	Work, Studies, and Play distinct.	6 to 6½. 12 to 12½. 6 to 6½.
	No interchange of Labors.	Sleeping Hours
		8 to 5. 8½ to 5.

[illegible] Silence and [illegible]

Order of Indoor Duties for the (Alcott) children, Hillside, 1846.
Courtesy of the Louisa May Alcott Memorial Association.

They all drew to the fire, mother in the big chair, with Beth at her feet; Meg and Amy perched on either arm of the chair, and Jo leaning on the back. — Page 13.

LITTLE WOMEN

OR,

MEG, JO, BETH AND AMY

BY LOUISA M. ALCOTT

ILLUSTRATED BY MAY ALCOTT

BOSTON
ROBERTS BROTHERS
1868

Title – Page from *Little Women* by Louisa May Alcott.
Illustration by May Alcott. (Boston: Roberts Brothers, 1869)
Courtesy of Louisa May Alcott Memorial Association.

A Louisa May Alcott Timeline (1832–1888)

1832 Louisa May Alcott (LMA) is born on November 29 in Germantown, PA to Amos Bronson Alcott (ABA) from Wolcott, CT and Abigail (Abby) May from Boston, MA

1834 The Alcotts move to Boston. Bronson opens the Temple School in Boston.

1835 Elizabeth Peabody Alcott born.

1839 Temple School closed on March 23.

1840 Family moves to Concord's Hosmer cottage. Abba May Alcott is born.

1842 ABA travels to England; returns with Charles Lane and Henry Wright. They make plans to form a utopian community together.

1843 Alcott family, Charles Lane and Henry Wright move to Fruitlands in Harvard, MA on June 1.

1844 Fruitlands experiment fails. Family moves to Still River, MA on January 14; They return to Concord on November 12; where they stay with the Hosmers.

1845 Alcotts move to Hillside house in Concord (now called Wayside).

1848 Louisa opens a school in a barn. Family returns to Boston, where Abby starts a social service agency to help the poor.

1851 Boston, High Street: LMA's poem, "Sunlight," is published in *Peterson's Magazine.* Louisa works "out to service."

1852 LMA's first story, "The Rival Painters," published in *Olive Branch.* Boston, Pinckney St: Louisa and Anna hold classes in their parlor.

1854 Told by publisher, James Fields, "Stick to your teaching. . . You can't write."
Flower Fables published from stories LMA wrote for Ellen Emerson.

1856 Walpole, N.H.: Elizabeth and May fall ill with scarlet fever.

1857 Family moves back to Concord. ABA purchases Orchard House.

1858 Elizabeth died in March. Then the family lives temporarily at Hillside. Ann becomes engaged to John Pratt. The Family moves to Orchard House in July. LMA returns to Boston in October.

1859 Boston: sewing, writing, and teaching.

1860 LMA's play, *Nat Bachelor's Pleasure Trip,* is produced in Boston. Anna Alcott and John Pratt are married in Orchard House. LMA writes *Moods* in four weeks.

1861 The Civil War begins.

1862 Boston: LMA teaches kindergarten. On December 13, she arrives in Washington, D.C. and volunteers as an army nurse at a Union acute care hospital. She continues to keep her journal,

1863 Taken home by train by ABA on January 24, ill with typhoid and pneumonia. Recuperates in Concord. "Hospital Sketches" published. in *Commonwealth Magazine.*

1864 Concord: She finishes revisions for *Moods*, which is published.

1865 LMA sails for Europe on July 19; where she meets Ladislas Wisniewski.

1866 Visits Nice, Paris, London. Returns to Concord in July.

1867 Boston: Thomas Niles asks her to write a "book for girls."

1868 Boston: Becomes editor of *Merry's Museum*. Concord: Begins *Little Women* in May; she finishes Part I in July, and publishes it in October. She begins a sequel, Part II, in November.

1869 Boston: Part II of *Little Women* is published in April.

1870 Boston: *An Old Fashioned Girl* is published. She sails to Europe with sister May and Alice Bartlett in April. John Pratt dies.

1871 Begins *Little Men* in January. Visits Italy and Rome. Comes home. *Little Men* is published in June.

1873 Boston, Allston St.: *Success,* renamed *Work,* is published, as is "Transcendental Wild Oats."

1874 Leads counter demonstration of local women at Concord's Bicentennial on April 19. Boston: Bellevue Hotel: *Eight Cousins* published. Attends Women's Congress in Syracuse, N.Y. Spends Christmas in New York City.

1876 Boston: Publishes *Rose in Bloom.* Buys the Main St. Thoreau House in Concord for Anna and her two sons.

1877 Concord: LMA moves into Bellevue Hotel. Moves into Thoreau House, November 14. Abba Alcott dies on November 25. *A Modern Mephistopheles* is published.

1878 Concord: *Under the Lilacs* is published. May Alcott marries Ernest Nieriker in Paris.

1879 LMA is the first woman to register to vote in Concord. Louisa May Nieriker (Lulu) is born in Paris, November 8. May dies, December 29, leaving her daughter Lulu to LMA. ABA's School of Philosophy opens in the Orchard House parlor.

1880 Boston: Publishes *Jack and Jill.* Lulu arrives in Boston.

1881 Concord: LMA writes only short stories, since she is absorbed in Lulu's care.

1882 Emerson dies. ABA suffers a stroke.

1884 LMA and ABA both receive medical care in Boston.

1886 *Jo's Boys* is published.

1888 ABA died on March 4. LMA died on March 6. Both are buried at Sleepy Hollow Cemetery in Concord, on Authors' Ridge.

[**Sources**: Alcott, LM. *Letters of LMA,* as quoted in Cheney (See below)
MacDonald, Ruth K. *Louisa May Alcott.* Boston: Twane, 1983
Meigs, Cornelia. *Invincible Louisa,* Little, Boston: Little Brown, 1968.
Cheever, Susan. *Louisa May Alcott: A Personal Biography.* New York, Simon & Schuster, 2010; *American Bloomsbury,* 2006.
Cheney, Ednah D., *Louisa May Alcott: Her Life, Letters and Journals,* Little, Brown, Boston, 1889 and 1928.
Turnquist, Jan. Review of LMA Timeline, 2014..]

The Alcott Family in front of Orchard House c. 1865.
Courtesy of the Louisa May Alcott Memorial Association.

The Alcott Family's Orchard House

In 1857 Amos Bronson Alcott, Louisa's father, bought twelve acres of woodland with apple trees and two buildings, an early seventeenth century farm house and an ell-shaped tenants' building on Lexington Road in Concord. To meet the $950 purchase price he borrowed $500 from Ralph Waldo Emerson and $450 from friends. The ownership of the buildings and land can be traced back to 1672 to John Hoar, brother of the Harvard President and member of a prominent Concord family.

Instead of taking down the old buildings, Mr. Alcott decided to join them together to create a single home for his family. He had one building propped on logs and rolled down a small hill to join the second structure. After a year of renovations the family moved in.

The unique structure that resulted was described by author Lydia Marie Child as a "house full of queer nooks and corners. . . as if the spirit of some old architect had brought it from the middle age and dropped it down in Concord." The apple trees dotting the land led Bronson Alcott to christen the house **"Orchard House."** However, Louisa, less enamored of the old and saggy house, dubbed it "Apple Slump." Despite her dislike of Orchard House, Louisa used it as the model for the March's house in *Little Women.*

The resulting house has nine rooms. In the spacious ground floor south facing front, parlor guests often gathered to watch the four Alcott sisters perform plays. Here the eldest sister Anna was married in 1860. At the left of the front center hall is Bronson Alcott's book lined study. Behind it is artist May Alcott's north facing studio with a skylight. May's original pencil sketches still enliven its walls.

Louisa often retired to her own second floor bedroom. Here she wrote *Little Women, Moods* and *Work* at a small desk facing the wall. Windows on either side look out to the Concord countryside beyond.

Today the house, at 399 Lexington Road, is operated by the Louisa May Alcott Memorial Association. Visitors pay a small fee for a guided house tour. Further information is at *www.louisamayalcott.org* or at 978-369-4118. There is a **Museum Shop**, where visitors can purchase Louisa's books and mementos, as well as books by other Concord authors.

Behind Orchard House is a wooden structure built by Bronson Alcott in 1879, **The Concord School of Philosophy.** Here he conducted a summer school for adults, which, encouraged study of original creative thought, most significantly, Transcendentalism,

According to a history of the school,. women as well as men attended the lectures and discussions. This was unusual for the era, since women were not admitted into universities. The School of Philosophy was the forerunner of today's adult education programs. Subjects included philosophy, mysticism, literature, art, education and social reform. For example, Emerson lectured on *Memory* in 1879 and on *Aristocracy* in 1880. Elizabeth Peabody talked on *Childhood* in 1882, Julian Hawthorne on *Novels* in 1883 and Julia Ward Howe, best known as creator of "The Battle Hymn of the Republic," is said to have created a sensation with her lecture on *Modern Society* in 1880. The school flourished for nine summers until Bronson Alcott's death in 1888.

Nathaniel Hawthorne

CHAPTER 4

A Puritan's Progress: Nathaniel Hawthorne

Having spent twelve years as a recluse living and writing in his mother's family house in his native Salem after college, Nathaniel Hawthorne at age thirty five became engaged to Sophia Peabody, a woman from a prominent Salem family. Three years later in 1842, on the day of their marriage, the couple moved into the Old Manse in Concord, the house built by Ralph Waldo Emerson's grandfather, Rev. William Emerson in 1770. Here the couple spent the next three years on what turned out to be a prolonged, happy honeymoon. Here they celebrated the birth of their first child, Una.

Thus, it wasn't until his mid-thirties that the previously shy, introverted and house-bound Hawthorne, who is best known today for his brooding, dark novel, *The Scarlet Letter,* which focuses on sin, guilt, angst, shame, and retribution so central to the lives of his New England Puritan ancestors, came into his own. It was in Concord that he developed a sexual and social passion for his new wife, and a zest for walking out of doors, rowing on the nearby Concord River in a boat made by and sold to him by Henry Thoreau and for spending hours outside, walking, and gardening.

The couple was soon befriended by members of Concord's literary coterie, Thoreau, Emerson, Bronson Alcott, Ellery Channing, and Margaret Fuller. (Hawthorne was characteristically reserved in the assessment he wrote in his journal about his new acquaintances.) It was during this time in Concord that he compiled a collection of short stories, published in 1846 as *Mosses from the Old Manse.*

Interestingly, in his Preface to *Mosses,* titled *The Old Manse*, he expresses disappointment at his meager literary output during this his first Concord stay, even as he tells of his great pleasure with his new family and with his idyllic Concord surroundings:

The treasure of intellectual gold, which I hoped to find in our secluded dwelling, had never come to light. No profound treatise of ethics—no philosophic history—no novel, even that could stand, unsupported, on its edges. All that I had to show, as a man of letters, were these few tales and essays, which had blossomed out like flowers in the calm summer of my heart and mind.

For myself the book will always retain one charm, as reminding me of the (Concord) river, with its delightful solitudes, and of the avenue, the garden, and the orchard, especially the dear old Manse, with the little study on its western side, and the sunshine glimmering through the willow-branches while I wrote.

Visitors to the Old Manse today are delighted to find that inscriptions that Nathaniel and Sophia Hawthorne scratched on to the Manse's windows with their diamond rings over 170 years ago still await their discovery today.

These exuberant observations still remain, etched on the window of Hawthorne's study:

Man's accidents are God's purposes.
Sophia A. Peabody 1843
Nat'n Hawthorne
This is his study.
1843

The smallest twig
Leans clear against the sky.
Composed by my wife
And written with her diamond.
Inscribed by my
Husband at sunset
April 3, 1843
On the gold light—SAH

To really understand Nathaniel Hawthorne we must go back to his beginnings. He was born on the fourth of July in 1804 in Salem, Massachusetts to Nathaniel and Elizabeth Manning Hathorne. (Nathaniel changed his name to Hawthorne in about 1825, because he wanted to disassociate himself from a Salem ancestor, his great-grandfather, John Hathorne, who had been a notorious hanging judge in the infamous Salem Witchcraft Trials of the 1690's.) Hawthorne's father, a ship's captain died from yellow fever in Surinam (Dutch Guiana) in 1808, when Nathaniel was four years old. His mother, now facing poverty, moved with Nathaniel and his two sisters into her parents, the Mannings' house in Salem. When Nathaniel was nine he injured his foot and became unable to attend school or walk for two years. He spent his time indoors reading, which fostered his lifetime affinity for literature.

When Nathaniel was fourteen he moved with his family to his Uncle Richard Manning's house in Raymond, Maine. There he thrived, hiking, hunting, and fishing in the forests around nearby Sebago Lake. In the winter of 1819, he was sent to board at a school in Portland, Maine. However, because he was homesick, he was then sent back to live with the Manning family and to study in Salem, under the tutelage of his guardian, his Uncle Robert Manning.

In 1821, Hawthorne entered Bowdoin College, a small liberal arts college in Brunswick, Maine. While in college he decided not to prepare himself for any of the most common learned professions of the day, ministry, law or medicine. He preferred, he wrote, "becoming an Author, and relying for support upon my pen," as reported by biographer Brenda Wineapple. Although not noted for literary achievements at Bowdoin, he did make lifelong friends: Franklin Pierce, who with some help from Hawthorne, became the fourteenth President of the United States, and Horatio Bridge, who later helped underwrite *Twice Told Tails,* Hawthorne's first published volume of short stories. Another classmate was the poet and future Harvard professor, Henry Wadsworth Longfellow. Hawthorne was a middling student at Bowdoin, graduating eighteenth in a class of thirty-five.

After college he returned to the Manning house in Salem and lived there with his mother, his two sisters and his three Manning aunts and five uncles. He lived in obscurity for the next twelve years. In Salem he led a secluded life as a recluse, living "under the eaves," most often staying indoors during the day, as he wrote at his desk. He ventured outside to walk only in the dark of night. He wrote short stories. He burned those that displeased him. He suffered from "unfocused depression, unrealized ambition and embarrassing penury," according to Wineapple.

Hawthorne wrote his first novel *Fanshawe* in 1828, which he published anonymously at his own expense (for about $100). It is about a doomed young man, very much like himself. But, displeased with his creation, he burned all the copies that he could find. (The novel was not re-published until 1876, well after his death.) During this time Hawthorne also published over seventy tales and sketches in newspapers, magazines, and annuals. Some were re-published also in later collections, such as *Twice-Told Tales,* published in 1837.

In 1839 Hawthorne became engaged to Sophia Peabody, a comely young woman from a prominent Salem family. He had met her better known sister, activist Elizabeth Peabody, first. Elizabeth was a pioneering intellectual and an educator who had taught with Bronson Alcott at the ill-fated Temple School. However, Hawthorne later fell in love with her shyer, almost reclusive sister Sophia. From 1839 to 1841, to supplement his meager income as a then little known author, Hawthorne was appointed as a salt and coal Weigher and Gauger at the Boston Custom House.

In 1841 he resigned this post and joined Brook Farm, a utopian farming community in the Boston suburb of West Roxbury. Hawthorne stayed at Brook Farm for only eight months. He soon discovered that his initial idealism and curiosity were supplanted by his insight that at his core he was not cut out to be either a farm laborer or a socialist. He found out that shoveling manure and hoeing in an isolated community were not activities that he truly enjoyed. He felt that he could best attain the higher ends of life by retaining the ordinary relation to society.

Some years later, in 1852 he published *The Blithedale Romance,* a fictional narrative based loosely on his experiences and on the personalities he had encountered earlier at Brook Farm. In his Preface Hawthorne writes:

> The Author has ventured to make free with his old, and affectionately remembered home, at BROOK FARM, as being, certainly, the most romantic episode of his own life—essentially a day-dream, and yet a fact—and thus offering an available foot hold between fiction and reality.

The novel follows the relationships between a quartet of Blithedale commune members, modeled after actual Brook Farm, members. The narrator, Miles Cloverdale, the Minor Poet (probably standing in for Hawthorne) encounters the Woman, Zenobia. She was modeled after Hawthorne's real life object of distinct but distant desire, Margaret Fuller. Biographer Susan Cheever in *American Bloomsbury* reveals that, "During the three years of his secret engagement to (Sophia) Peabody and the two years (in Concord) after their marriage, Hawthorne continued to pursue Fuller in his imagination and, as a friend, in life. . . *The Blithedale Romance* (published two years after Fuller's death) is warmed by the presence of an electrifying, truth–speaking female presence."

The narrator admits that "Zenobia's aspect. . . impressed itself on me so distinctly, that I can now summon her up like a ghost." Zenobia/ Fuller is described as a beautiful, passionate, mature woman:

> She was dressed as simply as possible. . . but with a silken kerchief between which and her gown there was one glimpse of white shoulder. It struck me as a great piece of good fortune that there should be just that glimpse. Her hair—which was dark, glossy, and of singular abundance—was put up rather soberly and primly without curls or other ornament except a single flower. It was an exotic of rare beauty. And as fresh as if the hothouse gardener had just clipt it from the stem. That flower has struck deep root in my memory.

Zenobia is pursued by Hollingsworth, the Philanthropist, whom Hawthorne describes as a hard working idealist and reformer of the wicked, who has a scheme to convert convicted prisoners to lead a worthier life. The self-admittedly dismal narrator, Cloverdale, admits at the end of the novel that he is secretly in love with Priscilla, the "weakly Maiden" described in his preface, a seamstress who encompasses youth, gaiety, and joy.

Zenobia is an early feminist, as was Fuller. She forcefully protests "the injustice that the world did to women" and proclaims that "society throttles us." She acts independently, displaying "native power and influence, for whatever Zenobia did was generally acknowledged as right for her to do."

In the end of the novel Zenobia drowns. In a macabre scene her rigid body is retrieved from a pond. (It is noteworthy that in 1850, two years before Hawthorne published *The Blithedale Romance,* Zenobia's prototype, Margaret Fuller Ossoli and her (probable) husband, Count Ossoli, along with their child, were on a voyage from Europe to America. During a fierce storm, their ship was wrecked on a sandbar off the coast of Fire Island. All three drowned. Only the baby's body was ever recovered.)

Hollingsworth, the Philanthropist, is said to represent masculine egotism. Cloverdale judges that, although Hollingsworth's efforts at reforming sinners are "useful to society at large, they are perilous in individuals and ruin the heart."

Literary critic Alfred Kazin points out insightfully that the *Blithedale Romance* is the only one of Hawthorne's four major novels that concerns itself wholly with issues and personalities of Hawthorne's own nineteenth century America, still suffering with pastoral issues of itself, soon to be destroyed in the fires of the Civil War. His other novels deal with aspects of evil and guilt, the dark legacy of his Puritan ancestors. *The Scarlet Letter,* is set in seventeenth century Boston and is steeped in witchcraft, guilt, and sin. Kazin writes: "*The House of Seven Gables,* though set in nineteenth century Salem, is about the hold of the past on some elderly characters and the struggle of the young to free them from the 'grip' (a favorite word in Hawthorne) and curses of their Puritan past. The last novel Hawthorne published in his lifetime, *The Marble Faun,* laid in contemporary Italy, is really about the unlovable past, the baleful and ominous past that stands in the way of two pairs of ill-matched and unbelievable lovers."

Another critic, A.N. Kaul, points out that, "In the *Scarlet Letter,* Hawthorne had noted the utopian aspect of the Puritan migration to New England," whereas, "in the *Blithedale Romance* he presents the utopian experiment of Brook Farm as an extension of the Puritan tradition. The backward glance of comparison runs like a rich thread through the latter novel, making explicit the significance. . . of the otherwise quixotic enterprise" of Brook Farm. Blithedale represents withdrawal from a corrupt society to form a regenerate community."

In November 1841, having spent seven months at Brook Farm, his fictional Blithedale, Hawthorne resigned from that utopian farming community. On July 9, 1842, after a three year engagement, he married Sophia Peabody of Salem. On the very day of their marriage the couple moved into The Old Manse in Concord, where they lived happily for the next three years, as we observed earlier at the beginning of this chapter.

Friendships with his Bowdoin chums Franklin Pierce and Horatio Bridge, both influential in the Democratic Party, helped him to secure the appointment as Surveyor in the Salem Custom House, where he worked mornings for the next three years. During this period his son Julian was born and in 1846 Hawthorne published *Mosses from An Old Manse,* as has been discussed at the beginning of this chapter.

Following the election of the Whig President, Zachary Taylor, in 1849 Hawthorne was dismissed from his post at the Salem Custom House for political reasons. Next he began writing what was to become his most famous novel, *The Scarlet Letter,* which he published the next year.

In Hawthorne's long introduction to *The Scarlet Letter*, "The Customs House," he invokes his feeling for old Salem, which is assignable to (his family's) deep roots there, going back over two hundred years. He claims that "The figure of my first ancestor (John Hathorne). . . still haunts me. . . He was a soldier, legislator, judge; he was a ruler in the Church; he had all the Puritanic traits, both good and evil. He was a bitter persecutor. . . His son too inherited the persecuting spirit and made himself so conspicuous in the martyrdom of the witches, that their blood may fairly be said to have left a stain upon him. . . I, the present writer, as their representative, hereby take shame upon myself for their sakes, and pray that any curse incurred by them. . . may be now and henceforth removed."

Hawthorne's concern for his Puritan Salem ancestors, explains why in much of his writing he looks backward to the somber past and focuses on the themes of sin, guilt, shame, punishment, and repentance, arising from what he describes as "the severity of the Puritan character," amongst whose people "religion and law were almost identical."

The dramatic opening scenes of *The Scarlet Letter* are set in the rigid, newly established community of seventeenth century Puritan Boston. The heroine, Hester Prynne, emerges from behind prison doors with a baby in her arms. She stands before a crowd of spiteful townsfolk, who stare at the scarlet letter "A" embroidered on the bosom of her dress. It was a mark of shame, her punishment for previous adultery. Spectators are surprised to observe that "her beauty shone out and made a halo of the misfortune and ignominy in which she was enveloped." She is led to the town scaffold by "an irregular procession of unkind men and unkindly visaged women." There she stands for three hours, holding her sin-born infant in her arms, with all the eyes of the vengeful crowd focused on her.

As Hawthorne's tale proceeds, the narrator tells us about Hester's secret contacts with the mysterious Roger Chillingsworth, who eventually is revealed to be her lost husband. We learn of her attraction to the minister, Arthur Dimmesdale. We observe her love for her infant, Pearl, who was "sprung out of the rank luxuriance of guilty passion" and is a "born outcast. . . an imp of evil, emblem and product of sin. . . demon origin. . . an elf child."

We learn of Chillingsworth's jealous hate for and torment of the minister Dimmesdale and of Hester's continuing love for Dimmesdale. We eventually learn that he is father of her child. Rejected by both her vengeful husband and by her fearful lover, Hester is left to build her own life all by herself. She is able to steer between the harsh judgments of her Puritan neighbors and her growing confidence in herself as a woman and mother. She changes herself over time from an outcast of society to an empathetic responder to calamities, where "her nature showed itself warm and rich, a wellspring of human tenderness." Such helpfulness caused many people to "refuse to interpret the scarlet A by its original signification, Adultery; they said that it meant Able; so strong was Hester Prynne with a woman's strength." Her resilience and courage in the face of harsh circumstances makes her one of the first true heroines in American literature.

Hawthorne has Chillingworth, who is a physician, explain that Dimmesdale's "bodily illness may be due to. . . trouble in (his) soul" and that "guilt can arise from "a strong sympathy between soul and body." Hawthorne's insights in recognizing psychosomatic causes of illness are clearly ahead of his time. Ironically, at the end of his novel Hawthorne reveals that Rev. Dimmesdale has his own scarlet A, imprinted in the flesh of his chest. The author leaves it to the reader to explain whether the red stigma originated by the minister inflicting it on himself, whether it was caused by Chillingsworth's magic or whether it was caused by Dimmesdale's "remorse, gnawing from the inmost heart outwardly."

Hawthorne moved his family to Lenox, MA in 1850 to a red cottage at Tanglewood, which overlooks the Berkshire Mountains. (It is now adjacent to the summer site of the Boston Symphony Orchestra.) Here he became friends with Herman Melville, the author of *Moby Dick,* who lived in nearby Pittsfield. Melville wrote a laudatory review about Hawthorne and dedicated *Moby Dick* to him.

In 1851, one year after he had published *The Scarlet Letter,* Hawthorne published his second best known novel, *The House of Seven Gables.* As in his previous novel Hawthorne focuses on the themes of sin, guilt, and shame as they relate to many generations of an ancient Puritan family, the Pyncheons of Salem. The first builder of the house is executed for witchcraft, "one of the martyrs to that terrible delusion. . . a passionate error that has always characterized the maddest mob!" Just before he faces the hangman's noose, the accused wizard, builder Mathew Maule, casts a curse on his accuser, Colonel Pyncheon: "God will give him blood to drink!."

Colonel Pyncheon is later discovered to have died suddenly under mysterious circumstances. Blood is found on his throat and sleeve. Several generations later his elderly descendents, Hepzibah and her feeble brother Clifford still live in porverty in Colonel Pyncheon's dark, old house. A distant cousin, Phoebe, a lively young woman, comes to stay with them. Hawthorne contrasts Hepzibah, who symbolizes the Old Gentility with Phoebe, who represents the New Plebeianism. Phoebe is pert, cheerful, energetic, rosy, an angel, a maiden. Her cousin Hepzibah, is a gentlewoman, who considers that work is beneath her. In contrast to lively, young Phoebe, Hepzibah is old and pale, a recluse, whose only facial expression is a constant scowl.

Holgrave, a boarder, declaims to Phoebe that "We live in Dead Men's houses. . . the house is expressive of that odious and abominable Past. . . I dwell in it for awhile that I might better know how to hate it. Deploring the unfairness of the power that people who lived in the past still have over those who live in the present," he exclaims. "A Dead Man sits on all our judgment-seats; and living judges do but search out and repeat his decisions. We read the Dead Man's books! We laugh at the Dead Man's jokes. . . We are sick of the Dead Man's diseases, physical, and moral. . . We worship the living Deity according to the Dead Man's forms and creeds!" Holgrave thus channels Hawthorne's dislike of the power of the past on current affairs. He does so in words that could well be written by Hawthorne's Concord neighbor, Ralph Waldo Emerson, who frequently criticized the power of the past to limit the creativity, understanding, and actions of humans in the present.

Judge Jaffrey Pyncheon, an evil throwback to his ancestor Colonel Pyncheon, is a duplicitous manipulator who bullies Hepzibah and Clifford. Upon his death it becomes clear that the Judge has unjustly convicted Clifford of a murder and misinterpreted a family will by trickery. His "inward criminality. . . sin. . . guilt" are now revealed. In the end Hepzibah and Clifford abandon the House of Seven Gables and move instead into Judge Pyncheon's now vacant country manor.

In 1852, one year after he published *The House of Seven Gables,* Hawthorne published *The Blithedale Romance.* As we have seen, this novel was based on his 1841 sojourn at Brook Farm. He also published a campaign biography of his Bowdoin classmate and friend Franklin Pierce, which helped Pierce get elected President. Hawthorne agreed with Pierce that, although slavery was evil, it should not be ended by human contrivance, which they believed would only bring on war and bloodshed and result in a divided nation. Hawthorne felt that slavery would eventually vanish like a dream. Hawthorne's support of Pierce alienated his Concord Transcendentalist and abolitionist neighbors, who supported immediate abolition of slavery and therefore opposed Pierce's election, as well as his Presidency.

The same year Hawthorne moved his family back to Concord, to the Wayside, the house he purchased from Bronson Alcott. It was the only house that Hawthorne ever owned. He constructed a cupola atop the house, so he could write at his standing desk and at the same time enjoy views overlooking the surrounding Concord countryside.

The following year President Pierce appointed Hawthorne the American Consul in Liverpool, England, most likely as a reward for the campaign biography he wrote for Pierce. Hawthorne moved his family to Liverpool where they remained for the next four years, until he resigned his Consulship in 1857. The family then traveled in France and Italy in 1858 and returned to England for a year in 1859 after his daughter Una became ill.

In 1860 Hawthorne published *The Marble Faun,* inspired by his travels in Italy. He returned with his family to live again at the Wayside in Concord. Over the next four years he began four different romance novels, all of which remained unfinished at his death. He did publish an article in *The Atlantic*, "Chiefly About War Matters," which criticized Lincoln's conduct of the Civil War. Hawthorne believed that the main results of the War would be bloodshed, death, and a divided nation. His Concord neighbors, most of whom favored speedy abolition of slavery, were not amused. He also published *Our Old Home* in 1864, impressions about England.

Hawthorne took a carriage trip to visit New Hampshire in 1864 in the company his old friend, former President Franklin Pierce. The next morning Pierce discovered that Hawthorne had died peacefully in his sleep. Hawthorne's funeral was attended by Concord notables, such as Emerson, as well as by fellow members of Boston's Saturday Morning Club, including Henry Wadsworth Longfellow and Oliver Wendell Holmes, both of whom served as pallbearers. His three children, Una, Julian, and Rose rode in a coach with their mother along side of the funeral procession. Hawthorne was buried in his family's plot on Authors' Ridge in Sleepy Hollow Cemetery in Concord. (Several years ago the bodies of his wife Sophia and his daughter Una were disinterred from a London cemetery, transported to America and re-buried next to Nathaniel.)

Hawthorne's obituary in *The New York Times* of May 20, 1864 reads: "The telegraph brings us the mournful and unexpected death of the most charming of America's novelists and one of the foremost descriptive writers in the language."

Concord literary historian, Jayne Gordon believes that Hawthorne was forced to maintain a tricky balance between living a literary life as an author and earning a living any way he could, in order to support his family. In the latter role he "lost 100 percent of his friends" due to his support of Pierce and opposition to abolition, and was even accused of "bartering his brain."

Among his contemporaries Emerson, the Transcendental essayist, had little understanding of Hawthorne, the Romantic novelist (and visa-versa.) Emerson remarked on "the painful solitude of the man." Oliver Wendell Holmes in a poem asked, "Who is he?" and went on to describe Hawthorne as an "artist, who broods alone. . . hidden behind his veil. . . from shyness." Most of his Boston and Concord acquaintances regretted that they had not had the opportunity to really know the shy and retiring Hawthorne during his life time. Longfellow described Hawthorne as "unfinished. . . inscrutable and unknowable."

However, a more recent assessment is more generous about Hawthorne's life and works. Respected literary critic Alfred Kazin believes that: "A century after his death Hawthorne is still the most interesting artist in fiction whom New England has produced—he is the only New England artist in fiction whose works constitute a profound imaginative world of their own. . . His 'tales' and 'romances' of New England have a depth of interest that we do not find in representations of the fixity and eccentricity of the New England character [in other authors.]"

A Hawthorne Timeline (1804–1864)

1804 Nathaniel Hathorne (after 1825, Hawthorne) was born in Salem, MA to Nathaniel and Elizabeth Manning Hathorne.

1808 His father, a ship's captain, dies from yellow fever in Surinam. His mother and her children, now facing poverty, move into her parents' house in Salem.

1813 Injures foot while playing ball; unable to go to school for two years.

1818 Hathornes move to family property in Raymond, Maine.

1821-25 Attends Bowdoin College in Brunswick, Maine. Classmates include Henry W. Longfellow and Franklin Pierce. Begins writing fiction. Graduates eighteenth in a class of thirty five.

1825-35 Returns to Salem; lives at the Manning house with his mother and his sisters. Lives in seclusion "under the eaves." Writes stories: publishes some, burns others.

1828 Publishes *Fanshawe* anonymously at his own expense. Ashamed, he destroys most copies. Novel not re-published until 1876, after his death.

1830's Publishes over seventy tales and sketches in newspapers, magazines and annuals.

1832 Visits New Hampshire and Vermont; starts work on "The Story Teller" series about an itinerant narrator.

1833 Publisher Goodrich rejects "The Story Teller." Some of the tales are published elsewhere.

1836 Named editor of a magazine, so moves briefly to Boston. When publisher becomes bankrupt, Hawthorne moves back to Salem.

1837 Publishes *Twice-Told Tales,* a collection of previously published stories.

1839 Becomes engaged to Sophia Peabody of Salem.

1839-41 Works in the Boston Custom House as salt and coal Measurer. Publishes three children's books.

1841 Joins Brook Farm, a socialist utopian community in West Roxbury, MA. Stays only for seven months from April to November. Leaves because he becomes disillusioned.

1842 On July 9 he marries Sophia Peabody and moves into "The Old Manse" in Concord. Here the couple shares a three year honeymoon and are befriended by Emerson, Thoreau, Bronson Alcott, Ellery Channing, and Margaret Fuller.

1844 Daughter Una is born.

1846 Publishes *Mosses from the Old Manse.* Son Julian is born. Appointed Surveyor in the Salem Custom House with the help of Franklin Pierce and other Democrats.

1849 Removed from post as Surveyor after Whig, Zachary Taylor, is elected President. Mother dies. Begins *The Scarlet Letter.*

1850 Publishes *The Scarlet Letter.* Moves to Lenox, MA. Becomes friends with Herman Melville, who lives in nearby Pittsfield, who writes a laudatory review about Hawthorne.

1851 Publishes *The House of Seven Gables* and *A Wonder-Book for Girls and Boys.*

1852 Publishes *The Blithedale Romance,* which is based on his 1841 sojourn at Brook Farm. Publishes a campaign biography for Franklin Pierce. Purchases Bronson Alcott's former house, the Wayside, and moves his family back to Concord. His sister Louisa dies in a steamboat accident on the Hudson River.

1853 Publishes *Tanglewood Tales.* President Pierce appoints him American Consul in Liverpool. He moves his family to Liverpool in July.

1857 Resigns his Consulship

1858 Hawthorne family travels in France and Italy.

1859 Returns to England, when Una becomes seriously ill. Remains there for a year.

1860 Publishes *The Marble Faun.* Family returns to the Wayside in Concord. During the next four years he begins four romances, all of which remain unfinished at the time of his death.

1861 Publishes "Chiefly About War Matters," in the *Atlantic,* which becomes controversial, since it criticizes Lincoln's conduct in the Civil War.

1863 Publishes *Our Old Home,* about his impressions of England.

1864 During a carriage trip in New Hampshire with his friend, former President Franklin Pierce, he dies in his sleep. He is buried in Sleepy Hollow Cemetery.

[**Sources**: Bloom, H. *Modern Critical Views of Nathaniel Hawthorne,* Chelsea House, *1986.* Levine Robert, Editor, *The House of Seven Gables,*
Norton, *2006.* Pearce, Roy, Editor, *Hawthorne: Tales and Sketches,* Literary Classics, 1982.]

The Old Manse, home to Emersons and Hawthornes
Photo by Joseph L. Andrews, 2011.

The Wayside, formerly called Hillside, home to Alcotts and Hawthornes. Photo by Joseph L. Andrews, 2011.

Hawthorne Sites in Concord

The Old Manse

The Old Manse is one of the most interesting Concord authors' house to visit. It has close associations with both the Emerson family and with Hawthorne. Also, since it was owned by members of the Emerson-Ripley family for 169 years, it still houses much original furniture and many heirlooms, reminding us of the notable personages who lived there.

The Manse (Scottish for minister's house) was silent witness to two revolutions. Members of the Emerson family looked out of their second story windows and witnessed the nearby battle of the North Bridge, where colonial militia and minutemen clashed with British redcoats on April 19, 1775 to start the American Revolution. A little more than a half century later its families and their visitors were deeply involved in the intellectual revolution or American Renaissance, whose proponents declared intellectual independence from Europe.

The Manse was built in 1770, by Rev. William Emerson, Ralph Waldo Emerson's grandfather, who was then Concord's minister. He volunteered as Chaplain of Continental Army and died in 1776 of camp fever in Vermont after the army's march to Fort Ticonderoga. A new minister, Ezra Ripley, assumed the Concord pulpit in 1778 and would not relinquish it until sixty three years later, upon his death in 1841. William Emerson's widow, Phebe Bliss Emerson, married the new Concord minister in1780. Together with their children they continued to live in the Manse.

Although Ralph Waldo Emerson spent only one year, 1836, living in the Manse with his grandmother and step-grandfather, a year between his two marriages, it was an extremely important time for him. For it was here that he wrote his first essay, "Nature" which, according to Paul Brooks, was "for Emerson the ultimate source of strength, the root of his doctrine of self-reliance."

Nathaniel Hawthorne and his new wife Sophia moved into the Old Manse on their wedding day, July 9, 1842, for what was to be a blissful three year honeymoon. In his introduction to *Mosses from the Old Manse* he describes what visitors can still see today:

"Between two tall gateposts of rough-hewn stone. . . we beheld the gray front of the old parsonage. . . From these quiet windows the figures of passing travelers looked too remote and dim to disturb the sense of privacy. . ."

A month after his arrival he described his happiness:

"We seem to have been translated to the other state of being, without having passed through death. . . (The Manse) is two stories high, with a third story of attic chambers in the gambrel roof."

The newly-weds made the dreary interior brighter by painting walls, hanging pictures, and displaying flowers throughout the house. Hawthorne built a standing desk against a wall in his second floor study, so that he would not be distracted by the scenic views from its windows of the Concord River and the Old North Bridge. Today's visitors can appreciate original furniture, portraits, books, and kitchen hardware, which is unusual for a historic house.

Visitors today still enjoy the etchings which Nathaniel and Sophia scratched with Sophia's diamond ring on their window panes. The etchings on the window of the first floor dining room read: "Una Hawthorne stood on this windowsill January 22, 1845, while the trees were all glass chandeliers, a goodly show which she liked much tho only ten months old." The etchings on the second floor window are described in the beginning of this chapter.

In 1939, descendants of the Emerson-Ripley family sold the Old Manse to the Trustees of the Reservations, a Massachusetts conservation organization, which manages it today. The Old Manse is at 269 Monument Street in Concord. Guided tours are held daily from mid-April to October 31 and weekends only from November 1 to mid-April. Admission is charged. Details are found at *www.oldmanse.org*.

The Wayside

The Wayside was home to three famous Concord authors from three different eras.

The Alcott family lived there from 1845 to 1848 called their house Hillside. It was the setting for many of the Alcott family events that

Louisa May Alcott wrote about so warmly in *Little Women.* Bronson Alcott had renovated the original early eighteenth century, four roomed farm house by adding a wing on the west side, which contained a study and two small rooms. He built a bathhouse and woodhouse on the east side. When the Alcotts moved, it was only a few hundred yards down Lexington Road to Orchard House.

After moving at least seven times in the first ten years of their marriage, Nathaniel and Sophia Hawthorne, bolstered by earnings from several of his novels, were anxious to own a home of their own. So they bought the Wayside in 1852 from the Bronson Alcott for $1500 It was the only home ever owned by Nathaniel Hawthorne.

Less than a year later his friend President Franklin Pierce offered Hawthorne the position as Consul to Liverpool, England, which he gratefully accepted. On July 6, 1853, the ship Niagra sailed out of the Boston Harbor bound for England with the Hawthornes on board.

After seven years abroad in England and Italy, the Hawthornes returned to the Wayside in 1860. They undertook renovations of their old house. A second story bedroom was built above what had originally been Hawthorne's study and the study was changed into a library. Hawthorne also directed that a third story tower be built as his writing room, so as he stood at his standing desk he faced out the window, enabling him to view the Concord countryside below.

The renovations were a disaster. The new bedroom with its very high ceiling looked like a deep narrow box. The tower-study required difficult access up very steep stairs. It was very hot in summer and freezing in winter. Hawthorne used the study only in spring and fall, then not at all.

After Hawthorne's death in 1864, his son Julian and his family lived in the Wayside. His daughter Rose sold it to Daniel Lothrop in 1883. Lothrop's wife Harriet, (pen name Margaret Sidney) was the author of children's books. Her best known book was *The Five Little Peppers and How They Grew.* Harriet Lothrop was also the founder of Children of the American Revolution.

The Wayside, at 455 Lexington Road in Concord, is now owned and administered by the National Park Service as part of Minute Man National Historical Park. There is a nominal admission charge for guided tours. Detailed information can be found at *www.nps.gov/mima/wayside.*

Margaret Fuller

Chapter 5

Woman Interrupted. . .: Margaret Fuller

"Margaret Fuller?" "Who is she?" "I never heard of her."

These are the most frequent responses from both visitors to Concord and from resident Concordians who participate in my Concord Guides Walking Tour, when I ask them if they have read any thing by or about Margaret Fuller, or even if they ever heard of her.

By contrast, in 1902 a popular magazine poll to select twenty American women for a Hall of Fame for Great Americans in New York City, Margaret Fuller was voted sixth, behind Harriet Beecher Stowe, but ahead of Abigail Adams, Louisa May Alcott, and Betsy Ross.

So who *was* Margaret Fuller? And why do most people today know nothing about her?

Born Sarah Margaret Fuller in Cambridge in 1810, she was one of the few women to be judged to be an intellectual by Emerson, as well as a brilliant conversationalist, "the most entertaining in America." After her tragic death Emerson's grief-stricken reaction was: "I have lost in her my audience."

She was a pioneer feminist. Early on she demanded and practiced equal rights for women, while living in tradition-bound New England during an era when most women stayed at home and were denied equal rights. They were denied entrance into most professions, and did not have the right to vote or to enter universities. She broke the glass ceiling for women with a solid record of achievement firsts: the first editor of the *Dial,* the Concord journal of Transcendentalism; the first author of a book about the history of women in the nineteenth century; the first woman editor, then the first foreign combat correspondent for a major American newspaper.

So who *was* Margaret Fuller?

Margaret Fuller was born the first of nine children. Five of her brothers became lawyers.

She was a girl prodigy, fluent in Latin by age six and in Greek by age ten.

She was coached by her ambitious and demanding lawyer father, Timothy Fuller, who was to become a four-term Congressman. He urged her: "To excel at all things should be your constant aim; mediocrity is obscurity."

And yet, as a teen living in Groton, Massachusetts, she felt she was a misfit. In her "Autobiographical Romance" written in 1840, she described her childhood situation:

My father, all of whose feelings were now concentrated on me (after her sister's death), instructed me himself. . . I was put at once under discipline of considerable severity, and at the same time had a more than ordinary high standard presented to me. . . He hoped to make me heir of all he knew. . . At the beginning he made one great mistake. . . He thought to gain time by bringing forward the intellect as early as possible. Thus, I had tasks given to me, as many and various as the hours would allow, on subjects beyond my age . . . The consequence was a premature development of my brain, that made me a 'youthful prodigy' by day, and by night a victim of spectral illusions, nightmares and somnambulism. . . (and it) induced continual headache, weakness, and nervous affections, of all kinds.

William Henry Channing, later a Unitarian minister and a long time friend, described his first meeting with Margaret in a "Memoir," compiled after her death by her brother, R.H. Fuller in 1851:

My earliest recollection of Margaret is as a schoolmate of my sisters, in Boston. At that period she was considered a prodigy of talent and accomplishment; but a sad feeling prevailed, that she had been overtasked by her father, who wished to train her like a boy, and that she was paying the penalty for undue application, in nearsightedness, awkward manners, extravagant tendencies of thought, and a pedantic style of talk, that made her a butt for the ridicule of frivolous companions.

Some time later a less than impressed Channing commented that: "At first, her vivacity, decisive tone, downrightness, and contempt of conventional standards, continued to repel. She appeared too *intense* in expression, action, emphasis to be pleasing. . ." However, he soon recognized and then extolled a much more positive side of Fuller: "Soon I was charmed, unaware, with the sagacity of her sallies, the profound thoughts carelessly dropped by her on transient topics, the breadth and richness of culture manifested in her allusions or quotations, her easy comprehension of new views, her just discrimination, and, above all, her *truthfulness.* 'Truth at all cost,' was plainly her ruling maxim."

In 1836 Margaret visited Ralph Waldo Emerson's family in Concord for three weeks. Thus, she began a life long friendship with Emerson, who served as her mentor, her friend, and later her colleague. To support herself after her father's death, she worked as a teacher. She started working as an assistant to Bronson Alcott at his Temple School in Boston, which failed the next year. Margaret also taught literature and language to young women in the evening. The next year she began teaching in Providence, Rhode Island at the Greene Street School.

At age thirty she began Conversations for women in Boston, in which women were encouraged to think and act for themselves and to express themselves clearly. She was appointed Editor of the new Concord Transcendental journal, the *Dial.* In this role at which she worked for two years, she screened and edited contributions by Emerson, Henry Thoreau and many other New England Transcendentalists, as well as printing some of her own essays and poems.

In 1841 at age thirty one she joined Brook Farm, a utopian community outside of Boston. (In Nathaniel Hawthorne's 1852 novel *The Blithedale Romance,* based on his short sojourn there, Margaret appears as the lovely but tragic character Zenobia, who ends her life by drowning. Hawthorne's fictional description of Zenobia's demise is most likely a reflection of Margaret's sad fate, two years earlier.)

Margaret had a Transcendental epiphany. "I saw that there was no self; that selfishness was all folly." She then asked four key questions:

1. "How came I here?
2. How is it that I seem to be this (woman) Margaret Fuller?
3. What does it mean?
4. What shall I do about it?"

At age thirty four in 1844 she wrote her landmark *Women in the Nineteenth Century*, a pioneering feminist work, which explored both the many barriers to achievement that most women then faced, as well as their successes. Here she laments "the idea that Man, however imperfectly brought out, has been far more so than that of Woman, that she, the other half of the same thought, the other chamber of the heart of life, needs now to take her turn in the full pulsation, and that improvement to the daughters will best aid in the reformation of the sons of this age."

She conjures up a dialogue with an unnamed, imaginary male chauvinist, to support her call for equality between the sexes:

"Is it not enough,' cries the (imaginary) irritated trader, 'that [because of her plea for the abolition of slavery] you have done all you could to break up the national union, and thus destroy the prosperity of our country, but now you must be trying to break up family union, to take my wife away from the cradle and the kitchen hearth to vote at the polls, and preach from the pulpit. Of course, if she does such things, she cannot attend to those of her own sphere. She is happy enough as she is. She has more leisure than I have every means of improvement and indulgence.'"

"Have you asked her whether she was satisfied with these *indulgences*?"

". . .Am I not the head of my house?"

"You are not the head of your wife. God has given her a mind of her own. . ."

Critics of Fuller at the time carped that, since she was not married, Fuller was incapable of assessing the experiences of most American women. Sarcastically, they commented that Fuller might as well proclaim about women's potential: "Let them be sea captains!"

Fuller biographer, Megan Marshall, points out that Fuller repeatedly also called for equal treatment for men, as well as for women.

In 1844 Margaret moved to New York City after she accepted the positions of literary editor and journalist for Horace Greeley's *New York Daily Tribune*, an unusually important position for a woman at the time. Here she reviewed works of prominent writers, such as Poe, Longfellow and Emerson.

Here is Margaret reviewing favorably the second volume of essays by her mentor and colleague, Emerson: ". . .we may hail as an auspicious omen the influence Mr. Emerson has there [in New England] obtained, which is deep rooted, increasing, and, over the younger portion of the community, far greater than that of any other person.

His books are received there with a more ready intelligence than elsewhere because his range of personal experience and illustration applies to that region, partly because he has prepared the way for his books to be read by his great powers as a speaker."

If Rev. W.H. Channing faulted a younger Ms. Fuller for being too abstract, idealistic, and clueless as to what happened in the real world, her work as a muckraking and crusading journalist in New York City, put these shortcomings to rest. In an article which she wrote for the March 19, 1845 *Tribune* she exposed unsavory conditions of "the pauper establishments" that "admonish us of stern realities" in a dispatch headlined: "A Visit to Bellevue Alms House, to the Farm School, the Asylum for the Insane, and the Penitentiary on Blackwell's Island."

In her description of the denizens of the Alms House, she follows her observations of the inmates of city institutions with her ideas for improving their lot: "The want of suitable and sufficient employment is a great evil. The persons who find here either a permanent or temporary refuge have scarcely any occupation provided except to raise vegetables for the establishment, or prepare clothing for themselves. The men especially have a vagrant and degraded air and so much indolence must tend to confirm them in every bad habit. . . Employment of various kinds must be absolutely needed, if only to counteract the bad effects of such a position. Every establishment in aid to the poor should be planned with a view to their education."

At the Asylum for the Insane she reports: "But *here*, insanity appeared in its more stupid, wild, or despairing forms. They crouched in corners; they had no eye for the stranger, no heart for hope, no habitual expectation of light. Just as at the Farm School, where the children show by their unformed features and mechanical movements that they are treated by wholesale, so do these poor sufferers. It is an evil incident to public establishments, and which only a more intelligent public attention can obviate."

In 1846, at the age of thirty six she voyaged from New York City to Europe as a journalist for the *Tribune,* thus serving as the first American foreign correspondent. In England she interviewed William Wordsworth, Thomas Carlyle and in France she talked to George Sand. The next year she traveled to Italy, where she covered the Italian Revolution. She befriended Giuseppe Mazzini, the exiled leader of the Italian republican movement.

She met a republican fighter, an Italian noble, Giovanni Angelo Ossoli, in Rome. Together they shared a passion for a republican victory, and later for each other. They created a son together, out of wedlock, Angelo Ossoli (Nino). She may or may not become married to Giovanni Ossoli later. Her dispatches for the *Tribune* extolled the new Roman Republic that was proclaimed in February, 1849. During the following combat, the French siege of Rome, she volunteered as director of a hospital that treated soldiers wounded in battle. She also wrote an extensive history of the Italian revolution, which, most unfortunately, never saw the light of day.

In her final dispatch to the *Tribune* on February 13, 1850, after the Roman republic failed, a bitter, disillusioned Fuller wrote:

The barbarities of reaction have reached their height in the Kingdom of Naples and Sicily. Bad government grows daily worse in the Roman dominions. The French have degraded themselves enough to punish them even for the infamous treachery of which they were guilty. . . President, envoys, ministers, officers have all debased themselves, have told the most baseless lies, have bartered the fair fame. . . for a few days of brief authority, in vain. . . The seeds for a vast harvest of hatreds and contempt are sown over every inch of Roman ground. . .

After the Revolution failed, Fuller, Ossoli, and their young son, Nino, escaped from Rome to Florence. Then, because they could not afford passage on a passenger ship, they embarked on a merchant ship, which was heading to New York. Two months later on July 19, 1850 during a fierce storm their ship struck a reef off the coast of Fire Island. Tragically, although they were in eye sight of the nearby shore, all three were drowned along with many of the crew. Henry Thoreau was delegated to travel to the Fire Island beach closest to the wreck, but found nothing of value. Baby Nino's body washed ashore, and was buried in a trunk on the beach by sailors. However, no trace of Fuller or Ossoli was ever found. Fuller's manuscript about the Italian Revolution was also lost to the stormy ocean and never retrieved.

Margaret Fuller was only forty when she perished.

Fuller biographer, Megan Marshall, postulates that the reason Fuller is not better known today for her pioneering exploits may be because, when she perished in 1850, it was two years before the Seneca Falls convocation that jumpstarted the movement for women's rights in America. (Fuller had been invited to participate but, tragically, was unable to.)

So who was this remarkable, brilliant woman, whose life and pioneering achievements were tragically cut so short?

Sarah Margaret Fuller.

And how much more might she have achieved, if she had lived out a normal life span?

Probably very much more.

And how many Americans today have ever heard about this extraordinary lady?

Very, very few.

Many, many too few.

Some Concluding Thoughts

We have looked closely, but separately and individually, at the different lives and unique creations of five of the most prominent nineteenth century Concord (and American) authors. What can we say about them as a group?

How important are their differences? Their similarities? How relevant are they today?

An overview of their lives reveals important differences. Henry D. Thoreau, the only native Concordian of the group, was a vigorous outdoorsman and an enthusiastic naturalist. He spent many hours every day walking through Concord's forests, over its meadows and farmlands and along its ponds and rivers, continually observing changing seasonal details of animal and plant life. Then he wrote his carefully worded field observations in his journal, which later became the basis for his lectures and later his essays and books like *Walden.* He was a lifelong bachelor with a penchant for living a solo life. According to Thoreau, he traveled much, but mostly within the borders of his home town, Concord.

Thoreau's prose is often graphic and memorable. His sentences and paragraphs can be understood on several levels, as vivid descriptions of Concord's flora and fauna or as seasonal changes in the appearance of his favorite spots in Concord, and often simultaneously on a spiritual level, whose significance lies behind and beyond his immediate natural descriptions.

Ralph Waldo Emerson, descendent of a long line of Concord ministers, tried being a minister himself, then a teacher. Not enjoying either occupation and having inherited money from the estate of his late first wife Ellen, he was free to pursue life as a philosopher, poet, lecturer, and essayist. Unlike Thoreau, Emerson was a family man with four children by his second wife, whom he called Lidian. Also, unlike Thoreau, Emerson was a social man, the center of a coterie of New England intellectuals, many of them newly minted Transcendentalists, who were drawn to Concord mostly by Emerson's intellectual, conversational, social (and sometimes monetary) magnetism. Emerson spent much more time indoors than Thoreau, the keen outdoor saunterer. In his role as a lecturer on a very wide range of topics Emerson traveled widely, both in New England and throughout America.

Of the group, Emerson was by far the most famous celebrity, much read, much heard and, much quoted in his life time. . . and beyond. The basic unit of expression in Emerson's essays was the sentence. Each of his sentences is packed with Emerson's beliefs and often with philosophical content, usually on a more abstract and less observational and less witty level than Thoreau.

Louisa May Alcott was a hardworking woman, writing obscurely for up to fourteen hours a day before her breakthrough, semi-autobiographical novel *Little Women,* based on her own childhood, growing up with three sisters, a loving mother, and an impecunious father. Like Thoreau, on whom she had a crush as a girl (along with Emerson), she remained unmarried, preferring to "paddle her own canoe." Her family meant the world to her and she devoted most of the money she earned from writing to help support them. In her life Louisa worked as a teacher, a seamstress, an actress, a nanny and a maid, as well as a writer. She incorporated her work experiences into her novels. For her time she was truly a pioneering feminist, in life as well as in literature.

Nathaniel Hawthorne was by birth and temperament a native of Salem, thus (as today's Concordians will point out) not a true man of Concord, although he lived in Concord on three separate occasions for a total of eight years. He married late in life to a fellow native of Salem, Sophia Peabody. After being a morose recluse in his twenties, he became a much happier family man, enjoying his wife and three children in his thirties and beyond. His best novels, *The Scarlet Letter* and *The House of Seven Gables* and many of his short stories looked backward to earlier, darker Puritan times and were concerned with the effects of sin, guilt shame, punishment and repentance on past generations of New Englanders, including his own ancestors, as well as their long term effects on current generations. In comparison with Thoreau, Emerson, and Fuller, Hawthorne was by far the most psychological writer of the Concord authors, frequently analyzing the underlying hidden motivations of his characters.

Margaret Fuller was also only an episodic resident of Concord. Much like Thoreau and Alcott, she was single and childless until two years before her tragic shipwreck drowning death. Her dispatches as a journalist covered wider geographical and topical subjects than any other Concord author but Hawthorne. Her varied first hand descriptions included prisoners in New York, Indians in the Midwest, and revolutionaries in Italy. Her seminal book, *Women in the Nineteenth Century,* established her as an outspoken, unapologetic feminist. She also supported equal rights for men from all levels of society. Fuller's prose in her dispatches are those of a journalist, but an opinionated one, passing judgment on the events she observed and then prescribing remedies to correct difficult social problems. .

Just how relevant are these famous nineteenth century Concord authors today?

As I pointed out, when I was in high school and college in the 1950's, Emerson was generally recognized as the man to read. Both in school and outside, his essays, such as "Self Reliance" provided guideposts to live by for generations of Americans. (The one book that Robert Frost usually carried with him was a collection of Emerson's essays.) However, in the turbulent 1960's Thoreau, and especially his writings about civil disobedience, became more relevant and decidedly more popular than Emerson among younger readers. *The Night Thoreau Spent in Jail* was a timely play then, because it granted permission for civil disobedience to opponents of the war in Viet Nam.

Today Thoreau is increasingly appreciated also for his role as a scientific observer of natural phenomena. As he wrote in his journal in 1851, "The question is not what you look at, but what you see." His precise observations and recording of the spring dates that specific plants and birds returned to Walden Pond are used now by ecologists as a baseline to compare similar arrivals today. The fact that many plants and animals return roughly two to three weeks earlier than they did in the 1850's is thought by many scientists to provide evidence of global warming on the environment.

Louisa May Alcott's progression from writing potboilers under a male pseudonym to writing popular novels under her own name that still resonate with readers today provides evidence of the real progress that women started to make in the mid-nineteenth century. Similarly, as Margaret Fuller becomes better known through recent biographies, her achievements as a pioneering woman essayist and journalist are becoming better appreciated by women and men alike.

And what do we make of Hawthorne and his melancholy novels and short stories? They continue to be assigned by both high school teachers and college professors. His two most widely read novels, *The Scarlet Letter* and *The House of Seven Gables,* are often viewed as windows on New England's Puritan history from the 1600's and onward. However, his savvy psychological insights into his characters' motivations and their resulting actions are still relevant and are increasingly appreciated by his readers today.

As my last chapter, Literary Concord Today," reveals, prominent current Concord authors admit to being very influenced by their Concord predecessors. The five mid-nineteenth century Concord authors that I have profiled in this book still continue to be read both for the distinct insights that they reveal about the lives and beliefs of their contemporaries and for the enjoyment that they continue to bring to their many readers today.

Appendix A

Transcendentalism

Among the renowned nineteenth century Concord authors, essayists, poets, and lecturers, Ralph Waldo Emerson, Henry Thoreau, and Margaret Fuller were self-proclaimed Transcendentalists. Writers of fiction, novelists, and short story tellers Louisa May Alcott and Nathaniel Hawthorne were not.

For Emerson and other Transcendentalists "revelation was supplanted by intuition, soul by self, and God by the over-soul or more broadly by nature," according to literary critics Wesley Mott and David Robinson. Both Emerson and Thoreau championed the individual, self-reliance, and innovation.

What is Transcendentalism? Writers and literary critics answer this question in many different ways. It might be easier to state what Transcendentalism was not. It was not a religion. It was not a specific philosophy marked by a manifesto or by clearly stated principles. It was not a formal organization characterized by specific rules of membership.

"Transcendentalism was a movement in New England in the 1830's and 1840's which resulted in theological innovation and in literary experimentation," according to Mott and Robinson. To understand this fully one must see it in the perspective of Protestant religious evolution in America. Puritans, who settled New England in the 1600's, had firm Calvinist beliefs: that man was born in sin. Salvation was predestined and was available only to a pre-chosen few (the select) by God's grace, irrespective of how good or bad the life that men lived.

Historically, across generations, most New England Puritans became Congregationalists, who rejected the Calvinist doctrine of predestination. Then many Congregationalists became Unitarians, who accepted a greater diversity of beliefs and believed in the unity, rather than in the trinity of God. Transcendentalists, mostly "Harvard Brahmins," were "all young Unitarians, who. . . revolted against Unitarianism," which was "indigenous to eastern Massachusetts," according to Perry Miller, author of *The Transcendentalists.* Their protest was an "assertion that men of New England, and so in the New World, will refuse to live by sobriety and decorum alone, that there are requirements of the soul which demand satisfaction even though respectability must be defied and shocked." It was, Miller continues, "a protest of the human spirit against emotional starvation." Transcendentalism "differed from its New England background of Calvinism in celebrating not the omnipotence of God, but the limitless possibilities of the self," observes literary historian Norman Foerster.

Unitarianism was too doctrinaire and overly authoritative for Emerson, who resigned from his Unitarian pulpit in 1832 and published "Nature" in 1836. In this essay and in his Harvard Divinity School address in 1838 he challenged the authority of both the Church and the Bible. He felt that society and its institutions, such as organized religion and political parties, corrupted the purity of the individual. He believed that each individual remained purer and truer to himself when he communicated directly with God (or the Oversoul or Nature, terms which Emerson used almost synonymously). This world view is expressed in the epitaph Emerson wrote for his own tombstone:

"The passive master lent his hand
To the vast soul which o'er him planned."

Emerson, and Thoreau as well, believed that each individual becomes the best he can become when he remains self-reliant and independent.

The term Transcendentalism was originally coined by Immanuel Kant (1724–1804), a German philosopher. Emerson in his essay "The Transcendentalist" (1843), points out that human thinkers are "divided into two sects, materialists and idealists; the first class founded on experience, the second on consciousness; the first class beginning to think on the data of the senses, the second class perceives that the senses are not final and say the senses give us representations of things, but what are the things themselves, they cannot tell."

Thoreau, on the other hand, insisted on a sense of mystery, declaring that "we require that all things be mysterious and unexplorable, that land and sea be infinitely wild, unsurveyed and unfathomed by us, because unfathomable." Thoreau in his journal famously labeled himself, "a Transcendentalist, a mystic and a natural philosopher to boot."

Postscript

Literary Concord Today

The rich tradition of Concord as an active literary town persists today, over 170 years after its literary apogee. A variety of authors make their homes here today. It is rumored that over 400 active authors write from their Concord homes today, in a town where the current population is approximately 16,000. This may well be, but is impossible to confirm, though amazing if it is true.

Some of the better known contemporary authors who are current residents of Concord include Doris Kearns Goodwin and her husband Richard Goodwin, Gregory Maguire, Robert Coles, Alan Lightman, Kate Flora, David Sibley, Peter Alden, and John Mitchell.

Doris Kearns Goodwin is a prominent Presidential historian, who has written biographies about Lyndon Johnson, Franklin and Eleanor Roosevelt, the Kennedy family, Lincoln and his cabinet and most recently about Presidents Teddy Roosevelt and William Howard Taft. In between these serious Presidential histories, she wrote a delightful book about growing up as a Brooklyn Dodgers baseball fan. She is also well known for her TV commentary about current Presidents and about modern politics, as viewed from the perspective of past American Presidential history. Her husband Richard Goodwin was an advisor and speech writer for President John F. Kennedy and is an essayist and playwright. A recently produced Richard Goodwin play highlighted the conflict between Galileo and the Catholic Church.

Robert Coles, a physician, has explored the effects of war and trauma on children in many parts of the world. Gregory Maguire's novel *Wicked,* based on the Wizard of Oz, provided the basis for a hugely successful, long running Broadway musical of the same name.

Alan Lightman, is both an astrophysicist at M.I.T. and a novelist. For many years he was the only M.I.T. professor to hold dual appointments, both in science and in humanities departments. He writes about the interstices between science and human behavior. *Einstein's Dreams* is an exploration about the effect of the laws of modern quantum physics on the every day lives of villagers today. In an interview Professor Lightman stated that he has a wonderful feeling living in a town with such a rich literary heritage, where he can share perspectives with a "community of writers, like Doris Kearns Goodwin and Gregory Maguire." He says that several of his essays, such as "A Sense of the Mysterious" and "Prisoners of the Wired World," were inspired by Thoreau. In these essays he expresses regrets that modern technology separates so many people from the daily immediate contact with nature, as was similarly described by Thoreau.

Kate Flora is a mystery writer. Many of her thrillers are set in Maine, where her heroine, sleuth Thea Kozak, solves violent crimes. Ms. Flora considers it "a real privilege to be a Concord author, because people here care about writers and writing, which is not true elsewhere. Here they talk about books in parking lots and in the drug store and take great pride in the Concord literary tradition."

Peter Alden, a native of Concord, whose roots go back to the Mayflower, is an avid birder. He writes field guides about indigenous plants and animals for the national Audubon Society, when he isn't leading field trips to Central and South America. He considers himself the "spiritual descendent of Henry Thoreau, when I go a-naturing." Thoreau's clear descriptions of Concord's natural sites stimulated him to explore when he was a boy, "to find new places I didn't know about, to find a great blue heron or hawk, or to get across a flooded brook." He also feels a strong affinity to Emerson, "who was less of a loner, who enjoyed travel and giving lectures."

David Sibley is best known for his meticulously illustrated books, which serve as field guides for identifying and learning about North American birds and trees. John Mitchell, a resident of nearby Littleton, the Editor of the Massachusetts Audubon Society magazine *Sanctuary,* is the author of several books extolling New Englanders' sense of place and the importance of supporting conservation, as he does in his book *Walking Towards Walden.*

Concord's present day ambience is very supportive of authors. The Concord Free Public Library is the destination of many writers and academic researchers from all over the world, as well as from Concord, who research Concord's earlier literary, historic, and environmental heritage. Its Special Collections encompasses many of the original publications of Concord's nineteenth century literati, including Emerson, Thoreau, the Alcotts, Hawthorne and Fuller. It's Curator, Leslie Perrin Wilson, is an author in her own right, having recently updated Allen French's local history, *Historic Concord and the Lexington Fight* by appending a new section, describing significant historic and literary sites to visit in Concord.

The Walden Woods Project in nearby Lincoln, in its the Don Henley Library houses extensive collections of original Thoreau books, many of them belonging to the Thoreau Society collection. Its Curator, Jeffrey Cramer has written several books about Thoreau, including *The Quotable Thoreau*, a compendium of his pithiest quotes.

Concord still has lively independent book shops, which unfortunately recently have vanished from many nearby towns (including Lexington.) The Concord Book Shop on Main Street has a complete section of books by past and current Concord authors, as well as a busy schedule of book talks and signings by recently published authors. The Barrow Book Store off of Main Street sells used books, many by major Concord authors. The Thoreau Society Book Store at Walden Pond stocks a myriad of books by and about Concord's classic authors, especially Thoreau and Emerson. Barefoot Books in the Concord Depot area both publishes and sells original books for children.

Concord hosts a well attended Festival of Authors each autumn. Authors read from, then sell and sign their new books at a variety of local venues, including libraries, book stores, schools, churches, and a synagogue. The Festival's founder and organizer, Rob Mitchell, firmly believes that good books have not just a past and present, but also—despite, or perhaps in addition to the rise of e-books—a strong future, both in Concord and well beyond.

The Concord Museum hosts an annual Holiday event where trees are decorated with themes from popular children's books. The Museum also presents many exhibits about major Concord authors and houses

Emerson's original study, as was described in an earlier chapter, as well as Thoreau possessions such as his flute and telescope..

Concord also hosts meetings of the Thoreau Society around Thoreau's July 12 birthday. The Thoreau Society is an unusual amalgam of literary academics and amateur literary aficionados from all over the world, who gather annually to give and to listen to presentations about various aspects of Thoreau's life and letters and to visit many of Concord's unique literary sites. The Emerson Society and the Thoreau Society share common meeting dates and are also both responsible for a full slate of literary talks and symposiums throughout the year. The First Parish Church sponsors a Transcendentalist Council, which also organizes literary talks and discussions about Concord's classic authors.

The Concord authors' houses sponsor many historic events and symposiums about their former inhabitants. For example, The Alcotts' Orchard House hosts a Christmas reception where costumed actors portraying Bronson Alcott and his wife and four daughters play music, dance, have a party, and generally re-enact events both from the Alcott family's life and from *Little Women.* At the Old Manse actors portray the Emerson and Hawthorne families, who are visited annually by uniformed Union Army troop re-enactors who announce that they are about to march off to combat in the Civil War, just as many Concord young men, who were Union Army volunteers, actually did so many generations ago.

[Appendix B]

Concord Area Web Sites

Alcotts' Orchard House	*www.louisamayalcott.org*
Best Western Hotel	*www.bestwesternconcord.com*
Colonial Inn	*www.concordscolonialinn.com*
Chamber of Commerce/ Visitors' Center	*www. concordchamberofcommerce.org*
Concord Guides Walking Tours	*www.concordguides.com*
Concord Press (Guide Books)	*www.concordpress.com*
Concord: Official Town web site	*www.concordnet.org*
Concord Book Shop	*www.concordbookshop.org*
Concord Museum	*www.concordmuseum.org*
Concord Community web site	*www.concordma.com*
Emerson House	*www.rwe.org*
Festival of Authors	*www.concordfestivalofauthors. com*
Great Meadows Wildlife Refuge	*www.fws.gov/gov/northeast/ greatmeadows*
Greater Boston Convention And Visitors' Bureau	*www.bostonusa.com*

Greater Merrimack Valley Convention & Visitors' Bureau	***www.merrimackvalley.org***
Hawthorne Inn	***www.concordmass.com***
Liberty Ride: Lexington-Concord	***www.libertyride.us***
Library, Concord Free Public	***www.concordlibrary.org***
Library Network, Minute Man	***www.min.lib.ma.us/***
MA Office Travel & Tourism	***www.mass-vacation.com***
Minute Man National	***www.nps.gov/mima***
Historical Park North Bridge Inn	***www.northbridgeinn.com***
North Bridge Visitors' Center	***www.nps.gov/mima***
Old Manse	***www.oldmanse.org***
Thoreau Society	***www.thoreausociety.org***
"Bookshop @ Walden Pond	***www.shopatwaldenpond.org***
Thoreau Farm/ Birth House	***www.thoreaufarm.org***
Walden Pond State Reservation	***www.massgov/dcr***
Walden Woods Project/ Thoreau Institute	***www.walden.org***
Wayside	***www.nps.gov/mima/wayside***

ACKNOWLEDGMENTS

I would like to thank Professor Leo Marx, formerly of the English and American Studies departments at Amherst College, who was my English Honors thesis advisor at Amherst in 1959, for first kindling my interest in American literature and in especially about the major Concord authors. Prof. Marx is now Senior Lecturer and Kenan Professor of American Cultural History, Emeritus at M.I.T. I am also grateful to Tom Blanding, an independent Thoreau scholar in Concord and a former President of the Thoreau Society. After I moved to Concord in 1995 I took many stimulating courses and seminars about Henry Thoreau and his writings with Tom.

I would like to thank both Richard Smith, who frequently portrays Henry Thoreau and is a sales associate at the Thoreau Society book shop at Walden Pond, and Michael Frederick, the Director of the Thoreau Society, for their careful review of my chapter on Thoreau. Thanks also to Michael Frederick for his stimulating course on *Walden* in 2014. Thanks also goes to Jeffrey Cramer, the Curator of the Don Henley Library at the Walden Woods Project, for helping me locate background material about Thoreau.

I also extend thanks to Jayne Gordon, formerly Director of the Thoreau Society and now Director of Education for the Massachusetts Historical Society, for reviewing my chapters on both Thoreau and Emerson and to Charles Phillips, convener of the Emerson book group, for reviewing my chapter on Emerson. Jan Turnquist, Director of the Alcott Family's Orchard House, was kind enough to carefully review my chapter on Louisa May Alcott. I would also like to thank Tom Beardsley, Director of the Old Manse, for reviewing my chapter about Nathaniel Hawthorne. Leslie Perrin Wilson, Director of Special

Collections, and other staff members of the Concord Free Public Library were most helpful to me in my research into books by and about the major Concord authors.

My thanks also go to members of my family, particularly to my daughter Sara K. Andrews and to my niece Barbara D. Paxton, for their hard work and diligence as my excellent chapter editors. I am also grateful to my sister Dale Andrews Eldridge, to my late sister Lynn Andrews Kotzen, to my daughter Jennifer Andrews Burke, and my son Joe Andrews for their helpful suggestions. I am indebted also to Sophie Wadsworth, Director of the Concord Nature Connection, to Elaine Inker and to Natasha Shabat, Carol Coutrier, Carol Connor, Elizabeth Goldring, and to Anne Gray for reviewing various chapters of my book. I am also indebted to Stephen Sackowich of Sackowich Design in Lincoln for his help in designing this book's covers and for other graphic designs in the book.

I have attended many lectures and seminars over the past twenty years by preeminent Thoreau scholars at meetings of the Thoreau Society in Concord, as well as about other Concord authors at book signings and lectures. I am particularly thankful to Professor Robert Richardson of Wesleyan University for his many insightful lectures on both Thoreau and Emerson; to Professor Robert Gross of the University of Connecticut for seminars on Transcendentalism and on historic Concord; to Prof. Joel Myerson of the University of South Carolina for sessions on Transcendentalism; to Professors E.O. Wilson of Harvard University and Richard Primack of Boston University for talks assessing the relevance of Thoreau's nature descriptions to modern biology, and to Professor John Matteson of John Jay College for his talks and books about the Alcott family and about Margaret Fuller. My thanks also goes to Megan Marshall, biographer of Margaret Fuller and the Peabody sisters of Salem, for her talks and books about these outstanding women.

Bibliography

By and About Henry Thoreau

Andrews, Joseph L. "Town Officials Should Lead Efforts to Save Thoreau's Birthplace," *Concord Journal,* June 8, 1996; *Middlesex News,* June 26, 1996.

______. "Sauntering Along Thoreau's Path," *Concord Journal.* August 9, 2007;

"Sauntering Along Thoreau's Path on Brister's Hill," *TSB 261:* Winter, 2008.

______. "There's Many Reasons to Swim at Walden." *Concord Journal:* Sept. 11, 2008: 9; "Swimming in Walden Pond: Thoreau's Way and Today." *TSB 274:* Spring, 2011: 1-3

Blanding, Tom. "Lectures on *Walden; or, Life in the Woods."* Concord: February-April,1998.

Concord Museum. "Early Spring: Henry Thoreau and Climate Change," exhibit. 2013.

Emerson, Edward W. *Henry Thoreau As Remembered by a Young Friend.* Concord: Thoreau Foundation, 1968.

"Fire in the Woods." Concord Freeman, May 3, 1844.

Frederick, Mike. Lectures on *Walden.* Concord: November, 2013.

Marx, Leo. "Relevance of *Walden.*" Lecture to Thoreau Society. Concord: July 10, 2004.

______. "Lectures on 19th Century American Literature," Amherst, MA.Amherst College, 1958-1959.

Meltzer, Milton and Harding, Walter. *A Thoreau Profile.* Concord: Thoreau Fdn,: 1962.

Pipkin, John. *Woodsburner.* New York: Anchor House, 2009.

Porter, Eliot.[Photos] *"In Wildness is the Preservation of the World."* San Francisco: Sierra Club, 1962.

Primack, Richard. "Thoreau and Timing of the Seasons," Talk to the Thoreau Society, Concord: July 12, 2012.

Richardson, Robert D. *Henry Thoreau: A Life of the Mind.* Berkeley: California UP, 1986.

Robbins, Roland W. *Discovery at Walden.* Stoneham: Barnstead, 1947.

Smith, Tim. *Thoreau's Walden.* Charleston: Arcadia, 2002.

Thoreau, Henry D. *Cape Cod.* New York: Bramhill, 1951.

______. *Civil Disobedience and Other Essays.* New York: Dover, 1993.

______. *Faith in a Seed: The Dispersion of Seeds and Other Natural History Writings.* Bradley P. Dean, ed. Washington, D.C.: Island Press, 1993.

______. *The Heart of Thoreau's Journals.* Odell Shepard, ed. New York: Dover, 1961.

______. *The Maine Woods.* New York: Apollo, 1966.

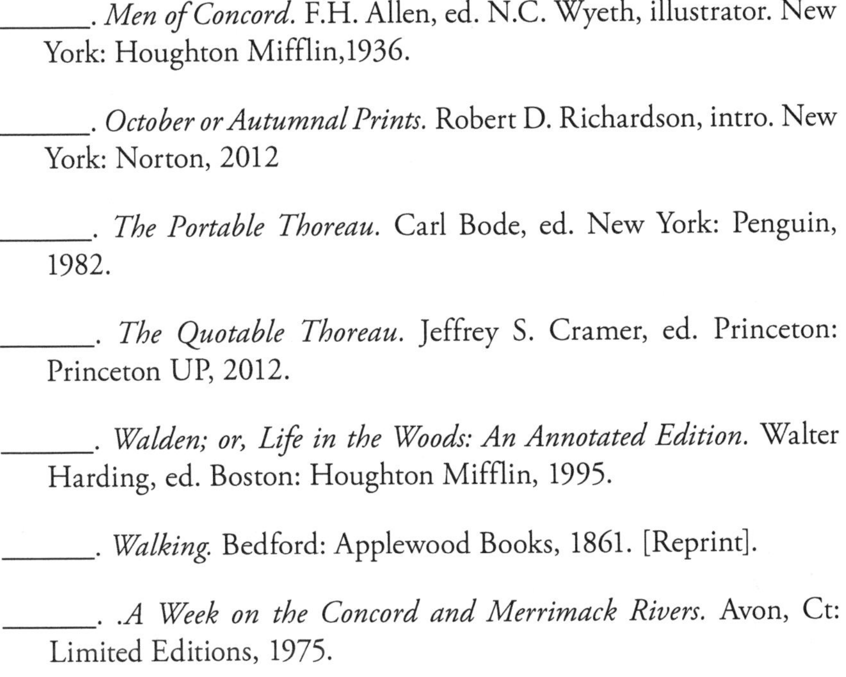

______. *Men of Concord.* F.H. Allen, ed. N.C. Wyeth, illustrator. New York: Houghton Mifflin,1936.

______. *October or Autumnal Prints.* Robert D. Richardson, intro. New York: Norton, 2012

______. *The Portable Thoreau.* Carl Bode, ed. New York: Penguin, 1982.

______. *The Quotable Thoreau.* Jeffrey S. Cramer, ed. Princeton: Princeton UP, 2012.

______. *Walden; or, Life in the Woods: An Annotated Edition.* Walter Harding, ed. Boston: Houghton Mifflin, 1995.

______. *Walking.* Bedford: Applewood Books, 1861. [Reprint].

______. .*A Week on the Concord and Merrimack Rivers.* Avon, Ct: Limited Editions, 1975.

Wilson, E.O. "Address to the Thoreau Society." Concord: July, 2012.

Wawrzonek, John. [Photos] *The Illuminated Walden: In the Footsteps of Thoreau.* New York: Barnes and Noble, 2002.

"Woods Burner." *Boston Globe* April 12, 2009

By and About Ralph Waldo Emerson

Baker, Carlos. *Emerson Among the Eccentrics.* New York: Penguin, 1996.

Buell, Lawrence. *Emerson.* Cambridge: Harvard UP, 2003.

Emerson, Ralph Waldo. *Essays: First and Second Series.* Mt Vernon: Peter Pauper Press.

______. *The Heart of Emerson's Essays.* Bliss Perry, ed. Boston: Houghton Mifflin, 1933.

______. *Essays and Lectures.* New York: Library of America, 1983

______. *An Emerson Garland: Twelve Poems of Ralph Waldo Emerson Set to Hymn Tunes.* Concord: Unitarian Universalist Association, for the Emerson Bicentennial, 2003.

______. *Emerson in His Journals.* Joel Porte, ed. Cambridge: Belknap Press, 1982.

______. The Dial: A Magazine for Literature, Philosophy, Religion. Boston: Weeks, 1840–44

______. *The Collected Works of RWE.* Cambridge: Belknap Press, 1971–.

______. *The Concord Hymn and Other Poems.* Toronto: Dover, 1996

Richardson, Robert D. *Emerson: The Mind on Fire.* Berkeley: California UP, 1995.

______. *First We Read and Then We Write: Emerson on the Creative Process.* Iowa City: Iowa UP, 2009.

Schulman, J. Frank. *Emerson and the Ministry.* Houston: Emerson Church, 1983

Sciaiabba, George. "America's Oracle." [book review} Boston Globe, June 1, 2003

"The Emerson House in Concord." Concord: R.W. Emerson Memorial Assoc., 2003.

Wilson, Leslie. *Thoreau, Emerson and Transcendentalism.* Foster City: IDG Books, Cliffsnotes c. 2000.

______. "Ralph Waldo Emerson's Roots, Inspiration Ran Deep in Concord." Concord Journal, January 30, 2003.

By and About Louisa May Alcott

Alcott, Louisa May. *Little Women.* New York: Simon & Shuster Pocket Books, 2003.

______. *Transcendental Wild Oats.* Harvard MA: Harvard Common Press, 1981.

______. *Hospital Sketches.* Bedford, MA: Applewood Books, 1993.

______. *Work: A Story of Experience.* Joy Kassan, Ed. Thorndike, ME: G.K.Hall, 2001.

______. *Journal Excerpts in* Cheney, Ednah D. *Louisa May Alcott: Her Life, Letters and Journals.* Boson: Little Brown, 1889.

______. *A Double Life: Recently Discovered Thrillers of Louisa May Alcott.* Intro., M. Stern. Boston: Little Brown, 1988.

______. *The Early Short Stories of Louisa May Alcott: 1852-1860.* Intro, Monika Elbert. New York: Ironwood Press, 2000.

______. *The Concord Centennial: The Town Delegation; Unofficial Incidents Overlooked by the Reporters.* [reprint.] Concord: The Women's Journal, May 1, 1875.

______. *Louisa May Alcott Unmasked.: Collected Thrillers.* M. Stern, Ed. Boston: Northeastern UP, 1995.

______. *Moods.* New Brunswick, N.J.: Rutgers UP, 1991.

Brooks, Geraldine. *March.* New York: Viking, 2005.

Cheever, Susan. *Louisa May Alcott: A Personal Biography.* New York: Simon & Shuster, 2010

Cheney, Ednah D. *Louisa May Alcott: Her Life, Letters and Journals,* Boston: Little Brown, 1889.

Dapper, Julie. *The Concord School of Philosophy: A Short History.* Concord, LMA Memorial Association, 1991.

LaPlante, Eve. *Marmee & Louisa: The Untold Story of Louisa May Alcott and Her Mother.* Free Press, 2012.

Macdonald, Ruth K. *Louisa May Alcott.* Boston: Twane, 1983.

Mattison, John. *Eden's Outcasts: The Story of Louisa May Alcott and Her Father.* New York: W.W. Norton, 2008.

Meigs, Cornelia. *Invincible Louisa.* Boston: Little Brown, 1968.

Saxton, Martha. *Louisa May Alcott: A Modern Biography.* New York: Farrar, Strauss,1995.

Smith, David F. *Little Women* [play/program.] Concord: Concord Players, April 27– May 13, 2012

Stern, Madeleine B. *Louisa May Alcott: A Biography.* Boston: Northeastern UP, 1999.

______. Ed. *Critical Essays on Louisa May Alcott.* Boston: C.K. Hall, 1984.

By and About Nathaniel Hawthorne

Bloom, Harold Ed. and Kaul, K.N. *Modern Critical Views of Nathaniel Hawthorne.* New York: Chelsea House, 1986.

Brooks, Paul. *The Old Manse and the People Who Lived There.* Carlisle, MA: Applewood Books, 1983.

Gordon, Jayne. "Mourning at Hawthorne's Funeral." Talk to the Friends of Sleepy Hollow Cemetery. Concord: March 29, 2014.

Hawthorne, Nathaniel. *Tales and Sketches.* New York: Library of America, 1982.

______. *Novels.* New York: Library of America, 1983.

______. *The House of Seven Gables.* Robert S. Levine, Ed. New York: Norton, 2006.

______. *Hawthorne's Short Stories.* New York: Dodd Mead, 1962.

______. *Young Goodman Brown and Other Short Stories.* Mineola, N.Y.: Dover, 1992.

______. *The Scarlet Letter.* New York: Hyperion, 1995.

______. *Selected Short Stories of Nathaniel Hawthorne.* Alfred Kazin, Ed. New York, Random House, 1983.

______. *Selections from Mosses From An Old Manse.* Carlisle, MA: Applewood Books, 2012.

Reynolds, Larry J., Ed. *A Historical Guide to Nathaniel Hawthorne.* New York, Oxford, 2001.

Sciacca, Jane and Derry, Robert. *The Wayside and the People Who Made It.* Concord: Eastern National, 1997.

Wagenecht, Edward. *Nathaniel Hawthorne: The Man, His Tales and Romances.* New York: Continuum, 1989.

By and About Margaret Fuller

Andrews, Barry. *The Spirit leads: Margaret Fuller in Her Own Words.* Skinner House, 2010.

Fuller, Margaret. *Women in the Nineteenth Century.* New York: Norton, 1971.

______. *The Dial.* M.F. Ed. Boston: Weeks Jordan, 1840–1842.

______. *The Essential Margaret Fuller.* Jeffrey Steele, Ed. New Brunswick, NJ: Rutgers UP, 1992.

______. *Love Letters of Margaret Fuller, 1845–6.* New York: Greenwood Press, 1969.

______. *Journal, 1842.* http://pds.lib.harvard.edu/pds/view/257335?n=10013&s=6.

______. *"My Heart is a Large Kingdom Selected Letters by Margaret Fuller."* Robert Hudspeth, Ed. Ithaca: Cornell UP, 2001.

______. *Memoirs of Margaret Fuller.* Ralph Waldo Emerson, Ed. Boston: Roberts Bros., 1859.

______. *Memoirs of Margaret Fuller Ossoli. Vol. II.* R.F. Fuller, Ed. Boston: Phillips, Sampson & Co., 1851. [Digital Reprint by the University of Michigan Library.]

Kornfield, Eve. *Margaret Fuller: A Brief Biography.* Boston: Bedford Books, 1987.

Loviglio, Lorraine. *Who Was Margaret Fuller?* Concord: Transcendentalism Council, 2010.

Marshall, Megan. *Margaret Fuller: A New American Life.* New York: Houghton Mifflin, 2013

Mattison, John. *The Lives of Margaret Fuller.* New York: W.W. Norton, 2012.

Miller, Perry. *Margaret Fuller: American Romantic: A Selection of Writings and Correspondence.* Garden City, NY: Doubleday, 1963.

Watson, David. *Margaret Fuller.* New York: Berg, 1988.

About Literary New England and Concord

Andrews, Joseph L. *Literary Concord: Visiting with Emerson, Thoreau, Alcott and Hawthorne.* Concord: Concord Guides & Press, 1996

Brooks, Paul. *The Old Manse and the People Who Lived There.* Carlisle, MA: Applewood Books, 1983.

Brooks, Van Wyck. *The Flowering of New England: 1815–1865.* New York, E.P. Dutton, 1936.

Brooks, Van Wyck and Bettmann, Otto. *Our Literary Heritage: A Pictorial History of the Writer in America.* New York: Dutton, 1956.

Burke, Michelle. *The Ideals Guide to Literary Places in the U.S.* Nashville:Ideals, 1998.

Cheever, Susan. *American Bloomsbury.* New York: Simon & Schuster, 2006.

Commager, Henry Steele. *The American Mind.* New Haven: Yale UP, 1950.

Felton, Todd. *A Journey Into the Trascendentalist's New England.* Berkeley: Roaring Forties Press, 2006.

Foerster, Norman, Ed. *American Poetry and Prose.* Boston: Houghton Mifflin, 1957.

Friends of Sleepy Hollow Cemetery. *Obituaries of Concord Luminaries.* Concord: 2010.

Kazin, Alfred. *An American Procession: Major American Writers from 1830–1930.* New York: Vantage Press, 1985.

Levine, Miriam. *A Guide to Writers Homes in New England.* Carlisle: Applewood, 1984

Marx, Leo. *The Machine in the Garden.* New York: Oxford UP, 1964

Miller, Perry. *The Transcendentalists, An Anthology.* Cambridge: Harvard UP, 1950.

Morrison, Samuel. *Oxford History of the American People.* New York: Oxford UP, 1955

Mott, Wesley. *Encyclopedia of Transcendentalism.* Westport: Greenwood Press, 1996

Schreiner, Samuel. *The Concord Quartet: Alcott, Emerson, Hawthorne and Thoreau: The Friendship That Freed the American Mind.* Hoboken: Wiley, 2006.

Spiller, Robert, Ed. *Literary History of the United States.* New York: Macmillan, 1957.

Wilson, Susan. *Literary Trail of Greater Boston.* Boston: Houghton Mifflin, 2000.

Books about Concord, Massachusetts

Andrews, Joseph L. *Revolutionary Boston, Lexington and Concord: The Shots Heard 'Round the World!* Third Edition. Beverly, MA: Commonwealth Editions, 2002.

______. "Environmentalist Mecca Faces New Battle in Wake of 'Rescue.'" *New Hampshire Sunday News:* November 26, 1995: Section 1 G.

______. "The Struggle for Walden." *The Humanist.* 57:1, February, 1997, pages 30–39.

______. "Revolutionary Concord." *New Hampshire Sunday News.* Manchester: April 14, 1996.

______. "Revolutionary Lexington and Concord. *S.A.R. Magazine.* Louisville: Spring, 1997.

______. "Concord and Roxbury Find Nature Connection." *Concord Journal,* June 23, 2011.

Barber, John W. *Massachusetts Towns: An 1840 View.* Barre Publishers: 1963 [Reprint]

Bartlett, George. *Concord: Historic, Literary and Picturesque.* Boston: Cupples, 1885.

Bemis, Allie. *Notes on the Land and on the People of Estabrook Woods.* Concord: 1974.

Brooks, Paul. *The People of Concord: American Intellectuals and their Timeless Ideas.* Chester, CT: Globe Pequot Press, 1990.

Cameron, Walter C. Ed. *The Massachusetts Lyceum During the American Renaissance.* Hartford: Transcendental Books, 1969.

Chamberlain, Samuel. *Lexington and Concord: A Camera Impression.* New York: Hastings House, 1939.

Chapin, Sarah. *Concord, MA: Images of America.* Dover, N.H.: Arcadia, 1997.

Concord Historical Commission. *Historic Resources Masterplan.* Concord: 1995.

Ells, Stephen F. *The Seasons of Estabrook Country.* Concord: 1999.

Fenn, Mary R. *Old Houses of Concord.* Concord: D.A.R., 1974.

Fischer, David H. *Paul Revere's Ride.* New York: Oxford U.P., 1994.

Greeley, Dana, Ed. *The Meeting House on the Green: A History of the First Parish In Concord and its Church.* Concord: First Parish, 1985.

Gross, Robert A. *The Minutemen and Their World.* New York: Hill & Wang, 1976.

Henley, Don & Marsh, Dave, Editors. *Heaven Under Our Feet: A Book for Walden Woods.* Stamford, CT: Longmeadow Press, 1991.

Jarvis, Edward. *Traditions and Reminiscences of Concord, Massachusetts, 1779–1878.* Sarah Chapin, Ed. Amherst: Massachusetts U.P., 1993.

Kennard, John. *Concord, Massachusetts.* Beverly, MA: Commonwealth Editions., 2002.

McAdow, Ron. *The Concord, Sudbury and Assabat Rivers.* Marlborough: Bliss, 1990.

Mitchell, John H. *Walking towards Walden: A Pilgrimage in Search of Place.* Reading, MA: Addison-Wesley, 1995.

Montague, Bill. *Concord Guidebook: Tourist Information.* Concord: Mousetrap, 1995.

Moss, Marcia. *A Wreath of Joy: Selected Holdings from the Special Collections of the Concord Free Public Library.* Concord: C.F.P.L., 1996.

National Park Service. *Walden Pond and Woods: Special Resource Study.* Boston, 2002.

Nordblum, Roger & Mary. *Concord: Its Poets & Its Places.* Concord: Odin Press, 1996.

Richardson, Lawrence E. *Concord Chronicle: 1865–1899.* Concord: Library, 1967.

Shattuck, Lemuel. *History of the Town of Concord.* Boston: Russell, 1835. [Reprint.]

Walden Woods Project. *Brister's Hill Interpretive Site.* Lincoln, MA: 2002.

Wheeler, Marion. *Old Burying Grounds of Concord.* Concord: Historical Comm., 1997.

Wheeler, Ruth. *Concord: Climate for Freedom.* Concord: Antiquarian Society, 1967.

Wilson, Leslie P. *Historic Concord and the Lexington Fight: A Brief Concord History.* Concord: Friends of the Concord Free Public Library, 2010.

Zwinger, Ann and Teale, Edwin Way. *A Conscious Stillness: Two Naturalists on Thoreau's Rivers.* New York: Harper and Row, 1982.

Index

Z

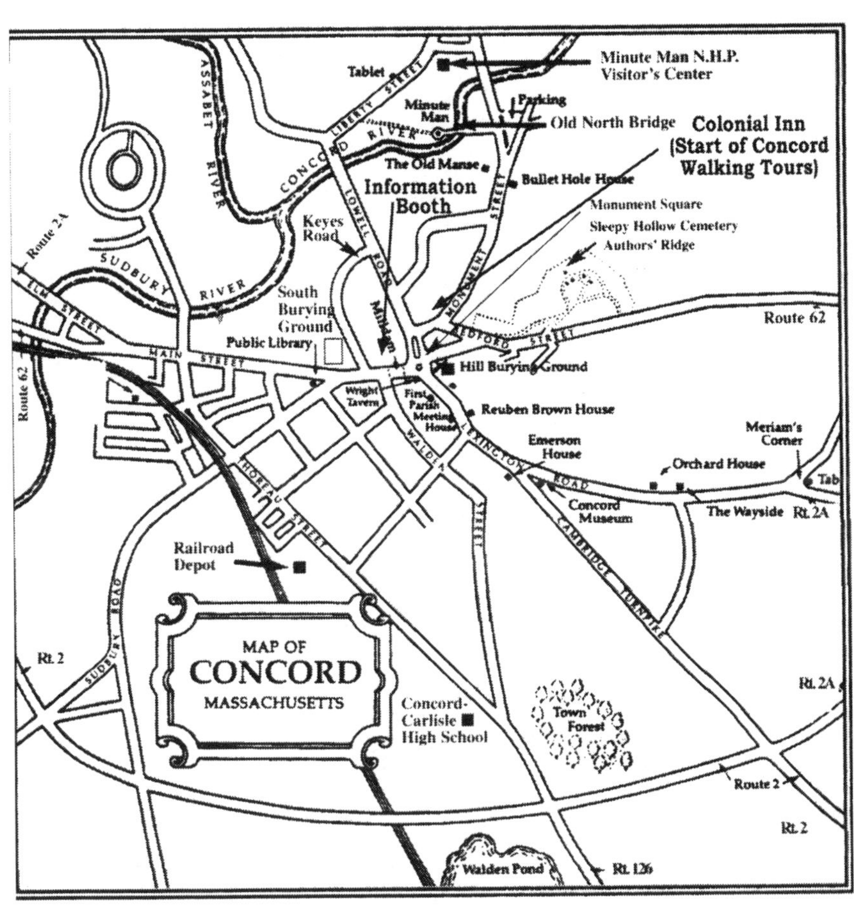

Map of Concord. Update of map by David A. Niles in *Concord '75 – Bicentennial Celebration*. (Concord Town, 1975), published in *Revolutionary Boston, Lexington & Concord: The Shots Heard 'Round the World! (Second Edition)* by Joseph L. Andrews (Concord: Concord Guides Press, 1999.)

Edwards Brothers Malloy
Oxnard, CA USA
August 19, 2014